Debate in Tibetan Buddhism

Debate in Tibetan Buddhism

Daniel E. Perdue

Snow Lion Publications
Ithaca, New York, U.S.A.

Snow Lion Publications
P.O. Box 6483
Ithaca, New York 14851

Printed in the USA

ISBN 0-937938-76-9 paper
ISBN 0-937938-84-X cloth
Textual Studies and Translations in Indo-Tibetan Buddhism
Series ISBN 0-937938-98-X

Library of Congress Cataloging-in-Publication Data

Perdue, Daniel.
  Debate in Tibetan Buddhism / Daniel E. Perdue.
    p. cm. — (Textual Studies and Translations in Indo-Tibetan Buddhism)
  Based on the author's thesis (University of Virginia, 1983)
  Includes bibliographical references and index.
  Includes Tibetan text with English translation and commentary of:
Tshad ma'i gźuṅ don 'byed / by Phur-bu-lcog Byams-pa-rgya-mtsho.
  ISBN 0-937938-76-9
    1. Phur-bu-lcog Byams-pa-rgya-mtsho. 1825-1901.   Tshad ma'i gźuṅ
don 'byed.   2. Buddhist logic.   3. Debates and debating—Religious
aspects—Buddhism.   4. Buddhism—China—Tibet—Doctrines.   I. Phur
-bu-lcog Byams-pa-rgya-mtsho. 1825-1901.   Tshad ma'i gźuṅ don 'byed.
English & Tibetan.   1991 II. Title.
BC25.P44   1992
160—dc20   91-35266
                                                                 CIP

Contents

Technical Note ix
Preface xiii

PART ONE: INTRODUCTION

1 The Place of Reasoning 3
   THE PURPOSE FOR DEBATE 6
   THE MATURATION OF CONSCIOUSNESS 13
   COURSE OF STUDY 21
   THE DEBATERS 24
2 Syllogisms and Consequences 33
   SYLLOGISMS 34
      THE ELEMENTS OF A SYLLOGISM 35
      CORRECT SIGNS 38
         The Property of the Subject 39
         Forward Pervasion 41
         Counter-Pervasion 47
      SUMMARY 49
   CONSEQUENCES 54
3 Definitions and Definienda 61
4 The Subjects 75
   QUANTIFICATION 85
   THE CATEGORIES OF SUBJECTS 88

5 The Procedure in Debate 99
   REMARKS 130
6 The Comparison of Phenomena 133
   MUTUALLY INCLUSIVE PHENOMENA 138
   THREE POSSIBILITIES 142
   FOUR POSSIBILITIES 153
   MUTUALLY EXCLUSIVE PHENOMENA............................. 159
   REMARKS 162

PART TWO: TRANSLATION AND COMMENTARY

7 Translation Introduction 169
   OBEISANCE 173
   EXPRESSION OF WORSHIP 177
8 Colors and So Forth 185
   INTRODUCTION 185
     EXTERNAL FORMS 192
      Visible Forms 192
      Sounds 200
      Odors.. 206
      Tastes 208
      Tangible Objects 210
     INTERNAL FORMS 217
   REFUTATION OF MISTAKEN VIEWS 222
   PRESENTATION OF THE AUTHOR'S OWN SYSTEM 248
   DISPELLING OBJECTIONS TO THE AUTHOR'S SYSTEM.. 252
   REMARKS 263
9 Established Bases.. 267
   INTRODUCTION 267
     ESTABLISHED BASES 269
      Functioning Things 272
      Permanent Phenomena 279
     SPECIFICALLY AND GENERALLY CHARACTERIZED
     PHENOMENA 284
      Thought Consciousnesses 287
      Direct Perceivers.. 290
      The Enumeration of Valid Cognizers 295

    Eliminative Engagers and Collective Engagers 297
    The Mixture of Place, Time, and Nature 300
    A GE-LUK-ḄA/ŚA-ḠYA-ḄA DEBATE 304
    REFUTATION OF MISTAKEN VIEWS 317
    PRESENTATION OF THE AUTHOR'S OWN SYSTEM 394
    DISPELLING OBJECTIONS TO THE AUTHOR'S SYSTEM..398
    REMARKS 407
10 Identifying Isolates...411
    INTRODUCTION 411
    THE NATURE OF ISOLATES 414
    THE TYPES OF ISOLATES...417
    THE PURPOSE OF IDENTIFYING ISOLATES 420
    THE PHENOMENA COEXTENSIVE WITH AN ISOLATE 422
    REFUTATION OF MISTAKEN VIEWS 440
    PRESENTATION OF THE AUTHOR'S OWN SYSTEM 472
    DISPELLING OBJECTIONS TO THE AUTHOR'S SYSTEM..472
    REMARKS 477
11 Opposite-From-Being-Something
    and Opposite-From-Not-Being-Something 481
    INTRODUCTION 481
    REFUTATION OF MISTAKEN VIEWS 489
    PRESENTATION OF THE AUTHOR'S OWN SYSTEM 525
    DISPELLING OBJECTIONS TO THE AUTHOR'S SYSTEM..526
    REMARKS 529
12 The Introductory Presentation of Causes and Effects............531
    INTRODUCTION 531
    DIRECT AND INDIRECT CAUSES AND EFFECTS 540
    SUBSTANTIAL CAUSES AND COOPERATIVE
    CONDITIONS..544
    REFUTATION OF MISTAKEN VIEWS 549
    PRESENTATION OF THE AUTHOR'S OWN SYSTEM 598
    DISPELLING OBJECTIONS TO THE AUTHOR'S SYSTEM..600
    REMARKS 614
13 Generalities and Instances 617
    INTRODUCTION 617
    THE THREE CHARACTERISTICS QUALIFYING A
    PHENOMENON AS AN INSTANCE OF A CERTAIN
    GENERALITY 621

THE DIVISIONS OF GENERALITIES 629
REFUTATION OF MISTAKEN VIEWS 632
PRESENTATION OF THE AUTHOR'S OWN SYSTEM 679
DISPELLING OBJECTIONS TO THE AUTHOR'S SYSTEM..681
REMARKS 692
14 Substantial and Isolate Phenomena 695
INTRODUCTION 695
THE FOUR REQUIREMENTS 701
THE NECESSITY FOR POSITING THE SIMILITUDES 707
Debate G.1 729
REMARKS 770

PART THREE: CONCLUSION

15 Conclusion 775
COPULATIVE ASSOCIATIONS 778
PERVASIONS 790
THE ALLIANCE OF COPULATIVE ASSOCIATIONS AND
PERVASIONS IN THE COLLECTED TOPICS TRADITION 795
THE CONTEXTS IN WHICH P IS A Q 795
THE CONTEXTS IN WHICH P IS NOT A Q 819
COMPARISON OF THE SYLLOGISMS USED IN THE
COLLECTED TOPICS AND ARISTOTELIAN SYSTEMS
OF REASONING 836
APPLICATIONS 849

Glossary 861
Bibliography 893
Index 901
Tibetan Text of "The Introductory Path of Reasoning"
in Pur-bu-jok Jam-ba-gya-tso's *The Presentation of
Collected Topics Revealing the Meaning of the Texts on
Valid Cognition, the Magical Key to the Path of Reasoning* 939

Technical Note

The system for transliteration of Tibetan used here is that formulated by Turrell Wylie ("A Standard System of Tibetan Transliteration", *Harvard Journal of Asian Studies* 22 [1959], pp. 261-267). Tibetan words are represented in this scheme of transliteration in parenthetical citations either by themselves or before citation of Sanskrit terms. In this work Tibetan citations are given before Sanskrit ones as an indication that I have worked primarily with Tibetan language sources.

In addition to this system of transliteration, a one-to-one correspondence of Tibetan and English letters, this work also employs a system of "essay phonetics" formulated by Prof. Jeffrey Hopkins of the University of Virginia. The Hopkins system is designed to facilitate a roughly accurate pronunciation of the Tibetan sounds as they are spoken in the central dialect but does not represent the Tibetan letters in a one-to-one correspondence since Tibetan syllables are so often loaded with unpronounced letters.

The conversion table from transliteration to "essay phonetics" is as follows, with the Wylie transliteration form on the left of each column and the Hopkins "phonetic" form on the right. Lines above letters indicate that the sound is high, sharp, and short:

ka = ḡa	kha = ka	ga = ga	nga = nga
ca = j̄a	cha = cha	ja = ja	nya = nya
ta = d̄a	tha = ta	da = da	na = na
pa = b̄a	pha = pa	ba = ba	ma = ma
tsa = d̄za	tsha = tsa	dza = dza	wa = wa
zha = sha	za = sa	'a = a	ya = ya
ra = ra	la = la	sha = s̄ha	sa = s̄a
ha = ha	a = a		

The phonetic system is derived by using the letters of the phonetic columns above and substituting *k* and *p* for *g* and *b* in the suffix position. Also, when *nga*, *nya*, *na*, *ma*, and *la* appear after a prefix or under a superscription, they are phoneticized as *n̄ga*, *ñya*, *ña*, *m̄a*, and *l̄a*, as they are pronounced with a high tone in such syllables. Similarly, *dbyang* is pronounced as *ȳang* and *dbang* as *w̄ang*. As regards the vowels, "a" indicates the vowel sound of "opt"; "i" indicates the vowel sound of "it" or "eat"; "u" indicates the vowel sound of "soon"; "ay" indicates the vowel sound of "bake"; "o" indicates the vowel sound of "boat"; and "ö" indicates the vowel sound of "er" (minus the "r"). Hyphens are supplied between syllables in the "phonetic" form so that the beginnings and ends of syllables may be easily distinguished.

The names of contemporary Tibetans who live or have published outside of Tibet have not been adopted to the Hopkins system; in most cases, their names are spelled as they spell them. Otherwise, all Tibetan names are rendered in the "phonetic" system in order to facilitate easy pronunciation and recollection.

Sanskrit equivalents for certain translation terms are given wherever possible; an asterisk before an entry indicates that it is a reconstruction. The transliteration scheme for Sanskrit is also aimed at easy pronunciation, using *sh*, *ṣh*, and *ch*, rather than *ś*, *ṣ*, and *c*; also, *chh* is used rather than *ch*. The intent of this style is to avoid excluding non-specialists or newcomers and to provide a basis for learning. For the same reasons, generally Sanskrit citations are provided in individual meaning units separated by hyphens rather than in compounds constructed according to Sanskrit rules of euphonic combination (*saṃdhi*). With the first mention of each Indian text, the Sanskrit title is provided. The full Sanskrit and Tibetan titles are found in the bibliography. Throughout this text, Sanskrit and Tibetan titles are translated into English; however, this is not meant to imply that the entire work has been translated into English.

Dedication
To those who may benefit from reasoning

Preface

Homage to Mañjushrī.

We are all born with a capacity for reasoning. Persons are of greater and lesser capacities, and the capacity is utilized to a greater or lesser extent, but in all cases the development of reasoning abilities is invariably linked to training.

This book is a presentation of the most introductory text used in one Tibetan system of training in reasoning. The heart and major portion of this work is a translation and annotation of an introductory debate manual. This text is the first portion of *The Presentation of Collected Topics Revealing the Meaning of the Texts on Valid Cognition, the Magical Key to the Path of Reasoning (tshad ma'i gzhung don 'byed pa'i bsdus grva'i rnam bzhag rigs lam 'phrul gyi lde mig)*. The author is Pur-bu-jok Jam-ba-gya-tso (*phur bu lcog byams pa rgya mtsho*), 1825-1901, here referred to as the Tutor (*yongs 'dzin*) Jam-ba-gya-tso because he was tutor to the Thirteenth Dalai Lama, for whose instruction he wrote the text. This source book of the various topics debated in the introductory study of logic and epistemology is currently used by the Jay (*byes*) College of Še-ra (*se ra*) Monastic University in Bylakuppe, Karnataka State, India; Jang-dzay (*byang rtse*) College of Gan-den (*dga' ldan*) Monastic University in Mundgod, Karnataka State, India; and Ñam-gyal (*rnam rgyal*) College in Dharamsala, Himachal Pradesh, India.

The Collected Topics of Valid Cognition (*tshad ma'i bsdus grva*) is essential introductory material for those seeking to learn Buddhist logic and epistemology. Rather than being a single work, the Collected Topics of Valid Cognition refers to any of a number of debate manuals written in Tibetan for the sake of introducing new students of Buddhist philosophy to a wide range of topics presented within a rigorous logical framework.

The Tutor's *Collected Topics* (*yongs 'dzin bsdus grva*) is divided into three major parts consisting of "The Introductory Path of Reasoning" (*rigs lam chung ngu*),[1] "The Middling Path of Reasoning" (*rigs lam 'bring*), and "The Greater Path of Reasoning" (*rigs lam che ba*). "The Greater Path of Reasoning" contains book-length presentations of "Awareness and Knowledge" (*blo rig*) and "Signs and Reasonings" (*rtags rigs*) as well as other collected topics which are listed below.

The division into introductory, middling, and greater paths of reasoning (*rigs lam*) accords with the capacity of the student. The debaters speak of "gaining the path of reasoning" meaning that one has developed a certain capacity and facility with the procedure in debate. Those who have the path of reasoning debate without hesitation and indecision, for they know well the implications of both their own and their opponent's assertions and immediately draw out those implications and possible interpretations of what was said.

One scholar noted that "reasoning" in the expression "The Path of Reasoning" has the same meaning as "correctness" and "suitability".[2] That water flows downhill accords with reasoning, correctness, and suitability. It is reasonable, correct, and suitable that fire exists on a smoky mountain pass.

---

[1] *Rigs lam chung ngu* could be translated more literally as "The Lesser Path of Reasoning" or "The Smaller Path of Reasoning".

[2] Kensur Jambel Shenpen, oral commentary.

Smoke exists on a smoky mountain pass, and wherever there is smoke there is fire. By the power of these facts one establishes reasonably, correctly, and suitably that fire exists on a smoky mountain pass. By this interpretation, a "path of reasoning" also means a "path of correctness" and a "path of suitability".

Generally in Buddhism, paths are consciousnesses, and like an ordinary path on the ground they lead one to another place or state. In the titles of these sections such as "The Introductory Path of Reasoning", however, the path is not only the conceiving consciousness but also that which is being thought about. In this sense, it is the Hindus' path that sound is a permanent phenomenon and it is the Buddhists' path that sound is an impermanent phenomenon.

That reasoning is interpreted to mean correctness and suitability indicates this system's commitment to the validity of reasoning. In the same way that whatever exists may be known, and whatever does not exist may not be known, just so whatever is established by the power of reasoning is correct and suitable. This does not mean that whatever one may think is correct, but that valid reasoning will establish only what is correct and concordant with valid cognition (*tshad ma, pramāṇa*). In the Collected Topics system, the qualities of phenomena and the differences between them are not asserted to be established merely by one's wish or even by mental imputation, but are taken to be established objectively by the power of the way that those phenomena exist.

In agreement with this view, a path of reasoning is a correct and suitable thought which, of course, accords with the fact, for otherwise it would not be suitable. The division of the Collected Topics of Valid Cognition into introductory, middling, and greater paths of reasoning indicates three levels of objects of thought and three levels of capacity. Having trained in "The Introductory Path of Reasoning" students are then able to study the more difficult topics of "The Middling Path of Reasoning" and "The Greater Path of Reasoning". Having completed the Collected Topics, one is then capable of studying and understanding the higher topics of Buddhist tenets. Although some students of greater capacity might begin with the later topics, most begin with "The Introductory Path of Reasoning" which forms the basis of this work.

"The Introductory Path of Reasoning" presents chapter by chapter seven different topics fundamental to Tibetan debate. In order, these are:

1 colors—white, red, and so forth (*kha dog dkar dmar sogs*)
2 established bases (*gzhi grub*)
3 identifying isolates (*ldog pa ngos 'dzin*)
4 opposite-from-being-something and opposite-from-not-being-something (*yin log min log*)
5 the introductory [presentation of] causes and effects (*rgyu 'bras chung ngu*)
6 generalities and instances (*spyi bye brag*)
7 substantial phenomena and isolate phenomena (*rdzas chos ldog chos*).

The translation and commentary presented here is of "The Introductory Path of Reasoning" in its entirety.

"The Middling Path of Reasoning" covers five main topics:

1 mutually exclusive phenomena and related phenomena (*'gal 'brel*)
2 realizing [something] as existent and realizing [something] as non-existent (*yod rtogs med rtogs*)
3 definitions and definienda (*mtshan mtshon*)
4 the greater [presentation of] causes and effects (*rgyu 'bras che ba*)
5 forward and counter-pervasions (*rjes 'gro ldog khyab*).

References to some of these topics occur in "The Introductory Path of Reasoning" and in the provided annotations, but they are not translated or covered in detail here.

"The Greater Path of Reasoning" explains four main topics and in addition technically includes the book-length

"Awareness and Knowledge"[1] and "Signs and Reasonings".[2] The Tutor Jam-ba-gya-tso includes these latter two, although suitable as independent works in their own rights, within "The Greater Path of Reasoning" because they, like the other subjects presented in the Collected Topics, are material traditionally covered in beginning studies of logic. Other than these two, the four topics presented in "The Greater Path of Reasoning" are:

1   the introductory [presentation of] consequences together with ancillary topics (*thal 'gyur chung ba zhar byung dang bcas pa*)
2   the greater [presentation of] consequences (*thal 'gyur che ba*)
3   negative phenomena and positive phenomena (*gzhan sel dgag sgrub*)
4   eliminative engagers and collective engagers (*sel 'jug sgrub 'jug*).

Again these topics are not translated and explained here, but occasional references do occur in "The Introductory Path of Reasoning" and the annotations.

Buddha himself never taught a system of logic as such; however, the system of reasoning presented in the Collected Topics tradition is said to have developed indirectly from Buddha's word. The Collected Topics texts draw their information and style of reasoning from the works of Dignāga (*phyogs glang*) (480-540 C.E.), Dharmakīrti (*chos kyi*

---

[1] Although the Tutor Jam-ba-gya-tso's explanation of "Awareness and Knowledge" is available only as an unpublished manuscript in English, a similar text by Ge-shay Jam-bel-sam-pel (*dge bshes 'jam dpal bsam 'phel*, d. 1975) appears in Lati Rinbochay's *Mind in Tibetan Buddhism*, trans., ed., with an introduction by Elizabeth Napper (Valois, New York: Gabriel Press, 1980).

[2] For a complete translation of the Tutor Jam-ba-gya-tso's "Signs and Reasonings" see Katherine Rogers, "Tibetan Logic: A Translation, with Commentary, of Pur-bu-jok Jam-ba-gya-tso's *The Topic of Signs and Reasonings from the 'Great Path of Reasoning'* in *The Magic Key to the Path of Reasoning, Explanation of the Collected Topics Revealing the Meaning of the Texts on Valid Cognition*" (M.A. thesis, University of Virginia, 1980).

grags pa) (600-660 C.E.),[1] and Vasubandhu (*dbyig gnyen*) (316-396 C.E.),[2] three major Indian Buddhist scholars who are said to have based their writings in a general way on the word of Buddha. From among their works the special sources of the Collected Topics texts are Dignāga's *Compendium of Valid Cognition* (*pramāṇa-samuchchaya*), Dharmakīrti's *Commentary on (Dignāga's) "Compendium of Valid Cognition"* (*pramāṇa-varttikakārikā*), and Vasubandhu's *Treasury of Knowledge* (*abhidharmakosha*). The Collected Topics texts gain their title by being presentations of assorted central points gathered mainly from these works of the Indian Buddhist tradition. They thereby introduce one to these texts by providing easy access to their complicated topics.

The first Collected Topics text was authored by the twelfth-century scholar Cha-ba-chö-ġyi-śeng-gay (*cha pa chos kyi seng ge*), 1109-1169, of the Ga-dam-ba (*bka' gdams pa*) sect.[3] This primary text is no longer extant, although at least some of the information presented in it is still studied. (The seventh chapter in "The Introductory Path of Reasoning" in the Tutor's *Collected Topics*, the presentation of substantial and isolate phenomena, was originally organized and presented by Cha-ba-chö-ġyi-śeng-gay.) In this work I do not undertake to trace the historical development of the Collected Topics literature and its sources or to describe the Indian antecedents to Tibetan debate, but have focused on the developed literature and present tradition of debate as given philosophical work.

---

[1] The dates for Dignāga and Dharmakīrti are as given in Masaaki Hattori, *Dignāga, On Perception, being the Pratyakṣapariccheda of Dignāga's 'Pramāṇasamuccaya' from the Sanskrit Fragments and the Tibetan Versions* (Cambridge, Massachusetts: Harvard University Press, 1968), pp. 4 and 14, who in turn takes these dates from E. Frauwallner.

[2] The dates for Vasubandhu are taken from Stefan Anacker, "Vasubandhu: Three Aspects" (Ph.D. dissertation, University of Wisconsin, 1970), p. 30.

[3] The dates for Cha-ba-chö-ġyi-śeng-gay are from L.W.J. Van de Kuijp, "Phya-Pa Chos Kyi Seng-Ge's Impact on Tibetan Epistemological Theory", *Journal of Indian Philosophy*, vol.5 (1978), p. 355.

Also, I make no attempt to compare the philosophical interpretations made in the Collected Topics texts with interpretations made in the vast Sa-ḡya literature on reasoning. Rather, I have tried to make a thorough investigation of the topics as they are seen in a variety of ways within the Ge-luk-ba tradition.

Thus, as an aid to understanding the Tutor's *Collected Topics* I have relied on four additional Collected Topics texts. These are:

1 Ra-dö *Collected Topics* (*rva stod bsdus grva*) by Jam-ȳang-chok-hla-ö-ser (*'jam dbyangs phyogs lha 'od zer*)
2 Go-mang *Collected Topics* (*sgo mang bsdus grva*) by Ngak-w̄ang-dra-shi (*ngag dbang bkra shis*)
3 Shar-dzay *Collected Topics* (*shar rtse bsdus grva*) by Dzemay Rinbochay (*dze smad rin po che*)
4 Lo-sel-ling *Collected Topics* (*blo gsal gling bsdus grva*) by Jam-bel-trin-lay-yön-den-gya-tso (*'jam dpal 'phrin las yon tan rgya mtsho*)

Citations are drawn from these texts and differences in interpretation are noted as a means for gaining broader access to the individual points of doctrine.

All of these texts are included in the literature of the Ge-luk-ba (*dge lugs pa*) order, the predominant order of Tibetan Buddhism in terms of numbers of monks and nuns, a tradition heralded for its rigorous scholarship. The appeal to reasoning is persistent and persuasive in the Ge-luk-ba order, and the study of reasoning begins with the Collected Topics. The Collected Topics texts and, more generally, the study of valid cognition are linked primarily to the system of the Proponents of Sūtra Following Reasoning, a Lesser Vehicle school of Buddhist tenets. Thus, the Collected Topics texts represent not only a study of the formal topics of reasoning but also indirectly a presentation of one system of Buddhist tenets.

The four systems of Buddhist tenets presented in Tibetan Buddhism are the Great Exposition School (*bye brag smra ba, vaibhāṣhika*) and the Sūtra School (*mdo sde pa, sautrāntika*), which are the two Lesser Vehicle (*theg dman, hīna-yāna*) systems, and the Mind Only School (*sems tsam, chitta-mātra*) and the Middle Way School (*dbu ma pa, mādhyamika*), which are the two Great Vehicle (*theg chen, mahā-yāna*) systems.

Proponents of the Sūtra School are divided into Followers of Scripture (*mdo sde'i rjes su 'brangs pa,* *āgamānusārin) and Followers of Reasoning (*rigs pa'i rjes su 'brangs pa,* *nyāyānusārin). From among these two, the Followers of Reasoning are so called because they follow Dharmakīrti's Seven Treatises on Valid Cognition (listed in the bibliography).[1] Although the tenets of the Proponents of Sūtra Following Reasoning are not accepted as final by the Ge-luk-b̄as, who take the Middle Way School as the highest system, the form of reasoning and the method for refutation and valid establishment is largely accepted by the Ge-luk-b̄as as applicable to the other schools. Thus, the translation offered here is one Ge-luk-b̄a interpretation of topics presented in the system of the Proponents of Sūtra Following Reasoning. As such, this work is by no means a presentation of the whole of Buddhist, Tibetan, or even Ge-luk-b̄a logic and epistemology.

The translation of the basic debate manual is supplemented with annotations on both the form and content of the debates, and these comprise the major part of this work. Prior to the translation and annotations I provide an introductory section designed to identify the place of reasoning within the Ge-luk-b̄a tradition and to give the reader some essential information for easier access to the text.

Throughout this work the debaters are referred to with masculine pronouns. The main reason for this is that, historically within the Tibetan tradition, debate was an activity primarily, though not exclusively, for monks rather than nuns. The problems with reliance on masculine references are not only social but also logical, for a

---

[1] See Anne C. Klein, *Knowledge and Liberation: Tibetan Buddhist Epistemology in Support of Transformative Religious Experience* (Ithaca, New York: Snow Lion Publications, 1986), p. 21.

Challenger or a Defender—one holding a philosophical position in debate—might equally well be a male or a female. Still, in the interest of saving some space in an already extensive volume, I have chosen not to use "he or she" and "his or her" in the countless references. Nevertheless, I would be remiss not to apologize up front for this obvious shortcoming. The omission of feminine pronouns is not meant to indicate in any way that females cannot perform well in debate or might not take a strong interest in it. Anyone who holds such a view need only be shown the nuns of Ge-den-chö-ling (*dge ldan chos gling*) in Dharamsala, India, who have in recent years shown great forcefulness in debate.

The third and final part of this book draws together the most important lessons on the structure of logical statements learned in "The Introductory Path of Reasoning" and offers comparisons with Western approaches to reasoning. In the conclusion I have used Euler diagrams to highlight points of a formal nature.

All comparisons with Western systems of thought are given in the conclusion in the interest of not mixing Western overlays into the indigenous understanding of these logical topics and in the interest of gathering together all of these comments in one place for easier access for those readers especially interested. Although the text presents many philosophical topics which could be cross-related with Western systems, such an enterprise, valuable as it might be, is beyond the scope of the present work.

Rather, here I have undertaken to lay out as clearly as possible the information and context of "The Introductory Path of Reasoning" of the Tutor's *Collected Topics*. In the interest of accomplishing this I have critically compared the interpretations presented in the root text with the interpretations presented in the Collected Topics texts of four other Ge-luk-ba authors. The thoroughgoing exegesis of this system is a prerequisite for serious comparative work because in order to compare two diverse systems one must first be equipped with an accurate understanding of both. Thus, in undertaking this first responsibility I have, for now, suspended judgment on relative values—which system is better and which worse, which system is richer and which poorer.

Here I do not undertake to draw comparisons with prior scholarship in the general field of Buddhist logic. This does not mean that I am unaware or even unappreciative of the work on Buddhist logic and epistemology that has been done from Sanskrit and Tibetan sources. Indeed, it is clear that some of the information presented here does contrast with earlier findings in this field, but it is beyond the scope of this work to emphasize these contrasts, except for citing two major examples in the conclusion. Also, although in general this work shares many topics with other well-known works in the field of Buddhist logic and epistemology, the specific subject-matter dealt with here is an entirely new and untapped source related to a different level of monastic education. Thus, I have limited the scope of this book to a critical exegesis of the tradition of education on debate in the Ge-luk-ba order of Tibetan Buddhism and within that to the most introductory texts.

Over the long history of indigenous scholarship on Buddhist logic and epistemology which began with Dignāga's work in the fifth and sixth centuries, the continuing trend is for the texts to become increasingly less terse and to include increasingly more of what had been oral explanation. Within the traditional educational framework of Indian and Tibetan monasteries, an essential component was the oral commentary of the teacher explaining the meaning of the text. Without the commentary of a qualified teacher it is quite difficult to gain access to the meaning of the terse writings on logic and epistemology. Furthermore, beyond passively receiving the oral commentary to the text, students are expected to debate the meaning and interpretation of passages in order to come to understand better the intent of the text. In keeping with this trend of recording increasingly more of the traditional oral explanation, in the annotations to the text I report the interpretations of several qualified Tibetan teachers in addition to drawing on my own understanding of the text gained from personal experience in debate.

PREPARATION

My study of the Collected Topics system of reasoning began at the University of Virginia in 1974 under the tutelage of Professor Jeffrey Hopkins who had gained an understanding of the essential forms of argument from Kensur Ngawang Lekden, a scholar of the highest (*lha ram pa*) rank and former abbot of the Tantric College of Lower Hla-ša (*rgyud smad*). During 1974-75 the whole of Prof. Hopkins' second year Tibetan language class undertook the study of logic and debate, using the Tutor's *Collected Topics* as the source. In the spring of 1975, during a short visit to Freewood Acres, New Jersey, I received instruction in elementary debate from Geshe Lobsang Tharchin of the May (*smad*) College of Še-ra Monastic University, and from Geshay Jambel Thardö of the Lo-šel-ling (*blo gsal gling*) College of Dre-bung Monastic University.

Continuing our study of the Collected Topics during the summer and fall of 1975, the Tibetan language class at the University of Virginia had about reached the limits of its capacities. Then in 1976 Lati Rinbochay (*bla ti rinpoche*), now former abbot of the Šhar-dzay (*shar rtse*) College of Gan-den Monastic University, came to the university as a Visiting Lecturer in the Department of Religious Studies. Also a scholar of the highest rank, he generously taught us the procedure in debate, explained the topics, and supervised our practice sessions. In the traditional style of teaching debate, Lati Rinbochay would present us with a quandary in the debate format and with great humor prod us in different directions to try to solve it but refuse to lay out the answer, thereby forcing us to figure it out ourselves. During his fifteen months in Virginia, he taught the whole of the Collected Topics from "The Introductory Path of Reasoning" through to the presentation of "Signs and Reasonings"—the five introductory texts on Buddhist logic and epistemology.

In 1978 after Lati Rinbochay had left, Denma Lochö Rinbochay (*ldan ma blo chos rinpoche*), a ge-shay of the Dre-bung Lo-sel-ling College and present abbot of Ñam-gyal College, came to the University of Virginia as a Visiting Lecturer. Rather than teaching from a text, he gave a summary overview of the whole of the Collected Topics. Teaching from amazingly detailed memory and a surpassing grasp of the material, he explained the procedure and content of debates and revealed the level of complexity that can be brought to even the most introductory material. In the beginning, Lochö Rinbochay often left us so stumped he had to suggest possible answers, but under his supervision our debating became more facile.

In February of 1979, prepared with a solid familiarity with the issues in the Collected Topics literature and with the essential procedure in debate, but lacking extensive practical experience, I left for India to pursue my study on a Fulbright Dissertation Research Abroad Grant. On the way, for one month I studied the Collected Topics at Tharpa Choeling Centre for Higher Tibetan Studies on Mont Pèlerin, Switzerland, with the permission of abbot Geshé Rabten. During this time I debated daily with the monks of Tharpa Choeling and benefitted greatly from discussions with Tom Tillemans, a lay associate of Tharpa Choeling, on the comparison of the Collected Topics and Western systems of reasoning.

Between March and November, 1979, I continued study of the Collected Topics in India with the kind cooperation of my academic advisor, Dr. A.K. Chatterjee of the Banaras Hindu University, Department of Philosophy, and Mr. C.S. Ramakrishnan, Director of the United States Educational Foundation in India. In New Delhi I studied the theoretical underpinnings of Buddhist logic and epistemology with Geshay Belden Drakba (*dge bshes dpal ldan grags pa*), a Lo-sel-ling ge-shay who is the scholar-in-residence at Tibet House and whom I found to be especially skilled in explaining Buddhist philosophy to Westerners.

In May of 1979 I set out for the Tibetan monasteries re-established in Karnataka State, southern India, where I was able to join in the daily debating sessions. This enabled me to continue the study and practice of debate begun in language classes in Virginia and furthered in Switzerland. During two and a half months at Dre-ḇung Monastic University I was able to study the practice and theory of Buddhist reasoning with Kensur Yeshay Tupḏen (*mkhan zur ye shes thub bstan*), former abbot of Lo-sel-ling College. I also enjoyed the skillful instruction of Ngak-wang Nyi-ma (*ngag dbang nyi ma*), then abbot of Go-mang College, on these same topics. With the support of these teachers and the many monks of Dre-ḇung, I was able to make progress toward understanding the procedure and intent of debate.

For one month I studied at Shar-dzay College of Gan-den Monastic University with Lati Rinbochay, the Tibetan teacher who had originally instructed our language class at Virginia in the Collected Topics. By this time I had collected a number of questions which Lati Rinbochay was able to clear away. Here too I pursued the daily practice of debate with the monks of Shar-dzay, distinguished in their effort at debate.

Finally, I studied for one month at the Jay College of Se-ra Monastic University with the kind permission of the abbot Ngakwang Lekden, the instruction of Ge-shay Ga-yang (*dge bshes bka' dbyangs*), and the encouragement of Ge-shay Dra-shi Bum (*dge bshes bkra shis 'bum*). I found the monks of Se-ra Jay well deserving of their reputation as assertive and competent debaters.

In Banaras, I consulted with Prof. T.R.V. Murti on a number of points in a series of valuable meetings. Prof. Murti discussed the Indian antecedents and descendants of Buddhist logic and epistemology as well as the position of reasoning within the soteriological perspective of religious motivation and activity.

I spent the last month of my research abroad in Japan where I met briefly with Prof. Yuichi Kajiyama of Kyoto University and Dr. Katsumi Mimaki of the Research Institute for Humanistic Studies of Kyoto University.

Despite the brevity, I benefitted greatly from meeting with these teachers, both Buddhologists with extensive knowledge of Indian logic and epistemology.

Having returned to the United States in December 1979, I worked until May 1983 writing up my research on the Collected Topics, which I submitted to the University of Virginia as my dissertation, entitled "Practice and Theory of Philosophical Debate in Tibetan Buddhist Education". During this period, in 1980-81 I was fortunate to be able to bring my final questions to Visiting Lecturer Kensur Jambel Shenpen (*mkhan zur 'jam dpal gzhan phan*), former abbot of the Tantric College of Lower Hla-ŝa and the present Gan-den Tri Rinbochay—the ninety-eighth holder of the throne of Dzong-ka-ba and head of the Ge-luk-ba order, who had completed his ge-ŝhay training at the Jang-dzay College of Gan-den Monastic University. Regardless of the thoroughness with which one researches, inevitably at the time of writing certain difficult questions arise, and Kensur Jambel Shenpen skillfully helped clear up many of these remaining questions. Finally, while at the University of Virginia in 1981-82 I relied on Kensur Yeshay Tupden, one of the lamas I had studied with in India during 1979 and a scholar renowned for his skill in the topics of valid cognition.

The present book is, for the most part, the dissertation submitted to the University of Virginia in 1983. I have made numerous changes, improving a number of translation terms, providing a glossary at the end, and so forth. Also, I have created an index, which the reader will find helpful for sorting through this vast volume—a work which William Magee, Instructor in Virginia's summer intensive in debate, calls "pound for pound, the best bargain in Buddhist texts".

I wish to express my heartfelt appreciation to all of the scholars on whom I have relied to produce this work. If anything outshines their wisdom, it is their kindness and patience in carefully and skilfully explaining and repeating the points in the Collected Topics tradition so that I might understand. I am also grateful to the monk-students of Drebung, Gan-den, and Se-ra who with great enthusiasm showed me the path of reasoning. Over the years I have studied with scholars from each of the six remaining colleges of these three main seats of Ge-luk-ba learning. I have found their understanding of the Collected Topics to be generally consistent, but given their view of the value of independent thought, it is clear that there is no monolithic presentation of these topics even within Ge-luk-ba.

I would like to thank each of my fellow students in Tibetan language courses at the University of Virginia—John Buescher, Anne Klein, Donald Lopez, Elizabeth Napper, Katherine Rogers, and Joe Wilson—who pursued debate with persistent enthusiasm to our mutual benefit. I am grateful to Georges Dreyfus (Geshay Sangyay Samdrup), former student in the School of Dialectics in Dharamsala, India, and the first Westerner to win the ge-shay degree, who advised me on several important points. Special thanks are due to Elizabeth Napper and Anne Klein for their recommendations on the preparation of this manuscript as well as for helping proofread the dissertation form. Also, I am grateful to Gareth Sparham (Ven. Tupden Tandö) for his proofreading, helping me locate quotations in the Tibetan canon, and helpful comments. I wish to thank Kimberly Bacon for drawing the illustration on p. xxviii, Nathaniel Garson for preparing the Tibetan in chapters 5 and 6, and Robert Clark for loaning his copy of the Tutor's *Collected Topics* which was photographed to provide the text at the end of this book. I would also like to thank Christina Curtis and Steven Weinberger for proofreading and offering helpful suggestions.

This work was greatly enhanced by free-flowing interchanges with Professors Julian Hartt, James Cargile, Harvey Aronson, and Paul Groner. Finally, my deepest gratitude is due to my thesis director, Professor Jeffrey Hopkins, who first showed me the door to Buddhist reasoning. At every stage Professor Hopkins has advised and helped, first encouraging me to undertake the study of Buddhist reasoning and throughout my study inspiring me, in word and deed, to complete this work.

The Challenger tests the Defender.

Part One
Introduction

1 The Place of Reasoning

Sentient beings (*sems can, sattva*) suffer continuously in the prison of cyclic existence (*'khor ba, saṃsāra*) due to the force of ignorance (*ma rig pa, avidyā*). There is no possibility for sentient beings to escape the repeated round of birth, aging, sickness, and death without actualizing in their own continuums the realizations that destroy ignorance. Buddha said:

> Buddhas neither wash sins away with water,
> Nor remove beings' sufferings with their hands,
> Nor transfer their realisations to others; beings
> Are freed through the teachings of the truth, the
> nature of things.[1]

Buddhas cannot grant liberation to suffering sentient beings. Rather, they teach them the nature of phenomena and thereby enable them to escape the suffering of cyclic existence by their own attainment of wisdom (*shes rab, prajñā*). Ignorance is the root cause of all suffering, and wisdom is

---

[1] Tenzin Gyatso (*bstan 'dzin rgya mtsho*), The Fourteenth Dalai Lama, *The Buddhism of Tibet and The Key to the Middle Way*, The Wisdom of Tibet Series 1, trans. by Jeffrey Hopkins and Lati Rimpoche (New York: Harper & Row, 1975), p. 46.

4 *Debate in Tibetan Buddhism*

the antidote to ignorance. Through learning one eventually becomes established in wisdom. "Putting far away ... a foolish doctrine which pleases laziness, one ought to do at first, as well as one can, an extensive learning of the doctrine." [1] Ashvaghosha's *Garland of the Life Tales* (*jātaka-mālā*) says:

> Learning is like a lamp for eliminating the darkness of ignorance.[2]

Just as a lamp illumines a house so that one can see colors and shapes, so learning and wisdom enable one to see the nature of phenomena. According to Lati Rinbochay, "There is no phenomenon which cannot be understood. There is no doctrine which, if studied well, cannot be learned, and there is no person who, if he or she studies well, cannot become wise."[3]

The essence of Buddha's doctrine and the source of all monastic studies is the four noble truths.[4] The first of these is true sufferings (*sdug bsngal bden pa, duḥkha-satya*), that all sentient beings are constantly beset by suffering. Padmasambhava, a great Indian Buddhist scholar and adept, said that life in cyclic existence is like living on the point of a needle.[5] No matter which way one turns within cyclic existence there is no relief of suffering and no happiness. The second truth is true origins (*kun 'byung bden pa, samudaya-satya*) which is ignorance, the root cause of suffering. Ignorance is not merely not knowing something, but is an active misconception.[6] Third is true cessations (*'gog bden, nirodha-satya*), the fact that there is an utter eradication of

---

[1] Geshe Lhundup Sopa, *Lectures on Tibetan Religious Culture* (University of Wisconsin, unpublished manuscript, 1972), Part 1, p. 180.
[2] Ashvaghosha, *Jātakamālā*, reported in Sopa, p. 166.
[3] Lati Rinbochay, oral commentary.
[4] Geshé Rabten, *The Life and Teaching of Geshé Rabten, A Tibetan Lama's Search for Truth*, trans. and ed. by B. Alan Wallace (Gelong Jhampa Kelsang), (London: George Allen & Unwin, 1980), p. 14.
[5] Khetsun Sangbo Rinbochay, *Tantric Practice in Nying-Ma* (London: Rider, 1982), p. 83.
[6] Denma Lochö Rinbochay, oral commentary.

suffering. The fourth is true paths (*lam bden, mārga-satya*), the wisdom knowing the opposite of what ignorance conceives, which leads one to the cessation of suffering.

The religious practitioner is compared to a patient and Buddha to a doctor.[1] Buddha administers the medicine of doctrine (*chos, dharma*) to sentient beings who suffer the illness of ignorance. The purpose for debate and all Buddhist practice directed toward one's own liberation is to abandon the first two truths, suffering and origin, and to attain the latter two, cessation and path.

Specifically, in the system of the Proponents of Sūtra Following Reasoning, the point of view from which the Collected Topics literature is written, the subtle ignorance that is the cause of sentient beings' suffering is identified as the conception of oneself as a self-sufficient (*rang rkya ba*) or substantially existent (*rdzas su yod pa, dravya-sat*) person. This is the view of the person as like a lord and master who controls the subjects, mind and body. The lack of being a self-sufficient or substantially existent person is a selflessness of persons (*gang zag gi bdag med, pudgala-nairātmya*).

In the view put forth in this system, sentient beings under the influence of this root ignorance are drawn into contaminated (*zag bcas, sāsrava*) actions and afflictions and powerlessly impelled again and again into birth, aging, sickness, and death. Just as a cattleman can lead a strong bull by a nose-ring, so sentient beings are lead into suffering by the nose-ring of ignorance.[2]

The medicine for the illness of ignorance is wisdom, the knowledge that persons lack the nature of being self-sufficient or substantially existent. Wisdom is the actual antidote to ignorance and the cure for suffering. One can temporarily suppress hatred by cultivating a loving attitude, desire by seeing the faults of the object of desire, and so forth, but in order to break the continuous cycle of suffering

---

[1] For instance, see Geshey Ngawang Dhargyey, *Tibetan Tradition of Mental Development* (Dharamsala, India: Library of Tibetan Works & Archives, 1974), p. 78.
[2] Lati Rinbochay, oral commentary.

one must utterly destroy the root cause, ignorance.[1] All of the study in debate is directed toward this goal, the eradication of ignorance. Depending upon one's motivation, one's efforts at debate and learning may be directed toward just one's own liberation or, for those more capable, toward the liberation of all sentient beings, oneself and others.

Ignorance and the afflictive emotions of desire and hatred which it induces are not inherent in the nature of the mind. Rather, the essential nature of the mind is pure, though for sentient beings it is stained with defilements. Just as clouds block the sun but the sky remains free of obstructions, so the defilements stain the mind but the mind remains essentially pure.[2] Cyclic existence did not begin as the sport of a deity or by an originally pure mind's becoming impure, for the cause of cyclic existence is beginningless ignorance. Once ignorance is removed, cyclic existence vanishes.

THE PURPOSE FOR DEBATE

The central purposes of Tibetan monastic debate are to defeat misconceptions, to establish the correct view, and to clear away objections to that view. To these ends, with great effort, the Ge-luk-ba monks engage in debate diligently seeking to learn well the words and to understand fully the meaning of the Buddhist doctrine.

Within this context, in the greater Tibetan monasteries the principal means of learning is debate. The monastery is the center of the Buddha's doctrine and a gathering place for those seeking inward peace and spiritual growth. In the monastery the sole purpose for study is to put the Buddha's

---

[1] As suggested by Tsong-ka-pa, *Tantra in Tibet, The Great Exposition of Secret Mantra*, trans. and ed. by Jeffrey Hopkins (London: George Allen & Unwin, 1977), p. 211.

[2] See Khetsun Sangbo Rinbochay, p. 141-142, and *Nāgārjuna's Letter to King Gautamiputra*, trans. by Ven. Lozang Jamspal, Ven. Ngawang Samten Chophel, and Peter Della Santina (Delhi: Motilal Banarsidass, 1978), stanza 14, p. 9.

teachings into practice in order to attain enlightenment.[1] Great emphasis is placed on the knowledge to be gained through debate. Debate for the monks of Tibet is not mere academics but a way of using direct implications from the obvious in order to generate an inference of the non-obvious state of phenomena. The diligent debaters are seeking to understand the nature of reality through careful analysis of the state of existence of ordinary phenomena, the bases of reality. This is the essential purpose for religious debate. As renunciates of worldly paths, having abandoned that which will not help, the monks seek to attain an incontrovertible understanding. Religious practitioners must be like bees gathering honey, taking only the essential and leaving the rest.

All Buddhist practices are based on the trilogy of hearing (*thos pa, shruta*) the teaching of the doctrine, thinking (*bsam pa, chintā*) about its meaning, and meditating (*sgom pa, bhāvana*) on it. Philosophical debate fits into all three of these levels of practice, but is mainly included in the level of thinking. One hears teaching on the topics of debate, this teaching often being given in the debating form. Then one reads the texts, memorizes the definitions and divisions, and on one's own thinks about the meaning of what one is studying. After this preparation one is able to debate the topic with others. One puts forth one's own view or understanding of a point of doctrine, and others raise objections to that view. Similarly, one raises objections to others' interpretations or understandings. This debating of the points of doctrine with others is included in the level of thinking. Further, the debating process may be utilized in the level of meditation as when one is pursuing analytical meditation and raising qualms as if one were debating with oneself. Analytical meditation is the main type of meditation, and debate is able to help this process by sharpening the reasoning capacities and providing one with a procedure for orderly investigation and analysis. Thus, debate may be

---

[1] See, for instance, Rabten, pp. 13ff.

included in all three practices of hearing, thinking, and meditating.

His Holiness, the Fourteenth Dalai Lama, the religious and secular leader of Tibet, affirms that the real significance of monastic training, including debate, is in its usefulness in helping one to extinguish all faults and to attain all auspicious attributes, including the generation of Buddhahood itself. If we apply his more general advice to the topic at hand, the immediate purpose for philosophical debate is practical application of the knowledge, not mere learnedness. If one can have both learnedness and a sense of practical application, then that is best. But if one were to have to choose, then: "A sense of practical application would be more important, for one who has this will receive the full benefit of whatever he knows."[1] It is better to apply thoroughly even just one stanza of the excellent doctrine than to learn merely the words of the great texts and not to understand them. Mere learnedness is not sufficient and may be detrimental if one uses his knowledge of the words to defeat others and not to help them, but practical application and thorough understanding together will only help. It will help oneself, it will help others.[2]

In a series of private meetings during February of 1975, Geshe Lobsang Tharchin, a Tibetan scholar of the highest rank, discussed his view on the purpose and application of monastic debate. After many years of study and debate at Śe-ra monastery near Hla-śa in Tibet he earned the title of Hla-ram-ba Ge-śhay, the highest of four rankings of the Ge-śhay degree. "Ge-śhay" (*dge bshes, kalyāna-mitra*), meaning "virtuous friend" or "spiritual guide", is a title earned much as a Doctorate of Philosophy and indicates a high order of proficiency in religious debate as well as an extensive and thorough knowledge of central Buddhist doctrines in the sūtra systems. Here are summarized Geshe Lobsang

---

[1] Tenzin Gyatso, *The Key to the Middle Way*, p. 56.
[2] *Ibid.*, pp. 56-57.

Tharchin's remarks on Tibetan monastic debate as translated into English by Artemus B. Engle:

> The purpose for debate is not to defeat and embarrass a mistaken opponent, thereby gaining some victory for oneself; rather, the purpose is to help the opponent overcome his wrong view. The real meaning of debate, its true significance, has three parts. The first lies in the refutation of mistaken conceptions or invalid reasoning. It is the nature of things that mistaken conceptions are prevalent; so, the first purpose for debate is to dispel wrong views. Such views are not to be given place. This is the predominant usage of debate, for usually the reasoning is used to overcome fallacies and misunderstandings.
>
> The second significance of debate is that of positing the correct view. Debate is not merely a means of refutation, but also serves to present the unmistaken. The third significance is that of clearing up uncertainties about the validity of the position which has been stated. If there is an apparent inconsistency in the correct view that was posited, then that must be resolved. This consists of being able to defend successfully one's own correct position from any possible inappropriate criticism. Formal debate has these three aspects, and the subject of debate has these three areas.
>
> Primarily one uses debate to overcome the abundant misconceptions in one's own and other's thought. The most outstanding feature of non-Buddhist beliefs is the acceptance of an entity which is permanent in nature and yet an entity which performs a function. Such a view is radically unacceptable to the Buddhists. The Buddhists define a permanent phenomenon as something which exists but is not of an instantaneous nature. Such a phenomenon is not something which is created, abides, and disintegrates. It is not acceptable for a thing which performs a

function to be permanent. As a permanent phenomenon, it would have to be something which remained in existence for more than an instant. The basic criticism of the non-Buddhist view that there could be a permanent functioning thing is that if that creative principle produced all other phenomena, then it would have to have either produced the phenomena all at the same moment or at different moments. There is no third possibility. If they were all produced in the same moment, then they would by necessity have existed for all time in the same manner or they would have never come into being at all. But it is obvious from experience that phenomena do exist and that they have not always existed in the same way. If phenomena were produced at different moments, then the creator of phenomena would be something which performed one function in one instant and another function at another instant; therefore, the creator would be changing and impermanent. Thus, the Buddhists conclude that a phenomenon which is both permanent and functioning cannot exist.

A thing which performs a function must by its very nature exist at one time and not exist at another time. This is the way that impermanent phenomena are defined. They come into being when the causes which produce them converge and they disappear when those causes are no longer present. Just so, the imperfections of the mind, the afflictions, are said to be removed by virtue of the fact that the causes and conditions which produced them can be removed. Then those afflictions will likewise disappear. But this theory of cause and effect, fundamental to the Buddhists, is not held to be so by the non-Buddhists.

Corresponding to the fact that when one removes the causes of mental afflictions, those imperfections will be extinguished, is the Buddhist assertion that when the causes which bring about liberation arise, then that liberation will be attained. This too does not fit with the non-Buddhist systems.

Because the Buddhist positions do not accord with the non-Buddhist ones, the non-Buddhist traditions therefore deny some of these fundamental qualities of Buddhist philosophy. Some deny the relationship between actions and their effects. In a similar way, some deny the existence of past lives and future lives. These fundamental principles the Buddhists hold to be correct. Yet the non-Buddhists deny them; so, the Buddhists must take the fundamental principles of the non-Buddhist schools and show the fallacies which lie in them in order to be able to substantiate the validity of their own. If their fundamental principles do not apply to another system, either their principles are mistaken or those of the other system are mistaken. Thus, if the Buddhists are going to show that their principles are right, they must somehow show that the principles of others are mistaken.

If one opponent cannot point out how the other is mistaken, then he cannot force the other to give up that mistaken position which he holds to be correct. Unless he is able to do that, the mistaken opponent will be denied the correct view. This would obviously necessitate that he would not be able to achieve that higher consciousness which is not mistaken. Although non-Buddhist schools do assert some kind of liberation which is a deliverance from the helpless condition of cyclic existence, this is the only similarity with Buddhists on this point. Exactly what that liberation consists of and how it is actually attained differ quite radically between the two.

If the non-Buddhists' fundamental principles are mistaken, then their view of what liberation actually is must also be mistaken. Their conception of what the pursuit of liberation consists of will then be misconceived, and their method of attaining that liberation must likewise be mistaken. Therefore, if one should undertake to pursue such a path, the effort would not bring about the attainment of what is conceived to be liberation.

In this way, the most important point, the primary purpose for debate, is to establish the validity of the law of cause and effect. This is the first of many levels, and it is the most important. Why is this of such primal importance? If one considered actions and their fruits, causes and their effects, to have any permanent quality throughout them or if one believed that all things which exist are permanent in nature, then it would naturally follow that one would adhere to the existence of a permanent self. Such a concept of a permanent self denies that the individual as such will undergo any form of death or destruction. If one does not have a clear idea of how death represents the end of a particular individual, then one will lose sight of the idea of the reemergence of another individual subsequent to death. Therefore, it follows that one would not place any importance on how this particular life determines what manner of future lives will arise. This would also mean that one would not exert effort in any way to try to bring about a superior form of life in the future and to avoid the misery of taking an inferior form of life. Then one is at a point where one entertains no concern for what is of fundamental importance in a person's life.

Therefore, one of the first things that one must understand and appreciate is that one's state of being is something that is impermanent. What a person presently is has arisen in dependence on the aggregation of certain causes and conditions, and when those causes and conditions are exhausted, that person will no longer exist in the same manner.

In order to establish the impermanence of the self, one begins by positing the impermanence of external things. For example, the impermanence of sound is established. Sound is impermanent because of being a thing which is produced from causes and conditions. This is one of the starting points. It is one of the most fundamental subjects of Buddhist epistemology.

The means of being able to show the inconsistencies of wrong views and to establish the validity of correct ones was formulated by Dharmakīrti. Dharmakīrti is the most renowned of all Buddhist logicians. He wrote seven texts, three main and four lesser, which represent branches of the main texts. Buddha never taught a system of logic as such, but the logic which was devised by Dharmakīrti was based entirely on what Buddha said.[1]

THE MATURATION OF CONSCIOUSNESS

As evidenced above, the Ge-luk-bas present a path to liberation which invariably involves reasoning. All Buddhists agree that in order to stop the cycle of birth, aging, sickness, and death in which sentient beings suffer, one must defeat the foe of ignorance. Sentient beings have since beginningless time assented to normal appearances and conceptions and thereby been drawn into contaminated actions and afflictions which lead to suffering. Here, the Ge-luk-bas emphasize that the principal weapon to be used in the battle against ignorance is reasoning. Despite the fact that in this tradition they often put tremendous emphasis on an appeal to even blind faith, when they teach the Collected Topics, they ask the students to follow only reasoning. Here the Ge-luk-bas issue a resounding call to analysis.

The process of abandoning a wrong consciousness and developing an unmistaken realization may pass through seven stages:[2]

---

[1] Geshe Lobsang Tharchin, oral commentary trans. by Artemus B. Engle.
[2] The sources for this section on the maturation of consciousness are Tsong-ka-pa, *Tantra in Tibet*, pp. 189-191, and Lati Rinbochay, *Mind in Tibetan Buddhism*, pp. 25-28.

1 wrong view (*log rtog, mithyā-saṃkalpa*)[1]
2 doubt tending to the non-factual (*don mi 'gyur gyi the tshom*)
3 equal doubt (*cha mnyam pa'i the tshom*)
4 doubt tending to the factual (*don 'gyur gyi the tshom*)
5 correct assumption (*yid dpyod, *manaḥ-parīkṣha*)
6 inferential cognition (*rjes dpag, anumāna*)
7 direct perception (*mngon sum, pratyakṣha*).

Using the most profound example according to the Proponents of Sūtra Following Reasoning, one may begin with the wrong view that there is a self-sufficient or substantially existent person. This is the most important of all wrong views to be defeated. Although selflessness is not a specific subject of debate in the Tutor's *Collected Topics*, the points that are debated are important topics designed to lead one into the reasoning on selflessness.

A wrong consciousness (*log shes, viparyaya-jñāna*) is necessarily discordant with the fact. Such a consciousness cannot realize its object, and it is mistaken with respect to it. Wrong consciousnesses are either non-conceptual, such as seeing snow on a distant mountain as blue, or conceptual, such as conceiving the existence of a substantially existent self. Non-conceptual wrong consciousnesses are merely mistaken with regard to their objects of engagement (*'jug yul, *pravṛtti-viṣhaya*), such as seeing white snow as if it were blue. However, conceptual wrong consciousnesses are doubly mistaken, for they are mistaken with regard to their objects of engagement, such as conceiving a person as substantially existent whereas no such person exists, and they are also mistaken with regard to their appearing objects (*snang yul, *pratibhāsa-viṣhaya*) which in this case is an internal mental image of a substantially existent self. All conceptual consciousnesses, wrong and otherwise, are

---

[1] The source for the Sanskrit, here and throughout this work, for most terms associated with consciousness is Lati Rinbochay, *Mind in Tibetan Buddhism*.

necessarily mistaken in this way, for what appears to them is only an image which serves to represent what it understands but is not the actual object. In the example at hand, the ignorance conceiving a substantially existent self is a conceptual wrong consciousness. Initially, debate functions to defeat wrong conceptions. It is to be noted that thought in general is not what is to be refuted, only wrong thought. Moreover, according to the Ge-luk-bas, debate may also act to defeat all wrong consciousnesses, conceptual and non-conceptual. Only Buddhas are beyond all wrong consciousnesses; still, in so far as debate may be a cause of Buddhahood, it also serves to defeat all wrong consciousnesses, though initially the focus is on wrong conceptions.

Subsequently, through hearing teachings on the selflessness of the person, one might generate doubt about whether or not there is a substantially existent person. At first one would likely still feel that there probably is a substantially existent person, but the firmness of conviction is gone though one still bears a conception which is factually discordant. Through repeatedly taking to mind the teaching on selflessness, one then develops equal doubt thinking perhaps there is such a person and perhaps there is not. Subsequently, the doubt tilts toward the factual, thinking probably there is no substantially existent self. Still there is no firmness of conviction and although the view is factual it may be reversed.

On the basis of doubt tending to the factual and through the power of repeated familiarization with the logical establishment of selflessness, one then generates a correctly assuming consciousness. This is a consciousness having conviction in accordance with the fact, but lacking actual realization of what it believes. Although this correctly assuming consciousness arises through reasoning, it is not an inferential cognition. It is not unshakable and incontrovertible, though it is decisive. The method for maturing a correctly assuming consciousness to the level of an incontrovertible inferential cognition is only repeated familiarization with the reasoning on selflessness.

As the result of this repeated familiarization, one eventually generates an inferential cognition which realizes selflessness. Such knowledge is incontrovertible and unshakable. The difference between a correctly assuming consciousness and an inferential cognition is, in a sense, a difference of acuity or sharpness. An inferential cognizer knows its object with great keenness and conviction, to an extent lacking in a correctly assuming consciousness.

Within the Ge-luk-ba view, inferential cognition is a necessary component of the process establishing one in liberation, but it is not sufficient. As a conceptual consciousness, inference is still hampered to some degree, for it realizes its object only through the medium of an internal image. Thus, it is necessary to mature the consciousness even further to the point of direct perception which does not depend on the appearance of an internal image.

According to the Proponents of Sūtra Following Reasoning and all the Lesser Vehicle systems, ordinary beings cannot directly realize selflessness or any permanent phenomenon (*rtag pa, nitya*), although the Great Vehicle systems disagree with this assertion. Rather, according to the Proponents of Sūtra, what appears to a wisdom consciousness realizing selflessness and what it directly contacts are the mind and body, which are impermanent phenomena (*mi rtag pa, anitya*), *qualified* as lacking substantial existence. For this reason, "Some scholars make a distinction between 'directly realize' (*mngon sum du rtogs pa*) and 'realize by means of a direct perceiver' (*mngon sum gyis rtogs pa*)."[1] Thus, they say that there is direct realization of selflessness in that one may realize selflessness *by means of* a direct perceiver (for the correctly apprehending consciousness does not depend on the appearance of an internal image), but one does not directly realize selflessness

---

[1] Lati Rinbochay, *Mind in Tibetan Buddhism*, p. 124.

(for selflessness does not actually appear to the wisdom consciousness).

Direct perception observing selflessness is the actual antidote to ignorance. Through knowing the person's lack of being a substantially existent person one counters and destroys the possibility of the conception of such a person. If realization of selflessness by means of a direct perceiver is cultivated well, it is able to obliterate completely the conception of a substantially existent self. In that way, through empowering the consciousness to destroy the foe of ignorance—the root cause of cyclic existence, it enables one to gain liberation.

The process for transforming an inferential cognition of selflessness into a realization of selflessness by a direct perceiver involves repeatedly familiarizing with the appearance of selflessness in thought and meditation. Similar to the process by which a correctly assuming consciousness is brought into focus such that it is seen with the acuity of an inferential cognition, so an inferential cognition is developed so that the image is known more and more clearly until finally the knowledge gained through an internal image of selflessness is so clear that the need for an image is transcended. One then has a realization of selflessness by means of a direct perceiver apprehending the mind and body as empty of substantial existence. According to the Proponents of Sūtra, this mature consciousness is the effective destroyer of ignorance. Still, one must continue to cultivate the direct realization of selflessness in meditative practice, and as the knowledge of selflessness grows in strength, it is able to defeat the subtler stains on the mind until finally the mind is free of defilements. At this point one gains liberation.

"The process of passing from wrong views to the incontrovertible knowledge of cognition, be it inferential or direct, depends on study, analysis, meditation, and acquaintance with a spiritual guide."[1] In the Ge-luk-ba view, it is not possible to gain a direct perception of selflessness without all

---

[1] Tsong-ka-pa, *Tantra in Tibet*, p. 191.

four of these essentials. Before seeing selflessness by means of a direct perceiver one must first engage in the process of reasoning and analysis leading to an inferential cognition seeing selflessness in a general, representative way. Through continued effort and meditation this can be matured to the point of clarity such that one can see selflessness by means of a direct perceiver, not in a vague and general way, but just as it is. Equally essential to the process of maturing a consciousness is acquaintance with a spiritual guide or lama. Without someone to teach selflessness, there would be no hope of even maturing a consciousness from wrong view to doubt tending toward the non-factual. Buddha is revered as the one who reveals the doctrine. Ontologically, selflessness always exists as the nature of persons, but epistemologically one cannot understand it unless someone teaches it.

It is clear from this description of the maturation of the consciousness that, at least in the Ge-luk-ba interpretation, reasoning has an essential and irreplaceable place on the path to liberation. Even so, the Ge-luk-bas place a tremendous emphasis on devotion. When one visits a Ge-luk-ba monastery, one sees that the main activity there is prayer, not study and debate. Indeed, they identify the limits of reasoning, for even this essential component is to be transcended by the development of direct perception. Reasoning itself and the inference it produces are not the actual antidotes to cyclic existence. Only direct realization of selflessness is able to eradicate the foe of ignorance. Thus, in the attainment of liberation, reasoning is a necessary but not a sufficient component. The Ge-luk-ba interpretation of the place of reasoning accords with what the *Kāshyapa Chapter Sūtra* says:

> Kashyapa, it is this way: For example, fire arises when the wind rubs two branches together. Once the fire has arisen, the two branches are burned. Just so, Kashyapa, if you have the correct analytical intellect, a Superior's ['phags pa, ārya] faculty of wisdom is gen-

erated. Through its generation, the correct analytical
intellect is consumed.[1]

Inferential cognition overcomes wrong views, and eventually the need for thought is surpassed. The practitioner's
intellect becomes so imbued with the knowledge of selflessness that in time this mind transcends the need for a representative image and becomes mixed with it.

The Buddhists assert only two types of valid cognizers
(*tshad ma, pramāṇa*), inferential valid cognizers (*rjes dpag
tshad ma, anumāna-pramāṇa*), and direct valid cognizers
(*mngon sum tshad ma, pratyakṣha-pramāṇa*).[2] "Within
Buddhism, there is a threefold terminological division of
pramāṇa into persons such as Buddha, scriptures such as the
teaching of the four noble truths, and minds—direct perceivers and inferential cognizers."[3] However, from among
the three—valid persons, valid scriptures, and valid
minds—only the minds are actual valid cognizers; the
others are merely called that.

Valid cognizers, both direct and inferential, are distinguished among consciousnesses in that they are incontrovertible (*mi slu ba, avisaṃvādin*). In the seven stage maturation of a consciousness, only inferential cognition and direct
perception yield incontrovertible knowledge. Knowledge
gained by either of these two types of valid cognizers is
unassailable and irreversible.

---

[1] *Ibid.*, p. 192.

[2] Prof. M. Nagatomi of Harvard University reports that in its Sanskrit
original the term *pramāṇa*, translated here as "valid cognizer", refers to the
scales with which one weighs or measures commodities. Both the Sanskrit
and Tibetan terms suggest a measure, but I have never found anything in
the literature of this tradition which supports this etymology. Still, it is
interesting that both terms suggest this interpretation. Perhaps the terms
indicate a measuring or estimation, as a correct consciousness which
estimates and comprehends its object. In Kensur Yeshay Tupden's
opinion, *tshad ma* means "the measure of existence and non-existence"
(*yod med kyi tshad*), for valid cognizers know what does and what does not
exist.

[3] Lati Rinbochay, *Mind in Tibetan Buddhism*, p. 117.

Direct perception consists of the realization of an object by any of the five sense consciousnesses (*dbang shes, indriya-jñāna*), a self-knower (*rang rig, svasaṃvedana*), or a non-conceptual mental consciousness (*rtog med yid shes, nirvikalpaka-mano-jñāna*) including yogic direct perception (*rnal 'byor mngon sum, yogi-pratyakṣha*). An instance of direct perception is the direct realization of fire by an eye consciousness. Seeing fire, one has the knowledge of fire's existing there. Inference, on the other hand, consists of an incontrovertible conceptual cognition of a phenomenon (*chos, dharma*) generated in dependence on a correct logical sign (*rtags yang dag, *samyak-liṅga*). This is, for instance, the knowledge of (unseen) fire generated in dependence on seeing billowing smoke.

There are those who feel that the serious pursuit of religion must involve the suicide of the intellect. Indeed, it is asserted that a Buddha is beyond all conception, totally without thought. On the basis of this, some may say that the way to the distant shore of liberation must be by severing all thought. However, in the Ge-luk-ba understanding, the raft that is able to carry one to the other shore (direct perception) must first be built on the shore of conceptuality and reasoning. To take the abandonment of conceptuality and reasoning as one's first goal is to destroy all hope of gaining one's goal. Nonetheless, some argue that white clouds (correct thoughts) and black clouds (wrong thoughts) both block the sun and the path to liberation is thus the removal of all conception.[1] The Ge-luk-bas deny that the removal of conception is the path, although they accept this as a fruit of the path. Rather, as indicated in the seven-stage maturation of consciousness and the passage in the *Kāshyapa Chapter Sūtra*, conceptuality is eventually consumed only by the path of reasoning and analysis. Thus, the Ge-luk-bas conclude that

---

[1] Ārya Maitreya, *The Sublime Science (Uttaratantra)* trans. by E. Obermiller, "The Sublime Science of the Great Vehicle to Salvation, being a Manual of Buddhist Monism". *Acta Orientalia*, vol. IX (1931), see especially Chapter 2, verses 3-7, pp. 242-244.

reasoning is an essential religious practice, necessary for the abandonment of suffering and the attainment of happiness.

Further, in noting that inferential cognition must be transcended, the Ge-luk-bas present a view that reasoning is not self-originating, self-sustaining, or self-complete. Rather, reasoning is presented as a route to something else—to liberation. Debate and the art of reasoning are not practiced in Ge-luk-ba monasteries as ends in themselves. The purpose for debate is, in the deepest sense, only for the sake of establishing sentient beings in liberation free from the round of suffering. Some may feel that the Ge-luk-bas, caught up in intellectual pursuits, are blind to the passion of religious pursuits. This might be valid criticism if the Ge-luk-bas saw intellectual pursuit as an end in itself. However, in debate, passion and intellect are unified in the battle against the causes of suffering.

COURSE OF STUDY

The mode of procedure in Tibetan monastic debate involves judging the capacity of one's opponent as well as the nature of that person's misunderstanding. The form of the reasoning, the purely logical aspect, is not complicated (except for the treatment of the subject-predicate relationship as will be discussed at length in this work). Monastic debate is a matter of learning a few basic, solidly established forms of reasoning and then taking that knowledge and applying it to many different subjects. This vigorous application sharpens one's intellect and increases the capacity for understanding.

The monks practicing debate study within a well developed system beginning with basic logic and working up to the great texts of India, both the sūtras and commentaries but mostly the latter.[1] Monks studying in the colleges of the three great monasteries of the Ge-luk-ba order (Dre-bung,

---

[1] The sources for this section on the course of study leading to the degree of Ge-shay are Rabten pp. 37-38, Sopa pp. 41-43, and Lati Rinbochay, *Mind in Tibetan Buddhism*, p. 161.

Śe-ra, and Gan-den) work toward the degree of "Ge-shay". In order to attain this, one must pass through a rigorous program of studies consisting of fifteen or possibly sixteen classes, some lasting for two years each. Listed in order, these classes are arranged according to five quintessential topics:

1 Collected Topics of Valid Cognition (*bsdus grva*); [three classes—the Introductory, Middling, and Greater Paths of Reasoning]
2 Perfection of Wisdom (*shes rab kyi pha rol tu phyin pa, prajñā-pāramitā*); [five classes]
3 Middle Way (*dbu ma, madhyamaka*); [two classes]
4 Discipline (*'dul ba, vinaya*); [two classes]
5 *Treasury of Knowledge* (*chos mngon pa'i mdzod, abhidharmakosha*); [two classes]

Beyond these classes devoted to particular topics, there are two retainer classes, Ka-ram and Hla-ram, in which the monks engage in lengthy review prior to their examinations for the degree of Ge-shay.

The program of studies begins with instruction in basic logic, learning the way of reasoning introductory to study-ing the texts on valid cognition. "The major points of termi-nology, classification, and so forth are arranged by Tibetan scholars who have composed many books which are like keys to the door of entry into the treasury of the logical texts."[1] The preliminary study of logic is compared to the study of the alphabet and grammar in primary school which enable one to understand greater things later.[2]

> Logic is studied to train the mind in subtle reasoning, enabling later appreciation of the great scriptures. After developing his intelligence and discriminatory powers in this way, the monk is able to apply as many as twenty logical arguments to just one point of teaching. Like monkeys that can run freely in and out

---

[1] Sopa, p. 41.
[2] Rabten, p. 38.

through a dense forest, our minds must be very supple before we can comprehend the depth of the concepts presented in the texts. If our minds are rigid like the antlers of a deer ... we will never be able to reach to this depth.[1]

In Śe-ra Jay, for instance, the three classes on the Collected Topics of Valid Cognition last for three years. The five classes on the Perfection of Wisdom total five years. The six classes on the Middle Way, Discipline, and the *Treasury of Knowledge* last for two years each. This is a total of twenty years of study.

At the end of these fourteen classes one takes an examination to determine which of the four ranks of higher and lower Ge-shay titles one will compete for—corresponding to the grade of the examination. Depending upon the quality of one's studies one remains in the fifteenth, the lower class of completion called Ka-ram, or one is moved to the sixteenth and highest class called Hla-ram.

Having successfully passed this examination, the monks remain in one of the two classes while awaiting their turns for the Ge-shay disputation. Consequently, according to the size of the class there is a varying number of years of waiting for the final examination. The monks of the lower Ka-ram class arrange their disputations within the individual monasteries and are awarded the Ge-shay title by those monasteries. The monks of the higher Hla-ram classes of the three main Ge-luk-ba monasteries were traditionally examined together during the Great Prayer Festival (*smon lam chen mo*) held annually in Hla-śa at the beginning of the Tibetan New Year; each year sixteen become Hla-ram-ba Ge-shays. "Depending upon the quality of the examination, a numerical order of merit in the disputation—first, second, and so on is assigned by the Tibetan government."[2] Altogether, from the beginning study of logic through to the

---

[1] *Ibid.*
[2] Sopa, p. 43.

final Hla-ram-ba Ge-shay disputation the program of studies may take as long as thirty-five years.

THE DEBATERS

One obvious evidence of the religious intent of debate is that it is preserved and practiced in monasteries. Within the Geluk-ba monasteries, debate is the main intellectual focus. The educational process involves three major branches: (1) study with a learned elder using a text as a guide, (2) memorization and study of definitions, divisions, illustrations, and even whole texts on one's own, and (3) debate of the topics studied in the first two branches. From among these three, debate is often the most rigorous, and the learning gained in the other two branches is generally focused toward the practice of debate.

The predispositions for adhering to the conception of a substantially existent self are very strong and in order to defeat this foe of ignorance one's knowledge must be incontrovertible. The style and ambience of debate as well as the total atmosphere of the monastery are designed to help initiates in the battle against ignorance. Development of the wisdom realizing selflessness requires not only sharp intellect and sustained effort at reasoning but also the amassing of great virtue and subsequent empowerment of the mind. In this regard, all the monastic activities from early morning prayers through evening recitations, including debate, are aimed at gaining virtue. Like warriors preparing for battle, the monks train and develop their capacities in order to defeat the enemy of ignorance.[1] As evidenced by the number of years spent in the course of study leading to the Geshay degree, the study and practice of the Buddhist doctrine is a slow and gradual process which demands great courage and effort.

Having assumed the two hundred fifty-three vows of a Buddhist monk, according to the Sarvāstivādin discipline,

---

[1] Suggested by Rabten, p. 24.

the religious initiates live in an ordered environment designed to facilitate sincere study and practice of the Buddhist doctrine. As evidence of this design, even the monk's clothing is symbolically related to the abandonment of the first two truths, sufferings and origins, and the attainment of the latter two, cessations and paths. As one Tibetan scholar, Geshé Rabten of the Jay College of Śe-ra Monastic University, explains:

> Take, for instance, the monk's boots. They symbolize the three mental poisons and their eradication. These poisons are attachment, hatred, and confusion. The shape of the boots bears a resemblance to a rooster, a snake, and a pig. They have a curved-up tip symbolizing the snout of a pig; on both sides of each shoe are two bumps resembling the upper part of a rooster's wing; and the curve from the top to the tip of the boot is like the curve of a snake. Buddha spoke of these three animals as being symbolic of the three mental poisons. The pig stands for confusion, the rooster for attachment, and the snake for hatred. He declared that all suffering in the world arises in dependence upon these mental distortions. The monk wears them on his feet, symbolizing his suppression of the poisons and is thus reminded always to avoid them.
>
> The boots themselves, aside from their symbolic significance, are neither comfortable nor stylish. In fact, when first seeing them, one is likely to think they are the boots of a barbarian. The reason for their unattractiveness is to counteract attachment for them. Most harmful actions are due to attachment; so there is a great need to prevent its arisal.
>
> Buddha commanded his ordained followers to wear their skirt-like lower garment; for when a monk puts it on, it reminds him of his vows and the duties resulting from his ordination. ... The way it is worn also symbolizes the four realities of realized beings. On the right side are two folds facing outwards,

symbolizing the two realities to be abandoned; on the left two folds face inwards, and represent the two realities to be attained. The harmonious practice and unification of method and wisdom is needed in order to abandon the first two realities and to attain the other two; and this is symbolized by the two folds facing each other in front. Thus, this robe not only reminds the monk of his ordination; but also of the need to turn away from the first two realities, to follow the latter two, and to practice the method and wisdom aspects of the Dharma together.

One of the upper garments is the vest. Although not very attractive, it is important symbolically. For the success of one's Dharma practice, joyful effort is essential, and this is gained by developing an understanding of impermanence. In some of the scriptures, this effort is compared to a horse and understanding to a rider's whip. The vest symbolizes impermanence. On each side are two pointed streaks crossing each other by the armpit. These represent the fangs of the Lord of Death, and the middle of the vest his mouth. Thus we live between his jaws, liable to die at any moment.

Joyful effort by itself is not enough. We need to hear and contemplate the teachings, and then to meditate. The hat symbolizes the practice and results of these three activities. The subject to be heard is the teachings of the Buddha, the entire body of which may be classified in twelve groups. To symbolize these, there are twelve stitches sewn in the handle of the hat. These twelve groups are more simply known as the three vessels of teaching [*sde snod gsum, tripiṭaka*]. They are represented by three blue tassels hanging down from the handle. Thus, when one picks up the hat, one is reminded of the subjects that are to be learned. When wearing it, the handle is folded inside, and when carrying it, is left outside. The outside is yellow, the inside white, and the rest of the lining is blue. The yellow, white, and blue colours symbolize wisdom, compassion, and power. When seeing them, one recalls these three qualities and meditates on them. They also stand for Mañjuśrī, Avalokiteśvara, and Vajrapāni, who embody the Buddha's wisdom, compassion, and power. By relying on these three divine beings, we receive a special power to develop their three virtues. The thousands of threads streaming out from the top of the hat represent the full development of wisdom, compassion, and power—the attainment of buddhahood. They also serve to remind us of the thousand buddhas of this fortunate eon. Because these are symbols of the ultimate refuge to which we entrust ourselves, they are worn on the highest part of the body—the top of the head. When the monk has the proper motivation and understanding of the significance of his garments, they constantly remind him and act as his teachers. ...

Some people may think that a monk's spiritual practice primarily concerns the proper use of these articles of clothing. But this is not so. What is most important is that his attitude, mindfulness, and way of life be in accordance with the meaning of the symbols. When a monk takes notice of these clothes, he is reminded of his monkhood and the teachings of the Buddha. ... In books many illustrations are given to aid understanding; but they will appear to be meaningless if their significance is not known. The same is true for the monk's garments. ...

When a monk first comes to the monastery, he does not know what these symbols mean; so every few weeks, at the beginning of a debating session, the disciplinarian of the college explains them, so that all know their meaning. Most of a monk's belongings are designed to aid him in dispelling his faults, and in cultivating noble qualities.[1]

---

[1] Rabten, pp. 14-19, 24.

As Geshé Rabten indicates, the monk's environment is designed to facilitate sincere study and practice of the Buddhist doctrine. The mere wish to learn is not adequate, for one needs effort sustained over many years. The symbolic meaning of the monk's clothing serves to enhance the development of sustained effort and constantly remind the monk of his situation and purposes, increasing his mindfulness and awareness and aiding his motivation.

An actual session of debate involves two people, a Defender (*dam bca' ba*) or "one [defending] a thesis" who sits and gives answers to the Challenger (*rigs lam pa*) or "one with the path of reasoning" who stands and asks questions. The Defender puts forth assertions for which he is held accountable. The Challenger raises qualms to the Defender's assertions and is not subject to reprisal for the questions he raises. The debates usually take place outside in winter as well as in summer. The daily schedule of the monasteries re-established in India include two hours of debate in the morning and two hours in the evening after dinner, although advanced classes may extend these sessions.[1]

The disputants come to the debating courtyard (*chos ra*) with no aid but their own understanding. One does not peruse books at the time of debating, and books may not be brought to the debating courtyard. There is a joke among debaters that if one has studied a topic and knows where to find the information in a text or in one's notes but is not able to explain it, then such a person "has his learning in a box" (where the books are stored). Rather, the debaters must depend on their memorization of the points of doctrine— definitions, divisions, illustrations, and even whole texts— together with their own measure of understanding gained from instruction and study.

At the opening of a session of debate, the standing Challenger claps his hands together and recites the seed syllable of Mañjushrī, "*Dhīḥ*". Mañjushrī is the manifestation of the wisdom of all the Buddhas and as such is the special

---

[1] See Rabten, especially pp. 50ff.

deity of debate. In debate, one must have a good motivation, the best of which is to conceive the special motivation of the Great Vehicle, the thought to establish all sentient beings in liberation. "But to fulfill this wish is not easy. You must have great knowledge and wisdom; and for this you recite *'dhīḥ'*, asking Mañjuśrī to pour down a torrent of wisdom upon you. ... The seed syllable *'dhīḥ'* has a very special effect upon Mañjuśrī."[1] Together with the seed syllable of Mañjushrī the Challenger begins the debate with the statement, "*Dhīḥ*! The subject, in just the way [Mañjushrī debated] (*dhīḥ ji ltar chos can*)." According to Denma Lochö Rinbochay, the meaning of this statement is: "Just as Mañjushrī stated subjects in order to overcome the wrong views and doubts of opponents, so I with a good mind will do also."[2]

Upon first seeing a debate, the most striking characteristic is the hand gestures. When the Challenger first puts his question to the sitting Defender, his right hand is held above the shoulder at the level of his head and the left hand is stretched forward with the palm turned upward (see Illustration I). At the end of his statement the Challenger punctuates by loudly clapping together his hands and simultaneously stomping his left foot. Then he immediately draws back his right hand with the palm held upward and at the same time holds forth his left hand with the palm turned downward. This motion of drawing back and clapping is done not in two sharp movements, but with the flow of a dancer's movements.

Holding forth the left hand after clapping symbolizes closing the door to rebirth in the helpless state of cyclic existence. The drawing back and upraising of the right hand symbolizes one's will to raise all sentient beings up out of cyclic existence and to establish them in the omniscience of Buddhahood. The left hand represents wisdom which alone is able to overcome powerless cyclic existence, for the wis-

---

[1] Rabten, pp. 40-41.
[2] Denma Lochö Rinbochay, oral commentary.

dom cognizing selflessness is the actual antidote to cyclic existence. The right hand represents method which for the Great Vehicle is the altruistic intention to become enlightened, called the "mind of enlightenment (*byang chub kyi sems, bodhi-chitta*)", motivated by great love and compassion for all sentient beings. The clap represents a union of method and wisdom. In dependence on the union of method and wisdom one is able to attain the auspicious rank of a Buddha.[1]

It might seem to an observer that the monks debating are perhaps angry with each other, for they speak loudly with confidence, clap their hands with fervor, and occasionally (when a wrong answer is given) scold and mock the opponent. However, this is normal procedure in debate and does not necessarily suggest anger. Since the generation of final wisdom is not easy and one must be strong, the debaters assert firmly their learning, seeking to become solid in their knowledge. Indeed, even when the Defender gives consistent answers in accordance with accepted interpretation, the Challenger will draw on his powers of persuasion and skill in debate to trick, test, and befuddle his opponent. This sort of procedure may seem devious, but if the purpose for debate is to generate knowledge in one's own continuum, then that knowledge must be firm and sure. If a Defender can be coerced away from a correct position by a clever Challenger, then his understanding is not solid.

Further, there is a strong tradition in debate of leaving a confused Defender to figure out on his own just what the correct position is. That is, very often the Challenger will leave the Defender with the question and show him his inconsistencies, but he will not sit down and explain the answers to him. This is sometimes because of the emphasis on making one's own understanding and sometimes because the Challenger himself does not know the answer

---

[1] Lati Rinbochay, oral commentary. The union of wisdom and method represented by a pressing together of the palms has to do with subtle wind channels of wisdom in the wrists which meet when the debater claps his hands together.

but is able to express the problem. The Challenger's role is often the easier one, for seeing apparent inconsistencies in others' positions may be accomplished without a firm understanding of the topic. However, the Defender must be able to put forth the correct position and, holding it firmly, defend it against the attacks of the Challenger. As evidence of this, one proceeds through the normal program of studies, passing from one class to the next, by taking examinations in the role of Defender before the assembled community. One must be able to set forth a correct view and hold it against objections in order to demonstrate knowledge of a topic and readiness to pass to the next level. When one is being examined before passing to a higher class, anyone capable in debate, not just one's classmates, may challenge the candidate on topics in the class just completed. When one sits for the final examination in candidacy for the ge-shay degree, anyone—from the newest novice to the most learned scholar—may challenge the examinee on any topic covered in the entire program of studies.

The emphasis on learning to hold a position against the assertions of others does not mean that the monks are learning precisely the same things. Nor does it mean that they are learning an accepted dogma which is to be defended against all possible objections. Rather, debate is an intense and imaginative critical analysis. In debate one learns to make one's own conclusions and to check one's own and other's assertions for sense. Of course, there is guidance for an interpretation of the material. The debaters rely on the great texts and commentaries of India, the works accepted by their own colleges, and oral instruction from their own teachers, but ultimately the understanding is only one's own. Debate is not a matter of mere rote repetition of former disputes, but an active intellectual exercise.

If debate were just repetition, then the disputants would not be able to muster a great deal of enthusiasm for the progress of the debate, for the outcome would be known beforehand. However, debates frequently become very heated.

Often when one Challenger is unable to shake a Defender from his position, another debater will push the first aside and pursue his own line of reasoning with the Defender. If the first Challenger is particularly intent on the debate, he may push back and indeed many debates have degenerated into brawls. Even long after the studies are completed the same sort of enthusiasm for debate will remain. Often when discussing a topic of debate, an old ge-shay's eyes will light up and he will again become animated.

Passive acceptance and lackluster performance are totally anathema to the Tibetan tradition of debate. "In their culture aggressive competition is a value as it has been in the culture of their forefathers before the advent of Buddhism. It should therefore be pointed out that monastic debate is not a marginal phenomenon in Tibetan culture, but part of the cultural focus."[1] Students are exhorted to debate with strength and intensity. Also, the cadence of debate aids the intensity with which it is pursued, for both the Challenger and the Defender are to respond immediately with respectively either a new question/consequence or an answer. If the Defender delays in his response, the Challenger quickly demands an answer. Hesitation on either part is a failure of reasoning.

Tibetan monastic debate is both physically and verbally aggressive. This assertiveness as well as the procedure and tradition of debate are all aimed at increasing the disputants' capacities, better enabling them to make progress toward the goal of liberation. The defilements that stain the mind have been accumulated over countless eons, and if they are to be removed it must be by the most intense and definite knowledge. The environment of the monastery and the technique of debate, complete with its trappings of verbal combat, are aimed at the development of this intense and definite knowledge which is able to destroy the enemy, ignorance.

---

[1] K. Sierksma, "Rtsod-pa: The Monachal Disputation in Tibet", *Indo-Iranian Journal*, Vol. 8 (1964), no. 2, p. 141.

2 Syllogisms and Consequences

In this system of reasoning, two forms of argument are used to defeat wrong conceptions and generate clear understanding. These are syllogisms (*prayoga*), consisting of a thesis and a reason stated together in a single sentence, and consequences (*thal 'gyur, prasaṅga*), an argument structurally similar to a syllogism but containing a word indicating a logical outflow of an opponent's own assertions (*thal, prasajyate*).[1] The Proponents of Sūtra Following Reasoning say that an inferential cognizer must be generated in dependence on a syllogism. In contrast to this view, the Consequence School (*thal 'gyur ba, prāsaṅgika*), the system predominantly accepted within Tibetan Buddhism as the highest, asserts that "although those of dull faculties can generate an inference only in dependence on a correct sign, those of sharpest faculties can generate one merely in dependence on a consequence".[2]

A valid argument may take the form of either a syllogism or a consequence. However, an argument that is valid as a

---

[1] The source for the Sanskrit terms provided in this chapter is Katherine Rogers, *Tibetan Logic*.

[2] Lati Rinbochay, *Mind in Tibetan Buddhism*, p. 75.

consequence is not necessarily valid if straightforwardly reformulated as a syllogism, for the argument forms reflect different approaches. Moreover, syllogisms and consequences are not valid arguments in the sense of being valid by all interpretations. Rather, here an argument is determined to be valid only in relation to certain persons at certain times. Further, an argument is not determined to be valid merely by its form, for validity is inextricably linked with the possibility of epistemological verification of that argument. Thus, a "logical" argument is determined to be valid only in a certain restricted sense. The limits of validity will be explained.

SYLLOGISMS

Although the text translated here mainly uses consequences, they are best approached through understanding syllogisms; thus, let us consider the latter first. The form of a syllogism generally used in the Ge-luk-ba literature consists of a thesis and a reason, both what is to be proven and the proof, in one sentence. Thus, the appellation "syllogism" is used here not in the sense of a series of sentences consisting of the premises and a conclusion, but in the sense of a deductive argument form. For example, a syllogism is stated:

> The subject, sound, is an impermanent phenomenon because of being a product (*sgra chos can mi rtag pa yin te byas pa yin pa'i phyir*).

The thesis (*dam bca'*, *pratijñā*) or what is to be proven (*bsgrub bya*, *sādhya*), sound is an impermanent phenomenon, is framed: the subject, sound, is an impermanent phenomenon. The reason (*gtan tshigs*, *hetu*) or proof (*sgrub byed*, *sādhana*), product, is framed: because of being a product. Although the form of syllogism used in the Collected Topics tradition is contained in a single sentence, this argument form is a condensation of a multi-sentence form in the works of

Dignāga and Dharmakīrti.[1] Consequently, this terse argument form implies a series of premises and a conclusion which form a more recognizable syllogistic form, as will be shown.

THE ELEMENTS OF A SYLLOGISM

The series of sentences implied by this terse form of syllogism is predicated by cross-relating the three basic units of a syllogism. These three are the subject (*chos can, dharmin*), the predicate to be proven (*bsgrub bya'i chos, sādhya-dharma*), and the sign (*rtags, liṅga*). In the sample syllogism:

> The subject, sound, is an impermanent phenomenon because of being a product

the subject is *sound*, the predicate to be proven (or predicate of the probandum) is *impermanent phenomenon*, and the sign (mutually inclusive with reason) is *product*. Anything, be it existent or non-existent, is suitable to be stated as a subject, predicate to be proven, or sign.

The fifth and final major section of the Tutor's *Collected Topics* is the book-length presentation of "Signs and Reasonings" (*rtags rigs*) in which the nature and types of reasons, valid and invalid, are systematically explained.[2] There are many such presentations of Signs and Reasonings within the Ge-luk-ba literature. One of these, a text used by the Lo-sel-ling College of Dre-bung Monastic University, is the *Presentation of Signs and Reasonings, A Mirror Illuminating All Phenomena* (*rtags rigs kyi rnam bzhag chos kun gsal ba'i me long*) by Mi-nyak Ge-shay Tsul-trim-ñam-gyel (*mi nyag dge bshes tshul khrims rnam rgyal*). A rigorous presentation of signs and reasonings is beyond the scope of this work, but by relying on Ge-shay Tsul-trim-ñam-gyel's text to illuminate some of the important points of this presentation, the

---

[1] See Jeffrey Hopkins, *Meditation on Emptiness* (London: Wisdom Publications, 1983), pp. 729-733.

[2] See Katherine Rogers' *Tibetan Logic* for a complete translation of the Tutor's "Signs and Reasonings" together with commentary.

essential form of syllogism used in the Collected Topics tradition can be understood.

The subject is the basis with respect to which one is seeking to learn something. According to the text, a proper subject (*chos can, dharmin*) of a syllogism, also known as a basis of debate (*rtsod gzhi*) or a basis of inference (*dpag gzhi*), must meet two requirements, one formal and one epistemological.[1] First, the subject must be held as a basis of debate in a syllogism as sound is held as the subject in the proof of sound as an impermanent phenomenon. In other words, a subject must occupy the first position in a syllogism. Second, as in the sample syllogism, there must be a person who has ascertained that sound is a product and is engaged in wanting to know whether or not it is an impermanent phenomenon. That a person has understood that sound is a product indicates that he or she is already involved in the reasoning process. That the person is now seeking to determine whether or not sound is an impermanent phenomenon indicates that the reasoning process is not complete, for the person is still seeking to learn something about the basis of inference, sound.

From this epistemological requirement one can understand that the form of syllogism used in this system is not valid in the sense of being valid for all persons. There must be a person who, within having certain knowledge, is seeking to know something that was not formerly known. Thus, although formally solid, the sample syllogism is not asserted to be valid in all contexts. For instance, it is not valid for a person who is unable to understand. Nor is it valid for a Buddha or anyone else who has already completed the understanding and has not forgotten it. Neither the unprepared person nor one who has already realized this is seek-

---

[1] Mi-nyak Ge-shay Tsul-trim-ñam-gyel (*mi nyag dge bshes tshul khrims rnam rgyal*), *The Presentation of Signs and Reasonings, A Mirror Illuminating All Phenomena* (*rtags rigs kyi rnam bzhag chos kun gsal ba'i me long*) of *The First Magical Key Opening a Hundred Doors to the Path of Reasoning* (*rigs lam sgo brgya 'byed pa'i 'phrul gyi lde mig dang po*), (Mundgod, India: Drepung Loseling Library, 1979), pp. 32-33.

ing to know whether or not sound is an impermanent phenomenon.

In the sample syllogism sound is the subject about which something is sought to be known; what one is seeking to know is whether or not sound is an impermanent phenomenon. In this syllogism, *impermanent phenomenon* is the predicate to be proven with respect to the basis of inference, sound. Thus, the thesis of the sample syllogism, that which is to be proven (*bsgrub bya, sādhya*), is *that sound is an impermanent phenomenon*. Anything may be stated as a predicate to be proven. For instance, one might state a proof of sound as a permanent phenomenon (*rtag pa, nitya*). This does not imply that one can prove sound as being anything, but that one can *state* anything as a predicate to be proven of sound.

In the proof of sound as an impermanent phenomenon, that which is to be negated (*dgag bya, pratiṣhedhya*) is *that sound is a permanent phenomenon*. This is the opposite of the thesis, that sound is an impermanent phenomenon. The predicate to be negated (*dgag bya'i chos, *pratiṣhedhya-dharma*) is *permanent phenomenon*, the opposite of the predicate to be proven. Being a permanent phenomenon is to be negated with respect to the basis of inference, sound. In explicitly proving that sound is an impermanent phenomenon, one implicitly proves that it is not a permanent phenomenon.

In the sample syllogism, the sign or reason is *product*. The thesis, sound is an impermanent phenomenon, is justified by the reason, product. Sign (*rtags, liṅga*) is mutually inclusive with reason (*gtan tshigs, hetu*) and proof (*sgrub byed, sādhana*). Anything may be put as a sign, although it may or may not be a valid reason. In the proof of sound as an impermanent phenomenon by the sign, product, it is product alone which is put as the sign.

Although one may state anything as the sign in the proof of sound as an impermanent phenomenon, only some reasons will justify the thesis ontologically. Moreover, certain epistemological requirements must be satisfied in order for a reason to be correct.

CORRECT SIGNS

Signs are of two types: correct signs (*rtags yang dag*, *samyak-linga*) and counterfeit signs (*rtags ltar snang*, *linga-ābhāsa*). These are valid and invalid reasons. The definition of a correct sign is:

> that which is the three modes.[1]

The three modes (*tshul gsum*, *trirūpa*) are three criteria that a correct sign must satisfy. These are its being:

1 the property of the subject (*phyogs chos*, *pakṣha-dharma*)
2 the forward pervasion (*rjes khyab*, *anvaya-vyāpti*)
3 the counter-pervasion (*ldog khyab*, *vyatireka-vyāpti*).[2]

An example of a correct sign is *product* in the syllogism:

> The subject, sound, is an impermanent phenomenon because of being a product.

Here product is the three modes, for it is the property of the subject, the forward pervasion, and the counter-pervasion. A correct sign is not something which has the three modes, but it *is* the three modes. The definition of the correct sign in the proof of sound as an impermanent phenomenon by the sign, product, is:

> that which is the three modes in the proof of sound as an impermanent phenomenon by the sign, product.[3]

This is not a definition of product but a definition of the correct sign in the proof of sound as an impermanent phenomenon by the sign, product. Product alone is the correct sign in this proof, but product as such is not what is being defined. There are definitions of each of the three modes in the proof of sound as an impermanent phenomenon.

---

[1] *Ibid.*, p. 36.
[2] *Ibid.*
[3] *Ibid.*

The Property of the Subject

The property of the subject, or the presence of the sign in the subject, requires that the subject must have the quality of the reason. In a proof such as this, the subject and the sign must be such that it is accurate to state them together in a copulative sentence, a sentence of the form, "That subject is that sign." For instance, sound and product are like this, for it is accurate to say that sound is a product. Sound is a product in that it is produced from causes and conditions. It does not arise adventitiously.

The definition of something's being the property of the subject in the proof of sound as an impermanent phenomenon is:

> that which is ascertained (by a person for whom it has become the property of the subject in the proof of sound as an impermanent phenomenon) as just existing, in accordance with the mode of statement, with sound.[1]

Product is the property of the subject in the proof of sound as an impermanent phenomenon by the sign, product, because product is ascertained (by a person for whom product has become the property of the subject in the proof of sound as an impermanent phenomenon by the sign, product) as just existing, in accordance with the mode of statement, with sound. The property of the subject is reckoned between the sign and its basis of relation (*ltos gzhi*), the subject. Thus, although technically only the sign, product, is the property of the subject in the sample syllogism, the first mode of the correct sign in this syllogism is *formulated*: sound is a product.

Reflecting this formulation, the definition specifies the association between the sign and the subject saying that the property of the subject must be "ascertained as just existing,

---

[1] *Ibid.*

in accordance with the mode of statement, with sound". The mode of statement (*'god tshul*) in the proof of sound as an impermanent phenomenon by the sign, product, is an "is" (*yin*) or copulative statement. The reason is framed, "because of *being* a product". Thus, the reason is saying something about the manner of being of sound. Sound *is* a product. This type of statement is to be distinguished from "exists" (*yod*) statements, reasons that justify the existence of something by the sign. For example, in the syllogism:

> The subject, on that mountain pass, there is fire because there is smoke,

the mode of statement is existential. The reason is stated in a manner to prove the existence or presence of one thing, fire, by the existence of another, smoke. This is not the same as saying, as implied by the definition, that the sign must *exist with* the subject. For example, in the proof of sound as an impermanent phenomenon by the sign, product, product exists with sound in accordance with the mode of statement, for sound has the quality of *being* a product.[1]

Also, the definition specifies that in order for something to be the property of the subject in the proof of sound as an impermanent phenomenon it must be ascertained by a person for whom it has become the property of the subject in the proof of sound as an impermanent phenomenon. A reason is not correct, it does not meet even the first requirement of a correct sign, unless it is ascertained by a certifying consciousness. In this system a syllogism cannot be valid merely by its form.

The heart of this definition is that the property of the subject is *ascertained as just existing* with sound.[2] The specification that the sign must be *ascertained* with sound serves to eliminate an indefinite understanding. Product is not the property of the subject in the proof of sound as an impermanent phenomenon either for a person who is wondering

---

[1] See Katherine Rogers, pp. 43ff.
[2] See Mi-nyak Ge-shay Tsul-trim-ñam-gyel, pp. 36-38.

whether or not sound is a product or a person who firmly holds that sound is not a product. The person must ascertain definitely that sound is a product. Again, it is emphasized that the validity of an argument is bound with the epistemological verification of that sign. A sign is the property of the subject only in relation to individual persons. The requirement that the sign must *exist* with the subject insures that the sign is a property of the subject, as productness is a property of sound. In saying that the property of the subject is ascertained as *just existing* with the subject, the definition insures that the sign must exist with the subject, though not exclusively with the subject. That is, the sign must actually be a property of the subject, as sound has the property of being a product. Yet, in order to be the property of the subject, the sign need not exist exclusively with the subject but may apply to other things as well. Not only sound is a product, for other phenomena such as chairs, tables, and so forth are products as well.

In summary, product is the property of the subject in the proof of sound as an impermanent phenomenon by the sign, product, because of being ascertained (by a person for whom it has become the property of the subject in the proof of sound as an impermanent phenomenon by the sign, product) as just existing, in accordance with the mode of statement, with sound. The property of the subject in this syllogism is formulated: sound is a product. However, whatever is a property of sound is not necessarily suitable as a correct sign in the proof of sound as an impermanent phenomenon because of the epistemological reasons given above concerning the person for whom the syllogism is stated and because of the requirements of the other two modes of a correct sign, the forward and counter-pervasions.

Forward Pervasion

Whereas the property of the subject is predicated between the sign and the subject, the pervasions are predicated between the sign and the predicate to be proven, the predicate of the thesis. More technically, in the case of the forward pervasion (*rjes khyab, anvaya-vyāpti*), it is a relationship between the sign and the similar class (*mthun phyogs, sapakṣha*). The similar class is the basis of relation (*ltos gzhi*) of the forward pervasion just as the subject is the basis of relation of the property of the subject.

In the proof of sound as an impermanent phenomenon, the class of impermanent phenomena is the similar class. The definition of the similar class in the proof of sound as an impermanent phenomenon is:

> that which is not empty of impermanence, in accordance with the mode of proof, in the proof of sound as an impermanent phenomenon.[1]

Anything which is an impermanent phenomenon is a member of the similar class in the proof of sound as an impermanent phenomenon. The mode of proof referred to here is the copulative mode, for the sample syllogism seeks to show that sound *is* an impermanent phenomenon, as opposed to the "exists" or existential mode of proof. Thus, in accordance with the mode of proof, all things which *are* "not empty of impermanence" (i.e., *are* impermanent phenomenon) are members of the similar class—matter, consciousness, and so forth.[2]

The sign's being the forward pervasion in the proof of something refers to its relating to the similar class in a certain way. For instance, the definition of something's being the forward pervasion in the proof of sound as an impermanent phenomenon is:

> that which is ascertained (by a person for whom it has become the second mode of the sign in the proof of sound as an impermanent phenomenon) as existing in

---

[1] Mi-nyak Ge-shay Tsul-trim-ñam-gyel, p. 33.
[2] For more information see Katherine Rogers, pp. 43ff.

only the similar class in the proof of sound as an impermanent phenomenon.[1]

In order for a sign to be the forward pervasion it must exist in only the similar class. In the sample syllogism, this means that product must exist only among impermanent phenomena. According to the tenets of the Proponents of Sūtra Following Reasoning, this is so, for "productness" exists only in impermanent phenomena. There are no products which are not impermanent phenomena.

The heart of the definition of forward pervasion is that the sign is *ascertained as existing in only* the similar class.[2] The requirement of ascertainment serves to eliminate a dubious cognition. The sign is the forward pervasion only for a person who realizes definitely that the sign exists only among members of the similar class. Again epistemological verification is required as a component of validity.

That the sign must *exist* in the similar class serves to eliminate contradictory reasons (*'gal ba'i gtan tshigs, viruddha-hetu*) as in the syllogism:

> The subject, sound, is a permanent phenomenon because of being a product.

Here the sign, product, does not exist in the similar class of permanent phenomena, for it exists only in the dissimilar class (*mi mthun phyogs, vipakṣa*) of impermanent phenomena. If being the property of the subject were the only requirement of a correct sign, then the foregoing syllogism would be a correct proof of sound as a permanent phenomenon. However, since a correct sign must be the forward pervasion and the forward pervasion requires that the sign must *exist* in the similar class, this syllogism is not valid.

Moreover, a correct sign must exist in *only* the similar class and cannot be present in the dissimilar class. The dissimilar class in the proof of sound as an impermanent phe-

---

[1] Mi-nyak Ge-shay Tsul-trim-ñam-gyel, p. 38.
[2] *Ibid.*, pp. 38-40.

nomenon includes the class of permanent phenomena. The requirement in the definition of forward pervasion that the sign must exist in *only* the similar class serves to eliminate indefinite reasons (*ma nges pa'i gtan tshigs, anaikāntika-hetu*) as in the syllogism:

> The subject, sound, is an impermanent phenomenon because of being an existent.

Here the reason, existent (*yod pa, sat*), exists not only in the similar class of impermanent phenomena but also in the dissimilar class of permanent phenomena, for both permanent and impermanent phenomena equally exist. Thus, in the definition of forward pervasion, the word "only" functions in the sense of "exclusively", for it entails that the sign must exist *exclusively* in the similar class.

However, although the sign must exist exclusively in the similar class, the definition does not specify that the similar class must exist exclusively in the sign. Rather, there are two types of correct signs in this regard: (1) those such that the sign and the similar class are equal in extent and (2) those such that the similar class is greater in extent than the sign.[1] In the sample syllogism:

> The subject, sound, is an impermanent phenomenon because of being a product,

the sign and the similar class are equal in extent. All products are impermanent phenomena and all impermanent phenomena are products. There is nothing which is the one but not the other. However, in the syllogism:

> The subject, sound, is an impermanent phenomenon because of being an object of hearing,

the similar class is greater in extent than the sign. There are impermanent phenomena such as consciousnesses which are not objects of hearing. The definition requires that the sign exist *exclusively but not necessarily universally* in the simi-

---

[1] See Katherine Rogers, pp. 142-143.

lar class. The extent of the sign may be equal to or lesser than the similar class, but it cannot be greater. Consequently, the extent of the similar class may be equal to or greater than that of the sign, but it cannot be less.

"Pervasion" means that the reason is *pervaded* by the predicate to be proven. The extent of the reason is either less than or equivalent to the extent of the predicate to be proven. In general, if the subject has the quality of being that sign and whatever is that sign is that predicate to be proven, then the subject must have the predicate to be proven. Applied to the sample syllogism, sound is a product and whatever is a product is an impermanent phenomenon; thus, sound is an impermanent phenomenon. In a valid syllogism, the *sign* is the *pervaded* (*khyab bya*), for its extent is less than or equal to the extent of the predicate to be proven which pervades it, and it is the *proof* (*sgrub byed*), for the sign proves the thesis. Conversely, in such a syllogism, the *predicate to be proven* is the *pervader* (*khyab byed*), for its extent is greater than or equal to the extent of the sign which is pervaded by it, and it is the *proven* (*bsgrub bya*), for the reason proves it as a predicate of the subject.

In this system of translation pervasion statements are generally formulated: whatever is that reason is necessarily that predicate to be proven. For example, the forward pervasion of the sample syllogism is formulated: whatever is a product is necessarily an impermanent phenomenon. Translated more literally, the general formula would be rendered: if something is that sign, then it is *pervaded* by being that predicate to be proven. If this is applied to the sample syllogism, the pervasion is formulated literally: if something is a product, then it is pervaded by being an impermanent phenomenon. For all statements in which the mode of statement is copulative—an "is" statement—it is suitable to translate a statement of pervasion into the form of an English conditional sentence, a sentence of the form: if something is a p, then it is necessarily a q. This conditional form is often relied upon in the translation, though usually pervasions are translated in the form: whatever is a p is necessarily a q. For syllogisms in which the mode of statement is existential—an "exists" statement—the translation is always of the form: if a *p* exists, then a *q* necessarily exists.

It is important to understand the nature of pervasion as associative and not copulative.[1] Although the sign *exists* in only the similar class in the sense that whatever is the sign *is* such and such, this does not mean that the sign itself is that predicate (although it may be). More correctly, pervasion indicates that the sign is *associated* with that predicate. For instance, products exist exclusively among impermanent phenomena. Products and impermanent phenomena are inextricably, necessarily associated. If something is a product, it is necessarily impermanent. In this case, it is also true that since product itself is a product, it is also an impermanent phenomenon. That is, here it may be said that the sign, product, is an example of the predicate to be proven, impermanent phenomenon, in the sense that product *is* an impermanent phenomenon. However, as will be seen, there are many cases for which, although there is pervasion, it cannot be said that the particular sign *is* that predicate in the sense that the sign has the quality of, demonstrates the being of, and exemplifies that predicate. Pervasion does not mean that the sign *is* the predicate to be proven. Rather, the meaning of pervasion is that the predicate to be proven encompasses the sign and is invariably associated with it.

The procedure of translating statements of pervasion in sentences of the form, "Whatever is a *p* is necessarily a *q*," serves to express this nature of pervasion. In saying that whatever is a product is necessarily an impermanent phenomenon, the point of emphasis is not so much on product itself but on *those things which are* products. This statement of pervasion says that product is an impermanent phenomenon, since product is itself a product, in that it says that *everything which has the quality of being* a product is also an impermanent phenomenon. Thus, those things—such as

---

[1] The term "associative" is suggested by *The Science of the Sacred Word* (Adhyar Madras, India: Vasanta, 1911), Vol. II, pp. 168-170 note.

pots, persons, consciousnesses, and so forth as well as product itself—which are products are also impermanent phenomena. Being a product is invariably associated with being an impermanent phenomenon. In the statement of pervasion, "Whatever is a product is necessarily an impermanent phenomenon," the word "whatever" stands in place of the points of emphasis, these things which are products—pots, persons, consciousnesses, and so on. Ascertaining this is essential for understanding the system of reasoning presented in the Collected Topics texts.

Counter-Pervasion

The third mode of a correct sign is the counter-pervasion (*ldog khyab, vyatireka-vyāpti*). This type of pervasion is a necessary outflow of the forward pervasion, for in all cases in which the sign is the forward pervasion it is also the counter-pervasion.

The basis of relation of the counter-pervasion is the dissimilar class (*mi mthun phyogs, vipakṣha*) which in the proof of sound as an impermanent phenomenon is the class of non-impermanent phenomena. The definition of the dissimilar class in the proof of sound as an impermanent phenomenon is:

> that which is empty of impermanence, in accordance with the mode of proof, in the proof of sound as an impermanent phenomenon.[1]

Anything which is not an impermanent phenomenon is a member of the dissimilar class in the proof of sound as an impermanent phenomenon. Thus, any permanent phenomenon or any non-existent (*med pa, asat*) is a member of this dissimilar class.

The dissimilar class is the basis of relation of the counter-pervasion, the third mode of a correct sign. The sign's being the counter-pervasion refers to its being distinct from the

---

[1] Mi-nyak Ge-shay Tsul-trim-ñam-gyel, p. 33-34.

dissimilar class in a particular way. For instance, the definition of something's being the counter-pervasion in the proof of sound as an impermanent phenomenon is:

> that which is ascertained (by a person for whom it has become the third mode of the sign in the proof of sound as an impermanent phenomenon) as just non-existent in the dissimilar class in the proof of sound as an impermanent phenomenon.[1]

If a sign is the counter-pervasion in the proof of something, it is ascertained as just non-existent in the dissimilar class. For the sample syllogism, this means that product is ascertained as just non-existent among non-impermanent phenomena. This is established, for products exist only among impermanent phenomena. There are no products which are non-impermanent phenomena.

In the definition of counter-pervasion, as in the definitions of the other two modes of the sign, there is an epistemological requirement—of how and by whom a sign must be ascertained—and an ontological requirement—of how the sign must exist in relation to its basis of relation. The sign must be ascertained as the counter-pervasion by a person who is actively involved in the reasoning process. In this case, the ontological requirement is that the sign must be *universally absent* in the dissimilar class and, although (according.to the requirements of the forward pervasion) it must exist in the similar class, it may or may not be universally present in the similar class.[2] This is to say that the extent of the sign may be lesser than the extent of the predicate to be proven.

As in the cases of the property of the subject and the forward pervasion, only the sign is the counter-pervasion. Still, counter-pervasion is *formulated* between the sign and its basis of relation, the dissimilar class. In general, this is: whatever is not that predicate to be proven is necessarily not

---

[1] *Ibid.*, p. 40.
[2] See Mi-nyak Ge-shay Tsul-trim-ñam-gyel, pp. 40-41.

that sign. Applied to the sample syllogism, the counter-pervasion is formulated: whatever is not an impermanent phenomenon is necessarily not a product. Since all products are impermanent phenomena, anything which is not an impermanent phenomenon cannot be a product.

The nature of counter-pervasion is reflective of and resultant from the nature of forward pervasion. For any syllogism in which the sign is established as the forward pervasion, that sign will also be the counter-pervasion. Still, the values of these two types of pervasion are somewhat different. The main requirement of the forward pervasion is that the sign must exist exclusively in the similar class whereas the main requirement of the counter-pervasion is that the sign must be universally absent in the dissimilar class. Also, the ascertainment of the forward pervasion and the ascertainment of the counter-pervasion are different sorts of realizations. If one explicitly realizes the forward pervasion, one implicitly realizes the counter-pervasion. And if one explicitly realizes the counter-pervasion, one implicitly realizes the forward pervasion. From this point of view, the two types of pervasions are different requirements. Although they are ontologically concomitant—for if the sign is the one then it is also the other as well—*explicitly* they are ascertained separately.

SUMMARY

Given the above information, one can understand that the single-sentence syllogism used in the Collected Topics tradition implies the more familiar syllogistic form consisting of a series of sentences leading to a conclusion. For instance, the sample syllogism:

> The subject, sound, is an impermanent phenomenon because of being a product

implies a series of three sentences and a conclusion:

Sound is a product.
Whatever is a product is necessarily an impermanent phenomenon.
Whatever is not an impermanent phenomenon is necessarily not a product.

Therefore, sound is an impermanent phenomenon.

The first three sentences in this implied syllogism are premises only in the sense that once they are true, then the conclusion too must be true. For any *valid* syllogism, the implied premises are not just assumptions that may or may not be true. Rather, according to the way the three modes of the sign are defined in this system of reasoning, the three sentences implied by any *valid* argument must be true and they must be ascertained as true by a person for whom the argument is valid.

However, in general the premises implied by a syllogism may or may not be true. For instance, there is the argument:

The subject, sound, is a permanent phenomenon because of being a product

which implies the series of premises and a conclusion:

Sound is a product.
Whatever is a product is necessarily a permanent phenomenon.
Whatever is not a permanent phenomenon is necessarily not a product.

Therefore, sound is a permanent phenomenon.

This syllogism is determined to be invalid by the Ge-luk-ba logicians simply because the second and third premises are not *true*. That is, productness is not ascertained as existing only in the class of permanent phenomena. Thus, one can say that in general the premises implied by a single-sentence argument are assumptions that may or may not be true, but for a valid argument the premises must be true.

The fact that this second argument, the proof of sound as a permanent phenomenon by the sign, product, is determined to be invalid emphasizes a major aspect of this system of reasoning. One criterion of validity is that the premises must be verifiably true, certified as concordant with fact by an ascertaining valid cognizer. This argument is sound in the sense that *if* the premises were true then the conclusion would be true. However, it is not factually true according to the assertions of this system of philosophy; thus, it is not valid. In this system of reasoning, soundness of argument does not entail validity. A valid argument must be sound, but a sound argument is not necessarily valid.[1]

Furthermore, even arguments which are formally sound and factually true may or may not be valid, for a valid argument must meet the epistemological requirements concerning the person faced with the argument. The person must be one who is actively seeking to understand the thesis/conclusion of the syllogism. An argument is not valid for all persons at all times. For one who has already ascertained the conclusion or for one who is unable to ascertain the conclusion, the argument is not valid even though it may be sound and the premises and conclusion factually true.

By way of review, Table I shows the components of a syllogism:

---

[1] See Benson Mates, *Elementary Logic* (New York: Oxford University Press, 1972), pp. 5ff.

Table I: Components of a Syllogism

Sample Syllogism: The subject, *sound*, is an *impermanent phenomenon* because of being a *product*.

1   2   3

1 subject (*chos can, dharmin*): sound

2 predicate to be proven (*bsgrub bya'i chos, sādhya-dharma*): impermanent phenomenon

3 sign (*rtags, liṅga*): product

4 that which is to be proven (*bsgrub bya, sādhya*): sound is an impermanent phenomenon
    Formulated in general: that subject is that predicate to be proven

5 predicate to be negated (*dgag bya'i chos, *pratiṣhedhya-dharma*): permanent phenomenon

6 that which is to be negated (*dgag bya, pratiṣhedhya*): sound is a permanent phenomenon
    Formulated in general: that subject is non-that predicate to be proven

7 similar class (*mthun phyogs, sapakṣha*): impermanent phenomenon

8 dissimilar class (*mi mthun phyogs, vipakṣha*): non-impermanent phenomenon

9   property of the subject (phyogs chos, pakṣha-dharma): product
    Defined: that which is ascertained (by a person for whom it has become the property of the
        subject in the proof of sound as an impermanent phenomenon by the sign, product) as just
        existing, in accordance with the mode of statement, with sound
    Formulated in general: that subject is that sign
    Formulated for the sample syllogism: sound is a product

10 forward pervasion (rjes khyab, anvaya-vyāpti): product
    Defined: that which is ascertained (by a person for whom it has become the second mode of
        the sign in the proof of sound as an impermanent phenomenon by the sign, product) as
        existing in only the similar class in the proof of sound as an impermanent phenomenon
    Formulated in general: whatever is that sign is necessarily that predicate to be proven
    Formulated for the sample syllogism: whatever is a product is necessarily an impermanent
        phenomenon

11 counter-pervasion (ldog khyab, vyatireka-vyāpti): product
    Defined: that which is ascertained (by a person for whom it has become the third mode of the
        sign in the proof of sound as an impermanent phenomenon by the sign, product) as just
        non-existent in the dissimilar class in the proof of sound as an impermanent phenomenon
    Formulated in general: whatever is not that predicate to be proven is necessarily not that sign
    Formulated for the sample syllogism: whatever is not an impermanent phenomenon is
        necessarily not a product

CONSEQUENCES

The predominant form of argument used in this text as well as in this tradition of debate is the consequence (*thal 'gyur, prasaṅga*).[1] For any position that one may set forth, there are certain consequences of that view. If a position is fundamentally correct, then the consequences of that view will be consistent and acceptable. If a position is fundamentally incorrect, through relying on consequences a debater is able to demonstrate to his opponent the inconsistency and invalidity of his position. When an opponent expresses a mistaken view, the debater states to him a logical consequence of that view for the sake of defeating his misconception.

The main system of philosophical tenets in Tibetan Buddhism is the Middle Way Consequentialist School (*dbu ma thal 'gyur ba, prāsaṅgika-mādhyamika*); the followers of this system are called Consequentialists (*thal 'gyur ba, prāsaṅgika*) due to their assertion that through reliance on consequences alone a consciousness understanding the correct view can be generated in an opponent.

> Non-Prāsaṅgikas also use consequences to break down the pointedness of the opponent's adherence to his own view. However, they do not accept that a consequence *alone* can generate in the opponent a consciousness inferring the implied thesis. Prāsaṅgikas assert that the statement of a consequence alone is sufficient, provided the opponent is intelligent and ready. To such an opponent, a further explicit statement of a syllogism is purposeless.[2]

---

[1] For more information on consequences see Pur-bu-jok Jam-ba-gya-tso (*phur bu lcog byams pa rgya mtsho*, 1825-1901), "The Greater Path of Reasoning" (*rigs lam che ba*) of *The Presentation of Collected Topics Revealing the Meaning of the Texts on Valid Cognition, the Magical Key to the Path of Reasoning* (*tshad ma'i gzhung don 'byed pa'i bsdus grva'i rnam bzhag rigs lam 'phrul gyi lde mig*), (Buxa, India: n.p., 1965), 1b.3-23a.6. See also Jeffrey Hopkins, *Meditation on Emptiness*, pp. 443-451.

[2] Jeffrey Hopkins, *Meditation on Emptiness*, p. 445.

The reason for the priority of consequences in Ge-luk-b̄a debate is pedagogical. It is frequently easier to bring forth the desired effect in debate if one uses the terminology and assertions already accepted by an opponent. In stating a consequence to an opponent one deals with that party on his own grounds, using views already accepted by the other party in order to contradict his assertions by drawing out their inconsistencies. In any disputation, if one is to defeat the views of an opponent, it is necessary to address accurately his assertions as he understands them. Otherwise, one is defeating merely a straw man.

Consequences are structurally similar to syllogisms, for both consist of a "thesis" and a reason. For instance, there is the consequence:

> It follows that the subject, sound, is an impermanent phenomenon because of being a product (*sgra chos can mi rtag pa yin par thal byas pa yin pa'i phyir*).

In terms of the manner of expression, consequences are different from syllogisms only in that they include the words "it follows that" which, in this translation, come at the beginning of the argument. However, this difference alone does not indicate the vast chasm dividing syllogisms and consequences.

The disputant who states a syllogism to an opponent must accept the three modes of the sign expressed in that syllogism. However, in stating a consequence to an opponent, a disputant is not bound to accept the establishment of the reason, the pervasion, or the "thesis". The argument put forth in a consequence is in accordance with and *follows* from the views expressed by the opponent. The Challenger who gives voice to that argument is not in the least obligated to accept it as his own view. Consequences are an effective form of argument which, while reflecting an opponent's own views, force the opponent to accept unwanted results and thereby lead to the dissolution of erroneous conceptions.

Also, consequences are to be distinguished from syllogisms in that some correct consequences, if straightforwardly reformulated as syllogisms, would not be valid according to the rules of syllogisms. That is, by simply removing the introductory words "it follows that" from some consequences that are correct according to the rules of consequences, the syllogism that would result would not be valid according to the rules of a syllogism. Again this is because the argument expressed in a consequence follows from the views of an opponent. The argument may be correct as a consequence in the sense that *if* the opponent's assertions are true, then the consequence will be true. However, this does not entail that the argument would be valid as a syllogism, for opponents sometimes present mistaken positions.

"The Greater Path of Reasoning", the third book in the Tutor's *Collected Topics*, includes a presentation of consequences. In that chapter consequences are divided into the two, correct consequences (*thal 'gyur yang dag, samyak-prasaṅga*) and counterfeit consequences (*thal 'gyur ltar snang, prasaṅga-ābhāsa*).[1] A correct consequence must be such that there is a person for whom it is a correct consequence and, moreover, this person is not able to give a factually concordant response to it. Arguments do not exist in a void but are related to persons and their assertions. Consequences are designed to address actual views held to be true. In order to defeat a wrong view a correct consequence must be such that an opponent cannot give an effective answer, thus forcing him to understand an implied thesis. A counterfeit consequence is one to which an opponent is able to give an effective answer or one that does not address views held by the opponent.

One type of consequence used in "The Introductory Path of Reasoning", the text translated and annotated in this work, is a consequence of which the sign is established by valid cognition and the pervasion is established only by the

---

[1] Pur-bu-jok Jam-ba-gya-tso , "The Greater Path of Reasoning", 11a.4-5.

"opponent's" assertion. For instance, in the first debate in "The Introductory Path of Reasoning"—the most introductory debate on colors—a hypothetical opponent asserts that whatever is a color is necessarily red. Of course, it is not the case that whatever is a color is necessarily red, for some colors are not red. Still, this absurd position is used as an example to demonstrate the argument form. In response to this assertion, a Challenger posits the counterexample of the color of a white religious conch (*chos dung dkar po'i kha dog*). A religious conch is a shell used as a horn in religious ceremonies. The shells are cut open on the broad end to produce a serviceable horn. The color of a white religious conch is, of course, white. However, according to the hypothetical opponent's assertion that whatever is a color is necessarily red, since the color of a white religious conch is a color, it too must be red. The Challenger may state the consequence:

It follows that the subject, the color of a white religious conch, is red because of being a color.

Here this example is explained in only a general and theoretical way, but in the chapter on the procedure in debate it will be discussed in detail as a paradigm for the method of applying consequences of an opponent's views. In this consequence, the sign is established by valid cognition, for the color of a white religious conch is a color. The pervasion, that whatever is a color is necessarily red, is established merely by the opponent's assertion and is not factually true. Still, this consequence is a genuine reflection of the assertions of the person to whom it is addressed.

The thesis implied by this consequence directly contradicts the "thesis" of the stated consequence. The implied thesis is:

The subject, the color of a white religious conch, is *not* red.

The consequence stated to the opponent may or may not be a correct consequence depending on the progress the opponent has made toward understanding the implied thesis, that the color of a white religious conch is not red.

If the opponent realizes by valid cognition that the color of a white religious conch is not red or even if he merely comes to assert that the color of a white religious conch is not red without having understood it by valid cognition, then for that person the stated consequence is a correct consequence.[1] In either case the opponent has clearly settled the implied thesis, that the color of a white religious conch is not red; thus, he is left without a factually concordant answer to the consequence. He cannot deny the establishment of the sign of the consequence, that the color of a white religious conch is a color, for this is factually concordant. He holds by assertion that whatever is a color is necessarily red; so, he cannot question the pervasion of the consequence. Finally, since the opponent has come to realize that the color of a white religious conch is not red or at least to hold this by assertion, he cannot accept the consequence that the color of a white religious conch is red.

At this point the Challenger who stated the consequence would shout, "The three spheres (*'khor gsum*)." This means that the opponent cannot deny the reason or the pervasion, yet he cannot accept the thesis. He is due to understand the implied thesis, that the color of a white religious conch is not red.

However, if the opponent neither realizes by valid cognition that the color of a white religious conch is not red nor comes to hold this by assertion, then for him the stated consequence is a counterfeit consequence. In this situation the opponent has not clearly settled the implied thesis, that the color of a white religious conch is not red. He is still left without a factually concordant answer, but since he neither realizes nor merely asserts that the color of a white religious conch is not red, he is not a person for whom this consequence is correct. For such a person, the statement of this

---

[1] See Pur-bu-jok Jam-ba-gya-tso, "The Greater Path of Reasoning", 18a.1-5.

consequence is not able to cause him to generate a new understanding, that the color of a white religious is not red, and the consequence is ineffective and counterfeit.

Here again the value of an argument is determined by its epistemological efficacy, its ability to cause a person to generate an understanding not previously held. A consequence is correct or counterfeit in dependence on the opponent's level of understanding of the implied thesis. The procedure for giving consequences of an opponent's view as well as this particular example will become clearer in the chapter on the procedure in debate and through the detailed study of "The Introductory Path of Reasoning".

A second, more predominant, type of consequence used in "The Introductory Path of Reasoning" is a consequence of which both the sign and the pervasion are established by valid cognition. For example, another consequence which appears in the first debate is:

> It follows that the subject, the color of a white religious conch, is a color because of being white.

In this consequence, the sign is established by valid cognition, for the color of a white religious conch is white. Also, the pervasion, whatever is white is necessarily a color, is established by valid cognition. Here the implied thesis (that is to be understood as incorrect) is that the color of a white religious conch is not a color.[1] If the opponent holds this implied thesis by assertion, then for him the above consequence is a correct consequence, and he is left without a factually concordant answer. He cannot deny effectively the establishment of the sign, that the color of a white religious conch is white, or the pervasion, that whatever is white is necessarily a color, for these are both established by valid cognition. Also, he cannot accept the "thesis" of the stated consequence, that the color of a white religious conch is a color, for he asserts its opposite, that the color of a white

---

[1] See Pur-bu-jok Jam-ba-gya-tso, "The Greater Path of Reasoning", 17a.6-17b.3.

religious conch is not a color. Thus, he is left without an effective answer and, for this person, the consequence is a correct one.

However, if the opponent to whom this consequence is stated does not assert that the color of a white religious conch is not a color, then for him this is a counterfeit consequence. He is able to accept the correct "thesis" of the stated consequence, that the color of a white religious conch is a color. Also, if the opponent does not assert that the color of a white religious conch is not a color, then there is no purpose in stating to him a consequence proving that the color of a white religious conch is a color, and he is not a person for whom the consequence is correct. For such a person, there is nothing new to be understood by the statement of the above consequence.

Both types of argument forms used in this system of reasoning, syllogisms and consequences, are aimed at defeating wrong consciousnesses and creating new, clear understanding. These forms are designed to address actual doubts or misconceptions held by the persons for whom they are stated. Debate, in this tradition, is not mere scholasticism for the sake of embarrassing and defeating opponents, but is rigorous analysis for the sake of eliminating faults and establishing clear, correct insight.

3 Definitions and Definienda

In Tibet the study of philosophy is known as the study of definitions (*mtshan nyid, lakṣhana*). Definitions are truly the focal point for the study of philosophy. They serve to identify the essential characteristics of phenomena and/or to distinguish, for instance, the Collected Topics position on the topic at hand from that of other systems, Buddhist and non-Buddhist. As with many topics in this tradition, some of the essential points in the presentation of definitions and definienda are taught in the oral tradition and usually are not related by the introductory texts.

First of all, a particular definition, or characterizer, and its definiendum (*mtshon bya, lakṣhya*), or that characterized, are mutually inclusive (*don gcig, ekārtha*). In this system, mutual inclusion has two components. First, the things mutually inclusive must be phenomena which are different (*tha dad, nānātva*); that is, they must be existents which are not *exactly* the same in both name and meaning. Obviously, any two mutually inclusive phenomena must be different in name, but their meaning, all the phenomena which they include or all those things to which their names can properly refer, must be just the same. The second requirement of mutually inclusive phenomena is that they be mutually pervasive;

whatever is the one is necessarily the other. Both of these requirements of mutually inclusive phenomena obtain for any particular definition and its definiendum.

For instance, in the first chapter, the presentation of colors, in "The Introductory Path of Reasoning", the Tutor Jam-ba-gya-tso posits as the definition of color (*kha dog, varṇa*):

> that which is suitable as a hue (*mdog tu rung ba*).

Color and that which is suitable as a hue are different, for they are existents which are not exactly the same in both name and meaning. They have just the same meaning in that they both include or refer to all the same phenomena, but they are designated by different terms. Also, for color and that which is suitable as a hue, whatever is the one is necessarily the other. They have a relationship of equivalence in the sense that they are mutually pervasive.

The definition of color is an appeal to obvious experience. A color is anything which is suitable to be shown or pointed out to an eye consciousness as a hue. The Collected Topics logicians do not have or need anything further to say at this point. It is a tenet of this system that all reasoning eventually meets back to obvious experience; one cannot give reasons endlessly. Beyond positing the meaning of color as that which is suitable as a hue, one can only appeal to ordinary experience. A person without the experience of that which is suitable as a hue will temporarily have to be taught in other ways.[1]

In this system, the definition is the actual object, and the definiendum is the name designated to that object. The definition is not a mere description, but the object itself. For the

---

[1] It is interesting that in a similar vein Ludwig Wittgenstein points out: "When we're asked 'What do "red", "blue", "black", "white" mean?' we can, of course, immediately point to things which have these colours, — but that's all we can do: our ability to explain their meaning goes no further." See Ludwig Wittgenstein, *Remarks on Colour*, ed. by G.E.M. Anscombe, trans. by Linda L. McAlister and Margarete Schättle, (Berkeley, California: University of California Press, 1978), p. 29e.

sake of convenience, we designate that which is suitable as a hue with the name "color".

Although color and that which is suitable as a hue are mutually inclusive, it cannot be said that definition, as such, and definiendum, as such, are mutually inclusive. The relationship of mutual inclusion that holds between any particular definition and its definiendum does not exist between definition and definiendum in general. In fact, definition and definiendum are mutually exclusive ('gal ba, virodha). Whatever is one is necessarily not the other because there is no one thing that is both a definition and a definiendum. Definitions are not themselves definienda, for they are not in turn defined—they may be described or explained but are not defined by their own definitions.

Indeed, that which is suitable as a hue is a definition and color is a definiendum, and, for instance, red is suitable as a hue and a color. However, this does not say that red is something which is both a definition and a definiendum. Rather, red is suitable as a hue (and suitable as a hue is in turn a definition), and red is a color (and color is in turn a definiendum).

One of the most important processes in debate is the positing of definitions. The debaters report the definitions as given in the texts and then analyze each component to ascertain its purpose, identifying what is included by a particular component and what is excluded. Also, the debaters posit alternative definitions to determine whether or not they stand up under analysis. By this method the students learn something of the differences between their own and other systems' assertions on philosophical topics.

In positing a definition it is necessary that one find just that which applies to the defined. A proper definition must not include more than what is being referred to, and, similarly, it must not exclude any portion of what it purports to define. In general, there are three possible faults of a definition. Sa-ġya Paṇḍita's *Treasury of Reasoning about Valid Cognition* (tshad ma rigs gter) says:

The three: non-pervasion, pervasion that is too
   extensive, and non-occurrence
Are the three general fallacies of definitions.[1]

According to Denma Lochö Rinbochay's explanation of this
passage, the fallacy of non-pervasion (*ma khyab pa'i skyon*) is,
for instance, positing as the definition of sound:

   an object of hearing caused by elements conjoined
   with consciousness (*zin pa'i 'byung ba las gyur pa'i nyan
   bya*).

An object of hearing caused by elements conjoined with
consciousness is, for instance, the sound of a voice.
However, it is not the case that whatever is a sound is
necessarily an object of hearing caused by elements
conjoined with consciousness because there are objects of
hearing caused by elements *not* conjoined with
consciousness (*ma zin pa'i 'byung ba las gyur pa'i nyan bya*),
such as the sound of a waterfall. Therefore, this definition of
sound incurs the fallacy of non-pervasion. The definiendum,
sound, and its proposed definition, an object of hearing
caused by elements conjoined with consciousness, are not
mutually pervasive. Whatever is the one is not necessarily
the other. Thus, they do not have the relationship of a
definition and its definiendum. The fallacy of non-pervasion
may also be referred to as the fallacy of a pervasion that is
too restricted. That is, the extension of the definition is too
restricted and it does not pervade the entire definiendum.

   The fallacy of a pervasion that is too extensive (*khyab che
ba'i skyon*) is, for instance, positing as the definition of
sound:

   the momentary (*skad cig ma, kṣhanika*).

The momentary is the definition of impermanent phenomenon (*mi rtag pa, anitya*) and as such properly includes
not only sound but also visual objects, odors, conscious-

---

[1] Reported by Denma Lochö Rinbochay.

nesses, and so forth—every impermanent phenomenon. Thus, whatever is momentary is not necessarily a sound. In this case, the definition, the momentary, is too extensive (for its extension is greater than that of the definiendum), and the definiendum, sound, does not pervade the definition (for its extension is lesser than that of the definition). Thus, positing the momentary as the definition of sound incurs the fallacy of a pervasion that is too extensive.

The fallacy of non-occurrence (*mi srid pa'i skyon*) is, for instance, positing as the definition of sound:

> an object of hearing which is a quality of space (*nam mkha'i yon tan gyi nyan bya*).

In the Buddhist systems sound is not asserted as a quality of space; therefore, sound which is a quality of space is not admitted to exist, and does not occur. Similarly, if one were to posit as the definition of sound:

> an object of hearing which is uncomposed (*'dus ma byas kyi nyan bya*),

then this too would have the fallacy of non-occurrence. Since an object of hearing is a product and all products are composed phenomena (*'dus byas, saṃskṛta*), an object of hearing which is uncomposed does not occur. Neither of these proposed definitions suitably characterize the definiendum, sound, for they do not exist and thereby incur the fallacy of non-occurrence.

In the Collected Topics texts, the definition of sound is:

> an object of hearing (*nyan bya*).

As a proper definition of sound, *object of hearing* does not incur any of the three fallacies of a definition. The pervasion is neither too restricted nor too extensive because whatever is a sound is necessarily an object of hearing and whatever is an object of hearing is necessarily a sound. Also, this definition does not have the fallacy of non-occurrence because an object of hearing does exist.[1]

Leading out of the discussion of the introductory definitions, the novitiate monks learn the method for establishing the relationship between a particular definition and its definiendum.[2] This information is generally communicated in the oral tradition and does not appear in the Tutor's *Collected Topics*. Using the example of color and its definition, that which is suitable as a hue, the method of establishment may be stated in the form of a syllogism:

> The subject, that which is suitable as a hue, is the definition of color because (1) it and color are ascertained as having the eight approaches of pervasion [that exist between] a definition and definiendum and also (2) it and color are established in the relationship of a definition and definiendum (*mdog tu rung ba chos can kha dog gi mtshan nyid yin te khyod kha dog dang mtshan mtshon gyi khyab pa sgo brgyad nges pa gang zhig mtshan mtshon gyi 'brel ba yang grub pa'i phyir*).

The first main component of the reason of this syllogism is that "that which is suitable as a hue and color are ascertained as having the eight approaches of pervasion [that exist between] a definition and definiendum". The eight approaches of pervasion that exist between color and that which is suitable as a hue are:

1 whatever is a color is necessarily suitable as a hue
2 whatever is suitable as a hue is necessarily a color
3 whatever is not a color is necessarily not suitable as a hue
4 whatever is not suitable as a hue is necessarily not a color
5 if a color exists, then that which is suitable as a hue necessarily exists

---

[1] Denma Lochö Rinbochay, oral commentary.
[2] Lati Rinbochay, oral commentary.

6   if that which is suitable as a hue exists, then color necessarily exists
7   if a color does not exist, then that which is suitable as a hue necessarily does not exist
8   if that which is suitable as a hue does not exist, then color necessarily does not exist.

The eight approaches of pervasion play on the facts that if something is the one then it is necessarily the other and that the presence of the one necessitates the presence of the other. Any particular definition and its definiendum are necessarily coextensive in terms of pervasions of being (*yin khyab*) and pervasions of existence (*yod khyab*).

More generally, these eight pervasions exist between any two mutually inclusive phenomena whether or not they are a definition and its definiendum. For instance, product (*byas pa, kṛta*) and impermanent phenomenon (*mi rtag pa, anitya*) are mutually inclusive but not a definition and its definiendum. Thus, whatever is a product is necessarily an impermanent phenomenon and vice versa, and if a product exists then an impermanent phenomenon exists, and so forth. Since the eight approaches of pervasion obtain not only between a definition and its definiendum but also between any two mutually inclusive phenomena, the above reason (on p. 66) given to justify that suitable as a hue is the definition of color specifies that the two "are ascertained as having the eight approaches of pervasion that exist between *a definition and definiendum*". In this way, the reason excludes other mutually inclusive phenomena such as product and impermanent phenomenon which, although they have the eight approaches of pervasion, are not a definition and definiendum.

Moreover, in order to distinguish in another way a definition and its definiendum from other types of mutually inclusive phenomena, the above reason (on p. 66) specifies in the second part that "suitable as a hue and color are established in the relationship of a definition and definiendum". According to Lati Rinbochay, this specification means that in order to ascertain color with valid cognition one must first ascertain that which is suitable as a hue with valid cognition. Thus, correct understanding of the definition, the actual object, must come before one can have correct understanding of the definiendum, understood as the conventionality or name which designates that object. In order to understand with valid cognition the meaning of the term "color" one must first be acquainted with these existents which are suitable to be demonstrated to an eye consciousness as a hue—blue, yellow, white, red, and so forth. There are persons who have ascertained that which is suitable as a hue with valid cognition but have not ascertained color with valid cognition because, for instance, a child untrained in language or a cow might know correctly phenomena which are suitable as a hue but not know correctly the name "color". On the other hand, a person who correctly knows the meaning of "color" yet does not know that which is suitable as a hue does not exist and is not possible.[1]

Although specific definitions are not in turn defined, there is a definition of definition, for definition is defined as:

> that which is a triply qualified substantial existent (*rdzas yod chos gsum tshang ba*).

A definition is called a "substantial existent" (*rdzas yod, dravya-sat*) because it is the actual object, the meaning or referent of its definiendum. The third chapter in "The Middling Path of Reasoning" of the Tutor's *Collected Topics* is a presentation of definitions and definienda. In that chapter, the Tutor Jam-b̄a-gya-tso presents, in the syllogistic form, the three qualities of a definition:

> There is a way to adduce the three qualities of a substantial existent because it is reasonable to adduce the three: (1) in general, it is a definition, (2) it is established with its illustrations [*mtshan gzhi*], and (3) it

---

[1] *Ibid.*

does not define anything other than that which is its own definiendum.[1]

For example, *that which is suitable as a hue* is the triply qualified substantial existent of color because (1) in general, it is a definition, (2) it is established with its illustrations, and (3) it does not define anything other than color. First, in general, that which is suitable as a hue is renowned as a definition, not a definiendum. Second, that which is suitable as a hue is established with its illustrations such as that which is suitable as a blue hue, that which is suitable as a red hue, and so forth. One knows that which is suitable as a hue in dependence on knowing its illustrations. Third, that which is suitable as a hue is not the definition of anything other than color. A definition cannot have more than one definiendum.

Just as there is a definition of definition, in general, so there is a definition of definiendum, in general. Definiendum is defined as:

> that which is a triply qualified imputed existent (*btags yod chos gsum tshang ba*).

A definiendum is called an "imputed existent" (*btags yod, prajñapti-sat*) because it is the name imputed to its definition. However, this does not mean that whatever is a definiendum is necessarily a name. For instance, color is not a name, for it is not a sound but a visible object. However, the word "color" is a name or conventionality commonly accepted as meaning that which is suitable as a hue.

In the Tutor Jam-ba-gya-tso's presentation of definitions and definienda there is also a description of the three qualities of a definiendum:

> There is a way to adduce the three qualities of an imputed existent because it is reasonable to adduce

---

[1] Pur-bu-jok Jam-ba-gya-tso, "The Middling Path of Reasoning" (*rigs lam 'bring*) of *The Presentation of Collected Topics Revealing the Meaning of the Texts on Valid Cognition, the Magical Key to the Path of Reasoning* (*tshad ma'i gzhung don 'byed pa'i bsdus grva'i rnam bzhag rigs lam 'phrul gyi lde mig*), (Buxa, India: n.p., 1965), 9b.2-3.

the three: (1) in general, it is a definiendum, (2) it is
established with its illustrations, and (3) it is not the
definiendum of anything other than just its own
definition.[1]

For example, *color* is the triply qualified imputed existent of
that which is suitable as a hue because (1) in general, it is a
definiendum, (2) it is established with its illustrations, and
(3) it is not the definiendum of anything other than that
which is suitable as a hue. In general, color is renowned as a
definiendum, and it is established with its illustrations such
as blue, green, and so forth.

It is said that a definiendum may not have more than one
definition, but in some cases alternate, plausible definitions
are given for the same definiendum. For example, two
slightly different definitions are offered for color. These are:

1   that which is suitable as a hue (*mdog tu rung ba*)
2   that which is suitable to be shown as a hue (*mdog tu
     bstan du rung ba*).

In debate, nevertheless, one must hold one or the other of
these as the definition of color because if it were accepted
that both of these qualify as the definition of color then color
would not satisfy the standards of a proper definiendum.
However, the requirement that a definition must not define
anything other than its own definiendum is stringently
observed, for it seems that indeed there is no case of a definition having more than one definiendum.

Both definitions and definienda are established with their
illustrations (*mtshan gzhi*). An illustration of a color is, for
instance, red. An illustration of an impermanent phenomenon is, for instance, a pot. An illustration is defined as:

that which serves as a basis for illustrating the appropriate definiendum by way of [its] definition (*mtshan*

---

[1] *Ibid.*, 9b.1.

nyid kyis skabs su bab pa'i mtshon bya mtshon pa'i gzhir gyur pa).[1]

The definition includes the qualification that it must illustrate the *appropriate* definiendum. This specification is being added because the definition is being stated in general. In order to avoid the possible fallacy of indicating that an illustration might suitably illustrate just any definiendum, it is specified that it must illustrate the *appropriate* definiendum.

This qualification need not be stated in the definition of an illustration for which the definiendum is specified. For instance, the definition of an illustration of color is:

> that which serves as a basis for illustrating color by way of [being] suitable as a hue (*mdog tu rung bas kha dog mtshon pa'i gzhir gyur pa*).

Red serves as a basis for illustrating color by way of being something which is suitable as a hue. Red is suitable as a hue, and it illustrates the meaning of color.

Just as a definition must be something that one might have ascertained without necessarily having ascertained its definiendum, so an illustration must be something that one might have ascertained without necessarily having ascertained that which it illustrates; otherwise, there would be no need for an illustration. For instance, it is conceivable that one might know red without knowing color in general or one might know a pot without knowing impermanent phenomena in general. An illustration serves as a basis for *illustrating* something. If it embodied all of the particular qualities of what it illustrates or if merely by knowing it one would have to know what it purports to illustrate, then it would not be a proper illustration. An illustration must serve as a basis which is able to cause one to know something. For instance, even though a gold pot is an instance (*bye brag, visheṣha*) of a pot, it is not an illustration of a pot because if one has ascertained a gold pot by valid cognition

---

[1] *Ibid.*, 10a.1.

then one necessarily has ascertained a pot by valid cognition.

Definitions and definienda must be established with their illustrations. Something which has no illustrations cannot be either a definition or a definiendum. This rule is related to the third possible fault of definitions, the fallacy of non-occurrence. For instance, some say that the definition of non-existent (*med pa*) is:

> that which is not observed by valid cognition (*tshad mas ma dmigs pa*).

According to Denma Lochö Rinbochay, this proposed definition incurs the fallacy of non-occurrence. Non-existent is not an existent and is not experienced as an existent; thus, it does not occur.[1] Something such as non-existent which has no illustrations is neither a definition nor a definiendum, for all definitions and definienda have illustrations and are existents.

In general, definitions are of two types: (1) definitions which eliminate discordant types (*rigs mi mthun sel ba'i mtshan nyid*) and (2) definitions which eliminate wrong ideas (*log rtog sel ba'i mtshan nyid*).[2] However, a single definition may be both one which eliminates discordant types and one which eliminates wrong ideas. For instance, the definition of a direct prime cognizer (*mngon sum tshad ma, pratyakṣha-pramāṇa*) is:

> that which is (1) a new, incontrovertible consciousness and (2) a non-mistaken consciousness free from conceptuality.[3]

---

[1] Denma Lochö Rinbochay, oral commentary.

[2] The source for this description of the two types of definitions is Pur-bu-jok Jam-ba-gya-tso, "The Middling Path of Reasoning", 10a.5-10b.4.

[3] Here *tshad ma* is translated as "prime cognizer" rather than "valid cognizer", which is the preferred translation in this work, because this section involves discussion of the assertion that a consciousness is a *tshad ma* only in its *first* moment of correctly apprehending an object. Thus, the definition specifies that a direct prime cognizer must be *new*. The term "prime cognizer" is better able to convey this factor of newness. For a

A direct prime cognizer is a sense or non-conceptual mental direct perceiver in its first moment of correctly apprehending its object. For example, an eye consciousness newly and correctly seeing a patch of blue is a direct prime cognizer. The above definition of a direct prime cognizer is one which eliminates both discordant types and wrong ideas.

It is a definition which eliminates discordant types because, from among consciousnesses, non-prime cognizers and inferential prime cognizers are the only discordant types of direct prime cognizers. The qualification in the definition that a direct prime cognizer must be *new and incontrovertible* eliminates non-prime cognizers, for only prime cognizers are new and incontrovertible. Either of the qualifications *free from conceptuality* or *non-mistaken* is able to eliminate inferential prime cognizers. This is so because inferential prime cognizers are *conceptual* consciousnesses which, although new and incontrovertible, are *mistaken* with respect to their appearing objects (*snang yul,* *pratibhāsa-viṣhaya*), internal mental images which merely serve to represent the actual objects being comprehended.

The definition of a direct prime cognizer also eliminates wrong ideas because, even though either of the qualifications *free from conceptuality* or *non-mistaken* eliminate discordant types, both of these are stated in order to eliminate wrong ideas. Since, for instance, even a sense consciousness to which a single moon appears as double is free from conceptuality, the qualification *non-mistaken* is stated in order to eliminate the wrong idea considering such a wrong sense consciousness as a direct perceiver and, thus, non-mistaken. In addition, the qualification *free from conceptuality* is stated for the sake of eliminating wrong ideas such as the assertions by the Naiyāyikas (Logicians) and so forth that direct perceivers can be conceptual consciousnesses. Thus, the definition of a direct prime cognizer both eliminates discordant types and eliminates wrong ideas.

detailed discussion of prime cognizers, see Lati Rinbochay, *Mind in Tibetan Buddhism*, pp. 116-129.

Essential to the study of Tibetan debate is an understanding of definitions and definienda—their properties, relations, and purposes. Definitions which eliminate discordant types function to identify clearly the essential characteristics of phenomena. Definitions which eliminate wrong ideas function to set off a system's assertions on a topic as distinguished from the assertions of other systems. As an indication of the importance of definitions and definienda, in the second debate in "The Introductory Path of Reasoning", the Tutor Jam-ba-gya-tso introduces this topic by citing the definition of color. Although the presentation of definitions and definienda is not taken up in detail until the third chapter of "The Middling Path of Reasoning", the topic is introduced in the first chapter of the book. In addition, a large part of the explanation of definitions and definienda is supplied, at least initially, by the oral commentary of teachers and is not taught from the texts. Thus, as is evidenced in both the texts and the oral tradition, the topic of definitions and definienda is vitally important to understanding the Collected Topics system of logic and epistemology.

4 The Subjects

The subjects of debate, or bases of disputation, are the things under discussion. Within the context of "The Introductory Path of Reasoning" the subjects are frequently used more to illustrate the broader principles and categories of this form of Buddhist reasoning than as genuine sources of argumentation.

Lati Rinbochay tells the story of one fellow's misunderstanding of the nature of the subjects of debate. At the time of the Great Prayer Festival (*smon lam chen mo*) traditionally held annually in Hla-ša at the beginning of the Tibetan New Year, around February 20, the monks and nuns of all the great Ge-luk-ba monasteries gather for several days of community prayer, celebration, and the Hla-ram-ba Ge-šhay examinations. During this time, even the monks who were not taking their examinations would naturally find opportunities for practicing debate. A layman who encountered two monks in heated disputation understood that they were arguing about a gold pot but nothing else about what was being said. Not understanding their debate, he worried about these two monks' arguing over material possessions.

The next year at the Great Prayer Festival when he again encountered these same two monks in disputation about a gold pot, he moved to intercede. Reprimanding them he said, "Last year I saw you here arguing about a gold pot, and now this year you are here arguing about it again. Please stop arguing about this thing! I will give you each a gold pot if you will just stop arguing."[1]

What this fellow failed to understand is that rather than arguing over the possession of a gold pot, the monks were debating about the nature of a gold pot—just what it is and in what manner it exists. In order to avoid this type of misunderstanding concerning the subjects of debate, a brief discussion is in order.

The subjects being discussed here are not the various areas or topics of debate but those things which occupy the subject position in a syllogism or consequence. For instance, sound is the subject in the syllogism:

> The subject, *sound*, is an impermanent phenomenon because of being a product.

In the text translated here there are fifty-three different subjects, several of which are used repeatedly. These subjects range from existents to non-existents, from forms to consciousnesses, and from impermanent phenomena to permanent phenomena. Any existent, or any non-existent as well, is suitable to assume the position of a subject in a syllogism or consequence. Of course, the focus of this chapter is not all subjects of debate, but the ones used in this text. However, in a broader sense the principles and categories that may be deduced by a study of these fifty-three subjects effectively serve to express the nature of all subjects. There are infinite characteristics of each and every phenomenon; thus, the same subject may be used in many different contexts to exemplify various characteristics.

The fifty-three subjects together with a brief description of each and a notation on their places of occurrence in the text are:

---

[1] Lati Rinbochay, oral commentary.

1 *The horn of a rabbit* (*ri bong rva*) is the favorite example of a non-existent (*med pa, asat*). (Appears as the subject in debates B.5 and C.13.)

2 *Only-a-permanent-phenomenon* (*rtag pa kho na*) is a non-existent, but being only a permanent phenomenon does exist.[1] Only-a-permanent-phenomenon does not exist because impermanent phenomena exist. If only-a-permanent-phenomenon existed, then nothing else, including impermanent phenomena, could exist. Even so, there is *something which is* only a permanent phenomenon. Any permanent phenomenon is only a permanent phenomenon, for it is not sometimes a permanent phenomenon and sometimes an impermanent phenomenon. Nor is a permanent phenomenon partially a permanent phenomenon and partially an impermanent phenomenon. Rather, it is only a permanent phenomenon. Thus, only-a-permanent-phenomenon does not exist, but being only a permanent phenomenon does exist. (Appears as a subject in debate D.4.)

3 *Functioning thing* (*dngos po, bhāva*) or *thing* is a general phenomenon, mutually inclusive with impermanent phenomenon (*mi rtag pa, anitya*), and the preferred way of referring to impermanent phenomena.[2] Impermanent phenomena are called "functioning things" because they perform the function of producing effects (*'bras bu, phala*), especially their own continuation of the next moment. (*Functioning thing* or *thing* appears as a subject in debates B.4, C.2, C.3, C.4, C.8, E.6, E.18, F.1, and F.2.)

---

[1] In this translation system, hyphens are used to tie some phrases together as single expressions when those phrases are used in the subject position. However, when used in the predicate position, hyphens are not needed.

[2] The word "thing" is used primarily in this work as a translation of *bhāva* (Tib. *dngos po*), meaning *functioning thing*, and referring to impermanent phenomena only. In other contexts, the word "thing" is used in its normal English usage to refer to any impermanent or permanent phenomenon; the meaning is clear by context.

4 *That which is able to perform a function (don byed nus pa, *kriyā-shakti) is the definition of thing. The Things perform the function of producing effects, as opposed to permanent phenomena which neither produce effects nor perform functions. (Appears as a subject in debates C.1, C.2, C.3, C.4, C.7, and F.2.)

5 *A functioning thing (ngos po, bhāva),* in the sense of *any* functioning thing, does not refer exclusively to functioning thing in general, but as it is used in several debates refers to each and every functioning thing including functioning thing in general. (Appears as the subject in debates E.2, E.3, E.4, and E.13.)

6 *Impermanent phenomenon (mi rtag pa, anitya)* is, along with permanent phenomenon, one of only two types of existents *(yod pa, sat).* Impermanent phenomena are characterized as:

   the momentary *(skad cig ma, kṣhaṇika)*

   because they are produced, abide, disintegrate, and cease moment by moment, as opposed to permanent phenomena which do not change moment by moment. (Appears as a subject in debate F.3.)

7 *The color of a white religious conch (chos dung dkar po'i kha dog)* is a simple subject and the subject in debate A.1, the first in the Tutor's "The Introductory Path of Reasoning".

8 *The color of the Buddha Amitāyus (sangs rgyas tshe dpag med kyi kha dog)* is a simple subject and, for new students, an introduction to the colors of the five lineages of the Buddhas. (Appears as the subject in debate A.2.)

9 *The color of a sapphire (in dra ni la'i kha dog)* is a simple subject. (Appears as the subject in debate A.3.)

10 *The color of refined gold (gser btso ma'i kha dog)* is a simple subject. (Appears as a subject in debate A.4.)

11 *The color of green Amoghasiddhi (don yod grub pa ljang khu'i kha dog)* is a simple subject and another indication of the colors of the Buddhas of the five lineages. (Appears as the subject in debate A.5.)

12 *The color of orange Mañjughoṣha ('jam dbyangs dmar ser gyi kha dog)* is a simple subject and also an indication of the color of a Buddha. (Appears as the subject in debate A.6.)

13 *Color-form (kha dog gi gzugs)* is mutually inclusive with color *(kha dog, varṇa)* and one of the two types of visible forms or form-sources *(gzugs kyi skye mched, rūpa-āyatana)*, for visible forms consist of only color-forms and shape-forms *(dbyibs kyi gzugs)*. (Appears as the subject in debate A.7.)

14 *A round form (zlum po'i gzugs)* is one of the eight types of shape and exemplifies a visible form which is a shape as opposed to a color. (Appears as the subject in debate A.8.)

15 *A white religious conch (chos dung dkar po)* is a subject which one might take to be a color, but it is given to point out that *the color of* a white religious conch is a color but a white religious conch is not. (Appears as a subject in debate A.9.)

16 *A white horse (rta dkar po)*, similar to a white religious conch, is not a color, but one might take it to be a color. (Appears as a subject in debate A.9.)

17 *Wind (rlung, vāyu)* is one of the four elements *('byung ba, bhūta)* or tangible objects which are elements *('byung bar gyur pa'i reg bya, bhūta-spraṣhtavya)*. These four are earth *(sa, pṛthivī)*, water *(chu, ap)*, fire *(me, teja)*, and wind. (Appears as the subject in debate A.10).

18 *A pot (bum pa, ghaṭa or kumbha)* is the favorite example of an impermanent phenomenon. (Appears as a subject in debates B.1, B.6, E.8, E.16, F.1, and G.1.)

19 *Pot (bum pa, ghaṭa or kumbha)* refers to pot as such, the singular generality, and not to each and every pot. (Appears as a subject in debates C.9, C.10, C.11, and D.2.)

20 *A gold pot (gser bum)* is a simple subject. (Appears as the subject in debate B.8.)

21 *Pot-which-is-one-with-pot (bum pa dang gcig tu gyur pa'i bum pa)* is a quality of pot, considered alone, for only pot

is one with pot; that is, exactly the same as pot in both name and meaning. (Appears as a subject in debate C.9.)

22   *A pillar (ka ba)* is a simple subject. (Appears as a subject in debates B.3, B.9, and D.5.)

23   *Sound (sgra, shabda)* is a simple subject. (Appears as the subject in debate C.6.)

24   *A prior arising of functioning thing (dngos po'i snga logs su byung ba)* is a cause *(rgyu, hetu)* of functioning thing. A prior arising of functioning thing or any cause of functioning thing is a functioning thing because it is able to perform the function of producing effects. However, it is surprising that in this system a cause of functioning thing is not the same entity *(ngo bo gcig pa, eka-rūpatā)* as functioning thing because a cause and its effect do not abide at the same time. (Appears as the subject in debate E.14.)

25   *A prior arising of a prior arising of functioning thing (dngos po'i snga logs su byung ba'i snga logs su byung ba)* is an indirect cause *(brgyud rgyu, *pāraṃparya-kāraṇa)* of functioning thing, for it is the cause of the direct cause *(dngos rgyu, sākṣhāt-kārana)* of functioning thing. (Appears as the subject in debate E.5.)

26   *A subsequent arising of functioning thing (dngos po'i phyi logs su byung ba)* is an effect *('bras bu, phala)* of functioning thing. (Appears as a subject in debate E.6.)

27   *Functioning-thing-which-is-one-with-functioning-thing (dngos po dang gcig tu gyur pa'i dngos po)* is a property of functioning thing, as such, and means that it is exactly the same as functioning thing in both name and meaning. (Appears as the subject in debate C.5.)

28   *A being who is a cause of a pot (bum pa'i rgyur gyur pa'i skyes bu)* is a non-substantial cause or cooperative condition *(lhan cig byed rkyen, sahakāri-pratyaya)* of a pot. (Appears as the subject in debate E.7.)

29   *The mud which is a cause of a pot (bum pa'i rgyur gyur pa'i 'jim pa)* is a substantial cause *(nyer len gyi rgyu, upādāna-kāraṇa)* of a pot, for it is a main producer of a pot as a

continuation of its own substantial entity (*rang gi rdzas rgyun*). (Appears as a subject in debate E.8.)

30 *The flame of a butter lamp in its last moment* (*mar me skad cig tha ma*) is something which has no continuation of its own substantial entity because it is the flame in its *last* moment, although it does have effects such as smoke. (Appears as the subject in debate E.9.)

31 *The two—the color of sandalwood and the odor of sandalwood—* (*tsan dan gyi kha dog dang tsan dan gyi dri gnyis*) are established, abide, and disintegrate simultaneously because they are both part of the same mass, but they are not the same substantial entity (*rdzas gcig, eka-dravya*) because they are not produced from the same substantial cause. (Appear as the subjects in debate E.10.)

32 *The two—a large and a small barley grain produced from one barley head which is their substantial cause—* (*nyer len nas rdog gcig las skyes pa'i nas 'bru che chung gnyis*) are the same type of substantial entity (*rdzas rigs gcig*) because they are produced from the same substantial cause, but they are not the same substantial entity because they are not the same entity. (Appear as the subjects in debate E.11.)

33 *The two—a white horse and a black horse—* (*rta dkar nag gnyis*) are the same type (*rigs gcig, eka-jāti*) because, upon seeing a white horse and a black horse, one might spontaneously think that they are alike (in that they are both horses), but they are not the same entity. (Appear as the subjects in debate E.12.)

34 *The two—a pillar and a pot—* (*ka bum gnyis*) are the favorite examples of objects of knowledge of which being [them] is not possible (*yin pa mi srid pa'i shes bya*). These phenomena are objects of knowledge (*shes bya, jñeya*) or existents because a pillar exists and a pot exists; yet there is nothing which is this set because there is no one thing or group of things which is both a pillar and a pot. (Appear as subjects in debates B.3, E.15, and F.9.)

35   *The two—matter and consciousness—* (*bem shes gnyis*) are another set which exists, but being both matter and consciousness does not exist (i.e., there is nothing which is both matter and consciousness). (Appear as the subjects in debate B.7.)

36   *The two—a gold pot and a copper pot—* (*gser bum zangs bum gnyis*) also comprise a set which exists, but a set of which being it does not exist. (Appear as the subjects in debate C.12.)

37   *The three—matter, consciousnesses, and non-associated compositional factors—* (*bem shes ldan min 'du byed gsum*) are the three types of functioning things. (Appear as subjects in debate B.4.)

38   *The two—a prime cognizer and a subsequent cognizer—which are causes of functioning thing* (*dngos po'i rgyur gyur pa'i tshad ma dang bcad shes gnyis*) are an instance of an awareness (*blo, buddhi*) or a consciousness (*shes pa, jñāna*), but are not an instance of functioning thing because of being causes of functioning thing and, thus, not the same entity as functioning thing. (Appear as the subjects in debate F.8.)

39   *Existent* (*yod pa, sat*) is a general phenomenon including all permanent phenomena and impermanent phenomena. Phenomena (*chos, dharma*) are existents because they are observed by valid cognition (*tshad mas dmigs pa, *pramāṇa-ālambīta*). (Appears as the subject in debate F.15.)

40   *Object of knowledge* (*shes bya, jñeya*) is mutually inclusive with existent and phenomenon. All existents are objects of knowledge because they are known by consciousnesses. Non-existents, however, are not objects of knowledge, for one cannot know that which does not exist. (Appears as a subject in debates A.11, D.1, D.4, E.1, F.10, and F.13.)

41   *Sound-impermanent-phenomenon* (*sgra mi rtag pa*) is a grammatical subject and predicate of a sentence without a verb. When the verb "to be" is supplied, the grammatical subject and predicate are unified in a copulative sen-

tence, "Sound is an impermanent phenomenon." This subject is a verbal trick used in a debate having little philosophical content. (Appears as the subject in debate F.7.)

42 *Permanent phenomenon (rtag pa, nitya)* is a general phenomenon including all existents which are not functioning things. In this system, permanent phenomena are not necessarily eternal but are permanent because they do not change moment by moment. (Appears as the subject in debate F.4.)

43 *Different-from-impermanent-phenomenon (mi rtag pa dang tha dad)* is a permanent phenomenon including every existent which is not exactly the same as impermanent phenomenon from the point of view of both name and meaning. Thus, every existent is different from impermanent phenomenon except for impermanent phenomenon itself. (Appears as a subject in debate F.3.)

44 *Uncomposed space ('dus ma byas kyi nam mkha')* is the favorite example of a simple permanent phenomenon. Uncomposed space is a mere absence of obstructive contact. (Appears as the subject in debates B.2 and B.12.)

45 *Definiendum (mtshon bya, lakṣhya)* is the triply qualified imputed existent of any particular definition. It is the meaning of the convenient name designated to that existent which is a definition. (Appears as the subject in debate D.6.)

46 *Generality (spyi, sāmānya)* is defined as:

> that which encompasses its manifestations
> (*rang gi gsal ba la rjes su 'gro ba'i chos*).

A generality is a general phenomenon which is manifest through its instances. (Appears as the subject in debate F.5.)

47 *The definiendum of that which is able to perform a function (don byed nus pa'i mtshon bya)* is a property of thing. Thing is the definiendum of that which is able to perform a function, but the definiendum of that which is able to perform a function is not a thing because it is a

permanent phenomenon, an appearing object of a thought consciousness (*rtog pa'i snang yul*). (Appears as a subject in debate C.1.)

48 *The triply qualified imputed existent of that which is able to perform a function* (*don byed nus pa'i btags yod chos gsum tshang ba*) is also a property of thing. Thing, and only thing, is the triply qualified imputed existent (i.e., the definiendum) of that which is able to perform a function. (Appears as a subject in debate C.2.)

49 *The definition of functioning thing* (*dngos po'i mtshan nyid*) is a property of that which is able to perform a function. (Appears as a subject in debate C.3.)

50 *The triply qualified substantial existent of functioning thing* (*dngos po'i rdzas yod chos gsum tshang ba*) is also a property of that which is able to perform a function, for that which is able to perform a function, and only it, is the triply qualified substantial existent (i.e., definition) of thing. (Appears as a subject in debate C.4.)

51 *One-with-pot* (*bum pa dang gcig*) is a property of pot as such, for pot, and only pot, is exactly the same as pot in both name and meaning. That is, pot alone is one with pot. (Appears as a subject in debate C.10.)

52 *Pot's isolate* (*bum pa'i ldog pa*) is also a property of pot alone and means that pot is non-non-one with pot (i.e., is one with pot). (Appears as a subject in debate C.11.)

53 *Pillar's isolate* (*ka ba'i ldog pa*) is a quality of pillar as pot's isolate is a quality of pot. (Appears as the subject in debate D.3.)

The debates are designated A.1, A.2, and so forth. The letters indicate the topic and chapter in the order in which they appear in the debate manual. The numbers indicate the individual debates within the chapters. For easy reference, the chapters in "The Introductory Path of Reasoning" with their designated letters are:

A. Colors—White, Red, and So Forth
B. Established Bases
C. Identifying Isolates
D. Opposite-From-Being-Something and Opposite-From-Not-Being-Something
E. The Introductory [Presentation of] Causes and Effects
F. Generalities and Instances
G. Substantial Phenomena and Isolate Phenomena.[1]

QUANTIFICATION

In some sense the quantification of the subjects as used in this system of debate is indefinite. It is not suitable to say that in every case the subject in a syllogism or consequence is modified by a universal quantifier "all" or "every kind of" or that it is modified by a particular quantifier "some", "a", or "the".

For instance, in the chapter on definitions and definienda (see pp. 61-74) it is mentioned that definition is not itself a definition. Rather, it is a definiendum because there is a definition of definition. This may be stated as the syllogism:

The subject, definition, is a definiendum because of being a triply qualified imputed existent.

One cannot say that this subject is universally quantified, for it is not the case that all definitions are definiendums. In fact, no definitions are definiendums. In this system of reasoning, there is nothing which is both a definition and a definiendum; definitions are not defined. For the same reason, one cannot say that some definitions are definiendums. Also, it is not suitable to use the indefinite article "a" or the definite article "the", for these modifiers would indicate that there is some definition which is a definiendum. Such does not exist, for even though definition itself is a definiendum it is not both a definition

---

[1] For the Tibetan of these chapter titles, see "Translation Introduction" p. 170.

and a definiendum because it is not a definition. Since none of these quantifiers accurately modify the subject, what is intended is only that *definition,* as such, is a definiendum.

In this sense, the subject, definition, is to be understood as a singular collective entity, as *definition which is exactly the same as definition.* This is definition in isolation from all of its instances and all the phenomena mutually inclusive with it. That definition, as such, is a definiendum may or may not be true of the phenomena mutually inclusive with it and is certainly not true for any of its instances. In this form of Buddhist reasoning, there are many such subjects which must be understood as collective entities, here referred to in the singular in order to set them off from their individual instances.

Although it is true for the subject, definition, that one cannot say that it is quantified either as a universal or as a particular, this is not true for all subjects. The quantification of some subjects seems to be universal. For instance, there is the syllogism:

> The subject, sound, is an impermanent phenomenon because of being a product.

One can accurately say that *all* sounds are impermanent phenomena. However, it must be noted that appending the quantifier "all" to the subject, sound, is an addition to the subject that is not in the Tibetan original and is predicated merely from knowledge of other assertions held in this system.

There are no cases of subjects in correct syllogisms or consequences in this system which are quantified as particulars and may not be reasonably interpreted as universals. That is, in no case may a subject be accurately modified by the quantifier "some" but not by the quantifier "all". For instance, it is true that some but not all impermanent phenomena are sounds, but this fact may not be formulated in a correct syllogism, for the syllogism:

> The subject, impermanent phenomenon, is a sound because of being an object of hearing

is unacceptable according to the rules of this system. Also, it would be misleading to say that the subject, *a n impermanent phenomenon*, is a sound, for this would indicate that each and every impermanent phenomenon is a sound. The information that some impermanent phenomena are sounds and some are not is communicated by other means which will be discussed later in this introduction.

The subject in the form of syllogism or consequence used in this tradition may be interpreted in one of two ways: (1) only as a singular, in the sense that definition is used in the above syllogism (see p. 85) or (2) as suitable to be universally quantified as in the case of sound given above (see p. 86). However, technically all subjects are to be understood only as singulars. For the syllogism:

> The subject, sound, is an impermanent phenomenon because of being a product,

it is suitable and does not entail any logical fault to interpret this syllogism to mean that all sounds are impermanent phenomena because of being products. However, for the syllogism:

> With respect to the subject, sound, it is a generality of the sound of water because the sound of water is an instance of it,

it is not suitable to interpret this same subject, sound, to mean that all sounds are generalities of the sound of water, for such is not true. The sound of fire, for instance, is a sound but it is not a generality of the sound of water because the sound of water is not a sound of fire.

Thus, even though some subjects may be interpreted as universally quantified, it is almost as if by coincidence. There is no logical necessity for a subject to be interpretable as universally quantified, for the same subject in a different context may not be suitable for such an interpretation. However, in all cases the subject may be interpreted in the singular sense, and this is often the required interpretation.

Because of the nature of the subjects of debate as singular collective entities, the translation and annotation offered here often tenders expressions that are at odds with normal English grammar. However, a failure to reflect the singular nature of subjects would result in logical absurdities. In this translation some of the subjects are modified with an indefinite article "a" or "an", for *within the context* of the debates in which those subjects appear it is suitable and logically accurate to modify the subjects in that way. However, this is done only out of deference for English grammar and *technically* does not reflect either the Tibetan original or the full potency of the subjects.

THE CATEGORIES OF SUBJECTS

In this system of reasoning there is a difference in meaning between existence and being. If something exists as such and such, then it must be that thing. For instance, sound *exists* as an impermanent phenomenon and it *is* an impermanent phenomenon. However, being such and such does not necessarily imply existing as that thing. For instance, the horn of a rabbit *is* a non-existent, but it does not *exist* as a non-existent.

Both the claim that something exists and the claim that something is such and such are ontological statements having epistemological implications. That is, both claims say something about what exists and imply something about the possibility of knowing that existent. The claim that something *exists* explicitly asserts the existence of something and, within the view that all existents are objects of knowledge, implies that the existent may be known. For example, the claim that a pot *exists* says something about what exists and implies that, since it exists, one may have knowledge of a pot.

The claim that something *is* such and such asserts that being such exists, and as an existent, being such is an object of knowledge. For example, the claim that sound *is* an impermanent phenomenon says that being an impermanent phenomenon exists, and thus may be known. However, the claim that something is such and such merely postulates the existence of the subject's *being* such and such and does not necessarily imply the subject's *existing* as such and such. For example, the horn of a rabbit is a non-existent; thus, its *being* a non-existent is an existent. However, this does not imply its *existing* is a non-existent. The difference between existence (*yod pa*) and being (*yin pa*) in the copulative sense is a very important distinction in this form of Buddhist reasoning.

Further, the claim that something exists does not necessarily imply that there is anything which is that thing. For example, red and blue exist because red exists and blue exists; however, nothing is both red and blue. Something that is dotted or striped such as the American flag might *have* both red and blue colors, but no color on the American flag is both red and blue. Even red and blue are not red and blue because they are not, on the one hand, red and, on the other hand, blue.

Also, the claim that something is such and such implies that being such and such exists but does not necessarily imply that such and such itself exists. For example, uncomposed space is only a permanent phenomenon, for it is not partially or occasionally either an impermanent phenomenon or a non-existent. Thus, being only a permanent phenomenon exists. However, one cannot say that only-a-permanent-phenomenon exists because impermanent phenomena exist as well.

Using this theory as a basis, one can organize all the subjects of the syllogisms and consequences that appear in this text into eight categories. This arrangement of the subjects is not found in the Collected Topics tradition, but is clearly implied by the assertions made in this system. The fifty-three subjects that occur in this text illustrate seven of the eight categories, and an illustration of the eighth is provided in the text although it is not used as a subject. Any subject used in this text is just one of these eight types of subjects.

The eight categories of subjects listed with an example of each are:

1   a subject which is a non-existent and nothing is it (example: the horn of a rabbit)
2   a subject which is a non-existent but something is it (example: only-a-permanent-phenomenon)
3   a subject which is an impermanent phenomenon and every impermanent phenomenon is it (example: functioning thing)
4   a subject which is an impermanent phenomenon and some but not all impermanent phenomena are it (example: a pot)
5   subjects which are impermanent phenomena but nothing is them (example: the two—a pillar and a pot)
6   a subject which is a permanent phenomenon and every phenomenon is it (example: object of knowledge)
7   a subject which is a permanent phenomenon and some but not all phenomena are it (example: uncomposed space)
8   subjects which are permanent phenomena but nothing is them (example: the two—a definition and a definiendum).

In order to gain easier access to these eight categories it will be helpful to correlate each category with the subjects it includes from among the fifty-three subjects listed on pp. 77-84.

A SUBJECT WHICH IS A NON-EXISTENT AND NOTHING IS IT (EXAMPLE: THE HORN OF A RABBIT)

The only example of this category included among the fifty-three subjects is the horn of a rabbit, the first subject (p. 77). Other examples of this category are the child of a barren woman (*mo gsham gyi bu*), the flower of a dry tree (*shing skam po'i me tog*), and a sky flower (*nam mkha'i me tog*). None of these exist, and there is nothing which is any of them.

A SUBJECT WHICH IS A NON-EXISTENT BUT SOMETHING IS IT (EXAMPLE: ONLY-A-PERMANENT-PHENOMENON)

From among the fifty-three subjects the only one included in this category is only-a-permanent-phenomenon, the second subject (p. 77). As has been explained, only-a-permanent-phenomenon does not exist, but being only a permanent phenomenon does exist because there are things which are it.

Another example of this category, which is somewhat different from only-a-permanent-phenomenon, is non-existent. Although non-existent is not used as one of the fifty-three subjects in this text, it is important to note just how it is different from other examples of this category, such as only-a-generality (*spyi kho na*), only-an-impermanent-phenomenon (*mi rtag pa kho na*), only-red (*dmar po kho na*), and so forth. Non-existent does not exist, but being a non-existent does exist because, for instance, the child of a barren woman is a non-existent. However, even though the child of a barren woman *is* a non-existent, it does not *exist* as a non-existent. This is the difference between non-existent and only-a-permanent-phenomenon. Whatever is only a permanent phenomenon necessarily exists as only a permanent phenomenon, but whatever is a non-existent necessarily does not exist as a non-existent. There is a distinction between being something and existing as something.

A SUBJECT WHICH IS AN IMPERMANENT PHENOMENON AND EVERY IMPERMANENT PHENOMENON IS IT (EXAMPLE: FUNCTIONING THING)

From among the fifty-three different subjects used in the text, only four are included in this category, but it is the second most prevalent category in terms of usage. The four subjects are three through six in the above list (pp. 77-78): functioning thing, that which is able to perform a function, a functioning thing, and impermanent phenomenon. Functioning thing is mutually inclusive with impermanent phenomenon and that which is able to perform a function is the definition of functioning thing. As such, that which is able to perform a function is also mutually inclusive with impermanent phenomenon. These three are all impermanent phenomena and whatever is an impermanent phenomenon is necessarily all three of these. For instance, a pot is an impermanent phenomenon, it is a functioning thing, and it is able to perform a function. These subjects exist, and being these subjects exists.

A functioning thing, in the sense of *any* functioning thing, too must be included in this category, for it is an impermanent phenomenon and everything which is an impermanent phenomenon is a functioning thing. However, clearly there is a difference between *a* functioning thing and functioning thing, as such, that is not reflected in the Tibetan original. This difference arises in the translation into English; still, the debaters and their philosophical tradition as a whole clearly note the difference between functioning thing, the singular generality, and a functioning thing, meaning any functioning thing, but the Tibetan term is the same for both of these subjects. When translated into English, the bifurcation of this one term into both a singular sense and a general sense is something of an aberration of the Tibetan original.

A SUBJECT WHICH IS AN IMPERMANENT PHENOMENON AND SOME BUT NOT ALL IMPERMANENT PHENOMENA ARE IT (EXAMPLE: A POT)

From among the fifty-three different subjects used in this text more fit into this category than any other single category. Also, this category is the most prevalent in terms of usage. There are twenty-four different subjects included in this category, subjects seven through thirty in the above list (pp. 78-81): six types of color (the color of a white religious conch, the color of the Buddha Amitāyus, the color of a sapphire, the color of refined gold, the color of green

Amoghasiddhi, and the color of orange Mañjughoṣha), color-form, a round form, a white religious conch, a white horse, wind, a pot, pot, a gold pot, pot-which-is-one-with-pot, a pillar, sound, two types of causes of functioning thing (a prior arising of functioning thing and a prior arising of a prior arising of functioning thing), a subsequent arising of functioning thing, functioning-thing-which-is-one-with-functioning-thing, two types of causes of a pot (a being who is a cause of a pot and the mud which is a cause of a pot), and the flame of a butter lamp in its last moment.

All of these subjects are impermanent phenomena and each is such that there is something which is it, but it is not the case that everything which is an impermanent phenomenon is it. For instance, some impermanent phenomena are sounds and some are not. This is true for each of the subjects in this category.

The subjects included in this category may be subdivided into two types. Any of these subjects is either a subject for which many phenomena are it or a subject for which only one phenomenon is it. An example of the former is a pot. There are many different kinds of pot and each of them is a pot. A gold pot is a pot, a copper pot is a pot, a clay pot is a pot, and so forth. One would not want to say that many pots are *a* pot, for *a* pot is only singular; however, what is intended by this division is that there are many different things which can be used accurately as the grammatical subject in a copulative sentence ending with the predicate, "is a pot".

This sort of logical subject is to be distinguished from the remaining type in this category, a subject for which only one phenomenon is it. An example of this type of subject is pot-which-is-one-with-pot. "One-with-pot" means that which is *exactly* the same as pot from the point of view of both name and meaning. Pot is the only thing which has both exactly the same name and exactly the same meaning as pot. Thus, pot is one with pot and pot is pot which is one with pot. Other than pot, there is nothing which is pot which is one with pot. For this reason, pot-which-is-one-with-pot is a subject for which only one phenomenon is it. There are many such subjects.

SUBJECTS WHICH ARE IMPERMANENT PHENOMENA BUT NOTHING IS THEM (EXAMPLE: THE TWO—A PILLAR AND A POT)

The eight subjects in this category and the corresponding category for permanent phenomena most clearly enunciate the distinction between being and existence in this system of reasoning. Several of the subjects included in this category are not used in debates to demonstrate subjects for which nothing is them; still, they must be included here. Each of these subjects is a grouping of two or three different and mutually exclusive impermanent phenomena. These are subjects thirty-one through thirty-eight in the above list (pp. 81-82): the two—the color of sandalwood and the odor of sandalwood, the two—a large and a small barley grain produced from one barley head which is their substantial cause, the two—a white horse and a black horse, the two—a pillar and a pot, the two—matter and consciousness, the two—a gold pot and a copper pot, the three—matter, consciousnesses, and non-associated compositional factors, and the two—a prime cognizer and a subsequent cognizer—which are causes of functioning thing. Each of these subjects exists, but there is nothing which is any of them.

For instance, the two—a pillar and a pot—exist as impermanent phenomena, but there is no one thing or group of things which is the two—a pillar and a pot. A pillar and a pot are mutually exclusive. This means that there is nothing which is both of them. The same is true for each of these subjects; since they are groupings of mutually exclusive phenomena, there is nothing which is both or all of them. Thus, these subjects exist, but being any of these subjects does not exist.

Although all of these phenomena are such that they exist but there is nothing which is any of them, they are not all used in the debate manual to demonstrate this sort of exis-

tence. Several of these subjects are used in debates developing from the consideration of the various types of sameness
and difference that may be predicated between phenomena.
Thus, the focus on this type of subject is not merely on their
mutual exclusion but also on their similarities and differences. For instance, the two—a white horse and a black
horse—are the same type of phenomena in that they are
both horses, but they are not the same entity but diverse
entities produced from separate substantial causes.

A SUBJECT WHICH IS A PERMANENT PHENOMENON AND EVERY PHENOMENON IS IT (EXAMPLE: OBJECT OF KNOWLEDGE)

Of the fifty-three subjects which occur in this text only two,
subjects thirty-nine and forty in the above list (p. 82), are
included in this category: object of knowledge and existent.
(A questionable third, sound-impermanent-phenomenon,
may also be put in this category.) These are permanent phenomena because they are not produced from causes and
conditions and abide unchangingly. Being them exists
because whatever exists—for instance, a pillar, a pot, etc.—is
necessarily an object of knowledge. Even though these subjects themselves are permanent phenomena this does not
imply that whatever is an object of knowledge or an existent
is a permanent phenomenon. Rather, what is meant is that
all phenomena, permanent and impermanent alike, are
existents and objects of knowledge. In other words, object of
knowledge itself is permanent, but a table, although an
object of knowledge, is not permanent, but impermanent.

The case of sound-impermanent-phenomenon is different
from the others in this category. As will be explained later
(pp. 670-675), sound-impermanent-phenomenon is an
incomplete sentence consisting of a grammatical subject and
a predicate without a verb. When the verb "to be" is supplied, the grammatical subject and predicate are unified in
the copulative sentence, "Sound is an impermanent phenomenon." This is what is meant by saying that every

phenomenon is sound-impermanent-phenomenon, for no matter what one states this verbal trick will work. For whatever exists, sound is an impermanent phenomenon.

A SUBJECT WHICH IS A PERMANENT PHENOMENON AND SOME BUT NOT ALL PHENOMENA ARE IT (EXAMPLE: UNCOMPOSED SPACE)

There are twelve subjects included in this category which can be subdivided into three types. Any of these twelve is either (1) a subject which is a permanent phenomenon such that all permanent phenomena are it but not all existents are it, (2) a subject which is a permanent phenomenon such that some but not all permanent phenomena are it, or (3) a subject which is a permanent phenomenon such that only an impermanent phenomenon is it.

A Subject Which Is a Permanent Phenomenon Such That All Permanent Phenomena Are It But Not All Existents Are It

Subjects of the first type are permanent phenomenon and different-from-impermanent-phenomenon, subjects forty-two and forty-three above (p. 83). (There are many phenomena mutually inclusive with permanent phenomenon such as generally characterized phenomenon (*spyi mtshan, sāmānya-lakṣaṇa*) and conventional truth (*kun rdzob bden pa, samvṛti-satya*) which are included in this category, but none of them appear as subjects in this text.) Permanent phenomenon exists and being it exists, for there are many things which are permanent phenomena. However, since permanent phenomenon includes only permanent phenomena, it does not include all existents.

"Different-from-impermanent-phenomenon" is to be understood as a single expression which refers to everything which is not exactly the same as impermanent phenomenon from the point of view of name and meaning; thus, all permanent phenomena are different from impermanent phenomenon.

A Subject Which Is a Permanent Phenomenon Such That Some But Not All Permanent Phenomena Are It

Three subjects used in this text are included in the second subdivision of this category, subjects forty-four through forty-six (p. 83): uncomposed space, definiendum, and generality. Each of these is a permanent phenomenon such that some but not all permanent phenomena are it. For instance, definiendum itself is a permanent phenomenon, and some permanent phenomena are definienda and some are not; for example, that which is observed by valid cognition, as the definition of an existent, is a permanent phenomenon but not a definiendum. The same is also true for space and generality.

Also included here, although not used as a subject in the basic text, are subjects such as one-with-definiendum. One-with-definiendum is a permanent phenomenon and the only thing which is it is definiendum (which is itself a permanent phenomenon). Thus, some, in the sense of at least one, but not all permanent phenomena are one with definiendum.

A Subject Which Is a Permanent Phenomenon Such That Only an Impermanent Phenomenon Is It

Of the subjects used in this text, seven are included in the third subdivision of this category, subjects forty-seven through fifty-three (pp. 83-84): the definiendum of that which is able to perform a function, the triply qualified imputed existent of that which is able to perform a function, the definition of functioning thing, the triply qualified substantial existent of functioning thing, one-with-pot, pot's isolate, and pillar's isolate. Each of these is a permanent phenomenon such that only an impermanent phenomenon is it. These subjects exist, and being each of them exists. In each case, there is one and only one impermanent phenomenon which is that subject. For instance, that which is able to perform a function is the definition of functioning thing, but other than that which is able to perform a function there is nothing which is the definition of functioning thing. Even though whatever is the definition of functioning thing is necessarily an impermanent phenomenon, the definition of functioning thing, as such, is a permanent phenomenon. (See below, pp. 413-414.) This is true in the same way for the six others in this group as well.

SUBJECTS WHICH ARE PERMANENT PHENOMENA BUT NOTHING IS THEM (EXAMPLE: THE TWO—A DEFINITION AND A DEFINIENDUM)

Although there are no phenomena of this category which are actually used as subjects in the debate manual translated here, this category must be postulated in order to complete the description of subjects. Furthermore, subjects of this category are implied in the text. Just as in the cases of the impermanent subjects listed in the fifth category, there are permanent phenomena which exist but being them does not exist. An example is the two—a definition and a definiendum. Both definition and definiendum are permanent phenomena, and they are mutually exclusive. There is nothing which is both a definition and a definiendum. Any pair of mutually exclusive phenomena such that one or both of the pair is a permanent phenomenon is included in this category of subjects.

There are countless subjects included in each of these eight categories as well as in each of the subdivisions of the categories. The subjects of debate are not rare.

5 *The Procedure in Debate*

Essential for debate on the nature of phenomena is a solid procedure or strategy for analysis. More than merely asking and answering questions, debate is a process for establishing what is irrefutable. What is validly established will be borne out by debate and what is specious will be revealed and destroyed.

The purpose for this chapter is to supply a detailed annotation to the textual form of the debates, not so much to prepare one for actual debate as to prepare one to absorb the debates translated in this work.[1] There is a marked discrepancy between the forms of the debates as they appear in the Collected Topics texts and the forms of the debates as they would actually be spoken in the debating courtyard (*chos ra*). The textual form is a terse notation of the essential points in a possible debate, which is meant not to represent a debate as it would be spoken, but to supply the student with information, to suggest debate, to demonstrate

---

[1] The procedure given here for applying the textual form of the debates to actual spoken debate is in accordance with Lati Rinbochay's oral commentary.

patterns of debate, to clarify points of doctrine, to dispel possible qualms, and so forth.

The procedure for transferring or applying this information to actual spoken debate is explained only in the oral tradition. One does not learn how to debate merely through reading texts but by studying with an experienced debater and then practicing in the debating courtyard. In the traditional setting, the oral explanation of a teacher is essential. Thus, in order to understand the issues and reasoning expressed in the debates translated here it is necessary to understand to some extent the procedure in debate and just how the terse textual notations imply a longer form of spoken debate.

In this chapter, the basis for demonstrating the procedure in debate is the first debate in the Tutor's *Collected Topics*, the most introductory debate on colors, referred to herein as debate A.1. First, the whole of debate A.1, just as it appears in the text, is provided with the text indented in order to mark it as translation and to distinguish it from the longer implied form of debate A.1 and from annotations. Second, in a line-by-line explanation, the text is mixed together with the spoken form of the debate. Here again the text is indented and the statements of the implied spoken form of the debate are set to the margin in order to distinguish them from the textual statements. Finally, the whole of the implied debate, just as it might be spoken in the debating courtyard, is provided alone. In the spoken form the statements are assigned to either the Challenger (C), the Buddhist Proponent of Sūtra[1] standing and asking questions, or the Defender (D), the non-Proponent of Sūtra sitting and answering. Thus, the debate will be given in both its terse textual form and in a longer form suggested by the text and closer to actual practice. However, in no case would one speak both forms of the debate.

---

[1] Here the description of the Challenger as a "Proponent of the Sūtra School" must be understood to mean a Proponent of the Sūtra School Following Reasoning as interpreted by the Tutor Pur-bu-jok Jam-ba-gya-tso.

Debate A.1 begins with the non-Proponent of Sūtra Defender's putting forth the absurd view that "Whatever is a color is necessarily red." Obviously, it is not the case that everything which is a color is red, for blue is a color which is not red, white is a color which is not red, and so forth. Still, an imaginary Defender is put in this position in the first debate in "The Introductory Path of Reasoning" in order to help one understand the formal procedure. Supplemented with implied information in brackets, the entire text of debate A.1 is:

> If someone [a hypothetical Defender] says, "Whatever is a color is necessarily red," [the Sūtra School Challenger responds to him,] "It [absurdly] follows that the subject, the color of a white religious conch, is red because of being a color. You asserted the pervasion [that whatever is a color is necessarily red]."
>
> If he says that the reason[1] [i.e., that the color of a white religious conch is a color] is not established, [the Sūtra School Challenger responds,] "It follows that the subject, the color of a white religious conch, is a color because of being white."
>
> If he says that the reason [i.e., that the color of a white religious conch is white] is not established, [the Sūtra School Challenger responds,] "It follows that the subject, the color of a white religious conch, is white because of being one with the color of a white religious conch."
>
> If he accepts the basic consequence [that the color of a white religious conch is red, the Sūtra School Challenger responds,] "It follows that the subject, the color of a white religious conch, is not red because of being white."

---

[1] Here the text says simply, "Not established (*ma grub*)," meaning, "The reason is not established (*rtags ma grub*)." Note that in this context *rtags* is translated as "reason" rather than as "sign".

If he says there is no pervasion [i.e., even though it is true that the color of a white religious conch is white, it is not the case that whatever is white is necessarily not red, the Sūtra School Challenger responds,] "It follows that there is pervasion [i.e., whatever is white is necessarily not red] because a common locus of the two, white and red, does not exist; because those two [white and red] are mutually exclusive."

The Tibetan original of Debate A.1, as in the Tutor's *Collected Topics*, follows:

ཁ་དོག་ཡིན་ན་དམར་པོ་ཡིན་པས་ཁྱབ་ཟེར་ན། ཆོས་ཅན་དཀར་པོའི་
ཁ་དོག་ཆོས་ཅན། དམར་པོ་ཡིན་པར་ཐལ། ཁ་དོག་ཡིན་པའི་ཕྱིར།
ཁྱབ་པ་ཁས།

མ་གྲུབ་ན། ཆོས་ཅན་དཀར་པོའི་ཁ་དོག་ཆོས་ཅན། ཁ་དོག་ཡིན་
པར་ཐལ། དཀར་པོ་ཡིན་པའི་ཕྱིར།

མ་གྲུབ་ན། ཆོས་ཅན་དཀར་པོའི་ཁ་དོག་ཆོས་ཅན། དཀར་པོ་ཡིན་
པར་ཐལ། ཆོས་ཅན་དཀར་པོའི་ཁ་དོག་དང་གཅིག་ཡིན་པའི་ཕྱིར།

རྩ་བར་འདོད་ན། ཆོས་ཅན་དཀར་པོའི་ཁ་དོག་ཆོས་ཅན། དམར་
པོ་མ་ཡིན་པར་ཐལ། དཀར་པོ་ཡིན་པའི་ཕྱིར།

མ་ཁྱབ་ན་ཁྱབ་པ་ཡོད་པར་ཐལ། དཀར་པོ་དང་དམར་པོ་གཉིས་
ཀྱི་གཞི་མཐུན་མེད་པའི་ཕྱིར་ཏེ། དེ་གཉིས་འགལ་བ་ཡིན་པའི་ཕྱིར།

The text begins with only the conditional, "If someone says, 'Whatever is a color is necessarily red.' " This means that a hypothetical Defender asserts this view. However, the *spoken* form of the debate actually begins with the Challenger's questioning the Defender whose view becomes clear through his answer. Thus, the first to speak in actual debate is the Challenger. He begins with the auspicious seed syllable of Mañjushrī, the special deity of debate. The text says:

> If someone [a hypothetical Defender] says, "Whatever is a color is necessarily red,"

This implies the spoken debate:

C: *Dhiḥ*! The subject, in just the way [Mañjushrī debated]. Is whatever is a color necessarily red?
D: I accept [that whatever is a color is necessarily red].
C: It follows that whatever is a color is necessarily red.
D: I accept it.

The Sūtra School Challenger begins the debate with the statement, "*Dhiḥ*! The subject, in just the way [Mañjushrī debated] (*dhiḥ ji ltar chos can*)." "*Dhiḥ*", the seed syllable of Mañjushrī, is usually uttered in a high-pitched voice and the rest at normal pitch. As an auspicious portent, at the beginning of every session of debate the Challenger declares that like Mañjushrī, the manifestation of the wisdom of the Buddhas, he will state subjects and consequences in order to defeat the wrong views and doubts of opponents.[1] In practice this statement is said only once by each Challenger upon beginning each new debating session, thus once or twice a day.

Having spoken the auspicious seed syllable of Mañjushrī, the Challenger asks, "Is whatever is a color necessarily red (*kha dog yin na dmar po yin pas khyab pa'i phyir*)?" The attitude is like that of one approaching another to find what he thinks. At this point the Defender must decide how he wishes to answer the Challenger's question. He may answer affirmatively, accepting that whatever is a color is necessarily red, or he may answer negatively, denying that whatever is a color is necessarily red. If he answers affirmatively, he says, "I accept it (*'dod*)," meaning, "I accept that whatever is a color is necessarily red." If he answers negatively, he says,

---

[1] Denma Lochö Rinbochay, oral commentary. Some scholars would not agree with Lochö Rinbochay's explanation of this point.

"There is no pervasion (*ma khyab* or *khyab pa ma byung*)," meaning, "Whatever is a color is not necessarily red."[1] Accepting the pervasion means that the Defender asserts that colors exist only among red things. Denying the pervasion means that the Defender asserts that colors do not exist exclusively among red things. This is the first point of decision for the Defender, the first fork in the path of Debate A.1.

The Defender gives an affirmative answer, an answer that is not concordant with fact, for some colors are not red. At this point the Challenger repeats what has been accepted, but now he puts it into the form of a consequence, "It follows that whatever is a color is necessarily red." He is repeating the statement for clarity and introducing the former question into the formal framework of a logical consequence. This is the point at which the text begins. In actual practice, the Defender has answered affirmatively the Challenger's question and then accepts its restatement as a consequence. To repeat, the text says:

> If someone [a hypothetical Defender] says, "Whatever is a color is necessarily red,"

This implies the spoken debate:

C: *Dhīḥ*! The subject, in just the way [Mañjushri debated]. Is whatever is a color necessarily red?
D: I accept [that whatever is a color is necessarily red].
C: It follows that whatever is a color is necessarily red.
D: I accept it.

When the Defender accepts that whatever is a color is necessarily red, he is asserting a pervasion. That is, colors exist

---

[1] Alternatively, if the Defender accepts the Challenger's question, he may answer, "There is pervasion (*khyab*)," and if he disagrees, he may say, "The reason is not established (*rtags ma grub*)." The latter answer is given because the Challenger has framed his question within a reason as "because whatever is a color is necessarily red". As usual, to disagree with a reason—even one with an imbedded pervasion, one says that it is not established.

exclusively among red things, or, colors are pervaded by being red. Obviously, it is not the case that all colors are red; however, this absurd position is being used as a basis for illustrating a formal debating procedure which may then be applied to more difficult issues.

The procedure involves stating to the mistaken opponent a contradictory consequence of his own position in order to draw out its absurdities. This process is used from the beginning of the rudimentary "Introductory Path of Reasoning" through to the presentations of the higher topics, such as the philosophy of the Middle Way School. For whatever position one holds there are logical consequences, and if the view is mistaken, through reliance on consequences the flaws in that view will become manifest. However, if the view accords with fact and is well-founded, a thorough analysis of its consequences will bear this out.

In order to demonstrate to his opponent that it is not the case that all colors are red, the Sūtra School Challenger must choose a counterexample. To show that some colors are not red the counterexample must be something which is a color but is not red. The Challenger points out the case of the color of a white religious conch. The conch shell is one of the eight good luck symbols (*bkra shis rtags brgyad*).[1] It "signifies the promulgation of the Buddha's precepts, or *Dharma*".[2] The shells are made into horns by cutting open the broad end and then used within the monastery "for assembling the monks for prayers or for meals".[3] The color of a white religious conch is, of course, white. However, since the hypothetical Defender asserts that whatever is a color is necessar-

---

[1] According to Detlef Ingo Lauf, *Tibetan Sacred Art, The Heritage of Tantra*, (Berkeley: Shambala, 1976), p. 89, the eight good luck symbols are: "victory sign, fish, vessel of water of life, lotus, conch-shell, eight-fold knot, umbrella of dignity, and wheel of doctrine".

[2] Hugh R. Downs, *Rhythms of a Himalayan Village*, (San Francisco: Harper & Row, 1980), p. 38.

[3] "Inaugural Exhibition Catalogue", of the Tibet House Museum (New Delhi: Statesman Press, 1965), p. 78.

ily red, according to his view the color of a white religious conch too must be red, for it is a color. The text says:

> [the Sūtra School Challenger responds to him,] "It [absurdly] follows that the subject, the color of a white religious conch, is red."

The spoken form of this is exactly the same:

C: It [absurdly] follows that the subject, the color of a white religious conch, is red.

The Challenger must carefully state the subject as the *color* of a white religious conch rather than simply positing a white religious conch as the counterexample. For, a white religious conch would not serve as a suitable subject because, being a hard tangible object, it *has* color but is not a color.

Further, the Challenger must choose a subject which, although a color, is not red in order to have a viable counterexample which can suitably reveal the absurdities of the Defender's error. The second position of the statement of pervasion, red, is put as the predicate of the consequences. That the color of a white religious conch is red is not established by valid cognition; so the "thesis" of the consequence is factually false.

In this way, the debate manual gives the instruction that if someone says that whatever is a color is necessarily red, in response to that mistaken view the Challenger may fling back a logical consequence using the counterexample of the color of a white religious conch.

It accords with normal disputation even in ordinary conversation that when one states a position, others will seek to test that assertion by giving examples in support or counterexamples to refute. Also, as in this system one will seek to support reasons by giving other reasons and so on. Normally, such disputation is not done within a formalized framework as is Tibetan debate, but it can be said that the Collected Topics tradition is a formalized system developed in accordance with the procedure of disputation in ordinary conversation.

At this point in the debate, once the Challenger has given a consequence, the Defender must give an answer. He is faced with a consequence having only two components of subject and predicate, and he is limited to one of only two possible answers:

1   I accept it (*'dod*).
Formulated in this case: I accept that the color of a white religious conch is red (*chos dung dkar po'i kha dog dmar po yin par 'dod*).
Formulated in general: I accept that that subject is that predicate of the consequence (*chos can de gsal ba de yin par 'dod*).
2   Why (*ci'i phyir*)?
Formulated in this case: Why is the color of a white religious conch red (*chos dung dkar po'i kha dog dmar po yin pa ci'i phyir*)?
Formulated in general: Why is that subject that predicate of the consequence (*chos can de gsal ba de yin pa ci'i phyir*)?

These answers have the force of agreement and disagreement with the consequence. Given the Defender's view that whatever is a color is necessarily red, it is an accurate consequence of his position that the color of a white religious conch would be red. Still, this is manifestly an unwanted consequence (*mi 'dod pa'i thal 'gyur*), for no one would wish to assert that white is red. Nonetheless, if the Defender is consistent in his view, he would accept this consequence, and the text eventually considers this possible answer.

Before taking up the debate that develops from the Defender's accepting the consequence, the text considers the possibility of his answering, "Why?" in response to the consequence. In a sense, this is both an answer and a question. It is obviously a question, but it is an answer too in that the Defender has made a decision that the consequence is unacceptable and seeks the Challenger's reasons for drawing this absurdity. When the Defender asks for a reason to justify the consequence, he is implicitly asserting that the opposite of the consequence is true. That is, he has decided that the color of a white religious conch is *not* red. The Challenger may hold him to this implicit assertion or he may give the Defender a reason why, according to his view that whatever is a color is necessarily red, the color of a white religious conch must be red.

The text moves first to consider the debate that develops from the Defender's answering, "Why?" to the consequence. Thus, in the spoken form of the debate, in response to the Challenger's stating the consequence that the color of a white religious conch is red, the Defender answers:

D: Why [is the color of a white religious conch red]?

In response, the Challenger gives him the reason that accords with his original false assertion. The text says:

> "Because of being a color. You asserted the perva-
> sion [that whatever is a color is necessarily red]."

The spoken form of this is just the same:

C: Because of being a color. You asserted the pervasion [that
   whatever is a color is necessarily red].

In this section the Challenger is giving a reason only. It is understood that this reason is being given as justification for the basic consequence (*rtsa ba'i thal 'gyur*), that the color of a white religious conch is red. Thus, the entire consequence, together with the reason, is stated:

> It follows that the subject, the color of a white
> religious conch, is red because of being a color. You
> asserted the pervasion [that whatever is a color is
> necessarily red].

It must be clearly understood that this argument is an accurate conclusion drawn from the Defender's position. The Challenger supplied the subject, but the predicate of the consequence, red, and the reason, color, are implied by the Defender's assertion that whatever is a color is necessarily red. In applying the Defender's accepted pervasion to a consequence, the relative positions of the two main components, color and red, are switched. That is, in the statement of pervasion color is stated before red, whereas in the consequence red is stated before color. This may be illustrated thus:

Whatever is *a color* is necessarily *red*

It follows that the subject is *red* because of being *a color*.

This manner of applying the pervasion is accurate. In the chapter on syllogisms and consequences it was explained that the reason is the pervaded, for its extent must be less than or equal to the extent of the predicate to be proven or the predicate of the consequence. Conversely, the extent of the predicate to be proven or, in this case, the predicate of the consequence must be greater than or equal to the extent of the reason; thus, the predicate is the pervader. That the subject has the quality of the reason, the pervaded, proves that it has the quality of the predicate, the pervader. The reverse would not be accurate for the cases in which the extent of the predicate is greater than the extent of the reason.

At this point in the debate, the Challenger has stated a logical consequence of the Defender's view. This is a properly formulated consequence having the three units of subject, predicate, and reason. As explained in the chapter on syllogisms and consequences (see pp. 33-60), a valid *syllogism* must have a reason which is the three modes: (1) the property of the subject, (2) the forward pervasion, and (3) the counter-pervasion. However, a valid or correct *consequence (thal 'gyur yang dag)*, as opposed to a syllogism, need not be a valid statement; rather, it is such that the opponent, due to his own assertions, cannot effectively object to the reason or the pervasion and also cannot accept the consequence. For a person who asserts that whatever is a color is necessarily red, the consequence:

It follows that the subject, the color of a white
religious conch, is red because of being a color,

is a correct consequence. The Defender cannot deny the pervasion without immediately contradicting himself, for he
has just asserted it. The Challenger reminds him of this by
saying, "You asserted the pervasion [that whatever is a color
is necessarily red]." This warning is comparable to inform-
ing a chess opponent that his king is in check. Also, in this
consequence, the Defender cannot effectively deny the reason, for the declaration that the color of a white religious
conch is a color is true. Finally, the Defender cannot sensibly
accept the basic consequence, that the color of a white religious conch is red, for such is not factually concordant. The
opponent is left without an effective answer, a state which
he is gradually shown by internally running through the
possible answers.

Thus, in this first consequence the Sūtra School
Challenger is putting forth a statement which would be
invalid if straightforwardly reformulated as a syllogism. It is
by virtue of its factual invalidity that the Challenger is able
to show the Defender his error, for the absurd consequence
stated to him is a logical conclusion drawn from the
Defender's own position. The Challenger's statement of a
correct consequence is able to suppress or overwhelm the
opponent's wrong ideas when he comes to realize the faults
of his assertions' logical consequences as they are stated to
him.

A correctly formulated consequence may or may not be
valid when straightforwardly reformulated as a syllogism.
In this introductory section on colors all of the Sūtra School
Challenger's consequences may be reformulated straightforwardly as valid syllogisms except in the cases of the first
one given in each debate.

At this point in the debate, having been given a contradictory consequence complete with subject, predicate, and
reason, the Defender has a choice of three possible answers:

1 I accept that the color of a white religious conch is red
(*chos dung dkar po'i kha dog dmar po yin par 'dod*).
Formulated in general: I accept that that subject is that
predicate of the consequence (*chos can de gsal ba de yin
par 'dod*).

2 The reason is not established (*rtags ma grub*).
Formulated in this case: The reason, that the color of a
white religious conch is a color, is not established (*chos
dung dkar po'i kha dog kha dog yin pa rtags ma grub*).
Formulated in general: The reason, that that subject is
that reason, is not established (*chos can de rtags de yin pa
rtags ma grub*).

3 There is no pervasion (*ma khyab* or *khyab pa ma byung*).
Formulated in this case: Whatever is a color is not
necessarily red (*kha dog yin na dmar po yin pas ma khyab*).
Formulated in general: Whatever is that reason is not
necessarily that predicate of the consequence (*rtags de
yin na gsal ba de yin pas ma khyab*).

Again, the Defender may accept the consequence that the
color of a white religious conch is red. When faced with the
two-part basic consequence:

It [absurdly] follows that the subject, the color of a
white religious conch, is red,

one of the Defender's two possible answers is to accept the
consequence. Now when faced with a complete three-part
consequence having subject, predicate, and reason, acceptance is again a possible answer.

However, in response to a full three-part consequence the
Defender spells out his acceptance by saying, "I accept that
the color of a white religious conch is red," or, "I accept that
it is red (*dmar po yin par 'dod*)," whereas in response to a two-
part consequence he says simply, "I accept it." According to
the etiquette of formal debate as explained by some
scholars, it is considered embarrassing to say simply, "I
accept it," to a full consequence having all three components

of subject, predicate, and reason.[1] Such is not the case when the Challenger has stated a two-part consequence, when it is suitable simply to accept the statement without spelling out the meaning of that acceptance.

In either case, if the Defender accepts the consequence, he is held to this view and is given further consequences of his acceptance or is dissuaded from his acceptance by reasoning explaining why the color of a white religious conch is not red. The text eventually explains the line of reasoning developing from the Defender's giving this answer.

If in response to the three-part consequence the opponent defends his assertion by saying that the reason is not established, he is held to the position that the opposite of the reason is established as a quality of the subject. For instance, when he answers that the reason, that the color of a white religious conch is a color, is not established, the Challenger may fling back at him the consequence of his answer by saying, "It follows that the subject, the color of a white religious conch, is *not* a color." Or, as is the usual case in "The Introductory Path of Reasoning", the Challenger will go on to explain his statement of the reason by giving another reason to justify the former, "It follows that the subject, the color of a white religious conch, is a color because of ... ."

The Defender's third possible answer to a three-part consequence is to deny the pervasion, thus rejecting the Challenger's consequence as indefinite. That is, he might now claim that, "Whatever is a color is not necessarily red" (sometimes translated here as, "It is not the case that whatever is a color is necessarily red"). However, the Defender has only just asserted that whatever is a color *is* necessarily red, and he is not likely to reverse immediately his position. Still, the Defender has at this point been given a contradictory consequence of his position, and he is not bound to continue to assert that all colors are red. To deny the pervasion is the correct response to this first basic consequence, but the Defender fails to do this as yet. If he

[1] Denma Lochö Rinbochay, oral commentary.

were to deny the pervasion now, he would be contradicting his own basic position, and this would signal the end of the debate. However, for purposes of instruction, the debate continues.

If the Defender disclaims the presence of the pervasion, by the rules of formal debate he implicitly accepts the establishment of the reason—in this case, that the color of a white religious conch is a color. Therefore, he may not return later, after having denied the pervasion, to deny the reason. Thus, when the Defender denies the pervasion, although explicitly his answer only indicates he accepts that whatever is a color is *not* necessarily red, the answer carries the force of saying, "Although it is true that the color of a white religious conch is a color, it is not the case that whatever is a color is necessarily red."

An alternative fourth possible answer to this consequence is:

4   The pervasion is opposite (*khyab log*).
    Alternatively: It is a contradictory pervasion (*'gal khyab*).
    Formulated in this case: Whatever is a color is necessarily not red (*kha dog yin na dmar po ma yin pas khyab*).
    Formulated in general: Whatever is that reason is necessarily not that predicate of the consequence (*rtags de yin na gsal ba de ma yin pas khyab*).

The force of this answer is technically included within the third answer, "There is no pervasion," for in every case of which the pervasion is opposite, the response that there is no pervasion also is appropriate. For, if it is the case that whatever is that reason is necessarily not that predicate, then it naturally follows that it is also the case that whatever is that reason is not necessarily that predicate. For instance, if a Challenger were to state the consequence, "It follows that the subject, the color of a white religious conch, is an object of hearing because of being a color," then the appropriate response would be, "The pervasion is opposite," meaning whatever is a color is necessarily not an object of hearing. Since it is the case that whatever is a color is necessarily not an object of hearing, it naturally follows that it is also the case that whatever is a color is not necessarily an object of hearing. To say it another way, pointing out that the pervasion is opposite has the force of asserting, "No colors are objects of hearing," whereas pointing out that there is no pervasion has the force of asserting, "Some colors are not objects of hearing." Naturally, if no colors are objects of hearing, then some (in fact, all) colors are not objects of hearing. If a Defender is faced with a consequence to which he might answer that the pervasion is opposite, this is a stronger and more specific answer than merely pointing out that there is no pervasion.

In the case at hand, the Defender is faced with the consequence:

> It follows that the subject, the color of a white religious conch, is red because of being a color.

If the Defender answers to this consequence that the pervasion is opposite, he would be asserting that whatever is a color is necessarily not red. Such an answer would be factually false, for some colors are red. Also, this answer would be at odds with his original assertion that whatever is a color is necessarily red, and thus he does not make it.

In all cases the Defender is limited to just one of these possible answers. During the course of a debate, however, he may respond differently to the same consequence posed at different times. In summary, it will be helpful to gather in one place the Defender's possible answers together with their general formulas. Table II shows these:

Table II: The Defender's Answers

In response to a two-part consequence:

It follows that that subject is that predicate.

1   I accept it (*'dod*).
Formulated: I accept that that subject is that predicate (*chos can de gsal ba de yin par 'dod*).
2   Why (*ci'i phyir*)?
Formulated: Why is that subject that predicate (*chos can de gsal ba de yin ba ci'i phyir*)?

In response to a three-part consequence:

It follows that that subject is that predicate because of being that reason.

1   I accept that that subject is that predicate (*chos can de gsal ba de yin par 'dod*).
2   The reason is not established (*rtags ma grub*).
Formulated: The reason, that that subject is that reason, is not established (*chos can de rtags de yin pa rtags ma grub*).
3   There is no pervasion (*ma khyab* or *khyab pa ma byung*).
Formulated: Whatever is that reason is not necessarily that predicate (*rtags de yin na gsal ba de yin pas ma khyab*).
4   The pervasion is opposite (*khyab log*).
Alternatively: It is a contradictory pervasion (*'gal khyab*).
Formulated: Whatever is that reason is necessarily not that predicate (*rtags de yin na gsal ba de ma yin pas khyab*).

In the course of debate A.1 as it is implied in the longer spoken form, the Defender gives three of these possible answers in response to the same basic three-part contradictory consequence. This corresponds to the intent of the text and is done for the sake of illustration; however, this does not imply that all such debates follow this course.

For a valid syllogism, the first mode of the sign is the property of the subject, that the subject has the quality of being that reason. Reflecting the priority of establishing the reason, the text proceeds first to the line of reasoning developing from the Defender's possible answer that the reason of the basic consequence is not established. That is, he defends his basic assertion against the Challenger's consequence by claiming that the reason, that the color of a white religious conch is a color, is not established. The text says:

> If [the Defender] says that the reason is not established,

This means:

D: The reason, that the color of a white religious conch is a color, is not established.

In response to the Defender's answer the Challenger moves to establish the reason in relation to the subject by stating a subsequent reason to justify that the color of a white religious conch is a color. In so doing, the reason from the first consequence, color, becomes the predicate of the second consequence, the old predicate drops out, and a new reason is given in support of the new predicate. The text says:

> [the Sūtra School Challenger responds to him,] "It follows that the subject, the color of a white religious conch, is a color because of being white."

The spoken form of this is exactly the same:

C: It follows that the subject, the color of a white religious conch, is a color because of being white.

To repeat, here the reason of the first consequence has become the predicate of the second consequence. In the first consequence:

> It follows that the subject, the color of a white religious conch, is red because of being a color,

the Challenger was trying to show that in accordance with the Defender's view that whatever is a color is necessarily red, then being red would be a property of the color of a white religious conch. Once the Defender denies the establishment of the reason, that the color of a white religious conch is a color, the Challenger moves to prove to his opponent that the subject is a color. The issue of whether or not the subject is red is set aside for the moment while the Challenger addresses the Defender's present doubt, whether or not the subject is a color. Thus, the new consequence, given in response to the Defender's qualm, takes color as the predicate to be proven as a quality of the subject. The former reason has become the new predicate, the old predicate drops out, and a new reason is given in support of the new consequence. This flow may be illustrated:

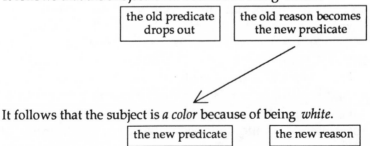

It follows that the subject is *red* because of being *a color.*

| the old predicate drops out | the old reason becomes the new predicate |

It follows that the subject is *a color* because of being *white.*

| the new predicate | the new reason |

This procedure illustrates the pragmatic approach of Tibetan monastic debate, as it accords with normal discussion and disputation for persons to seek to justify their claims which are being denied. The form may be seen as uncomplicated. This system of debate is a matter of learning a basic form and procedure and then applying what one has learned to many different topics. The complication comes in the meaning.

In seeking to establish color as a quality of the subject, the Challenger's consequence:

> It follows that the subject, the color of a white religious conch, is a color because of being white,

is an example of a consequence which, if straightforwardly reformulated as a syllogism, would have a reason which is all three modes of the sign. Assuming the epistemological requirements are met, since the color of a white religious conch is white, the reason is a property of the subject. There is positive pervasion because whatever is white is necessarily a color; consequently, there is also counter-pervasion, for it is true that whatever is not a color is necessarily not white.

Both the first and second consequences are equally correct consequences. There is someone for whom each is a correct consequence, and in either case the opponent is not able to give a factually concordant answer. The difference is that the second consequence may be straightforwardly reformulated as a correct consequence whereas the first may not. The first consequence is one for which the reason, that the color of a white religious conch is a color, is established by valid cognition, but the pervasion, that whatever is a color is necessarily red, is established merely by assertion. For the second consequence, the reason, that the color of a white religious conch is white, and the pervasion, that whatever is white is necessarily a color, are both established by valid cognition. In this introductory section on colors all of the Sūtra School Challenger's consequences may be reformulated as valid syllogisms except in the cases of the first one given in each debate.

The important information in the second consequence is in the pervasion, whatever is white is necessarily a color. In a sense, this is not very revealing, but it does teach about terminology and how to use it. The author, the Tutor Jam-ba-gya-tso, is indicating to the student that although the color of a thing is a color and a white conch is commonly said to be white, it itself is not a color. We commonly say that a house or a person is white, but this is loose and factually incorrect terminology; rather, the *color* of a house or a person's complexion is white.

Still the Defender is not convinced that the color of a white religious conch is a color because of being white. He denies that the reason is established. The text says:

> If [the Defender] says that the reason is not established,

Or, in other words:

D: The reason, that the color of a white religious conch is white, is not established.

As before in the previous consequence, when the Challenger responds, he takes the old reason which has been denied and makes it the predicate in the new consequence and then supplies a new reason in support of the new predicate. Here the Challenger justifies his assertion of the subject as white by the reason that it is one with the color of a white religious conch. Again this is a properly formulated consequence which as a syllogism would have a reason which is the three modes of a logically valid sign. The text says:

> [the Sūtra School Challenger responds to him,] "It follows that the subject, the color of a white religious conch, is white because of being one with the color of a white religious conch."

The spoken form of this is exactly the same:

C: It follows that the subject, the color of a white religious conch, is white because of being one with the color of a white religious conch.

The only thing which is one with the color of a white religious conch is the color of a white religious conch. Being one (*gcig, ekatva*) with something means being *exactly* the same in both name and meaning. Any variation between two phenomena means that they are not one, but different (*tha dad, nānātva*). Even mutually inclusive phenomena, though they include all the same phenomena, are different because of being different in name.

Whatever exists is one with itself and cannot be different from itself. Consequently, whatever exists is different from anything other than itself, for it is one only with itself. In the case at hand, the reason is established, for the color of a white religious conch is one with the color of a white religious conch. Also, there is pervasion, for whatever is one with the color of a white religious conch is necessarily white, as the color of a white religious conch, the only thing which is one with the color of a white religious conch, is white.

At this point, the next notation *in the text* has the Defender accepting the basic consequence:

> It follows that the subject, the color of a white religious conch, is red because of being a color.

That is, the Defender accepts that the color of a white religious conch is red. This is the first consequence, the one posited in response to the Defender's asserting that whatever is a color is necessarily red.

In actual debate as it might be spoken in the debating courtyard, from the point of the Challenger's stating the third consequence:

> It follows that the subject, the color of a white religious conch, is white because of being one with the color of a white religious conch,

the debate would proceed back through the reasons just given and once denied by the Defender up to the point of the Defender's accepting the basic consequence. That the text ceases to pursue the line of reasoning resulting from the Defender's questioning the reason of the basic consequence indicates that the Defender has come to accept that line of reasoning. From the point of the Defender's accepting the final consequence, the Challenger reviews in reverse order the line of reasoning that has brought the Defender to the point where he can accept the argument. In the reviewing process, the Defender must accept all of the Challenger's statements or, upon objection, will receive further justification for those reasons until he can accept them. In this way the debate can go any number of routes, one consequence leading the discussion to an ancillary topic, then eventually returning to proceed ahead on the route of the primary topic. Formal debate is not an argument, nor is it a matter of one opponent's merely trying to embarrass the other. The method of procedure in actual debate gives the discussion more of a flavor of seeking to establish the truth.[1]

Once the Defender has accepted the last consequence, that the color of a white religious conch is white, the Challenger then moves back to the reason of the immediately preceding consequence which the Defender had earlier questioned but is now likely to accept. Thus, the spoken form of this debate follows:

D: I accept that the color of a white religious conch is white.
C: It follows that the subject, the color of a white religious conch, is a color.
D: I accept it.

As mentioned earlier (pp. 111-112), according to some scholars the etiquette of debate requires that when a Defender accepts the "thesis" of a full three-part consequence, he must give a full answer spelling out his acceptance. However, when the Challenger has stated a two-part consequence, it is suitable simply to accept the statement without spelling out the answer. Thus, in accordance with this etiquette, in his response to the Challenger's third consequence the Defender spells out his acceptance by saying, "I accept that the color of a white religious conch is white," whereas in his response to the Challenger's next consequence he says simply, "I accept it."

The procedure for reviewing the line of reasoning which led to the Defender's acceptance is reported only in the oral

---

[1] Geshe Wangyal (*dge bshes dbang rgyal*), oral commentary.

tradition. The texts, for obvious reasons of space limitation, do not spell out the entire implied or spoken form of the debates. Rather, the texts serve as notations on possible debates and, while teaching the form of debate, primarily relay the content of philosophical issues, clarify difficult points, and suggest debates.

Once the Defender has accepted the qualities of the subject that he had formerly denied, the basic consequence is posed for a second time. He himself has asserted the pervasion, that whatever is a color is necessarily red. He has come to accept the establishment of the reason, that the color of a white religious conch is a color. He will opt now for the only remaining alternative, accepting the consequence. This acceptance ushers in the second branch of the debate, often the more revealing one. The text says:

If [the Defender] accepts the basic consequence,

This implies, in its spoken form, that the Challenger has once again posed the basic consequence and that the Defender now accepts it, spelling out his answer fully in response to a three-part consequence:

C: It follows that the subject, the color of a white religious conch, is red because of being a color.

D: I accept that the color of a white religious conch is red.

Now that the Defender has accepted the basic consequence, that the color of a white religious conch is red, the Challenger refutes this position by again pointing out that the subject is white. The text says:

[the Sūtra School Challenger responds to him,] "It follows that the subject, the color of a white religious conch, is not red because of being white."

The spoken form of this is exactly the same:

C: It follows that the subject, the color of a white religious conch, is not red because of being white.

Whatever is white is necessarily not red. This the Defender proceeds to deny when he claims that there is no pervasion, trying to defend against this consequence by asserting that it is not the case that whatever is white is necessarily not red, perhaps thinking that there is at least one color which is both white and red. The text says:

> If [the Defender] says there is no pervasion,

Meaning:

> D: There is no pervasion [i.e., even though it is true that the color of a white religious conch is white, it is not the case that whatever is white is necessarily not red].

The subject now drops out of the consequence, and the existence of the denied pervasion becomes the subject and predicate, as it were. The Challenger moves to support the pervasion of his former consequence, that whatever is white is necessarily not red, in opposition to the Defender's assertion. He gives a reason why whatever is white is necessarily not red: " ... because a common locus of the two, white and red, does not exist". A common locus (*gzhi mthun pa, samāna-adhikaraṇa*) of white and red would be a color which is both white and red. Pink, though a mixture of white and red, is not both white and red. Something that is spotted or striped *has* two colors, but it is not two colors. At this point the text gives two reasons: " ... because a common locus of the two, white and red, does not exist; because those two are mutually exclusive". This implies that the Defender says, "The reason is not established," to the first reason and a second reason is being given in support. The text says:

> [the Sūtra School Challenger responds to him,] "It follows that there is pervasion because a common locus of the two, white and red, does not exist; because those two are mutually exclusive."

In other words:

C: It follows that whatever is white is necessarily not red because a common locus of the two, white and red, does not exist.

According to the text, the Defender now denies the reason, that a common locus of the two, white and red, does not exist. The Challenger justifies his reasoning, "because those two, white and red, are mutually exclusive". This means that the two colors are different and that a common locus, something which is both white and red, is not possible. White and red are mutually exclusive and, more generally, individual colors are mutually exclusive. The spoken form of this debate proceeds:

D: The reason—that a common locus of the two, white and red, does not exist—is not established.
C: It follows that a common locus of the two, white and red, does not exist because those two are mutually exclusive.

The last part of debate A.1 *in the text* has the Challenger giving this final reason: " ... because those two are mutually exclusive". This indicates that the Defender does not deny this last consequence, but accepts the "thesis" that a common locus of the two, white and red, does not exist. *In actual debate* as it might be practiced in the debating courtyard, the Sūtra School Challenger now leads the Defender back through this line of reasoning and once again, for the third and final time, states to him the basic consequence. The Challenger first calls for the Defender's acceptance of the reasoning showing that the color of a white religious conch is not red. The spoken form of the debate proceeds:

D: I accept that a common locus of the two, white and red, does not exist.
C: It follows that whatever is white is necessarily not red.
D: I accept it.

C: It follows that the subject, the color of a white religious conch, is not red.

D: I accept it.

In his last statement the Defender has accepted that the color of a white religious conch is not red. The Challenger immediately opposes this acceptance by stating the basic consequence for the third time. He insists that, in accordance with the Defender's original assertion, the color of a white religious conch *is* red because of being a color. The Defender finally answers correctly, "There is no pervasion," abandoning his own original position. He had asserted earlier that whatever is a color is necessarily red, but he now reverses his position saying that whatever is a color is not necessarily red. The Sūtra School Challenger throws this denial back to him in the form of a consequence, "It follows that whatever is a color is not necessarily red." The Defender accepts what he has just asserted and in so doing contradicts his basic position stated at the beginning of the debate.

At this point the Challenger shouts, "Finished (*tshar*)!" This means that the Defender's original assertion from the beginning of the debate is now finished because he has contradicted his basic position or that his original misconception is ended.[1] According to other scholars, what the Challenger shouts at this point is "Amazing (*mtshar*)!" That a person would first say one thing and then later contradict his own assertion is amazing![2] One piece of evidence for the understanding of this syllable as "finished" is that often at this point the debaters will laugh, "[Your] basic thesis is finished (*rtsa ba'i dam bca' tshar*)!" The understanding of the last syllable as "amazing" would not make sense in this context.[3]

---

[1] The understanding of this syllable as *tshar*, "finished", is predominant in the tradition.

[2] Lati Rinbochay, oral commentary.

[3] In the course of the debate the Defender reverses his position on many of the consequences as when the Challenger reviews the line of reasoning that the Defender had earlier denied. At those points too it is suitable for the Challenger to say, "Finished!" When the Defender contradicts his

The spoken form of the end of debate A.1 is as follows:

C: It follows that the subject, the color of a white religious conch, is red because of being a color.

D: There is no pervasion [i.e., even though it is true that the color of a white religious conch is a color, it is not the case that whatever is a color is necessarily red].

C: It follows that whatever is a color is not necessarily red.

D: I accept it.

C: Finished!

In summary, the forms of the debates as they appear in the Collected Topics texts do not fully report the debates as they might actually be spoken in the debating courtyard. Rather, the terse textual notations on the debates serve to supply the student with the essential points in a possible debate. In order to understand Tibetan philosophical debate, it is necessary to understand the application of this terse textual information to actual spoken debate. To this end, it will be helpful to gather in one place all of the implied form of debate A.1 as it might be spoken:

C: *Dhiḥ*! The subject, in just the way [Mañjushrī debated]. Is whatever is a color necessarily red?

D: I accept [that whatever is a color is necessarily red].

C: It follows that whatever is a color is necessarily red.

D: I accept it.

C: It [absurdly] follows that the subject, the color of a white religious conch, is red.

D: Why [is the color of a white religious conch red]?

C: Because of being a color. You asserted the pervasion [that whatever is a color is necessarily red].

D: The reason [that the color of a white religious conch is a color] is not established.

---

basic assertion, in this case that whatever is a color is necessarily red, then the Challenger will shout "Finished!" three times. Also, when saying "Finished!" the Challenger does not clap his hands as usual but slaps the right hand with palm upraised into the left palm.

C: It follows that the subject, the color of a white religious conch, is a color because of being white.

D: The reason [that the color of a white religious conch is white] is not established.

C: It follows that the subject, the color of a white religious conch, is white because of being one with the color of a white religious conch.

D: I accept that the color of a white religious conch is white.

C: It follows that the subject, the color of a white religious conch, is a color.

D: I accept it.

C: It follows that the subject, the color of a white religious conch, is red because of being a color.

D: I accept that the color of a white religious conch is red.

C: It follows that the subject, the color of a white religious conch, is not red because of being white.

D: There is no pervasion [i.e., even though the color of a white religious conch is white, it is not the case that whatever is white is necessarily not red].

C: It follows that whatever is white is necessarily not red because a common locus of the two, white and red, does not exist.

D: The reason [that a common locus of the two, white and red, does not exist] is not established.

C: It follows that a common locus of the two, white and red, does not exist because those two are mutually exclusive.

D: I accept that a common locus of the two, white and red, does not exist.

C: It follows that whatever is white is necessarily not red.

D: I accept it.

C: It follows that the subject, the color of a white religious conch, is not red.

D: I accept it.

C: It follows that the subject, the color of a white religious conch, is red because of being a color.

D: There is no pervasion [i.e., even though the color of a white religious conch is a color, it is not the case that whatever is a color is necessarily red].

C: It follows that whatever is a color is not necessarily red.

D: I accept it.

C: [Your] basic thesis is finished!

The Tibetan version of the implied form of debate A.1 follows:

C: རྡྲྀ་ཇེ་སྐྱར་ཚོས་ཅན། ཁ་དོག་ཡིན་ན་དམར་པོ་ཡིན་པས་ཁྱབ་པའི་ཕྱིར།

D: [ཁ་དོག་ཡིན་ན་དམར་པོ་ཡིན་པས་ཁྱབ་པར་] འདོད།

C: ཁ་དོག་ཡིན་ན་དམར་པོ་ཡིན་པས་ཁྱབ་པར་ཐལ།

D: འདོད།

C: ཚོས་དང་དཀར་པོའི་ཁ་དོག་ཚོས་ཅན། དམར་པོ་ཡིན་པར་ཐལ།

D: [ཚོས་དང་དཀར་པོའི་ཁ་དོག་དམར་པོ་ཡིན་པ་] ཅིའི་ཕྱིར།

C: ཁ་དོག་ཡིན་པའི་ཕྱིར། [ཁ་དོག་ཡིན་ན་དམར་པོ་ཡིན་པས་] ཁྱབ་པ་ ཁས།

D: [ཚོས་དང་དཀར་པོའི་ཁ་དོག་ཁ་དོག་ཡིན་པ་] དགོས་མ་གྲུབ།

C: ཚོས་དང་དཀར་པོའི་ཁ་དོག་ཚོས་ཅན། ཁ་དོག་ཡིན་པར་ཐལ། དཀར་ པོ་ཡིན་པའི་ཕྱིར།

D: [ཚོས་དང་དཀར་པོའི་ཁ་དོག་དཀར་པོ་ཡིན་པ་] དགོས་མ་གྲུབ།

C: ཚོས་དང་དཀར་པོའི་ཁ་དོག་ཚོས་ཅན། དཀར་པོ་ཡིན་པར་ཐལ། ཚོས་ དང་དཀར་པོའི་ཁ་དོག་དང་གཅིག་ཡིན་པའི་ཕྱིར།

D: ཚོས་དང་དཀར་པོའི་ཁ་དོག་དཀར་པོ་ཡིན་པར་འདོད།

C: ཚོས་དང་དཀར་པོའི་ཁ་དོག་ཚོས་ཅན། ཁ་དོག་ཡིན་པར་ཐལ།

D: འདོད།

C: ཆོས་ཅན་དཀར་པོའི་ཁ་དོག་ཆོས་ཅན། དམར་པོ་ཡིན་པར་ཐལ། ཁ་
དོག་ཡིན་པའི་ཕྱིར།

D: ཆོས་ཅན་དཀར་པོའི་ཁ་དོག་དམར་པོ་ཡིན་པར་འདོད།

C: ཆོས་ཅན་དཀར་པོའི་ཁ་དོག་ཆོས་ཅན། དམར་པོ་མ་ཡིན་པར་ཐལ།
དཀར་པོ་ཡིན་པའི་ཕྱིར།

D: [དཀར་པོ་ཡིན་ན་དམར་པོ་མ་ཡིན་པས་] མ་ཁྱབ།

C: དཀར་པོ་ཡིན་ན་དམར་པོ་མ་ཡིན་པས་ཁྱབ་པར་ཐལ། དཀར་པོ་དང་
དམར་པོ་གཉིས་ཀྱི་གཞི་མཐུན་མེད་པའི་ཕྱིར།

D: [དཀར་པོ་དང་དམར་པོ་གཉིས་ཀྱི་གཞི་མཐུན་མེད་པ་] རྟགས་མ་གྲུབ།

C: དཀར་པོ་དང་དམར་པོ་གཉིས་ཀྱི་གཞི་མཐུན་མེད་པར་ཐལ། དཀར་པོ་
དང་དམར་པོ་གཉིས་འགལ་བ་ཡིན་པའི་ཕྱིར།

D: དཀར་པོ་དང་དམར་པོ་གཉིས་ཀྱི་གཞི་མཐུན་མེད་པར་འདོད།

C: དཀར་པོ་ཡིན་ན་དམར་པོ་མ་ཡིན་པས་ཁྱབ་པར་ཐལ།

D: འདོད།

C: ཆོས་ཅན་དཀར་པོའི་ཁ་དོག་ཆོས་ཅན། དམར་པོ་མ་ཡིན་པར་ཐལ།

D: འདོད།

C: ཆོས་ཅན་དཀར་པོའི་ཁ་དོག་ཆོས་ཅན། དམར་པོ་ཡིན་པར་ཐལ། ཁ་
དོག་ཡིན་པའི་ཕྱིར།

D: [ཁ་དོག་ཡིན་ན་དམར་པོ་ཡིན་པས་] མ་ཁྱབ།

C: ཁ་དོག་ཡིན་ན་དམར་པོ་ཡིན་པས་མ་ཁྱབ་པར་ཐལ།

D: འདོད།

C: ཙ་བའི་དམ་བཅའ་ཚར།

REMARKS

One essential lesson learned at the time of studying the Collected Topics of Valid Cognition is that of the basic procedure or strategy of debate. According to one teacher, what one learns here is not the answers but the questions.[1] In other words, the thrust of the pedagogy in introductory debate is on learning how to assume the role of the Challenger, the one who questions his opponent's assertions.

It may appear that the role of the Challenger is the more difficult one because he has more to say in the debates. Actually, the role of the Defender is the more difficult one, for he is required to put forth assertions that can be defended against the qualms and deceit of the Challenger. Also, the ultimate priority of the Defender's role is evidenced by the fact that in proceeding from one class to the next, the debaters are required to pass examinations in the role of the Defender. However, initially the main lesson in debate is in how to question the validity of an assertion, testing that view through drawing out its consequences. Thus, according to the way this system of scholarship is taught, before one can proceed to the higher topics such as the Middle Way School and so forth it is of paramount importance to develop in the beginning a serviceable critical procedure, this being illustrated more in the role of the Challenger.

The aim is to be able to identify any error in an opponent's position and then to refute that mistaken view, thereby affording that person an opportunity to overcome misconception. This is accomplished by the strategy of first giving a consequence of the Defender's assertions and then forcing him to contradict himself by systematically closing

---

[1] Losang Gyatso (*blo bzang rgya mtsho*), Principal of the School of Dialectics in Dharamsala, India, oral commentary reported by B. Alan Wallace (Gelong Jhampa Kelsang).

off his possible answers, leaving him with no reasonable defense of his original error. As represented in the text, the Challenger first closes off that route of possible defense beginning with the Defender's denying the establishment of the reason of the basic consequence. Then, he closes off the route in which the Defender accepts the basic consequence. Finally, having asserted the pervasion and the establishment of the reason and being unable to accept the basic consequence, the Defender is obligated to pierce his mistaken conception and to contradict his own original assertion.

In order for this strategy to work, it is necessary that the Defender be limited to the four responses:

1 I accept it (*'dod*).
2 Why (*ci'i phyir*)?
3 The reason is not established (*rtags ma grub*).
4 There is no pervasion (*ma khyab*).

These are a finite, certain, yet adequate number of responses with which the Defender is able to test the validity of the Challenger's argument. This procedure for testing the Challenger's arguments eventually either will reveal the Defender's own error by causing him to contradict his earlier position or will dispel the Challenger's defective arguments by identifying his failures of reasoning.

Also important for the procedure in debate is the process for working back through the chain of reasoning because in this way one is able to continue to address the central problem. If one just stopped after proving the establishment of the reason, then the central mistaken view would be left unresolved. This strategy is the heart of the study of the Collected Topics and serves as a prerequisite for subsequent debate of the higher topics. The students are, of course, learning the terminology, definitions, divisions, and so forth, but the most important lesson in the beginning is the basic procedure.

6 *The Comparison of Phenomena*

One main purpose of debate is to establish the boundaries of pervasion (*khyab mtha'*) between phenomena.[1] The boundaries of pervasion or extension of a phenomenon is its range—what it pervades, what it includes, and what it excludes. By understanding clearly a phenomenon's boundaries of pervasion one is able to ascertain the scope of that phenomenon. The essential tool in this investigation is the analytical comparison of phenomena. By comparing two phenomena and establishing their relative boundaries of pervasion, the limits of each phenomenon in relation to the other, one comes to understand the points of similarity and dissimilarity between them.

The nature of debate vitally depends on this comparative or associative aspect, for the normal process of debate involves establishing the relative differences between phenomena. In the chapter on procedure the implied debate ends when the Sūtra School Challenger has forced the Defender to contradict his main thesis; however, this need not necessarily signal the end of the debate. Frequently at

---

[1] Lati Rinbochay is the main source for this section, and the paradigm debates are structured in accordance with his explanations.

the end of such a debate the Challenger asks the Defender to describe the difference between the two principals of the debate. This process is not a mere afterthought, but serves to address directly the Defender's mistaken view. If an opponent asserts that whatever is a color is necessarily red, he obviously has not understood the difference between color and red. Moreover, the form of debate described in the procedure chapter is used as a process for supporting or denying claims that arise out of analysis of the differences between phenomena. If an opponent incorrectly discerns the comparison of phenomena, then the Challenger will employ the previously described strategy of consequences to point out his error. The analysis of differences between phenomena is not a separate strategy of debate that supersedes the other, but is one procedural framework within which reasoning by consequences may be employed.

The comparison of phenomena presupposes that those phenomena are different (*tha dad*) in the sense that they are not *exactly* the same from the point of view of name and meaning. Phenomena which are not different are one. A pot is the only thing which is one with a pot, for it is exactly the same as a pot in name and meaning. The investigation of differences does not address the cases of phenomena which are exactly the same. There is no difference between a pot and a pot. Every existent other than a pot is different from it—a pillar, a person, a gold pot, and so forth.

Any two different phenomena must compare in one of five ways. Expressed in terms of their relative pervasions and represented by Euler diagrams, these five ways of comparison are the following:

The Comparison of Phenomena

1 Whatever is a *p* is necessarily a *q*, and whatever is a *q* is necessarily a *p*.

2 Whatever is a *p* is necessarily a *q*, but whatever is a *q* is not necessarily a *p*.

3 Whatever is a *q* is necessarily a *p*, but whatever is a *p* is not necessarily a *q*.

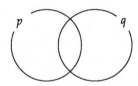

4 Whatever is a *p* is not necessarily a *q* and it is not the case that whatever is a *p* is necessarily not a *q*. Whatever is a *q* is not necessarily a *p* and it is not the case that whatever is a *q* is necessarily not a *p*.

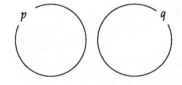

5 Whatever is a *p* is necessarily not a *q*, and whatever is a *q* is necessarily not a *p*.

Any two different phenomena must compare in one of these five ways. There is no sixth possible way.

In the first case the relative boundaries of pervasion or extensions of the two phenomena are absolutely concomitant. They pervade exactly the same things. This is represented by two circles combined into one—one is superimposed over the other.

In debate, the second and third cases are collapsed into one. Though in reference to p and q there are two separate cases, in reference to the two principals in general, such that the order does not matter, there is only one case. Here there is a uni-directional pervasion between the two. Whatever is a p is necessarily a q, but whatever is a q is not necessarily a p (or vice versa). This is represented by a smaller circle wholly included within the perimeter of a larger one. There is something (inside the smaller circle) which is both a p and a q, and there is something (inside the larger circle but outside the smaller) which is one but not the other. The relative sizes of the circles may or may not represent the relative extensions of the two principals being considered. What is being shown is that the larger circle includes at least one phenomenon the smaller does not.

In the fourth case there is an intersection of the relative extensions of the two phenomena, but there is no pervasion between the two. This is represented by two overlapping circles. There is something which is both a p and a q (in the overlapping area), there is something which is a p but not a q (inside the circle p but outside the circle q), and there is something which is a q but not a p (inside the circle q but outside the circle p).

Particular-form sentences, the information that some A's are B's and some are not, are communicated by either the second, third, or fourth cases above. For instance, the information that some impermanent phenomena are sounds and some are not is handled by stating their relative pervasions. Whatever is a sound is necessarily an impermanent phenomenon, but whatever is an impermanent phenomenon is not necessarily a sound.

In the fifth case above the relative extensions of the two phenomena do not correlate at all. There is neither any pervasion between the two nor is there any overlapping at all. There is nothing which is both a *p* and a *q*. This is represented by two separate circles.

When a debate is focused on an analysis of the differences between two phenomena, the Challenger asks the Defender to identify how the two compare in terms of the ways noted above. The Defender will give one of four answers:

1 They are mutually inclusive (*don gcig yin*).
2 There are three possibilities (*mu gsum yod*).
3 There are four possibilities (*mu bzhi yod*).
4 They are mutually exclusive (*'gal ba yin*).

The subsequent debate serves to establish or refute the Defender's decision on the comparison of the two phenomena. In the course of this debate the Defender must prove his assertion by positing subjects that exemplify the relative points of similarity and dissimilarity and by giving reasons that justify his assertions. In the context of such a debate the Defender is not limited merely to objecting to the Challenger's reasoning, but must justify his own reasoning as well.

The debate that develops in response to the Defender's answer follows one of several patterns. Examples of these patterns are provided below. The focus of this chapter is only the form of these debates; the content will be discussed in detail in the annotations to the translation. There are many different styles for debating the comparison of phenomena. The approach varies even between monasteries within the Ge-luk-ba order. Moreover, in a very real sense each debate is individual, for the development of that debate depends on the answers that the Defender gives and upon the knowledge, skill, and cleverness of the Challenger.

As with the implied debate provided in the procedure chapter, these examples are mere sketches of the patterns and do not accurately reflect the vibrant and versatile nature of actual debate. For instance, here the Defender's answers are all correct according to the assertions of the Proponents of Sūtra, but in actual debate Defenders do make errors and subsequent debate arises from those errors. Still, these paradigm debates contain all the essential points to demonstrate the procedure in the most straightforward style possible for debating the differences between phenomena. One can understand that in actual debate many opportunities arise for detailed discussion of the individual points of these arguments.

MUTUALLY INCLUSIVE PHENOMENA

Mutually inclusive phenomena are represented by the first diagram above (p. 135), one circle superimposed over another of equal size. The extension of p is precisely equivalent to the extension of q. Things which are mutually inclusive are different phenomena which have all eight approaches of pervasion. The Tibetan term for "mutually inclusive" (*don gcig*) literally means "the same meaning". Mutually inclusive phenomena are different only in the sense of not having exactly the same name, for their meanings—the objects which are included within the extension of each—are exactly the same. Also, any two mutually inclusive phenomena have all eight approaches of pervasion. That is, whatever is a p is necessarily a q (and vice versa), if a p exists, then a q exists (and vice versa), and so on. These are the same eight approaches of pervasion that exist between a definition and its definiendum (see pp. 66-67).

That mutually inclusive phenomena have all eight approaches of pervasion entails that there is a common locus; that is, there is something which *is* those two mutually inclusive phenomena. A common locus is not something that exists halfway between the two and is neither. Rather, it is something which is both of them. For instance, product and impermanent phenomenon are mutually inclusive, and there is a common locus of these two, for a pot is such a common locus. A pot is a product, and it is also an impermanent phenomenon. It is something which is both. Such a common locus exists for any set of mutually inclusive phenomena.

In the pattern of debate provided here for establishing mutually inclusive phenomena the two principals being compared are thing and that which is able to perform a function. That which is able to perform a function is the definition of thing, and, as is the case for any definition and its definiendum, they are mutually inclusive. The debate proceeds as follows:

C: What is the difference between the two, thing and that which is able to perform a function?

D: They are mutually inclusive.

C: It follows that the subjects, the two—thing and that which is able to perform a function, are mutually inclusive.

D: I accept it.

C: The subjects, the two—thing and that which is able to perform a function, are mutually inclusive—

D: Because of (1) being different and (2) having all eight approaches of pervasion.

C: It follows that the subjects, the two—thing and that which is able to perform a function, are different.

D: I accept it.

C: The subjects, the two—thing and that which is able to perform a function, are different—

D: Because of (1) being existents and (2) not being one.

C: It follows that if they (1) are existents and (2) are not one, then they are necessarily different.

D: I accept it.

C: It follows that the subjects, the two—thing and that which is able to perform a function, have all eight approaches of pervasion.

D: I accept it.

C: The subjects, the two—thing and that which is able to perform a function, have all eight approaches of pervasion—

D: Because (1) whatever is a thing is necessarily able to perform a function, (2) whatever is able to perform a function is necessarily a thing, (3) whatever is not a thing is necessarily not able to perform a function, (4) whatever is not able to perform a function is necessarily not a thing, (5) if a thing exists, then that which is able to perform a function necessarily exists, (6) if that which is able to perform a function exists, then a thing necessarily exists, (7) if a thing does not exist, then that which is able to perform a function necessarily does not exist, and (8) if that which is able to perform a function does not exist, then a thing necessarily does not exist.

C: It follows that if those eight are established, then thing and that which is able to perform a function necessarily have all eight approaches of pervasion.

D: I accept it.

The Tibetan for this paradigm follows:

C: དངོས་པོ་དང་དོན་བྱེད་ནུས་པ་གཉིས་ལ་ཁྱད་པར་ག་རེ་ཡོད།

D: དོན་གཅིག་ཡིན།

C: དངོས་པོ་དང་དོན་བྱེད་ནུས་པ་གཉིས་ཆོས་ཅན། དོན་གཅིག་ཡིན་པར་ཐལ།

D: འདོད།

C: དངོས་པོ་དང་དོན་བྱེད་ནུས་པ་གཉིས་ཆོས་ཅན། དོན་གཅིག་ཡིན་ཏེ།

D: ས་དད་ཡིན་པ་གང་ཞིག །ཁྱབ་པ་སྐྱོ་བཅུད་ཅང་བའི་ཕྱིར།

C: དངོས་པོ་དང་དོན་བྱེད་ནུས་པ་གཉིས་ཆོས་ཅན། ས་དད་ཡིན་པར་ཐལ།

D: འདོད།

C: དངོས་པོ་དང་དོན་བྱེད་ནུས་པ་གཉིས་ཆོས་ཅན། ས་དད་ཡིན་ཏེ།

D: ཡོད་པ་གང་ཞིག །གཅིག་མ་ཡིན་པའི་ཕྱིར།

C: ཡོད་པ་གང་ཞིག །གཅིག་མ་ཡིན་ན་ན་ཐ་དད་ཡིན་པས་ཁྱབ་པར་ཐལ།

D: འདོད།

C: དངོས་པོ་དང་དོན་བྱེད་ནུས་པ་གཅིས་ཚོས་ཅན། ཁྱབ་པ་སྐྱ་བཅྱད་ཚང་
བར་ཐལ།

D: འདོད།

C: དངོས་པོ་དང་དོན་བྱེད་ནུས་པ་གཅིས་ཚོས་ཅན། ཁྱབ་པ་སྐྱ་བཅྱད་ཚང་
 སྟེ།

D: དངོས་པོ་ཡིན་ན་དོན་བྱེད་ནུས་པ་ཡིན་པས་ཁྱབ། དོན་བྱེད་ནུས་པ་ཡིན་
ན་དངོས་པོ་ཡིན་པས་ཁྱབ། དངོས་པོ་མ་ཡིན་ན་དོན་བྱེད་ནུས་པ་མ་ཡིན་
པས་ཁྱབ། དོན་བྱེད་ནུས་པ་མ་ཡིན་ན་དངོས་པོ་མ་ཡིན་པས་ཁྱབ།
དངོས་པོ་ཡོད་ན་དོན་བྱེད་ནུས་པ་ཡོད་པས་ཁྱབ། དོན་བྱེད་ནུས་པ་ཡོད་
ན་དངོས་པོ་ཡོད་པས་ཁྱབ། དངོས་པོ་མེད་ན་དོན་བྱེད་ནུས་པ་མེད་པས་
ཁྱབ། དོན་བྱེད་ནུས་པ་མེད་ན་དངོས་པོ་མེད་པས་ཁྱབ་པའི་ཕྱིར།

C: བཅྱད་པོ་དེ་གྲུབ་ན་དངོས་པོ་དང་དོན་བྱེད་ནུས་པ་ལ་ཁྱབ་པ་སྐྱ་བཅྱད་
ཚང་བས་ཁྱབ་པར་ཐལ།

D: འདོད།

When the Challenger asks the Defender for a reason in support of his assertions, he provides the Defender with the
subject and predicate of a *syllogism* and the Defender supplies the reason. This is stated in the syllogistic form to indicate to the Defender that he must give a *correct* reason.
Consequences may or may not be valid by the rules of syllogisms, but a syllogism must be supplied with a correct reason. Therefore, in the format of comparing phenomena, the
Challenger uses the syllogistic form. When the Defender has
given a reason, he is held accountable for the establishment

of the reason, the pervasion, and the thesis. Should he fail to give a correct reason, the Challenger would pursue this point of misunderstanding by stating absurd consequences of his view.

In this paradigm, after the Defender has given a reason the Challenger always moves to check the pervasion. However, in actual debate this need not be done. If the establishment of the reason is more interesting, he is free to challenge the Defender on that count. Actual debate is much more fluid and versatile than the paradigms might indicate. Still, these patterns do represent the essential framework of actual debate.

THREE POSSIBILITIES

If there are three possibilities between two phenomena, there must be a common locus of the two and there are two points of difference, at least one of which is something which is one of the two phenomena but not the other. In this context the term "possibility" refers to a subject which exemplifies the various qualities under discussion. The subject does not have to be an existent, but must be something which demonstrates the various points of difference and similarity of the two phenomena that are being compared. For example, the horn of a rabbit may be used as a subject, a "possibility", to demonstrate something which is not one with a pot and also is not a permanent phenomenon. However, the etiquette of debate requires that if there is an existent which exemplifies the qualities, one should posit that. Also, it is considered a fine point of debate to posit subjects which, while demonstrating the two qualities of a point, are the more interesting or difficult cases. In so doing the Defender shows his command of the topic and also provides the Challenger with the more fertile bases for debate. For instance, a better subject to demonstrate the qualities of something which is not one with a pot and also is not a permanent phenomenon is a gold pot because it is an existent and it shows that the Defender understands that even though a gold pot is a pot, it is not one with a pot.

Phenomena having three possibilities compare in two ways. The first, which is represented by the second and third diagrams above (p. 135) is such that:

1 There is something which is both a p and a q.
2 There is a uni-directional pervasion between the two because whatever is a p is necessarily a q, but whatever is a q is not necessarily a p (or the other way around).
3 There is something which is neither a p nor a q.

These three points represent the three possibilities—something which is both, something which is one but not the other, and something which is neither.

This first type of three possibilities is exemplified in the comparison of color and red, the two principals of Debate A.1. The paradigm debate is:

C: What is the difference between the two, color and red?
D: There are three possibilities.
C: It follows that there are not three possibilities.[1] Posit something which is both.
D: There is something. The subject, the color of a ruby.
C: It follows that the subject, the color of a ruby, is a color.
D: I accept it.
C: The subject, the color of a ruby, is a color—
D: Because of being suitable as a hue.
C: It follows that whatever is suitable as a hue is necessarily a color.
D: I accept it.
C: It follows that the subject, the color of a ruby, is red.
D: I accept it.
C: The subject, the color of a ruby, is red—
D: Because of being an instance of red.

---

[1] When the Challenger says, "It follows that there are not three possibilities," he is stating something which is false. This is done only for the sake of riding the Defender in an attempt to make him unsure of his position.

C: It follows that whatever is an instance of red is necessarily red.

D: I accept it.

C: Now which is necessarily the other? Which is not necessarily the other? Posit something which is one but not the other.

D: Whatever is red is necessarily a color. Whatever is a color is not necessarily red. The subject, the color of a white religious conch.[1]

C: It follows that the subject, the color of a white religious conch, is a color.

D: I accept it.

C: The subject, the color of a white religious conch, is a color—

D: Because of being white.

C: It follows that whatever is white is necessarily a color.

D: I accept it.

C: It follows that the subject, the color of a white religious conch, is not red.

D: I accept it.

C: The subject, the color of a white religious conch, is not red—

D: Because of being white.

C: It follows that whatever is white is necessarily not red.

D: I accept it.

C: Now posit something which is neither.

D: There is something. The subject, a round form.

C: It follows that the subject, a round form, is not a color.

D: I accept it.

C: The subject, a round form, is not a color—

D: Because of being a shape.

C: It follows that whatever is a shape is necessarily not a color.

D: I accept it.

---

[1] If at this point the Defender had made the mistake of saying that whatever is a color is necessarily red, all of the implied debate of A.1 might be played out here.

C: It follows that the subject, a round form, is not red.

D: I accept it.

C: The subject, a round form, is not red—

D: Because of not being a color.

C: It follows that whatever is not a color is necessarily not red.

D: I accept it.

The Tibetan for this paradigm debate follows:

C: ཁ་དོག་དང་དཀར་པོ་གཉིས་ལ་ཁྱད་པར་ག་རེ་ཡོད།

D: སྤྱི་གསུམ་ཡོད།

C: སྤྱི་གསུམ་མེད་པར་ཐལ། གཉིས་ཀ་ཡིན་པའི་སྤྱི་ཞིག

D: ཡོད། པད་མའི་རྫ་གའི་ཁ་དོག་ཆོས་ཅན།

C: པད་མའི་རྫ་གའི་ཁ་དོག་ཆོས་ཅན། ཁ་དོག་ཡིན་པར་ཐལ།

D: འདོད།

C: པད་མའི་རྫ་གའི་ཁ་དོག་ཆོས་ཅན། ཁ་དོག་ཡིན་ཏེ།

D: མདོག་ཏུ་རུང་བ་ཡིན་པའི་ཕྱིར།

C: མདོག་ཏུ་རུང་བ་ཡིན་ན་ཁ་དོག་ཡིན་པས་ཁྱབ་པར་ཐལ།

D: འདོད།

C: པད་མའི་རྫ་གའི་ཁ་དོག་ཆོས་ཅན། དམར་པོ་ཡིན་པར་ཐལ།

D: འདོད།

C: པད་མའི་རྫ་གའི་ཁ་དོག་ཆོས་ཅན། དམར་པོ་ཡིན་ཏེ།

D: དམར་པོའི་རྗེ་བྲག་ཡིན་པའི་ཕྱིར།

C: དམར་པོའི་རྗེ་བྲག་ཡིན་ན་དམར་པོ་ཡིན་པས་ཁྱབ་པར་ཐལ།

D: འདོད།

C: གང་གིས་གང་ལ་ཁྱབ་གང་གིས་གང་ལ་མ་ཁྱབ་པའི་སྤྱི་ཞིག

D: དམར་པོ་ཡིན་ན་ཁ་དོག་ཡིན་པས་ཁྱབ། ཁ་དོག་ཡིན་ན་དམར་པོ་ཡིན་
པས་མ་ཁྱབ། ཆོས་ཅན་དཀར་པོའི་ཁ་དོག་ཆོས་ཅན།

C: ཆོས་ཅན་དཀར་པོའི་ཁ་དོག་ཆོས་ཅན། ཁ་དོག་ཡིན་པར་ཐལ།

D: འདོད།

C: ཆོས་ཅན་དཀར་པོའི་ཁ་དོག་ཆོས་ཅན། ཁ་དོག་ཡིན་ཏེ།

D: དཀར་པོ་ཡིན་པའི་ཕྱིར།

C: དཀར་པོ་ཡིན་ན་ཁ་དོག་ཡིན་པས་ཁྱབ་པར་ཐལ།

D: འདོད།

C: ཆོས་ཅན་དཀར་པོའི་ཁ་དོག་ཆོས་ཅན། དམར་པོ་མ་ཡིན་པར་ཐལ།

D: འདོད།

C: ཆོས་ཅན་དཀར་པོའི་ཁ་དོག་ཆོས་ཅན། དམར་པོ་མ་ཡིན་ཏེ།

D: དཀར་པོ་ཡིན་པའི་ཕྱིར།

C: དཀར་པོ་ཡིན་ན་དམར་པོ་མ་ཡིན་པས་ཁྱབ་པར་ཐལ།

D: འདོད།

C: ད་གཅིས་ཀ་མ་ཡིན་པའི་མུ་ཞིག

D: ཡོད། རྒྱལ་པོའི་གཟུགས་ཆོས་ཅན།

C: རྒྱལ་པོའི་གཟུགས་ཆོས་ཅན། ཁ་དོག་མ་ཡིན་པར་ཐལ།

D: འདོད།

C: རྒྱལ་པོའི་གཟུགས་ཆོས་ཅན། ཁ་དོག་མ་ཡིན་ཏེ།

D: དཔྱིབས་ཡིན་པའི་ཕྱིར།

C: དཔྱིབས་ཡིན་ན་ཁ་དོག་མ་ཡིན་པས་ཁྱབ་པར་ཐལ།

D: འདོད།

C: རྒྱལ་པོའི་གཟུགས་ཆོས་ཅན། དམར་པོ་མ་ཡིན་པར་ཐལ།

D: འདོད།

C: རྒྱུ་མཚན་གཟུགས་ཚོས་ཅན་ན། དམར་པོ་མ་ཡིན་ཏེ།

D: ཁ་དོག་མ་ཡིན་པའི་ཕྱིར།

C: ཁ་དོག་མ་ཡིན་ན་དམར་པོ་མ་ཡིན་པས་ཁྱབ་པར་ཐལ།

D: འདོད།

In this debate the hypothetical Defender has the responsibility of positing three subjects, each of which exemplify two separate qualities—a subject which is both, a subject which is one but not the other, and a subject which is neither. He also must give six reasons, one in support of each of the two qualities of the three subjects. As always, the Challenger functions to check his opponent's reasoning for validity and to test his command of the topic at hand.

The essential points in this last debate may be represented diagrammatically. The chart below shows two columns, one for color and one for red. In the columns there are three rows, one for each of the three possibilities. The three subjects that the Defender posited in this debate are given to the right of the columns, and under the headings of "Color" and "Red", checks (✓) and X's represent, respectively, whether the subject is or is not an example of that phenomenon:

Color	*Red*	
✓	✓	The color of a ruby.
✓	X	The color of a white religious conch.
X	X	A round form.

The chart shows that the color of a ruby is both a color and red, that the color of a white religious conch is a color but not red, and that a round form is neither a color nor red. There is nothing which is red but not a color.

In a sense, this chart also suggests the procedure in such a debate. The debate follows the course of having the

Defender posit subjects to exemplify the various points of comparison, and then the Challenger and Defender together investigate whether or not the subjects have the properties they are supposed to exemplify. The Defender's positing of subjects is represented by the list of subjects on the right of the chart, and the analysis of the properties of those subjects is represented by the checks and X's under the headings of the two main principals of this debate.

The second type of comparison called "three possibilities", which is represented by the fourth diagram above (p. 135), is such that:

1 There is something which is both a *p* and a *q*.
2 There is something which is a *p* but not a *q*.
3 There is something which is a *q* but not a *p*.

In this case there is nothing one can posit which is neither a *p* nor a *q*. Such comparisons necessarily involve two phenomena that together include all existents and non-existents as well.

A comparison of this type of three possibilities is exemplified by object of knowledge (*shes bya, jñeya*), which is mutually inclusive with existent, and non-impermanent phenomenon (*mi rtag pa ma yin pa*). The debate is:

C: What is the difference between the two, object of knowledge and non-impermanent phenomenon?
D: There are three possibilities without there being something which is neither.
C: It follows that there are not three possibilities. Posit something which is both.
D: There is something. The subject, a permanent phenomenon.
C: It follows that the subject, a permanent phenomenon, is an object of knowledge.
D: I accept it.
C: The subject, a permanent phenomenon, is an object of knowledge—
D: Because of being an existent.

C: It follows that whatever is an existent is necessarily an object of knowledge.

D: I accept it.

C: It follows that the subject, a permanent phenomenon, is a non-impermanent phenomenon.

D: I accept it.

C: The subject, a permanent phenomenon, is a non-impermanent phenomenon—

D: Because of not being produced from causes and conditions.

C: It follows that whatever is not produced from causes and conditions is necessarily a non-impermanent phenomenon.

D: I accept it.

C: Now posit something which is an object of knowledge but not a non-impermanent phenomenon.

D: There is something. The subject, a pot.

C: It follows that the subject, a pot, is an object of knowledge.

D: I accept it.

C: The subject, a pot, is an object of knowledge—

D: Because of being an impermanent phenomenon.

C: It follows that whatever is an impermanent phenomenon is necessarily an object of knowledge.

D: I accept it.

C: It follows that the subject, a pot, is not a non-impermanent phenomenon.

D: I accept it.

C: The subject, a pot, is not a non-impermanent phenomenon—

D: Because of being produced from causes and conditions.

C: It follows that whatever is produced from causes and conditions is necessarily not a non-impermanent phenomenon.

D: I accept it.

C: Now posit something which is a non-impermanent phenomenon but not an object of knowledge.

D: The subject, the horn of a rabbit.

C: It follows that the subject, the horn of a rabbit, is a non-impermanent phenomenon.

D: I accept it.

C: The subject, the horn of a rabbit, is a non-impermanent phenomenon—

D: Because of being a non-existent.

C: It follows that whatever is a non-existent is necessarily a non-impermanent phenomenon.

D: I accept it.

C: It follows that the subject, the horn of a rabbit, is not an object of knowledge.

D: I accept it.

C: The subject, the horn of a rabbit, is not an object of knowledge—

D: Because of not being an existent.

C: It follows that whatever is not an existent is necessarily not an object of knowledge.

D: I accept it.

The Tibetan for this debate follows:

C: ཤེས་བྱ་རྡང་མི་རྟག་པ་མ་ཡིན་པ་གཉིས་ལ་ཁྱད་པར་ག་རེ་ཡོད།

D: གཉིས་ཀ་མ་ཡིན་པ་མེད་པའི་མུ་གསུམ་ཡོད།

C: མུ་གསུམ་མེད་པར་ཐལ། གཉིས་ཀ་ཡིན་པའི་མུ་ཞིག།

D: ཡོད། རྟག་པ་ཆོས་ཅན།

C: རྟག་པ་ཆོས་ཅན། ཤེས་བྱ་ཡིན་པར་ཐལ།

D: འདོད།

C: རྟག་པ་ཆོས་ཅན། ཤེས་བྱ་ཡིན་ཏེ།

D: ཡོད་པ་ཡིན་པའི་ཕྱིར།

C: ཡོད་པ་ཡིན་ན་ཤེས་བྱ་ཡིན་པས་ཁྱབ་པར་ཐལ།

D: འདོད།

C: རྟག་པ་ཆོས་ཅན། མི་རྟག་པ་མ་ཡིན་པ་ཡིན་པར་ཐལ།

D: འདོད།

C: རྟག་པ་ཆོས་ཅན། མི་རྟག་པ་མ་ཡིན་པ་ཡིན་ཏེ།

D: རྒྱུ་རྐྱེན་ལས་སྐྱེས་པ་མ་ཡིན་པའི་ཕྱིར།

C: རྒྱུ་རྐྱེན་ལས་སྐྱེས་པ་མ་ཡིན་ན་མི་རྟག་པ་མ་ཡིན་པ་ཡིན་པས་ཁྱབ་པར་
ཐལ།

D: འདོད།

C: ད་ཤེས་བྱ་ཡིན་ལ་མི་རྟག་པ་མ་ཡིན་པ་མ་ཡིན་པའི་མུ་ཞིག

D: ཡོད། བུམ་པ་ཆོས་ཅན།

C: བུམ་པ་ཆོས་ཅན། ཤེས་བྱ་ཡིན་པར་ཐལ།

D: འདོད།

C: བུམ་པ་ཆོས་ཅན། ཤེས་བྱ་ཡིན་ཏེ།

D: མི་རྟག་པ་ཡིན་པའི་ཕྱིར།

C: མི་རྟག་པ་ཡིན་ན་ཤེས་བྱ་ཡིན་པས་ཁྱབ་པར་ཐལ།

D: འདོད།

C: བུམ་པ་ཆོས་ཅན། མི་རྟག་པ་མ་ཡིན་པ་མ་ཡིན་པར་ཐལ།

D: འདོད།

C: བུམ་པ་ཆོས་ཅན། མི་རྟག་པ་མ་ཡིན་པ་མ་ཡིན་ཏེ།

D: རྒྱུ་རྐྱེན་ལས་སྐྱེས་པ་ཡིན་པའི་ཕྱིར།

C: རྒྱུ་རྐྱེན་ལས་སྐྱེས་པ་ཡིན་ན་མི་རྟག་པ་མ་ཡིན་པ་མ་ཡིན་པས་ཁྱབ་པར་
ཐལ།

D: འདོད།

C: ད་མི་རྟག་པ་མ་ཡིན་ལ་ཤེས་བྱ་མ་ཡིན་པའི་མུ་ཞིག

D: རི་བོང་རྭ་ཆོས་ཅན།

C: རི་བོང་རྭ་ཆོས་ཅན། མི་རྟག་པ་མ་ཡིན་པ་ཡིན་པར་ཐལ།

D: འདོད།

C: རི་བོང་རྭ་ཆོས་ཅན། མི་རྟག་པ་མ་ཡིན་པ་ཡིན་ཏེ།

D: མེད་པ་ཡིན་པའི་ཕྱིར།

C: མེད་པ་ཡིན་ན་མི་རྟག་པ་མ་ཡིན་པ་ཡིན་པས་ཁྱབ་པར་ཐལ།

D: འདོད།

C: རི་བོང་རྭ་ཆོས་ཅན། ཤེས་བྱ་མ་ཡིན་པར་ཐལ།

D: འདོད།

C: རི་བོང་རྭ་ཆོས་ཅན། ཤེས་བྱ་མ་ཡིན་ཏེ།

D: ཡོད་པ་མ་ཡིན་པའི་ཕྱིར།

C: ཡོད་པ་མ་ཡིན་ན་ཤེས་བྱ་མ་ཡིན་པས་ཁྱབ་པར་ཐལ།

D: འདོད།

In this type of three possibilities the three points are something which is both, something which is a *p* but not a *q*, and
something which is a *q* but not a *p*. A fourth possibility,
something which is neither, is inconceivable. Something
which is, on the one hand, not an object of knowledge and,
on the other, a non-non-impermanent phenomenon, i.e., an
impermanent phenomenon cannot be posited. As indicated
by the use of the horn of a rabbit as the subject in the third
point above, it is not necessary that the individual
"possibilities" be existents. It is only necessary that there be
a subject which exemplifies the two qualities of the individual point. In this sense, something which is not an object of
knowledge but is an impermanent phenomenon is not
possible.

The essential points of this debate too may be shown in
chart form:

Object of Knowledge	Non-Impermanent Phenomenon	
√	√	A permanent phenomenon.
√	X	A pot.
X	X	The horn of a rabbit.

The chart shows that a permanent phenomenon is both an object of knowledge and a non-impermanent phenomenon, that a pot is an object of knowledge but not a non-impermanent phenomenon (i.e., is an impermanent phenomenon), and that the horn of a rabbit is not an object of knowledge but is a non-impermanent phenomenon. There is nothing which is not an object of knowledge (i.e., is not an existent) and is not a non-impermanent phenomenon (i.e., is an impermanent phenomenon).

FOUR POSSIBILITIES

If there are four possibilities between two phenomena, all the points of similarity and difference are exemplified. In this case, there is no pervasion between the two principals; whatever is a p is not necessarily a q, and whatever is a q is not necessarily a p. The four possibilities are represented by the fourth diagram above (p. 135), as is the second type of three possibilities. The difference is that whereas with the above second type of three possibilities there is nothing outside the two circles, here in the case of four possibilities something outside both circles can be posited. The four possibilities are such that:

1 There is something which is both a p and a q.
2 There is something which is a p but not a q.
3 There is something which is a q but not a p.
4 There is something which is neither a p nor a q.

A comparison of four possibilities is demonstrated by blue and the color of cloth. The debate is:

C: What is the difference between the two, blue and the color of cotton cloth?

D: There are four possibilities.

C: It follows that there are not four possibilities. Posit something which is both.

D: There is something. The subject, the color of blue cotton cloth.

C: It follows that the subject, the color of blue cotton cloth, is blue.

D: I accept it.

C: The subject, the color of blue cotton cloth, is blue—

D: Because of being suitable as a blue hue.

C: It follows that whatever is suitable as a blue hue is necessarily blue.

D: I accept it.

C: It follows that the subject, the color of blue cotton cloth, is a color of cotton cloth.

D: I accept it.

C: The subject, the color of blue cotton cloth, is a color of cotton cloth—

D: Because of being an instance of the color of cotton cloth.

C: It follows that whatever is an instance of the color of cotton cloth is necessarily a color of cotton cloth.

D: I accept it.

C: Now posit something which is blue but not a color of cloth.

D: There is something. The subject, the color of a blue sky.

C: It follows that the subject, the color of a blue sky, is blue.

D: I accept it.

C: The subject, the color of a blue sky, is blue—

D: Because of being suitable as a blue hue.

C: It follows that whatever is suitable as a blue hue is necessarily blue.

D: I accept it.

C: It follows that the subject, the color of a blue sky, is not a color of cloth.

D: I accept it.

C: The subject, the color of a blue sky, is not a color of cloth—

D: Because of being a color of the sky.

C: It follows that whatever is a color of the sky is necessarily not a color of cloth.

D: I accept it.

C: Now posit something which is a color of cotton cloth but not blue.

D: There is something. The subject, the color of yellow cotton cloth.

C: It follows that the subject, the color of yellow cotton cloth, is a color of cotton cloth.

D: I accept it.

C: The subject, the color of yellow cotton cloth, is a color of cotton cloth—

D: Because of being suitable as a hue of cotton cloth.

C: It follows that whatever is suitable as a hue of cotton cloth is necessarily a color of cotton cloth.

D: I accept it.

C: It follows that the subject, the color of yellow cotton cloth, is not blue.

D: I accept it.

C: The subject, the color of yellow cotton cloth, is not blue—

D: Because of being yellow.

C: It follows that whatever is yellow is necessarily not blue.

D: I accept it.

C: Now posit something which is neither.

D: There is something. The subject, the color of a ruby.

C: It follows that the subject, the color of a ruby, is not blue.

D: I accept it.

C: The subject, the color of a ruby, is not blue—

D: Because of being red.

C: It follows that whatever is red is necessarily not blue.

D: I accept it.

C: It follows that the subject, the color of a ruby, is not a color of cotton cloth.

D: I accept it.

C: The subject, the color of a ruby, is not a color of cotton cloth—

D: Because of being a color of a jewel.

C: It follows that whatever is a color of a jewel is necessarily not a color of cotton cloth.

D: I accept it.

The Tibetan for this debate follows:

C: སྟོན་པོ་དང་རས་ཀྱི་ཁ་དོག་གཉིས་ལ་ཁྱད་པར་ག་རེ་ཡོད།

D: སུ་བཞི་ཡོད།

C: སུ་བཞི་མེད་པར་ཐལ། གཉིས་ཀ་ཡིན་པའི་སུ་ཞིག

D: ཡོད། རས་སྟོན་པོའི་ཁ་དོག་ཆོས་ཅན།

C: རས་སྟོན་པོའི་ཁ་དོག་ཆོས་ཅན། སྟོན་པོ་ཡིན་པར་ཐལ།

D: འདོད།

C: རས་སྟོན་པོའི་ཁ་དོག་ཆོས་ཅན། སྟོན་པོ་ཡིན་ཏེ།

D: སྟོན་པོའི་མདོག་ཏུ་རུང་བ་ཡིན་པའི་ཕྱིར།

C: སྟོན་པོའི་མདོག་ཏུ་རུང་བ་ཡིན་ན་སྟོན་པོ་ཡིན་པས་ཁྱབ་པར་ཐལ།

D: འདོད།

C: རས་སྟོན་པོའི་ཁ་དོག་ཆོས་ཅན། རས་ཀྱི་ཁ་དོག་ཡིན་པར་ཐལ།

D: འདོད།

C: རས་སྟོན་པོའི་ཁ་དོག་ཆོས་ཅན། རས་ཀྱི་ཁ་དོག་ཡིན་ཏེ།

D: རས་ཀྱི་ཁ་དོག་གི་རེ་བྲག་ཡིན་པའི་ཕྱིར།

C: རས་ཀྱི་ཁ་དོག་གི་རེ་བྲག་ཡིན་ན་རས་ཀྱི་ཁ་དོག་ཡིན་པས་ཁྱབ་པར་ཐལ།

D: འདོད།

C: ད་སྟོན་པོ་ཡིན་ལ་རས་ཀྱི་ཁ་དོག་མ་ཡིན་པའི་སུ་ཞིག

D: ཡོད། ནམ་མཁའ་སྟོན་པོའི་ཁ་དོག་ཆོས་ཅན།

C: ནམ་མཁའ་སྟོན་པོའི་ཁ་དོག་ཆོས་ཅན། སྟོན་པོ་ཡིན་པར་ཐལ།

D: འདོད།

C: ནམ་མཁའ་སྟོན་པོའི་ཁ་དོག་ཆོས་ཅན། སྟོན་པོ་ཡིན་ཏེ།

D: སྟོན་པོའི་མདོག་ཏུ་རུང་བ་ཡིན་པའི་ཕྱིར།

C: སྟོན་པོའི་མདོག་ཏུ་རུང་བ་ཡིན་ན་སྟོན་པོ་ཡིན་པས་ཁྱབ་པར་ཐལ།

D: འདོད།

C: ནམ་མཁའ་སྟོན་པོའི་ཁ་དོག་ཆོས་ཅན། རས་ཀྱི་ཁ་དོག་མ་ཡིན་པར་ཐལ།

D: འདོད།

C: ནམ་མཁའ་སྟོན་པོའི་ཁ་དོག་ཆོས་ཅན། རས་ཀྱི་ཁ་དོག་མ་ཡིན་ཏེ།

D: ནམ་མཁའི་ཁ་དོག་ཡིན་པའི་ཕྱིར།

C: ནམ་མཁའི་ཁ་དོག་ཡིན་ན་རས་ཀྱི་ཁ་དོག་མ་ཡིན་པས་ཁྱབ་པར་ཐལ།

D: འདོད།

C: ད་རས་ཀྱི་ཁ་དོག་ཡིན་ལ་སྟོན་པོ་མ་ཡིན་པའི་མུ་ཞིག

D: ཡོད། རས་སེར་པོའི་ཁ་དོག་ཆོས་ཅན།

C: རས་སེར་པོའི་ཁ་དོག་ཆོས་ཅན། རས་ཀྱི་ཁ་དོག་ཡིན་པར་ཐལ།

D: འདོད།

C: རས་སེར་པོའི་ཁ་དོག་ཆོས་ཅན། རས་ཀྱི་ཁ་དོག་ཡིན་ཏེ།

D: རས་ཀྱི་མདོག་ཏུ་རུང་བ་ཡིན་པའི་ཕྱིར།

C: རས་ཀྱི་མདོག་ཏུ་རུང་པོ་ཡིན་ན་རས་ཀྱི་ཁ་དོག་ཡིན་པས་ཁྱབ་པར་ཐལ།

D: འདོད།

C: རས་སེར་པོའི་ཁ་དོག་ཆོས་ཅན། སྟོན་པོ་མ་ཡིན་པར་ཐལ།

D: འདོད།

C: རས་མེར་པོའི་ཁ་དོག་ཆོས་ཅན། སྟོན་པོ་མ་ཡིན་ཏེ།

D: མེར་པོ་ཡིན་པའི་ཕྱིར།

C: མེར་པོ་ཡིན་ན་སྟོན་པོ་མ་ཡིན་པས་ཁྱབ་པར་ཐལ།

D: འདོད།

C: དཔྱད་ས་ཀ་མ་ཡིན་པོའི་མུ་ལེགས།

D: འོད། པད་མའི་རྩ་གའི་ཁ་དོག་ཆོས་ཅན།

C: པད་མའི་རྩ་གའི་ཁ་དོག་ཆོས་ཅན། སྟོན་པོ་མ་ཡིན་པར་ཐལ།

D: འདོད།

C: པད་མའི་རྩ་གའི་ཁ་དོག་ཆོས་ཅན། སྟོན་པོ་མ་ཡིན་ཏེ།

D: དམར་པོ་ཡིན་པའི་ཕྱིར།

C: དམར་པོ་ཡིན་ན་སྟོན་པོ་མ་ཡིན་པས་ཁྱབ་པར་ཐལ།

D: འདོད།

C: པད་མའི་རྩ་གའི་ཁ་དོག་ཆོས་ཅན། རས་ཀྱི་ཁ་དོག་མ་ཡིན་པར་ཐལ།

D: འདོད།

C: པད་མའི་རྩ་གའི་ཁ་དོག་ཆོས་ཅན། རས་ཀྱི་ཁ་དོག་མ་ཡིན་ཏེ།

D: རིན་ཆེན་གྱི་ཁ་དོག་ཡིན་པའི་ཕྱིར།

C: རིན་ཆེན་གྱི་ཁ་དོག་ཡིན་ན་རས་ཀྱི་ཁ་དོག་མ་ཡིན་པས་ཁྱབ་པར་ཐལ།

D: འདོད།

Shown in the form of a chart, the essential points of this debate are:

Blue	The Color of Cotton Cloth	
√	√	The color of blue cotton cloth.
√	X	The color of a blue sky.
X	√	The color of yellow cotton cloth.
X	X	The color of a ruby.

The chart shows that the color of a blue cotton shirt is both blue and a color of cloth, that the color of a blue sky is blue but is not a color of cloth, that the color of a yellow cotton robe is a color of cloth but not blue, and that the color of a ruby is neither blue nor a color of cloth. Each of the four possibilities are exemplified.

The pattern for debating four possibilities is just the same as that for the second type of three possibilities except that here one also posits something which is neither of the two principals. In debating either of the types of three possibilities or the four possibilities the Defender must posit subjects which exemplify the various facets of similarity and difference between the two principals, and he must give valid reasons which justify those subjects as having the prescribed qualities.

MUTUALLY EXCLUSIVE PHENOMENA

Mutually exclusive phenomena are those which are different and a common locus of them is not possible. The first requirement, that they be different, assures that mutually exclusive phenomena are existents and that they are not exactly the same in name and meaning. Different phenomena are of two types: (1) those which have a common locus and (2) those which do not have a common locus. An example of the first type is color and blue. Color and blue are different and there are things such as the color of a blue cotton shirt which exemplify both of them. Different phenomena which have a common locus may be mutually inclusive (for example, product and impermanent phenomenon), either type of three possibilities (for example, in the first case, color and blue, and, in the second, existent and non-impermanent phenomenon), or four possibilities (for example, red and the color of ink). Moreover, whatever phenomena compare in any of these ways must be different phenomena which have a common locus. Different phenomena which do not have a common locus are mutually exclusive. There is nothing which is both of them. Mutually exclusive phenomena are represented by the fifth diagram above (p. 135), two circles which do not overlap and do not have a common boundary of pervasion.

The pattern for debating mutually exclusive phenomena is shown by this comparison of definition and definiendum:

C: What is the difference between the two, definition and definiendum?

D: They are mutually exclusive.

C: It follows that the subjects, the two—definition and definiendum, are mutually exclusive.

D: I accept it.

C: The subjects, the two—definition and definiendum, are mutually exclusive—

D: Because (1) they are different and (2) a common locus of the two is not possible.

C: It follows that a common locus of the two, definition and definiendum, is not possible.

D: I accept it.

C: A common locus of the two, definition and definiendum, is not possible—

D: Because (1) whatever is a definition is necessarily not a definiendum and (2) whatever is a definiendum is necessarily not a definition.

C: It follows that if (1) whatever is a definition is necessarily not a definiendum and (2) whatever is a definiendum is necessarily not a definition, then a common locus of the two, definition and definiendum, is not possible.

D: I accept it.

The Tibetan for this paradigm follows:

C: མཚན་ཉིད་དང་མཚོན་བྱ་གཉིས་ལ་ཁྱད་པར་ག་རེ་ཡོད།

D: འགལ་བ་ཡིན།

C: མཚན་ཉིད་དང་མཚོན་བྱ་གཉིས་ཆོས་ཅན། འགལ་བ་ཡིན་པར་ཐལ།

D: འདོད།

C: མཚན་ཉིད་དང་མཚོན་བྱ་གཉིས་ཆོས་ཅན། འགལ་བ་ཡིན་ཏེ།

D: ཕ་དད་ཡིན་པ་གང་ཞིག །དེ་གཉིས་ཀྱི་གཞི་མཐུན་མི་སྲིད་པའི་ཕྱིར།

C: མཚན་ཉིད་དང་མཚོན་བྱ་གཉིས་ཀྱི་གཞི་མཐུན་མི་སྲིད་པར་ཐལ།

D: འདོད།

C: མཚན་ཉིད་དང་མཚོན་བྱ་གཉིས་ཀྱི་གཞི་མཐུན་མི་སྲིད་དེ།

D: མཚན་ཉིད་ཡིན་ན་མཚོན་བྱ་མ་ཡིན་པས་ཁྱབ་པ་གང་ཞིག ། མཚོན་བྱ་ ཡིན་ན་མཚན་ཉིད་མ་ཡིན་པས་ཁྱབ་པའི་ཕྱིར།

C: མཚན་ཉིད་ཡིན་ན་མཚོན་བྱ་མ་ཡིན་པས་ཁྱབ་པ་གང་ཞིག ། མཚོན་བྱ་ ཡིན་ན་མཚན་ཉིད་མ་ཡིན་པས་ཁྱབ་ན་མཚན་ཉིད་དང་མཚོན་བྱ་གཉིས་ ཀྱི་གཞི་མཐུན་མི་སྲིད་པས་ཁྱབ་པར་ཐལ།

D: འདོད།

The reason the Defender gives here is obvious. Once the two are mutually exclusive, whatever is the one is necessarily not the other. This sort of reason is possible and suitable for all cases of mutually exclusive phenomena. Still, by stating the reasons the Defender is asserting a view and provides the Challenger with a source of debate. In many cases other reasons prove more demonstrative. For instance, the Defender may link the two principals with other mutually exclusive phenomena, saying, for instance, "(1) Whatever is a p is necessarily a permanent phenomenon and (2) whatever is a q is necessarily an impermanent phenomenon." In any case the Defender has the responsibility of showing that a common locus of the two different phenomena is not possible.

REMARKS

As with almost everything in the Collected Topics tradition, there are various approaches to comparing phenomena—the way the questions are framed, the order in which the points are considered, the description of the different comparisons, and so on. For instance, Kensur Yeshay Tupden describes two of the comparisons between phenomena somewhat differently than Lati Rinbochay, whose commentary served as the basis for this chapter. In comparing two things such as non-pot (*bum pa ma yin pa*) and functioning thing, Lati Rinbochay designates the difference as "three possibilities without there being something which is neither" (*gnyis ka ma yin pa'i mu med pa'i mu gsum*). The three points of comparison are:

1   Something which is a functioning thing and a non-pot is a pillar, a person, or a consciousness.
2   Something which is a functioning thing but not a non-pot (that is to say, is also a pot) is a gold pot.
3   Something which is not a functioning thing and is a non-pot is uncomposed space.

Something which is neither would have to be a pot but not be a functioning thing; thus, nothing may be posited as neither.

Kensur Yeshay Tupden prefers to call this comparison *"four* possibilities without there being something which is neither" (*gnyis ka ma yin pa'i mu med pa'i mu bzhi*) rather than three possibilities. In his opinion, comparisons which are called "three possibilities" must be limited to those cases such that there is something which is both a p and a q and there is a one-directional pervasion between the two, as is the case with pot and functioning thing. However, both Lati Rinbochay and Kensur Yeshay Tupden agree that a comparison of three possibilities does not necessarily entail that there be something which is neither. For example, both of these scholars agree that object of knowledge and the selfless have three possibilities without there being something which is neither:

1 Something which is both an object of knowledge and selfless is a pot.
2 Whatever is an object of knowledge is necessarily selfless, but whatever is selfless is not necessarily an object of knowledge, as in the case of a horn of a rabbit.

Something which is neither an object of knowledge nor selfless is not possible, for the selfless alone includes all existents and non-existents.

In a sense, the interpretation given by Kensur Yeshay Tupden is preferable. If one designates both comparisons such as (1) that between non-pot and functioning thing and (2) that between object of knowledge and the selfless as "three possibilities without there being something which is neither", then this designation is ambiguous. Kensur Yeshay Tupden avoids this ambiguity by designating the former as "four possibilities without there being something which is neither" and the latter as "three possibilities without there being something which is neither".

By whatever designation for any of these comparisons of phenomena, it is interesting to consider just what is being compared in this process. When reckoning the differences between phenomena, the two principals such as color and red in debate A.1 are stated as singulars and without articles. This style reflects the Tibetan original and is done in the interest of preserving the integrity of the format.

The principals are not stated as plurals but as singulars because, for instance, if it were said that there are three possibilities between colors and red colors, this might be taken to imply that there are three possibilities between *each and*

every color and *each and every* red color. However, such is not
the case because, for example, there are not three possibilities between the color of a white cloud and the color of
a red shirt, for they are mutually exclusive.

Also, the principals of the debates are not stated with articles because this too would be misleading. For instance, if
one said that there are three possibilities between *a* color
and *a* red color, this too might suggest that *each and every*
color and *each and every* red color compare with three
possibilities. Alternatively, the use of the indefinite articles
"a" and "an" might indicate that there are three possibilities
between some particular but unspecified color and some
other particular red color. However, this is not at all the
intention of the comparison of phenomena. Moreover, it
would seem to be pointless to undertake a process of
comparing two different particular but unspecified things
because, for instance, any particular color such as the color
of a page and any other color such as the color of the next
page are just mutually exclusive. More generally, any two
individual colors and any two individual things would, it
seems, be mutually exclusive. Nothing is both itself and
something other than itself. Indeed, any particular red color,
specified or not, is also *a* color and might be posited as the
first possibility, something which is both a color and red.
However, one could not say that the particular red color is
also the other particular color. It is *a* color but not the other
color to which it is being compared.

Also, the two principals of a debate are not modified with
a definite article "the" because, for instance, the process of
comparing *the* color and *the* red color carries with it too all
the problems of suggesting that what is being discussed are
two particular things. Thus, the principals of debates are not
stated in the plural and are not modified with articles.

What is being discussed in the comparison of color and
red are the abstract singular, color, and the abstract singular,
red. It is not any particular color but the whole sphere of
colors, referred to in the singular in order to set it off as a
collective entity. In establishing the various points of com-

parison and difference between color and red, one points out those things which take (1) both, (2) one but not the other, and (3) neither of these two as a *predicate*. That is, one demonstrates *something which is* both a color and red, *something which is* a color but not red, and *something which is* neither. Thus, the point of comparison between two principals is those two as *predicates*. Terminologically, it is being asked, "May both 'color' and 'red' be appropriately applied as predicates of some subject, may one but not the other be applied as a predicate of some subject, and so on?" The process of comparing color and red involves finding those subjects and thereby delineating the difference between color and red as grammatical and logical predicates and as general entities—phenomena having extension over some sphere. In order to convey this sense of comparison, it is helpful to state the two principals as singulars and without articles.

In the Collected Topics classes and all subsequent study, one of the main sources of debate is the comparison of different phenomena. If an opponent does not know whether or not the boundaries of pervasion of the two phenomena overlap and in what ways those boundaries are distinct, he will hold mistaken views concerning the natures of those phenomena. Due to his misunderstanding he will put forth faulty assertions. In the Tibetan tradition, debate on the comparison of phenomena is an essential process for drawing out those faulty assertions, and reasoning by consequences is the method for dispelling them.

Part Two
Translation and Commentary

The Explanation of
"The Introductory Path of Reasoning"
in Pur-bu-jok Jam-ba-gya-tso's
*The Presentation of Collected Topics
Revealing the Meaning of the Texts on Valid Cognition,
the Magical Key to the Path of Reasoning*

7 Translation Introduction

Note: The Tutor Jam-ba-gya-tso's "The Introductory Path of Reasoning" is intermingled with line-by-line annotations. The text is indented and supplemented with information in brackets indicating the intended meaning or what is actually spoken in debate. Explanatory commentary is put to the left margin to distinguish it from the text.

The text translated here is "The Introductory Path of Reasoning" (*rigs lam chung ngu*), the first major part of *The Presentation of Collected Topics Revealing the Meaning of the Texts on Valid Cognition, the Magical Key to the Path of Reasoning* (*tshad ma'i gzhung don 'byed pa'i bsdus grva'i rnam bzhag rigs lam 'phrul gyi lde mig*). (See the Preface for a description of the overall layout of this Collected Topics text.) The author is Pur-bu-jok Jam-ba-gya-tso (*phur bu lcog byams pa rgya mtsho*), 1825-1901, referred to as the Tutor Jam-ba-gya-tso because he was tutor to the Thirteenth Dalai Lama, for whose instruction he wrote the text.

"The Introductory Path of Reasoning" has seven chapters. Together with a brief description of each, in their order of appearance, these are:

1   "Colors—White, Red, and So Forth" (*kha dog dkar dmar sogs*) is the essential introductory presentation of forms (*gzugs, rūpa*) or matter (*bem po, kanthā*)—visible forms, sounds, odors, tastes, and tangible objects—in the Collected Topics system.

2   "Established Bases" (*gzhi grub*) is the main study of ontology, the nature of existence, in the Collected Topics system as well as an introductory indication of epistemological concerns focusing on the consciousnesses which are able to observe the types of phenomena.

3   "Identifying Isolates" (*ldog pa ngos 'dzin*) is a study of one type of negation in the Collected Topics system, built up primarily on the assertion that any phenomenon is one with itself alone.

4   "Opposite-From-Being-Something and Opposite-From-Not-Being-Something" (*yin log min log*) is also a presentation of a type of negation in the Collected Topics system and, in addition, includes a section of verbal debates which play on the manner of expressing something.

5   "The Introductory [Presentation of] Causes and Effects" (*rgyu 'bras chung ngu*) is the primary introduction to causes and effects focusing on direct and indirect causes and effects, substantial causes, cooperative conditions, and substantial and cooperative effects.

6   "Generalities and Instances" (*spyi bye brag*) is a study of the natures of generalities and instances approached primarily through a description of the requirements a phenomenon must meet in order to be an instance of some generality.

7   "Substantial Phenomena and Isolate Phenomena" (*rdzas chos ldog chos*), first formulated by Cha-ba-chö-ḡyi-śeng-gay, is an arrangement of phenomena predicated essentially on the basis of whether it is or is not an example of itself and whether non-that phenomenon is or is not an example of itself.

Each chapter is subdivided into three separate sections which together serve to present and clarify the Collected Topics position on colors, established bases, and so forth as well as related topics. Representing three methods of approach to the central topic, the sections involve refutation of mistaken views (*'khrul ba dgag pa*), presentation of our own system (*rang lugs bzhag pa*), and dispelling objections (*rtsod pa spong ba*) to that system. These three approaches reflect the important uses of debate: to refute mistaken views and fallacious reasoning, to posit the correct position, and to overcome objections to the position which has been stated. Formal debate and philosophical discussion in general have these three approaches. Not only do the debate manuals incorporate this technique but also an important portion of the Tibetan commentarial tradition incorporates the format of these three approaches to a central topic as a principal means of explaining philosophy.

The first of these three sections, refutation of mistaken views or refutation of others' systems (*gzhan lugs dgag pa*), uniformly consists of the statement of mistaken views by a hypothetical opponent and the refutation of those views by the use of contradictory consequences (*thal 'gyur, prasaṅga*) to draw out their internal absurdities. In these first sections the non-Proponent of Sūtra opponent assumes the position of the Defender, for he is stating a basic assertion which he must *defend* against the objections of the Challenger, the Buddhist Proponent of Sūtra.

There are logical consequences of any assertion. If the assertion is factually concordant, then reasoned analysis will only bear this out, for the consequences of that view will not conflict with the basic assertion. However, if the Defender asserts a factually mistaken position, the Challenger will draw out the discordant consequences of that view for the sake of causing him to overcome his error. For any mistaken view, the logical consequences will destroy the basic assertion. By revealing the inner contradictions of a position one is able to suppress the manifestation of wrong views.

The second section, presentation of the "correct" system called "our own system" (*rang lugs*), details the Ge-luk-ba author's interpretation of the basic position of the Proponents of Sūtra Following Reasoning by means of giving definitions, divisions, mutually inclusive phenomena, and illustrations for the objects under discussion, colors or whatever. In "The Middling Path of Reasoning" and "The Greater Path of Reasoning", the presentation of the author's system often takes the form of a debate between two opponents with the definitions and so forth being presented as a part of their discussion, but in "The Introductory Path of Reasoning" this section is usually in the form of an organized explanation outside the framework of formal debate.

The third section is called "dispelling objections" to the correct system that has been posited in the previous section. In this final section the Proponent of Sūtra initially assumes the role of Defender in taking on the Challenger's objections to what has been said concerning the topics at hand. The defense against these objections is made by pointing out the opponent's failure of reasoning manifest in his misinterpretation or misconception of the system that has been posited. Having given a defense of his own system, again in this section the Proponent of Sūtra is often put into the role of Challenger stating absurd consequences of the former non-Proponent of Sūtra Challenger's misconceptions or challenging the answers given by a hypothetical second Defender.

Each chapter has these three sections representing diverse methods of approach to the central topic. Moreover, in this work, in addition to these three sections each chapter is supplemented with an explanatory introduction. Traditionally, upon beginning a new topic, the teachers expand a great deal on the issues that are raised. Thus, drawing from explanations given by scholars within the tradition, materials from other Collected Topics texts, my own personal experience with debate, and so forth, at the beginning of each chapter I lay out in some detail the topics that are presented in that chapter. This is done in the interest of leading the reader into the subject-matter so that the translation is easier and more accessible. This approach reflects a pedagogical technique, common in this tradition, of previewing the material, thereby allowing one to gain gradually a familiarity with the topics. Also, the explanatory introductions provided with each chapter reflect the technique of the oral tradition and the system of debate through giving a broader presentation of the topics than does the actual text.

As a means of coming to understand the Collected Topics of Valid Cognition, study of the text itself is the best guide. Thus, the translation augmented by point-by-point annotations here serves to illustrate both the procedure and content of this introductory book on Tibetan Buddhist debate.

OBEISANCE

> I bow down to the lamas and to the Protector Mañjushrī.

The Tutor's *Collected Topics* begins with obeisance to the lamas (*bla ma, guru*) who preserved and transmitted the teachings on valid cognition and to the Protector Mañjushrī. Paying homage to Mañjushrī indicates that this text is included in the scriptures on Knowledge (*chos mngon pa, abhidharma*). Mañjushrī is the manifestation of all the Buddhas' wisdom and is the special deity of debate, logical and epistemological studies, and all topics of philosophy. "In order to penetrate the subtle meaning of Buddha's teaching it is necessary to have the wisdom discriminating phenomena, and Mañjushrī along with Sarasvatī [*dbyang can ma*] are the two deities that bestow wisdom to others."[1] Mañjushrī (*'jam dpal*) is also called Mañjughosha (*'jam dbyang*), and in this passage, literally rendered, the author is paying homage to Mañjushrīghosha (*'jam dpal dbyang*):

---

[1] Denma Lochö Rinbochay, oral commentary.

He is called *mañju*—gentle, agreeable, soft—because
he is free from the harshness of afflictive and non-
afflictive obstructions. He is called *ghoṣha*—speech,
sound, melody—because he is the lord of speech and
his speech possesses the sixty qualities of vocalization.
He is called *shrī*—glorious—because he has the glory
of the completion of the two collections, merit and
wisdom.[1]

Mañjushrī is usually depicted in the form of a youth of
sixteen years who holds a scripture of the Perfection of
Wisdom (*shes rab kyi pha rol tu phyin, prajñā-pāramitā*) at his
heart indicating that "he sees all objects just as they are with
his pure and clear intelligence".[2] The Perfection of Wisdom
Sūtras "express the superior of all of Buddha's teachings
and are the main of the 84,000 masses of doctrine".[3] He
holds the scripture on his left side, the side associated with
wisdom, showing that his wisdom is in accordance with
Buddha's highest teachings of the most profound emptiness
(*stong pa nyid, shūnyatā*).

In his right hand, associated with method, he holds a
flaming sword "which clears away the darkness of ignorance and cuts every sprout of suffering".[4] The sword is an
indication of Mañjushrī's method (*thabs, upāya*), the motivation of the Great Vehicle seeking to establish all sentient
beings in Buddhahood. It is in flames, for just as the light of
a flame is able to clear away darkness in a room so is the
light of wisdom able to clear away the darkness of ignorance. This flaming sword "cuts every sprout of suffering",

---

[1] Lati Rinbochay, *Mind in Tibetan Buddhism*, p. 44.

[2] This line is from a popular prayer to Mañjushrī. For the Tibetan of this
prayer, see "Daily Recitations of Preliminaries" (Dharamsala: Library of
Tibetan Works and Archives, 1975), p. 4. According to Kensur Yeshay
Tupden this prayer was composed by a group of Indian Buddhist pandits
who one day planned that the next day each would bring a prayer to
Mañjushrī. When they gathered the next day, they found that each had
composed the same prayer.

[3] Denma Lochö Rinbochay, oral commentary.

[4] Mañjushrī prayer.

for wisdom is the actual antidote of ignorance, the root cause of all suffering. Wisdom destroys the causes of suffering, making it impossible for it to arise.

In the obeisance Mañjushri is called a Protector (*mgon po*). A Protector is a Buddha, one who protects sentient beings from suffering and establishes them in happiness.

> The Protector Mañjushri, who has great love and compassion for sentient beings suffering in cyclic existence, dispels the darkness of ignorance in their minds through the rays of light of his wisdom as sunlight dispels darkness. Mañjushri will clear away the darkness of mind of all those who pray to him.[1]

When Dzong-ka-ba (*tsong kha pa*), the founder of the Ge-luk-ba order of Tibetan Buddhism, heard that Mañjushri is able to bestow wisdom upon trainees, he resolved not to turn away from him.

> When a trainee pleases him, Manjushri can, with merely a glance, bestow the wisdom discriminating the truth in the sense of quickly increasing realisation, like lighting a flame. Tsong-ka-pa says that having heard such a marvellous account, he has relied on Manjushri as his special deity over a long time and will not forsake him in the future.[2]

With great effort Dzong-ka-ba sought and actually achieved a meeting with the Protector Mañjushri.

> There was a painting of Manjushri on the wall of Tsong-ka-pa's Ga-wa-dong retreat, and upon improvement of his meditation a great light emitted from Manjushri's heart. That was the first time Tsong-ka-pa saw Manjushri, and thereafter at his wish he met with Manjushri, who taught him the difficult points of the stages of the path.[3]

---

[1] Lati Rinbochay, oral commentary, trans. by Joe Wilson, Jr..

[2] Tsong-ka-pa, *Tantra in Tibet*, p. 27.

[3] *Ibid.*, p. 24.

It is said that Mañjushrī is able to bestow wisdom on disciples in the way that a spark is able to ignite a fire.[1]

The author pays homage first to the lamas. It is only in dependence on the lamas or teachers that the tradition of logic and debate is transmitted. "The lama is one who unerringly teaches the path."[2] "Lama" is the Tibetan translation for "guru". "Guru" means "heavy" and indicates one who is heavy with good qualities (*yon tan, guṇa*). A guru is a spiritual guide, one who has previously developed good qualities and traversed the path. He is able to lead his disciples to enlightenment because he knows the path. The word "lama" is etymologized in two ways. "*La*" means "high" and "*ma*" means "not", so "lama" means "not high" which in Tibetan expresses "none higher", for the lama is taken as the supreme of all beings. In another way, "*la*" means "high" and "*ma*" means "mother", for a lama is like a spiritual mother who nourishes one's good qualities. The lama or guru is the conduit of the Buddhist doctrine. In dependence on the kindness of a lama who teaches the doctrine one is able to hear the Buddha's doctrine, think about its meaning, and achieve superior qualities of body, speech, and mind.

"A true lama is like a channel through which the blessings of all Buddhas flow."[3] Through reliance on a spiritual guide one is able to destroy non-virtues accumulated in the past and actualize virtuous qualities of body, speech, and mind. Mañjushrī is said to be able to destroy one's non virtues in a moment.

> The Venerable Mañjushrī has great compassion and wisdom, but because we have great obstructions we are not able to actually meet with him. Rather, we must meet him through the lama. For example, the sun is very hot, but the trees and other material objects

---

[1] Lati Rinbochay, oral commentary.
[2] Denma Lochö Rinbochay, oral commentary.
[3] Khetsun Sangbo Rinbochay, *Tantric Practice in Nying-Ma*, p. 103.

do not burst into flames. However, if one uses a magnifying glass to focus the sun's rays, then one can create a fire. The one who holds the magnifying glass is like the lama, the fiery sun is like the Venerable Mañjushrī, and we are like the magnifying glass. Through focusing the sun's rays with a magnifying glass, one is able to create a fire. The sun is very far away and we need someone to focus its light.[1]

Thus, in the beginning the Tutor Jam-ba-gya-tso pays obeisance to the lamas and to the Protector Mañjushrī

Here the author is making the three types of homage, through body, speech, and mind. Physical homage means to raise with a pure mind even one finger or bow the head in respect; a verbal homage is any praise spoken with a pure mind; mental homage is a pure mind of respect itself.[2]

EXPRESSION OF WORSHIP

Homage to the former scholars and adepts of the country of Superiors and Tibet,[3]
The great beings Dignāga, Dharmakīrti, and so forth
Who clarified with valid cognition the path of reasoning well spoken
By the Valid Teacher seeing the meaning of reality.

The expression of worship pays reverence to the former scholars and adepts of India and Tibet who organized and clarified the teachings of Buddha, the Valid Teacher (*ston pa tshad ma*). The principal formulators of Buddhist logic were the Indians Dignāga (circa C.E. 480-540) and Dharmakīrti (circa C.E. 600-660) who organized a system of logic and formulated a theory of knowledge in accordance with scrip-

---

[1] Lati Rinbochay, oral commentary, trans. by Joe Wilson, Jr..
[2] Lati Rinbochay, *Mind in Tibetan Buddhism*, pp. 44-45.
[3] The "country of Superiors" is India.

ture.[1] Although Buddha himself never taught a formal system of logic as such, a path of reasoning said to have been taught by him was organized by later Indian and Tibetan scholars. Thus, this text on one form of Buddhist reasoning pays homage indirectly to Buddha who first indicated the path of reasoning, and directly to the scholars who organized and preserved the Buddha's path of reasoning.

Here Buddha is called the Valid Teacher. One purpose of Buddhist reasoning is to establish Buddha as a Valid Teacher. "By showing Buddha as a Valid Teacher, we can then take his sayings as validly established."[2] It becomes of essential importance to establish Buddha as valid and reliable. One difference between Buddhist and non-Buddhist schools of tenets is from the point of view of teacher. The Buddhist schools have the distinguishing trait of having a teacher who has extinguished all faults and completed his good qualities.[3]

Buddha exhorted his followers to develop their reasoning capacities in order to avoid faulty views and to adopt correct ones. Buddha said, "Monks and scholars should analyze well, like analyzing gold through scorching, cutting, and rubbing. My words are not to be adopted for the sake of respect."[4] A gold assayer tests metal to determine its value by scorching, cutting, and rubbing it. Similarly, Buddha's words are to be tested by the three analyses or the three valid cognizers: direct valid cognizers (*mngon sum tshad ma, pratyaksha-pramāṇa*), inference through the power of the fact

---

[1] For source of dates for Dignāga and Dharmakīrti, see note 5 above.

[2] Samdong Rinbochay, oral commentary.

[3] Paraphrased from Geshe Lhundup Sopa and Jeffrey Hopkins, *Practice and Theory of Tibetan Buddhism*, (New York: Grove Press, Inc., 1976), p. 54.

[4] The source of this passage in sūtra is indefinite, but it is reported by several authors as being from sūtra. For instance, see Den-dar-hla-ram-ba (*bstan dar lha ram pa*), *Notes Helping with the Difficult Points in Signs and Reasoning, Clear Sunlight of New Explanation* (*rtags rigs kyi dka' ba'i gnas la phan pa'i zin bris gsar bshad nyi ma'i 'od zer*), Collected Works of Bstan-dar Lha-ram of A-lag-sha, Vol. 1 (New Delhi: Lama Guru Deva, 1971), 70.4-5. Also, see Tenzin Gyatso, *The Buddhism of Tibet and The Key to the Middle Way*, p. 55.

(*dngos stobs rjes dpag*, **vastu-bala-anumāna*), and inference through belief (*yid ches rjes dpag*, **āpta-anumāna*). The above passage from sūtra indicates that "even though something is the speech of Buddha, one should not just accept it but investigate it and, having analyzed it, then [one may] accept it. It also teaches the method of analysis by the example of analyzing gold."[1]

The three valid cognizers are correct consciousnesses which incontrovertibly realize the three types of objects of comprehension (*gzhal bya*, *prameya*): manifest phenomena (*mngon gyur*, *abhimukhī*), slightly hidden phenomena (*cung zad lkog gyur*, *kimchid-parokṣha*), and very hidden phenomena (*shin tu lkog gyur*, *atyartha-parokṣha*). Manifest objects of comprehension are impermanent phenomena such as visible forms, sounds, and so forth which can be apprehended by ordinary direct perceivers. Slightly hidden phenomena such as the impermanence of sound are accessible to inferential cognizers through the power of the fact, that is, by the power of the nature of the object such as the heat of fire. Very hidden phenomena are accessible only to inferential cognizers through the power of belief, that is, through scriptural inference.

The process of testing Buddha's words involves thorough investigation for non-contradiction. That is, the teaching must not contradict the three analyses: direct perception, inference through the power of the fact, and inference through belief. The assayer's three tests for gold—scorching, cutting, and rubbing—are correlated to the three valid cognizers and their objects of comprehension.

> This scripture identifies passages which are pure by way of the three analyses because it indicates respectively the three: (1) non-damage [i.e., non-contradiction] and establishment by direct perception with respect to a passage in which Buddha teaches manifest phenomena—sounds, visible forms, and so forth, (2)

---

[1] Ḍen-dar-hla-ram-ba, *Notes Helping with the Difficult Points in Signs and Reasoning, Clear Sunlight of New Explanation*, 70.5-6.

non-damage and good establishment by inference through the power of the fact with respect to its teaching slightly hidden phenomena such as the impermanence of sound, and (3) non-contradiction of earlier and later assertions [within the passage] with regard to its teaching very hidden phenomena such as [in the scripture], "From giving, resources [arise]," and non-damage by explicit or implicit contradiction within one's own words.[1]

The correlation between the assayer's three tests of gold and the three analyses by valid cognizers of their objects of comprehension is made because of a special similarity between them. It is said that scorching is qualitatively similar to direct perception, cutting is qualitatively similar to inference through the power of the fact, and rubbing is qualitatively similar to inference through belief.[2]

An assayer tests gold by burning, and disciples test Buddha's teachings on manifest phenomena through analysis by direct perception. "Just as the manifest flaws in gold are analyzed by analyzing its color after scorching, so one analyzes the object of expression of a passage with a direct valid cognizer."[3] If a passage teaching manifest phenomena is not contradicted by direct perception, then it is suitable to accept it. For instance, if Buddha had said that fire is cold, this is contradicted by direct perception and could not be accepted. "One can establish with direct perceivers what the Buddha taught about the objects of comprehension of direct perceivers."[4]

"One can establish with direct perceivers that an object is a form, that it is a shape, and so forth. However, in order to

---

[1] Bel-jor-hlün-drup (*dpal 'byor lhun grub*), *Commentary on the Difficult Points in (Dzong-ka-ba's) "The Essence of the Good Explanations", Lamp for the Teaching* (*legs bshad snying po'i dka' 'grel bstan pa'i sgron me*) (Delhi: Rong tha mchog sprul, 1969), 5b.4-6a.1.

[2] *Ibid.*, 6a.1-2.

[3] Den-dar-hla-ram-ba, *Notes Helping with the Difficult Points in Signs and Reasoning, Clear Sunlight of New Explanation*, 70.6.

[4] Kensur Jambel Shenpen, oral commentary.

establish an object as an impermanent phenomenon, in the beginning one must rely on a logical sign."[1] The manifest faults of gold are quickly shown by scorching, but some faults are more subtle and more difficult to find, requiring close investigation. Testing for these faults the assayer cuts the gold ore into sections.

> Just as one analyzes the slightly hidden faults of gold by analyzing the internal faults through cutting and sectioning, so one analyzes the object of expression of some passage by an inferential cognizer through the power of the fact.[2]

If a passage concerning slightly hidden phenomena is not contradicted by inference through the power of the fact, then it is suitable to accept it. "If one cannot see externally by direct perceivers, then one must see internally by logical signs."[3]

Initially, one is not able to realize by direct perception that a form is an impermanent phenomenon, this must first be established through dependence on a logical sign. A form is an impermanent phenomenon because of being a product. A form is a product, and whatever is a product is necessarily an impermanent phenomenon. Therefore, a form is an impermanent phenomenon. The subtle impermanence of products is the first of the four seals which identify a view as being Buddhist. These are:

1 all products are impermanent phenomena
2 all contaminated things are miserable
3 all phenomena are selfless
4 *nirvāṇa* is peace.[4]

These four are slightly hidden phenomena which must initially be investigated through dependence on logical signs.

---

[1] *Ibid.*

[2] Ḍen-dar-hla-ram-ba, *Notes Helping with the Difficult Points in Signs and Reasoning, Clear Sunlight of New Explanation*, 70.6-71.1.

[3] Kensur Jaṃbel Shenpen, oral commentary.

[4] Sopa and Hopkins, *Practice and Theory of Tibetan Buddhism*, pp. 68-69.

Eventually one can know these phenomena too by direct perceivers, but at first one can only approach them internally through signs. Like testing the value of gold by cutting, one must analyze Buddha's teachings on slightly hidden phenomena by looking, as if inside, with careful, reasoned analysis.

Very hidden objects of comprehension must be realized by an inferential cognizer through belief. This is scriptural inference. Examples of very hidden phenomena are the specific causes of one's resources in this lifetime. Nāgārjuna's *Precious Garland of Advice for the King* (*rājaparikathā-ratnamālā*) says, "From giving, resources [arise]," which indicates that by accumulating an action of giving in a former lifetime, one is able to enjoy resources in a later one.[1] "One does not need inference through belief to realize just that through giving, resources are achieved, for this is not a very hidden phenomenon; [however], to realize the very hidden phenomenon such as the specific action of giving, its entity, its object, the giver, the time of giving, and so forth involved in giving rise to a specific resource, one needs inference through belief."[2]

Again, inference through belief relies on non-contradiction by direct perception, non-contradiction by inference through the power of the fact, and non-contradiction by earlier and later passages.

> Just as one analyzes the faults or good qualities of gold that are very difficult to realize by analyzing whether it is good or bad through rubbing it on a black stone, so one analyzes the words of a certain passage by searching for earlier and later explicit and implicit contradictions and so forth. If the passage is

---

[1] Nāgārjuna, *The Precious Garland of Advice for the King* (*rājaparikathā-ratnamālā*), in Nagarjuna and Kaysang Gyatso, the Seventh Dalai Lama, *The Precious Garland* and *The Song of the Four Mindfulnesses*, The Wisdom of Tibet Series 2, trans. by Jeffrey Hopkins and Lati Rimpoche with Anne Klein (New York: Harper & Row, 1975), stanza 438, p. 83.

[2] Lati Rinbochay, *Mind in Tibetan Buddhism*, p. 77.

without fallacies, that is to say, if it is purified by the three analyses, then it is appropriate to accept it.[1]

The third type of valid cognizer relies on other factors to establish validity. Like rubbing gold on a black stone to see, perhaps, if it is pure and malleable enough to leave a shine on the dark surface of a black stone, inference through belief requires reflection on earlier and later passages. However, this is not merely a test for internal consistency, but a rigorous, reasoned analysis. "Scriptures teaching very hidden topics ... are proved to be unmistaken with respect to their contents by reasoning purified through the three analyses. The establishment of the modes of the process is done through reasoning; one does not rely on asserting scripture as proof."[2]

Reasoning is able to establish even very hidden phenomena. "The only way of proving very hidden phenomena is if we can take the word of Buddha as valid. To do this we must establish Buddha as a Valid Teacher."[3] Thus, in Dharmakīrti's *Commentary on (Dignāga's) "Compendium of Valid Cognition"* (*pramāṇavarttikakārikā*), one of the main sources of Buddhist logic and epistemology, there is a proof of Buddha as a Valid Teacher. Buddha, as a Valid Teacher, taught a path of reasoning which was formulated by the scholars and adepts of India and Tibet—Dignāga, Dharmakīrti, and so forth. Here, in the expression of worship of this book on one form of Buddhist reasoning, the author pays homage to the Valid Teacher and those who organized and preserved his teaching of a path of reasoning.

---

1 Den-dar-hla-ram-ba, *Notes Helping with the Difficult Points in Signs and Reasoning, Clear Sunlight of New Explanation*, 71.1-2.

2 Tsong-ka-pa, *Tantra in Tibet*, p. 89.

3 Samdong Rinbochay, oral commentary.

8 *Colors and So Forth*

INTRODUCTION

Before examining the first debates, an introductory overview of the topics considered in the presentation of colors and so forth will be beneficial. This is done in order to give the reader a broader perspective on the issues, thereby rendering the debates more accessible.

All of the Collected Topics debate manuals begin with a presentation of colors (*kha dog, varṇa*). In the Tutor's *Collected Topics*, this first chapter is an examination of not only colors but also all types of external forms—visible forms (*gzugs, rūpa*), sounds (*sgra, shabda*), odors (*dri, gandha*), tastes (*ro, rasa*), and tangible objects (*reg bya, spraṣṭavya*). The topics are asserted in accordance with the philosophical tenets of the Buddhist system of the Proponents of Sūtra Following Reasoning as interpreted by the Tibetan Ge-luk-ba order.

The first few debates in this text are indeed limited to a consideration of colors, and this topic is precisely where the traditional study of Buddhist reasoning commences for the novice monks as Geshé Rabten recalls:

> We were first taught the easiest subject—the relation-
> ships between the four primary and the eight secon-
> dary colours. They were explained carefully; and we
> learned how to apply simple logical reasoning to
> them. ... While the subject of colours and their rela-
> tionships is very simple, it is the manner of phrasing
> the question in debate that trains the mind. This be-
> comes very interesting and challenging. Once we had
> mastered it, our intelligence developed somewhat.[1]

These debates on colors and so forth, as the first introduction to debate and formalized reasoning, are simple and
straightforward. Beyond teaching the form and procedure of
the debating process, they offer little content. Still, there is a
purpose for beginning the reasoning texts with a presentation of colors and other forms because, using this as a basis,
one is able to progress toward higher, more profound topics:

> The purpose is to train the potency of the mind so that
> one will be able to penetrate the difficult topics. At the
> beginning of the study of reasoning it would be diffi-
> cult to prove the existence of omniscience or the exis-
> tence of liberation. For the sake of understanding, one
> initially settles such topics as impermanent phenom-
> ena, non-impermanent phenomena, and objects of
> comprehension. In order to understand in debate the
> extension of pervasions [*khyab pa che chung*] with
> regard to such topics, it is necessary to first settle this
> in relation to phenomena that can be seen with the
> eye—colors and shapes—as well as others such as
> sounds, odors, tastes, and tangible objects. That is, in
> relation to the objects of direct perception. From
> among these, we are most involved with color; thus,
> the study begins with color.[2]

---

[1] Rabten, pp. 38-39.
[2] Denma Lochö Rinbochay, oral commentary.

Underlying this pedagogy is the Buddhist view that sentient beings caught in cyclic existence are constantly involved with forms, being distracted by colors, shapes, and so forth while not mixing their minds with reasoning. Due to this, sentient beings remain confused with respect to the ultimate and conventional natures of phenomena and are powerlessly imprisoned in cyclic existence. Thus, the textbooks on introductory reasoning take forms as the first topic of debate in order to lead trainees to the path of reasoning through first analyzing the familiar. What is familiar is more accessible. An examination of forms requires no special introduction, and so it is an easy and suitable topic with which to begin training young monks, usually between the ages of seven and fifteen.

> By training in easier topics, one advances and is eventually able to handle the more difficult. This is the reason why the presentation of white and red colors is given at the beginning. If this purpose is not understood, one might think it is senseless to talk about white and red colors.[1]

As mentioned above, in the Tutor's *Collected Topics* this first chapter is more generally an examination of all types of external form (*phyi'i gzugs, bahirdhā-rūpa*). One of the main sources of the Collected Topics texts is Vasubandhu's *Treasury of Knowledge* (*abhidharmakosha*) which presents form in the following passage:

> Forms are the five sense powers, the five
> Objects, and non-revelatory forms only.
> The bases of the consciousnesses of these types—
> The eye [sense] and so forth—are forms.
> [Visible] forms are of two types or twenty types.
> Sounds are of eight types.

---

[1] *Ibid.*

Tastes are of six types. Odors are of four types.
Tangible objects are of just eleven [types].[1]

In sūtra Buddha said, "Monks, it is called the appropriated
aggregate of form because it exists as form and it is suitable
as form."[2] Ajitamitra, in his commentary on Nāgārjuna's
Precious Garland, reports that *rūpa* (form) means "that which
is breakable", for form may be broken.

All forms are impermanent phenomena because they are
produced in dependence on causes and conditions and,
once produced, disintegrate. As such, forms may be
perceived by direct perception. In this system, the various
types of forms serve as the fields of activity of the five sense
consciousnesses (*dbang shes, indriya-jñāna*)—eye, ear, nose,
tongue, and body consciousnesses.

According to the *Treasury of Knowledge*, form is divided
into eleven types: the five physical sense powers (*dbang po,
indriya*), the five external objects (*phyi'i don, *bahirdhā-artha*)
of those senses, and non-revelatory form (*rnam par rig byed
ma yin pa'i gzugs, avijñapti-rūpa*), also called form for the
mental consciousness (*chos kyi skye mched pa'i gzugs, dharma-
āyatana-rūpa*), which is not any of the other five external
forms and is an object apprehended by the mental consciousness only.[3] These are:

1   eye sense power (*mig gi dbang po, chakṣhur-indriya*)
2   ear sense power (*rna ba'i dbang po, shrotra-indriya*)
3   nose sense power (*sna'i dbang po, ghrāṇa-indriya*)
4   tongue sense power (*lce'i dbang po, jihvā-indriya*)

---

[1] Vasubandhu, *Treasury of Knowledge* (*abhidharmakosha*), P5590, Vol. 115,
117.2.5-117.2.6.
[2] Gen-dün-drup-ba (*dge 'dun grub pa*), *Commentary on (Vasubandhu's)
"Treasury of Knowledge", Illuminating the Path to Liberation (dam pa'i chos
mngon pa'i mdzod kyi rnam par bshad pa thar lam gsal byed)* (Sarnath, India:
Pleasure of Elegant Sayings Press, 1973), p. 28.
[3] In the system of the Proponents of the Sūtra School Following Reasoning
non-revelatory form or form for the mental consciousness is asserted but
not as fully qualified form. It is probably included among non-associated
compositional factors because it is impermanent but neither a
consciousness nor actual form.

5   body sense power (*lus kyi dbang po, kāya-indriya*)
6   visible form (*gzugs, rūpa*)
7   sound (*sgra, shabda*)
8   odor (*dri, gandha*)
9   taste (*ro, rasa*)
10 tangible object (*reg bya, spraṣhṭavya*)
11 non-revelatory form (*rnam par rig byed ma yin pa'i gzugs, avijñapti-rūpa*).[1]

In the system of the Proponents of Sūtra, form (*gzugs, rūpa*) and matter (*bem po, kanthā*) or material phenomenon are mutually inclusive. Whatever is the one is necessarily the other. In accordance with the above passage from sūtra (p. 188), form is defined as:

> that which is suitable as form (*gzugs su rung ba, rūpaṇa*).

This definition is more tautological than descriptive and is an appeal to ordinary experience.

Matter is defined as:

> what which is atomically established (*rdul du grub pa, *aṇusiddha*).

A material phenomenon is generally a collection of many atoms or particles, though a single atom too is matter. Matter is divided into two types: external matter (*phyi'i bem po, bahirdhā-kanthā*) and internal matter (*nang gi bem po, ādhyātmika-kanthā*). The division into external and internal varieties can also be made for form.[2] External matter is defined as:

> that which is atomically established and is not included within the continuum of a person (*skyes bu'i rgyud kyis ma bsdus pa'i rdul du grub pa*).

---

[1] The source for the Sanskrit in this list is Jeffrey Hopkins, *Meditation on Emptiness*, p. 221.
[2] Lati Rinbochay, oral commentary.

External matter consists of visible forms, sounds, odors, tastes, and tangible objects. The definition of internal matter is:

> that which is atomically established and is included within the continuum of a person (*skyes bu'i rgyud kyis bsdus pa'i rdul du grub pa*).

Internal matter is included within the continuum of a person in the sense of being appropriated as the body or form of a person and being a sensate portion of the body. Thus, internal matter includes the fleshy body—though not the hair or nails beyond where they may be felt—as well as the five sense powers: eye sense power, ear sense power, and so forth.

> The five sense powers are neither the course organs, which are the eyes, ears, nose, tongue, and body, nor are they consciousnesses. They are clear matter located in the coarse organs which cannot be seen by the eye but can be seen by certain clairvoyants. They give their respective consciousnesses dominance or power with respect to certain objects and thus are called "powers" (*indriya*).[1]

Indeed, the five "external" forms also exist as internal forms included within a person's continuum because what is internal for one person is external for another and because internal form has color, shape, and so forth as does external matter. Still, the Collected Topics logicians do not assert ten internal forms including visible forms, sounds, odors, and so forth in addition to the five sense powers, probably because it would be repetitious to enumerate the five "external" sources again.

The subtle internal sense powers cannot be perceived by anyone's sense consciousnesses—they do not appear to the senses. Thus, the texts assert only five internal forms. Given this apparent inconsistency, forms may be posited as three

---

[1] Jeffrey Hopkins, *Meditation on Emptiness*, pp. 221-222.

types: internal forms, external forms, and forms which are both internal and external. Material phenomena which are both internal and external are, for instance, the loci of the senses: the eyes, ears, and so forth. For example, the fleshy eye, not the sense power, is an internal form because of being a material phenomenon which is included within the continuum of a person, and it is an external form because of being matter which is an object of others' sense consciousnesses.[1]

It should be noted that even though the above passage from Vasubandhu's *Treasury of Knowledge* identifies eleven types of form (see pp. 188-189), in the system of the Proponents of Sūtra there are only ten because non-revelatory form is not asserted as actual form. Jang-gya Rol-bay-dor-jay (*lcang skya rol pa'i rdo rje*) explains in his presentation of tenets, "Those who assert non-revelatory form as fully qualified form are definitely the two, Proponents of the Great Exposition and Consequentialists."[2] An example of a non-revelatory form in the system of the Great Exposition School, the point of view of the *Treasury of Knowledge*, is a form arising from promises.[3] Such a form is said to be a subtle physical entity which arises at the moment of first taking a vow and remains with the person until losing the vow or death.[4] In the system of the Proponents of Sūtra, non-revelatory forms or forms for the mental consciousness are asserted but not as fully qualified forms; thus, they are not generally discussed in the Collected Topics texts. Still, the Lo-sel-ling *Collected Topics* does list form for the mental consciousness as the sixth type of external form and defines it as:

---

[1] Lati Rinbochay, oral commentary.
[2] Jang-gya (*lcang skya*) *Presentation of Tenets/Clear Expositions of the Presentations of Tenets, Beautiful Ornament for the Meru of the Subduer's Teaching* (*grub pa'i mtha'i rnam par bzhag pa gsal bar bshad pa thub bstan lhun po'i mdzes rgyan*) (Sarnath, India: Pleasure of Elegant Sayings Press, 1970), p. 88.
[3] Kensur Yeshay Tupden, oral commentary.
[4] Jeffrey Hopkins, *Meditation on Emptiness*, p. 234.

that which is suitable as a form which appears only to a mental consciousness (*yid shes kho na la snang ba'i gzugs su rung ba*).[1]

Since non-revelatory forms are objects only of the mental consciousness, they are not form-sources (*gzugs kyi skye mched, rūpa-ayatana*) but are phenomena-sources (*chos kyi skye mched, dharma-āyatana*).[2]

Even though forms are technically of three types—external, internal, and both external and internal—a study of just external and internal varieties, apart from a separate consideration of forms which are both, is adequate to assess the presentation of forms in the Collected Topics tradition. Following the pedagogical technique of beginning with more familiar topics, we will first consider external forms.

EXTERNAL FORMS

The five external forms—visible forms, sounds, odors, tastes, and tangible objects—are the objects of experience of the five sense consciousnesses—eye, ear, nose, tongue, and body sense consciousnesses. External forms are the five sources (*skye mched, āyatana*), the five objects (*yul, viṣhaya*), the five meanings (*don, artha*), and the five object-sources (*yul gyi skye mched, viṣhaya-āyatana*). An external form is called a "source" because of being a form that is a *door, cause, condition,* or *source* of a sense consciousness.[3]

Visible Forms

A form-source (*gzugs kyi skye mched, rūpa-āyatana*), meaning a visible form, is defined as:

---

[1] Jam-b̄el-trin-lay-yön-d̄an-gya-tso (*'jam dpel 'phrin las yon tan rgya mtsho*), Lo-šel-ḷing *Collected Topics* (*blo gsal gling bsdus grva*), (Mundgod, India: Drepung Loseling Press, 1978), p. 4.
[2] Jeffrey Hopkins, *Meditation on Emptiness*, p. 232.
[3] *Ibid.*, p. 223.

an object apprehended by an eye consciousness (*mig shes kyi gzung bya*)

and is the first of the five types of external sources. The term "form-source" is "to be distinguished from the general term 'form' (*rūpa*) which is the basis of the division into eleven types of forms".[1] Form-sources include only the two types of visible forms—that is, just colors and shapes—whereas forms include sounds, odors, tastes, and tangible objects as well. The Go-mang *Collected Topics* lists form-source (*gzugs kyi skye mched*), form-constituent (*gzugs kyi khams*), and demonstrable form (*bstan yod kyi gzugs*) as mutually inclusive phenomena. Any color or shape is called a "demonstrable form" because it may be demonstrated as an object for the eye consciousness.[2]

Very often the Collected Topics texts begin a new chapter with citation of some relevant passages from source literature. One source-quote cited at the beginning of the colors chapter in several Collected Topics texts is a passage from the chapter on inference for oneself (*rang don rjes dpag, svārtha-anumāna*) in Dharmakīrti's *Commentary on (Dignāga's) "Compendium of Valid Cognition"* which says:

> Because the individual potencies, blue and so forth,
> Are seen by the eye consciousness.[3]

According to Kensur Yeshay Tupden, the meaning of this passage is that blue produces an eye consciousness apprehending blue in the sense of serving as a cause of that consciousness; thus, here blue is called a "potency". Similarly, yellow serves as a cause of an eye consciousness apprehending yellow, and so on. Thus, an eye consciousness is established in dependence on the individual potencies.[4]

---

[1] *Ibid.*

[2] Ngak-ẘang-d̄ra-s̄hi (*ngag dbang bkra shis*), Go-mang *Collected Topics* (*sgo mang bsdus grva*), (n.p., n.d.), p. 13.

[3] Dharmakīrti, *Commentary on (Dignāga's) "Compendium of Valid Cognition"* (*pramāṇavārttikakārikā*), P5709, Vol. 130, 79.5.6.

[4] Kensur Yeshay Tupden, oral commentary.

The *Commentary on (Dignāga's) "Compendium of Valid Cognition"* does not present an organized explanation of colors as such but does refer to colors in this and other passages. The presentation of colors and, more generally, forms in the Collected Topics debate manuals issues from passages in this text, the *Treasury of Knowledge*, and other Indian Buddhist sources.

The above passage from Vasubandhu's *Treasury of Knowledge* (see pp. 187-188) says, "[Visible] forms are of two types or twenty types."[1] This sentence indicates the types of form-sources, not forms in general. Form-sources are divided briefly into two types, colors (*kha dog, varṇa*) and shapes (*dbyibs, saṃsthāna*). If divided extensively, there are twelve types of color and eight types of shape, totaling twenty types of form-sources. The twelve types of color consist of four primary colors and eight secondary colors:

1   primary color (*rtsa ba'i kha dog, mūla-varṇa*)
    blue (*sngon po, nīla*)
    yellow (*ser po, pīta*)
    white (*skar po, avadāta*)
    red (*dmar po, lohita*)
2   secondary color (*yan lag gi kha dog, aṅga-varṇa*)
    cloud (*sprin, abhra*)
    smoke (*du ba, dhūma*)
    dust (*brdul, rajaḥ*)
    mist (*khug sna, mahikā*)
    illumination (*snang ba, āloka*)
    darkness (*mun pa, andhakāra*)
    shadow (*grib ma, chhāyā*)
    sunlight (*nyi ma'i 'od ser, ātapa*).[2]

The definition of a color is:

that which is suitable as a hue (*mdog tu rung ba*).

---

[1] Vasubandhu, *Treasury of Knowledge*, P5590, Vol. 115, 117.2.5.
[2] The source for the Sanskrit in this list is Jeffrey Hopkins, *Meditation on Emptiness*, p. 224.

As in the case of the definition of a form (p. 189) this definition relies on ordinary empirical experience indicating that the Collected Topics logicians do not have or need anything further to say at this point. The definition of a color is extended similarly to the many types of color—that which is suitable as a secondary hue (*yan lag gi mdog tu rung ba*) being the definition of a secondary color, that which is suitable as a blue hue (*sngon po'i mdog tu rung ba*) being the definition of blue, and so forth.

A primary color is defined as:

> that which is suitable as a primary hue (*rtsa ba'i mdog tu rung ba*).

According to Lati Rinbochay, primary colors may be divided into natural, or innate, primary colors (*lhan skyes kyi rtsa ba'i kha dog, sahaja-mūla-varṇa*) and manufactured primary colors (*sbyar byung gi rtsa ba'i kha dog, sāṃyogika-mūla-varṇa*). A natural color is something that is not made by a person; it is not the result of someone's having dyed it into the material or such but is a color arisen through natural causes. A manufactured color is something made by a person by dyeing and so forth. For example, the color of a flower is a natural color and the color of a red car is a manufactured color.[1]

More frequently, primary colors are divided into the four—blue, yellow, white, and red. The four primary colors are associated with the elements which exist in all forms. "Wind is blue; earth, yellow; water, white; and fire, red."[2]

Generally, in the scientific description of colors white is not included among the primary colors, these being only red, blue, and yellow. White, in terms of pigments, is an absence of color, and what is called white light is a light having all colors of the spectrum. Still, it is unmistakable that white is something that appears to the eye consciousnesses and is normally taken as a color. It is not, as in the

---

[1] Lati Rinbochay, oral commentary.
[2] Jeffrey Hopkins, *Meditation on Emptiness*, p. 223.

case of pigments, an absence of colors like a desert without water. If the primary colors are taken to be those root colors that are "not derivable from other colors",[1] then is it not the case that white is a primary color? As pigment, white cannot be derived from any combination of other pigments. As light, what is called white is a *clear* appearance of illumination, but by no combination of light rays can one derive truly white light. If primary colors are taken as those root colors from which all other colors are derived, then white must be considered a primary color because some colors are derived from white in combination with other colors, such as pink which is a mixture of white and red. When the Collected Topics texts enumerate the primary colors as four, it is indefinite whether they are indicating colors on the basis of pigment or light. Still, the basis of the division into primary and secondary colors is color, that which is suitable as a hue. It is that object apprehended by an eye consciousness, and it is what is suitable to be demonstrated as a hue to the eye consciousness. Within this framework, it is unmistakable that white is a color, and here it is asserted to be a primary color.

The eight secondary colors of cloud, smoke, and so forth (p. 194) do not include all secondary colors because mixtures of colors, such as green which is a mixture of blue and yellow, are also secondary colors. The Lo-śel-ling *Collected Topics* says, "Those which arise from a mixture of two or three primary colors are secondary colors."[2]

Cloud etc. are the eight famous secondary colors indicated in Vasubandhu's *Treasury of Knowledge*. Gen-dün-drup-ba's (*dge 'dun grub pa*) *Commentary on (Vasubandhu's) "Treasury of Knowledge"* lists these: "There are eight secondary colors because there are shadow, sunlight, illumination, darkness, cloud, smoke, dust and mist."[3] This

---

[1] *Webster's Seventh New Collegiate Dictionary* (Springfield, Mass.: G. & C. Merriam Company, 1963), p. 675.

[2] Jam-ḃel-trin-lay-yön-ḋan-gya-tso, Lo-śel-ling *Collected Topics*, p. 2.

[3] Gen-dün-drup-ba, *Commentary on (Vasubandhu's) "Treasury of Knowledge"*, p. 29.

enumeration is not taken to mean that clouds, smoke, dust, and mist are colors, but that the colors of these are colors and may be secondary colors. For instance, the color of a gray cloud is a secondary color. Technically, these eight "secondary colors" must be *specified* as secondary colors; thus, the debate manuals qualify these as, for instance, "a cloud color which is that" (*der gyur pa'i sprin gyi kha dog*) referring to a cloud which is a secondary color. Some cloud colors are secondary colors and some are not. For instance, the color of a gray cloud is a secondary color because of being gray, not because of being a cloud color. However, the color of a white cloud is a primary color because of being white. Taken as adjectives—cloudy, smoky, and so on— these describe characteristics of colors and identify them as secondary colors.

Unlike cloud, smoke, dust, and mist, some scholars assert that illumination, darkness, shadow, and sunlight themselves are secondary colors.[1]

> Illumination refers to the light of the moon, stars, fire, medicine, and jewels. Darkness refers to a form that obscures other forms and causes one to see gloom and blackness. Darkness obscures other forms such that they cannot be seen, whereas shadow makes other forms a little unclear but still perceivable; thus, darkness and shadow have a difference of density. Sunlight refers to the illumination of other forms when the sun appears.[2]

Of the twenty types of form-sources indicated in Vasubandhu's *Treasury of Knowledge* twelve are colors and the remaining eight are shapes (*dbyibs, saṃsthāna*). The eight types of shape are:

1   long (*ring ba, dīrgha*)
2   short (*thung ba, hrasva*)
3   high (*mtho ba, unnata*)

---

[1] Jeffrey Hopkins, *Meditation on Emptiness*, p. 224.
[2] *Ibid.*, pp. 224-225.

4   low (*dma' ba, avanata*)
5   square (*lham pa, vṛtta*)
6   round (*zlum po, parimaṇḍala*)
7   level (*phya le ba, shāta*)
8   non-level (*phya le ba ma yin pa, vishāta*).[1]

A shape is defined as:

> that which is suitable to be shown as a shape (*dbyibs su bstan du rung ba*).

As before in the case of secondary colors, it seems this list is not exhaustive of all shapes because shapes such as those of a triangle or an octagon are apparently not included.

Concerning long, short, high, and low, Lati Rinbochay explains that they may be posited even in terms of where one is; that is, in relation to other shapes. Thus, a long or tall form is, for instance, the shape of Mount Meru, the mountain at the center of the world system. A short form is, for instance, the shape of a single atom. Since in relation to our land the fourth concentration—the highest level of form lands where sentient beings live—is high, the shape of an immeasurable palace in the fourth concentration may be posited as a high shape. Similarly, it is asserted that below our land there is a *maṇḍala* of wind which is the lower basis of the world system. Since it is below our land, its shape may be posited as a low shape. In the same way, if one is in a valley, the shape of a mountain is high, and if one is on a mountain,the shape of a valley is low.[2] Since some shapes may be posited in relation to other shapes, such figures as triangles and octagons, which are not otherwise included, may be included among long, short, high, or low forms depending on one's perspective.

A square (*lham pa*) is designated as being four-sided (*gru bzhi*), and the Ra-dö, Lo-sel-ling, and Shar-dzay Collected Topics texts list four-sided in place of square. However, it

---

[1] The source for the Sanskrit in this list is Jeffrey Hopkins, *Meditation on Emptiness*, p. 226.
[2] Lati Rinbochay, oral commentary.

seems either designation is not meant literally, for the category includes not only proper squares but also other plane figures such as rectangles and even cubes and other rectangular solids. An example of a "square" is the shape of a square house.

Similarly, round shapes include not only circles but also spheres and other ellipsoids and, according to the Go-mang *Collected Topics*, even egg-shaped figures. Thus, a round form is, for instance, the shape of a round ball.[1]

A level form is the shape of an even surface (*ngos mnyam pa'i dbyibs*). A non-level form is the shape of an uneven surface. The Lo-śel-ling *Collected Topics*, rather than listing level (*phya le ba*) and non-level (*phya le ba ma yin pa*) shapes, lists attractive (*phya legs pa*) and unattractive (*phya legs pa ma yin pa*) ones.[2] An attractive shape is, for instance, the shape of a Buddha's Complete Enjoyment Body (*saṃbhoga-kāya*). An unattractive shape is, for instance, the shape of a rotting corpse. This assertion seems to be unique to Lo-śel-ling, as none of the other Collected Topics texts lists attractive and unattractive shapes. Also, Gen-dün-drup-ba's *Commentary on (Vasubandhu's) "Treasury of Knowledge"* gives level and non-level, not attractive and unattractive, as the seventh and eighth type of shapes. Such a division is theoretically acceptable, as some of the other divisions of forms are done, at least in part, on the basis of attractiveness and unattractiveness. Still, such an assertion is at odds with the bulk of the tradition. The difference in interpretation could have arisen easily out of an error in the oral tradition as the two terms, "*phya le ba*" meaning even and "*phya legs pa*" meaning attractive, sound quite similar in Tibetan.

Generally, color and shape are taken to be mutually exclusive. Each appears to the eye consciousness, but what is the one is necessarily not the other. However, the Go-mang *Collected Topics* takes a stance at odds with this position in asserting that any of the four—cloud, smoke,

---

[1] Examples are from Lati Rinbochay, oral commentary.
[2] Jam-bel-trin-lay-yön-dan-gya-tso, Lo-śel-ling *Collected Topics*, p. 2.

dust, or mist—is both a color and a shape.[1] This Go-mang view is in accordance with Vasubandhu's *Treasury of Knowledge* and the system of the Great Exposition School. Bel-den-chö-jay's *Presentation of the Two Truths* says, "In the Sūtra School, one designates the conventions of long and so forth to certain different arrangements of particles of color."[2] This means that the Proponents of Sūtra assert shapes as imputedly existent (*btags yod, prajñapti-sat*) because they are merely imputed to arrangements of color particles. However, the Proponents of the Great Exposition assert shapes as substantially existent (*rdzas su yod pa, dravya-sat*) because they are not merely imputed to arrangements of color particles but are established as an independent type of form-source. Following the Great Exposition School interpretation, the Go-mang *Collected Topics* asserts red as a color but not a shape, long as a shape but not a color, and a cloud as something which is both a color—suitable to be shown to an eye consciousness as a hue—and a shape— suitable to be shown to an eye consciousness as a shape.

Sounds

The second of the five types of external form is sound (*sgra, shabda*). "Sound, sound-constituent [*sgra'i khams, shabda-dhātu*], and sound-source [*sgra'i skye mched, shabda-āyatana*] are synonyms."[3] A sound is defined as:

> an object of hearing (*nyan bya*).

The definition of a sound-source is:

> an object of hearing of an ear consciousness (*rna shes kyi nyan bya*).

---

[1] Ngak-wang-dra-shi, Go-mang *Collected Topics*, p. 12.
[2] Bel-den-chö-jay (*dpal ldan chos rje*) a.k.a. Ngak-wang-bel-den (*ngag dbang dpal ldan*), *Explanation of the Meaning of Conventional and Ultimate in the Four Tenet Systems* (*grub mtha' bzhi'i lugs kyi kun rdzob dang don dam pa'i don rnam par bshad pa*), (New Delhi: Lama Guru Deva, 1972), 21.7.
[3] Jeffrey Hopkins, *Meditation on Emptiness*, p. 226.

All sounds are included within the eight types of sound:

1 pleasant articulate sound caused by elements conjoined with consciousness (*zin pa'i 'byung ba las gyur pa'i sems can du ston pa'i sgra snyan pa, upātta-mahābhūta-hetuka-sattvākhya-yasha-shabda*)

2 unpleasant articulate sound caused by elements conjoined with consciousness (*zin pa'i 'byung ba las gyur pa'i sems can du ston pa'i sgra mi snyan pa, upātta-mahābhūta-hetuka-sattvākhya-ayasha-shabda*)

3 pleasant inarticulate sound caused by elements conjoined with consciousness (*zin pa'i 'byung ba las gyur pa'i sems can du mi ston pa'i sgra snyan pa, upātta-mahābhūta-hetuka-asattvākhya-yasha-shabda*)

4 unpleasant inarticulate sound caused by elements conjoined with consciousness (*zin pa'i 'byung ba las gyur pa'i sems can du mi ston pa'i sgra mi snyan pa, upātta-mahābhūta-hetuka-asattvākhya-ayasha-shabda*)

5 pleasant articulate sound caused by elements not conjoined with consciousness (*ma zin pa'i 'byung ba las gyur pa'i sems can du ston pa'i sgra snyan pa, anupātta-mahābhūta-hetuka-sattvākhya-yasha-shabda*)

6 unpleasant articulate sound caused by elements not conjoined with consciousness (*ma zin pa'i 'byung ba las gyur pa'i sems can du ston pa'i sgra mi snyan pa, anupātta-mahābhūta-hetuka-sattvākhya-ayasha-shabda*)

7 pleasant inarticulate sound caused by elements not conjoined with consciousness (*ma zin pa'i 'byung ba las gyur pa'i sems can du mi ston pa'i sgra snyan pa, anupātta-mahābhūta-hetuka-asattvākhya-yasha-shabda*)

8 unpleasant inarticulate sound caused by elements not conjoined with consciousness (*ma zin pa'i 'byung ba las gyur pa'i sems can du mi ston pa'i sgra mi snyan pa, anupātta-mahābhūta-hetuka-asattvākhya-ayasha-shabda*).[1]

---

[1] The source for the Sanskrit in this list is Jeffrey Hopkins, *Meditation on Emptiness*, p. 227.

Sounds may be divided simply into the two, sounds caused by elements conjoined with consciousness and sounds caused by elements not conjoined with consciousness. Each of these two may then be divided into articulate and inarticulate types, thereby yielding articulate and inarticulate sounds caused by elements conjoined with consciousness and articulate and inarticulate sounds caused by elements not conjoined with consciousness. These four types of sound may then be divided into pleasant and unpleasant varieties, yielding eight types of sound which together include all sounds. In much simpler fashion, the Shar-dzay *Collected Topics* divides sounds into pleasant and unpleasant types, and the Tutor's *Collected Topics* divides sounds into those caused by elements conjoined with consciousness and those caused by elements not conjoined with consciousness.

All sounds are caused by the four elements of earth, water, fire, and wind. Sounds themselves are non-elemental in the sense that they are not any of the four elements, but they are caused by or arisen from the elements. Elements may be conjoined with consciousness or not. For instance, a person's tongue is conjoined with consciousness because it is a form held within one's continuum. The sound of a person's voice is a sound conjoined with consciousness, if the person is speaking directly and the voice is not being relayed by some other medium. However, if a voice is conveyed indirectly as when amplified or transmitted by a telephone, the sound one hears is not conjoined with consciousness . In the case of a person's speaking directly, as in a room, the sound is caused by elements conjoined with consciousness because of arising in dependence upon the vocal chords, tongue, palate, the upward moving wind enabling speech, and so forth. In the case of a person's voice conveyed on the telephone or in a recording, the sound heard is caused by elements not conjoined with consciousness because it is voice reproduction accomplished by electricity, wires, transmitters, speakers, and so forth. Of course, the person's voice is caused by the vocal chords and so forth, but what is actually heard on the telephone is produced by inanimate matter. A more obvious example of a sound caused by elements not conjoined with consciousness is the sound of a waterfall.

Sounds are also divided into articulate and inarticulate types. Articulate sounds indicate meaning to sentient beings and inarticulate sounds do not. "Sound which indicates meaning to a sentient being [*sems can la ston pa'i sgra*] and expressive sound [*brjod byed kyi sgra*] are mutually inclusive. An example is the expression, 'Sound is impermanent.' "[1] This is revelatory sound, for it reveals meaning to sentient beings. Articulate and inarticulate sounds are of both types, those caused by elements conjoined with consciousness and those caused by elements not conjoined with consciousness. Articulate sounds caused by elements not conjoined with consciousness are, for instance, "the words of doctrine taught by trees rustled by a Buddha's extraordinary powers".[2] It is said that in certain Pure Lands the residents hear the teaching of Buddha's doctrine even from the movement of tree leaves. Such sound is articulate in that it indicates meaning to sentient beings, but it is caused by elements not conjoined with consciousness because it is produced from the rustling of trees.

In the Pure Land of the Buddha Amitābha the waters moving in the rivers produce pleasant sounds.

> The sound which issues from these great rivers is as pleasant as that of a musical instrument, ... which, skilfully played, emits a heavenly music. It is deep, commanding, distinct, clear, pleasant to the ear, touching the heart, delightful, sweet, pleasant, and one never tires of hearing it.[3]

Music is inarticulate sound as is the sound of water because it does not reveal meaning.

---

[1] Ngak-w̄ang-ḡra-s̄hi, Go-mang *Collected Topics*, p. 14.

[2] Jeffrey Hopkins, *Meditation on Emptiness*, p. 227.

[3] Edward Conze, *Buddhist Scriptures* (Harmondsworth, Middlesex, England: Penguin, 1973), p. 233.

These four types of sound, articulate and inarticulate sounds caused by elements conjoined with consciousness and articulate and inarticulate sounds caused by elements not conjoined with consciousness, are further divided into pleasant and unpleasant types. Sounds are pleasant if they appeal to the listener and are attractive. Unpleasant sounds do not appeal to the listener and are unattractive. The eight types of sound with examples of each are:

1   pleasant articulate sound caused by elements conjoined with consciousness, e.g., words teaching the the doctrine
2   unpleasant articulate sound caused by elements conjoined with consciousness, e.g., the sound of harsh words
3   pleasant inarticulate sound caused by elements conjoined with consciousness, e.g., the sound of snapping fingers
4   unpleasant inarticulate sound caused by elements conjoined with consciousness, e.g., the sound of a fist on impact
5   pleasant articulate sound caused by elements not conjoined with consciousness, e.g., the words of an unembodied emanation (*sprul pa'i gang zag*) teaching the doctrine or the words of doctrine taught by trees rustled by a Buddha's extraordinary powers
6   unpleasant articulate sound caused by elements not conjoined with consciousness, e.g., the sound of harsh words spoken by an unembodied emanation or words of scolding conveyed by trees rustled by a Buddha's extraordinary powers
7   pleasant inarticulate sound caused by elements not conjoined with consciousness, e.g., the sound of a gong or the sound of a drum[1]

---

[1] Gen-dün-drup-ba's *Commentary on (Vasubandhu's) "Treasury of Knowledge"* lists the sound of a tabor, a small drum, as a pleasant inarticulate sound caused by elements conjoined with consciousness and gives the sound of a gong as a pleasant inarticulate sound caused by elements *not* conjoined with consciousness. It would seem there is no

8   unpleasant inarticulate sound caused by elements not conjoined with consciousness, e.g., the sound of crashing stones, the sound of water, the sound of a house falling down, or the sound of wind.[1]

Sound is the second of the five external sources; therefore, it is matter, atomically established. This assessment of sound does not accord with the physicist's view of sound as itself non-material though depending on matter, such as air or water, as a medium to relay audible vibrations. Indeed, even within this Buddhist presentation, sound is not materially established in precisely the same way that some other material phenomena are. In the system of the Proponents of Sūtra Following Reasoning, material particles are compositions of at least eight potencies: the four elements of earth, water, fire, and wind together with visible form, odor, taste, and tangibility arisen from the elements.[2] If sound is present, in addition to these eight which exist in all material phenomena there is a ninth potency of sound.[3] Thus, sound is materially established but not in the same sense that other forms are. Also, sound has an extremely short duration. It does not

difference, for each is directly arisen from inanimate matter and indirectly from conscious effort. Perhaps in the case of the tabor the player slaps the hand directly against the drumskin, whereas in the case of a gong one uses an inanimate instrument to hit the playing surface. Still, in both cases the sound is produced directly from inanimate matter.

[1] Some of the examples in this list are from Gen-dün-drup-ba, *Commentary on (Vasubandhu's) "Treasury of Knowledge"*, pp. 29-30, and some are from Jeffrey Hopkins, *Meditation on Emptiness*, p. 227.

[2] Jeffrey Hopkins, *Meditation on Emptiness*, p. 230.

[3] Gen-dün-drup-ba's *Commentary on (Vasubandhu's) "Treasury of Knowledge"*, 97.4-9, explains that, in the Desire Realm, an atom located in a place where a sense power and sound are not present is composed of eight particle substances. However, if it is located in a place where a body sense power is present, there are nine (the ninth being the body sense power); if in addition to that the atom is in a place where the eye, ear, nose, or tongue sense power is located, then there are ten particle substances (the tenth being the potency of that sense power); and if it is in a place where there is also sound, there are eleven (the eleventh being sound). Thus, if an atom is in a place where there are none of the sense powers and sound is present, then sound is the ninth particle substance.

exist continuously as a potency of atoms as does visibility, for forms do not constantly hum or produce a sound whereas a color may remain as a potency in form for a long period.

Odors

The third of the five types of external forms is odor (*dri, gandha*). "Odor, odor-constituent [*dri'i khams, gandha-dhātu*], and odor-source [*dri'i skye mched, gandha-āyatana*] are synonyms."[1] The definition of an odor-source is:

> an object experienced by a nose consciousness (*sna shes kyi myong bya*)

or

> an object smelled by a nose consciousness (*sna shes kyi snom bya*).[2]

According to Vasubandhu's *Treasury of Knowledge* odors are of four types, and most sources agree with this although the way in which they are divided varies somewhat. Gen-dün-drup-ba's *Commentary on (Vasubandhu's) "Treasury of Knowledge"* says, "Odors are of four types because there are fragrant, unfragrant, equal, and unequal odors."[3] Thus, according to this source the four types of odor are:

1 fragrant odor (*dri zhim pa, sugandha*), e.g., the odor of a rose
2 unfragrant odor (*dri mi zhim pa, durgandha*), e.g., the odor of manure

---

[1] Jeffrey Hopkins, *Meditation on Emptiness*, p. 226.
[2] The first definition is from Pur-bu-jok Jam-ba-gya-tso, "The Introductory Path of Reasoning" (*rigs lam chung ngu*) of *The Presentation of Collected Topics Revealing the Meaning of the Texts on Valid Cognition, the Magical Key to the Path of Reasoning* (*tshad ma'i gzhung don 'byed pa'i bsdus grva'i rnam bzhag rigs lam 'phrul gyi lde mig*), (Buxa, India: n.p., 1965), 4b.6, and the second is from Lati Rinbochay, oral commentary.
[3] Gen-dün-drup-ba, *Commentary on (Vasubandhu's) "Treasury of Knowledge"*, p. 30.

3   equal odor (*dri mnyam pa, sama-gandha*), e.g., the odor of
     sesame seeds
4   unequal odor (*dri mi mnyam pa, visama-gandha*), e.g., the
     odor of gasoline.[1]

Fragrant and unfragrant odors are attractive and unattractive ones. "An equal odor is very faint and will not infuse what it is near with its smell. Uncooked rice and sesame seeds have equal odors. An unequal odor is a strong infusive odor such as that of garlic."[2]

Odors may also be enumerated as four by first dividing them into fragrant and unfragrant types and then subdividing each of those into equal and unequal types:

1   equal fragrant odor (*zhim pa'i dri mnyam pa, sama-sugandha*), e.g., the odor of fresh air
2   unequal fragrant odor (*zhim pa'i dri mi mnyam pa, visama-sugandha*), e.g., the odor of cinnamon
3   equal unfragrant odor (*mi zhim pa'i dri mnyam pa, sama-durgandha*), e.g., the odor of ammonia
4   unequal unfragrant odor (*mi zhim pa'i dri mi mnyam pa, visama-durgandha*), e.g., the odor of garlic.[3]

This division of odors is, of course, in accord with Gen-dün-drup-ba's explanation of the four types of odor. However, the four odors Gen-dün-drup-ba lists—fragrant, unfragrant, equal, and unequal—are not each mutually exclusive with the others because for instance, some fragrant odors are equal and some are not, but in the second division each of the four odors is mutually exclusive with all the others. In this sense, the second division may be said to be a refinement of the first.

The Tutor's and Shar-dzay Collected Topics texts divide odors simply into the two, natural (*lhan skyes, sahaja*) and manufactured (*sbyar byung, sāṃyogika*). The Go-mang

---

[1] The source for the Sanskrit in this list is Jeffrey Hopkins, *Meditation on Emptiness*, p. 228.
[2] Lati Rinbochay, oral commentary.
[3] Jeffrey Hopkins, *Meditation on Emptiness*, p. 228.

Collected Topics expands this division to four by subdividing natural and manufactured odors into fragrant and unfragrant types:

1   fragrant natural odor (*zhim pa'i lhan skyes kyi dri, sahaja-sugandha*), e.g., the odor of sandalwood
2   unfragrant natural odor (*mi zhim pa'i lhan skyes kyi dri, sahaja-durgandha*), e.g., the odor of decaying flesh
3   fragrant manufactured odor (*zhim pa'i sbyar byung gi dri, sāmyogika-sugandha*), e.g., the odor of bread
4   unfragrant manufactured odor (*mi zhim pa'i sbyar byung gi dri, sāmyogika-durgandha*), e.g., the odor of formaldehyde.[1]

As in the second division above, each of these four types of odors is mutually exclusive with the others.

All odors are probably included within any of these three divisions, especially if odors which are not fragrant are considered unfragrant. In that way all neutral odors would be counted as unfragrant or non-fragrant.

Tastes

The fourth type of external form is taste (*ro, rasa*) which is defined as:

> an object experienced by a tongue consciousness (*lce shes kyi myong bya*).

Tastes are divided into six types, and all of the different Collected Topics texts agree in their presentations of these:

1   sweet (*mngar ba, madhura*)
2   sour (*skyur ba, āmla*)
3   bitter (*kha ba, tikta*)
4   astringent (*bska ba, kaṣhāya*)
5   pungent (*tsha ba, kaṭuka*)

---

[1] Ngak-ẅang-ḏra-śhi, Go-mang *Collected Topics*, p. 14.

6   salty (*lan tshva ba, lavaṇa*).¹

A sweet taste is, for instance, the taste of molasses.² Sour tastes are, for example, the tastes of lemons, olives, and yogurt. A bitter taste is, for instance, the taste of *gentiana chiretta*, "a bitter plant growing in the Himalayas which is largely used as an antidote against fever and liver complaints",³ called "*ḍik-ḍa*" (*tig ta*) in Tibetan, the Sanskrit word for bitter. An astringent taste is, for instance, the taste of the myrobalan fruit or the taste of bread. Pungent tastes are like the taste of three-pungency-medicine or the taste of pepper. Salty is, for instance, the taste of "*bay*" (*pad*) salt or Mongolian salt.

The six tastes are correlated to relative predominances of combinations of the four elements.

> Sweetness arises from a predominance of earth and water; sourness, from a predominance of fire and earth; bitterness, from a predominance of water and wind; pungency, from a predominance of fire and wind; and saltiness, from a predominance of water and fire.⁴

Table III shows the six types of tastes with an example of each and correlation to the predominant elements:

---

¹ The source for the Sanskrit in this list is Jeffrey Hopkins, *Meditation on Emptiness*, p. 228.
² These examples of tastes are from Ngak-ẉang-ḍra-shi Go-mang *Collected Topics*, pp. 15-16, and Lati Rinbochay, oral commentary.
³ Chandra Das, *Tibetan-English Dictionary*, compact edition (Kyoto, Japan: Rinsen, 1979), p. 515.
⁴ Jeffrey Hopkins, *Meditation on Emptiness*, pp. 228-229.

Table III: Tastes

Taste	Example	Predominant Elements
1 sweet	taste of honey	earth and water
2 sour	taste of lemons	fire and earth
3 bitter	taste of coffee	water and wind
4 astringent	taste of persimmons	earth and wind
5 pungent	taste of chili peppers	fire and wind
6 salty	taste of sea water	water and fire

Tangible Objects

The fifth and final group of external forms are tangible objects (*reg bya, sprashtavya*). A tangible object is defined as:

> an object experienced by a body consciousness (*lus shes kyi myong bya*)

or

> an object felt by a body consciousness (*lus shes kyi reg bya*).

These are divided into tangible objects which are elements (*'byung bar gyur pa'i reg bya, bhūta-sprashtavya*) and tangible objects arisen from the elements (*'byung 'gyur gyi reg bya, bhautika-sprashtavya*). Tangible objects which are elements are the four: earth, water, fire, and wind. These are the bases and causes for the seven remaining tangible objects which are arisen from the elements: smoothness, roughness, heaviness, lightness, cold, hunger, and thirst. Thus, in accordance with the passage from the *Treasury of Knowledge* which says, "Tangible objects are of just eleven [types]," these are:

1 earth (*sa, prthivi*)
2 water (*chu, ap*)
3 fire (*me, tejaḥ*)

4 wind (*rlung, vāyu*)
5 smoothness (*'jam pa, shlakṣhṇatva*)
6 roughness (*rtsub pa, karkashatva*)
7 heaviness (*lci ba, gurutva*)
8 lightness (*yang ba, laghutva*)
9 cold (*grang ba, shīta*)
10 hunger (*bkres pa, bubhūkṣhā*)
11 thirst (*skom pa, pipāsā*).[1]

The four elements serve as the bases for all material phenomena. Matter which is not one of the four elements is arisen from the elements. Yet, the elements do not occur in strictly irreducible units. Rather, they can exist as *potencies* within physical particles, the atoms which compose all internal and external matter. Each atom is an aggregate of at least eight components: earth, water, fire, wind, visible form, odor, taste, and tangibility arisen from the elements. Thus, the four elements exist together.

Earth is defined as:

> that which is hard and obstructive (*sra zhing 'thas pa*).

As with many definitions, the definition of earth identifies its nature and function, for the nature of earth is hardness and its function is to obstruct. Similarly, the definition of water is:

> that which is wet and moistening (*rlan zhing gsher ba*).

The definition of fire is:

> that which is hot and burning (*tsha zhing sreg pa*).

The definition of wind is:

> that which is light and moving (*yang zhing g.yo ba*).

As was mentioned above, all material phenomena are constructed of particles which, rather than being only one element alone, are composites of at least eight potencies

---

[1] The source for the Sanskrit in this list is Jeffrey Hopkins, *Meditation on Emptiness*, p. 229.

including all four of the elements. Therefore, material phenomena are composites which do not have one simple nature. "Wherever one of the elements exists, the other three also exist, but there is a difference of strength and, thus, dominance."[1]

The four elements are like principles of material nature. The earth element is manifest as stability or as a basis. The predominance of the earth element in a stone is shown by its stability. Indeed, water, fire (as heat), and wind (as motility) do exist as characteristics of a stone, but the stability of the earth element is manifest predominantly. This means that physical stability is a sign of the presence of the earth element. Wherever there is physical stability, there is the earth element. Greater or lesser stability indicates greater or lesser manifestation of the earth element.

The water element is manifest as cohesiveness. A wet cloth will pick up dirt whereas a dry one will not. The adherence of dirt to moisture indicates the presence of the water element manifest as cohesiveness. Still, ordinary water is not the water element separate from the remaining elements, for the other elements also exist in water. For instance, a single drop of water shows greater resistance to one's finger than the same amount would show as internal fluid in a greater volume of water. In this system of Buddhist physics, the ability of water to form drops and its stability in that form indicate the presence of the earth element in water. Also, "That the water element can serve as a support for boats, leaves, and so forth indicates that the earth element is present in the water element."[2]

Further, dry sand at the beach will not serve as a support in the same way that wet sand will. One can easily kick into dry sand whereas wet sand, like concrete, gives full support even for a car. This ability of wet sand to give greater support is, in one way, due to the surface tension of the water increasing resistance of the sand. As described in this pre-

---

[1] Jeffrey Hopkins, *Meditation on Emptiness*, p. 230.
[2] *Ibid.*, 230.

sentation of the Buddhist physics, the water's manifestation as cohesiveness causes the individual grains of sand to bond together. Thus, the predominance of the earth element temporarily increases, this being manifest as greater stability and resistance and enabling the sand to serve as a better basis of support.

The fire element is manifest as heat. Wherever there is heat, there is the fire element. According to this system, a complete absence of heat means that, rather than the fire element's having become completely non-existent in matter, it has become completely non-manifest. As with the other elements, the fire element exists even where the others are predominant. For instance, "That sparks are produced when two stones meet indicates the presence of the fire element [in the earth element]."[1]

The wind element is manifest as motility. Similar to the others, any manifestation of motility indicates the presence of the wind element. Wherever there is wind there is motility, and wherever there is motility there is wind. The rustling leaves and branches of a tree serve as an effective sign of the presence of wind. Also, even the ability of living beings to move is due to the presence of wind within them.

The internal wind in living beings is, of course, not like the gross external wind which moves leaves and branches nor is it like the external breath. Rather, it is that factor enabling motility of substances within the body—food, blood, etc. Furthermore, internal wind serves as the basis for consciousness. It is said within tantra that the mind rides on wind as a man rides on a horse, thus wind is referred to as the mount of consciousness.[2] "The ultimate science of the Buddhists is the science of the winds."[3] In the advanced practices of the Tantra Vehicle, meditators cultivate control of the internal winds in order to attain special feats of body and mind and eventually to attain the supreme feat of Bud-

---

[1] *Ibid.*

[2] For instance, see Tsong-ka-pa, *Tantra in Tibet*, p. 39.

[3] Jeffrey Hopkins, discussion.

dhahood itself. In the very beginning of Ge-luk-b̄a philosophical studies wind is defined as *that which is light and moving*, and this identification is not surpassed or replaced at any point, even in the highest final practices.

Also, the body—as a material phenomenon—is composed of elements. In this instance, the elements are enumerated as five with space (*nam mkha'*, *ākāsha*) being included as the fifth. Space here does not refer to just the absence of obstruction, but to the "element" of the open spaces in one's body such as the nasal passages. Space itself is non-material; thus, it is not included as an element in the presentation of form.

> The Tibetan medical system is based on a view of the body as composed of five elements.[1] Animate and inanimate phenomena have for their physical basis the five elements—earth, water, fire, wind, and space. ... The earth element acts as the basis or foundation of everything, animate and inanimate. Water is that element which provides cohesion, enabling things to hold together. Fire is that element, or factor, which helps things to mature or ripen. Wind helps things to grow. Space provides an opportunity or place for things to grow. It is within the context of the five elements that one should understand the humors.[2]

The Tibetan medical system presents a humoral theory of disease based on three humors—wind, bile, and phlegm. When the humors are in a state of complete balance, one has good health. If the humors are in a state of unbalance or disharmony, one suffers poor health.

The humors are affected by the food that one eats and may be thrown into a state of unbalance by a diet having a strong predominance of one or another of the elements. This is not to say that certain foods will cause ill health for all,

---

[1] The source for this section on Tibetan medicine is Dr. Yeshi Donden, oral commentary.

[2] Dr. Yeshi Donden, oral commentary.

but that too much of certain foods will be harmful for certain persons.

For instance, for a person given to obesity caused by an excess of the phlegm humor, sweet foods are harmful. The theory underlying this rule is that, as noted above in the discussion of tastes, sweet tastes are caused by a predominance of earth and water. Similarly, the humors, as material phenomena, are correlated to relative predominances of a particular element or elements. The phlegm humor is characterized as heavy, stabilizing, and sticky (i.e., cohesive) and has a predominance of the earth and water elements. Thus, sweet foods, strongly manifesting earth and water, serve to further increase the predominance of those elements in a phlegmatic patient and contribute to the humoral imbalance. On the other hand, pungent foods, having a predominance of fire and wind elements, are helpful for the decrease of phlegm because the heat of the fire in those foods serves to counteract the coolness of water in phlegm and the lightness of wind counteracts the heaviness of earth.

Similarly, the bile humor has a predominance of fire or heat. Pungent tastes, having a predominance of fire and wind, increase excessive bile whereas sweet foods, countering with a predominance of earth and water, are helpful for the decrease of bile. Wind disorders caused by an increase of the wind element are also helped by sweet foods. The stability and cohesiveness of the earth and water elements in sweet foods helps to settle the motility of wind. By regulating the foods, and thereby the elements, that one eats one can help to keep the humors in balance and maintain health.

The remaining tangible objects are the seven arisen from the elements: smoothness, roughness, heaviness, lightness, cold, hunger, and thirst. These are tangible objects, objects experienced by a body consciousness, which are not elements but are arisen from or caused by the elements. As in the cases of the different tastes which arise in dependence on relative predominances of certain elements, so these tangible objects arise in dependence on predominance of certain elements.

216 Debate in Tibetan Buddhism

> Smoothness arises from a preponderance of water and
> fire. Roughness arises from a preponderance of earth
> and wind. Heaviness arises from a preponderance of
> earth and water. Lightness arises from a preponder-
> ance of fire and wind. Cold arises from a preponder-
> ance of water and wind. Hunger arises from a pre-
> ponderance of wind. Thirst arises from a preponder-
> ance of fire.[1]

Furthermore, all material phenomena which are not elements are arisen from elements. Visible forms, sounds,
odors, tastes and tangible objects which are not the elements
themselves are all caused by the elements. "The colors of
particles depend upon the element that is predominant. If
the earth element is predominant, the color is yellow; if
water, white; if fire, red; and if wind, blue."[2] Shapes are
arrangements of color particles and in that way are caused
by the elements. Sounds are divided into those caused by
elements conjoined with consciousness and those caused by
elements not conjoined with consciousness; in either case,
they are arisen from the elements. Odors and tastes too are
caused by the elements, and tangible objects which are not
the elements themselves are caused by the relative prepon-
derances of the elements.

All form, the elements and that arisen from the elements,
is atomically established. Form is constructed of atoms or
particles of matter which in turn are composed of eight
factors—earth, water, fire, wind, visible form, odor, taste,
and tangibility arisen from the elements. This means that
even in a stone the wind element exists, in wind the earth
element exists, and so forth. Among forms there is a difference of relative dominance of the elements. Obviously, the
earth element predominates in a stone, the water element
predominates in milk, and so on. Still, because of the perva-
siveness of all four elements in every form, the water, fire,

---

[1] Jeffrey Hopkins, *Meditation on Emptiness*, pp. 230-231.
[2] *Ibid.*, p. 231.

and wind elements exist in a more or less dormant state in a stone. The earth, fire, and wind elements exist in a more or less dormant state in water, and so forth for the fire and wind elements as well.

Since all the elements exist in all forms, skillful yogis are said to be able to utilize the potencies of form in any way, using a wall as an open passageway, drawing water from a rock, using air as a platform, and so on. This does not mean that yogis can counteract the nature of phenomena by, perhaps, using fire to quench thirst. Rather, they are able to transform matter from one state to another by drawing on the potencies that are present but dormant in phenomena and using them in a "miraculous" way. The Indian Buddhist saint Chandrakīrti is said to have been able to use the potencies of forms, as in the story of his taking milk from the painting of a cow by means of his special powers.[1]

INTERNAL FORMS

The internal forms are the bases of a person's feelings of physical pleasure and pain.[2] In addition to the fleshy material phenomena within a person's continuum—organs, skin, and so forth—which are technically both internal and external matter, internal forms include the five sense powers (*dbang po, indriya*).

The eye sense power gives the eye consciousness (*mig shes, *chakṣhur-jñāna*) dominance over visible forms, colors and shapes. The three causes of a visual perception are the eye sense power, the external visible object, and the former moment of the eye consciousness. Sense powers are not consciousnesses and cannot know an object. Rather, the eye consciousness, empowered by the eye sense power and observing an external color or shape, is generated in the aspect of that object and an eye consciousness apprehending the object is produced. The sense powers give their respec-

---

[1] Khetsun Sangbo Rinbochay, oral commentary.
[2] Kensur Yeshay Tupden, oral commentary.

tive consciousnesses dominance with respect to only certain external objects. For instance, the nose consciousness is empowered with respect to odors but not with respect to sounds and so forth. It is said that a Buddha's consciousnesses are cross-functional such that his eye consciousness can perceive sounds, his ear consciousness can perceive colors, and so forth, but for ordinary persons this is not so.

The definition of an eye sense power is:

> a clear internal form which is the uncommon empowering condition for its own effect, an eye consciousness (*rang 'bras mig gi rnam shes kyi thun mong ma yin pa'i bdag rkyen du gyur pa'i nang gi gzugs can dvang ba*).

An illustration of an eye sense power is a clear internal form having a shape like a *zar-ma* flower, this form being in the continuum of a person. A sense power is *clear internal form* because it is matter within the physical body of a person and cannot be perceived by any sense consciousness. The eye sense power is located in the eye and is in the shape of a flower. The other sense powers have different shapes. A sense power is an *uncommon empowering condition* (*thun mong ma yin pa'i bdag rkyen, asādhāraṇa-adhipati-pratyaya*) because it alone can give its consciousness power with respect to its field of perception. That is to say, it is a necessary but not sufficient condition for its effect which is an eye consciousness.

The Go-mang *Collected Topics* lists eye (*mig*), eye sense power (*mig dbang*), and eye-constituent (*mig gi khams*) as mutually inclusive phenomena. Also, that text divides eye sense powers into two types: eye sense powers which are bases (*rten bcas kyi mig dbang*) and eye sense powers which are like bases (*rten mtshungs kyi mig dbang*). An example of the first type is an eye sense power seeing white, blue, and so on. An example of the second type is an eye sense power at the time of sleep.[1] The eye sense power exists whether one

---

[1] Ngak-wang-dra-shi, Go-mang *Collected Topics*, p. 17.

is perceiving external colors and shapes or not. When one is engaged in visual perception, the eye sense power is a basis of perception. When sleeping, however, one is not engaged in perceiving external colors and shapes, and the eye sense power is merely "like a basis".

The definitions, divisions, and illustrations for the remaining sense powers are similar to those for the eye sense power. The definition of an ear sense power is:

> a clear internal form which is the uncommon empowering condition for its own effect, an ear consciousness.

An illustration of an ear sense power is a clear internal form having a shape like a cut bundle of wheat, this form being in the continuum of a person. The bundle of wheat seems as if cut off on one end and has the shafts oriented toward the outside of the ear.

The definition of a nose sense power is:

> a clear internal form which is the uncommon empowering condition for its own effect, a nose consciousness.

An illustration of a nose sense power is a clear internal form having a shape like two copper needles, this form being in the continuum of a person.

The definition of a tongue sense power is:

> a clear internal form which is the uncommon empowering condition of its own effect, a tongue consciousness.

An illustration of a tongue sense power is a clear internal form having a shape like a cut half moon, this form being in the continuum of a person.

The definition of a body sense power is:

> a clear internal form which is the uncommon empowering condition of its own effect, a body consciousness.

An illustration of a body sense power is a clear internal form having a shape like smooth skin, this form being in the continuum of a person.

The five sense powers are clear internal forms located within the coarse seats of the senses, the eye sense power being in the eyes, the ear sense power in the ears, etc. The body sense power pervades the body.

The five internal forms, in combination with the five external forms, are necessary to give rise to the five sense consciousnesses—eye, ear, nose, tongue, and body consciousnesses. The sense powers and consciousnesses are always cited in the same order: eye, ear, nose, tongue, and body. Some scholars say that they are given in this order because that is the order of certifiability or reliability. That is, the eye consciousness is least reliable and the body consciousness is most reliable. If one is unable to see clearly the form of a person, hearing that person's voice can serve as certification of the person's presence. Also, if the eye consciousness cannot discriminate clearly some form, one naturally seeks to verify with the hand. Others point out that the given order of the sense powers and consciousnesses merely reflects the physical placement of those senses within the body. Roughly, the eye is above the ear, the ear above the nose, and so forth. However, the body consciousness is present throughout the body and may not be said to exist predominantly in any one part of the body as do the other consciousnesses. Still other scholars say that the forms and consciousnesses are listed in this order because it reflects the range of perception, visible objects being perceptible from the greatest distance and tangible objects being perceptible only in direct contact with the body. One can perceive a visual object as far away as the stars. A sound must be much closer, within a few miles or so. Odors must be still closer, and tastes and tangible objects must be in direct contact.

Each sense has domain over its own field of operation: the eye consciousness being empowered with respect to colors and shapes; the ear consciousness, with respect to sounds, and so forth. However, each consciousness is totally insensitive with respect to the objects of the other consciousnesses. Thus, upon meeting an object such as a flower the eye consciousness alone is able to perceive its colors and shape; the nose consciousness, its odor, and so on. In this way one perceives an object through the various doors of perception with each consciousness perceiving one aspect. But what is the object itself? It is commonly said that one sees, for instance, a pot, but does this mean that a pot is an object apprehended by an eye consciousness? It is the color and shape, the visible form, of a pot that an eye consciousness sees, not the pot itself. In this regard, the Collected Topics debaters make a distinction between what the eye consciousness sees (*mig shes kyi mthong rgyu*) and an object apprehended by the eye consciousness (*mig shes kyi gzung bya*). The former is whatever one may be said to see—a pot, a flower, a person, and so on. The latter is only those visual forms that the eye consciousness has domain over—the color and shape of a pot, the color and shape of a person's body, and so on.

Some scholars say that particular forms are classified as one of the five types of external matter on the basis of its predominant purpose or usage. Thus, a painting is a visible form; bread is an object of the tongue consciousness; flesh and bones are earth and thus tangible objects, and so forth. Others say that pots, bread, flowers, and so forth are tangible objects because of being objects experienced by the body consciousness. Indeed, the eye consciousness perceives the color and shape of a pot, but by this interpretation the pot itself is earth and thus a tangible object. Seeing fire is a case of seeing the color and shape of fire, but the element fire, that which is hot and burning, is apprehended solely by the body consciousnesses.

REFUTATION OF MISTAKEN VIEWS CONCERNING COLORS
AND SO FORTH (2A.3)

In the Tutor's *Collected Topics* this first section in the presentation of colors and so forth consists of eight debates. In each
case, a hypothetical Defender asserts a mistaken view concerning colors and so forth. In response, a Challenger,
assuming the stance of a Proponent of Sūtra Following
Reasoning in accordance with the interpretation of the Tutor
Jam-ba-gya-tso, refutes that mistaken view in order to expli-
cate the correct understanding of the topic at hand. In this
translation, each of these debates is identified as a "mistaken
view" as opposed to the debates in the third section of each
chapter which are identified as "objections".

Debate A.1, First Mistaken View (2a.3)

The first debate in the Tutor's *Collected Topics* has a Defender
asserting that whatever is a color is necessarily red. The
commentary and explanation for this debate is provided in
the earlier chapter on procedure in debate (pp. 99-131).

To reiterate, in this translation the actual text of the
Tutor's *Collected Topics* is uniformly indented and the annotations, interwoven with the text, are set to the margin to
distinguish them from the translation. Also, after the original designation of the sections and each debate, the page
and line reference for the Tibetan text is provided. Here the
lower case letters "a" and "b" identify respectively whether
the page is the front or reverse of the folio. The second number, to the right of the decimal point, identifies the line on
which the debate begins. Thus, the notation of 2a.3 indicates
that debate A.1 begins on line three of the front side of page
two. The text says:

> If someone [a hypothetical Defender] says,
> "Whatever is a color is necessarily red," [the Sūtra
> School Challenger responds to him,] "It [absurdly]
> follows that the subject, the color of a white

religious conch, is red because of being a color. You asserted the pervasion [that whatever is a color is necessarily red]."

If he says that the reason [that the color of a white religious conch is a color] is not established, [the Sūtra School Challenger responds,] "It follows that the subject, the color of a white religious conch, is a color because of being white."

If he says that the reason [that the color of a white religious conch is white] is not established, [the Sūtra School Challenger responds,] "It follows that the subject, the color of a white religious conch, is white because of being one with the color of a white religious conch."

If he accepts the basic consequence [that the color of a white religious conch is red, the Sūtra School Challenger responds,] "It follows that the subject, the color of a white religious conch, is not red because of being white."

If he says there is no pervasion [i.e., even though it is true that the color of a white religious conch is white, it is not the case that whatever is white is necessarily not red, the Sūtra School Challenger responds,] "It follows that there is pervasion [i.e., whatever is white is necessarily not red] because a common locus of the two, white and red, does not exist; because those two [white and red] are mutually exclusive."

Debate A.2, Second Mistaken View (3a.2)

Debate A.2 closely parallels A.1 in form. Here the Defender is holding that whatever is a color is necessarily white. The Sūtra School Challenger flings at him the unwanted consequence that the color of the Buddha Amitāyus (*tshe dpag med*), which is actually red, would then be white. The Buddha Amitāyus, whose name means "infinite life", is an aspect of the Buddha Amitābha (*'od dpag med*), meaning "infinite light". Amitābha is the master of one of the five Buddha lineages, his lineage being associated with the western direction and the color red. He is lord of the pure land called "Land of Happiness" (*bde ba can, sukhā-vatī*).

> Just as Amitābha is radiant with infinite light, so "the duration of the life of this Bhagavat Amitābha, the Tathāgata, is infinite, so that it is not easy to comprehend its duration." And because the extent of this Tathāgata's life is infinite he is also known as Amitāyus (Infinite Life).[1]

Since the color of the Buddha Amitāyus is red, it is a suitable counterexample to demonstrate to the Defender that it is not the case that all colors are white. The text says:

> If someone [a hypothetical Defender] says, "Whatever is a color is necessarily white," [the Sūtra School Challenger responds to him,] "It [absurdly] follows that the subject, the color of the Buddha Amitāyus, is white because of being a color. You asserted the pervasion [that whatever is a color is necessarily white]."

Here, as in debate A.1, the Defender first moves to deny the reason. In response, the Challenger proves the subject as a color by the sign of its being suitable as a hue, the definition of a color. The text says:

> If he says that the reason [that the color of the Buddha Amitāyus is a color] is not established [the Sūtra School Challenger responds,] "It follows that the subject, the color of the Buddha Amitāyus, is a color because of being suitable as a hue."

The Challenger has stated a consequence which, if straightforwardly re-formulated as a syllogism, would still be a valid argument. The reason, that the color of the Buddha Amitāyus is suitable as a hue, is established. Also, there is

---

[1] Detlef Ingo Lauf, *Tibetan Sacred Art, The Heritage of Tantra*, p. 99.

pervasion because whatever is suitable as a hue is necessarily a color.

Still, the Defender's response to this last consequence is to deny the pervasion. The Challenger justifies the pervasion by the reason that suitable as a hue is the definition of color. Once this is the case, as explained in the chapter on definitions and definienda (pp. 61-74) the relationship between a definition and its definiendum entails that the eight approaches of pervasion must exist between them. This means, in part, that whatever is the one is necessarily the other. Thus, in the case at hand, whatever is suitable as a hue is necessarily a color.

> If he says there is no pervasion [i.e., even though it is true that the color of the Buddha Amitāyus is suitable as a hue, it is not the case that whatever is suitable as a hue is necessarily a color, the Sūtra School Challenger responds,] "It follows that there is pervasion in that [i.e., whatever is suitable as a hue is necessarily a color] because suitable as a hue is the definition of color."

The next notation *in the text* has the Defender accepting the basic consequence, that the color of the Buddha Amitāyus is white, even though it is actually red. In this way the text signals the end of the line of reasoning justifying the subject as a color. This means that the Defender has accepted the "thesis" of the third consequence, that whatever is suitable as a hue is necessarily a color. The procedure from here is the same as in debate A.1. (See pp. 120-122.) That is, the Challenger now leads his opponent back through the arguments he had earlier denied. If the Defender still cannot accept the individual points of the argument, the Challenger will give him further arguments until he can accept them. Finally, the Defender accepts that the color of the Buddha Amitāyus is a color. Having gotten the Defender to accept this, the Challenger again poses the basic consequence, that the subject is white because of being a color. The Defender originally asserted the pervasion, that whatever is a color is necessarily white, and he has come to accept the reason, that the color of the Buddha Amitāyus is a color. He will now accept the basic consequence:

> If he accepts the basic consequence [that the color of the Buddha Amitāyus is white, the Sūtra School Challenger responds,] "It follows that the subject, the color of the Buddha Amitāyus, is not white because of being red."

The Challenger refutes the Defender's acceptance of the subject as white by making it clear that the color of the Buddha Amitāyus is red. The pervasion of this consequence supports what was indicated in debate A.1, whatever is one primary color is necessarily not another one. That is, nothing is both white and red, and, more generally, there is no common locus of two primary colors. The Defender now questions the establishment of the reason:

> If he says that the reason [that the color of the Buddha Amitāyus is red] is not established, [the Sūtra School Challenger responds,] "It follows that the subject, the color of the Buddha Amitāyus, is red because of being the isolate of the color of the Buddha Amitāyus."

The Challenger establishes the subject as red by the sign of its being the isolate (*ldog pa*) of the color of the Buddha Amitāyus. The reason of this consequence indicates that the color of the Buddha Amitāyus is the isolate of the color of the Buddha Amitāyus. Technically, an isolate of something is identified as "that which is reversed from what is not one with it" (*khyod dang gcig ma yin pa las ldog pa*). Thus, the isolate of the color of the Buddha Amitāyus is identified as that which is reversed from (i.e., opposite from) what is not one with the color of the Buddha Amitāyus. This means that it is non-non-one with itself; that is, it is one with itself. The color of the Buddha Amitāyus or any existent is one with itself in the sense that it is *exactly* the same as itself in both name and meaning. This description is an appeal to self-identity. A phenomenon is exactly the same as itself, and it is different from all else. It is from this point of view that such an abstraction is called an "isolate", for it refers to a phenomenon in *isolation* from all else. Therefore, the color of the Buddha Amitāyus, and only that, is one with the color of the Buddha Amitāyus, and thereby it alone is also the isolate of the color of the Buddha Amitāyus.

The Defender moves to deny the reason of this last consequence, claiming that the color of the Buddha Amitāyus is not the isolate of the color of the Buddha Amitāyus. In response, the Challenger generalizes the quality predicated to the subject at hand—that it is its own isolate—as it applies to all established bases (*gzhi grub*, *vastu-siddha*) or existents, for each and every established base has the quality of being its own isolate. The text says:

> If he says that the reason [that the color of the Buddha Amitāyus is the isolate of the color of the Buddha Amitāyus] is not established, [the Sūtra School Challenger responds,] "It follows with respect to the subject, the color of the Buddha Amitāyus, that it is its own isolate because it is an established base."

The color of the Buddha Amitāyus is an established base, that is, an existent. If something is an established base, then it is necessarily its own isolate. Therefore, the color of the Buddha Amitāyus is its own isolate.

It is a characteristic of whatever exists that it is its own isolate. This does not say that, for instance, a pot's isolate is a pot, but that a pot is a pot's isolate. A pot's isolate is a permanent phenomenon because it is a conceptual abstraction, and so it is not a pot. However, a pot is its own isolate because it is one with a pot—exactly the same as a pot in both name and meaning. If we must posit a pot's isolate, then what is there to posit but a pot itself? The third section of "The Introductory Path of Reasoning" deals with this topic of isolates in depth. It is only alluded to in this one portion of the presentation of colors.

In the last consequence, all specification or statement of particulars is taken out of the predicate and the reason. This is done in order to keep the pervasion general—applying to more than the subject at hand—and to avoid a possible verbal fault. The pervasion, i.e., if something is an established base, then it is necessarily its own isolate, is stated in the general in order to apply to all existents. Indeed, the pronoun "it" does refer to the subject, such that if the color of the Buddha Amitāyus is an established base, then the color of the Buddha Amitāyus is necessarily the isolate of the color of the Buddha Amitāyus. However, the pronoun "it" is employed here in order to keep the pervasion general and to avoid a faulty consequence.

When spelling out the meaning of what is being said, the subject is put back in place of the pronouns. Thus, if the Defender were to accept the consequence, he would fill in the specification saying, "I accept that the color of the Buddha Amitāyus is the isolate of the color of the Buddha Amitāyus." Or, if the Defender were to attack the establishment of the reason, in spelling out his answer he would again put the subject in place of the pronoun "it" saying, "The reason, that the color of the Buddha Amitāyus is an established base, is not established."

The Challenger states the predicate and the reason in this general way in order to avoid the fallacy of a consequence such that if one has understood the premises, one would have already understood the conclusion. Spelling out the consequence, it would read, "It follows that the color of the Buddha Amitāyus is the isolate of the color of the Buddha Amitāyus," filling in the specific subject at hand for the nonspecific pronouns. This subject and predicate form what is to be understood—the conclusion, as it were. However, if the predicate and the reason of this consequence had been stated specifically with their referents, the pervasion would be, "If the color of the Buddha Amitāyus is an established base, then the color of the Buddha Amitāyus is necessarily the isolate of the color of the Buddha Amitāyus." Thus, when the Defender understands the pervasion, he would

also simultaneously understand the "thesis" of this consequence—that the color of the Buddha Amitāyus is the
isolate of the color of the Buddha Amitāyus. This would be
faulty reasoning, for, although the premises of an argument
must logically entail the conclusion, the premises cannot
include what they purport to prove. Therefore, in order to
avoid this fallacy, the predicate and the reason are stated
generally.

Furthermore, it should be noted that the predicate of the
above consequence contains both a *grammatical* subject, "it"
(*khyod*), and predicate nominative, "its own isolate" (*khyod
kyi ldog pa*). When this is the case, the translation format
must be switched from, "It follows that the subject is such
and such," to the form, "It follows *with respect to* the subject
that it is such and such," in order to state the grammatical
subject and predicate in addition to the logical subject. Both
must be included in order to avoid a verbal fault. For
instance, if the grammatical subject were dropped out of the
predicate of the consequence, the resultant consequence
would be stated, "It follows that the subject, the color of the
Buddha Amitāyus, is its isolate because it is an established
base." Such is not the case because the color of the Buddha
Amitāyus is not the isolate of "it" since "it" is the isolate of
"it". The color of the Buddha Amitāyus is the isolate of the
color of the Buddha Amitāyus and only that, and the only
thing that is the isolate of "it" is "it".

Moreover, if the predicate of the consequence were stated
specifically and the reason were left with both a
grammatical subject and predicate, the following faulty
consequence would result, "It follows that the subject, the
color of the Buddha Amitāyus, is the isolate of the color of
the Buddha Amitāyus because it is an established base." The
consequence, that the color of the Buddha Amitāyus is the
isolate of the color of the Buddha Amitāyus, is true.
However, there is no pervasion, i.e., it is not the case that if
something is an established base, then [it] is necessarily the
isolate of the color of the Buddha Amitāyus If the pervasion
were held to be true, it would absurdly follow that the

subject, an eye consciousness, would be the isolate of the color of the Buddha Amitāyus because of being an established base. In order to avoid these verbal faults the Challenger very carefully states the predicate of the consequence and the reason generally and each with both a grammatical subject and predicate.

The Defender now accepts the Challenger's reasoning proving that the subject is not white (pp. 226-227), and is led back through the reasons he formerly denied. The subject is the isolate of the color of the Buddha Amitāyus, it is red, it is not white. The Challenger then states the basic consequence, that the subject is white because of being a color, to the Defender for the third time. The Defender himself originally asserted the pervasion of the basic consequence, and the Challenger has proven the reason to him and shown him that he cannot accept the consequence. Thus, the Defender's options have been effectively removed. As before in debate A.1, he will now have to deny his original assertion of the pervasion.

Just as there are three possibilities between the two principals of debate A.1, color and red, so there are three possibilities between color and white, the two principals of debate A.2.

1   Something which is both a color and white is, for instance, the color of a white religious conch, the color of a snow mountain, or the color of white cloth.
2   Whatever is white is necessarily a color, but whatever is a color is not necessarily white. For instance, the color of the Buddha Amitāyus, the color of blue ink, or the color of a ruby is a color but not white.
3   Something which is neither a color nor white is, for instance, the sound of water, a sweet taste, an eye consciousness, any permanent phenomenon, or any non-existent.

Debate A.3, Third Mistaken View (3a.5)

Debate A.3 is quite similar to the former two debates in form and content. The hypothetical Defender is now asserting that whatever is a color is necessarily yellow whereupon the Challenger takes the counterexample of the color of a sapphire (*indranīla*), a blue corundum. The text says:

> If someone [a hypothetical Defender] says, "Whatever is a color is necessarily yellow," [the Sūtra School Challenger responds to him,] "It [absurdly] follows that the subject, the color of a sapphire, is [yellow] because of [being a color]. You asserted the pervasion [that whatever is a color is necessarily yellow]."

At this point the text has changed from the introductory style of spelling out the entire consequence to the standard form of stating merely the demonstrative pronoun "that" (*de*) in the places of the predicate of the consequence, the reason, and, in the next consequence, the subject. That is, whereas the text reads, "It follows that the subject, the color of a sapphire, is that because of that," what is implied is the consequence, "It follows that the subject, the color of a sapphire, is yellow because of being a color." The predicate of the consequence and the reason are supplied from the pervasion the Defender has asserted. The text employs pronouns in the places of their longer referents for the sake of brevity. In the earlier chapters of this translation, the implied complete form is supplied in brackets. The debate continues:

> If he says that the reason [that the color of a sapphire is a color] is not established, [the Sūtra School Challenger responds,] "It follows that the subject [the color of a sapphire] is [a color] because of being a primary color."

Blue is a primary color. Primary colors are a proper division of colors. Thus, whatever is a primary color is necessarily a color.

> If he says that the reason [that the color of a sapphire is a primary color] is not established, [the Sūtra School Challenger responds,] "It follows that the subject [the color of a sapphire] is [a primary color] because of being one of the four—blue, yellow, white, and red."

Blue, yellow, white, and red are the four primary colors. Whatever is any of these four is necessarily a primary color. However, on the other hand, one cannot say that whatever is a primary color is necessarily any of the four—blue, yellow, white, or red. This is so because whereas primary color itself is a primary color, one cannot say that it is either blue, yellow, white, or red.

> If he accepts the basic consequence [that the color of a sapphire is yellow, the Sūtra School Challenger responds,] "It follows that the subject [the color of a sapphire] is not yellow because of being blue."
> [If he says there is no pervasion, i.e., even though it is true that the color of a sapphire is blue, it is not the case that whatever is blue is necessarily not yellow, the Sūtra School Challenger responds, "It follows that] there is pervasion [i.e., whatever is blue is necessarily not yellow] because the two, blue and yellow, are mutually exclusive."

Whatever is blue is necessarily not yellow, and whatever is yellow is necessarily not blue. There is nothing which is both blue and yellow; green, for instance, is neither blue nor yellow despite being a mixture of the two.

The Defender now accepts that whatever is blue is necessarily not yellow. He is led back through the reasoning for the third statement of the basic consequence. He now denies his earlier basic thesis that whatever is a color is necessarily yellow. (See p. 231.)

There are three possibilities between the two principals of debate A.3, color and yellow:

1 Something which is both is the color of a yellow cloth, the color of a yellow flower, or the color of purified gold.
2 Whatever is yellow is necessarily a color, but whatever is a color is not necessarily yellow. For example, the color of a sapphire and the color of a white religious conch are colors but are not yellow.
3 Something which is neither is a sound, an odor, a taste, a tangible object, a consciousness, and so on.

Debate A.4, Fourth Mistaken View (3b.2)

In debate A.4 the Defender asserts that all colors are blue. The first four debates play on someone's asserting that whatever is a color is necessarily one of the four primary colors. The debates occur in the reverse order of the normal list of primary colors. That is, the four primary colors—blue, yellow, white, and red—are debated in the reverse order— red, white, yellow, and blue. The text says:

> If someone [a hypothetical Defender] says, "Whatever is a color is necessarily blue," [the Sūtra School Challenger responds to him,] "It [absurdly] follows that the subject, the color of refined gold, is [blue] because of [being a color]. You asserted the pervasion [that whatever is a color is necessarily blue]."
>
> If he says that the reason [that the color of refined gold is a color] is not established, [the Sūtra School Challenger responds,] "It follows that the subject [the color of refined gold is [a color] because of being an instance of color."

The Challenger proves that the subject is a color by virtue of its being an instance (*bye brag, viśeṣa*) of the generality (*spyi, sāmānya*), color. Whatever is an instance of color is necessarily a color.

This point does not suggest that whatever exists is an instance of something, but that whatever is an instance of something is necessarily that thing. The sixth section of "The Introductory Path of Reasoning" is the presentation of generalities and instances where it is made clear that existent, for instance, is only a generality and not an instance. Here again the author makes a brief reference to a topic that is later presented extensively in this same work.

> If he accepts the basic consequence [that the color of refined gold is blue, the Sūtra School Challenger responds,] "It follows that the subject [the color of refined gold] is not blue because of being yellow."
>
> If he says that the reason [that the color of refined gold is yellow] is not established, [the Sūtra School Challenger responds,] "It follows that the subject [the color of refined gold] is [yellow] because of being the color of refined gold."
>
> If he says that the reason [that the color of refined gold is the color of refined gold] is not established, [the Sūtra School Challenger responds,] "It follows that the color of refined gold is the color of refined gold because the color of refined gold exists."

This last consequence is not strictly correct if reformulated as a general principle. That is, the generalized statement, "It follows that it is itself because it exists," is not correct. For, although it is true as it applies to the color of refined gold, there are many counterexamples to the generalized consequence. Definition, for instance, is not itself [that is, it is not a definition] because it is a definiendum. There is a definition of definition; thus, definition is a definiendum and not itself a definition. Many counterexamples to the generalized statement that whatever exists is itself will be brought out in later chapters. Though whatever is an existent is necessarily one with itself, it is not necessarily itself in the sense of being an exemplifier of itself.

Still, it is true that the color of refined gold exists and that it is itself. Although this last consequence may not be strictly correct if re-formulated as a *general* principle, it is correct as it stands.

Similar to the preceding debates, there are three possibilities between the two principles of debate A.4, color and blue:

1 Something which is both is the color of a sapphire, the color of a blue sky, or the color of a blue cloth.
2 Whatever is blue is necessarily a color, but whatever is a color is not necessarily blue. For instance, the color of refined gold, the color of a ruby, and the color of a white religious conch are colors but not blue.
3 Something which is neither is pot, a pillar, or the horn of a rabbit.

Debate A.5, Fifth Mistaken View (3b.4)

Debate A.5 plays on the division of colors into primary colors and secondary colors. A hypothetical Defender asserts that all colors are primary colors, and in response the Challenger points out that a secondary color is a color but not a primary color. Further, primary colors and secondary colors are mutually exclusive. Whatever is one is necessarily not the other. All colors except for the four primary colors are secondary colors. Secondary colors consist of the eight famous secondary colors (see pp. 194, 196-197) and any color which is a mixture of colors. Green, for instance, is a secondary color because of being a mixture of blue and yellow. The text says:

> If someone [a hypothetical Defender] says, "Whatever is a color is necessarily a primary color," [the Sūtra School Challenger responds to him,] "It [absurdly] follows that the subject, the color of green Amoghasiddhi, is [a primary color] because of [being a color. You asserted the pervasion that whatever is a color is necessarily a primary color]."

Amoghasiddhi (*don yod grub pa*), meaning accomplishing the purposeful, is master of one of the five Buddha lineages. He is associated with the color green, the northern direction, and the exalted wisdom of accomplishing activities (*bya grub ye shes, kṛtyanushthāna-jñāna*).[1]

> If he says that the reason [that the color of green Amoghasiddhi is a color] is not established, [the Sūtra School Challenger responds,] "It follows that the subject [the color of green Amoghasiddhi] is [a color] because of being that subject."

The reason phrase, "because of being that subject", means, "because of being the color of green Amoghasiddhi", but it is stated as it is because, technically speaking, the subject cannot be given as the reason. The meaning is that the color of green Amoghasiddhi is a color because of being the color of green Amoghasiddhi. This consequence offers little but indicates that the subject is itself and whatever is the color of green Amoghasiddhi is necessarily a color. It seems to be an appeal to common sense.

> If he accepts the basic consequence [that the color of green Amoghasiddhi is a primary color, the Sūtra School Challenger responds,] "It follows that the subject [the color of green Amoghasiddhi] is not a primary color because of being a secondary color."
> "It follows that [the color of green Amoghasiddhi is a secondary color] because of being the secondary color composed of the two, blue and yellow."

For this last consequence the text says simply, "That follows" or "It follows in that way" (*der thal*) implying that the Defender has said that the reason is not established. In all the previous occasions the text said, "If [he says that the reason is] not established (*ma grub na*)," explicitly indicating the Defender's answer. Here and in many other cases, the Defender's answer is not explicitly indicated, but is to be understood implicitly. Similarly, the text often reads simply, "[There is] pervasion," (*khyab ste*) implicitly indicating that

---

[1] Detlef Ingo Lauf, *Tibetan Sacred Art, The Heritage of Tantra*, p. 130.

the Defender has said there is no pervasion by supplying only the Challenger's response to that unstated answer.

> "It follows that [the color of green Amoghasiddhi is the secondary color composed of the two, blue and yellow] because of being green; because of being the color which is a mixture of blue and yellow."

Here again the author employs another shortened form for presenting the debates. Having given one reason, the text then immediately gives another separated by only a continuative (here, *te*) in Tibetan and by a semicolon in English. This form was used earlier in debate A.1 (see pp. 123-124). Such a notation does not mean that the author is offering an alternative reason for the first consequence; rather, this form indicates that the Defender has said that the first reason is not established and the Challenger is giving the second reason in support of the first. The text continues:

> "[There is] pervasion [i.e., whatever is a color which is a mixture of blue and yellow is necessarily green] because a mixture of blue and yellow is posited as green, a mixture of red and yellow is posited as orange, and a mixture of red and blue is posited as black."

Here, the text says, "[There is] pervasion" (*khyab ste*), rather than, "It follows that there is pervasion" (*khyab par thal*). The Challenger's response is being given in the syllogistic form rather than in the form of a consequence. Unlike the statement of a consequence, for which the Challenger need not hold the reason, pervasion, or predicate to be established, when the Challenger states a syllogism he must hold the statement to be accurate in all respects.

There are three possibilities between the two principals of debate A.5, color and primary color:

1 Something which is both is blue, yellow, white, or red.
2 Whatever is a primary color is necessary a color, but whatever is a color is not necessarily a primary color as, for instance, the color of green Amoghasiddhi.

3   Something which is neither a color nor a primary color is, for instance, a white horse. A white horse is not a form but a person and, thus, could not be a color. The color of a white horse is a color, but persons, including animals, are not colors.

Debate A.6, Sixth Mistaken View (3b.6)

In debate A.6 the Defender asserts that whatever is a secondary color is necessarily one of the eight secondary colors indicated in Vasubandhu's *Treasury of Knowledge*. (See pp. 194, 196-197.) However, not all secondary colors are one of the eight famous secondary colors (cloud, smoke, dust, and so on), for colors which are mixtures are also secondary colors. The text says:

> If someone [a hypothetical Defender] says, "Whatever is a secondary color is necessarily one of the eight secondary colors," [the Sūtra School Challenger responds to him,] "It [absurdly] follows that the subject, the color of orange Mañjughoṣa, is one of the eight secondary colors because of being a secondary color. You asserted the pervasion [that whatever is a secondary color is necessarily one of the eight secondary colors]."
>
> If he says that the reason [that the color of orange Mañjughoṣa is a secondary color is not established, [the Sūtra School Challenger responds,] "It follows that the subject, the color of orange Mañjughoṣa, is a secondary color because of being a secondary color composed of the two, red and yellow."
>
> If he accepts the basic consequence [that the color of orange Mañjughoṣa is one of the eight secondary colors, the Sūtra School Challenger responds,] "It follows that the subject, the color of orange Mañjughoṣa, is not any of the eight secondary colors because of (1) not being any of the four colors—cloud, smoke, dust, and mist—and (2)

also not being any of the four colors—illumination, darkness, shadow, and sunlight."

The Challenger has given a two-part reason to show that the subject is not any of the eight secondary colors. The Defender can deny the combined reason, the first part alone, the second part alone, or each part individually.

In this reason the Challenger is laying out just what the eight secondary colors are, and in so doing he may be providing the Defender with new information. However, in many cases this form is used not so much to provide new information as to separate the predicate at hand into simpler parts that can more easily be considered. That is, the Defender accepts that something has a certain quality p, and the Challenger moves to show that the subject is not a p because of not being any of the proper subdivisions of p. For instance, the subject is not a p of the first type nor a p of the second type, there being only two types. In this case, the Challenger is proving that the subject is not any of the eight secondary colors because of not being any of the first four and also not being any of the second four. Thus, he is providing the Defender with the opportunity to say which he feels is it.

Similarly, this form is used to establish something positively as being both a p and a q. For instance, if a Defender denied that the color of a white religious conch is a common locus of color and white, the Challenger might prove that it is so because of (1) being a color and (2) also being white. In this way the Defender can more specifically identify how he disagrees with the Challenger. The debate continues:

> The reasons are established individually because of being one with the color of orange Mañjughoṣa.

Thus, the text indicates that the Defender attacks each part of the two-part reason in turn and is told that the subject is not any of the first four secondary colors nor any of the second four secondary colors for the same reason—because of being one with the color of orange Mañjughoṣa. Whatever is one with the color of orange Mañjughoṣa is necessarily not any of the eight secondary colors. The appeal is to the obvious fact that the color of a Buddha is not a cloud color, not a smoke color, nor any of the other eight famous secondary colors. The color of orange Mañjughoṣa is orange and not any of those.

The procedure for debating a two-part reason is somewhat more involved than the procedure for a single-unit reason. The implied debate is:

C: It follows that the subject, the color of orange Mañjughoṣa is not any of the eight secondary colors because of (1) not being any of the four colors—cloud, smoke, dust, or mist—and also (2) not being any of the four colors—illumination, darkness, shadow, and sunlight.

D: The first part of the reason is not established (*rtags dang po ma grub*).

C: Spell it out (*rtsis*).

D: The reason, that the color of orange Mañjughoṣa is not any of the four colors—cloud, smoke, dust, or mist, is not established.

C: It follows that the subject, the color of orange Mañjughoṣa is not any of the four colors—cloud, smoke, dust, or mist—because of being one with the color of orange Mañjughoṣa.

D: I accept that it is that (*de yin par 'dod*). The second part of the reason is not established (*rtags gnyis pa ma grub*).

Here the Defender accepts the establishment of the first reason only. His answer is carefully worded in order to avoid possible misunderstanding of what he means to accept and what he means to deny. He declares, "I accept that it is that," meaning that he accepts the first reason, that the subject is not any of the four colors—cloud, smoke, dust, or mist. If he had said simply, "I accept it," this would have signaled acceptance of the whole line of reasoning. He immediately moves on to attack the second part of the two-part reason. The implied debate continues:

C: Spell it out.

D: The reason, that the color of orange Mañjughoṣha is not any of the four colors—illumination, shadow, darkness, or sunlight, is not established.

C: It follows that the subject, the color of orange Mañjughoṣha, is not any of the four colors—illumination, darkness, shadow, or sunlight—because of being one with the color of orange Mañjughoṣha.

D: I accept that it is that.

The Defender has accepted the second part of the reason and in so doing has implicitly accepted the whole line of reasoning.

As the implied debate proceeds, the Challenger now states to him the consequence that the second reason is established. In terms of content, this is no different from what the Defender has just accepted, that the subject is none of the second four secondary colors. Still, the Challenger gives this consequence for the sake of pointing out to the Defender that he has now asserted the second part of the reason as established:

C: It follows that the second part of the reason is established.

D: I accept it.

C: It follows that the subject, the color of orange Mañjughoṣha, is not any of the four colors—cloud, smoke, dust, or mist.

D: I accept it.

C: It follows that the first part of the reason is established.

D: I accept it.

C: It follows that the subject, the color of orange Mañjughoṣha, (1) is not any of the four colors—cloud, smoke, dust, or mist—and also (2) is not any of the four colors—illumination, darkness, shadow, and sunlight.

D: I accept it.

On the way back through the reasoning the Challenger must combine the two-part reason again in order to provide the Defender the opportunity for denying the combined reason. The answer, "The combined reason is not established (*sdoms rtags ma grub),"* may be given when the individual parts of a reason are established or, at least, may not be effectively questioned, yet the two parts of the reason in combination are not established. For instance, for the consequence:

> It follows that sound is both an impermanent phenomenon and a permanent phenomenon because of (1) sound's being an impermanent phenomenon and (2) being a permanent phenomenon,

the correct response is that the combined reason is not established. The first part of the reason, that sound is an impermanent phenomenon, is established. The second part of the reason is a grammatical predicate without a subject and so may not effectively be questioned, for denial of a quality apart from a basis is not sensible.

There are three possibilities between the two principals of debate A.6, secondary color and any of the eight secondary colors:

1   Something which is both is the color of an orange cloud. It is one of the eight secondary colors because of being a cloud color which is a secondary color. It is a secondary color because of being orange, a color which is a mixture of red and yellow.
2   Whatever is any of the eight secondary colors is necessarily a secondary color, but whatever is a secondary color is not necessarily any of the eight secondary colors, for the color of orange Mañjughoṣa is a secondary color but not any of the eight secondary colors.
3   Something which is neither is the color of a ruby or any primary color.

Whereas there are three possibilities between secondary color and any of the eight secondary colors, there are four possibilities between secondary color and cloud color:

1   Something which is both is the color of an orange cloud. It is a secondary color because of being orange, and it is a cloud color because of being suitable as a hue of a cloud.

2 However, it is not the case that whatever is a cloud color is necessarily a secondary color. The color of a white cloud, for instance, is a cloud color, but it is not a secondary color because of being a primary color—white.
3 Since it is not the case that whatever is a secondary color is necessarily a cloud color, there is something which is a secondary color but not a cloud color such as the color of green Amoghasiddhi or the color of brownish dust.
4 There are many things which are neither a secondary color nor a cloud color—the color of white cloth, a house, etc.

Similarly, there are four possibilities between cloud color and primary color, between smoke color and secondary color, and between smoke color and primary color. This reasoning applies similarly to the others of the eight secondary colors except, perhaps, to darkness and shadow which appear to be always black or gray.

Because, for instance, whatever is a cloud color is not necessarily a secondary color, when the eight secondary colors are enumerated, they must be posited as cloud colors which are that (*der gyur pa'i sprin gyi kha dog*), smoke colors which are that (i.e., secondary colors) and so forth. The qualification "which are that" is added to specify cloud colors which are secondary colors and to eliminate cloud colors which are primary colors.

Since cloud colors, smoke colors, etc. are not definitely secondary colors, one might wonder why whatever is any of the eight secondary colors is necessarily a secondary color and, thus, why there are three possibilities between these two. There is no fault in this because any of the eight secondary colors is, just that, a secondary color. When the eight secondary colors are posited, they are posited as secondary colors. Thus, whatever is any of the eight secondary colors is necessarily a secondary color.

Debate A.7, Seventh Mistaken View (4a.3)

In debates A.7 and A.8, the focus switches from colors alone to the two subdivisions of visible forms, colors and shapes or color-forms (*kha dog gi gzugs*) and shape-forms (*dbyibs kyi gzugs*). Color and color-form are mutually inclusive. Whatever is one is necessarily the other, as is the case with shape and shape-form. In debate A.7, when the Defender accepts that whatever is a form is necessarily a shape-form, the Challenger posits the counterexample of a color-form. A color-form is any color; it is a form but not a shape-form. He could have stated any subject which is a form but not a shape-form such as a sound, an odor, a taste, or a tangible object. The text says:

> If someone [a hypothetical Defender] says, "Whatever is a form is necessarily a shape-form," [the Sūtra School Challenger responds to him,] "It [absurdly] follows that the subject, a color-form, is [a shape-form] because of [being a form]. You asserted the pervasion [that whatever is a form is necessarily a shape-form]."
>
> If he says that the reason [that a color-form is a form] is not established, [the Sūtra School Challenger responds,] "It follows that the subject [a color-form] is [a form] because of being matter."
>
> If he says that the reason [that a color-form is matter] is not established [the Sūtra School Challenger responds,] "It follows that the subject [a color-form] is [matter] because of being atomically established."

In the Sūtra School system, form (*gzugs, rūpa*) and matter (*bem po, kanthā*) are mutually inclusive. Thus, the subject is a form because of being matter, and it is matter because of being atomically established—the definition or meaning of matter. The pervasion is correct because, applying the rules of the relation between definition and definiendum, whatever is atomically established is necessarily matter and whatever is matter is necessarily atomically established.

> If he accepts the basic consequence [that a color-form is a shape-form, the Sūtra School Challenger responds,] "It follows that the subject [a color-form] is not a shape-form because of being one with a color-form."

Shape-form and color-form are mutually exclusive in this interpretation of the system of the Proponents of Sūtra. Whatever is one is necessarily not the other. Though this is the most frequent assertion on this point among the Collected Topics texts, the Go-mang *Collected Topics*, in accordance with the system of the Great Exposition School, asserts that color and shape are not mutually exclusive, that there is a common locus of the two (see pp. 199-200).

It should be noted here that even though the subject is stated as "a color-form" and the reason is stated, "one with a color-form", the indefinite article "a" is added in English and is not specified in the Tibetan original. Indefinite articles are often added to the English translation for reasons of grammatical correctness and clarity of meaning. Though it is true that any color-form is not a shape-form, the point being made here is that color-form itself is not a shape-form. The subject does not refer to any particular color-form, but just color-form as such. Here, "a color-form" is to be understood in this sense, not as meaning *any* particular color-form.

As discussed earlier (see pp. 85-88), when articles, either definite or indefinite, are used in the English translation, they introduce a problem which does not exist in the Tibetan original. We have to say that the only phenomenon which is one with color-form is color-form, not even *a* color-form. *A* color-form is one with a color-form. In the last consequence, the reason might better have been translated, "Because of being one with color-form", leaving out the indefinite article. However, in order to avoid the verbal fault of saying that a color-form is one with color-form, the reason is stated, "Because of being one with a color-form".

In any case, in this translation system, even "a color-form" should be understood as referring to color-form itself; the article is used just for convenience of expression.

> If he says that the reason [that a color-form is one with a color-form] is not established, [the Sūtra School Challenger responds,] "It follows with respect to the subject [a color-form] that it is one with itself because it is an existent."

If something is an existent, then is it necessarily one with itself. This does not say that whatever is an existent is necessarily itself in the sense of being an exemplifier of itself, but that whatever exists is necessarily one with itself. The topic of one (*gcig, ekatva*) and different (*tha dad, nānātva*) or the various types of sameness and difference will be discussed in greater detail in later chapters.

There are three possibilities between the two principals of debate A.7, form and shape-form:

1   Something which is both is the shape of a house or the shape of a triangle.
2   Whatever is a shape-form is necessarily a form, but whatever is a form is not necessarily a shape-form. For instance, a color-form, the color of a sapphire, a bitter taste, the sound of a voice, and so forth are forms but not shape-forms.
3   There are many phenomena which are neither a form nor a shape form, such as a consciousness, a person, uncomposed space, non-cow, and so forth.

Debate A.8, Eighth Mistaken View (4a.5)

In debate A.8, the final debate in this first section of the presentation of colors and so forth—refutation of mistaken views, the Defender takes the opposite stand to that of debate A.7, now asserting that all forms are color-forms. The Challenger refutes this view using the counter-example of a round form, a form which is not a color-form.

If someone [a hypothetical Defender] says, "Whatever is a form is necessarily a color-form," [the Sūtra School Challenger responds to him,] "It [absurdly] follows that the subject, a round form, is [a color-form] because of [being a form]. You asserted the pervasion [that whatever is a form is necessarily a color-form]."

If he says that the reason [that a round form is a form] is not established, [the Sūtra School Challenger responds,] "It follows that the subject [a round form] is [a form] because of being a form-source."

(See pp. 192ff.) Form-source refers to visible forms, a proper subdivision of forms; thus, whatever is a form-source is necessarily a form. Form-sources are divided into color-forms and shape-forms. Thus, whatever is either a color-form or a shape-form is necessarily a form-source and thereby is necessarily a form. However, it is not the case that whatever is a form is necessarily a color-form or a shape-form. For example, a sound or a taste is a form but not a form-source and thus neither a color-form nor a shape-form.

If he says that the reason [that a round form is a form-source] is not established, [the Sūtra School Challenger responds,] "It follows that the subject [a round form] is [a form-source] because of being an object apprehended by an eye consciousness."

A round form is an object apprehended by an eye consciousness; it is a form-source, a visible form. Form-sources are defined as objects apprehended by an eye consciousness. This does not imply that whatever is a form-source is always being apprehended by an eye consciousness, but that whatever is a form-source is an object that an eye consciousness is capable of apprehending and, further, only form-sources are objects that an eye consciousness is capable of apprehending.

> If he accepts the basic consequence [that a round form is a color-form, the Sūtra School Challenger responds,] "It follows that the subject [a round form] is not a color-form because of not being a color."
>
> "[It follows that] there is pervasion [i.e., whatever is not a color is necessarily not a color-form] because color-form and color are mutually inclusive and the two, shape-form and shape, are mutually inclusive."

As before (see p. 237), the text reads simply, "There is pervasion," indicating that the Defender has answered to the last consequence that there is no pervasion. However, since color-form and color are mutually inclusive, there is pervasion, i.e., whatever is not a color is necessarily not a color-form. This is so because the eight approaches of pervasion (see pp. 66-67) exist between any two mutually inclusive phenomena as well as between any definition and its definiendum.

There are three possibilities between the two principals of debate A.8, form and color-form:

1 Something which is both is, for instance, the color of purified gold, the color of a red flower, or any color.
2 Whatever is a color-form is necessarily a form, but whatever is a form is not necessarily a color-form. For instance, the shape of a house, a round form, a pleasant smell, or a salty taste is a form but not a color-form.
3 Something which is neither is, for instance, a consciousness or a permanent phenomenon.

PRESENTATION OF THE AUTHOR'S OWN SYSTEM OF
COLORS AND SO FORTH (4B.1)

The second major section of the three in "Colors and So Forth" is the presentation of the Tutor Jam-ba-gya-tso's own system, presented from the point of view of the Proponents of Sūtra Following Reasoning. In the first section, refutation of mistaken view, coarse misconception is cleared away. In the second section, the Tutor Jam-ba-gya-tso lays out the "correct" interpretation of the topics, mainly giving the definitions and divisions of form and so forth.

The procedure or style in this section generally involves beginning with the broadest category under discussion, form in this case, which is defined and divided. Each of the divisions is then defined and subdivided in turn. Often illustrations of each division are given in order to exemplify what is included within the category.

> There is a definition of a form because that which is suitable as a form is the definition of a form. The two, form and matter, are mutually inclusive. If forms are divided, there are five consisting of form-sources, sound-sources, odor-sources, taste-sources, and tangible-object-sources.
>
> There is a definition of a form-source because an object apprehended by an eye consciousness is the definition of a form-source. If form-sources are divided, there are two because there are the two, shapes and colors.
>
> There is a definition of a shape because that which is suitable to be shown as a shape is the definition of a shape. If [shapes] are divided, there are eight because there are the eight consisting of long, short, high, low, square, round, level, and non-level forms. A square has four corners. A round [shape] is circular or spherical. Level is, for instance, a shape of even surface.
>
> The definition of a color is what which is suitable to be shown as a hue. If colors are divided, there are two because there are the two, primary colors and secondary colors. If primary colors are divided, there are four because there are the four—blue, yellow, white, and red. If secondary colors are divided, there are eight because there are the eight consisting of the colors of cloud, smoke, dust, mist, illumina-

tion, darkness, shadow, and sunlight which are secondary colors.

There is a definition of a sound-source because an object heard by an ear consciousness is the definition of a sound-source. If sounds are divided, there are two because there are the two, sounds caused by elements conjoined with consciousness and sounds caused by elements not conjoined with consciousness.

There is definition of an odor-source because an object experienced by a nose consciousness is the definition of an odor-source. If odors are divided, there are two because there are the two, natural odors and manufactured odors.

There is a definition of a taste-source because an object experienced by a tongue consciousness is the definition of a taste-source. If tastes are divided, there are six because there are the six—sweet, sour, bitter, astringent, pungent, and salty.

There is a definition of a tangible-object-source because an object experienced by a body consciousness is the definition of a tangible-object-source. If tangible objects are divided, there are two because there are the two, tangible objects which are elements and tangible objects arisen from the elements. If tangible objects which are elements are divided, there are four because the four—earth, water, fire, and wind—are tangible objects which are elements. There is a definition of earth because hard and obstructive is the definition of earth. There is a definition of water because wet and moistening is the definition of water. There is a definition of fire because hot and burning is the definition of fire. There is a definition of wind because light and moving is the definition of wind. If tangible objects arisen from the elements are divided, there are seven because there are the seven consisting of smoothness, roughness, heaviness, lightness, cold, hunger, and thirst which are tangible objects arisen from the elements.

Within the explanation of the author's own interpretation, the definitions and divisions are presented in the syllogistic form, "There is a definition of ... because ... is the definition of ... "

Although in this section the one presenting the definitions does not have to defend his assertions, the definitions are presented within a debate form in order to show that they are suitable as bases of debate. In some later chapters the presentation of the author's own system takes the form of debate, but here the information is given straightforwardly within a reasoning form.

This second section of each chapter, in which the "correct" interpretation is explained, generally serves as the basis of new students' study and understanding. All of the definitions and divisions must be memorized. The meaning of these is then debated. What is included by the definition? What is excluded? Do the divisions include all phenomena of that type? If not, what is not included within the stated divisions? Even without employing creative debate, the beginners may use the debate format simply as a framework for positing the definitions, divisions, and illustrations.

Also, one main way of using the information in this section is a basis for considering the differences between phenomena. For instance, there are three possibilities between color and form. Form-sources and sound-sources are mutually exclusive. Color and primary color have three possibilities. Secondary color and any of the eight secondary colors have three possibilities. The color of cloth and blue have four possibilities. The color of blue cloth and blue have three possibilities. Non-color and visible form have four possibilities. Secondary color and the color of a cloud have four possibilities. Primary color and the color of a cloud have four possibilities.

Often in beginning a new topic the teacher will first guide the student through the second section of the chapter explaining the author's interpretation, and then teach the first section refuting mistaken views. In so doing, the students are initially equipped with an overall understanding of the topic which they can then apply to understand the specific debates.

DISPELLING OBJECTIONS TO THE AUTHOR'S SYSTEM OF COLORS AND SO FORTH (5A.4)

The third and final major section of the presentation of colors and so forth is the forum in which the Tutor Jam-ba-gya-tso is "dispelling objections" (*rtsod pa spong ba*), literally "abandoning debate", to the system of the Proponents of Sūtra he has posited. Now that the "correct" presentation of the topic has been given in the second section, hypothetical objections are cleared away. In the first section the Proponent of Sūtra assumed the role of Challenger in order to refute others' mistaken views, but in the third section the Proponent of Sūtra initially assumes the role of Defender holding the "correct" position against the Challenger's objections.

Here the hypothetical Challenger states consequences of the Sūtra School position, and the Proponent of Sūtra defends against these objections by pointing out the opponent's failure of reasoning which led to a misconception of the Sūtra School system. Moreover, often in this section, after the Sūtra School disputant has defended his position against possible objections, he again assumes the role of Challenger stating absurd consequences of the former hypothetical Challenger's misinterpretations or refuting answers given by a second hypothetical Defender.

This section in which the author dispels others' possible objections is obviously helpful as a teaching aid, for it serves to increase debate and clarifies his own interpretation. The debates given here hint at possible weaknesses in the text's position and function to guide the students' thought toward creative debate. This section serves to clarify the given interpretation by more clearly identifying what is being asserted and by setting the Sūtra School position in contradistinction to others. Together with the other sections, "dispelling objections" serves to establish the scope of the topic at hand. What is included? What is excluded? How does this part relate to that? Is there something which is this and not that? In the presentation of colors and so forth this section consists of three debates.

Debate A.9, First Objection (5a.4)

Debate A.9 serves to emphasize the difference between what was said earlier in this text and what is said in ordinary language. In debate, one must carefully say, for instance, that the *color* of a white religious conch is white, not as in ordinarily speech that a white religious conch is white. The text says:

> Someone [a hypothetical Challenger] might say, "It follows that the subject, a white religious conch, is a color because of being white."

A white religious conch is not a color at all but earth (since it is hard and obstructive) and thus a tangible object. Therefore, the correct response to this consequence is that the reason, that a white religious conch is white, is not established.

Next, an imagined Defender gives just this answer; however, within the forum of laying out the hypothetical Challenger's objections, such answers do not always represent the author's position. Rather, the author is guiding the discussion by merely providing possible answers, sometimes accurate and sometimes not, in order to draw out more fully the Challenger's objections.

> If [another] says that the reason [that a white religious conch is white] is not established, [the hypothetical Challenger will respond,] "It follows that the subject [a white religious conch] is [white] because of being a white religious conch."

At this point the text indicates the end of the hypothetical Challenger's line of reasoning with the conditional "if" (*na*), meaning that all that has come before in this debate is a supposition of a possible opponent's position. Sometimes the clause "if it is said" (*zer na*) is used in the same way to mark this transition from the hypothetical Challenger's debate to the author's response. The Sūtra School Defender's answer follows:

> [To this the Sūtra School Defender responds,] "The pervasion is opposite [i.e., whatever is a white religious conch is necessarily not white]."

The answer that the pervasion is opposite (*'gal khyab*) is a stronger, more specific answer for some cases in which there is no pervasion (see pp. 113-114). That is, here it is true that there is no pervasion because whatever is a white religious conch is *not necessarily* white; but beyond that, whatever is a white religious conch is *necessarily not* white. Thus, the answer that the pervasion is opposite is more decisive and informative. The hypothetical Challenger's consequence is wrong not merely because of being indefinite in the sense that perhaps some white religious conches are white and others are not, but it is clearly wrong because no white religious conch is white. The Defender is not required to give this answer whenever possible. It is a matter of how firmly he wishes to rebuke the Challenger.

At this point the debaters switch roles. The hypothetical Challenger becomes the Defender, and the Proponent of Sūtra, who was formerly the Defender accepting objections to his position, now becomes the Challenger in order to pose some questions/consequences to the opponent based on the problems he has raised.

> Then [the Proponent of Sūtra would become Challenger and fling these consequences] at him: "It [absurdly] follows that the subject, a white horse, is white because of being a white horse. The pervasion is parallel."

If, in accordance with his earlier statement, the hypothetical opponent asserts that whatever is a white religious conch is necessarily white, this pervasion is parallel to saying that whatever is a white horse is necessarily white.

> "You cannot accept the consequence [that a white horse is white] because of [the subject's] not being matter; because of being a person; because of being a horse."

Horses are persons, and persons are not matter. Since whatever is not matter is necessarily not a color, horses are not colors. Therefore, the hypothetical Defender cannot accept that a white horse is white. White and a white horse are mutually exclusive. There is nothing which is both because whatever is a white horse is necessarily a person, and whatever is white is necessarily not a person but matter.

The Sūtra School Challenger now addresses the hypothetical opponent's earlier objection more directly by posing the same consequence to him which he, of course, accepts. In this way the Proponent of Sūtra can explain why a white religious conch is not white.

> Furthermore, [there is this fault with the hypothetical opponent's position:] "It [absurdly] follows that the subject, a white religious conch, is a color because of being white. You asserted the reason [that a white religious conch is white]."
>
> If he accepts [that a white religious conch is a color, the Sūtra School Challenger responds,] "It follows that the subject [a white religious conch] is not a color because of not being arisen from the elements."
>
> "It follows that [a white religious conch is not arisen from the elements] because of being an element; because of being a religious conch."

Colors are arisen from the elements, but they are not tangible objects arisen from the elements—rather, visible forms arisen from the elements. A white religious conch is an element, for it is earth, hard and obstructive. Whatever is an element is necessarily not arisen from the elements, and whatever is not arisen from the elements is necessarily not a color; therefore, a white religious conch is not a color. The two, white and a white religious conch, are mutually exclusive. There is nothing which is both because whatever is a white religious conch is necessarily an element and whatever is white is necessarily not an element but arisen from the elements.

Debate A.10, Second Objection (5b.1)

Debate A.10 also plays on the fact that the elements and what is arisen from the elements are mutually exclusive. Here the hypothetical Challenger is asserting that the element wind is in fact arisen from the elements.

> Also, someone [a hypothetical Challenger] might say, "It follows that the subject, wind, is arisen from the elements because of being one of the seven tangible objects arisen from the elements."

Tangible objects (see pp. 210-217) are the four elements—earth, water, fire, and wind—and the seven arisen from the elements—smoothness, roughness, heaviness, lightness, cold, hunger, and thirst. This Challenger is claiming that wind is among the seven tangible objects arisen from the elements. The correct answer to his consequence is that the reason is not established, the answer that an imagined Defender now gives.

> If [another] says that the reason [that wind is one of the seven tangible objects arisen from the elements] is not established, [the hypothetical Challenger will respond,] "It follows that the subject, wind, is one of the seven tangible objects arisen from the elements because of being the tangible object lightness."
> "It follows that [wind is the tangible object lightness] because of being both a tangible object and light."

[To this the Sūtra School Defender responds,]
"There is no pervasion [i.e., even though it is true
that wind is both a tangible object and light, it is not
the case that whatever is both a tangible object and
light is necessarily the tangible object lightness]."

The element wind is light and a tangible object, but it is not
the tangible object lightness, which is arisen from the elements. Therefore, whatever is light and a tangible object is
not necessarily the tangible object lightness.

Extend this type of reasoning similarly to earth,
water, and fire.

The author directs the reader to apply this type of reasoning
to the other three elements. Earth, for instance, is not the
tangible object heaviness simply because it is heavy and a
tangible object. Whatever is an element is necessarily not
arisen from the elements. The elements and forms arisen
from the elements are mutually exclusive.

There are three possibilities between forms arisen from
the elements and the seven tangible objects arisen from the
elements:

1 Something which is both is smoothness, roughness,
   heaviness, lightness, cold, hunger, or thirst.
2 Whatever is any of the tangible objects arisen from the
   elements is necessarily a form arisen from the elements,
   but whatever is a form arisen from the elements is not
   necessarily any of the tangible objects arisen from the
   elements. Color, for instance, is a form arisen from the
   elements but not a tangible object. Also, shape, sound,
   odor, and taste are non-tangible forms arisen from the
   elements.
3 Something which is neither a form arisen from the elements nor a tangible object arisen from the elements is
   any of the four tangible objects which are elements
   (earth, water, fire, and wind), a consciousness, a permanent phenomenon, and so on.

Wind and form arisen from the elements are mutually exclusive. Also, wind and the seven tangible objects arisen from the elements are mutually exclusive. However, there are three possibilities between wind and that which is both a tangible object and light.

1   Something which is both is, for instance, the wind in the east. It is wind, a tangible object, and light to the touch.
2   Whatever is a wind is necessarily both a tangible object and light, but whatever is both a tangible object and light is not necessarily wind—for instance, a feather. Also, the tangible object lightness is both a tangible object and light, but it is not wind.
3   Of course, there are many things which are neither wind nor something which is both a tangible object and light—a car, for instance.

Debate A.11, Third Objection (5b.2)

In debate A.11, the final debate in the section on dispelling objections and thus the final debate in the presentation of colors and so forth, the subject of debate is object of knowledge (*shes bya, jñeya*), which is mutually inclusive with existent (*yod pa, sat*) and phenomenon (*chos, dharma*). This debate leads the student into the material of the second chapter, the presentation of established bases, which is an introductory description of the ontology of the Proponents of Sūtra Following Reasoning. The text says:

> Someone [a hypothetical Challenger] might say, "It follows that the subject, object of knowledge, is a shape because of being one of the two, level or non-level."
>
> [To this the Sūtra School Defender responds,] "There is no pervasion [i.e., even though it is true that object of knowledge is one of the two, level or non-level, it is not the case that whatever is one of the two, level or non-level, is necessarily a shape]."

Even though level and non-level are divisions of shape, not everything that is non-level is a shape. Level and non-level are a dichotomy that include everything, shapes and otherwise. Whatever is level is necessarily a shape but whatever is non-level is not necessarily a shape, as in the case of an eye consciousness which must be said to be non-level because of not being level. For this reason, in the second section of this chapter, the presentation of the author's own system of colors and so forth, the division of shapes specifies non-level *forms*. Thus, the text avoids the fallacy of including non-material things as shapes, and the Challenger's objection fails.

Object of knowledge, which is non-level but not a non-level shape, is a broadly inclusive phenomenon encompassing all existents. Whatever exists may be known and thus is an object of knowledge. Objects of knowledge include both permanent phenomena and impermanent phenomena, but object of knowledge itself is a permanent phenomenon. It is a fact of Buddhist ontology that something which has both permanent and impermanent instances is itself a permanent phenomenon. That is, some objects of knowledge are permanent phenomena; therefore, object of knowledge itself abides as a permanent phenomenon. This criterion is one of the ways by which one may judge whether or not a phenomenon is permanent.

Still, the fact that object of knowledge itself is permanent phenomenon does not mean that whatever is an object of knowledge is a permanent phenomenon because, for example, a pot is an object of knowledge but not permanent. For this reason, the subject of this debate is stated in English without an indefinite article as simply "object of knowledge", rather than as "an object of knowledge", in order to avoid the fault of implying that any and all objects of knowledge are permanent phenomena or of implying that only one object of knowledge is a permanent phenomenon. However, as mentioned earlier (pp. 85-88, 245-246), this translation technique is not always used. This is a problem of the English translation that does not exist in the Tibetan original, the indefiniteness of which causes its own problems as will be seen later. The text continues:

> If someone were to say that the reason [of the basic consequence, i.e., that object of knowledge is one of the two, level or non-level] is not established, [then the Proponent of Sūtra would become Challenger and respond to him,] "It follows that the subject, object of knowledge, is one of the two, level or non-level, because of being non-level."
>
> If he says that the reason [that object of knowledge is non-level] is not established, [then the Sūtra School Challenger responds,] "It follows that the subject, object of knowledge, is non-level because of not being level."
>
> If someone were to accept the basic consequence [that object of knowledge is a shape, the Sūtra School Challenger would respond to him,] "It follows that the subject, object of knowledge, is not a shape because of being a permanent phenomenon."

The difference between the two principals of the debate A.11, (1) either of the two, level or non-level, and (2) shape, is described as "three possibilities without their being anything which is neither" (*gnyis ka ma yin pa med pa'i mu gsum*). This is not the usual sort of three possibilities; nevertheless, such a situation is not that infrequent. (See pp. 142-153.)

1   There is a common locus of these two as in the case of the shape of an even surface. The shape of an even surface is one of the two, level or non-level, because of being level; and it is a shape because of being suitable to be shown as a shape.

2   It seems there is a uni-directional pervasion between these two, because whatever is a shape is necessarily one of the two, level or non-level.[1] The second possibility is

---

[1] This pervasion cannot be asserted with all confidence because it is conceivable that it is not the case that whatever is a shape is necessarily

something which is one but not the other. For instance, object of knowledge is one of the two, level or non-level, but it is not a shape.

3   A third possibility, something which is neither, cannot be posited. The two, level and non-level, include all phenomena. Further, non-existents are included within these two as non-level because of not being level. Thus, there is no existent or non-existent that can qualify as something which is neither level nor non-level.

Even though there are not three things to point at as the "possibilities" in this comparison, one still must say that there are three possibilities. Clearly the two principals are neither mutually exclusive nor mutually inclusive, and since there are not four points of comparison and difference, there are not four possibilities between them. Thus, there are three possibilities between them. The difference here is that because one of the two principals is an all inclusive dichotomy one cannot find anything as a possibility which is neither.

This problem of not being able to find something which is neither would not have arisen if the principals of the debate had been stated as the two: (1) either of the two, level or non-level *form*, and (2) shape. The hypothetical Challenger's original reasoning which gave rise to debate A.11 fails because he stated merely "either of the two, level or non-

---

one of the two, level or non-level. The possible counterexample is shape itself which is certainly a shape, but, in the opinion of Kensur Yeshay Tupden, whether it is level or non-level is indeterminate. Consistent with this view, he also said that one could say that color is a color but not that it is a primary color or a secondary color. To return to the case at hand, if whatever is a shape is not necessarily one of the two, level or non-level, these two principals would compare in this way:

1   The shape of an even surface is both a shape and one of the two, level or non-level.
2   Shape itself is a shape but neither of the two, level or non-level.
3   Object of knowledge is one of the two, level or non-level (that is, it is non-level), but is not a shape.

level", rather than specifying "level or non-level forms". He did not accurately reflect the text's position which was stated in the second section of the presentation of colors and so forth where the author specified the seventh and eighth types of shapes as "level and non-level *forms*". (See p. 249.)

If the two principals had been so specified, then there would be three possibilities between them including something which is neither one nor the other:

1   Something which is both (1) a level or non-level form and (2) a shape is again the shape of an even surface.
2   Whatever is a shape is necessarily either of the two, a level or non-level form, but whatever is either of the two, a level or non-level form, is not necessarily a shape. For instance, a color is one of the two—a level or non-level form—because of being a non-level form, but it is not a shape. This is, of course, also true for sounds, odors, tastes, and tangible objects.
3   In this case, any non-form—a consciousness, a person, a permanent phenomenon, and so forth—is neither a level nor non-level form and also not a shape.

In this second case it is possible to posit something which is neither because the two, level and non-level forms, dominate over all forms but do not include other phenomena. They are not a dichotomy which together exhaust all phenomena.

If the two principals of the debate were stated as the two: (1) either of the two, level or non-level *shape*, and (2) shape, they would be mutually inclusive. Every shape (with the possible exception of shape itself) is either a level or non-level shape, and whatever is either of the two, a level or non-level shape, is necessarily a shape. In this way the two, level and non-level shapes, refers to all shapes but not to other phenomena.

This fact points out a problem with the way that shapes are divided in the presentation of the author's own system of colors and so forth. Since the text specifies the seventh and eighth types of shape as "level and non-level *forms*", all non-forms are excluded but not all non-shapes are excluded. As above in the second reckoning of possibilities, whatever is either of the two, a level or non-level form, is not necessarily a shape. For instance, a color, an odor, a taste, or a tangible object is a non-level form but not a shape. Thus, the debate indicated by the hypothetical Challenger in A.11 could have been effective, if he had stated his objection in accordance with what the text says. He could have used the following line of reasoning to defeat the author's stated position: "It [absurdly] follows that the subject, a sweet taste, is a shape because of being one of the eight types of shape. It follows that a sweet taste is one of the eight types of shape because of being a non-level form; because of not being a level form."

Clearly it is not suitable to fail to specify level and non-level as forms, and the best solution would be to specify them as shapes. In this way, indeed, all shapes are included among just the last two of the eight types, but the problem of including non-shapes within the division of shapes would be avoided. In the Collected Topics tradition, there are precedents for divisions which include all the phenomena of the type being divided into one or two, but not all, of its divisions. However, there can be no case in which phenomena other than what is being divided—here non-shapes—may be included by any of the divisions.

REMARKS

One important pedagogical technique employed in the presentation of colors and so forth—and more generally in the whole of the monastic educational system—is that of briefly previewing topics that are later studied in great detail. In the first debate, the Tutor Jam-ba-gya-tso introduces in a general way the topic of oneness (*gcig, ekatva*) and difference (*tha dad, nānātva*) by justifying the color of a white religious conch as white by reason of its being "one with the color of a white religious conch". In the second debate, he broaches the subject of isolates (*ldog pa*) in saying that the color of the

Buddha Amitāyus is the isolate of the color of the Buddha Amitāyus and that whatever is an established base is necessarily its own isolate. In debate A.4, the Tutor first mentions the topics of generalities (*spyi, sāmānya*) and instances (*bye brag, visheṣha*) in noting that the color of refined gold is an instance of color. Also in debate A.4, the author touches on the topic of whether or not a phenomenon is an exemplifier of itself (as opposed to whether or not a phenomenon is one with itself, which all existents certainly are) in pointing out that the color of refined gold is the color of refined gold.

In each of these cases the author is merely touching on issues that will be taken up in detail later in "The Introductory Path of Reasoning". He is suggesting these topics in the first chapter so that later when they are presented the students will already have a vague notion of the subject-matter. Incorporating this previewing technique in the text supports the system of the oral tradition. Students at all levels receive instruction on topics and texts from qualified teachers who have previously studied and debated the subjects. Thus, through early on raising an issue in the text, the author provides the teacher with an opportunity to discuss these topics in a general way prior to the detailed study.

More manifestly, the presentation of colors and so forth has the purpose of instructing students on the nature of forms. By enumerating the five external sources in detail, the tradition imparts to students a sense of the finite number of types of existents. Also, teachers issue to novices the challenge to analyze well the presentation of material phenomena to find whether or not it breaks down at some point, thereby encouraging analysis. Consequently, this chapter gives the student a ground of reference. Whatever form he meets with, no matter how new or unique, may be understood.

Beginning debaters memorize the definitions, divisions, and illustrations of forms to prepare for debate and then apply their knowledge rigorously to test or confirm the assertions. This is accomplished not merely by rote recitation but by detailed investigations of the assertions and their implications. Upon contact with a form one can judge where it might be included in this system. To what is the eye consciousness paying attention? Is the sound that one is hearing conjoined with consciousness or not? By analyzing forms in this way students gain a grasp of the whole of external matter, decreasing the sense of discouragement that might arise when faced with the awesome task of investigating all that exists and increasing their confidence that the task can be accomplished.

9 Established Bases

INTRODUCTION

The single most important chapter in the Collected Topics texts is "Established Bases", the essential introductory description of ontology in the system of the Proponents of Sūtra Following Reasoning. All of the information on forms that has come before in "Colors—White, Red, and So Forth" could have been included in the discussion of established bases (*gzhi grub*, **vastu-siddha*). Moreover, this chapter serves as an important guide to all the chapters that follow. Without a thorough familiarity with the topics presented in this chapter, one cannot hope to understand the Collected Topics or Buddhist reasoning.

The broadest possible category, including all existents and non-existents as well, is that of the selfless (*bdag med*, *nairātmya*). All Buddhist tenet systems except perhaps for that of the Proponents of a Person (*gang zag yod par smra ba*, *pudgala-vādin*) assert selflessness as the main principle of their philosophies. What is selfless is empty of or lacks a certain type of self (*bdag*, *ātman*). A fundamental assertion in

Buddhism is that only through understanding selflessness, or emptiness (*stong pa nyid, shūnyatā*), can one gain liberation and thereby be relieved of powerless rebirth into the suffering of cyclic existence. The nature of selflessness is variously identified in the different Buddhist systems, but all agree that: "Phenomena are selfless in the sense that they are empty of being a permanent, partless, independent self or of being the object of use of such a self."[1] The higher philosophical schools describe some forms of selflessness that are more subtle, more difficult to pierce, than those asserted in the lower schools. Still, in each case the assertion of a lack of self is not a theory of nihilism, that phenomena do not exist at all, but an identification that phenomena lack certain qualities that they are incorrectly assumed to have. It is precisely these misapprehended, non-existent qualities that constitute the self the Buddhists deny in the theory of selflessness.

In the Great Vehicle schools, selflessness is divided into two types, the selflessness of persons (*gang zag gi bdag med, pudgala-nairātmya*) and the selflessness of phenomena (*chos kyi bdag med, dharma-nairātmya*). In all systems, the selflessness of persons is further divided into coarse (*rags pa, sthūla*) and subtle (*phra ba, sūkṣma*) varieties. In the two Lesser Vehicle systems, the Great Exposition School and the Sūtra School, the coarse selflessness of persons is a person's lack of being a permanent, partless, independent self (*rtag gcig rang dbang can bdag gis stong pa*) and the subtle selflessness of persons is the lack of being a substantially existent self in the sense of being self-sufficient (*rang rkya thub pa'i rdzas yod bdag gis stong pa*).[2] The subtler emptiness is more difficult to get at, more profound, and only by understanding persons as lacking the subtle self does one gain liberation. The Lesser Vehicle systems "both present an emptiness that must be understood in order to reach the goal, and in both systems this emptiness is the non-substantiality of persons. Through

---

[1] Sopa and Hopkins, *Practice and Theory of Tibetan Buddhism*, p. 68.
[2] Tsong-ka-pa, *Tantra in Tibet*, p. 180.

realizing and becoming accustomed to this insubstantiality, the afflictions and, thereby, all sufferings are said to be destroyed."[1]

The two Lesser Vehicle systems do not assert a selflessness of phenomena because they propound a view that external phenomena truly exist. Still, based on their assertion of persons as empty of being substantially existent, they assert that phenomena other than persons are empty of being objects of use of such a self. Therefore, it may be said that even for the Proponents of Sūtra all phenomena are selfless. Moreover, not only are all existents selfless, but also all non-existents are selfless, for they are neither substantially existent persons nor objects of use of such a person. Through understanding merely that they do not exist, one can understand that they lack any certain type of existence. However, the realization of the non-substantial establishment of a non-existent is not considered a realization, as the base does not exist at all. Still, the broadest possible category, the selfless, may be divided into the existent (*yod pa, sat*) and the non-existent (*med pa, asat*).

ESTABLISHED BASES

In order to understand selflessness, it is necessary to understand the phenomena that are the bases of selflessness. Therefore, in the beginning, students are taught what exists and how one can know those existents. The material presented in the chapter on established bases forms the essential bedrock on which one can build understanding.

Established base is mutually inclusive with object of knowledge, existent, phenomenon, object of comprehension, object, object of comprehension of an omniscient consciousness, and hidden phenomenon. Also, established base is mutually inclusive with its own definition as well as with the definitions of the phenomena mutually inclusive with it. Table IV gives this list:

---

[1] *Ibid.*, p. 175.

Table IV: Established Base and the Phenomena Mutually Inclusive With It

Definienda	Definitions
1 established base (*gzhi grub, *vastu-siddha*)	established by a valid cognizer (*tshad mas grub pa*)
2 object of knowledge (*shes bya, jñeya*)	suitable as an object of an awareness (*blo'i yul du bya rung ba*)
3 existent (*yod pa, sat*)	observed by a valid cognizer (*tshad mas dmigs pa*)
4 phenomenon (*chos, dharma*)	that which holds its own entity (*rang gi ngo bo 'dzin pa*)
5 object of comprehension (*gzhal bya, prameya*)	object realized by a valid cognizer (*tshad mas rtogs par bya ba*)
6 object (*yul, viṣhaya*)	object known by an awareness (*blos rig par bya ba*)
7 object of comprehension of an omniscient consciousness (*rnam mkhyen gyi gzhal bya, sarvākārā-jñāna-prameya*)	object realized by an omniscient consciousness (*rnam mkhyen gyis rtogs par bya ba*)
8 hidden phenomenon (*lkog gyur, parokṣha*)	object realized in a hidden manner by a thought consciousness apprehending it (*rang 'dzin rtog pas lkog tu gyur pa'i tshul gyis rtogs par bya ba*)

An established base is *established by a valid cognizer*. Valid cognizers are correct, certifying consciousnesses that incontrovertibly realize their objects. These are either direct perceivers (*mngon sum, pratyakṣha*), consciousnesses free from conceptuality which unmistakenly know their objects without depending on internal images, or inferential cognizers (*rjes dpag, anumāna*), conceptual consciousnesses which correctly realize their objects by way of the appearance of internal mental images. Whatever exists is certified as existing by a valid cognizer, and whatever is the object of comprehension of a valid cognizer is necessarily an existent.

Established bases are *objects of knowledge*; they are suitable as objects of awarenesses. Awareness (*blo, buddhi*) is mutually inclusive with consciousness (*shes pa, jñāna*) and knower (*rig pa, saṃvedana*). Existents are suitable to be known by awarenesses, and non-existents are not. It is not possible to *know* something that does not exist. Objects of knowledge are continually known by some awareness. "Without even considering the penetrating clairvoyances of Buddhas and yogis, the various hungry ghosts and unusual types of beings which exist everywhere insure that even particles in the centers of huge rocks are cognized by some being."[1] Established bases are constantly observed, realized, and known by awarenesses, be they consciousnesses of ordinary beings or consciousnesses of omniscient Buddhas.

Established bases are *phenomena*, for they hold or bear their own entities (*ngo bo, vastu*). This does not mean that phenomena are self-arisen without depending on any causes or conditions, but that each phenomenon is the bearer of its own entity; it is one with itself and distinct from all else. Also, though some phenomena may change, they do not radically transform from moment to moment. A table does not become an elephant, and then the next moment become a consciousness. Rather, phenomena hold their own entities and remain of a similar type for some time.

All established bases are *hidden phenomena*, objects realized in a hidden manner by the thought consciousnesses (*rtog pa, kalpanā*) apprehending them. Thought must realize its object in a hidden manner by taking cognizance of an

---

[1] Jeffrey Hopkins, *Meditation on Emptiness*, p. 215.

internal appearing object. Objects are hidden for a thought consciousness because it cannot apprehend them directly. Indeed, even something suitable as an appearing object of direct perception (*mngon sum gyi snang yul*) such as a patch of blue cannot be known directly by a thought consciousness, but must be known by means of a mental image. Thus, all existents are hidden phenomena in the sense that they are objects of thought consciousnesses.

Established bases are *objects*, objects known by awarenesses. One division of objects is into objects and object-possessors or subjects (*yul can, viṣhayin*). However, even though subjects, such as consciousnesses, are themselves knowers of objects, they too are objects and suitable to be known by awarenesses. This does not imply that all consciousnesses are self-knowing, conscious of themselves, but that all consciousnesses are known by some awareness, by some valid cognizer. Subjects, as existents, are objects as well.

Many divisions of established bases and the phenomena mutually inclusive with it are discussed in the Collected Topics tradition, but the chief of these is the exhaustive division of established bases into permanent phenomena (*rtag pa, nitya*) and functioning things (*dngos po, bhāva*). Functioning things or, simply, things are impermanent phenomena which are produced, abide, and disintegrate moment by moment. On the other hand, permanent phenomena in this system are not necessarily eternal but are those existents which are not momentary in the sense that they do not disintegrate moment by moment.

Functioning Things

A thing is defined as:

> that which is able to perform a function (*don byed nus pa, artha-kriyā-shakti* or *artha-kriyā-sāmarthya*).

The main function or the main object produced by a functioning thing is an effect which is the substantial continuum of that functioning thing itself in the next moment. Thus, functioning things principally perform the function of producing effects. Only such things, impermanent phenomena, are produced by their causes and conditions, abide for a single moment, and disintegrate only to be re-produced in the next moment. The main or substantial cause (*nyer len gyi rgyu, upādāna-karaṇa*) of the table of this moment is the table of the former moment which has produced a type similar to but not the same as itself. Reflecting this nature of functioning things, the phenomena mutually inclusive with it include cause, effect, created phenomenon, momentary phenomenon, and so forth. Table V shows functioning thing and the phenomena mutually inclusive with it:

Table V: Functioning Thing and the Phenomena Mutually Inclusive With It

Definienda	*Definitions*
1 functioning thing (*dngos po, bhāva*)	that which is able to perform a function (*don byed nus pa, artha-kriyā-shakti*)
2 impermanent phenomenon (*mi rtag pa, anitya*)	momentary phenomenon (*skad cig ma, kshaṇika*)
3 product (*byas pa, kṛta*)	created phenomenon (*skyes pa, utpanna*)
4 composed phenomenon (*'dus byas, saṃskṛta*)	disintegrating phenomenon (*'jig pa, vināsha*)
5 cause (*rgyu, hetu* or *kāraṇa*)	producer (*skyed byed, janaka*)
6 effect (*'bras bu, phala*)	object produced (*bskyed bya, janya*)

7 ultimate truth (*don dam bden pa, paramārtha-satya*)	phenomenon which is ultimately able to perform a function (*don dam par don byed nus pa'i chos*)
8 specifically characterized phenomenon (*rang mtshan, svalakṣhaṇa*)	a phenomenon which is established by way of its own character without being merely imputed by a term or thought consciousness (*sgra rtog gis btags tsam ma yin par rang gi mtshan nyid kyis grub pa'i chos*)
9 manifest phenomenon (*mngon gyur, abhimukhī*)	object explicitly realized by a direct valid cognizer (*mngon sum gyi tshad mas dngos su rtogs par bya ba*)

Things are *phenomena which are able to perform a function.* An example is a pot which is defined as:

a bulbous flat-based phenomenon able to perform the function of holding water (*lto ldir zhabs zhum chu skyor gyi don byed nus pa*).

According to this definition, a pot has the nature of being a bulbous flat-based thing. And, in addition to performing the function of producing a pot which is its own continuation of the next moment, a pot is able to perform the function of holding water. Functioning things are often defined, at least in part, in terms of their functions. Fire, for instance, is defined as:

that which is hot and burning.

Its nature is heat, and its function is to burn. Only functioning things, impermanent phenomena, are active entities which produce effects and perform functions.

That which performs a function necessarily undergoes change and is an impermanent phenomenon. This is so because, for instance, the pot of a former moment which produced the pot of the present moment must no longer exist, for a cause and its effect cannot exist simultaneously. Similarly, the pot of the present moment will no longer exist when it has produced the pot of the next moment. Thus, a pot performs one function in one moment, and the pot which is its effect performs another function in another moment.

Functioning things are *impermanent*, momentary phenomena. Impermanent phenomena are defined as momentary because they disintegrate moment by moment. This doctrine of subtle impermanence (*phra ba'i mi rtag pa, *sūkṣhma-anitya*) is to be distinguished from the doctrine of coarse impermanence (*rags pa'i mi rtag pa, *sthūla-anitya*). "All Buddhist schools agree that coarse impermanence is the production of a thing such as a table, its lasting for a period of time, and finally its disintegration such as its being consumed by fire."[1] All products openly display their nature of coarse impermanence. Tables, chairs, and even great mountain systems are produced in dependence upon certain causes and conditions, abide for some time, and inevitably decline into non-functionality. A human life comes into existence in dependence upon certain causes and conditions. One enjoys this life due to those causes, and when the power of the causes which impelled this life is exhausted, this life too will end. Thus, death is an example of coarse impermanence.

Moreover, all of the Buddhist tenet systems assert a subtle impermanence which is a momentary disintegration of products. A moment is identified as one sixtieth part of the time that it takes for a healthy person to snap the fingers or blink the eyes.[2] Functioning things are produced, abide, and disintegrate sixty times within the snapping of the fingers.

---

[1] Sopa and Hopkins, *Practice and Theory of Tibetan Buddhism*, p. 77.

[2] Kensur Ngawang Lekden, oral commentary (reported by Jeffrey Hopkins). According to Kensur Lekden, in the Consequence School the span of a moment is identified as one three hundred sixtieth part of the time it takes for a healthy person to snap the fingers or blink the eyes, not one sixtieth as it is in the Sūtra School system.

Although subtle impermanence does appear to ordinary beings, it is not ascertained except by advanced practitioners who are able to realize a single moment.

The Proponents of Sūtra assert that production alone is all that is required for momentary disintegration. However, in the Great Exposition School production, abiding, aging, and disintegration are four separate agents that act on the impermanent phenomena themselves. Because these four exist simultaneously with the impermanent phenomena but perform their functions serially, the Proponents of the Great Exposition identify momentariness as the period of these four instants.[1]

All other Buddhist systems, including the Sūtra School, assert that it is the impermanent phenomenon itself that is produced, abides, ages, and disintegrates. It requires no outside agents to cause aging and disintegration. The Proponents of Sūtra "hold that production is the new arising of what did not exist before, abiding is the remaining of a type similar to what preceded it, aging is the non-similarity in entity of a later moment and a former moment, and disintegration is a product's not remaining a second moment after its present."[2] Products last for only a moment and cannot last for a second moment. Their production alone is sufficient for their disintegration. The very nature, the defining characteristic, of impermanent phenomena is their momentariness.

Functioning things are *products* because they are made or created in dependence upon causes and conditions. They do not exist without being produced, and what is produced is impermanent. They are *composed phenomena* because they are composed after the aggregation of their causes. Once created, they abide for a moment and inevitably disintegrate, for they are not able to abide for a second moment.

As phenomena arisen in dependence upon their causes and conditions, functioning things are *effects*. Effects are

---

[1] Paraphrased from Jeffrey Hopkins, *Meditation on Emptiness*, p. 350.
[2] Jeffrey Hopkins, *Meditation on Emptiness*, p. 350.

objects produced from causes or objects helped (*phan gdags bya*) by causes. Functioning things are also *causes,* producers or helpers (*phan 'dogs byed*) of effects. Whatever is an impermanent phenomenon is necessarily both a cause and an effect. This does not imply that functioning things continue in a similar type or necessarily produce a phenomenon of similar type. For example, a seed produces a sprout,a different type of phenomenon which is unlike the seed. Also, the last moment of a flame causes only smoke, an effect of a different type, and does not continue its own substantial entity of fire. Still, all functioning things are effects of their causes that preceded them and are causes of their effects that arise subsequent to them.

Causes are of two types, substantial causes (*nyer len, upādāna-kāraṇa*) and cooperative conditions (*lhan cig byed rkyen, sahakāri-pratyaya*). A substantial cause is a cause which produces an effect which is a continuation of its own substantial entity, and a cooperative condition produces an effect which is not a continuation of its own substantial entity. Whatever is an effect necessarily has both a substantial cause and a cooperative condition. For instance, the substantial cause of a clay pot is the mud which serves as a cause for that pot, and a cooperative condition of a pot is a person who molds the clay and so forth. In the case of a person's present mind, the substantial cause is the mind of the immediately preceding life and the cooperative conditions include one's mother and father and the karmic action of ethics, performed in a former life, which impels this life.

The study of causes and effects is essential to the study of Buddhism. Buddha identified the causes of suffering and of liberation. Thus, Buddha is revered as one who taught causes and effects. The fifth chapter of "The Introductory Path of Reasoning" is an introductory presentation of causes and effects in which the topics of substantial causes and cooperative conditions are discussed in greater detail. The topic of causes and effects is introduced here only as an aid to understanding the nature of impermanent phenomena.

Functioning things are *ultimate truths*, phenomena which are ultimately able to perform functions. In all the Buddhist systems, existents are divided into ultimate truths and conventional truths. Ultimate truths are so called because of being truths for an undeceived ultimate awareness. An ultimate awareness (*blo don dam pa*) is a direct perceiver, a consciousness free from conceptuality and non-mistaken with respect to what appears to it—an ultimate truth. Ultimate truths are phenomena which appear just as they exist.

What is identified as ultimate truth varies from system to system, and only the Proponents of Sūtra Following Reasoning present ultimate truth as mutually inclusive with impermanent phenomenon. This interpretation of the system of the Proponents of Sūtra Following Reasoning and the issues surrounding their assertions on the two truths will be taken up below in greater detail.

Functioning things are *specifically characterized phenomena*, phenomena established by way of their own characters (*rang gi mtshan nyid kyis grub pa, svalakshana-siddhi*) without being merely imputed by terms or thought consciousnesses. They are truly established (*bden par grub pa, satya-siddha*) objects, for they exist from their own side (*rang ngos nas grub pa, *svarūpa-siddhi*) without depending on mental or verbal imputation. Rather, functioning things are capable of being explicitly known by direct perceivers. The emphasis is on the consciousnesses which know specifically characterized phenomena. Functioning things are specifically characterized because of being phenomena which appear together with all of their specific characteristics of impermanence and so forth. As opposed to permanent phenomena which are generally characterized phenomena known only in a general way by a thought consciousness, specifically characterized phenomena are known nakedly and directly as specific phenomena. This topic of specifically and generally characterized phenomena will be discussed in greater detail below.

Finally, functioning things are *manifest phenomena*, objects explicitly realized by direct valid cognizers. Again, the phenomena are defined in terms of the consciousnesses which realize them. The emphasis on consciousnesses illustrates the nature of this system of Buddhist logic as inseparable from its epistemology. Functioning things—forms, consciousnesses, and so forth—are manifest phenomena, explicitly realized by direct valid cognizers.

Permanent Phenomena

Other than functioning things, all remaining established bases are permanent phenomena. A permanent phenomenon is defined as:

> a common locus of a phenomenon and the non-momentary (*chos dang skad cig ma ma yin pa'i gzhi mthun pa*).

That is, permanent phenomena are both phenomena and non-momentary. The portion of the definition qualifying permanent phenomena as *phenomena* serves to include established bases and exclude non-existents. The portion of the definition which qualifies permanent phenomena as *non-momentary* excludes impermanent phenomena and includes permanent phenomena and non-existents because, indeed, non-existents are not momentary. The two portions of the definition together exclude non-existents and impermanent phenomena and include only permanent phenomena.

An example of a permanent phenomenon is uncomposed space (*'dus ma byas kyi nam mkha'*, *asaṃskṛta-akasha*), which is a mere absence of obstructive contact. "Space is all pervading because there is an absence of obstructive contact everywhere, even where solid objects exist, for without an absence of obstructive contact an obstructive object could not be there in the first place."[1] Such space is not produced from causes and conditions. Uncomposed space is to be dis-

---

[1] *Ibid.*, p. 217.

tinguished from composed space which results from removing objects to allow passage and so forth.

Another example of a permanent phenomenon is non-cow which refers to all non-existents as well as to all existents other than cows. Non-cow is a permanent phenomenon because of being a common locus of a phenomenon and the non-momentary. This is so because it both is an existent and, since it includes permanent phenomena such as uncomposed space, is not a momentary phenomenon. Furthermore, as is the case with all permanent phenomena, non-cow can only appear to a thought consciousness. It is an existent which must be brought to mind by means of an internal mental image and cannot be realized by a direct valid cognizer. Although it is true that many non-cows such as pots, pillars, horses, and so forth can be realized by direct valid cognizers, it is not the case that all non-cows or non-cow itself can be known by direct valid cognizers. Rather, non-cow depends on imputation by a thought consciousness or by the term "non-cow" in order to be understood.

In the system of the Proponents of Sūtra the most important permanent phenomenon is the subtle selflessness of the person, "a person's emptiness of being substantially existent or self-sufficient (able to exist by itself)".[1] Since selflessness itself, as a permanent phenomenon, cannot be directly realized, the Proponents of Sūtra say that the yogi realizing selflessness cognizes the mind and body as not qualified with such a substantially existent self. "Thus, it is products, the mental and physical aggregates, which are directly cognized, and thereby the emptiness of the personal self is implicitly realized. This fact greatly distinguishes the Sautrāntikas from the Mahāyāna schools which assert direct cognition of emptiness itself."[2]

In all of the Buddhist systems except Proponents of the Great Exposition School, permanent is not taken to mean lasting eternally. Rather, as in the definition, "permanent"

---

[1] Sopa and Hopkins, *Practice and Theory of Tibetan Buddhism*, p. 104.
[2] *Ibid.*, p. 105.

refers to phenomena that are not momentary. Thus, whatever lasts for even a second moment without changing is a permanent phenomenon. Permanent phenomena are of two types, those which are stable in time (*dus brtan pa'i rtag pa*) and those which are occasional (*res 'ga' ba'i rtag pa*).[1] Indeed, some permanent phenomena such as established base and the phenomena mutually inclusive with it, non-cow, and selflessness in general are stable in time and do last forever. However, some permanent phenomena are not eternal, but are occasional. For instance, the uncomposed space inside a pot is a permanent phenomenon but is not eternal. "When the pot is destroyed, the space is no longer suitable to be designated. Also, the space inside a pot does not change moment by moment and thus cannot be called impermanent. It is an occasional permanence because it does not disintegrate momentarily as do all impermanent phenomena and does not exist forever."[2]

Similarly, specific cases of selflessness are permanent phenomena which are occasional. For example, the selflessness of Thomas Jefferson came into existence when he was born and went out of existence when he died. This does not imply that Jefferson's selflessness was created by the same causes which impelled his birth or by any causes at all. Rather, since selflessness is a mere absence of a certain type of self, it abides as a nature of the person, uncreated and non-disintegrating. Yet, when the person who is the basis of selflessness dies, the selflessness is no longer suitable to be designated and goes out of existence when its basis is destroyed. Although specific cases of selflessness are occasional permanents, selflessness itself is an eternal permanent, for there is no time when the selflessness of persons does not exist.

The phenomena mutually inclusive with permanent phenomenon closely parallel those of functioning thing. For instance, just as functioning thing is mutually inclusive with

---

[1] Lati Rinbochay, oral commentary.
[2] Sopa and Hopkins, *Practice and Theory of Tibetan Buddhism*, p. 95.

282 Debate in Tibetan Buddhism

product, so permanent phenomenon is mutually inclusive with non-produced phenomenon. It must be noted, however, that permanent phenomenon is not mutually inclusive with non-product. This is so because non-product includes not merely permanent phenomena but also non-existents. Although they are not phenomena, non-existents are non-products because of not being impermanent phenomena produced from causes and conditions. Rather, it must be said that permanent phenomenon is mutually inclusive with non-produced *phenomenon (ma byas pa'i chos, akṛta-dharma)*, the qualification "phenomenon" being added for the sake of eliminating non-existents.

Table VI lists permanent phenomenon and the phenomena mutually inclusive with it:

Table VI: Permanent Phenomenon and the Phenomena Mutually Inclusive With It

Definienda	Definitions
1 permanent phenomenon (*rtag pa, nitya*)	common locus of a phenomenon and the non-momentary (*chos dang skad cig ma ma yin pa'i gzhi mthun pa*)
2 non-produced phenomenon (*ma byas pa'i chos, akṛta-dharma*)	non-created phenomenon (*ma skyes pa'i chos*)
3 uncomposed phenomenon ('*dus ma byas kyi chos, asaṃskṛta-dharma*)	non-disintegrating phenomenon (*mi 'jig pa'i chos*)
4 conventional truth (*kun rdzob bden ba, samvṛti-satya*)	phenomenon which is ultimately unable to perform a function (*don dam par don byed mi nus pa'i chos*)

5 phenomenon which is a non-thing (*dngos med kyi chos, abhāva-dharma*)

phenomenon which is empty of the ability to perform a function (*don byed nus stong gi chos*)

6 generally characterized phenomenon (*spyi mtshan, sāmānya-lakṣhana*)

phenomenon which is merely imputed by a term or though consciousness and is not established as a specifically characterized phenomenon (*sgra rtog gis btags pa tsam yin gyi rang mtshan du ma grub pa'i chos*)

Permanent phenomena are *non-produced phenomena;* they are not created from causes and conditions. They are *uncaused phenomena,* not effects, and not disintegrating phenomena.

Permanent phenomena are *non-things,* for they lack the ability to perform a function. They do not serve as causes and cannot perform the function of producing effects. Rather, they are static and inactive. The Great Exposition School alone says that permanent phenomena are things, able to perform a function. This is so, they claim, "because, for instance, a space performs the function of allowing an object to be moved. [However,] the other systems of tenets say that the presence or absence of another obstructive object is what allows or does not allow an object to be moved, not space itself."[1] Still, all of the Buddhist systems of tenets agree that permanent phenomena are not momentary.

Permanent phenomena are *conventional truths,* ultimately unable to perform a function. Again, in the system of the Proponents of Sūtra Following Reasoning only functioning things—those phenomena which are able to perform a function—are ultimate truths, and permanent phenomena—unable to perform a function—are conventional truths. Permanent phenomena are not truths for an ultimate mind,

---

[1] Jeffrey Hopkins, *Meditation on Emptiness*, p. 219.

a direct perceiver which is not mistaken with regard to the object appearing to it. In the system of the Proponents of Sūtra permanent phenomena are realized by thought consciousnesses only (with the exception of a Buddha's omniscient consciousness). As such, they are conventional truths, truths for a conventional [mind] or truths for an obscured [mind] (*kun rdzob bden ba, samvṛti-satya*). Thought consciousnesses are called "obscured minds" because they are prevented from taking impermanent phenomena as their appearing objects. Being unable to perceive their objects directly, they must apprehend their objects by means of a permanent internal image.

Permanent phenomena are *generally characterized phenomena*, phenomena which are merely imputed by terms or thought consciousnesses and are not established as specifically characterized phenomena. Generally characterized phenomena are not established by way of their own character but must be imputed by a thought consciousness or by a term such as "non-cow". Therefore, they are mere imputations. This does not mean that they do not exist, but that they are not established from their own side.

SPECIFICALLY AND GENERALLY CHARACTERIZED PHENOMENA

In the topic of specifically and generally characterized phenomena, one finds the essence of the presentation of permanent and impermanent phenomena and the two truths according to the Proponents of Sūtra Following Reasoning. The distinction between generally and specifically characterized phenomena turns on whether or not the phenomena must be understood by a thought consciousness. Generally characterized phenomena, all permanent phenomena, must be gotten at by means of a thought consciousness. On the other hand, specifically characterized phenomena, all impermanent phenomena, need not be cognized by a thought consciousness. As hidden phenomena—that is to say, as existents—specifically characterized phenomena *may* be understood by thought consciousnesses, but since they are also manifest phenomena, they may be realized by direct perceivers.

Since generally characterized phenomena and specifically characterized phenomena may be distinguished in this way as those phenomena which must be realized by thought consciousnesses and those which may be realized by direct perceivers, the presentation of these phenomena depends on the description of the differences between thought consciousnesses and direct perceivers. In this regard, the main avenue to understanding the differences between these two types of awarenesses is the account of the four main types of objects of consciousnesses:

1   object of engagement (*'jug yul, *pravṛtti-viṣhaya*)
2   determined object (*zhen yul, *adhyavasāya-viṣhaya*)
3   appearing object (*snang yul, *pratibhāsa-viṣhaya*)
4   apprehended object (*bzung yul, grāhya-viṣhaya*).[1]

The object of engagement or determined object of a consciousness is that object that it is actually getting at or understanding. "However, there is the qualification that the term 'determined object' is used only for conceptual consciousnesses, whereas 'object of engagement' is used for both conceptual and non-conceptual consciousnesses."[2] This difference in usage arises due to the fact that only thought consciousnesses are determinative knowers (*zhen rig, *adhyavasāya-saṃvedana*) because they determine, "This is such and such. That is such and such."[3] Thus, for both a direct perceiver apprehending blue and a thought consciousness conceiving blue the object of engagement is blue, and for such a thought consciousness it also may be said that blue is its determined object.

---

[1] Lati Rinbochay, *Mind in Tibetan Buddhism*, p. 28. For sources of Sanskrit given in *Mind in Tibetan Buddhism* see p. 163, note 24.
[2] *Ibid.*, pp. 28-29.
[3] *Ibid.*, p. 50.

The appearing object or apprehended object is the object that is actually appearing to the consciousness but is not necessarily what the consciousness is understanding.

> Since the actual object that appears to direct perception is what it realizes, its appearing object, apprehended object, and object of engagement are all the same—in the example of an eye consciousness apprehending blue, all three are blue. However, for a conceptual consciousness, although the object of engagement and determined object are the actual object the consciousness is understanding—i.e., blue for a thought consciousness apprehending blue—the appearing object and apprehended object are just an [internal mental] image of blue.[1]

By distinguishing the *appearing objects* of direct perceivers and thought consciousnesses one is led to understand the distinction between specifically characterized phenomena and generally characterized phenomena and thereby between ultimate truths and conventional truths in the system of the Proponents of Sūtra Following Reasoning. In the seventh debate in the presentation of established bases, permanent phenomena is identified as mutually inclusive with the appearing object of a thought consciousness (*rtog pa'i snang yul*) and functioning thing is identified as mutually inclusive with the appearing object of a direct perceiver (*mngon sum gyi snang yul*). Reflecting the importance of these alliances, in this system specifically characterized phenomena are ultimate truths, truths for an ultimate awareness (*blo don dam pa*), and generally characterized phenomena are conventional truths, truths for a conventional awareness (*blo kun rdzob pa*). Thus, here phenomena are called "ultimate" or "conventional" in dependence on the awarenesses that take them as their appearing objects.

This fact points up a central emphasis of the Buddhist systems—clear preference is given to direct perceivers over

---

[1] *Ibid.*, p. 29.

thought consciousnesses. (See pp. 13-21.) Although thought consciousnesses, specifically inferential cognizers, are an essential feature of the path leading to liberation, they are not able to carry one to the final attainment and eventually must be transcended. The reason for this is the nature of thought as a mistaken consciousness (*'khrul shes, bhrānti-jñāna*).

Thought Consciousnesses

Every thought consciousness (*rtog pa, kalpanā*) is mistaken with respect to its appearing object—an internal mental image which is a meaning-generality (*don spyi, artha-sāmānya*). A meaning-generality, necessarily a permanent phenomenon, is an image which, although it appears to be the actual object being understood, merely serves as an elimination of what is not that object. For instance, the thought consciousness conceiving of a table understands its object indirectly by means of a representative image, a meaning-generality of a table. A meaning-generality of a table is not an actual table, but is a mere mental image of a table which is an elimination of non-table.

Thus, thought proceeds by an essentially negative process. What appears to the thought consciousness apprehending a table is the elimination of non-table. That is, all that is not a table is eliminated, and thought understands table in a general way. In this way thought understands the generality of table rather than any particular instance. Therefore, permanent phenomena are called generally characterized phenomena because their characters are known only in a general way by an imputing thought consciousness, and since they depend on such imputation, they are not established from their own side. There is no way to realize a permanent or generally characterized phenomenon by way of its own specific entity.

One might wonder why, if these mental images are dependent upon having seen external phenomena of that type, are meaning-generalities permanent phenomena rather than products. "Each person's images or concepts do indeed come into existence in dependence on the person's having formed an image of such an object, but from the viewpoint of their being the exclusion of everything that is not that object, they are said to be permanent."[1]

The Collected Topics logicians present naming as an essentially arbitrary process. Whatever exists is suitable to be designated by any name. It is only by conditioning that we come to refer to these four-legged creatures with fur, wagging tails, and so forth as "dogs". One comes to learn the meaning of "dog" in dependence upon seeing a dog and being taught the name by one's mother and so forth. In this way a meaning-generality of dog, which may be an appearance of, perhaps, a golden retriever that serves as an elimination of all that is not a dog, comes into existence.

For instance, one sees a golden retriever and then later in another place the form of that animal is remembered clearly.[2] The image of the dog seen earlier appears to a conceptual consciousness and does not appear to a direct perceiver. That appearance of a golden retriever is a meaning-generality, not an actual dog. The meaning-generality cannot be an actual dog, for if it were, then when that golden retriever grew old and died the meaning-generality too would have to appear just as old and decrepit as the dog does. Such is not the case, for it is well known that the internal image of a youthful golden retriever can continue to appear clearly long after the actual external dog has grown old and died. Also, the conceptual or internal dog is not an actual dog because it would have to be able to perform the functions of a dog. Then it would be the case that wherever the thought of a dog existed, there would exist a dog. Or, if by thinking of gold one came to have actual gold, then no

---

[1] Jeffrey Hopkins, *Meditation on Emptiness*, p. 347.

[2] The source for this section on the process of thought is Den-dar-hla-ram-ba (*bstan dar lha ram pa*), *Beginnings of a Presentation of Generally and Specifically Characterized Phenomena* (*rang mtshan spyi mtshan gyi rnam gzhag rtsom 'phrol*), Collected Works of Bstan-dar Lha-ram of A-lag-sha, Vol. 1 (New Delhi: Lama Guru Deva, 1971).

one would be without gold. The meaning-generality of dog, although it appears to be a dog, is not an actual dog.

Therefore, a conceptual awareness is necessarily a mistaken consciousness (*'khrul shes, bhrānti-jñāna*), defined as:

> a knower which is mistaken with regard to its appearing object (*rang gi snang yul la 'khrul ba'i rig pa*),

because a meaning-generality of, for instance, a pot appears to a thought consciousness to be a pot although it is not.[1] Still, even though a thought consciousness is necessarily mistaken, it is not necessarily a wrong consciousness (*log shes, viparyaya-jñāna*), defined as:

> a knower which is mistaken with regard to its object of engagement (*rang gi 'jug yul la 'khrul ba'i rig pa*)

because a correct thought consciousness is able to realize validly and incontrovertibly its object of engagement, the actual object it is getting at or understanding.[2] That is, within the context of being mistaken with regard to its appearing object—a meaning-generality, a conceptual consciousness may be correct with regard to its object of engagement—the actual object it is cognizing. For instance, an inferential cognizer (*rjes dpag, anumāna*), necessarily a thought consciousness, realizing the impermanence of sound is mistaken with regard to its appearing object—a meaning-generality of impermanent sound which appears to be sound but is not. However, such a thought consciousness is not a *wrong* consciousness because it is not mistaken with regard to its object of engagement—the impermanence of sound—which it realizes correctly.

Thus, every thought consciousness is such that what appears to it and what it understands are different. This does not entail that thought is unreliable, but that it is only able to understand its object—impermanence, gold, pot, dog, and so forth—in an indirect manner, through the

---

[1] See Lati Rinbochay, *Mind in Tibetan Buddhism*, pp. 133ff.
[2] See Lati Rinbochay, *Mind in Tibetan Buddhism*, pp. 109-110.

appearance of an internal image. "Thought is a reliable way to ascertain objects."[1] As a sign of the reliability of thought, the Dignāga-Dharmakīrti schools of reasoning present inferential cognizers as one of the two types of valid cognizers (*tshad ma, pramāṇa*).

Direct Perceivers

The other type of valid cognizer is a direct perceiver (*mngon sum, pratyakṣha*), a consciousness able to realize specifically characterized phenomena. They are so called because they realize their objects *directly* without depending on the appearance of an internal image. The actual object appears to be a direct perceiver whereas a thought consciousness gets at its object only by means of an appearing meaning-generality. A direct perceiver is defined as:

> a non-mistaken knower that is free from conceptuality (*rtog pa dang bral zhing ma 'khrul ba'i rig pa*).[2]

The portion of the definition which specifies it as a *knower*—mutually inclusive with consciousness and awareness—serves to include all consciousnesses and exclude all else—forms, permanent phenomena, and so forth. The portion that specifies direct perceivers as *free from conceptuality* eliminates the possibility that there could be a direct perceiver that knows its object by way of an internal image rather than contacting its object directly.

Direct perceivers are non-mistaken (*ma 'khrul pa, abhrānta*) knowers, for they are not mistaken with regard to their appearing objects, specifically characterized phenomena which appear directly to the apprehending consciousness. Further, since the object of engagement of a direct perceiver is the same as its appearing object, it is not mistaken with regard to its object of engagement and thereby is not a wrong consciousness. The differences between the processes

---

[1] Lati Rinbochay, *Mind in Tibetan Buddhism*, p. 30.
[2] See Lati Rinbochay, *Mind in Tibetan Buddhism*, pp. 49ff.

of conception and direct perception may be illustrated in this way: Thought consciousnesses are limited to knowing their objects indirectly by the appearance of a representation of that object, like seeing an image reflected in a mirror. Direct perceivers, on the other hand, are not limited in this way, for their objects appear to them directly. Thus, direct perceivers are non-mistaken knowers.

Indeed, a specifically characterized phenomenon which is the appearing object of a direct perceiver appears to that consciousness just as it is. However, this does not mean that for the Proponents of Sūtra Following Reasoning the content of direct perception is wholly determined by the external object. Rather, the perception may also be influenced by the physical sense power or the consciousness of the one making the perception. For example, an eye consciousness which sees snow-covered mountains as blue, which sees a single moon as double, or which sees everything as red when one is embroiled in anger is a faulty perceiver due to subjective errors.

Such an eye consciousness, necessarily a non-conceptual consciousness (*rtog med kyi shes pa, nirvikalpaka-jñāna*), is nonetheless a *mistaken* consciousness because it is mistaken with respect to its appearing object and a *wrong* consciousness because it is mistaken with respect to its object of engagement. Since what appears to a non-conceptual consciousness is the same as what it is engaging or understanding, such consciousnesses which are mistaken with respect to both of these do not qualify as actual direct perceivers. Thus, in his *Compendium of Valid Cognition* (*pramāṇasamuchchaya*) Dignāga includes "dimness of sight" as one of the types of counterfeit direct perceivers (*mngon sum ltar snang, pratyakṣa-ābhāsa*) indicating all non-conceptual wrong consciousness as knowers which falsely appear to be direct perceivers but are not actually such.[1]

Still, since such wrong consciousnesses are not direct perceivers, they do not show that the content of actual direct

---

[1] See Lati Rinbochay, *Mind in Tibetan Buddhism*, pp. 72-73.

perception is not wholly determined by the object. In this regard, the Collected Topics logicians note that whereas a direct perceiver is necessarily a consciousness to which a specifically characterized phenomenon *appears* together with all of its uncommon characteristics, it does not necessarily *ascertain* those characteristics. For instance, a directly perceiving eye consciousness apprehending blue is a non-mistaken knower correctly ascertaining the color which appears to it, but it does not ascertain the subtle impermanence of that specifically characterized phenomenon which appears together with it. Thus, with respect to its appearing object, blue, it is a direct perceiver, but with respect to the subtle impermanence of blue it is an awareness to which an object appears but is not ascertained (*snang la ma nges pa, *aniyata-pratibhāsa*).[1] Such an eye consciousness is a non-mistaken non-conceptual knower of blue, but due to the fact that subtle impermanence is an object of engagement of a mental consciousness only it does not cognize all that appears to it. Thus, the content of direct perception is influenced by the perceiving consciousness.

Direct perceivers are of two types—sense direct perceivers (*dbang po'i mngon sum, indriya-pratyakṣa*) and mental direct perceivers (*yid kyi mngon sum, mānasa-pratyakṣa*). There are five types of sense direct perceivers corresponding to the five sense consciousnesses—eye, ear, nose, tongue, and body sense consciousnesses. Consciousnesses of all types are impermanent phenomena, and, in the case of directly perceiving consciousnesses, their explicit objects are also impermanent phenomena, objects which disintegrate moment by moment. Thus, some have raised the qualm that since consciousnesses last for only a moment and their objects too are momentary phenomena, how can a sense consciousness know any object? One Buddhist answer is: "What we experience as sense perception is a continuum of moments of consciousness apprehending a continuum of

---

[1] See Lati Rinbochay, *Mind in Tibetan Buddhism*, pp. 99-106.

moments of an object which is also disintegrating moment by moment."[1]

"Sense consciousnesses are also capable of comprehending their object's ability to perform a function; thus, an eye consciousness itself can perceive that fire has the ability to cook and burn."[2] Therefore, direct perceivers do not merely register sensory input, but are non-mistaken knowers which are capable of realizing their objects.

Although direct perceivers may induce conception, they themselves are totally non-conceptual. Such consciousnesses do not name or classify their objects, but experience them apart from *conceptually* determining types and so forth. Still, this does not mean that direct perceivers are not aware of their objects' qualities. "Sense consciousnesses can also be trained such that an eye consciousness can know not only that a person being seen is a man but also that that person is one's father."[3]

A sense consciousness would not *conceive* that its object is one's father, but it may induce a conceptual consciousness which affixes names, determines types, remembers associations, and so forth. In this way, people are drawn into conceptuality, quickly abandoning the richness of direct perception in favor of mental imagery and abstraction. Specifically characterized phenomena appear nakedly to direct perceivers; however, ordinary beings do not perceive them nakedly because (1) generally these objects maintain a continuum of similar type moment by moment and thereby appear to persist and (2) such beings are under the influence of predispositions for naming objects.

Mental direct perceivers are the second type of direct perceivers, and again these are of several types.[4] Included among these is mental direct perception in the continuums of ordinary beings. "The Ge-luk-ḃas assert that at the end of a continuum of sense direct perception of an object there is

---

[1] Lati Rinbochay, *Mind in Tibetan Buddhism*, p. 18.
[2] *Ibid.*
[3] *Ibid.*
[4] See Lati Rinbochay, *Mind in Tibetan Buddhism*, pp. 54-74.

generated one moment of mental direct perception; this in turn induces conceptual cognition of that object, naming it and so forth."[1] Such mental direct perceivers serve to link the knowledge of raw sense data to conceptual consciousnesses which notice, name, determine types, and so forth. Lasting only an instant, these mental direct perceivers are too ephemeral for an ordinary person to notice; however, they are ascertained by advanced practitioners who have more stable and insightful awarenesses.

The most important of direct perceivers is yogic direct perceivers (*rnal 'byor mngon sum, yogi-pratyakṣha*), a kind of mental direct perceiver which is a non-conceptual, direct realizer of such profound objects as subtle impermanence and selflessness or, more specifically, the mind and body qualified as selfless. Yogic direct perceivers do not occur in the continuums of ordinary beings but exist only in the continuums of Superiors (*'phags pa, ārya*)—those who have attained the path of seeing (*mthong lam, darshana-mārga*) in which the truth is realized directly.

Such yogic direct perceivers do not arise effortlessly but must be cultivated over a long period through engaging in extensive practice. The yogi first understands, for instance, subtle impermanence conceptually. Then through continued and sustained familiarization with that conceptual realization, he is able to bring the image appearing to that inferential cognizer—that is, a meaning-generality of subtle impermanence—into exceptionally clear focus. Having cultivated a conceptual understanding to the peak of its capacity, the yogi eventually passes beyond the need for a representative image of what is understood and develops a direct perception of the object. These yogic direct perceivers are the most exalted of all knowers; being able to realize the profound truths in a totally unmistaken manner, they are the actual antidote to ignorance, the source of all suffering in cyclic existence. The achievement of yogic direct perceivers is the goal of all Buddhist reasoning.

---

[1] Lati Rinbochay, *Mind in Tibetan Buddhism*, p. 18.

The Enumeration of Valid Cognizers

All established bases are divided exhaustively between the two, phenomena suitable to appear to direct perceivers and those which must appear to thought consciousnesses. The divisions as stated are mutually exclusive, for what must appear to a thought consciousness cannot appear to a direct perceiver and what is suitable to appear to a direct perceiver cannot be the *appearing* object of thought consciousnesses. This is not to say that what appears to direct perception cannot also be known by thought, for all phenomena are suitable to be known by thought. Both permanent and impermanent phenomena are hidden phenomena, one of the phenomena mutually inclusive with established bases, defined as:

> objects realized in a hidden manner by the thought consciousnesses apprehending them.

They are qualified as objects of thought, and they are hidden in the sense that they appear to the thought consciousnesses apprehending them only by way of an internal mental image which represents them. However, only impermanent phenomena are manifest phenomena as well in that they are also:

> objects explicitly realized by direct valid cognizers.

These are phenomena *suitable* to appear to direct perceivers. They are forms and so forth which are manifest for the five sense consciousnesses and mental direct perceivers. Still, manifest phenomena are hidden phenomena in the sense that they are objects realized in a hidden manner by the *thought consciousnesses* apprehending them. Thus, even though all phenomena are suitable to be realized by thought, phenomena may be divided without exception into those *suitable* to appear to direct perceivers and those which *must* appear to thought consciousnesses.

Specifically characterized phenomena are objects suitable to appear to direct perceivers, and generally characterized phenomena are objects which must appear to thought consciousnesses. These are the two types of objects of comprehension. Most Collected Topics texts begin the presentation of established bases with citation of a passage from the third chapter, on direct perceivers, of Dharmakīrti's *Commentary on (Dignāga's) "Compendium of Valid Cognition"* which says, "Because objects of comprehension are two, valid cognizers are two."[1] The intention of this passage is to establish the enumeration of two valid cognizers, direct valid cognizers and inferential valid cognizers, as definite in order to clear away the many Hindu assertions of fewer or more valid cognizers. In so doing, Dharmakīrti presents a quintessential instruction on Buddhist logic and epistemology. He proves conclusively that there are only two valid cognizers "by way of showing that more than two are unnecessary and less than two would not include them all".[2]

The Lo-śel-ling *Collected Topics* expresses the meaning of this passage in syllogistic form:

> With respect to the subject, valid cognizers, they are definitely enumerated as two, direct valid cognizers and inferential valid cognizers, because their objects of comprehension are definitely enumerated as two, manifest phenomena which are objects realized within taking a specifically characterized phenomenon as the apprehended object (*bzung yul, grāhya-viṣhaya*) and hidden phenomena which are objects realized within taking a generally characterized phenomenon as the apprehended object.[3]

All objects of comprehension, specifically and generally characterized phenomena, are suitable as objects of comprehension by a valid cognizer. Direct valid cognizers are able

---

[1] Dharmakīrti, *Commentary on (Dignāga's) "Compendium of Valid Cognition"*, P5709, Vol. 130, 88.3.4.

[2] Lati Rinbochay, *Mind in Tibetan Buddhism*, p. 118.

[3] Jam-ḃel-trin-lay-yön-ḋan-gya-tso, Lo-śel-ling *Collected Topics*, p. 2.

to realize specifically characterized phenomena which serve as their apprehended objects. Apprehended object is mutually inclusive with appearing object and "refers to the object which is actually appearing to the consciousness and not necessarily to what it is comprehending".[1] In the case of a direct perceiver the apprehended object and what is being comprehended are the same. In the case of a thought consciousness the apprehended object is a meaning-generality and the object comprehended is the actual object, any hidden phenomenon. Inferential valid cognizers, necessarily thought consciousnesses which are produced in dependence upon a correct sign, have the special ability to realize generally characterized phenomena. Although inferential cognizers are able to comprehend any hidden phenomenon, their apprehended object is necessarily a generally characterized phenomenon. Thus, by means of the two valid cognizers, direct and inferential, one is able to realize all objects of comprehension, specifically and generally characterized phenomena. The enumeration of valid cognizers as two is both necessary and sufficient; therefore, Dharmakīrti concludes, the enumeration is definite.

Eliminative Engagers and Collective Engagers

Corresponding to the division of consciousnesses into conceptual and non-conceptual types is the division into consciousnesses which are eliminative engagers (*sel 'jug, *apoha-pravṛtti*) and consciousnesses which are collective engagers (*sgrub 'jug, *vidhi-pravṛtti*). Thought consciousnesses are eliminative engagers and direct perceivers are collective engagers. "Whereas in the conceptual/non-conceptual division the emphasis is on what the consciousness sees, i.e., whether the actual object or an image of the object appears to it, here the emphasis is on the way in which that consciousness apprehends its object."[2]

---

[1] Lati Rinbochay, *Mind in Tibetan Buddhism*, p. 29.
[2] *Ibid.*, p. 34.

A direct perceiver is a collective engager, it engages its object in a collective manner because its object appears to it together with all of its uncommon characteristics.[1] For instance, a direct perceiver realizing blue does not comprehend its object by explicitly eliminating non-blue or anything else in order to understand blue. Rather, it realizes its object nakedly and directly. Beyond that, it is *capable* of realizing its object just as it is—that is to say, together with all of its uncommon characteristics. The "uncommon characteristics" of an impermanent phenomenon are those impermanent characteristics that are the same substantial entity in terms of being established, abiding, and disintegrating simultaneously with that thing. These are phenomena such as the individual particles that compose a material phenomenon, the impermanence of the object, its productness, and so forth that are produced together with the object, last one instant with the object, and disintegrate simultaneously with the object.

Although a direct perceiver is *capable* of realizing all of the uncommon characteristics of a specifically characterized phenomenon it does not necessarily do so. These characteristics appear to an ordinary direct perceiver, but such a consciousness is unable to notice them. Only a yogic direct perceiver notices and ascertains all of the uncommon characteristics together with its appearing object. If an ordinary direct perceiver realized all of the uncommon characteristics of a specifically characterized phenomenon, then in order to understand subtle impermanence it would be necessary merely to stop conception rather than to familiarize with the object first by means of inferential cognizers. Still, "In the Sautrāntika system all the qualities that are established, abide, and cease with a thing—such as its shape, colour, impermanence, nature of being a product,

---

[1] The sources for this section are Den-dar-hla-ram-ba, *Beginnings of a Presentation of Generally and Specifically Characterized Phenomena* and Ngak-wang-dra-shi, Go-mang *Collected Topics*.

and so forth—appear to any direct perceiver apprehending that object."[1]

Direct perceivers do not superimpose artificial characteristics on their objects. The appearing object of a direct perceiver is necessarily a specifically characterized phenomenon, "a thing with respect to which place, time, and nature are not mixed".[2] Essentially, the meaning of the assertion that specifically characterized phenomena, impermanent phenomena, functioning things, and so forth are phenomena with respect to which place, time, and nature are not mixed is that these phenomena appear to direct perceivers nakedly, just as they are, without being at all mixed or confused with phenomena of other places, times, or natures.

Specifically characterized phenomena have the character of appearing as they are, specifically, without depending on the appearance of a meaning generality. In the system of the Proponents of Sūtra, these are phenomena that are established by way of their own characters without depending on imputation by thought. Moreover, they appear together with all of their own characteristics of impermanence and so forth without being generally characterized in a rough way by association with phenomena of other places, times, and natures. "A specifically characterized phenomenon is so called because of being a phenomenon of which the entity is able to appear to a direct valid cognizer without depending on the elimination of an object of negation, the indirectness of a meaning-generality, and so forth."[3] Specifically characterized phenomena can appear without involving the errors of conceptuality.

Thought consciousnesses are not collective engagers but eliminative engagers. Thought does not comprehend its object together with all of its uncommon characteristics, but understands its object in a general way by a negative

---

[1] Lati Rinbochay, *Mind in Tibetan Buddhism*, p. 31.
[2] Ngak-ŵang-dra-shi, Go-mang *Collected Topics*, p. 411.
[3] *Ibid.*

process of eliminating all that is not that object. The thought consciousness apprehending a table does not comprehend a table just as it is, for it comprehends a mere mental imputation which is an elimination of non-table. Such a thought consciousness explicitly ascertains a table, but a table is not its appearing object. The meaning-generality of table is the appearing object, but it is not what the thought consciousness ascertains.

The Mixture of Place, Time, and Nature

The appearing object of a thought consciousness is necessarily a generally characterized phenomenon, a permanent phenomenon. Generally characterized phenomena are so called because their characters are realized not by way of their own entities but by way of a generality. They are realized in a general way. For instance, the thought consciousness apprehending ice cream understands it through the elimination of non-ice cream by way of the appearance of a mental image of something which is the opposite of non-ice cream. By this process ice cream is not understood together with all of its specific qualities but merely in a general way, as the elimination of non-ice cream. Thus, a conceptual consciousness can know something in only a general way rather than appreciating its object's freshness and fullness.

A meaning-generality of ice cream appearing to a thought consciousness apprehending ice cream is a phenomenon with respect to which place (*yul*), time (*dus*), and nature (*rang bzhin*) are mixed. That is, upon reading the word "ice cream" or contacting the actual object, what appears to the *thought* apprehending ice cream is an internal image of ice cream that was encountered in a different place, in an earlier time, and had a different nature.

For instance, when one was a child training in the use of language, upon going to the amusement park and first encountering this cold sweet chocolate food one's mother explained, "This is ice cream." Confirming the association the child thinks, "This cold sweet chocolate food is ice cream." Thus, an image of the cold sweet chocolate food appears to the thought consciousness as ice cream and as the opposite of non-ice cream. Then when one encountered a cold sweet strawberry food at the aunt's house, one immediately thought, "This is ice cream." In terms of what appears to that thought consciousness, factors of chocolate ice cream experienced earlier at the amusement park appear to be present also in the strawberry ice cream at the aunt's house. Thought is mixing or confusing *places*, for the factors which existed with an ice cream in one place appear to thought to be present also with an ice cream in another place. The mixing of *times* is that factors which existed with the ice cream of an earlier time appear to be present with the ice cream of the present time. The mixing of *natures* is thought's perception of the factor of chocolate ice cream's being ice cream and the factor of strawberry ice cream's being ice cream as being the same whereas they are different. Thus, thought takes cognizance merely of its object's general quality as ice cream and does not appreciate the freshness and fullness of its object as a vibrant, impermanent, specifically characterized phenomenon.

Thought is by its very nature a mistaken consciousness, and for ordinary people usual perception is dominated by thought. Upon meeting an old friend we say, "This is my friend from years ago," and in so doing we are apprehending the former friend and the later friend as if the same whereas there are doubtless changes. Such thought mixes objects of different places, times, and natures.

Still, as interpreted by the Ge-luk-ba order it is a fundamental and shared assertion of all the Buddhist tenet systems that thought is essential on the path leading to liberation. Eventually, the need for thought consciousnesses is transcended, but in order to attain a direct realization of the truths it is necessary to engage in rigorous analytical investigation over a long period of time. Through training in reasoning one can eventually progress to the point when conceptuality is no longer necessary.

The stated purpose for Buddhist reasoning is the development of yogic direct perceivers realizing subtle impermanence, the mind and body as selfless, etc. Only yogic direct perceivers can serve as the antidote to the ignorance that binds one in the suffering of cyclic existence. Such consciousnesses are produced in dependence on a very stable and insightful mind developed by the power of meditation, but some of the best qualities of this very special consciousness are shared by all direct perceivers, those in the continuums of ordinary beings as well as those in the continuums of Superiors. For instance, all direct perceivers are non-mistaken consciousnesses to which the appearing object, a specifically characterized phenomenon, appears just as it is together with all of its uncommon characteristics of impermanence and so forth. Still, even though subtle impermanence *appears* equally to all direct perceivers, it is only yogic direct perceivers which are able to take such impermanence as an object of *realization*. Direct perceivers in the continuums of ordinary beings are not able to notice the subtle impermanence which appears. This failure is due to the influence of both internal conditions—thick predispositions for adhering to permanence—and external conditions—the object's abiding in a similar type in former and later moments. By the power of these two conditions, a direct perceiver in the continuum of an ordinary being is unable to induce the ascertainment of subtle impermanence. The process of sharpening one's direct perception to the point of being able to realize all of the qualities that appear depends on thought consciousnesses, the analytical reasoning inducing inferential cognizers, which are like a tonic for empowering perception.

One good quality shared equally by all types of direct perceivers is that they are consciousnesses which do not mix place, time, and nature. Whereas thought consciousnesses understand their objects by the appearance of an associated object of a similar type which was encountered in a different place at an earlier time, direct perceivers experience their objects just as they are.

The meaning of non-mixture of place is not simply that what exists, for instance, in the east must necessarily not exist in the west, for if that were the correct interpretation it would absurdly follow that some phenomenon which is present everywhere such as object of knowledge would not exist in the west because it exists in the east.[1] Rather, the meaning of a non-mixture of place is that even though some functioning thing exists in both the east and west, just that factor which exists in the east does not exist in the west. Indeed, general phenomena such as functioning things and objects of knowledge do exist in both the east and west, but precisely what exists in the east does not also exist in the west. This is merely an appeal to the uniqueness of all specifically characterized phenomena.

Similarly, if one interprets the meaning of a non-mixture of time to be that what existed yesterday morning necessarily does not exist today, then it would absurdly follow that an unchanging phenomenon—a permanent phenomenon—would not exist today because it existed yesterday morning. More accurately, the meaning of a non-mixture of time is identified: Even though some functioning thing exists both this morning and this evening, just that factor which existed in the morning does not exist in the evening. The objects of direct perceivers are specifically characterized phenomena, momentary phenomena; therefore, precisely what existed this morning could not also exist this evening.

Finally, someone might mistakenly interpret the meaning of a non-mixture of nature to be that whatever encompasses a pot (in the sense of being a generality of a pot) necessarily does not encompass a pillar, and whatever encompasses a pillar necessarily does not encompass a pot. Such an interpretation is not correct because it would absurdly follow that the subject, functioning thing, would not encompass a pillar because it encompasses a pot. Functioning thing is a generality of both a pot and a pillar, and as such it equally

---

[1] The source for the meanings of the non-mixture of place, time, and nature is Ngak-w̄ang-d̄ra-s̄hi, Go-mang *Collected Topics*, pp. 406-408, 411.

encompasses each of them. Thus, the meaning of a non-mixture of natures is that although some functioning thing encompasses both a pot and a pillar, just that factor which encompasses a pot does not encompass a pillar. Again, this is an appeal to the uniqueness of specifically characterized phenomena. Although all functioning things share the nature of being able to perform functions as they are causes and so forth, there are certain qualities in the nature of, for instance, a pot that are not also present in the nature of a pillar.

A GE-LUK-BA/SA-GYA-BA DEBATE

All of the Buddhist systems agree with one voice that in the end direct perception is preferable to conceptuality. However, there are many interpretations of the nature of the objects suitable to be realized by direct perceivers and the nature of the objects that must be realized by thought consciousnesses. The interpretation that has been presented here is that of the Tutor Pur-bu-jok Jam-ba-gya-tso, author of the text translated in Part Two of this work. This is a Ge-luk-ba interpretation of the system of the Proponents of Sūtra Following Reasoning and is in great measure supported by other Ge-luk-ba Collected Topics manuals, commentaries, and so forth. However, in the general study of the tenet systems, the many commentators—both within Ge-luk-ba and between the traditions—have frequently disagreed. By considering the commentators' various stances in their interpretations of a point of doctrine one can come to understand the issues much more clearly.

In this regard, it is instructive to consider the differences between two interpretations of the doctrine of the two truths, a Ge-luk-ba view and an opposing view presented by at least some interpreters of the Ṡa-ḡya-ba (*sa skya pa*) order. This dialectic between two orders of Tibetan Buddhism arises within the framework of their interpretations of the system of the Proponents of Sūtra and focuses on the question of the relation between the two truths, or specifically and generally characterized phenomena, and impermanent and permanent phenomena. The presentation of the Ge-luk-ba interpretation is drawn from the Tutor's *Collected Topics*, a recent work which is consistent with the basic Ge-luk-ba stance established earlier. The Ša-ġya-ba position was formulated by the monk-scholar Ḍak-tsang (*stag tshang*, b. 1405) who raised several objections to the Ge-luk-ba interpretation of the system of the Proponents of Sūtra. Ḍak-tsang's interpretation is drawn from his general presentation of Buddhist tenets.[1]

The source of this Ge-luk-ba/Ša-ġya-ba controversy is a particular passage in Dharmakīrti's *Commentary on (Dignāga's) "Compendium of Valid Cognition"* (*pramāṇavarttika-kārikā*) which says:

> That which is ultimately able to perform a function
> Exists ultimately here [in this system]; other
> [phenomena, unable to do so] exist conventionally.
> These explain specifically characterized [phenomena]
> And generally characterized [phenomenon].[2]

Thus, Dharmakīrti identifies specifically characterized phenomena as those ultimately able to perform a function and explains that they ultimately exist, thereby indicating specifically characterized phenomena as ultimate truths. Also, he identifies generally characterized phenomena as those which exist and are other than those ultimately able to perform a function. Thus, generally characterized phenomena exist conventionally and are explained to be conventional truths.

Both the Ge-luk-bas and the Ša-ġya-bas agree that ultimate truth and specifically characterized phenomenon are

---

[1] Ḍak-tsang (*stag tshang lo tsā ba shes rab rin chen*), *Ocean of Good Explanations, Explanation of "Freedom From Extremes Through Understanding All Tenets"* (*grub mtha' kun shes nas mtha' bral grub pa zhes bya ba'i bstan bcos rnam par bshad pa legs bshad kyi rgya mtsho*), (Thim-phu: Kun-bzang-stobs-rgyal, 1976).

[2] Dharmakīrti, *Commentary on (Dignāga's) "Compendium of Valid Cognition"*, P5709, Vol. 130, 88.3.5-88.3.6.

mutually inclusive and that these two are mutually exclusive with generally characterized phenomenon. Also, they agree that conventional truth and generally characterized phenomenon are mutually inclusive and that these two are mutually exclusive with specifically characterized phenomenon. The differences in their interpretations are illustrated when the two truths are related to permanent and impermanent phenomena.

To review briefly the Ge-luk-ba interpretation as presented by the Tutor Pur-bu-jok Jam-ba-gya-tso: (1) the three—specifically characterized phenomenon, ultimate truth, and impermanent phenomenon—are mutually inclusive with each other; (2) the three—generally characterized phenomenon, conventional truth, and permanent phenomenon—are mutually inclusive with each other; and (3) any of the three in (1) is necessarily mutually exclusive with any of the three in (2). For instance, according to the Ge-luk-ba interpretation, there is nothing that is both an impermanent phenomenon and a conventional truth in the system of the Proponents of Sūtra Following Reasoning.

In "The Introductory Path of Reasoning" the Tutor Jam-ba-gya-tso gives the definition of an ultimate truth as:

> that which is ultimately able to perform a function.

This does not seem to agree with the passage from Dharmakīrti which identifies "that which is ultimately able to perform a function" as explaining specifically characterized phenomena. If Dharmakīrti's meaning is that this is the definition of a specifically characterized phenomenon, then although Jam-ba-gya-tso does not pair this definition with the same definiendum, since he asserts ultimate truth and specifically characterized phenomenon as well as their definitions to be mutually inclusive, he does not accrue the fault of stating a definition which is too broad or too narrow. In other Ge-luk-ba texts the definition of a specifically characterized phenomenon is identified as that which is ultimately able to perform a function. For instance, in Gön-chok-jik-may-wang-bo's (*dkon mchog 'jigs med dbang po*), 1728-1791,

Precious Garland of Tenets (*grub pa'i mtha'i rnam par bzhag pa rin po che'i phreng ba*), the theory section of Sopa and Hopkins' *Practice and Theory of Tibetan Buddhism*, the definition of a specifically characterized phenomenon in the system of the Proponents of Sūtra Following Reasoning is given as:

> a phenomenon which is ultimately able to perform a function.[1]

The *Precious Garland of Tenets* is a condensation of one of the textbooks of the Go-mang College of Dre-bung Monastic University, a Ge-luk-ba monastery.

Correspondingly, the Tutor Jam-ba-gya-tso defines a conventional truth as:

> a phenomenon which is ultimately unable to perform a function

whereas some interpret Dharmakīrti as identifying this as the definition of a generally characterized phenomenon. Again, since Jam-ba-gya-tso asserts conventional truth and generally characterized phenomenon to be mutually inclusive, the eight approaches of pervasion do exist between the definition and the definiendum as he has stated them. And in accordance with Dharmakīrti's original statement, Gön-chok-jik-may-wang-bo defines a generally characterized phenomenon as:

> a phenomenon which is ultimately unable to perform a function.

This disparity between the definitions as identified by some Ge-luk-bas, however, is not a source of debate between the Ge-luk-bas and the Ša-ǧya-bas.

In his discussion of the two truths in the system of the Proponents of Sūtra, Đak-tsang cites the same quote from Dharmakīrti's *Commentary on (Dignāga's) "Compendium of Valid Cognition"* which says:

---

[1] Sopa and Hopkins, *Practice and Theory of Tibetan Buddhism*, p. 96.

That which is ultimately able to perform a function
Exists ultimately here [in this system]; other
  [phenomena, unable to do so] exist conventionally.
These explain specifically characterized [phenomena]
And generally characterized [phenomena].[1]

In addition to this basic quote from Dharmakīrti, he cites a passage in Vasubandhu's *Treasury of Knowledge* which says:

That with respect to which, when it is broken or
Mentally separated into others [i.e., parts], an aware-
  ness [realizing]
It no [longer] operates, exists conventionally, like a pot
  or water.
That which exists ultimately is other.[2]

Dak-tsang takes these two statements as getting at the same meaning and works them together to formulate his view.

In his interpretation, these passages indicate two variant definitions of a conventional truth:

a phenomenon which is ultimately unable to perform
a function (*don dam par don byed mi nus pa'i chos*)

and

a phenomenon with respect to which a factually concordant awareness apprehending it is cancelled due to
[the object's] being destroyed by a destroyer [such as a
hammer] or separated into parts by an awareness
which is a separator (*chos gang la gzhig byed kyis gzhig
pa dang sel byed kyi blos cha gzhan bsal bas rang 'dzin gyi
blo don mthun 'dor pa*).[3]

Similarly, he interprets these passages as indicating two variant definitions of an ultimate truth:

---

[1] Dharmakīrti, *Commentary on (Dignāga's) "Compendium of Valid Cognition"*, P5709, Vol. 130, 88.3.5-88.3.6.

[2] Vasubandhu, *Treasury of Knowledge*, P5590, Vol. 115, 124.2.1-124.2.2.

[3] Dak-tsang, *Revelation of All Tenets*, unpublished translation by Jeffrey Hopkins, p. 6.

a phenomenon which is ultimately able to perform a
function (*don dam par don byed nus pa'i chos*)

and

a phenomenon with respect to which a factually concordant awareness apprehending it is not cancelled
due to [the object's] being destroyed by a destroyer
[such as a hammer] or separated into parts by an
awareness which is a separator (*chos gang la gzhig byed
kyis gzhig pa dang sel byed kyi blos cha gzhan bsal bas rang
'dzin gyi blo don mthun mi 'dor ba*).[1]

Both the Ge-luk-ḃas and the Ṡa-ġya-ḃas agree that the above
passage from Vasubandhu's *Treasury of Knowledge* indicates
the Great Exposition School's assertions on the two truths.
However, Ḋak-tsang takes this passage as concordant with
Dharmakīrti's statement, which the Ge-luk-ḃas interpret to
be written from the point of view of the Proponents of Sūtra
Following Reasoning. Jam-ḃa-gya-tso, in accordance with
the general Ge-luk-ḃa view, would not accept these statements as concordant because they are presentations of the
two truths from the points of view of two different systems,
but this difference is not the basic issue of the debate.

The central point of debate between Ḋak-tsang and the
Ge-luk-ḃas lies in their respective interpretations of the term
"ultimately" in the phrase "that which is ultimately able to
perform a function". Both agree that conventional truths, or
generally characterized phenomena, are imputed by a term
or a thought consciousness. Similarly, they agree that ultimate truths, or specifically characterized phenomena, are
truly established (*bden par grub pa, satya-siddha*), not merely
imputed by the mind, and objects established from their
own side (*rang ngos nas grub pa, *svarūpa-siddhi*). Jam-ḃa-gya-
tso asserts that all impermanent phenomena including a pot,
water, and so forth are ultimately able to perform a function,
but Ḋak-tsang denies this. He asserts that some

---

[1] *Ibid.*

impermanent phenomena—composite phenomena such as a pot, water, and so forth—are conventionalities because they are unable to perform functions as ultimate objects.

Pots, water, and so on are unable to perform functions as ultimate objects, Ḍak-tsang says, because that which is an object ultimately able to perform a function from its own side is a self-characterized actual object which unmistakenly generates a mind apprehending it. That is, there can be no chance that the consciousness apprehending an ultimate truth would be cancelled due to the breaking up of its object. Ḍak-tsang explains that a pot cannot unmistakenly generate a mind apprehending it because it depends on imputation by a term or a thought consciousness due to being a composite or gross phenomenon. Pots, and all gross composite material phenomena, can be broken into parts by force. Immaterial composite phenomena as well as subtler material composite phenomena can be mentally separated into parts.

A pot is a composite phenomenon because it consists of many parts, the individual particles that compose it, and in Ḍak-tsang's system, composite phenomena depend on imputation by a term or thought. Whatever depends on imputation by a term or thought cannot unmistakenly generate a mind apprehending it because whatever depends on imputation by a term or thought is necessarily not an ultimate truth and not established from its own side. It would seem that according to Ḍak-tsang, in order to apprehend a composite phenomenon such as a pot one must rely on the appearance of an internal mental image. This would mean that the impetus for the apprehension comes not from the side of the actual object but from the side of the imputing consciousness. Such a gross phenomenon is not able to unmistakenly generate a mind apprehending it. Therefore, composite phenomena—pots, water, and so forth—are not objects ultimately able to perform a function and are not ultimate truths. Still, even though a pot is unable to perform a function *ultimately*, it is *conventionally* able to perform the function of generating an apprehender of itself. Composite phenomena, Ḏak-tsang asserts, are conventional truths.

Since he takes the passage from the *Treasury of Knowledge* to be concordant with the passage from the *Commentary on (Dignāga's) "Compendium of Valid Cognition"*, for Ḏak-tsang the meaning of "ultimately" comes to entail that ultimate objects must not be composite or gross phenomena which can be broken up or mentally separated, thereby cancelling the consciousness apprehending it. Therefore, because many impermanent phenomena are such composite or gross phenomena, Ḏak-tsang concludes that ultimate truth and specifically characterized phenomena are not mutually inclusive with impermanent phenomenon.

Further, Ḏak-tsang denies the Ge-luk-ḇa interpretation of pots and so forth as ultimate truths in the system of the Proponents of Sūtra Following Reasoning on the basis that such a view is a deprecation of the Proponents of Sūtra. The Ge-luk-ḇa acceptance of all impermanent phenomena as ultimate truths is, for him, an acceptance of a self of phenomena more extensive than that of the Proponents of the Great Exposition. This would mean that in their respective assertions of the two truths, the Proponents of the Great Exposition, a lower system, would be presenting a doctrine which is subtler than that of the Proponents of Sūtra. This would go against the drift of the layout of the systems moving from lower to higher. The higher systems are called "higher" due to their assertions of subtler doctrines, progressively subtler as one moves up.

In the Great Exposition School, ultimate truths include spatially partless particles (*rdul phran phyogs kyi cha med*) and temporally partless moments (*skad cig cha med*). Partless particles are, for instance, the unbreakable units of form and odor that accompany a pot and partless moments are, for instance, indivisible moments of consciousness. In accordance with the passage from the *Treasury of Knowledge*, these phenomena cannot be broken or mentally separated, so the mind apprehending one of these would not cease due to the break-up or mental separation of its object.

Dak-tsang says that in the system of the Proponents of Sūtra as well ultimate truths must be identified as these partless particles and partless moments. He asserts that in their system composed phenomena such as pots must be identified as conventional truths because if a pot were broken or mentally separated into parts, the awareness apprehending it would no longer perceive a pot. The Proponents of the Great Exposition say that such gross collections are falsities and conventionalities, and the Ge-luk-bas agree with this interpretation of the Great Exposition School. However, in the Ge-luk-ba interpretation of the Sūtra School Following Reasoning such collections are said to be true existents and ultimates. Thus, Dak-tsang concludes that by this interpretation the Proponents of Sūtra would be asserting a self of phenomena more extensive than that of the Proponents of the Great Exposition, and if this were so, it would follow that their tenets would be lower than those of the Proponents of the Great Exposition.

Dak-tsang's interpretation of the two truths entails that ultimate truth is not mutually inclusive with impermanent phenomenon. Rather, they have three possibilities because some impermanent phenomena are ultimate truths and some are conventional truths:

1   Something which is both an ultimate truth and an impermanent phenomenon is a partless particle.
2   Whatever is an ultimate truth is necessarily an impermanent phenomenon, but whatever is an impermanent phenomenon is not necessarily an ultimate truth, such as a pot.
3   Also, there are phenomena which are neither ultimate truths nor impermanent phenomena. An illustration is uncomposed space which is a conventional truth and a permanent phenomenon.

Similarly, Dak-tsang disagrees with the Ge-luk-ba interpretation that conventional truth and permanent phenomenon are mutually inclusive in the system of the

Proponents of Sūtra Following Reasoning, for he takes these two as having three possibilities:

1 Any permanent phenomenon is both a conventional truth and a permanent phenomenon, for whatever is a permanent phenomenon is necessarily a conventional truth. This assertion of the Proponents of Sūtra, according to the Ge-luk-ba interpretation, is at odds with the Great Exposition School which takes permanent phenomena to be ultimate truths because they cannot be broken or mentally separated. The Proponents of Sūtra, under the influence of Dharmakīrti's criterion that ultimate truths must be ultimately able to perform a function, do not assert permanent phenomena as ultimate truths, for they do not produce effects.

2 As opposed to the Ge-luk-bas, however, Ḍak-tsang interprets that whatever is a conventional truth is not necessarily a permanent phenomenon because, for instance, water or a pot is an impermanent conventional truth.

3 A phenomenon which is neither a permanent phenomenon nor a conventional truth is a temporally partless moment.

The Ge-luk-ba response to Ḍak-tsang's interpretation was formulated much prior to Jam-ba-gya-tso's writing the Tutor's *Collected Topics* by many authors. Among the Ge-luk-bas who addressed this dispute is the Mongolian scholar Ḅel-den-chö-jay (*dpal ldan chos rje*, b. 1797) who took it up in his explanation of the two truths in the various Buddhist systems, the source text for this section.[1] In his discussion of the system of the Proponents of Sūtra Following Reasoning, Ḅel-den-chö-jay gives in syllogistic form his interpretation of the criteria of an ultimate truth:

---

[1] See Ḅel-den-chö-jay, *Explanation of the Meaning of Conventional and Ultimate in the Four Tenet Systems*, 17a.6-30b.2 for his explanation of the two truths in the system of the Proponents of Sūtra Following Reasoning.

The subject, a specifically characterized phenomenon, is ultimately existent [for four separate and adequate reasons]:

1 because of being able to perform the function of producing its own effects;
2 because of appearing in a dissimilar or uncommon manner to the awareness taking it as an appearing object;
3 because of being a phenomenon the entity of which is unable to appear fully as the object of an awareness from the mere empowering condition of an expressive sound; and
4 because of being a phenomenon with respect to which the awareness realizing it would not be produced if the object—established from the side of its own mode of subsistence—did not exist, even though other factors such as sense powers and mental application are present.[1]

Ḅel-den-chö-jay identifies ultimate truth, specifically characterized phenomenon, and impermanent phenomenon as mutually inclusive.[2] Thus, according to the Ge-luk-ḅa interpretation, in this system each and every impermanent phenomenon is both a specifically characterized phenomenon and an ultimate truth.

Further, Ḅel-den-chö-jay asserts that a pot (even though it is a composite material phenomenon) is an ultimate truth because of being a truth for the appearance factor (*snang ngor*) of an ultimate awareness (*blo don dam pa*).[3] "Ultimate awareness" here refers to a direct perceiver which is non-mistaken with respect to a specifically characterized phenomenon. An example is a direct perceiver apprehending blue which is non-mistaken with respect to the nature and

---

[1] Ḅel-den-chö-jay, *Explanation of the Meaning of Conventional and Ultimate in the Four Tenet Systems*, 17b.3-5.
[2] *Ibid.*, 17b.1.
[3] *Ibid.*, 18b.6-7.

specific character of blue.[1] This is the crucial point of the Ge-luk-ba interpretation: Ultimate truths are truths for an ultimate consciousness, one which is not mistaken with respect to the specifically characterized phenomenon appearing to it. The only appearing objects of such a consciousness are impermanent phenomena, all of which appear together with their specific characteristics just as they exist. Thus, the Ge-luk-bas conclude that since all impermanent phenomena qualify in this way, they are all ultimate truths.

In his explanation of conventional truths in the system of the Proponents of Sūtra Following Reasoning, Bel-den-chö-jay takes conventional truth, generally characterized phenomenon, and permanent phenomenon to be mutually inclusive.[2] Thus, all conventional truths are generally characterized and permanent phenomena. Bel-den-chö-jay explains that a generally characterized phenomenon is a phenomenon which must be realized through taking to mind a *general* aspect without their being an appearance of its uncommon signs to the awareness which takes it as an appearing object.[3] He gives his interpretation of the criteria of conventional existence:

> The subject, a generally characterized phenomenon, is conventionally existent [for four separate and adequate reasons]:
>
> 1 because of being unable to perform the function of producing its own effects;
> 2 because of appearing in a common manner [in a general way, devoid of specific character] to the awareness taking it as an appearing object;
> 3 because of being a phenomenon the entity of which is able to appear fully as the object of an awareness

---

[1] *Ibid.*, 18b.7.
[2] *Ibid.*, 17b.1.
[3] *Ibid.*, 18b.4-5.

from the mere empowering condition of an expressive sound; and

4 because the mere presence of the factors of sense powers and mental application [are sufficient to] produce an awareness realizing it.[1]

In the Ge-luk-ba understanding of this system, conventional truths must be generally characterized and permanent phenomena. An impermanent phenomena does not exist conventionally, for it is able to appear together with all of its *specific* characteristics to a consciousness which takes it as an appearing object. A permanent phenomenon such as the meaning-generality of pot is a conventional truth because of being a truth for the appearance factor of a conventional awareness (*blo kun rdzob pa*). Here "conventional awareness" refers to a conceptual consciousness to which natures appear as mixed.[2] Thus, conceptuality is a conventional consciousness. In this context, the Sanskrit word for "conventional" is "*saṃvṛti*" which here means "obscured". A conceptual consciousness is obscured in that the great richness of specifically characterized phenomena cannot appear to it. This does not mean that conceptuality is not rich, but that it is not able to perceive the full appearance of impermanent phenomena. Still, conceptuality is an essential component of the path, but eventually—after clear and sustained application—the need for it is surpassed.

This debate between Sa-ġya-ba and Ge-luk-ba commentators focuses on their respective interpretations of the Indian sources, the writings of Dharmakīrti, Vasubandhu, and so forth. Dak-tsang interprets Dharmakīrti's use of the word "ultimately" to intend an exclusion of functioning things which are able to perform functions merely conventionally. Also, by taking Vasubandhu's description in the *Treasury of Knowledge* of ultimate and conventional truths to be consistent with Dharmakīrti's description, Dak-tsang formulates a view that all Proponents of Sūtra, Followers of Scripture and

---

[1] *Ibid.*, 17b.7-18a.1.
[2] *Ibid.*, 19a.3-4.

Followers of Reasoning alike, must accord with the Proponents of the Great Exposition in asserting partless particles and moments as ultimate truths and composite phenomena as conventional truths.

The Ge-luk-bas deny both points of Dak-tsang's interpretation in saying that the Proponents of Sūtra Following Reasoning cannot be taken as asserting composite phenomena as conventional truths because all functioning things, composite and singular, equally share the characteristics of ultimate existents. All functioning things are ultimate truths, according to the Ge-luk-ba interpretation, in terms of producing effects, being objects which are suitable to appear together with all of their uncommon characteristics, being unsuitable to appear fully to a thought consciousness, and being established from their own side without depending on imputation by a term or a thought consciousness.

The presentation of phenomena which are suitable to appear to direct perceivers and those which must appear to thought consciousnesses is vitally important in the Collected Topics texts and all the literature on valid cognition. The Ge-luk-ba commentators neatly pair off the appearing objects of direct perceivers with all impermanent phenomena and the appearing objects of thought consciousnesses with all permanent phenomena. Dak-tsang disagrees with this interpretation, and his challenge raises some very important questions concerning the intent of the Indian formulators of the Buddhist logical systems.

REFUTATION OF MISTAKEN VIEWS CONCERNING
ESTABLISHED BASES (5B.4)

In the Tutor's *Collected Topics*, the refutation of mistaken views concerning established bases consists of nine debates. These debates present several topics important for the study of debate and serve as the essential introduction to ontology in the system of the Proponents of Sūtra.

Debate B.1, First Mistaken View (5b.4)

The chapter begins with a hypothetical Defender's assertion that whatever is an established base is necessarily a permanent phenomenon. Established base (*gzhi grub, *vastu-siddha*) is mutually inclusive with existent (*yod pa, sat*), and since both permanent and impermanent phenomena are included among existents, it is not the case that whatever is an established base is necessarily a permanent phenomenon. In order to convince his mistaken opponent that this is the fact, the Sūtra School Challenger uses the counterexample of a pot, an impermanent established base. Thus, this first debate serves to introduce students to the basic division of established bases into permanent and impermanent phenomena.

Moreover, the main intent of this debate is to illustrate the distinction that even though established base itself is a permanent phenomenon, whatever is an established base is not necessarily a permanent phenomenon. As an existent which includes both permanent and impermanent phenomena, established base itself is a permanent phenomenon because in order to apprehend the singular collective established base it is necessary to do so by a thought consciousness. Furthermore, established base, by its nature (*rang bzhin*), is a permanent phenomenon. Established base itself, whether with a permanent phenomenon or an impermanent one, is an appearing object of a thought consciousness. The factor of something's being an established base, its being an established base, or the established base with any existent is a permanent phenomenon. Thus, even on the basis of an impermanent established base such as a table, the factor of its being an established base, or the established base with the table, is an appearing object of a thought consciousness only. Thus, by its nature, established base is a permanent phenomenon. Yet, one cannot say that whatever is an established base is necessarily a permanent phenomenon, for there are impermanent established bases such as tables which are appearing objects of direct perceivers. The text says:

> If someone [a hypothetical Defender] says, "Whatever is an established base is necessarily a permanent phenomenon," [the Sūtra School Challenger responds to him,] "It [absurdly] follows that the subject, a pot, is a permanent phenomenon because of being an established base. You asserted the pervasion."

The Challenger has stated an unwanted consequence. If all established bases were permanent, then even a functioning thing such as a pot would be a permanent phenomenon.

> If he says that the reason [that a pot is an established base] is not established, [the Sūtra School Challenger responds,] "It follows that the subject [a pot] is [an established base] because of being established by a valid cognizer."
> "[It follows that] there is pervasion [i.e., whatever is established by a valid cognizer is necessarily an established base] because that which is established by a valid cognizer is the definition of an established base."

In the usual brief style the text reads simply, "There is pervasion because ... ," meaning that the Defender answered, "There is no pervasion," to the last consequence. The author does not spell out the answer that there is pervasion, but relies on the reader to internalize the systematic style.

> If he accepts the basic consequence [that a pot is a permanent phenomenon, the Sūtra School Challenger responds,] "It follows that the subject, a pot, is not a permanent phenomenon because of being an impermanent phenomenon."

The text implies that the Defender has now accepted the line of reasoning resulting from his earlier questioning the establishment of the reason of the basic consequence and the

Challenger has led him back to that consequence. In order to maintain his original assertion of the pervasion, he opts for his last possibility, accepting the basic consequence, whereupon the Challenger moves to contradict his acceptance. A pot is, of course, not a permanent phenomenon but an impermanent one.

> If he says that the reason [that a pot is an impermanent phenomenon] is not established, [the Sūtra School Challenger responds,] "It follows that the subject [a pot] is [an impermanent phenomenon] because of being a momentary phenomenon."
>
> "[It follows that] there is pervasion [i.e., whatever is a momentary phenomenon is necessarily an impermanent phenomenon] because a momentary phenomenon is the definition of an impermanent phenomenon."
>
> "It follows that [a momentary phenomenon is the definition of an impermanent phenomenon] because that which is able to perform a function is the definition of a thing [*dngos po, bhāva*], a disintegrating phenomenon is the definition of a composed phenomenon ['*dus byas, saṃskṛta*], and a created phenomenon is the definition of a product [*byas pa, kṛta*]."

Here again the author is condensing the meaning of the text into a terse style. The text says simply, "It follows that ... because ... ," indicating that the Defender has answered, "The reason is not established," to the last consequence. In the first two debates in the chapter on colors, the author spelled out the Challenger's consequences as an introductory instructional aid. His style has now evolved into the usual terse form which relies more on the active participation of the reader as interpreter rather than as mere passive receiver.

This last consequence in debate B.1 seems hardly correct as stated. Although the reason is established in that those three are put as the definitions of those three definienda, this does not seem to entail logically that a momentary phenomenon is the definition of an impermanent phenomenon. Is there any reason that an impermanent phenomenon could not then be defined as a produced phenomenon or as that which exists and is not a permanent phenomenon?

The author's intent here is likely more pedagogical than dialectic. The appeal of this consequence is that since that which is able to perform a function is the definition of a functioning thing, a disintegrating phenomenon is the definition of a composed phenomenon, and a created phenomenon is the definition of a product, then what is left as the definition of an impermanent phenomenon is a momentary phenomenon. This does not say that the definitions and definienda are paired arbitrarily; rather, it is as though, since we have heard that these are the definitions of these phenomena, and since these three are indeed the definitions of these three, then a momentary phenomenon must be the definition of an impermanent phenomenon.

Still, the consequence as stated is suspect. It is possible that it may be the error of a scribe. Throughout the whole of the Tutor's *Collected Topics* there are but a handful of such errors, some scholars' attributing them to the Tutor's wish to foster further debate.

There are three possibilities between the two principals of debate B.1, established base and permanent phenomenon:

1　The selflessness of persons, uncomposed space, non-cow, and so forth are both established bases and permanent phenomena.
2　Whatever is a permanent phenomenon is necessarily an established base, but whatever is an established base is not necessarily a permanent phenomenon as in the case of a pot.
3　Something which is neither must be a non-existent, for any existent is an established base.

Debate B.2, Second Mistaken View (5b.6)

Debate B.2 is similar to debate B.1 except that here the Defender is asserting that whatever exists is necessarily a functioning thing. Taking a stance opposite to that in debate B.1 the Defender is now implicitly denying the existence of all permanent phenomena. Some Western interpreters have taken this to be an accurate assertion of the Buddhist position. However, according to all Ge-luk-b̄a interpretations, all Buddhist systems assert the existence of both permanent and impermanent phenomena and thereby deny that all phenomena are impermanent. Indeed, according to the Ge-luk-b̄a interpretation, the Proponents of Sūtra Following Reasoning do assert impermanent phenomena as ultimately existent and permanent phenomena as conventionally existent, and this may be the source of some interpreters' misunderstanding. Although there is a difference between ultimate and conventional existence, one cannot say that therefore impermanent phenomena are thus more "real" and certainly not that only impermanent phenomena exist. Permanent phenomena verifiably exist, and are established by valid cognizers, accurate consciousnesses certifying the existence of phenomena. Thus, in debate B.2 when the Defender asserts that all existents are functioning things, the Challenger posits the counterexample of uncomposed space, a permanent existent.

> If someone [a hypothetical Defender] says, "Whatever is an existent is necessarily a functioning thing," [the Sūtra School Challenger responds to him,] "It [absurdly] follows that the subject, uncomposed space, is [a functioning thing] because of [being an existent]. You asserted the pervasion."
>
> If he says that the reason [that uncomposed space is an existent] is not established, [the Sūtra School Challenger responds,] "It follows that the subject

[uncomposed space] is [an existent] because of being observed by a valid cognizer."

If he says there is no pervasion [i.e., even though it is true that uncomposed space is observed by a valid cognizer, it is not the case that whatever is observed by a valid cognizer is necessarily an existent, the Sūtra School Challenger responds,] "It follows that there is pervasion in that [i.e., whatever is observed by a valid cognizer is necessarily an existent] because that observed by a valid cognizer is the definition of an existent."

The Defender now accepts the pervasion he had earlier denied and then accepts that uncomposed space is an existent, whereupon the Sūtra School Challenger states the basic consequence to him for a second time. In accordance with his original assertion that whatever exists is a functioning thing, he accepts the consequence.

If he accepts the basic consequence [that uncomposed space is a functioning thing, the Sūtra School Challenger responds,] "It follows that the subject [uncomposed space] is not a functioning thing because of being a non-thing."[1]

If he says that the reason [that uncomposed space is a non-thing] is not established, [the Sūtra School Challenger responds,] "It follows that the subject [uncomposed space] is [a non-thing] because of being empty of the ability to perform a function."

"[It follows that] there is pervasion [i.e., whatever is empty of the ability to perform a function is necessarily a non-thing] because that which is empty of the ability to perform a function is the definition of a non-thing [*dngos med, abhāva*], that which is non-disintegrating is the definition of the uncomposed ['*dus*

---

[1] Here *dngos med* is translated as "non-thing" rather than as "non-functioning thing" in order to avoid implying that there might be some existent which, although a thing, is not a functioning thing.

ma byas, asaṃskṛta], and that which is non-created is
the definition of a non-product [*ma byas pa, akṛta*]."

Here again the author is using the forum of a debate
refuting a mistaken view in order to present basic
information for the study of established bases. Except for
showing that some existents are not functioning things and
that uncomposed space is an existent non-thing, debate B.2
is essentially a layout of definitions.

This last consequence, as opposed to the last consequence
in debate B.1, is definitely correct as it is stated. That is,
debate B.1 ended with a consequence of the form:

It follows that p is the definition of q because r is the
definition of s, t is the definition of u, and v is the definition of w.

This form is suspect because the reason seems indefinite.
That r is the definition of s and so forth does not necessarily
entail that p is the definition of q. However, debate B.2 ends
with a consequence of the form:

It follows that whatever is a p is necessarily a q
because p is the definition of q, r is the definition of s,
and t is the definition of u.

This consequence is sound because if p is the definition of q
and so on, then whatever is a p is necessarily a q. That is, the
conclusion, as it were—that whatever is empty of the ability
to perform a function is necessarily a non-thing—is justified
by the reason that that which is empty of the ability to perform a function is the definition of a non-thing and so on.

It may seem as though this consequence incurs the fallacy
of incorporating the conclusion into the reason such that if
one has understands the reason, one would have already
understood the conclusion. However, there is no such fault
here. The reason gives the information that that which is
empty of the ability to perform a function is the definition of
a non-thing in order to justify the pervasion that whatever is
empty of the ability to perform a function is necessarily a
non-thing. This is true according to the rules of definitions

and definienda, but understanding the one does not necessitate that one would have understood the other. If this last consequence, or the one at the end of debate B.1, had been of the form:

> It follows that p is the definition of q because p is the definition of q, r is the definition of s, t is the definition of u, and v is the definition of w

it would incur the fallacy of incorporating the conclusion into the reason. Understanding the reason that p is the definition of q, r is the definition of s, and so on, one would have already understood that p is the definition of q. However, the author avoids this error.

It should be noted that these definitions and definienda are somewhat different from those in Table VI: Permanent Phenomenon and the Phenomena Mutually Inclusive With It (see pp. 282-283). For instance, here one definiendum is non-thing whereas in Table VI the corresponding definiendum is *phenomenon* which is a non-thing. Non-thing refers to what is not a functioning thing, both permanent phenomena and non-existents, whereas phenomenon which is a non-thing refers only to permanent phenomena. The qualification "phenomenon" serves to exclude non-existents. Non-thing is mutually inclusive with the uncomposed and non-product, but it is not mutually inclusive with uncomposed phenomenon or non-produced phenomenon. Phenomenon which is a non-thing is mutually inclusive with permanent phenomenon, uncomposed phenomenon, and so forth. One of the most interesting aspects of debate is in learning to express one's meaning carefully. In order to understand the differences between phenomena, to state proper theses and reasons, and to know the value of another's reasoning, debaters must become skilled in precise expression, knowing well what qualifications to state in order to exclude certain phenomena and to include others. The definitions and definienda presented in the last consequence are all mutually inclusive as they are stated, and they all become mutually inclusive with permanent phenomenon when the qualification "phenomenon" is added.

In debate B.2 the Defender's error is in thinking that existent and functioning thing are mutually inclusive, thereby implying that whatever is an existent is necessarily a functioning thing. Contradicting this, the Ge-luk-bas say that all of the Buddhist systems from the Sūtra School on up assert that there are three possibilities between existent and functioning thing:

1 Something which is both is a pot, a person, and so on.
2 Whatever is a functioning thing is necessarily an existent, but whatever is an existent is not necessarily a functioning thing. For instance, uncomposed space, permanent phenomenon, generally characterized phenomenon, or established base is an existent but not a functioning thing.
3 Something which is neither is a non-existent.

The two, existent and non-thing, have three possibilities without there being something which is neither:

1 Something which is both is a conventional truth.
2 Something which is an existent but not a non-thing is a pot.
3 Something which is a non-thing but not an existent is the child of a barren woman.

There is nothing which is neither an existent nor a non-thing because existent includes all existents and non-thing includes all non-existents; thus, nothing can be posited as that which is neither. The same comparison holds between existent and non-product, between existent and the uncomposed, between established base and non-thing, and so forth.

There are three possibilities between non-thing and permanent phenomenon:

1 Something which is both is, for instance, non-cow.
2 Whatever is a permanent phenomenon is necessarily a non-thing, but whatever is a non-thing is not necessarily

a permanent phenomenon as in the case of the horn of a rabbit.

3 Something which is neither is an ear consciousness, the shape of a stone, or an inferential cognizer.

Debate B.3, Third Mistaken View (6a.3)

In debate B.3 the Tutor Jam-ba-gya-tso introduces the interesting new topic of objects of knowledge of which being [them] is possible (*yin pa srid pa'i shes bya*) and objects of knowledge of which being [them] is not possible (*yin pa mi srid pa'i shes bya*).[1] The completely exhaustive division of objects of knowledge into these two types develops out of the consideration of phenomena in pairs and groups and, within that, out of the differences between the individuals within those pairs and groups.

The definition of an object of knowledge of which being it is possible is:

> that observed as a common locus which is (1) something of which being it exists and (2) also is suitable as an object of an awareness (*khyod kyi yin pa yod pa yang yin blo'i yul du bya rung ba yang yin pa'i gzhi mthun par dmigs pa*).

An example is a pot, for a pot is observed as a common locus which is (1) something of which being it exists and (2) also it is suitable as an object of an awareness. In the definition, *observed* means *observed by a valid cognizer*, the definition of an existent, and serves to specify the definiendum as an existent. Also, the definiendum, an object of knowledge of which being it is possible, must be observed as a *common locus*. In the definition, this portion

---

[1] In "objects of knowledge of which being [them] is possible" and "objects of knowledge of which being [them] is not possible", the word "them" is placed within brackets because the Tibetan, *yin pa srid pa'i shes bya* and *yin pa mi srid pa'i shes bya*, does not have these equivalent pronouns. However, in general discussion of these topics, since the pronoun is required in English to reflect the meaning, it is supplied without brackets.

serves to specify that an object of knowledge of which being it is possible such as a pot must be a phenomenon which brings together in one entity both of the defining qualities:

1   A pot is something of which being it exists; that is, there is something which is a pot, for a gold pot is a pot. This qualification in the definition means that an object of knowledge of which being it is possible must be suitable to serve as the predicate nominative (q) in a copulative sentence, a sentence of the form, p is a q, such that there is at least one phenomenon which is a q. In the case of a pot, a gold pot is a pot, a copper pot is a pot, a clay pot is a pot, and so forth. Since a gold pot is a pot, there is something which is a pot and a pot is something of which being it exists.

2   Also, a pot is suitable as an object of an awareness, the definition of an object of knowledge. Thus, the definition specifies that an object of knowledge of which being it is possible must be an object of knowledge and cannot be a non-existent.

Other examples of such objects of knowledge are a person, a consciousness, a functioning thing, a permanent phenomenon, an object of knowledge, and so forth. For instance, a permanent phenomenon, as an object of knowledge, is suitable as an object of an awareness and also there is something which is a permanent phenomenon because uncomposed space is a permanent phenomenon. In the case of a functioning thing, an eye consciousness is a functioning thing; therefore, something's being a functioning thing is possible. Further, since a functioning thing is an object of knowledge as well, it is an object of knowledge of which being it is possible. More generally, any singular phenomenon (*gcig, ekatva*) is an object of knowledge of which being it is possible. As phenomena, they are all objects of knowledge, and for each and every singular phenomenon such as a pillar, a pot, a person, and so forth there is something which is it.

The definition above is specified for the singular—an object of knowledge of which being it is possible. However, in relation to the plural—objects of knowledge of which being them is possible—the definition requires some rephrasing in English, though the Tibetan is the same for both singular and plural. Thus, the definition of *objects of knowledge* of which being them is possible is:

> those observed as a common locus of being (1) [phenomena] of which being them exists and (2) also being suitable as objects of awarenesses.

An example is the two—a product and an impermanent phenomenon (*byas pa dang mi rtag pa gnyis*). Something's being the two—a product and an impermanent phenomenon—is possible because, for instance, a pot is the two—a product and an impermanent phenomenon—*in the sense that* it is both a product and an impermanent phenomenon. Also, both a product and an impermanent phenomenon are suitable as objects of an awareness. Thus, the two—a product and an impermanent phenomenon—are objects of knowledge of which being them is possible.

It is interesting that among "objects of knowledge of which being them is possible" there are sets which include both existents and non-existents. For example, the two—a permanent phenomenon and only a permanent phenomenon (*rtag pa dang rtag pa kho na gnyis*), the two—an object of knowledge and only a generality (*shes bya dang spyi kho na gnyis*), or the two—a non-pot and only a non-pot (*bum pa ma yin pa dang bum pa ma yin pa kho na gnyis*)—are each such sets. Obviously, a permanent phenomenon is an existent; however, only-a-permanent-phenomenon (see pp. 504ff) does not exist because impermanent phenomena exist. If only-a-permanent-phenomenon existed, then impermanent phenomena could not exist. Still, something's being only a permanent phenomenon does exist, for there is something which is only a permanent phenomenon. For instance, uncomposed space is only a permanent phenomenon because it is not sometimes a permanent phenomenon and sometimes not, nor is it partially a permanent phenomenon and partially not. Uncomposed space is only a permanent phenomenon; thus, being only a permanent phenomenon does exist, but only-a-permanent-phenomenon does not exist.

This situation leads us to see that the two—a permanent phenomenon and only a permanent phenomenon—is a set including an existent and a non-existent of which being them is possible because they are observed as a common locus of being (1) selfless such that being them exists and (2) also (the set) is suitable as an object of an awareness. The two—a permanent phenomenon and only a permanent phenomenon—are selfless such that being them exists because there is something which is the two—a permanent phenomenon and only a permanent phenomenon, as in the case of uncomposed space. As for the second requirement specified in the definition, that of being suitable as an object of an awareness, in the case of a set including an existent and a non-existent such as the two—a permanent phenomenon and only a permanent phenomenon—it is only the combined set that is suitable as an object of an awareness, for it is not true that each of the two components is an object of knowledge.

For a collection including both existents and non-existents (such as the selfless which is divided into these two), existence predominates, and thus the collection is an existent. This rule is based on the fact that one may apprehend the set with a valid cognizer even though only one member of the set is so apprehensible.

Because it is only the *collection* of such sets as the two—a permanent phenomenon and only a permanent phenomenon—that is existent means that such sets must be referred in the singular as *an* object of knowledge of which being them is not possible. Further, this situation calls into question the intention of the second portion of the definition. Is it that each member of the set must be suitable as an object of an awareness or that only the combined set must be suitable as an object of an awareness? The Tibetan language version is not specific in number and so does not yield an answer. According to Kensur Yeshay Tupden, this is not a problem. If all the members of a set are existent, then each is suitable as an object of an awareness as is the collective set. If only one member of the set is an existent, then the collection is an existent, and in that way the set satisfies the second requirement of the definition. Kensur Yeshay Tupden denied that either is the *main* intention of the second requirement, but since a combined existent/non-existent set qualifies as an object of knowledge, this implies that the ontological status of the combination is the predominant concern. Still, as he points out, the question is moot in that if any of the set is an existent, then the whole set is too.

Since a combined set including an existent and a non-existent may qualify as an object of knowledge of which being them is possible, the above definition given for the plural, objects of knowledge of which being them is possible, may be thus revised to include all contingencies:

> those observed as a common locus of being (1) selfless such that being them exists and (2) also (at least one of the set is) suitable as an object of an awareness.

In considering pairs and groups of phenomena, some are objects of knowledge of which being them is possible and some are objects of knowledge of which being them is not possible. However, although some pairs or groups of things are objects of knowledge of which being them is not possible, no singular phenomenon can be such. All objects of knowledge of which being them is not possible must be either (1) a pair or group of different phenomena (*tha dad, nānātva*) or (2) a pair or group of one or more existents and one or more non-existents. The definition of objects of knowledge of which being them is not possible is:

> those observed as a common locus of being (1) [phenomena] of which being them does not exist and (2) also being suitable as objects of awarenesses (*khyod kyi yin pa med pa yang yin blo'i yul du bya rung ba yang yin pa'i gzhi mthun par dmigs pa*).

332 *Debate in Tibetan Buddhism*

An example is the two—a form and a consciousness (*gzugs shes gnyis*), for they are observed as a common locus of being (1) phenomena of which being them does not exist and (2) also being suitable as objects of awarenesses. In this definition, the qualification that objects of knowledge of which being them is not possible must be a *common locus* means that the collective set must bring together the two defining characteristics:

1 The two—a form and a consciousness—are phenomena of which being them does not exist, for there is no one thing or combination of things that is the two—a form and a consciousness. In order for something to be the two—a form and a consciousness—it would have to be *both* a form and a consciousness in the same way that John F. Kennedy was both an American and the President. Something's being a form exists and being a consciousness exists, but something's being both a form and a consciousness does not exist and is not possible.

   To repeat, being a certain object means that the word expressing that object must be suitable to serve correctly as the predicate (*q*) in a copulative sentence, a sentence of the form, *p* is a *q*, such that there is some thing or combination of things which is a *q*. However, in the case of the two—a form and a consciousness—there is nothing that one may say is the two—a form and a consciousness. A form is not both a form and a consciousness, and a consciousness is not both a form and a consciousness. Even the two—a form and a consciousness—are not the two—a form and a consciousness—because they are not on the one hand forms and on the other consciousnesses.

2 Although being the two—a form and a consciousness—does not exist, the individuals within that set as well as the set itself are suitable as objects of awarenesses A form is suitable as an object of an awareness, and also a consciousness is suitable as an object of an awareness; therefore, the two—a form and a consciousness—are

suitable as objects of awarenesses. It must be clearly seen
that the two—a form and a consciousness—are suitable
as objects of awarenesses, are objects of knowledge, and
do exist.

Here too, among objects of knowledge of which being them
is not possible there are sets including both an existent and a
non-existent. For example, the two—an existent and a non-
existent (*yod med gnyis*), the two—a pot and the horn of a
rabbit (*bum pa dang ri bong rva gnyis*), and the two—a boy
and the child of a barren woman (*bu dang mo gsham gyi bu
gnyis*)—are such sets.

As a case in point, the two—an existent and a non-
existent—are an object of knowledge of which being them is
not possible. The collective set is suitable as an object of an
awareness because one of the members, an existent, is so
suitable. Thus, the two—an existent and a non-existent—is
an object of knowledge. However, something's being the
two—an existent and a non-existent—is not possible, for
there is nothing among all selflessnesses that is on the one
hand an existent and on the other also a non-existent. The
selfless, which is divided into existents and non-existents, is
not itself both an existent and a non-existent because it is a
permanent phenomenon and thereby an existent. Even the
two—an existent and a non-existent—is not the two—an
existent and a non-existent—because the set is not both an
existent and a non-existent. Rather, the set is only an existent. Thus, being the two—an existent and a non-existent—
does not exist and is not possible; yet, the two—an existent
and a non-existent—together do exist. Therefore, the two—
an existent and a non-existent—are an object of knowledge
of which being them is not possible. Again, it is interesting
that even though the subject is grammatically plural, they
must be referred to in the singular as *an* object of
knowledge, for it is only the collective set that is existent
and not both of the members.

Since some objects of knowledge of which being them is
not possible are such combinations of existents and non-

existents, the definition may be revised more generally to read:

> those observed as a common locus of being (1) selfless such that being them does not exist and (2) also (at least one of the set is) suitable as an object of an awareness.

In their discussion of objects of knowledge of which being them is not possible, the Collected Topics logicians stress the point that they do exist, but *being*, for instance, the two—a form and a consciousness—does not exist in the sense that there is nothing which is the two—a form and a consciousness. At first glance it seems counterintuitive to say that there could be some things which exist, yet there is nothing which is those things. However, since forms exist and consciousnesses exist, as a result the two—a form and a consciousness—exist even though there is no one thing or set of things which one can put as being the two—a form and a consciousness.

To stress the importance of the fact that these objects do exist, if objects of knowledge of which being them is not possible were defined simply as:

> those of which being them does not exist (*khyod kyi yin pa med pa*),

failing to specify them as suitable as objects of awarenesses, one would incur the fault of including non-existents, singly or in sets without existents. For instance, the horn of a rabbit is something of which being it does not exist because there is nothing which is a horn of a rabbit, but since it is non-existent it is not an *object of knowledge* of which being it is not possible. Thus, objects of knowledge of which being them is not possible must exist, yet there can be nothing which demonstrates the being of that particular existent.

The stock example of objects of knowledge of which being them is not possible is the two—a pillar and a pot (*ka bum gnyis*). Other examples include the two—a gold pot and a copper pot (*gser bum dang zangs bum gnyis*), the two—a permanent phenomenon and a functioning thing (*rtag dngos gnyis*), and the two—a definition and a definiendum (*mtshan mtshon gnyis*). Each of these sets is comprised of different objects of knowledge and are suitable as objects of awarenesses, but for each of them there is nothing which demonstrates the two diverse qualities. For example, the two—a permanent phenomenon and a functioning thing—are objects of knowledge because a permanent phenomenon is such an object and so is a functioning thing. However, being the two—a permanent phenomenon and a functioning thing—is not possible. There is nothing which is both a permanent phenomenon and a functioning thing. Established base, which may be divided into permanent phenomena and functioning things, is not itself both a permanent phenomenon and a functioning thing, for it is only a permanent phenomenon. Also, the two—a permanent phenomenon and a functioning thing—are not both a permanent phenomenon and a functioning thing. Rather, as in the case of established base, since the set includes both a permanent phenomenon and a thing, it itself is a permanent phenomenon. Thus, the two—a permanent phenomenon and a functioning thing—are a permanent phenomenon, and being the two—a permanent phenomenon and a functioning thing—does not exist.

As mentioned earlier, any singular phenomenon is an object of knowledge of which being it is possible; however, among different phenomena, some are objects of knowledge of which being them is possible and some are objects of knowledge of which being them is not possible. The differentiation breaks along orderly lines. By applying the method of analyzing the differences between two phenomena one can see that the discrimination of whether two particular phenomena are objects of knowledge of which being them is possible or objects of knowledge of which being them is not possible corresponds to the type of difference that exists between those two phenomena. From among the four types of differences that can exist between two phenomena—three possibilities, four possibilities, mutually exclusive, and mutually inclusive—if two phenomena have three possibilities or four possibilities between them or are mutually inclusive, then they are objects of knowledge of which being them *is* possible. If and only if two phenomena are mutually exclusive, then they are objects of knowledge of which being them *is not* possible.

For example, the two—a pillar and a pot—are mutually exclusive because they are different phenomena which do not have a common locus. A common locus of a pillar and a pot would have to be something which is both a pillar and a pot, as a consciousness is a common locus of a functioning thing and an established base. However, no such common locus can be found; thus, being the two—a pillar and a pot— does not exist, and they are objects of knowledge of which being them is not possible.

As specified in the definition, objects of knowledge of which being them is not possible are common loci. In other words, even though there is no common locus of, for instance, the two—a pillar and a pot—they are a common locus of other qualities. Whatever exists is necessarily a common locus. Even the simplest phenomenon has a variety of qualities and is a common locus of those qualities. A chair, for instance, is a common locus of furniture and matter, of a functioning thing and an established base, and so forth. Anything which exists is at least a common locus of an existent and a phenomena. This is necessarily true, for existent and phenomenon are mutually inclusive. Whatever is the one must be the other as well, so whatever exists is both.

Furthermore, both objects of knowledge of which being them is possible and objects of knowledge of which being them is not possible, as existents, are also common loci. This is so because they are at least common loci of being objects of knowledge and phenomena. However, for any two phenomena which are objects of knowledge of which being them is not possible, there is no common locus which is the two of them. This is exactly the point: It is not that objects of knowledge of which being them is not possible are not a common locus of some other qualities, but that there is nothing which is a common locus of those two mutually exclusive phenomena. When combined, they are objects of knowledge of which being them is not possible. In describing these categories of objects of knowledge the Collected Topics logicians are making the point that in no case is there anything which shares two mutually exclusive qualities. This is the way that mutually exclusive phenomena are defined, they are existents for which there is no common locus. So, of course, any two mutually exclusive phenomena are objects of knowledge of which being them does not exist.

All other pairs of phenomena, those that are not mutually exclusive, are objects of knowledge of which being them is possible. If two phenomena are mutually inclusive, they are objects of knowledge of which being them is possible. For instance, product and impermanent phenomenon are mutually inclusive, and thereby the two—a product and an impermanent phenomenon (*byas pa dang mi rtag pa gnyis*)— are objects of knowledge of which being them is possible. A product exists and an impermanent phenomenon exists; therefore, the two—a product and an impermanent phenomenon—are suitable as objects of awarenesses. Also, being the two—a product and an impermanent phenomenon—exists because, for instance, a tongue consciousness, an eye sense power, and a tree are both products and impermanent phenomena.

If there are three possibilities between two phenomena, they too are invariably objects of knowledge of which being them is possible. For instance, there are three possibilities between pot and functioning thing; thus, the two—a pot and a functioning thing—are objects of knowledge of which being them is possible. Although it is not the case that whatever is a functioning thing is a pot, since there is a common locus of being a pot and a functioning thing, there is something which is the two—a pot and a functioning thing—such as a gold pot.

If there are four possibilities between two phenomena, those two are objects of knowledge of which being them is possible. For example, there are four possibilities between functioning thing and definition:

1   Something which is both is that which is able to perform a function, the definition of a functioning thing.
2   Something which is a functioning thing but is not a definition is a product, the definiendum of a created phenomenon.
3   Something which is a definition but is not a functioning thing is that which is established by a valid cognizer, the definition of an established base.
4   Something which is neither is easy to posit—for instance, uncomposed space.

The reason why any two phenomena that have four possibilities between them are objects of knowledge of which being them is possible is that there is necessarily a common locus of the two. In this case, there is something which is the two—a functioning thing and a definition—because that which is able to perform a function is such, a momentary phenomenon is such, a disintegrating phenomenon is such, and so forth.

It should be noted that these rules identified for sets of two phenomena apply equally well for sets of three or more phenomena. That is, all sets of phenomena including two or more that are mutually exclusive are each objects of knowledge of which being them is not possible, and all other sets not including mutually exclusive phenomena are each objects of knowledge of which being them is possible. For instance, the three—a functioning thing, a definition, and a definiendum—are objects of knowledge of which being them is not possible because, although they exist, since there is nothing which is both a definition and a definiendum there is nothing which is those three phenomena. However, the four—a color, a primary color, the color of cloth, and yellow—are objects of knowledge of which being them is possible because they are suitable as objects of awarenesses and, for instance, the color of a yellow cotton robe is all of these. This distinction seems to hold true for all sets that do not contain any mutually exclusive phenomena, but should be investigated.

The presentation of objects of knowledge of which being them is not possible, beyond being merely a result of a willingness to accept the consequence of their assertion of the individual existence of these, reflects the ordinary view of phenomena in groups and suggests a possible fault in that view. It is the nature of both direct perceivers and thought consciousnesses that they apprehend separate phenomena as if together. To an eye consciousness a chair may appear together with a desk, yet there is nothing which is both that chair and that desk. Also, upon hearing the names, "John and Mary", something appears very strongly to a thought consciousness apprehending them. They appear as if bound together, yet there is nothing which is both John and Mary. Who are John and Mary? John is not John and Mary because, even though he is John, he is not both John and Mary. By the same reasoning, Mary too is not John and Mary. It is difficult even to say that John and Mary are John and Mary. The understanding is this: Since the two parts of the predicate, "John" and "Mary", are joined by a conjunction and occur in a copulative sentence, both parts of the predicate must apply equally to both parts of the subject. This is the way that the sentence is understood in the Collected Topics tradition. For instance, in the statement, "John and Mary are Americans and taxpayers," one understands that John is an American and a taxpayer and that Mary as well is an American and a taxpayer.

However, what can one say is John and Mary? What can be put as the subject in a copulative sentence having John and Mary as the predicate? If one says that John and Mary are John and Mary, then it will have to be the case that John is John and Mary and that Mary is John and Mary. Since such is clearly not the case, even John and Mary are not John and Mary.

This situation shows that objects of knowledge of which being them is not possible are not themselves in the sense of being exemplifiers of themselves. For instance, the two—a pillar and pot—are not a pillar and a pot because of not being a common locus of a pillar and a pot. There is nothing among all existents that exemplifies two mutually exclusive phenomena.

The presentation of these two types of objects of knowledge serves to emphasize that even though one may perceive mutually exclusive phenomena together, there is nothing which is those phenomena and being them is not possible. Normal apprehension of phenomena constantly trades in these mutually exclusive objects. If someone asks for a pen and paper, one would not become befuddled. Yet is there anything which is a pen and paper? One example the debaters often use to illustrate objects of knowledge of which being them is not possible is the two hands. One can see that one has two hands, yet what is it that is the two hands? The left hand is not the two hands. The right hand is not the two hands. Even the left and the right hands are not the two hands. Still, the two hands exist as objects of one's use, though there is nothing that is the two hands.

This type of reasoning suggests and leads one into the Middle Way School reasoning on emptiness. In the Middle Way School, phenomena exist, are objects of use, and are able to perform functions, but they exist merely conventionally and are not findable among their bases of designation (*gdags gzhi*). Here it is being shown that although John and Mary or one's two hands exist, are objects of use, and can perform functions, there is no one thing or combination of things which is John and Mary or one's two hands. This sort of instruction early in the logical training sharpens one for the later, higher reasoning. One becomes accustomed to the idea that even though something might exist, one cannot find anything which is that phenomenon.

On first consideration, one may feel that if something exists, then there also must be something which is that thing. If this were the case, the apprehension of phenomena would be limited to either single phenomena or sets of non-mutually exclusive phenomena, for all others would not exist, being neither the objects of comprehension of direct perceivers nor of thought consciousnesses. Then it would follow that conceiving of John and Mary would be a case of taking to mind only a non-existent like apprehending the horns of a rabbit. Also, one could not make use of one's left and right hands because one's two hands would be empty of the ability to perform a function since they would be non-existent, as something which is one's two hands does not exist. Seeing the absurdity of this reasoning the Collected Topics logicians assert that the mere existence of sets of mutually exclusive phenomena does not necessarily entail that there is something which is those phenomena.

As has been seen, objects of knowledge of which being them is possible and objects of knowledge of which being them is not possible do not correspond at all to functioning things and permanent phenomena; rather, both are themselves permanent phenomena. However, like established base and the phenomena mutually inclusive with it, although they themselves are permanent, it is not the case that whatever is either of these two types of objects of knowledge is necessarily a permanent phenomenon, for they do include impermanent phenomena. For instance, objects of knowledge of which being them is not possible such as the two—a pillar and a pot—are functioning things. It may seem that if such phenomena exist, since there is nothing one can put as them, together they must be a permanent phenomenon, an appearing object of a thought consciousness and a mere imputation. However, the Collected Topics texts deny this. Since a pillar is a functioning thing and a pot is a functioning thing, when combined to form the two—a pillar and a pot—these objects of knowledge are still functioning things, causes, appearing objects of direct perception, and so forth. Grouping impermanent phenomena together does not give rise to permanent phenomena.

Further, sets of phenomena may be included not merely among permanent or impermanent phenomena but also into sub-categories of those phenomena. For instance, the two—a pillar and a pot—are matter because of being atomically established. The two—an eye consciousness and an ear consciousness—are consciousnesses because of being awarenesses. The two—a gold pot and a copper pot—are pots, and so on. Such distinctions depend on whatever the two have in common.

Since pairs of phenomena are included with whatsoever phenomena they both share qualities, the differentiation of objects of knowledge of which being them is possible and those of which being them is not possible can be used as a way of dividing permanent phenomena, functioning things, matter, consciousnesses, pots, and so forth. In the second section of this chapter, the layout of the author's own system of established bases, permanent phenomena are divided into those of which being them is possible and those of which being them is not possible. In that section, an object of knowledge is given as an illustration of a permanent phenomenon of which being it is possible, and the two—a permanent phenomenon and a functioning thing—are given as an illustration of a permanent phenomenon of which being them is not possible. Even though a functioning thing is not permanent, when put with a permanent phenomenon the set is permanent because it is a common locus of being a phenomenon and the non-momentary. Like established base itself, the two—a permanent phenomenon and a functioning thing—are a combination of the permanent and the impermanent, and since the combination includes a permanent phenomenon, it too is permanent and an appearing object of a thought consciousness. Since it is the combination of the two—a permanent phenomenon and a functioning thing— which is permanent and not both of the members individually they must be referred to in the singular as a permanent phenomenon of which being them is not possible rather than as permanent phenomena of which being them is not possible.

Debate B.3 begins with a hypothetical Defender's accepting that whatever are objects of knowledge are necessarily objects of knowledge of which being them is possible. He has not understood that objects of knowledge may be divided into those of which being them is possible and those of which being them is not possible. The Sūtra School Challenger posits the counterexample of the two—a pillar and a pot—which, although objects of knowledge, are not objects of knowledge of which being them is possible. The text says:

> If someone [a hypothetical Defender] says, "Whatever are objects of knowledge are necessarily objects of knowledge of which being [them] is possible," [the Sūtra School Challenger responds to him,] "It [absurdly] follows that the subjects, the two—a pillar and a pot, are [objects of knowledge of which being them is possible] because of [being objects of knowledge]."
>
> If he says that the reason [that the two—a pillar and a pot—are objects of knowledge] is not established, [the Sūtra School Challenger responds,] "It follows that the subjects [the two—a pillar and a pot] are [objects of knowledge] because of being existents."
>
> "[It follows that] there is pervasion [i.e., whatever is an existent is necessarily an object of knowledge] because object of knowledge, existent, object of comprehension, and established base are mutually inclusive."
>
> If he accepts the basic consequence [that the two—a pillar and a pot—are objects of knowledge of which being them is possible, the Sūtra School Challenger responds,] "It follows that the subjects [the two—a pillar and a pot] are not objects of knowledge of which being [them] is possible because of being objects of knowledge of which being [them] is not possible."

> If he says that the reason [that the two—a pillar and a pot—are objects of knowledge of which being them is not possible] is not established, the Sūtra School Challenger responds,] "It follows that the subjects [the two—a pillar and a pot] are [objects of knowledge of which being them is not possible] because of (1) being objects of knowledge and (2) being them does not exist."

The reason is perhaps a variant definition of objects of knowledge of which being them is not possible or, at least, expresses the essential features of such phenomena.

> The second part of the reason [that being the two—a pillar and a pot—does not exist] is easy.

The author notes simply that the second part of the reason is easy to establish and does not pursue that possible line of reasoning. This is not something that either disputant would say but is only a textual note. In spelling out the meaning of the second part of the reason, that being them does not exist, one puts the subjects in the place of the pronoun "them" (*khyod*) that represents the subjects, the two—a pillar and a pot, in the reason. When the pronoun *"khyod"* ("it" or "them") is used, one spells out the reason by filling in its referent, the subject, no matter where "it" or "them" occurs in the reason.

The Challenger uses a pronoun in the reason in place of spelling out the subject in order to keep the pervasion general. In this way if some things are (1) objects of knowledge and (2) being them does not exist, then they (any phenomena satisfying the qualities specified in the antecedent) are necessarily objects of knowledge of which being them is not possible. Rather than being limited to the subjects at hand (the two—a pillar and a pot), the pervasion applies generally.

If the Defender had questioned the second part of the reason, that being the two—a pillar and a pot does not exist, the Challenger might choose to force the Defender to justify his denial or he might choose to further justify his own reason.

When the Defender denies the establishment of the reason, he is asserting the opposite. Thus, the Challenger might state the implicit assertion to his opponent in the form of a consequence, "It follows with respect to the subjects, the two—a pillar and a pot, that being them does exist." When the Defender accepts this, the Challenger will ask him to posit something which is the two—a pillar and a pot—and the debate will develop out of his assertion.

On the other hand, the Challenger might choose to defend his reason saying, "It follows with respect to the subjects, the two—a pillar and a pot, that being them does not exist because there is no valid cognizer which realizes the existence of something's being them." What is not realized by a valid cognizer does not exist. This second approach, defending the reason, is the usual one seen in the literature as it generally serves to relay more information, but in the debating courtyard either approach will be taken according to the need of the Challenger. Here, however, the text does not follow out a line of reasoning developing from the Defender's denying the establishment of the second part of the reason—merely stating that the proof would be easy.

> If he says that the first part of the reason [that the two—a pillar and a pot—are objects of knowledge] is not established, [the Sūtra School Challenger responds,] "It follows that the subjects [the two—a pillar and a pot] are objects of knowledge because of being either one or different."

The Defender chooses to challenge the first part of the reason alone. When given a two part reason, one can question the establishment of the individual parts or of the combined parts. Here the Defender does not deny the second part of the reason, that being the two—a pillar and a pot—does not exist, which in many ways is more interesting. He denies that the two—a pillar and a pot—are objects of knowledge, the same as when he objected to the establishment of the reason of the basic consequence. So the Challenger again must prove that the two—a pillar and a pot—are objects of knowledge. He proves this by the reason of their being one or different. Whatever is either one or different necessarily exists.

Established bases may be divided exhaustively into the two, [phenomena which are] one (*gcig, ekatva*) and [those which are] different (*tha dad, nānātva*). Like established base and the phenomena mutually inclusive with it, both one and different are permanent phenomena, but whatever is one or different is not necessarily permanent, for each includes impermanent instances. The one, or a singular phenomenon, is defined as:

> a phenomenon which is not diverse (*so so ba ma yin pa'i chos, *aprthaktva-dharma*).

An example is an object of knowledge. Different phenomena are defined as:

> phenomena which are diverse (*so so ba'i chos, prthaktva-dharma*).

An example is the two—a gold pot and a copper pot— which are separate and distinct phenomena.

The division of established bases into one and different distinguishes singular phenomena from plural or diverse phenomena. Moreover, it serves as a guide for the comparison of phenomena in sentences of the form, "This particular phenomenon is *one* with that particular phenomenon," or, "This particular phenomenon is *different* from that particular phenomenon." Whatever is one with something must be one with that thing in both name and meaning. The only thing that is one with sound is sound. Sound is one with sound, and all other existents are different from sound. Oneness, here, is a case of self-identity. What is one with something must be *exactly the same as* that phenomenon. Even two mutually inclusive phenomena such as product and imper- manent phenomenon are not one, for, although they have the same meaning or referent, they do not have the same name; thus, they are different and mutually inclusive (*don gcig, ekārtha*), literally "one meaning". Also, "pot" and its

Tibetan language equivalent *"bum-ba"* (*bum pa*) are not one but are mutually inclusive because although their meaning is the same the terms expressing that meaning are different. Further, although two plus two equals four, since two plus two is not exactly the same as four, it is not one with four.

Whatever exists is necessarily one with itself and different from all else. A pot is one with itself, but only with itself. Oneness is a completely self-reflexive quality. Even objects of knowledge of which being them is not possible are one with themselves. For instance, the two—a pillar and a pot—are one with the two—a pillar and a pot. There is nothing which is the two—a pillar and a pot, but they are one with themselves. That they are one with themselves does not mean that they are themselves, for they are not. Rather, they are not different from themselves. This is in line with what the definition of a phenomenon suggests, that whatever exists bears its own entity. Phenomena may or may not be themselves in the sense of being exemplifiers of themselves, but without exception they are one with themselves and are not different from themselves.

Different phenomena may be different in terms of name, meaning, or both name and meaning. Thus, different phenomena may compare in any of the four possible ways—three possibilities, four possibilities, mutually inclusive, or mutually exclusive. The analytical comparison of phenomena presumes that they are different. As mentioned above, things which are mutually inclusive are different phenomena having the same meaning. Mutually exclusive phenomena, as well as phenomena having three possibilities or four possibilities, are different phenomena having different names and meanings. It is immediately apparent that two mutually exclusive phenomena such as functioning thing and permanent phenomena are different because there is nothing which is both of them; thus, they have both different names and different meanings. Also, two phenomena such as functioning thing and pot, which have a relationship of three possibilities, are different phenomena *even though* there is something such as a gold pot which is both of them. A pot is a functioning thing, but even so it is different from functioning thing. Being something does not mean being exactly the same as that thing. Also, if something is different from a particular phenomenon, that does not necessarily entail that it is not an example of that phenomenon, as a pot is different from functioning thing but it is still a functioning thing.

The above definitions stated for one and different in general may be applied to any particular phenomenon to yield definitions of what is one with that phenomenon and what is different from it. For instance, the definition of something which is one with sound (*sgra dang gcig*) is:

> a phenomenon which is not diverse from sound (*sgra dang so so ba ma yin pa'i chos*).

The only illustration is sound itself, for sound alone is a phenomenon which is not diverse from sound. Similarly, the definition of something which is different from sound (*sgra dang tha dad*) is:

> a phenomenon which is diverse from sound (*sgra dang so so ba'i chos*).

An illustration is the sound of a drum, a pot, or a consciousness, for each of these is a phenomenon which is diverse from sound.

The definitions of one and different specify them as phenomena (*chos, dharma*); thus, what does not exist is neither one nor different. The horn of a rabbit is grammatically singular, but it is not a phenomenon which is non-diverse because of not being a phenomenon. Also, the horn of a rabbit is not different from, for instance, a pot because of not being a phenomenon which is diverse from a pot.

On first consideration it may seem that two phenomena such as functioning thing and different-from-functioning-thing (*dngos po dang tha dad*) would be mutually exclusive, but there are four possibilities between them:

1 Something which is both is a pot, a pillar, a specifically characterized phenomenon, or any functioning thing other than functioning thing itself.
2 Something which is different from functioning thing but is not a functioning thing is uncomposed space, object of knowledge, or any permanent phenomenon.
3 Only functioning thing itself is a functioning thing but not different from functioning thing.
4 Something which is neither a functioning thing nor different from functioning thing is the horn of a rabbit.

Similarly, there are four possibilities between different-from-functioning-thing and non-thing (*dngos po ma yin pa*):

1 Uncomposed space or any permanent phenomenon is both different from functioning thing and a non-thing.
2 Something which is different from functioning thing but not a non-thing (that is, is a thing) is an eye consciousness.
3 Something which is a non-thing but is not different from functioning thing is a non-existent.
4 For something which is neither, one must posit functioning thing itself, as it alone is not a non-thing and also is not different from functioning thing.

Since there are four possibilities between these two, it is apparent that something's being different from functioning thing does not mean that it is not a functioning thing.

The division of established bases into phenomena which are one and those which are different is completely exhaustive. Established base and either of the two, one or different, are mutually inclusive. Unlike the division of colors into primary colors and secondary colors such that color itself is a color but neither a primary color nor a secondary color, established base is included within this division as something which is one. *All* established bases are one or different. Further, one is itself, it is one, for it is a phenomenon which is non-diverse. Also, different is one because it too is a phenomenon which is non-diverse. Different phenomena must be pairs or groups of phenomena, and since different itself is singular, it is one. Any different phenomena are necessarily not one, but different itself is one.

In the last consequence the Challenger introduced the topic of one and different in showing that the two—a pillar and a pot—are objects of knowledge because of being either one or different. Of course, the two—a pillar and a pot—are different because of being different in both name and meaning. A pillar is different from a pot, and a pot is different from a pillar.

> If he says that the reason [that the two—a pillar and a pot—are either one or different] is not established, [the Sūtra School Challenger responds,] "It follows that the subjects [the two—a pillar and a pot] are [either one or different] because of being different."
>
> If he says that the reason [that the two—a pillar and a pot—are different] is not established, [the Sūtra School Challenger responds,] "It follows that the subjects [the two—a pillar and a pot] are [different] because of being mutually different."

The Sūtra School Challenger justifies a pillar and a pot as different by reason of their being mutually different (*phan tshun tha dad*). As shown in the next consequence, mutual difference means that each is different from the other, a pillar is different from a pot and a pot is different from a pillar.

All phenomena which are different are mutually different, meaning that if *p* is different from *q*, then *q* is different from *p*. It could not be the case that one phenomenon is different from another and yet the other is not different from the one, for if one phenomenon is not different from another phenomenon, they must be one and the same.

The only way in which different phenomena and mutually different phenomena are not the same comes in the interface between a non-existent and an existent. For instance, the child of a barren woman and a functioning thing are different but not mutually different. However, one cannot say that the child of a barren woman and a functioning thing are different *phenomena*, for only one is a phenomenon. Still, one can say that a functioning thing is a different *phenomenon* from the child of a barren woman because of (1) being an existent and (2) not being one with the child of a barren woman. However, the child of a barren woman is not different and not a different *phenomenon* from a functioning thing because of not being a phenomenon which is diverse from a functioning thing. Thus, whatever is different from a non-existent is necessarily not mutually different from a non-existent.

> If he says that the reason [that the two—a pillar and a pot—are mutually different] is not established, [the Sūtra School Challenger responds,] "It follows that the two—a pillar and a pot—are mutually different because a pillar is different from a pot and a pot is different from a pillar."
>
> If he says that the first part of the reason [that a pillar is different from a pot] is not established, [the Sūtra School Challenger responds,] "It follows that the subject, a pillar, is different from a pot because of (1) being an existent and (2) not being one with a pot."

In justifying that a pillar is a different phenomenon from a pot, the Challenger specifies that it is an existent in the first part of the reason. This must be added in order to keep the pervasion accurate. It is not the case that whatever is not one with a pot is necessarily different from a pot because a non-existent is not one with a pot but it is also not different from a pot.

The Challenger has shown that the two—a pillar and a pot—are different. As a pair they are objects of knowledge and, within that, are objects of knowledge of which being them is not possible. Therefore, as opposed to the hypothetical Defender's original acceptance, whatever are objects of knowledge are not necessarily objects of knowledge of which being them is possible. These two principals of debate

B.3, objects of knowledge and objects of knowledge of which being them is possible, have three possibilities:

1   The two—a pot and a gold pot—or the two—a product and an impermanent phenomenon—are both.
2   Whatever are objects of knowledge of which being them is possible are necessarily objects of knowledge, but whatever are objects of knowledge are not necessarily objects of knowledge of which being them is possible. For instance, the two—a pillar and a pot, the two—a cow and a horse, or the two—a human and an animal—are objects of knowledge but are not objects of knowledge of which being them is possible.
3   Something which is neither is the flower of a dry tree.

Debate B.4, Fourth Mistaken View (6b.1)

In debate B.4 the hypothetical Defender takes a stand opposite to that taken in debate B.3. He now accepts that all existents are existents of which being them is *not* possible. The text says:

> If someone [a hypothetical Defender] says, "Whatever is an existent is necessarily an existent of which being [it] is not possible," [the Sūtra School Challenger responds to him,] "It [absurdly] follows that the subject, a functioning thing, is [an existent of which being it is not possible] because of [being an existent]. You asserted the pervasion."
>
> If he says that the reason [that a functioning thing is an existent, is not established, [the Sūtra School Challenger responds,] "It follows that the subject [a functioning thing] is [an existent] because of being either a permanent phenomenon or a functioning thing; because of being a functioning thing."
>
> If he accepts the basic consequence [that a functioning thing] is an existent of which being it is not possible, [the Sūtra School Challenger responds,] "It follows that the subject [a functioning thing] is not

an existent of which being it is not possible because
of being an existent of which being it is possible."

If he says that the reason [that a functioning thing
is an existent of which being it is possible] is not
established, [the Sūtra School Challenger responds,]
"It follows that the subject [a functioning thing] is
[an existent of which being it is possible] because (1)
[it] is an existent and (2) the three—matter [*bem po,
kanthā*], consciousness [*shes pa, jñāna*], and non-
associated compositional factors [*ldan min 'du byed,
viprayukta-saṃskāra*] are it."

Functioning things are divided into the three—matter, consciousnesses, and non-associated compositional factors—
which will be discussed in some detail below. Here the
Challenger is proving that a functioning thing is an existent
of which being it is possible by showing that it has the
defining characteristics of such a phenomenon. It is an existent and there is something which it is. Matter is a functioning thing, consciousnesses are functioning things, and non-
associated compositional factors are functioning things.
Therefore, a functioning thing is an existent of which being
it is possible.

If he says that the latter part of the reason [that the
three—matter, consciousnesses, and non-associated
compositional factors—are functioning things] is not
established, [the Sūtra School Challenger responds,]
"It follows that the subjects, the three—matter, consciousnesses, and non-associated compositional factors, are functioning things because of (1) being
existents and (2) not being permanent phenomena."

Here, in the last consequence in debate B.4, the subject has
changed to the three—matter, consciousnesses, and non-
associated compositional factors. In the former reason, "the
three ... are it," these three formed the grammatical subject.
The Defender questioned whether or not they are functioning things, so they became the basis of debate, and the
former subject, a functioning thing, which was the

grammatical predicate in the former reason, became the predicate of the consequence. In this way, the structure of the argument form is adaptable to the flow of debate.

In proving matter, consciousnesses, and non-associated compositional factors as functioning things, the Challenger specified them as *existents* which are not permanent phenomena. If this specification were left out, there would be no pervasion because it is not the case that whatever is not a permanent phenomenon is necessarily a functioning thing. This is so because a non-existent is not a permanent phenomenon, but it is also not a functioning thing. When stating negatives in a reason one must be careful to qualify that reason in such a way as to have pervasion.

As indicated above, functioning things are divided into three types:

1   matter (*bem po, kanthā*)
2   consciousnesses (*shes pa, jñāna*)
3   non-associated compositional factors (*ldan min 'du byed, viprayukta-saṃskāra*).

Without exception, every impermanent phenomena is included into one or another of these categories, and each of the three divisions is mutually exclusive with the other two.

Matter is defined as:

> that which is atomically established (*rdul du grub pa, *anusiddha*).

(See pp. 185-221.) In the system of the Proponents of Sūtra, matter and form (*gzugs, rūpa*) are mutually inclusive. Thus, functioning things also may be divided into forms, consciousnesses, and non-associated compositional factors. Matter is divided into internal matter and external matter as discussed above in the chapter on colors and so forth. In some Collected Topics texts the introductory chapter is limited to colors, and in those books the presentation of matter comes in later chapters. In the Tutor's *Collected Topics* the chapter on colors is more general. In any case, the layout of forms might suitably be included in the presentation of established bases as a portion of the discussion of functioning things.

The second branch of functioning things is that of consciousnesses.[1] The three—awareness, knower, and consciousness—are mutually inclusive. A consciousness is defined as:

> that which is clear and knowing (*gsal zhing rig pa*).

An awareness (*blo, buddhi*) is defined as:

> a knower (*rig pa, saṃvedana*).

The topic of consciousness is discussed in detail in the book-length section called "Awareness and Knowledge " (*blo rig*), the fourth major section in the Collected Topics, included as an internal division of "The Greater Path of Reasoning".

It is said that all schools of tenets agree that a knower is the definition of an awareness.[2] However, the definition of a consciousness is variously identified in different sources. The Go-mang *Types of Awarenesses* (*blo rigs*) textbook says, "The clear and non-material is the definition of a consciousness."[3] This definition is based on passages in Dharmakīrti's *Commentary on (Dignāga's) "Compendium of Valid Cognition"* such as, "The nature of the mind is clear light,"[4] on a passage in Shāntirakṣhita's *Ornament to the Middle Way* (*dbu ma rgyan, madhyamakālaṃkāra*) which says,

---

[1] The source for this section on the definitions of an awareness and a consciousness is Losang Gyatso, *Compendium of the Important Points in the Presentation of Types of Awarenesses, [an Internal Division of] the Greater Path of Reasoning* (*rigs lam che ba blo rigs kyi rnam bshag nye mkho kun btus*), (Dharamsala, India: Shes rig par khang, 1974), 4b.1-8a.6.

[2] Losang Gyatso, *Types of Awarenesses*, 4b.2-3.

[3] *Ibid.*, 4b.2. The majority of such introductory textbooks on consciousnesses are called "Awareness and Knowledge" (*blo rig*) with the "*rig*" (meaning knower or knowledge) not having an extra suffix. However, Losang Gyatso reports the title of the Go-mang text and gives his own title as "Types of Awarenesses" (*blo rigs*) with the second syllable "*rigs*" (type) having an extra suffix *sa*.

[4] Dharmakīrti, *Commentary on (Dignāga's) "Compendium of Valid Cognition"*, P5709, Vol. 130, 87.1.6.

"Consciousness is thoroughly generated as reversed from the nature of matter,"[1] and so forth.[2] However, this definition is denied by the followers of Panchen Sö-nam-drak-ba (*pan chen bsod nams grags pa*), 1478-1554, author of the monastic textbooks used by Gan-den Shar-dzay and Dre-bung Lo-sel-ling Colleges. This definition also is not used by Jam-ba-gya-tso in the Tutor's *Collected Topics*.

The clear and non-material is not suitable as the definition of a consciousness because a consciousness is a positive phenomenon (*sgrub pa, vidhi*) whereas the clear and non-material is a negative phenomenon (*dgag pa, pratiṣhedha*). Positive and negative phenomena, which are mutually exclusive, are distinguished by the way they appear to the conceptual awareness which knows them. Negative phenomena are known only after having explicitly eliminated some object of negation. For instance, in order to know the clear and non-material it is necessary to eliminate or mentally set aside *the material*, which is here the object of negation of the non-material. Positive phenomena, such as matter or consciousness, are those not realized in this way.

A definition and its definiendum must accord in this aspect of being negative or positive phenomena because an awareness knowing a positive phenomenon and an awareness knowing a negative phenomenon are so radically opposed. That is, one cannot be a positive phenomenon and the other a negative phenomenon, they must both be the same. For a thought consciousness knowing the relationship of a name or definiendum, such as a consciousness, and a meaning or definition, such as the clear and non-material, the aspects of those two, the definition and the definiendum, must accord in the manner of appearance. One cannot appear in the manner of a negative phenomenon and the other appear in the aspect of a positive phenomenon. If it were not so, there would be the resultant fallacy that a

---

[1] Shāntirakṣhita, *Ornament to the Middle Way* (*madhyamakālaṁkarakārikā*), P5284, Vol.101, 1.3.1.
[2] Losang Gyatso, *Types of Awarenesses*, 5b.3-4, 6a.4.

thought consciousness realizing a negative phenomenon and a thought consciousness realizing a positive phenomenon would not be mutually exclusive. For instance, when the hot and burning appears to a thought consciousness, the conventionality of fire is realized when a special ascertaining thought consciousness which joins name and meaning thinks "fire" with respect to just that hot and burning phenomenon. It is not possible for a thought consciousness relating name and meaning simultaneously to take to mind the aspects of both a positive and a negative phenomenon. Therefore, the clear and non-material is not suitable as the definition of a consciousness.[1]

In this system, the definition of a consciousness is posited as *that which is clear and knowing*. Many scholars interpret "clear" as referring to the entity of a consciousness and "knowing" as referring to its function. "Nevertheless, there are varying interpretations of its meaning. Some say that 'clear' refers to the object's appearing clearly from its own side to the appearance factor of the mind and 'knowing' refers to the subject, the awareness, apprehending or knowing the object. There are others who say that 'clear' and 'knowing' both refer to the subject's perceiving the object and thus the definition means 'that which illuminates and knows.'"[2]

Further, in this system *a knower* is posited as the definition of an awareness. The Go-mang *Types of Awarenesses* indicates that the meaning of "knower of an object" (*yul rig pa*) is that which, when an object appears (*'char ba*) perceives (*snang ba*) it.[3] Some scholars deny this interpretation pointing out that what does not appear to a consciousness and is not perceived by it may nonetheless be known by that consciousness. Thus, some argue that if such were the meaning of a knower of an object, it would absurdly follow that an inferential cognizer realizing the impermanence of

---

[1] *Ibid.*, 5b.5-6a.3.
[2] Lati Rinbochay, *Mind in Tibetan Buddhism*, p. 46.
[3] Reported by Losang Gyatso, *Types of Awarenesses*, 4b.6-5a.1.

sound would not know the sound's lack of permanence because a sound's lack of permanence does not appear to and is not perceived by an inferential cognizer realizing the impermanence of sound. What appears to and is perceived by an inferential cognizer realizing the impermanence of sound is a meaning-generality of impermanent sound; thus, a sound's lack of permanence does not appear to and is not perceived by such a consciousness. Still, such a consciousness *explicitly* realizes the impermanence of sound and *implicitly* realizes the sound's lack of permanence. (Although this is a cognition of a positive phenomenon, the impermanence of sound, and a negative phenomenon, the sound's lack of permanence, it is not like the case of a consciousness and the clear and non-material, for the latter is a case of a thought consciousness simultaneously associating positive and negative aspects whereas the former is a case of explicit and implicit realizations.) A sound's lack of permanence does not appear to and is not perceived by an inferential cognizer realizing the impermanence of sound. Yet, that consciousness knows through implicit realization the sound's lack of permanence.[1]

Further, there is another fault with saying that a knower of an object is that which, when an object appears, perceives it. If that were the meaning of a consciousness's being a knower of selflessness, it would absurdly follow that even a yogic direct perceiver realizing the selflessness of the person would not be a knower of selflessness. This is because the selflessness of the person does not appear to and is not perceived by a yogic direct perceiver realizing selflessness. In the system of the Proponents of Sūtra, whatever appears to a direct perceiver is necessarily a functioning thing, and since selflessness is a permanent phenomenon, it can appear only to a thought consciousness and not to a direct perceiver. Still, a yogic direct perceiver realizing selflessness does know its object. Again, it is the difference of an explicit

---

[1] *Ibid.*, 5a.2-3.

realization and an implicit one. Such a yogic perceiver explicitly realizes the body and mind as devoid of a self of persons and implicitly realizes the selflessness of persons. One cannot say that it *directly* realizes (*mngon sum du rtogs pa*) the selflessness of persons, but some say that it realizes its object *by means of a direct perceiver* (*mngon sum gyis rtogs pa*).[1] Even though selflessness does not appear ('*char ba*) to and is not perceived (*snang ba*) by a yogic direct perceiver realizing selflessness, it *knows* (*rig pa*) selflessness.[2]

In his *Presentation of Types of Awarenesses* (*blo rigs kyi rnam gzhag*), Losang Gyatso concludes that in the system of the Proponents of Sūtra the meaning of a knower is that which has the activity of discriminating ('*byed pa*) what are and what are not the qualities of just its own object *or* that which is holding ('*dzin pa*) or apprehending (*bzung pa*) by an awareness.[3] He is taking knower (and by extension consciousness, which is mutually inclusive with knower) in the broadest possible sense as that which discriminates or apprehends.

In the Awareness and Knowledge textbooks, consciousnesses are divided and discussed in many ways; as a portion of the presentation of established bases consciousness are divided exhaustively into two types:

1 mental consciousnesses (*yid shes, mano-jñāna*)
2 sense consciousnesses (*dbang shes, indriya-jñāna*).

The definition of a mental consciousness is:

> a knower that is produced in dependence on its own uncommon empowering condition, a mental sense power (*rang gi thun mong ma yin pa'i bdag rkyen yid dbang la brten nas skye ba'i rig pa*).

The definition of a sense consciousness is:

---

[1] Lati Rinbochay, *Mind in Tibetan Buddhism*, p. 124.
[2] Losang Gyatso, *Types of Awarenesses*, 5a.3-5.
[3] *Ibid.*, 5b.2-3.

a knower that is produced in dependence on its own uncommon empowering condition, a physical sense power (*rang gi thun mong ma yin pa'i bdag rkyen dbang po'i gzugs can pa la brten nas skye ba'i rig pa*).

Mental and sense consciousnesses are divided in terms of their special bases of dependence, their uncommon or unshared causes. Only mental consciousnesses are produced in dependence on an uncommon empowering condition which is a mental sense power, identified as a former moment of consciousness. Sense consciousnesses are produced in dependence on their own uncommon empowering conditions, physical sense powers such as the eye sense power (see pp. 217-220). Sense consciousnesses are of five types:

1 eye consciousnesses (*mig shes, chakṣhur-jñāna*)
2 ear consciousnesses (*rna shes, shrotra-jñāna*)
3 nose consciousnesses (*sna shes, ghrāṇa-jñāna*)
4 tongue consciousnesses (*lce shes, jihvā-jñāna*)
5 body consciousnesses (*lus shes, kāya-jñāna*).

The uncommon empowering condition of an eye consciousness is an eye sense power; the uncommon empowering condition of an ear consciousness is an ear sense power, and so forth.

The definition of an eye consciousness is:

a knower that is produced in dependence on its own uncommon empowering condition, the eye sense power, and an observed-object-condition, a visible form (*rang gi thun mong ma yin pa'i bdag rkyen mig dbang dang dmigs rkyen gzugs la brten nas skye pa'i rig pa*).

The remaining sense consciousnesses are defined similarly in relation to their own special sense powers and the objects which they are empowered to perceive. The definition of an ear consciousness is:

a knower that is produced in dependence on its own uncommon empowering condition, the ear sense power, and an observed-object-condition, a sound.

The definition of a nose consciousness is:

a knower that is produced in dependence on its own uncommon empowering condition, the nose sense power, and an observed-object-condition, an odor.

The definition of a tongue consciousness is:

a knower that is produced in dependence on its own uncommon empowering condition, the tongue sense power, and an observed-object-condition, a taste.

The definition of a body consciousness is:

a knower that is produced in dependence on its own uncommon empowering condition, a body sense power, and an observed-object-condition, a tangible object.

The observed-object-conditions (*dmigs rkyen, ālambana-pratyaya*) for the five sense consciousnesses are the forms themselves, colors and shapes for the eye consciousness, sounds for the ear consciousness, and so on. A form is a condition for a sense consciousness because in dependence on the appearance of such a material object a consciousness observing it is produced.

The uncommon empowering condition (*thun mong ma yin pa'i bdag rkyen, asādhārana-adhipati-pratyaya*) of a sense consciousness is a physical sense power (*dbang po gzugs can pa*) which is clear form (*gzugs dvang pa, rūpa-prasāda*). The eye sense power is that uncommon empowering condition for the eye consciousness, and so on with the other four sense powers and their respective consciousnesses. The uncommon empowering condition of a mental consciousness is the mental sense power which is any of the six consciousnesses in the immediately preceding moment. Thus, the eye consciousness of the last moment can serve as the mental sense power and uncommon empowering condition of a mental consciousness of the present moment. Moreover, as the substantial cause of the eye consciousness of the present moment, the eye consciousness of the last moment is also an empowering condition of the present eye consciousness, although not an *uncommon* empowering condition. Similarly, the eye sense power is an uncommon empowering condition of an eye consciousness and, if that eye consciousness induces a mental consciousness, the eye sense power is also an empowering condition of that mental consciousness, although not an *uncommon* one.

Within Buddhism there is great emphasis on the study and training of consciousness. "Buddhism presents a view of self-creation, that one's own actions create one's life situation. In this light, it has been said that Buddhism is not a religion, but a science of the mind."[1] This emphasis on the mind comes from knowing that though one can train the body extensively, eventually physical skills will only decline. On the other hand, if one trains the mind well, one's advancement will not be lost.

The third type of functioning thing is a non-associated compositional factor, variously defined as:

a functioning thing which is neither matter nor a consciousness (*bem shes gang rung ma yin pa'i dngos po*)

or

a functioning thing which is neither a form nor a consciousness (*gzugs shes gang rung ma yin pa'i dngos po*)

or

a composed phenomenon which is neither matter nor a consciousness (*bem shes gang rung ma yin pa'i 'dus byas*).

---

[1] Dalai Lama, "Spiritual Contributions to Social Progress", *The Wall Street Journal* (October 29, 1981), p. 22.

All impermanent phenomena which are neither matter nor consciousnesses are included among non-associated compositional factors. "They are called 'compositional factors' because of being factors that allow for the aggregation of causes and conditions and for the production, abiding, and cessation of products."[1] They are called "non-associated" because, unlike minds and mental factors which constantly accompany each other, they are not associated with, or not under the possession of, either minds or mental factors.[2] Non-associated compositional factors are of two types:

1 non-associated compositional factors which are persons (*gang zag yin par gyur pa'i ldan min 'du byed, pudgala-viprayukta-saṃskāra*)
2 non-associated compositional factors which are not persons (*gang zag ma yin par gyur pa'i ldan min 'du byed, apudgala-viprayukta-saṃskāra*).

Persons are non-associated compositional factors because of being impermanent phenomena which are neither forms nor consciousnesses. Rather, persons are imputed to a collection of form and consciousness. "Since this collection itself is neither form nor consciousness but impermanent, it can only be an instance of the remaining category of impermanent phenomena, non-associated compositional factor."[3] A person is defined as:

> a being who is imputed in dependence upon any of the five aggregates (*phung po lnga po gang rung la brten nas btags pa'i skyes bu*).

The five aggregates (*phung po, skandha*) together include all impermanent phenomena. In the Go-mang *Collected Topics* functioning things are divided into the five aggregates:

1 forms (*gzugs, rūpa*)
2 feelings (*tshor ba, vedanā*)

---

[1] Jeffrey Hopkins, *Meditation on Emptiness*, p. 268.
[2] *Ibid.*
[3] *Ibid.*, pp. 268-269.

3   discriminations (*'du shes, samjñā*)
4   compositional factors (*'du byed, saṃskāra*)
5   consciousnesses (*rnam shes, vijñāna*).

The five aggregates are the basis to which persons are imputed, but the aggregates include all impermanent phenomena, not just those within the continuums of persons. A person is imputed to a collection of the bases of a mind and body, the mental and physical aggregates. From seeing the color and shape of a person's face one thinks, "I saw a person." From hearing a voice one imputes that there is a person there. One does not need to contact all of the mental and physical aggregates of a person before being able to impute the presence of a person. Thus, the definition specifies that a person is a being imputed in dependence on *any* of the five aggregates. Mutually inclusive with non-associated compositional factor which is a person are non-associated compositional factor which has life (*srog dang ldan pa'i ldan min 'du byed*), being (*skyes bu*), person (*gang zag*), and self (*bdag*).[1]

All systems of Buddhist tenets assert selflessness. Even though self in general is a synonym of person, the meaning of "self" in the term "selflessness" is different; thus, this is not a doctrine that persons do not exist. Rather, persons do exist and are impermanent phenomena. The meaning of "selflessness" is variously identified in the different schools of philosophy, but all agree that, at least, the person is devoid of being a permanent, partless, independent self. It is such a "self" that does not exist. Persons exist, but a permanent, partless, independent self does not.

If persons are divided, there are two:

1   common beings (*so so'i skye bo, pṛthak-jana*)
2   Superiors (*'phags pa, ārya*)

The definition of a common being is:

---

[1] Geshe G. Lodrö, *Geschichte der Kloster-Universität Drepung* (Weisbaden, West Germany: Franz Steiner Verlag GmbH, 1974), p. 223.

a person who has not attained a Superior's path of any of the three vehicles (*theg pa gsum gang rung gi 'phags lam ma thob pa'i gang zag*).

A Superior is a person who has attained a Superior's path (*'phags pa'i lam, ārya-marga*) of any of the three vehicles and who, through extensive meditative practice, has realized selflessness by means of a direct perceiver. Each of the four systems of tenets assert three vehicles (*theg pa, yāna*):

1 Hearer Vehicle (*nyan thos kyi theg pa, shrāvaka-yāna*)
2 Solitary Realizer Vehicle (*rang sangs rgyas kyi theg pa, pratyeka-buddha-yāna*)
3 Bodhisattva Vehicle (*byang sems kyi theg pa, bodhisattva-yāna*).

They are called "vehicles" because, like a means of transportation, they are able to carry one to a higher state.[1] They are practices that serve as the bases for generating higher qualities in one's mental continuum. The Hearer and Solitary Realizer Vehicles are the Lesser Vehicle (*hīnayāna*) practices able to carry one to the fruit of liberation. The third, the Bodhisattva Vehicle, is the Great Vehicle (*mahāyāna*) practice able to bear the welfare of all beings and to establish one in the state of Buddhahood. Each of the three vehicles has five paths:

1 path of accumulation (*tshogs lam, sambhāra-mārga*)
2 path of preparation (*sbyor lam, prayoga-mārga*)
3 path of seeing (*mthong lam, darshana-mārga*)
4 path of meditation (*sgom lam, bhāvana-mārga*)
5 path of no more learning (*mi slob lam, ahaikṣha-marga*).

Generally in Buddhism paths are consciousnesses, and a person on any of these five paths is a person who has generated a certain level of consciousness. According to Denma Lochö Rinbochay, they are called "paths" because they are the way of proceeding to the fruits of the three vehicles. We

---

[1] Denma Lochö Rinbochay, oral commentary.

call the tracks of someone who has gone before a "path", for this is the way that will be followed by someone afterwards. The way the Buddhas of the past proceeded, the kinds of thoughts and consciousnesses that they generated, is the way that the people of the present must proceed in order to become Buddhas. And those in the future who wish to become Buddhas also will have to proceed in the same way. Thus, these consciousnesses are called "paths".[1]

Of these five paths the former two, accumulation and preparation, are paths of common beings and the latter three—seeing, meditation, and no more learning—are paths of Superiors. The point of entry into the Superior's paths is a direct realization of the truth, selflessness. The practitioner familiarizes with selflessness through the reasoning process, eventually transcends the need for inferential cognition, and generates a yogic direct perceiver "seeing" the meaning of selflessness. This first moment of direct realization is the first moment of the path of seeing. At this point one becomes a Superior, a person who has attained a Superior's path of any of the three vehicles. There are four types of Superiors, three corresponding to the three vehicles and also Buddha Superiors who have attained the path of no more learning of the Bodhisattva Vehicle and thus are no longer trainees in any vehicle:

1 Hearer Superiors (*nyan thos kyi 'phags pa, shrāvaka-ārya*)
2 Solitary Realizer Superiors (*rang sangs rgyas kyi 'phags pa, pratyeka-buddha-ārya*)
3 Bodhisattva Superiors (*byang sems kyi 'phags pa, bodhisattva-ārya*)
4 Buddha Superiors (*sangs rgyas 'phags pa, buddha-ārya*).[2]

On the basis of each of the three vehicles there are Superiors who have attained a path of no more learning and those who have not yet attained a path of no more learning. The

---

[1] *Ibid.*

[2] A Buddha is both a being (*skyes bu*) and a person (*gang zag*), but does not fit the Tibetan etymology of a person as one who, having become full (*gang*) of the afflictions, has fallen into cyclic existence.

former are the three liberated beings—Foe Destroyers (*dgra bcom pa, arhan*) who are Hearers, Solitary Realizers, or Buddhas.[1] According to the Great Vehicle schools of tenets (except for the Proponents of Mind Only Following Scripture), all Superiors and even all persons eventually enter the Great Vehicle and achieve the rank of a Buddha.

The *Treasury of Knowledge* says, "Those who have not attained a Superior path are common beings."[2] Common beings are of six types, each having the basis of a migrator (*'gro ba, gati*) in cyclic existence. Sentient beings, or non-Buddhas, are called "migrators" because, for the most part, they are constantly moving and travelling within cyclic existence. The six types of common beings having the basis of a migrator are:

1　common beings having the basis of a hell-being (*dmyal ba'i rten can gyi so so'i skye bo*)
2　common beings having the basis of a hungry ghost (*yi dvags kyi rten can gyi so so'i skye bo*)
3　common beings having the basis of an animal (*dud 'gro'i rten can gyi so so'i skye bo*)
4　common beings having the basis of a human (*mi'i rten can gyi so so'i skye bo*)
5　common beings having the basis of a demigod (*lha ma yin pa'i rten can gyi so so'i skye bo*)

---

[1] Some scholars argue that there are four types of Foe Destroyers including Bodhisattva Foe Destroyers as the fourth together with Hearer, Solitary Realizer, and Buddha Foe Destroyers. The Grounds and Paths (*sa lam*) literature written in accordance with the view of the Consequentialists of the Middle Way School (*prāsaṅgika-mādhyamika*) asserts that Bodhisattvas overcome the obstructions to liberation (*nyon mong pa'i sgrib pa, klesha-avaraṇa*) at the beginning of the eighth Bodhisattva ground. On the basis of this assertion, some say that such higher ground Bodhisattvas are Foe Destroyers, for they have destroyed the foe of afflictive ignorance. Others deny this interpretation pointing out that since the higher ground Bodhisattvas have not yet overcome the obstructions to omniscience (*shes bya'i sgrib pa, jñeya-avaraṇa*), which is the main object of abandonment of the Bodhisattva Vehicle, they are not yet Foe Destroyers in that they have not defeated their main foe.

[2] Vasubandhu, *Treasury of Knowledge*, P5590, Vol. 115, 118.3.6.

6   common beings having the basis of a god (*lha'i rten can gyi so so'i skye bo*).[1]

These persons are qualified as *common beings* having the basis of a migrator for the sake of eliminating Superiors having the basis of a migrator. Since Superiors and common beings are differentiated not by body type but by qualities of mind, beings having the bases of migrators are of both types. According to Lati Rinbochay, there are probably no Superiors having the basis of any of the three lower types of migrators, but there are cases of Superiors having the basis of a human, demigod, or god. These are Hearer, Solitary Realizer, and Great Vehicle trainees who, although they have attained a Superior's path, have not attained liberation and still take rebirth in cyclic existence as a person having the basis of a migrator. There are Superiors who intentionally take rebirth as, for instance, an animal in order to be able to help others; still, this is not a case of a Superior having the basis of an animal because the Superior is merely assuming that appearance and is not powerlessly reborn as an animal due to the effects of contaminated actions.[2]

Through the power of actions of desire, hatred, and ignorance common beings are born into cyclic existence as one of the six types of migrators.

> What is cyclic existence? ... It is like a bee caught in a jar. It can only go round and round in the same place. No matter how much it flies round inside, all it can do is dart to the top, the middle, or the bottom of the jar. Cyclic existence is like the jar, and our mind is like the bee because whether we are born as a god, demigod, human, animal, hungry ghost, or hell-being, we remain in cyclic existence.[3]

---

[1] The one exception to this division of migrators is the intermediate state beings (*bar do ba*), migrators who are between lives and searching for a suitable place of rebirth, who are not included among the six types of migrators even though they are migrators.

[2] Lati Rinbochay, oral commentary.

[3] Khetsun Sangbo Rinbochay, *Tantric Practice in Nying-Ma*, p. 64.

Each of the places of rebirth, the six migrations, is an impermanent, temporary state into which a person is born, lives for some time, and then dies only to be reborn into another state. Only liberated Superiors are free from the suffering of cyclic existence. The only way to become free of cyclic existence is to eliminate one's own desire, hatred, and ignorance. From among these, the root is ignorance. The antidote to ignorance, the actual medicine for the suffering of cyclic existence, is the wisdom realizing selflessness. In order to achieve this wisdom Buddhist practitioners put great effort into reasoning and debate.

In terms of physical suffering the least fortunate of all beings are the hell-beings (*dmyal ba, nāraka*) whose main suffering is extreme hot or cold. There are four types of hell-beings:

1 hot hell-beings (*tsha dmyal ba*)
2 cold hell-beings (*grang dmyal ba*)
3 neighboring hell-beings (*nye 'khor ba'i dmyal ba*)
4 lesser hell-beings (*nyi tshe'i dmyal ba*).

Within the first two, there are eight types of hot hell-beings and eight types of cold hell-beings. Altogether, there are eighteen types of hell-beings corresponding to the eighteen hells.

Suffering slightly less than the hell-beings are the hungry ghosts (*yi dvags, preta*) whose main suffering is unusual hunger and thirst. Living for a very long time, "they may search for food and water for hundreds of years without finding a scrap to eat or a drop to drink. ... To add to their troubles, in summer they suffer greatly from cold and in winter from heat."[1] There are three types of hungry ghosts:

1 hungry ghosts having external obstructions (*sgrib pa phyi na yod pa'i yi dvags*)
2 hungry ghosts having internal obstructions (*sgrib pa nang na yod pa'i yi dvags*)

---

[1] *Ibid.*, p. 74.

3 hungry ghosts having both external and internal obstructions (*sgrib pa phyi nang gnyis ka yod pa'i yi dvags*).

External obstructions are, for instance, being born into a dry and barren land where nothing grows or being kept from food and drink by guards. Internal obstructions are like physical deformities such as a throat as small as the eye of a needle or internal parasites feeding on one's flesh.

Animals (*dud 'gro, tiryañch*) are familiar. They suffer mainly from stupidity and from having their bodies used for other's purposes. The Buddhists divide animals into two types:

1 animals living in the depths (*dud 'gro bying na gnas pa*)
2 animals scattered [about the surface] (*dud 'gro kha 'thor ba*).[1]

"Those in the watery depths are especially prone to the suffering of the larger eating the smaller and the smaller latching onto the bodies of the larger and eating holes in them. Those on land suffer particularly from being used by others. ... Their minds are so obscured that they do not know what to do and what to avoid; they have no notion of how to engage in religious practice."[2]

Humans (*mi, manuṣhya*) suffer mainly from birth, aging, sickness, and death. Corresponding to the places where they live, there are two types of humans:

1 humans of the four continents (*gling bzhi'i mi*)
2 humans of the eight subcontinents (*gling phran brgyad kyi mi*).

The four continents are the eastern one called "Superior Body" (*lus 'phags po, videha*), the southern one called the "Land of Jambu" (*'dzam bu gling, jambu-dvīpa*), the western

---

[1] Generally, animals in the depths are explained as those in the *watery* depths as in the ocean. However, according to Kensur Yeshay Tupden, animals living in the depths includes not only those in water but also those under the surface of the earth such as worms.

[2] Khetsun Sangbo Rinbochay, *Tantric Practice in Nying-Ma*, p. 75.

one called "Using Oxen" (*ba gling spyod, godānīya*), and the
northern one called "Unpleasant Sound" (*sgra mi snyan,
kuru*).[1] Our land is the southern continent, the Land of
Jambu. Between each of the four major continents are two
smaller subcontinents which are also inhabited by humans.
In the middle of all the continents and subcontinents is
Mount Meru which is the place where the demigods and
some gods live. "This is described according to the way our
land is arranged, having four continents and eight subcontinents. There are many other world systems."[2]

The human life, as a mixture of relative comfort and dis-
comfort, is the most precious of all of the migrations because
it is the best basis for religious practice. Those born into the
lower migrations are too bothered by suffering and
stupidity to be able to engage in religious practice and those
born into the migrations higher than humans are too
involved in fighting or too distracted by objects of desire to
be able to engage in practice. Thus, the teachers and lamas
with one voice exhort their followers to practice now in
order to achieve happiness.

Demigods (*lha ma yin, asura*) suffer mainly under the
influence of jealousy (*phrag dog, irṣhyā*). They are born into a
situation where they can meet with the gods, whose lands
are located above their own. There is a wish-granting tree
that grows from the land of the demigods up into the land
of the gods. The roots and trunk of the tree are in the
demigods' land and the branches, which grant wishes, are in
the gods' land. Because the merit of the gods is greater, they
are able to enjoy whatever they wish from the tree. Seeing
this, the demigods become very jealous and battle with the
gods. The gods' vulnerability is so much less and their
strategic capacity so much greater that the demigods suffer

---

[1] The source for the Sanskrit names for the four human continents is Lati
Rinbochay, Denma Lochö Rinbochay, Leah Zahler, and Jeffrey Hopkins,
Meditative States in Tibetan Buddhism (London: Wisdom Publications,
1983).
[2] Lati Rinbochay, oral commentary.

great losses. The suffering resulting from this fighting is the main suffering of the demigods.[1]

Gods (*hla, deva*), in terms of prosperity and comfort, are the most fortunate of all sentient beings. They live very long lives enjoying great physical and mental comfort, but eventually when their great merit is consumed, they must die and again take rebirth in a lower state. "The dying god clairvoyantly sees where he is to be reborn. He knows that he will separate from the great fortune of gods, leave friends behind, and be reborn in far harsher conditions than those to which he has become accustomed—most likely in one of the bad migrations where he will suffer hunger, thirst, heat, and cold."[2] Seeing the state into which he will be reborn, the god suffers greatly. Mirroring the hell-beings in the lowest realms whose physical suffering is the greatest in cyclic existence, at the time of death the gods in the highest realms have mental suffering that is the greatest in cyclic existence. Corresponding to the places where they live there are three types of gods:

1   gods of the Desire Realm (*'dod khams kyi lha, kāma-dhātu-deva*)
2   gods of the Form Realm (*gzugs khams kyi lha, rūpa-dhātu-deva*)
3   gods of the Formless Realm (*gzugs med khams kyi lha, ārūpya-dhātu-deva*).

The three realms—Desire, Form, and Formless Realms—are differentiated essentially by the levels of concentration of the beings living with them. The Desire Realm (*kāma-dhātu*) is the place where all hell-beings, hungry ghosts, animals, humans, and demigods live as well as some types of gods. The beings living in the Desire Realm have a level of concentration (*bsam gtan, dhyāna*) that is characterized as constant distraction (*rnam par g.yeng ba, vikṣhepa*) interrupted

---

[1] Paraphrased from Khetsun Sangbo Rinbochay, *Tantric Practice in Nying-Ma*, p. 81.
[2] Khetsun Sangbo Rinbochay, *Tantric Practice in Nying-Ma*, p. 82.

by occasional moments of concentrative stability. Located above the Desire Realm is the Form Realm (*gzugs khams, rūpa-dhātu*) separated into four levels representing progressively greater states of concentration. All beings of the Form Realm are included among the gods. The beings having the greatest concentrative stability are those of the Formless Realm (*gzugs med khams, ārūpya-dhātu*). Because it is totally non-material the Formless Realm is not located anywhere although it is often described as being above the Form Realm. There are four levels of the Formless Realm. If divided extensively, there are twenty-seven types of gods— six types of gods of the Desire Realm, seventeen types of gods of the Form Realm, and four types of gods of the Formless Realm.

It may seem as though hell-beings, hungry ghosts, and animals suffer greatly while humans, demigods, and gods have happiness and comfort, but the Buddhists deny this saying that in truth there is not a moment of happiness in cyclic existence. Padmasambhava, a great Indian Buddhist teacher credited with bringing Buddhism to Tibet, said that life in cyclic existence is like living on the point of a needle.[1] No matter which way one turns—whether hell-being, human, or god—there is no happiness. Turning away from the marvels of cyclic existence, Buddhist practitioners seek a liberation free from powerless rebirth into suffering. Beyond this, the followers of the Great Vehicle seek to find not merely some peace and happiness for themselves, but to establish all suffering beings in liberation.

After persons, the remaining non-associated compositional factors are those which are not persons. Included here is functioning thing (*dngos po, bhāva*) itself as well as all of the phenomena mutually inclusive with it (see Table V, pp. 273-274). It is not the case that whatever is a functioning thing is necessarily a non-associated compositional factor, but functioning thing itself is a non-associated compositional factor because of a being an impermanent

---

[1] *Ibid.*, p. 83.

phenomena which is neither matter nor a consciousness. Although both matter and consciousness are functioning things, functioning thing as such is neither of them. Since functioning thing is an impermanent phenomenon, it must be a non-associated compositional factor. Unlike color which, although a color, is neither a primary color nor a secondary color, functioning thing is itself to be found among its divisions.

A non-associated compositional factor has to be something which is not any of the other kinds of functioning things. There are many such phenomena. For instance, an hour, a day, a week, a month, a year, and so forth—all times (*dus, kāla*)—are non-associated compositional factors which are not persons. Also, such phenomena as number (*grangs, saṃkhyā*) and order (*go rim, anukrama*) are non-associated compositional factors.[1] " 'Number' is designated to a condition of measure. 'Order' is designated to a serial state of former and later, high and low, and so forth."[2] Order, as a mere serial state, is an object of apprehension of any of the six consciousnesses and is something which is produced, abides for some time, and disintegrates.

Table VII shows the divisions of functioning things (*dngos po, bhāva*):

---

[1] Lati Rinbochay, oral commentary. Also, the Sanskrit for these terms is drawn from Jeffrey Hopkins, *Meditation on Emptiness*, p. 270.
[2] Jeffrey Hopkins, *Meditation on Emptiness*, p. 271.

Table VII: The Divisions of Functioning Things

I matter (*bem po, kanthā*)
  A. external matter (*phyi'i bem po, bahirdhā-kanthā*)
    1 visible forms (*gzugs, rūpa*)
    2 sounds (*sgra, shabda*)
    3 odors (*dri, gandha*)
    4 tastes (*ro, rasa*)
    5 tangible objects (*reg bya, sprashtavya*)
  B. internal matter (*nang gi bem po, ādhyātmika-kanthā*)
    1 eye sense powers (*mig gi dbang po, chakshur-indriya*)
    2 ear sense powers (*rna ba'i dbang po, shrotra-indriya*)
    3 nose sense powers (*sna'i dbang po, ghrāṇa-indriya*)
    4 tongue sense powers (*lce'i dbang po, jihvā-indriya*)
    5 body sense powers (*lus kyi dbang po, kāya-indriya*)

II consciousnesses (*shes pa, jñāna*)
  A. mental consciousnesses (*yid shes, mano-jñāna*)
  B. sense consciousnesses (*dbang shes, indriya-jñāna*)
    1 eye consciousnesses (*mig shes, chakshur-jñāna*)
    2 ear consciousnesses (*rna shes, shrotra-jñāna*)
    3 nose consciousnesses (*sna shes, ghrāṇa-jñāna*)
    4 tongue consciousness (*lce shes, jihvā-jñāna*)
    5 body consciousnesses (*lus shes, kāya-jñāna*)

(Table VII: The Divisions of Functioning Things cont.)

III non-associated compositional factors (ldan min 'du byed, viprayukta-saṃskāra)

A. non-associated compositional factors which are persons (gang zag yin par gyur pa'i ldan min 'du byed, pudgala-viprayukta-saṃskāra)

1 common beings (so so'i skye bo, pṛthak-jana)

  a. common beings having the basis of a hell-being (dmyal ba'i rten can gyi so so'i skye bo)

  b. common beings having the basis of a hungry ghost (yi dvags kyi rten can gyi so so'i skye bo)

  c. common beings having the basis of an animal (dud 'gro'i rten can gyi so so'i skye bo)

  d. common beings having the basis of a human (mi'i rten can gyi so so'i skye bo)

  e. common beings having the basis of a demigod (lha ma yin pa'i rten can gyi so so'i skye bo)

  f. common beings having the basis of a god (lha'i rten can gyi so so'i skye bo)

2 Superiors ('phags pa, ārya)

  a. Hearer Superiors (nyan thos kyi 'phags pa, shrāvaka-ārya)

  b. Solitary Realizer Superiors (rang sangs rgyas kyi 'phags pa, pratyeka-buddha-ārya)

  c. Bodhisattva Superiors (byang sems kyi 'phags pa, bodhisattva-ārya)

  d. Buddha Superiors (sangs rgyas 'phags pa, buddha-ārya)

B. non-associated compositional factors which are not persons (gang zag ma yin par gyur pa'i ldan min 'du byed, apudgala-viprayukta-saṃskāra)

Debate B.5, Fifth Mistaken View (6b.3)

In debate B.5 the hypothetical Defender makes the error of accepting that whatever is not a functioning thing is necessarily a permanent phenomenon. He is not carefully assessing what non-thing includes and what it excludes. Of course, it excludes only functioning things; it includes, however, not just permanent phenomena but also non-existents, for they too are not functioning things. The Defender has not been careful as regards the implications of a negative.

> If someone [a hypothetical Defender] says, "Whatever is not a functioning thing is necessarily a permanent phenomenon," [the Sūtra School Challenger responds to him,] "It [absurdly] follows that the subject, the horn of a rabbit, is [a permanent phenomenon] because of [not being a functioning thing]. You asserted the pervasion."
>
> If he says that the reason [that the horn of a rabbit is not a functioning thing] is not established [the Sūtra School Challenger responds,] "It follows that the subject [the horn of a rabbit] is [not a functioning thing] because of being neither a permanent phenomenon nor a functioning thing."
>
> If he says that the reason [that the horn of a rabbit is neither a permanent phenomenon nor a functioning thing] is not established, [the Sūtra School Challenger responds,] "It follows that the subject [the horn of a rabbit] is [neither a permanent phenomenon nor a functioning thing] because of not being an existent."
>
> If he says that the reason [that the horn of a rabbit is not an existent] is not established, [the Sūtra School Challenger responds,] "It follows that the subject [the horn of a rabbit] is [not an existent] because of being a non-existent."
>
> If he says that the reason [that the horn of a rabbit is a non-existent] is not established, [the Sūtra

School Challenger responds,] "It follows that the subject [the horn of a rabbit] is [a non-existent] because of not being established by a valid cognizer."

If he accepts the basic consequence [that the horn of a rabbit is a permanent phenomenon, the Sūtra School Challenger responds,] "It follows that the subject [the horn of a rabbit] is not a permanent phenomenon because of not being an existent."

If he says that the reason [that the horn of a rabbit is not an existent] is not established, [the Sūtra School Challenger responds,] "It follows that the subject [the horn of a rabbit] is [not an existent] because its entity does not exist."

If he says that the reason [that the entity of the horn of a rabbit does not exist] is not established, [the Sūtra School Challenger responds,] "It follows with respect to the subject [the horn of a rabbit that its entity does not exist] because of not being something that holds its own entity."

If he says that the reason [that the horn of a rabbit is not something that holds its own entity] is not established, [the Sūtra School Challenger responds,] "It follows that the subject [the horn of a rabbit] is [not something that holds its own entity] because of not being a phenomenon."

"[It follows that] there is pervasion [i.e., whatever is not a phenomenon is necessarily not something which holds its own entity] because that which holds its own entity is the definition of a phenomenon."

If that which holds its own entity is the definition of a phenomenon (*chos, dharma*), then whatever is not a phenomenon is necessarily not something which holds its own entity. This is true because the eight approaches of pervasion exist between any definition and its definiendum.

The two principals of debate B.5, permanent phenomenon and non-thing, have three possibilities:

1 Something which is both is uncomposed space or object of knowledge.
2 Whatever is a permanent phenomenon is necessarily not a functioning thing. However, it is not the case that whatever is not a functioning thing is necessarily a permanent phenomenon because any non existent is not a functioning thing but is also not a permanent phenomenon.
3 Something which is neither is a pot or a god of the Desire Realm. Any functioning thing is not a permanent phenomenon and is also not a non-thing because of being a functioning thing.

Debate B.6, Sixth Mistaken View (6b.6)

In this debate the Defender accepts that whatever is a phenomenon is necessarily not a phenomenon that has a basis of negation (*dgag gzhi can gyi chos*). A phenomenon that has a basis of negation is something which, although it exists, is not present everywhere. If there is a place where some phenomenon does not exist, then that phenomenon is one that has a basis of negation, for it is negated somewhere. An example is an elephant. Although in general elephants exist, there are places where an elephant does not exist; therefore, an elephant is a phenomenon which has a basis of negation.

> If someone [a hypothetical Defender] says, "Whatever is a phenomenon is necessarily not a phenomenon that has a basis of negation," [the Sūtra School Challenger responds to him,] "It [absurdly] follows that the subject, a pot, is [not a phenomenon that has a basis of negation] because of [being a phenomenon]. You asserted the pervasion."
>
> If he says that the reason [that a pot is a phenomenon] is not established, [the Sūtra School Challenger responds,] "It follows that the subject [a

pot] is [a phenomenon] because of being a composed phenomenon."

If he says that the reason [that a pot is a composed
phenomenon] is not established, [the Sūtra School
Challenger responds,] "It follows that the subject [a
pot] is [a composed phenomenon] because of being
a functioning thing."

If he says that the reason [that a pot is a functioning thing] is not established, [the Sūtra School
Challenger responds,] "It follows that the subject [a
pot] is [a functioning thing] because of being able to
perform a function."

If he says that the reason [that a pot is able to perform a function] is not established, [the Sūtra School
Challenger responds,] "It follows that the subject [a
pot] is [able to perform a function] because of being
a bulbous flat-based phenomenon able to perform
the function of holding water."

"It follows that [a pot is a bulbous flat-based phenomenon able to perform the function of holding
water] because of being a pot."

"[It follows that] there is pervasion [i.e., whatever
is a pot is necessarily a bulbous flat-based phenomenon able to perform the function of holding
water] because that is the definition of a pot."

The definition of a pot is a case of a description of the entity
and function of a phenomenon. The entity of a pot is bulbous and flat-based. Its function is that of holding water.
Often in debate this rather lengthy definition is condensed
for brevity into simply "the bulbous" (*lto ldir ba*). This does
not mean that the bulbous is suitable as a definition of a pot,
but, since it occurs so often in introductory debate, it is
stated in a brief way.

If he accepts the basis consequence [that a pot is not
a phenomenon that has a basis of negation, the Sūtra
School Challenger responds,] "It follows that the
subject [a pot] is a phenomenon that has a basis of

negation because (1) there is a basis of its negation and (2) it is a phenomenon."

The second part of the reason is easy. If he says that the first part of the reason [that there is a basis of a pot's negation] is not established, [the Sūtra School Challenger responds,] "It follows that there is a basis of pot's negation because there is a place where there is no pot."

If he says that the reason [that there is a place where there is no pot] is not established, [the Sūtra School Challenger responds,] "It follows that [there is a place where there is no pot] because whatever is selfless is not necessarily [a place where] there is a pot."

This last consequence, the last in debate B.6, is an appeal to the obvious fact that there are places where there are no pots. Not everything is a place where a pot exists. Therefore, a pot is a phenomenon that has a basis of negation.

The two principals of this debate, phenomenon and what is not a phenomenon that has a basis of negation, have three possibilities without their being something which is neither:

1   Something which is both is object of knowledge, existent, and so on as well as selflessness. There is no place where an object of knowledge or selflessness does not exist. Objects of knowledge do not exist among non-existents, of course, but this does not mean that non-existents are places where objects of knowledge do not exist, for they are not places.

Selflessness, although it includes both existents and non-existents, is a phenomenon because of being a permanent phenomenon. Also, among all existents and non-existents there is no place for negating selflessness; thus, selflessness is not a phenomenon that has a basis of negation.

2   Something which is a phenomenon but is not something which is not a phenomenon that has a basis of negation, i.e., *is* a phenomenon which has a base of negation, is a

pot, a pillar, any functioning thing, or any instance of
established base. Any functioning thing is a phenomenon that has a basis of negation because it is
negated on the basis of a permanent phenomenon such
as uncomposed space. Any permanent phenomenon
except for selflessness and established base and the phenomena mutually inclusive with it is negated on the
basis of a functioning thing such as a table.[1]

3   Something which is not a phenomenon that has a basis
of negation and is also not a phenomenon is any non-
existent.

These are the three possibilities. There is nothing which is
neither because it would have to be something which on one
hand is a phenomenon that has a basis of negation and on
the other hand is not a phenomenon. Such a thing cannot be
posited.

Debate B.7, Seventh Mistaken View (7a.3)

In debate B.7 the Sūtra School Challenger cross-applies
some of the vocabulary that comes up in this chapter. If
specifically characterized phenomenon is mutually inclusive
with functioning thing and functioning things are divided
into matter, consciousnesses, and non-associated
compositional factors, then specifically characterized
phenomena too must have these same three types. Thus,
when the hypothetical Defender accepts that whatever is a
specifically characterized phenomenon is necessarily a
consciousness, the Challenger posits the counterexample of
the two—a material phenomenon and a consciousness (*bem
shes gnyis*)—which is a functioning thing of which being
them is not possible.[2] He could posit, just as effectively,
matter alone or a pot.

---

[1] Kensur Yeshay Tupden, oral commentary.

[2] In this debate the subjects, the two—a material phenomenon and a
consciousness (*bem shes gnyis*), are treated as a unit and referred to in the
singular as *a* functioning thing. This is done because within this debate

If someone [a hypothetical Defender] says, "Whatever is a specifically characterized phenomenon is necessarily a consciousness," [the Sūtra School Challenger responds to him,] "It [absurdly] follows that the subjects, the two—a material phenomenon and a consciousness, are [a consciousness] because of [being a specifically characterized phenomenon]. You asserted the pervasion."

If he says that the reason [that the two—a material phenomenon and a consciousness—are a specifically characterized phenomenon] is not established, [the Sūtra School Challenger responds,] "It follows that the subjects [the two—a material phenomenon and a consciousness] are [a specifically characterized phenomenon] because of being established for the appearance factor of a direct perceiver."

That which is established for the appearance factor of a direct perceiver (*mngon sum gyi snang ngor grub pa*) is another phenomenon mutually inclusive with functioning thing. Functioning things are established for the appearance factor of direct perceivers in that they exist as that which is suitable to appear to a direct perceiver, and permanent phenomena do not.

If he says that the reason [that the two—a material phenomenon and a consciousness—are established for the appearance factor of a direct perceiver] is not

---

there is no play on the fact that they are functioning things of which being them is not possible and because the text qualifies them as a non-associated compositional factor. Since it is only the set of the two that is a non-associated compositional factor and not the individual members of the set, they must be referred to as a singular non-associated compositional factor. From this point of view, they are also *a* functioning thing, *a* specifically characterized phenomenon, and so forth. Thus, in this debate in order to keep the number consistent, they are referred to with singular predicate nominatives as "*a* non-associated compositional factor" and so on.

established, [the Sūtra School Challenger responds,] "It follows that the subjects [the two—a material phenomenon and a consciousness] are [established for the appearance factor of a direct perceiver] because of being an appearing object of a direct perceiver."

If he says that the reason [that the two—a material phenomenon and a consciousness—are an appearing object of a direct perceiver] is not established, [the Sūtra School Challenger responds,] "It follows that the subjects [the two—a material phenomenon and a consciousness] are [an appearing object of a direct perceiver] because of being a functioning thing."

"[It follows that] there is pervasion [i.e., whatever is a functioning thing is necessarily an appearing object of a direct perceiver] because appearing object of a direct perceiver [*mngon sum gyi snang yul*] and functioning thing [*dngos po, bhāva*] are mutually inclusive and appearing object of a thought consciousness [*rtog pa'i snang yul*] and permanent phenomenon [*rtag pa, nitya*] are mutually inclusive."

In the Sūtra School presentation only impermanent phenomena can be appearing objects of direct perceivers and only permanent phenomena can be appearing objects of thought consciousnesses. Functioning thing, appearing object of a direct perceiver, that which is established for the appearance factor of a direct perceiver, and specifically characterized phenomenon are all mutually inclusive. The subjects, the two—a material phenomenon and a consciousness, are a functioning thing because a material phenomenon is a functioning thing and a consciousness is a functioning thing. Thus, the two—a material phenomenon and a consciousness—are an appearing object of a direct perceiver, established for the appearance factor of a direct perceiver, and a specifically characterized phenomenon. According to the Defender's unfounded assertion, if something is a specifically characterized phenomenon, it must be a consciousness; thus:

> If he accepts the basic consequence [that the two—a material phenomenon and a consciousness—are a consciousness, the Sūtra School Challenger responds,] "It follows that the subjects [the two—a material phenomenon and a consciousness] are not a consciousness because of being a non-associated compositional factor."

Sets of phenomena are included as objects of knowledge, permanent phenomena, functioning things, matter, or within whatever group they share qualities. The two—a pillar and a pot—are objects of knowledge, functioning things, and even matter because both are forms, but that set is not a pot and not a pillar. In the same way, the two—a material phenomenon and a consciousness—share the qualities of being objects of knowledge and functioning things, but since it is not the case that both are material phenomena or both are consciousnesses, they are a non-associated compositional factor.

> "[It follows that] there is pervasion [i.e., whatever is a non-associated compositional factor is necessarily not a consciousness] because the three—material phenomenon, consciousness, and non-associated compositional factor—are only mutually exclusive with each other."

There is no common locus of any two of the three—material phenomenon, consciousness, and non-associated compositional factor. They are only mutually exclusive with each other.

The principals of B.7, specifically characterized phenomenon and consciousness, have three possibilities:

1 Something which is both is a mental consciousness.
2 Whatever is a consciousness is necessarily a specifically characterized phenomenon, but it is not the case that whatever is a specifically characterized phenomenon is

necessarily a consciousness, for any form or any non-associated compositional factor is a specifically characterized phenomenon but not a consciousness.

3 Something which is neither is any permanent phenomenon or any non-existent.

Debate B.8, Eighth Mistaken View (7a.6)

In this debate the Defender accepts that whatever is a hidden phenomenon is necessarily a generally characterized phenomenon. This is the equivalent of accepting that whatever exists is necessarily a permanent phenomenon, a position which no one supports. However, the debate is instructive, for one might think that since a hidden phenomenon is defined as an object realized in a hidden manner by the *thought consciousness* apprehending it and since a generally characterized phenomenon must be an appearing object of a thought consciousness, then probably all hidden phenomena are generally characterized phenomena. This is not correct. Indeed, they are hidden phenomena because of being known by thought consciousnesses in an indirect or hidden manner, but this means that all phenomena are hidden *to thought* not that all phenomena are hidden to all consciousnesses, for specifically characterized phenomena can appear directly to direct perceivers. Generally characterized phenomena are objects that *must* appear to thought consciousnesses, though this is not the case for all hidden phenomena. Still, all phenomena, permanent phenomena and functioning things alike, are hidden phenomena. Thought can know functioning things even though they do not appear to thought as functioning things, for they must be represented by a meaning-generality—a mentally appearing object which *must* be a generally characterized phenomenon. Thought can *know* impermanent phenomena, but only permanent phenomena are *appearing objects* of thought.

If someone [a hypothetical Defender] says, "Whatever is a hidden phenomenon is necessarily a generally characterized phenomenon," [the Sūtra School Challenger responds to him,] "It [absurdly] follows that the subject, a gold pot, is [a generally characterized phenomenon] because of [being a hidden phenomenon]. You asserted the pervasion."

If he says that the reason [that a gold pot is a hidden phenomenon] is not established, [the Sūtra School Challenger responds,] "It follows that the subject [a gold pot] is [a hidden phenomenon] because of being an object realized in a hidden manner by the thought consciousness apprehending it."

"[It follows that] there is pervasion [i.e., whatever is an object realized in a hidden manner by the thought consciousness apprehending it is necessarily a hidden phenomenon] because that is the definition of [a hidden phenomenon]."

If he says that the above reason [i.e., that a gold pot is an object realized in a hidden manner by the thought consciousness apprehending it] is not established, [the Sūtra School Challenger responds,] "It follows that the subject [a gold pot] is an object realized in a hidden manner by the thought consciousness apprehending it because of being an object of comprehension by the thought consciousness apprehending it."

Frequently, the texts will specify, "If he says that the *above* reason is not established (*gong du ma grub na*)," "If he says to the *above* that there is no pervasion (*gong du ma khyab na*)," or "If he accepts the *above* (*gong du 'dod na*)." In this way the author is offering an alternative response to a previous consequence. This technique serves to better instruct the reader on the topics being presented in that each component of a single consequence may be studied closely. Also, this technique reflects the actual procedure in debate, for the course of a debate routinely involves considering the same consequence more than once.

When such a textual note occurs, there are two ways to determine which of the "above" consequences is being referred to in the note. First, one must go back over the previous consequences to find the ones to which the alternative response might apply. In this case, there are three previous consequences, the basic consequence and two subsequent ones. The hypothetical Defender has already questioned the establishment of the reason of the basic consequence, and since the word "above" would never refer to the immediately preceding consequence, the referent must be the middle consequence. Previously the Defender did answer to the middle consequence that there is no pervasion. Therefore, the referent is definitely the middle consequence. The second way to determine which previous consequence is being referred to is to look ahead to the Challenger's response which often clearly identifies the point of issue by spelling out the disputed pervasion, putting the previous reason into the new predicate, and so forth. In cases where these textual notes come after a long line of reasoning, it is sometimes difficult to determine quickly which is the referent consequence, but by using the two search procedures outlined here one can find the referent.

In the last consequence the Challenger justifies a golden pot as an object realized in a hidden manner by the thought consciousness apprehending it by the sign of its being an object of comprehension of the thought consciousness apprehending it. An object of comprehension of the thought consciousness apprehending it (*rang 'dzin rtog pa'i gzhal bya*) is another phenomenon mutually inclusive with established base. All established bases are objects comprehended by the thought consciousnesses apprehending them because what a factually concordant thought consciousness apprehends, it comprehends.

> If he says that the reason [that a gold pot is an object of comprehension by the thought consciousness apprehending it] is not established, [the Sūtra School Challenger responds,] "It follows that the

subject [a gold pot] is [an object of comprehension by the thought consciousness apprehending it] because of being an established base."

This consequence is the last in the line of reasoning developing from the hypothetical Defender's denying the establishment of the reason of the basic consequence. In this line of reasoning, the author provided two different answers to the one consequence. This reflects the procedure in debate which provides the Defender with the opportunity to give different answers to the same consequence when it is posed to him at different times. Having denied the establishment of the reason when the consequence was first stated to him, when the Sūtra School Challenger is working his way back through the line of reasoning to the basic consequence, the Defender might accept or deny the pervasion of the same consequence when it is stated to him again.

When the Defender denies the pervasion, he implicitly accepts the establishment of the reason. The answer that there is no pervasion means that although the reason is true of the subject, this does not entail that whatever is that reason is necessarily that predicate. Thus, if the Defender is in a position where he has accepted the pervasion, he cannot deny the reason without contradicting his implicit acceptance of it. However, if he first denies the reason and thus is convinced by the Challenger that the reason is accurate, then he may accept the consequence or, if he is still not convinced, deny the pervasion without compromising his position. In the implied debate that follows, the Defender first denies the reason and then, when convinced that the reason is true, denies the pervasion. Finally, when the second consequence is stated to him for the third time, he accepts it. In this way, normal debate allows the Defender to question a consequence more than once and requires that the Challenger be able to justify what he is stating to the Defender. The implied debate, the statements of which are assigned to the Challenger and the Defender, is from the first statement of the basic consequence to the second statement of the basic consequence only and does not represent the whole debate:

C: It follows that the subject, a gold pot, is a generally characterized phenomenon because of being a hidden phenomenon. You asserted the pervasion.

D: The reason, that a gold pot is a hidden phenomenon, is not established.

C: It follows that the subject, a gold pot, is a hidden phenomenon because of being an object realized in a hidden manner by the thought consciousness apprehending it.

D: The reason, that a gold pot is an object realized in a hidden manner by the thought consciousness apprehending it, is not established.

C: It follows that the subject, a gold pot, is an object realized in a hidden manner by the thought consciousness apprehending it because of being an object of comprehension by the thought consciousness apprehending it.

D: The reason, that a gold pot is an object of comprehension by the thought consciousness apprehending it, is not established.

C: It follows that the subject, a gold pot, is an object of comprehension by the thought consciousness apprehending it because of being an established base.

D: I accept that a gold pot is an object of comprehension by the thought consciousness apprehending it.

C: Finished! It follows that the subject, a gold pot, is an object realized in a hidden manner by the thought consciousness apprehending it.

D: I accept it.

C: Finished! It follows that the subject, a gold pot, is a hidden phenomenon.

D: Why?

C: Because of being an object realized in a hidden manner by the thought consciousness apprehending it.

D: There is no pervasion.

C: It follows that whatever is an object realized in a hidden manner by the thought consciousness apprehending it is necessarily a hidden phenomenon because that is the definition of a hidden phenomenon.

D: I accept that whatever is an object realized in a hidden manner by the thought consciousness apprehending it is necessarily a hidden phenomenon.

C: Finished! It follows that the subject, a gold pot, is a hidden phenomenon.

D: I accept it.

C: It follows that the subject, a gold pot, is a generally characterized phenomenon because of being a hidden phenomenon.

> If he accepts the basic consequence [that a gold pot is a generally characterized phenomenon, the Sūtra School Challenger responds,] "It follows that the subject [a gold pot] is not a generally characterized phenomenon because of being a specifically characterized phenomenon."
>
> If he says that the reason [that a gold pot is a specifically characterized phenomenon] is not established, [the Sūtra School Challenger responds,] "It follows that the subject [a gold pot] is [a specifically characterized phenomenon] because of being a functioning thing."
>
> "[It follows that] there is pervasion [i.e., whatever is a functioning thing is necessarily a specifically characterized phenomenon] because functioning thing [*dngos po, bhāva*], specifically characterized phenomenon [*rang mtshan, svalakṣhana*], and ultimate truth [*don dam bden pa, paramārtha-satya*] are mutually inclusive and permanent phenomenon [*nitya, rtag pa*], generally characterized phenomenon [*spyi mtshan, sāmānya-lakṣhana*], and conventional truth [*kun rdzob bden pa, samvṛti-satya*] are mutually inclusive."

There are three possibilities between the two principals of debate B.8, hidden phenomenon and generally characterized phenomenon:

1 Something which is both is any permanent phenomenon—uncomposed space, permanent phenomenon itself, or object of knowledge.
2 Whatever is a generally characterized phenomenon is necessarily a hidden phenomenon, but it is not the case that whatever is a hidden phenomenon is necessarily a generally characterized phenomenon. For instance, a pot or the sound of a drum is a hidden phenomenon but not a generally characterized phenomenon.
3 Something which is neither must be a non-existent, such as the horn of a rabbit.

Debate B.9, Ninth Mistaken View (7b.3)

In debate B.9, the last in this first section—refutation of mistaken views concerning established bases, the hypothetical Defender accepts that whatever is a manifest phenomenon is necessarily not a hidden phenomenon. At first glance, this seems a reasonable assertion; one would think that manifest phenomena and hidden phenomena are mutually exclusive. Indeed, if hidden phenomena were those that must be known by thought consciousnesses and manifest phenomena were those that must be known by direct perceivers, then it would be the case that whatever is a manifest phenomenon would necessarily not be a hidden phenomena. However, such is not the case. Hidden phenomena are not those that must be known by thought consciousnesses, for only permanent phenomena *must* be known by thought whereas hidden phenomena include both permanent phenomena and functioning things. From just hearing the names "manifest phenomena" and "hidden phenomena" without knowing their meanings, one could easily make the mistake that the hypothetical Defender in B.9 has made.

If someone [a hypothetical Defender] says, "Whatever is a manifest phenomenon is necessarily not a hidden phenomenon," [the Sūtra School Challenger responds to him,] "It [absurdly] follows that the subject, a pillar, is [not a hidden phenomenon] because of [being a manifest phenomenon]."

If he says that the reason [that a pillar is a manifest phenomenon] is not established, [the Sūtra School Challenger responds,] "It follows that the subject [a pillar] is [a manifest phenomenon] because of being an object explicitly realized by a direct valid cognizer."

"[It follows that] there is pervasion [i.e., whatever is an object explicitly realized by a direct valid cognizer is necessarily a manifest phenomenon] because an object explicitly realized by a direct valid cognizer is the definition of a manifest phenomenon."

If he says that the above reason [i.e., that a pillar is an object explicitly realized by a direct valid cognizer] is not established, [the Sūtra School Challenger responds,] "It follows that the subject [a pillar] is an object explicitly realized by a direct valid cognizer because of being a functioning thing."

As before in debate B.8 the author is showing two possible answers to one consequence and provides two responses to those answers. Again it is clear that it is the second consequence begin referred to as the one "above" because it is the only one for which the alternative answer that the reason is not established is applicable and also because the Challenger's subsequent response is appropriate only to that consequence. However, in actual debate the Defender would have questioned the establishment of reason first and then later denied the pervasion.

> If he accepts the basic consequence [that a pillar is
> not a hidden phenomenon, the Sūtra School
> Challenger responds,] "It follows that the subject [a
> pillar] is a hidden phenomenon because of being an
> object realized in a hidden manner by the thought
> consciousness apprehending it."
>   The reason [that a pillar is an object realized in a
> hidden manner by the thought consciousness
> apprehending it] has been established.

The reason was established in debate B.8 (see pp. 387-388)
when the Defender denied both the pervasion and the
establishment of this same reason with respect to the subject
of that debate, a gold pot.

The two principals of debate B.9, manifest phenomenon
and non-hidden phenomenon, are mutually exclusive. There
is no common locus of these two because manifest phenomena are only impermanent phenomena and non-hidden
phenomena are only non-existents. A common locus of the
impermanent and the non-existent is not possible.

PRESENTATION OF THE AUTHOR'S OWN SYSTEM OF
ESTABLISHED BASES (7B.5)

The second section within the presentation of established
bases is the account of the author Pur-bu-jok Jam-ba-gya-
tso's own system of established bases. This is a Ge-luk-ba
interpretation of the system of the Proponents of Sūtra
Following Reasoning. Having refuted several mistaken
views concerning established bases and associated topics,
the author now moves to present the correct interpretation.
As in the presentation of colors, this section uniformly consists of a layout of definitions, divisions, and illustrations
given within the syllogistic form:

> Second, in our own system: There is a definition of
> an established base because what which is estab-
> lished by a valid cognizer is [the definition of an
> established base]. If established bases are divided,

there are two because there are the two, permanent phenomena and functioning things.

There is a definition of a permanent phenomenon because a common locus of a phenomenon and the non-momentary is the definition of a permanent phenomenon. If permanent phenomenon are divided, there are two because there are the two, permanent phenomenon of which being [them] is possible and permanent phenomena of which being [them] is not possible. There is something to be posited as a permanent phenomenon of which being [it] is possible because object of knowledge is such. There is something to be posited as a permanent phenomenon of which being [them] is not possible because the two—a permanent phenomenon and a functioning thing—are such.[1]

There is a definition of a functioning thing because that which is able to perform a function is [the definition of a functioning thing]. If functioning things are divided, there are three because there are the three—matter [or material phenomena], consciousnesses, and non-associated compositional factors.

There is a definition of matter because that which is atomically established is [the definition of matter]. If matter is divided, there are two because there are the two, external matter and internal matter.

There is a definition of external matter because that which is atomically established and is not included within a being's continuum is [the definition of external matter]. There are illustrations because a pot, a pillar, and the four—earth, water, fire, and wind—are such.

There is a definition of internal matter because that which is atomically established and is included

---

[1] See pp. 342 for an explanation of the two—a permanent phenomenon and a functioning thing.

> within a being's continuum is [the definition of
> internal matter]. There is an illustration because the
> contaminated form aggregate which is appropriated
> is such.

As mentioned above, all impermanent phenomena are
included in the five aggregates (see pp. 363-364), one of
which is the form aggregate (*gzugs kyi phung po, rūpa-
shandha*). It is called "contaminated" (*zag bcas, sāsrava*)
because of being an object which is suitable to serve as a
basis for the increase of the contaminations of desire, hatred,
and ignorance. Any form is a form aggregate and a contaminated phenomenon. For instance, the form of an
attractive partner may serve as an object of desire, thereby
increasing the afflictions or contaminations. Also, an inanimate object such as a gold pot is suitable to serve as a basis
for the increase of the contaminations such as desire or
miserliness (*ser sna, mātsarya*).

Since form aggregate is mutually inclusive with form,
there are many instances of contaminated form aggregates
which are not instances of internal form. Thus, the Tutor
Jam-ba-gya-tso has specified the illustration of an internal
form as an *appropriated* form aggregate. This means that the
form is an aggregate which the person appropriates in the
process of rebirth due to the force of contaminated actions
(*las, karma*) and afflictions (*nyon mongs, klesha*). The appropriated form aggregate includes all form within the personal
continuum—the five sense powers, blood, flesh, bones, and
so forth.

> There is a definition of a consciousness because that
> which is clear and knowing is [the definition of a
> consciousness]. There is an illustration because an
> eye consciousness is such.
>
> There is a definition of a non-associated composi-
> tional factor because a composed phenomenon
> which is neither matter nor a consciousness is [the
> definition of a non-associated compositional factor].
> There are illustrations because functioning things,

impermanence, and persons—a horse, an ox, and so forth are such.

If established bases are divided in another way, there are two because there are the two, one and different. There is a definition of [a phenomenon which is] one because a phenomenon which is not diverse is [the definition of one]. There are illustrations because object of knowledge, permanent phenomenon, and functioning thing are individually such.

There is a definition of [phenomena which are] different because those phenomena which are diverse is [the definition of different]. There are illustrations because the two—a permanent phenomenon and a functioning thing, the two—a definition and a definiendum, the two—a pillar and a pot, and the two—a gold pot and a copper pot—are such.

Although all of the provided illustrations of different phenomena are objects of knowledge of which being them is not possible they need not necessarily be so. Objects of knowledge of which being them is possible such as the two—a functioning thing and an established base—are also different phenomena.

If objects of knowledge are divided in another way, there are two because there are the two, specifically characterized phenomena and generally characterized phenomena. There is a definition of a specifically characterized phenomenon because a phenomenon which is established by way of its own character without being merely imputed by a term or a thought consciousness is [the definition of a specifically characterized phenomenon]. There is a definition of a generally characterized phenomenon because that which is merely imputed by a term or a thought consciousness and is not established as a

specifically characterized phenomenon is the definition of a generally characterized phenomenon.

Furthermore, a phenomenon which is ultimately
able to perform a function is the definition of an
ultimate truth. A phenomenon which is ultimately
unable to perform a function is the definition of a
conventional truth.

DISPELLING OBJECTIONS TO THE AUTHOR'S SYSTEM OF ESTABLISHED BASES (8B.3)

The third and final section of the presentation of established
bases in the Tutor's *Collected Topics* is the author's defense
against possible objections to his interpretations given in
two previous sections. As in the presentation of colors, here
in the chapter on established bases this section consists of
three debates. Again the essential format is that a hypothetical Challenger, who is outside the system explained in this
text, states consequences to the interpretations given by the
Tutor Jam-ba-gya-tso. The Sūtra School Defender, who is
inside the view presented in this text, answers these objections by pointing out the Challenger's failure of reasoning.
Beyond this, the debater who is defending the system presented in this book may again assume the role of Challenger
to state consequences against the former hypothetical
Challenger's objections or to respond to mistaken answers
that might be given by a second hypothetical Defender.

Debate B.10, First Objection (8b.3)

In this debate the Tutor Jam-ba-gya-tso is reacting against a
proposed alternative definition of an object of knowledge of
which being [it] is possible (*yin pa srid pa'i shes bya*) as:

that which is suitable as an object of an awareness of
which being [it] is possible (*yin pa srid pa'i blo'i yul du
bya rung ba*)

and a proposed definition of objects of knowledge of which being [them] is not possible (*yin pa mi srid pa'i shes bya*) as:

> those [phenomena] which are suitable as objects of awarenesses of which being [them] is not possible (*yin pa mi srid pa'i blo'i yul du bya rung pa*).[1]

The text says:

> Someone [a hypothetical Challenger] might say, "It follows that that which is suitable as an object of an awareness is not the definition of an object of knowledge because that which is suitable as an object of an awareness of which being [it] is possible is not the definition of an object of knowledge of which being [it] is possible."

This debate turns on the interpretation of the genitive case ending of the words "is possible" (*srid pa*), the ending which is translated as "of which" in English. If one defines an object of knowledge of which being it is possible in this way, the meaning intended must be "that which is suitable as an object of an awareness [*and* is an object] of which being it is possible". In this interpretation, the phrase "of which being [it] is possible" (*yin pa srid pa'i*) is an adjectival phrase modifying the understood "object" (*yul*). The Tutor Jam-ba-gya-tso points out that this phrase can easily be misinterpreted as modifying the contiguous word "awareness" (*blo*) in which case the definition is broader than the definiendum and therefore unsuitable. If a definition is such that by a valid interpretation of its grammar its meaning is broader or narrower than the definiendum it purports to define, then that definition is not suitable.

---

[1] Lati Rinbochay identified these definitions as being from Jam-yang-chok-hla-ö-ser (*'jam dbyangs phyogs lha 'ad zer*) in his Ra-dö *Collected Topics* (*rva stod bsdus grva*), (Dharamsala, India: Damchoe Sangpo, Library of Tibetan Works and Archives, 1980), but I have not been able to find these definitions in that text.

In this vein, according to the Tutor Jam-ba-gya-tso's interpretation, the definition as posited is not limited merely to objects of knowledge of which being them is possible but applies to all established bases because whatever is an established base is necessarily suitable as an object of an awareness of which being it is possible. This is so because whatever is an established base is necessarily an object of comprehension of an omniscient consciousness of which being it is possible (*yin pa srid pa'i rnam mkhyen*).

An omniscient consciousness of which being it is possible is, for instance, the omniscient consciousness of Shākyamuni Buddha. All established bases are objects of comprehension of the omniscient consciousness of Shākyamuni Buddha, and thereby are objects of comprehension of an omniscient consciousness of which being it is possible and suitable as objects of an awareness of which being it is possible. Therefore, that which is suitable as an object of an awareness of which being it is possible cannot be posited as the definition of an object of knowledge of which being it is possible.

Similarly, the Tutor argues that the definition of objects of knowledge of which being them is not possible cannot be those phenomena which are suitable as objects of awarenesses of which being them is not possible because whatever is an established base is necessarily suitable as an object of awarenesses of which being them is not possible. This is so because whatever is an established base is necessarily an object of comprehension of omniscient consciousnesses of which being them is not possible (*yin pa mi srid pa'i rnam mkhyen*). Omniscient consciousnesses of which being them is not possible are, for instance, the two—an omniscient consciousness in its first moment and in its second moment—or the two—the omniscient consciousness in the continuum of Amitābha Buddha and the omniscient consciousness in the continuum of Shākyamuni Buddha. All established bases are objects of comprehension of any of these omniscient consciousnesses singly or together with another, objects of knowledge of awarenesses of which being them is not possible, and suitable as objects of awarenesses of which being them is not possible. Thus, the definition of objects of knowledge of which being them is not possible is not posited as those phenomena which are suitable as objects of awarenesses of which being them is not possible.

> [The Sūtra School Defender answers,] "There is no pervasion [i.e., even though it is true that that which is suitable as an object of an awareness of which being it is possible is not the definition of an object of knowledge of which being it is possible, this does not entail that that which is suitable as an object of an awareness is not the definition of an object of knowledge]."
>
> "[It follows that there is no pervasion] because whatever is an established base is necessarily both suitable as an object of an awareness of which being [it] is possible and suitable as an object of awarenesses of which being [them] is not possible."
>
> "[It follows that it is so] because whatever is an established base is necessarily an object of comprehension of both an omniscient consciousness of which being [it] is possible and omniscient consciousnesses of which being [them] is not possible."

There are three possibilities between object of knowledge of which being it is possible and its purported definition, that which is suitable as an object of an awareness of which being it is possible:

1   Something which is both is a pot.
2   Whatever is an object of knowledge of which being it is possible is necessarily suitable as an object of an awareness of which being it is possible. However, whatever is suitable as an object of an awareness of which being it is possible is not necessarily an object of knowledge of which being it is possible, for the two—a permanent phenomenon and a functioning thing—are the former but not the latter.

3   Something which is neither must be a non-existent such as the flower of a dead tree.

Debate B.11, Second Objection (8b.5)

This debate is provided primarily for the sake of demonstrating an aspect of the reasoning form used in the Collected Topics tradition.

> Also, someone [a hypothetical Challenger] might say, "It follows that there is a common locus of impermanent phenomenon and permanent phenomenon because sound is both an impermanent phenomenon and a permanent phenomenon."

Of course, there is no common locus of impermanent phenomenon and permanent phenomenon. Here, rather than giving a different interpretation of the topics, the hypothetical Challenger is trying to force unwanted consequences on the Sūtra School Defender by manipulating the reasoning form.

> [If another says that the reason—that sound is both an impermanent phenomenon and a permanent phenomenon—is not established, the hypothetical Challenger will respond,] "It follows that [sound is both an impermanent phenomenon and a permanent phenomenon] because (1) sound is an impermanent phenomenon and (2) a permanent phenomenon."

The answer that the reason of the first consequence is not established is correct, for it is not true that sound is both an impermanent phenomenon and a permanent phenomenon.

In his response the hypothetical Challenger manipulates the reasoning form in order to try to prove the unwanted consequence. The standard procedure for proving that some phenomenon p is both a q and an r is by the reason that (1) p is a q and (2) p is an r. In this way the Challenger gives a valid reason in support of his thesis while providing the

Defender with an opportunity to deny only the part he doubts, to deny each part in turn, or to deny the combined reason. In the above consequence, however, the Challenger has not followed strictly the standard procedure, for his reason is of the form "because (1) p is a q and (2) r". Here the first part of the reason is properly stated with both a grammatical subject, "sound" (p), and predicate, "impermanent phenomenon" (q). However, the second part of the reason is indefinite in meaning as it has only one component, "permanent phenomenon" (r), which was a predicate nominative in the former consequence but here stands alone and does not function with the rest of the sentence. It would be suitable to leave the grammatical subject, "sound" (p), out of both parts of the reason or to include it in both, but it is mistaken to include it in one part and not in the other.

This second consequence is the end of the hypothetical Challenger's line of reasoning. The Sūtra School Defender now offers his answer:

> One gives the answer, "The combined reason [i.e., that (1) sound is an impermanent phenomenon and (2) a permanent phenomenon] is not established."

Only this answer is correct. The Defender cannot deny the first part of the reason, that a sound is an impermanent phenomenon, as this is true.

He cannot deny the second part of the reason alone, for this would lead him into unwanted consequences. The second part, lacking a grammatical subject and predicate, is so indefinite in meaning as to be open to many interpretations. For instance, if the Defender says that the second part of the reason—being a permanent phenomenon—is not established, the hypothetical Challenger might respond, "It follows that the reason—being a permanent phenomenon—is not established." When the Defender accepts that, the Challenger might respond,

> It follows that the subject, uncomposed space, is not a generally characterized phenomenon because of not

being a permanent phenomenon. You asserted the
reason.

The Defender is left with no effective answer. By denying
"being a permanent phenomenon" he is asserting the opposite, "not being a permanent phenomenon;" so he cannot
now deny the reason he has asserted. He also cannot effectively question the pervasion, for it is true that whatever is
not a permanent phenomenon is necessarily not a generally
characterized phenomenon. And he cannot accept the predicate of the consequence, that uncomposed space is not a
generally characterized phenomenon, as the opposite is true.
Thus, if the Defender questions the second part of the reason
alone, he is open to a barrage of unwanted consequences.

Also, he cannot deny the pervasion of the above consequence, for that would implicitly involve acceptance of the
combined reason as established. The only effective answer
to the hypothetical Challenger's consequence is that the
combined reason is not established (*sdoms rtags ma grub*), the
answer that the Tutor Jam-ba-gya-tso suggests.

This debate offers little in terms of philosophical content,
for it is well known to the debaters that there is no common
locus of impermanent phenomena and permanent phenomenon. Rather, the purpose of this debate is to instruct
students in the use of the answer that the combined reason
is not established and to suggest possibilities for
manipulating the reasoning form. This debate is provided
for the sake of increasing inquiry.

Debate B.12, Third Objection (8b.6)

In debate B.12, the last in the presentation of established
bases, the non-Sūtra School Challenger brings up the topic
of the ascertainment factor (*nges ngo*) and the appearance
factor (*snang ngo*) of direct perception. In debate B.7 (pp.
382-386) the Sūtra School Challenger spoke of "that which is
established for the appearance factor of a direct perceiver"
(*mngon sum gyi snang ngor grub pa*) and indicated it is
mutually inclusive with specifically characterized phe-

nomenon, appearing object of a direct perceiver, and impermanent phenomenon. Here the hypothetical Challenger suggests that whatever is established for the ascertainment factor of a direct perceiver (*mngon sum gyi nges ngor grub pa*) is necessarily established for the appearance factor of a direct perceiver.

Such is not the case. Only impermanent phenomena are established for the *appearance* factor of a direct perceiver, but all phenomena, impermanent and permanent alike, are established for the *ascertainment* factor of a direct perceiver. This is because all phenomena are objects of comprehension by omniscient consciousnesses, which are only direct perceivers. A Buddha has no thought consciousnesses whatsoever yet knows all phenomena. Although a permanent phenomenon does not *appear* to a Buddha's direct perceiver, that consciousness does *ascertain* or know the meaning of permanent phenomena, as is the case with a yogic perceiver knowing selflessness (see pp. 358-359).

There are three possibilities between what is established for the appearance factor of a direct perceiver and what is established for the ascertainment factor of a direct perceiver:

1 Something which is both is a pot or any other functioning thing.
2 Whatever is established for the appearance factor of a direct perceiver is necessarily established for the ascertainment factor of a direct perceiver. However, it is not the case that whatever is established for the ascertainment factor of a direct perceiver is necessarily established for the appearance factor of a direct perceiver, for any permanent phenomenon is unsuitable to appear to a direct perceiver but may be ascertained by a direct perceiver.
3 Something which is neither is any non-existent.

Also, someone [a hypothetical Challenger] might say, "It follows that the subject, uncomposed space, is an ultimate truth because of being established for the appearance factor of a direct perceiver."

If [another] says that the reason [that uncomposed space is established for the appearance factor of a direct perceiver] is not established, [the hypothetical Challenger responds,] "It follows that the subject [uncomposed space] is [established for the appearance factor of a direct perceiver] because of existing for the appearance factor of a direct perceiver."

The correct answer to the first consequence is that the reason is not established. Uncomposed space, as a permanent phenomenon, is not established for the appearance factor of a direct perceiver. The hypothetical Challenger tries to prove that it is so because of existing for the appearance factor of a direct perceiver (*mngon sum gyi snang ngor yod pa*). This too is mutually inclusive with functioning thing. Whatever *exists* for the appearance factor of a direct perceiver necessarily is *established* for the appearance factor of a direct perceiver. In general, existing (*yod pa, sat*) and being established (*grub pa, siddha*) are mutually inclusive. "Established" means "established by a valid cognizer" which is the definition of an established base and mutually inclusive with existent.

If [another] says that the reason [that uncomposed space exists for the appearance factor of a direct perceiver] is not established, [the hypothetical Challenger responds,] "It follows that the subject [uncomposed space exists for the appearance factor of a direct perceiver] because of existing for the ascertainment factor of a direct perceiver."

[To this the Sūtra School Defender answers,] "There is no pervasion [i.e., even though it is true that uncomposed space exists for the ascertainment factor of a direct perceiver, it is not the case that whatever exists for the ascertainment factor of a direct perceiver necessarily exists for the appearance factor of a direct perceiver]."

[If someone were to say that the reason of the last consequence—that uncomposed space exists for the ascertainment factor of a direct perceiver—is not established, then the Proponent of Sūtra would become Challenger and respond to him,] "The reason is established because of being an object of comprehension by a direct perceiver; because of being an object of comprehension by an omniscient consciousness."

If someone were to accept the above consequence [that uncomposed space is an ultimate truth, the Sūtra School Challenger would respond to him,] "It follows that the subject [uncomposed space] is not an ultimate truth because of being a conventional truth."

If he says that the reason [that uncomposed space is a conventional truth] is not established, [then the Sūtra School Challenger responds,] "It follows that the subject [uncomposed space] is [a conventional truth] because of being a permanent phenomenon."

Conventional truth is mutually inclusive with permanent phenomenon, and uncomposed space, as a permanent phenomenon, is a conventional truth.

REMARKS

"Established Bases" is the most important single chapter in the Tutor's *Collected Topics*. It is the foundation on which the structure rests. This chapter describes primarily the fundamental ontology in the system of the Sūtra School Following Reasoning, but that description of what exists is essentially framed within the requirement of epistemological verification of those existents by valid cognizers (*tshad ma, pramāṇa*). For example, an established base is defined as:

> that which is established by a valid cognizer

and an existent as:

> that observed by a valid cognizer.

Thus, in this system of Buddhist philosophy it is not sensible to postulate the existence of something that cannot be verified by a correct consciousness and, indeed, is not continuously observed by some such consciousness.

In this vein, established bases are designated as objects of knowledge (*shes bya, jñeya*), for whatever exists may be known. By asserting all existents to be objects of knowledge the Collected Topics logicians are emphasizing the vast capacity of awarenesses, thereby encouraging and fortifying students' efforts and determination.

The most important division of established bases, first explained in this seminal chapter, into permanent phenomena (*rtag pa, nitya*) and functioning things (*dngos po, bhāva*) also depends essentially on the description of the consciousnesses—thought consciousnesses (*rtog pa, kalpanā*) and direct perceivers (*mngon sum, pratyakṣha*) respectively—which take these two types of existents as their appearing objects. Since permanent phenomena are the appearing objects of thought consciousnesses and functioning things are the appearing objects of direct perceivers, all existents may be verified by the two types of valid cognizers, inferential valid cognizers and direct valid cognizers. However, the fact that only permanent phenomena are the appearing objects of thought consciousnesses and only functioning things are the appearing objects of direct perceivers does not mean that each of these types of consciousnesses is limited to knowing only those types of phenomena that are their appearing objects. Rather, all phenomena are hidden phenomena in the sense that they may be known by a thought consciousness in an indirect manner through the appearance of an internal imagistic representation. Also, all phenomena may be known by means of direct perception in that all existents are realized by a directly perceiving omniscient consciousness.

Still, even though any established base may be ascertained by either of the two types of valid cognizers, clear priority is given to direct perceivers. Permanent phenomena are described as conventional truths, truths for a conventional or obscured awareness, for they are the appearing objects of only thought consciousnesses which are unable to ascertain the specific characteristics of their objects. On the other hand, impermanent phenomena are acclaimed as ultimate truths, truths for an ultimate awareness, as they appear immediately and vibrantly to direct perceivers which are consciousnesses capable of ascertaining them unmistakenly.

In this educational system, the description of the appearance of specifically characterized phenomena to direct perception is for the sake of causing one to understand that the essential information on subtle impermanence and so forth—the raw data—is continuously available and that common beings, under the influence of thick predispositions for adhering to permanence, do not tap into the rich appearance of direct perception.

In addition to the fundamental division of established bases into permanent phenomena and functioning things, in this chapter they are also divided into objects of knowledge of which being them is possible (*yin pa srid pa'i shes bya*) and objects of knowledge of which being them is not possible (*yin pa mi srid pa'i shes bya*). This division functions to describe the status of phenomena in sets and forcefully emphasizes the distinction between existence (*yod pa, sat*) and being (*yin pa*) by showing that sets of mutually exclusive phenomena exist but *being* those phenomena does not exist.

Also in this chapter the Tutor first explains the division of established bases into those which are one (*gcig, ekatva*) and those which are different (*tha dad, nānātva*). This primary distinction rests on the doctrine of self-identity, that any existent is identical with itself and is different from all else.

For the novice monks studying "Established Bases" perhaps the most approachable lesson is the division of functioning things, which traditionally is supplied by the oral tradition and here is included in the annotations. The extensive division of functioning things serves to locate the information on external forms that came in "Colors and So Forth", to raise the important topic of consciousness which is later taken up in detail in the Awareness and Knowledge texts, and to give an initial indication of the path (*lam*, *mārga*) structure through the discussion of persons. Immediately, studying the division of functioning things serves to identify the range of ultimate truths in the system of the Proponents of Sūtra Following Reasoning, providing students with a handle on those existents and thereby strengthening their efforts toward gaining insight into the nature of phenomena.

10 *Identifying Isolates*

INTRODUCTION

In this system, mental abstractions are permanent phenomena. Even though the basis of an abstraction may be a functioning thing, a mental imputation with respect to that basis is necessarily a permanent phenomenon. For instance, although each and every pot is a functioning thing and pot itself—the singular generality—is a functioning thing, different-from-pot (*bum pa dang tha dad*) is a permanent phenomenon. From one point of view, it is easy to see that like established base, object of knowledge, and so forth different-from-pot has both permanent and impermanent instances, and therefore different-from-pot itself is a permanent phenomenon. Since it has permanent instances, different-from-pot itself is a common locus of a phenomenon and the non-momentary.

That different-from-pot is a permanent phenomenon is explained from another point of view as well. Like established base, different-from-pot is by its nature a permanent phenomenon (see p. 318). According to Kensur Yeshay Tupden, since different (*tha dad, nānātva*) itself is a permanent phenomenon, when it is applied to such things as a pot, a pillar, a functioning thing and so forth to yield different-from-pot and so on, then those phenomena too are permanent. The reason, in turn, why different itself is a permanent phenomenon is that it has both permanent and impermanent instances.[1] Thus, the collective abstract different is an appearing object of a thought consciousness only and different-from-something, whether a permanent phenomenon or an impermanent one, is also a mental abstraction and a permanent phenomenon.

However, also like established base itself, the fact that different-from-pot itself is a permanent phenomenon does not mean that whatever is different from pot is necessarily a permanent phenomenon, for some things which are different from pot such as a pillar are impermanent. Still, it must be clear that different-from-pot itself is an abstraction such that it cannot appear to a direct perceiver and must appear to thought consciousnesses only. Similarly, the definition of something which is different from pot:

> a phenomenon which is diverse from pot (*bum pa dang so so ba'i chos*)

is also a permanent phenomenon, as it has all the same permanent and impermanent instances. Both different-from-pot and phenomenon which is diverse from pot are abstractions that depend on imputation by a term or a thought consciousness and are not established by way of their own characters in the sense that they do not appear unmistakenly to an awareness knowing them but must be known through the appearance of a mental image.

Moreover, one-with-pot (*bum pa dang gcig*) is also a permanent phenomenon, and the definition of one-with-pot:

> a phenomenon which is not diverse from pot (*bum pa dang so so ba ma yin pa'i chos*)

---

[1] Kensur Yeshay Tupden, oral commentary.

too is a permanent phenomenon. However, these two permanent phenomena are in one important aspect quite distinct from different-from-pot and phenomenon which is diverse from pot. In the case of different-from-pot, it is not true that whatever is different from pot is necessarily a functioning thing because, for instance, uncomposed space is different from pot but is a permanent phenomenon. However, one-with-pot is not like this because even though it is itself a permanent phenomenon, whatever is one with pot is necessarily a functioning thing. Whatever is one with pot is necessarily a functioning thing because only pot itself is one with pot, and pot, since it is matter, is a functioning thing. Thus, unlike different-from-pot, one-with-pot cannot be justified as a permanent phenomenon by the reason of there being some permanent phenomena which are one with pot, for there are none. Still, since one (*gcig, ekatva*) itself is a permanent phenomenon as it has both permanent and impermanent instances, when applied to something such as a pot, one-with-pot is a permanent phenomenon, a mental abstraction merely imputed by a term or a thought consciousness.

In the same way, both definition and definiendum are permanent phenomena by reason of their each having both permanent and impermanent instances. Thus, just as different-from-pot and a phenomenon which is diverse from pot are permanent, so the definition of pot (*bum pa'i mtshan nyid*) and the definiendum of that which is a bulbous flat-based phenomenon able to perform the function of holding water (*lto ldir zhabs zhum chu skyor gyi don byed nus pa'i mtshon bya*) are both permanent phenomena too. This does not mean that a particular definition such as that which is a bulbous flat-based phenomenon able to perform the function of holding water is a permanent phenomenon, for it is not. Rather, an object such as the definition of pot, understood as a single expression of one phenomenon, is permanent. Also, as in the case of one-with-pot, whatever is the definition of a pot or the definiendum of that which is a bulbous flat-based phenomenon able to perform the function of holding water is necessarily a functioning thing, but they themselves are permanent phenomena.

THE NATURE OF ISOLATES

Pot's isolate (*bum pa'i ldog pa*) bears the same relationship to its basis, pot, as does one-with-pot and is also a permanent phenomenon. Pot itself is the only thing that may be posited as pot's isolate; thus, whatever is pot's isolate is necessarily a functioning thing, for *only* pot is pot's isolate. Even so, pot's isolate is not itself a functioning thing. Rather, like one-with-pot, it is a permanent phenomenon "because of being merely imputed by a nominal expression (*ming gi brjod pa*) or a thought consciousness and not being established from the side of the object itself".[1]

Pot's isolate is called an "isolate" (*ldog pa*) because it is just pot itself, that which is one with pot, in *isolation* from all else—its instances, its illustrations, the phenomena mutually inclusive with it, and everything that is not exactly the same as pot in both name and meaning. The Tibetan word "*ldog pa*" translated here as "isolate" literally means "reverse" and indicates a double reverse or double negation, not a single reverse or single opposition away from the object but a double reverse back to the object.

In debate C.13, the Tutor Jam-b̄a-gya-tso identifies the precise meaning of pot's isolate as:

> that which is reversed from not being one with pot
> (*bum pa dang gcig ma yin pa las ldog pa*),

meaning that which is non-non-one with pot. By the laws of negation, this reduces to that which is one with pot, which is pot itself. Thus, pot alone, the singular collective entity, is pot's isolate because it alone is reversed from not being one with pot. No other phenomenon nor any non-existent is reversed from not being one with pot, except pot itself.

---

[1] Denma Lochö Rinbochay, oral commentary.

Particular instances of pot such as a gold pot are not pot's isolate because a gold pot, for instance, is not reversed from not being one with pot. Rather, since it is not one with pot (as it is different from pot), it is reversed from being one with pot. Even phenomena mutually inclusive with pot are not pot's isolate because, having different names from pot, they are not one with pot but are different from pot.

In this tradition, a common description of the relationship between mutually inclusive phenomena is that they are the same entity but different isolates (*ngo bo gcig ldog pa tha dad*). For instance, product and impermanent phenomenon are mutually inclusive and thus are the same entity. They are the same entity because they are different phenomena such that whatever is the one is necessarily the other and one cannot find an impermanent phenomenon which is not a product nor a product which is not an impermanent phenomenon. However, they are different isolates. Product is product's isolate and impermanent phenomenon is the isolate of impermanent phenomenon. This is because they are each one with themselves and are not mutually one with each other. That product and impermanent phenomenon are different isolates implies that they are different for thought. A meaning-generality of product appears to the thought consciousness understanding product, but a meaning-generality of impermanent phenomenon appears to a conceptual consciousness thinking about impermanent phenomenon. Thus, although they are mutually inclusive and the same entity, they are different isolates and different for thought.

Whatever is pot's isolate is necessarily one with pot, and what is different from pot is necessarily not pot's isolate. Mutually inclusive phenomena are necessarily different; therefore, they are different isolates. For every phenomenon, it alone—and nothing else—is its isolate, for only it is one with it. For instance, pot is pot's isolate because pot is one with pot. However, this association cannot be reversed: It is not the case that pot's isolate is a pot because pot's isolate is a permanent phenomenon. Pot is reversed from not being one with pot, but what is reversed from not being one with pot is not a pot but a permanent phenomenon.

According to Denma Lochö Rinbochay, "What one understands by pot's isolate is that factor which is a negation of non-pot and which [exists] with pot (*bum pa'i steng tu bum pa ma yin pa'i dgag pa'i cha*)."[1] It is the nature of any phenomenon that merely by its existence it is a negation of what is not it. A phenomenon exists in contradistinction to what is not it, for it alone is one with itself.

The basic source for the topic of isolates is Dharmakīrti's *Commentary on (Dignāga's) "Compendium of Valid Cognition"* which says:

> Because all things naturally abide in their own
> entities,
> They have a dependence on isolation from other
> things.[2]

All phenomena abide naturally as themselves, not mixed with others.[3] Phenomena do not become distinct from themselves, but abide naturally in their own entities; therefore, they are isolated from all similar and dissimilar things. A phenomenon is defined as:

> that which bears its own entity (*rang gi ngo bo 'dzin pa*).

This implies that a phenomenon is one with itself, not different from itself, and is isolated from all that is not one with it. Because all phenomena abide in their own entities, they are not mixed with other phenomena. They depend on this non-mixture or isolation from other things in order to abide in their own entities.

One can posit limitless isolates, for whatever exists is isolated from all other phenomena in the sense that it alone is

---

[1] *Ibid.*

[2] Dharmakīrti, *Commentary on (Dignāga's) "Compendium of Valid Cognition"*, P5709, Vol. 130, 78.5.6-78.5.7.

[3] The source for this explanation of the cited passage from Dharmakīrti's *Commentary on (Dignāga's) "Compendium of Valid Cognition"* is Lati Rinbochay, oral commentary.

one with itself. As mentioned in debate A.2: if something is an established base, it is necessarily its own isolate. Every established base is reversed from not being one with itself. This is the essential meaning of isolates. An isolate brings the focus onto just that phenomenon itself that is one with itself, the singular aspect. All established bases are their own isolates because each is one with itself and only itself. Even phenomena which are not exemplifiers of themselves such as objects of knowledge of which being them is not possible are one with themselves and are their own isolates. For instance, the two—a pillar and a pot—are not the two—a pillar and a pot—but are one with and the isolate of the two—a pillar and a pot. Any phenomenon is one with itself; therefore, any phenomenon is reversed from not being one with itself and is its own isolate.

THE TYPES OF ISOLATES

There are four types of isolates (*ldog pa*, **vyatireka*):

1 self-isolates (*rang ldog*)
2 general-isolates (*spyi ldog*)
3 illustration-isolates (*gzhi ldog*)
4 meaning-isolates (*don ldog*).

The self-isolate or general-isolate of a phenomenon is its ordinary isolate and refers only to the phenomenon itself, alone. Self-isolate and general-isolate are mutually inclusive. The illustration-isolate of a phenomenon refers only to the illustrations (*mtshan gzhi*) of that phenomenon. The meaning-isolate of a phenomenon refers only to the definition of a phenomenon. If applied to a particular case such as a pot, pot is the self-isolate and the general-isolate of pot, a bulbous flat-based phenomenon which is made from gold and is able to perform the function of holding water is an illustration-isolate of pot, and a bulbous flat-based phenomenon which is able to perform the function of holding water is the meaning-isolate of pot.

418 Debate in Tibetan Buddhism

An illustration (see pp. 70-72) of a phenomenon is an illustration-isolate of that phenomenon. In general, an illustration is defined as:

> that which serves as a basis for illustrating the appropriate definiendum by way of [its] definition (*mtshan nyid kyis skabs su bab pa'i mtshon bya mtshon pa'i gzhir gyur pa*).

Applied to a particular phenomenon such as a pot, the definition of an illustration of a pot (*bum pa'i mtshan gzhi*) is:

> that which serves as a basis for illustrating pot by way of [being] a bulbous flat-based phenomenon which is able to perform the function of holding water (*lto ldir zhabs zhum chu skyor gyi don byed nus pas bum pa mtshon pa'i gzhir gyur pa*).

An example is a bulbous flat-based phenomenon which is made from gold and is able to perform the function of holding water (*gser las grub pa'i lto ldir zhabs zhum chu skyor gyi don byed nus pa*).

An illustration or an illustration-isolate must be something which is the object that it illustrates as a pot is a functioning thing, but it cannot be such that understanding the illustration effectively serves as understanding all of the essential characteristics of the illustrated object. That is, in order to be a valid illustrator (*mtshon byed*) of something, a phenomenon must be such that although someone might have realized the illustration, that person would not necessarily have realized that which it illustrates. For instance, a gold pot is a proper illustration of a functioning thing because it is a functioning thing and merely through having ascertained a gold pot with valid cognition, one would not necessarily have ascertained functioning thing itself with valid cognition. That is, it is possible that there be a person who has ascertained a gold pot with valid cognition but has not ascertained functioning thing with valid cognition. A gold pot indicates functioning thing by way of being able to perform a function; thus, it *illustrates* or *demonstrates* the meaning of functioning thing.

On the other hand, a gold pot is not a proper illustration of a pot because, although it is a pot, if someone has ascertained a gold pot with valid cognition, that person must have ascertained pot with valid cognition. It is not possible for one to know the meaning of a gold pot and not know the meaning of pot.

According to Lati Rinbochay, an illustration-isolate of pot is, for instance, a bulbous flat-based phenomenon which is made from gold and is able to perform the function of holding water. This is the definition and meaning of a gold pot. In the case of a definition and its definiendum, one might have ascertained with valid cognition a particular definition, such as that which is able to perform a function, without having ascertained with valid cognition its definiendum, functioning thing. Similarly, one might have ascertained with valid cognition a bulbous flat-based phenomenon which is made from gold and is able to perform the function of holding water without having ascertained with valid cognition pot, or even gold pot. This distinction turns on the difference between name (*ming*) and meaning (*don*). One might know the meaning without knowing the name, but one could not know the name of an instance, such as a gold pot, without knowing the name of the generality, pot, because knowing the name with valid cognition depends on knowing the meaning, and one cannot know the meaning of gold pot without knowing the meaning of pot.[1]

The meaning-isolate of a phenomenon refers to its definition; thus, only definienda have meaning-isolates. The definition of a phenomenon is referred to as its meaning-isolate because the definition is the meaning or actual object and the definiendum is the name. That which is able to perform a function is the meaning-isolate of functioning thing, the meaning of the appellation "functioning thing".

---

[1] Lati Rinbochay, oral commentary.

Each and every phenomenon has a self-isolate and a general-isolate, for whatever exists is necessarily its own isolate. In general, what is called the "isolate of a phenomenon" is the self-isolate or general-isolate of that phenomenon.

Thus, only definienda have all four types of isolates—a self-isolate, a general-isolate, an illustration-isolate, and a meaning-isolate. Objects of knowledge of which being them is not possible have only self-isolates and general-isolates. Definitions have three isolates—self-isolates, general-isolates, and illustration-isolates. Dual objects of knowledge of which being them is possible such as the two— functioning thing and that which is able to perform a function—have a self-isolate, a general-isolate, and an illustration-isolate.

THE PURPOSE OF IDENTIFYING ISOLATES

With regard to the intention of "Identifying Isolates", the Lo-šel-ling *Collected Topics* says:

> There is a purpose [for the presentation identifying isolates] because it indicates that there is a way of realizing objects by the power of the appearance of a specifically characterized phenomenon and a way of realizing self-isolates or illustration-isolates by the power of the appearance of an isolate, and thus that in terms of objects, specifically characterized phenomena are established as functioning things and that self-isolates and illustration-isolates, which are equal to the enumeration of objects of knowledge, are imputed by thought consciousnesses.[1]

As explained by Kensur Yeshay Tupden, the meaning of this passage is that functioning things, which are specifically characterized phenomena, appear to direct perceivers together with all of their uncommon characteristics and that

---

[1] Jam-ƀel-trin-lay-yön-ďan-gya-tso, Lo-šel-ling *Collected Topics*, p. 7.

appearance is cast from the side of the object whereas isolates, which are permanent and generally characterized phenomena, appear to thought consciousnesses in a general way and that appearance is imputed by the thought consciousness. A direct perceiver realizes its object by the power of the appearance of a specifically characterized phenomenon, and that awareness does not have to induce the appearance of its object. However, a thought consciousness may realize its object by the power of the appearance of an isolate, and that awareness must impute the appearance of its object, for the appearance is not cast from the object. (Although an isolate may appear to a thought consciousness, it is not the case that an isolate appears to every thought consciousness. For instance, an isolate does not appear to a doubting consciousnesses but appears only to a decisive thought consciousness.) For instance, an isolate appears to a thought consciousness contemplating table. It understands table through the appearance of that factor which is a negation of non-table. Thinking about the color of a table, color's isolate appears to such a thought consciousness. Also, in thinking about the shape, size, structure, and so forth of a table, isolates appear. However, there is a way of realizing all of these qualities of a table apart from the appearance of isolates; that is by the power of the appearance of a specifically characterized phenomenon, the table itself. This is the purpose of identifying isolates, to indicate these distinct ways of realizing objects.[1]

Since the above passage from the Lo-sel-ling *Collected Topics* explains that one way of realizing objects is by the power of the appearance of isolates and since thought consciousnesses understand their objects through the appearance of meaning-generalities, one is led to wonder how isolates and meaning-generalities compare. According to Kensur Yeshay Tupden, the isolate exists on the side of the object as a natural predicate of its being one with itself, and the meaning-generality is what appears to the conceptual

---

[1] Kensur Yeshay Tupden, oral commentary.

awareness. For instance, pot's isolate exists with pot as a corollary of its being one with pot and thereby reversed from not being one with pot, and the conceptual consciousness thinking about a pot understands its object through the appearance of a meaning-generality of pot (*bum pa'i don spyi*), which is defined as:

> that superimposed factor which appears like a pot to the thought consciousness apprehending pot although it is not a pot (*bum 'dzin rtog pa la bum pa ma yin bzhin du bum pa lta bur snang ba'i sgro btags kyi cha*).

Again, according to Lochö Rinbochay, "What one understands by pot's isolate is that factor which is a negation of non-pot and which [exists] with pot."[1] Through the appearance of a meaning-generality which has a nature of an elimination of all that is not pot, a thought consciousness understands pot. Thus, thought understands its object in a general way, for the meaning-generality which appears to such a consciousness is a superimposed factor which is mixed with objects of other places, times, and natures. The appearance of that image prevents thought from perceiving the actual specifically characterized phenomenon. Rather, thought focuses on the isolate, understanding the abstract rather than the specific object.

THE PHENOMENA COEXTENSIVE WITH AN ISOLATE

An important topic for debate taught in the section on isolates is that of the phenomena which are coextensive (*yin khyab mnyam*) with the isolate of a phenomenon. These are also referred to as the phenomena which are mutually inclusive with the isolate of a phenomenon. The coextensives are phenomena which, within being different from a phenomenon's isolate, are mutually pervasive with that phenomenon's isolate. They are said to be "coextensive" with the isolate because each pervades that isolate and that

---

[1] Denma Lochö Rinbochay, oral commentary.

isolate pervades each of them. Among the eight approaches of pervasion that exist between a definition and its definiendum there is a relationship of coextensiveness such that each pervades the other. The phenomena which are coextensive with an isolate compare to that isolate in the same way.

For instance, the four phenomena which are coextensive with the isolate of functioning thing (*dngos po'i ldog pa dang yin khyab mnyam bzhi*) are:

1 one-with-functioning-thing (*dngos po dang gcig*)
2 functioning-thing-which-is-one-with-functioning-thing (*dngos po dang gcig tu gyur pa'i dngos po*)
3 the definiendum of that which is able to perform a function (*don byed nus pa'i mtshon bya*)
4 the triply qualified imputed existent of that which is able to perform a function (*don byed nus pa'i btags yod chos gsum tshang ba*).

Each of these phenomena is mutually inclusive with *the isolate of functioning thing*, but none is mutually inclusive with *functioning thing*. For instance, according to the method outlined in the text for establishing a phenomenon as coextensive with an isolate:

> The subject, one-with-functioning-thing, is coextensive with the isolate of functioning thing because (1) it is different from the isolate of functioning thing and (2) whatever is it is necessarily the isolate of functioning thing and (3) whatever is the isolate of functioning thing is necessarily it (*dngos po dang gcig chos can dngos po'i ldog pa dang yin khyab mnyam yin te khyod dngos po'i ldog pa dang tha dad gang zhig khyod yin na dngos po'i ldog pa yin pas khyab dngos po'i ldog pa yin na khyod yin pas khyab pa'i phyir*).

First, an isolate and a phenomenon coextensive with it must be different phenomena; one-with-functioning-thing is different from the isolate of functioning thing because of being a phenomenon which is not one with the isolate of functioning thing. Second, it must be the case that whatever is that coextensive phenomenon is necessarily the isolate of that phenomenon. Thus, whatever is one with functioning thing is necessarily the isolate of functioning thing because the only thing that can be posited as one with functioning thing is functioning thing itself, which is also the isolate of functioning thing. Third, it must be the case that whatever is the isolate of that phenomenon is necessarily that coextensive phenomenon. Thus, whatever is the isolate of functioning thing is necessarily one with functioning thing because only functioning thing is the isolate of functioning thing, and it is also one with functioning thing. This type of reasoning applies in the same way to the other coextensives.

Each of these four coextensives is the same as the isolate of functioning thing in the sense that all that one can posit as any of them is functioning thing itself. What is the isolate of functioning thing? Functioning thing. In the same way, functioning thing is one with functioning thing. Also, functioning thing is the functioning thing which is one with functioning thing. From among all functioning things, which is the functioning thing which is one with functioning thing? Only functioning thing itself. Functioning thing and only functioning thing is also the definiendum of that which is able to perform a function. Thus, functioning thing is also the only thing which is the triply qualified imputed existent of that which is able to perform a function. A triply qualified imputed existent (see pp. 69-72) is the definition of a definiendum, and the triply qualified imputed existent of that which is able to perform a function is the definition of the definiendum of that which is able to perform a function.

Since they are mutually inclusive, there is a common locus of the isolate of functioning thing and one-with-functioning-thing, there is a common locus of one-with-functioning-thing and the definiendum of that which is able to perform a function, and so forth because functioning thing, and only functioning thing, is that common locus.

However, it cannot be said that the isolate of functioning thing or any of the phenomena themselves which are coextensive with the isolate of functioning thing *is* any of the others. For instance, even though whatever is one with functioning thing is necessarily the isolate of functioning thing, one-with-functioning-thing itself *is not* the isolate of functioning thing. Similarly, whatever is the definiendum of that which is able to perform a function is necessarily one with functioning thing, but the definiendum of that which is able to perform a function is not one with functioning thing. The reason for this situation is that whatever is any one of these—that is, functioning thing—is necessarily *one* with functioning thing, but any of these mutually inclusive phenomena—the isolate of functioning thing, one-with-functioning-thing, and so forth—is necessarily *different* from functioning thing.

It must be seen clearly that an assertion of a pervasion—such as whatever is the isolate of functioning thing is necessarily one with functioning thing—focuses on *those things which are* the isolate of functioning thing and *those things which are* one with functioning thing and does not range over the isolate of functioning thing itself (for it is neither the isolate of functioning thing nor one with functioning thing) or one-with-functioning-thing (for it too is neither the isolate of functioning thing nor one with functioning thing). If this is not understood clearly, one might mistakenly think that the assertion of pervasion—whatever is the isolate of functioning thing is necessarily one with functioning thing—means that the isolate of functioning thing is one with functioning thing whereas it is not, for it is different from functioning thing.

Thus, the case of an isolate and the phenomena coextensive with it present a very odd sort of mutual inclusion. Even though they are mutually pervasive, the one is not the other in the sense that the one does not demonstrate the being of the other. Whatever is the isolate of functioning thing is necessarily one with functioning thing and whatever is one with functioning thing is necessarily the isolate of functioning thing, *but* the isolate of functioning thing is not one with functioning thing and one-with-functioning-thing is not the isolate of functioning thing. This applies equally to all the coextensives. This situation forcefully points out the difference between statements of pervasion and copulative statements.

There is a precedent for this sort of mutual inclusion in the Collected Topics tradition, but perhaps not a parallel. For instance, the definition of a definition is:

that which is a triply qualified substantial existent.

In this case, whatever is either a definition or a triply qualified substantial existent is necessarily the other, and that which is a triply qualified substantial existent is a definition. However, definition itself is not a triply qualified substantial existent because it is a definiendum, for it is the definiendum of the triply qualified substantial existent. There are other similar cases of mutually inclusive phenomena for which one is the other and one is not the other, but they merely suggest and do not quite parallel the relationship that exists between an isolate and the phenomena which are coextensive with it because in such a case neither one is the other.

In the same way, the isolate of functioning thing and the four phenomena coextensive with it are not themselves in the sense that they are not exemplifiers of themselves. The isolate of functioning thing is not the isolate of functioning thing because only functioning thing itself is the isolate of functioning thing. One-with-functioning-thing is not one with functioning thing because of being different from functioning thing. It is different from functioning thing because of being a permanent phenomenon. One-with-functioningthing is a phenomenon which is different in both name and meaning from functioning thing. Because only functioning thing itself is any of these phenomena, they are not themselves in the sense that they do not demonstrate their own being.

Also, one can say that the isolate of functioning thing is coextensive and mutually inclusive with one-withfunctioning-thing, functioning-thing-which-is-one-with-functioning-thing, and so forth; however, one must say that the isolate of functioning thing is *mutually exclusive* with the phenomena which are coextensive with it. Whatever is the isolate of functioning thing is necessarily not a phenomenon coextensive with the isolate of functioning thing, and whatever is a phenomenon coextensive with the isolate of functioning thing is necessarily not the isolate of functioning thing; thus, there is no common locus of these. There is nothing to posit as a phenomenon coextensive with the isolate of functioning thing except one-with-functioning-thing, functioning-thing-which-is-one-with-functioning-thing, and so forth. Since, as noted above, none of these phenomena is an exemplifier of the others, the phenomena coextensive with the isolate of functioning thing are mutually exclusive with the isolate of functioning thing. From another point of view, a common locus of the isolate of functioning thing and a phenomenon coextensive with the isolate of functioning thing is not possible because whatever is the isolate of functioning thing is necessarily one with functioning thing, but whatever is a phenomenon coextensive with the isolate of functioning thing is necessarily not one with functioning thing but different from functioning thing.

Again, this is a very odd situation. The more usual case is like that between functioning thing and the phenomena mutually inclusive with it—product, impermanent phenomenon, specifically characterized phenomenon, cause, effect, and so forth—in which case any one of them is an exemplifier of any of the others. Functioning thing is a product, product is an impermanent phenomenon, impermanent phenomenon is a specifically characterized phenomenon, and so on. Therefore, functioning thing and the phenomena which are mutually inclusive with functioning thing (*dngos po dang don gcig pa'i chos*) have three possibilities:

1 Something which is both is product. Product is a functioning thing, and it is a phenomenon which is mutually
   inclusive with functioning thing.
2 Whatever is a phenomenon which is mutually inclusive
   with functioning thing is necessarily a functioning thing,
   but whatever is a functioning thing is not necessarily a
   phenomenon which is mutually inclusive with functioning thing. For instance, a pot is a functioning thing but
   not mutually inclusive with functioning thing.
3 Something which is neither is uncomposed space.

However, as has been explained, the isolate of functioning
thing and the phenomena coextensive with it do not compare in this way, for they are mutually exclusive. Thus, they
present an unusual sort of comparison between a phenomenon and the set of phenomena which are mutually
inclusive with it.

In general, the phenomena coextensive with the isolate of
functioning thing are enumerated as four; however, there
are many such phenomena. For instance, phenomenon
which is not different from functioning thing (*dngos po dang
tha dad ma yin pa'i chos*) is coextensive with the isolate of
functioning thing, but it is not enumerated among the four
coextensives. Still, "These four coextensives are able to illustrate the matter. There is nothing which one can posit that
cannot be included in these four."[1]

From among the four phenomena coextensive with the
isolate of functioning thing only one is an impermanent
phenomenon. Functioning-thing-which-is-one-with-
functioning-thing is an impermanent phenomenon because
it is qualified as being a functioning thing. From among all
functioning things, only functioning thing itself—the
generality—is one with functioning thing, and that is what
is being referred to here. It is not even suitable to express
this phenomenon as "impermanent-phenomenon-which-is-
one-with-functioning-thing" or as "product-which-is-one-

---

[1] Lati Rinbochay, oral commentary.

with-functioning-thing" because even though functioning thing is an impermanent phenomenon and a product, impermanent phenomenon and product as such are not one with functioning thing.

The other three phenomena coextensive with the isolate of functioning thing are permanent phenomena. One-with-functioning-thing, the definiendum of that which is able to perform a function, and the triply qualified imputed existent of that which is able to perform a function are phenomena merely imputed by a term or a thought consciousness. Also, the isolate of functioning thing, an illustration-isolate of functioning thing, and the meaning-isolate of functioning thing are permanent phenomena.

From among the four coextensives with the isolate of functioning thing one is a definiendum and one is a definition. The definiendum of that which is able to perform a function is a definiendum because of being the definiendum of the triply qualified imputed existent of that which is able to perform a function. Thus, from among the four coextensives, the triply qualified imputed existent of that which is able to perform a function is a definition, for it is the definition of the definiendum of that which is able to perform a function.

Some scholars assert that one-with-functioning-thing is also a definiendum because it is defined as:

a phenomenon which is not diverse from functioning thing (*dngos po dang so so ba ma yin pa'i chos*).

Since, in general, the definition of a phenomenon which is one is:

a phenomenon which is not diverse (*so so ba ma yin pa'i chos*),

the definition of one-with-functioning-thing must be posited as above. These scholars reason that the case of one-with-functioning-thing is parallel to the case of the definiendum of that which is able to perform a function. Since everyone agrees that the definiendum of that which is able to perform a function is itself a definiendum, then one-with-functioning-thing must be admitted as a definiendum as well.

Other scholars deny the assertion of one-with-functioning-thing as a definiendum by citing a passage in the Ra-dö *Collected Topics* which says:

> It follows with respect to the subject, pillar, that one-with-it is neither a triply qualified imputed existent nor a triply qualified substantial existent because of being selfless.[1]

One-with-pillar is neither a definiendum nor a definition, and, moreover, for whatever is selfless one-with-it is neither a definiendum nor a definition. This passage indicates that from among objects of knowledge there are phenomena which are neither definitions nor definienda and one-with-pillar, one-with-functioning-thing, and so forth are such phenomena.

Also, some scholars say that functioning-thing-which-is-one-with-functioning-thing (*dngos po dang gcig tu gyur pa'i dngos po*) is a definiendum because it is defined as:

> that which is able to perform a function which is one with functioning thing (*dngos po dang gcig tu gyur pa'i don byed nus pa*).

Since a thing is defined as that which is able to perform a function, they say that this must be the definition of functioning-thing-which-is-one-with-functioning-thing.

Most others deny this assertion. They reason that since that which is able to perform a function is not one with functioning thing, the expression "that which is able to perform a function which is one with functioning thing" does not refer to any phenomenon, and as a non-existent, it is neither a definition nor a definiendum. This view is based on a very strict interpretation of the expression, taking "that which is able to perform a function" to mean just that and thereby

---

[1] Jam-ȳang-chok-hla-ö-ser, Ra-dö *Collected Topics*, 14a.3-4.

not referring to each and every thing which is able to perform a function. By this account, since that which is able to perform a function is not itself one with functioning thing, "that which is able to perform a function which is one with functioning thing" does not express any phenomenon.

The main way of ascertaining the meaning of the four phenomena coextensive with the isolate of functioning thing is by determining their comparison with other phenomena. To repeat, these four coextensives are:

1 one-with-functioning-thing
2 functioning-thing-which-is-one-with-functioning-thing
3 the definiendum of that which is able to perform a function
4 the triply qualified imputed existent of that which is able to perform a function.

Individually, each of these four is mutually inclusive with each of the others and with the isolate of functioning thing, but as a group they are mutually exclusive with the isolate of functioning thing (see pp. 426-428). As a group, there are four possibilities between the four coextensives of the isolate of functioning thing and functioning thing:

1 The only thing which is both is functioning-thing-which-is-one-with-functioning-thing. It is one of the four coextensives and it is also a functioning thing.
2 Something which is one of the coextensives but is not a functioning thing is one-with-functioning-thing.
3 Something which is a functioning thing but is not one of the four coextensives is functioning thing itself. Functioning thing is a functioning thing, but it is not coextensive or mutually inclusive with itself because it is not different from itself.
4 Something which is neither is uncomposed space.

One can see that as a consequence of this last comparison, there are four possibilities between the four coextensives and permanent phenomenon:

1   Either one-with-functioning-thing, the definiendum of that which is able to perform a function, or the triply qualified imputed existent of that which is able to perform a function is both a permanent phenomenon and one of the four coextensives.
2   Only functioning-thing-which-is-one-with-functioning-thing is one of the four coextensives but not a permanent phenomenon.
3   Something which is a permanent phenomenon but not one of the coextensives is uncomposed space or object of knowledge.
4   Something which is neither is functioning thing or a pot.

Since at least one but not all of the four coextensives is a definition, there are four possibilities between the four coextensives and definition:

1   The only thing which is both is the triply qualified imputed existent of what which is able to perform a function. This is one of the four coextensives, and it is a definition because of being the definition of the definiendum of that which is able to perform a function.
2   Either one-with-functioning-thing, functioning-thing-which-is-one-with-functioning-thing, or the definiendum of what which is able to perform a function is one of the coextensives but not a definition.
3   Something which is a definition but is not one of these four coextensives is that which is able to perform a function.
4   Something which is neither is functioning thing or object of knowledge.

Similarly, since at least one but not all of the four coextensives is a definiendum, there are four possibilities between these four and definiendum:

1   The only one which all agree is both one of these coextensives and a definiendum is the definiendum of that which is able to perform a function, which is the

definiendum of the triply qualified imputed existent of that which is able to perform a function.

2 The clearest example of one of these four coextensives which is not a definiendum is the triply qualified imputed existent of what which is able to perform a function, which is a definition.

3 Something which is a definiendum but not one of these four coextensives is functioning thing or impermanent phenomenon.

4 Something which is neither is that which is able to perform a function or that which is suitable as an object of an awareness.

It should be understood that the phenomena coextensive with the isolate of a permanent phenomenon do not compare to functioning thing and permanent phenomenon as do the phenomena coextensive with the isolate of an impermanent phenomenon. For instance, the four phenomena coextensive with the isolate of permanent phenomenon (*rtag pa'i ldog pa dang yin khyab mnyam bzhi*) are:

1 one-with-permanent-phenomenon (*rtag pa dang gcig*)
2 permanent-phenomenon-which-is-one-with-permanent-phenomenon (*rtag pa dang gcig tu gyur pa'i rtag pa*)
3 the definiendum of that which is a common locus of a phenomenon and the non-momentary (*chos dang skad cig ma ma yin pa'i gzhi mthun gyi mtshon bya*)
4 the triply qualified imputed existent of that which is a common locus of a phenomenon and the non-momentary (*chos dang skad cig ma ma yin pa'i gzhi thun gyi btags yod chos gsum tshang ba*).

Since even permanent-phenomenon-which-is-one-with-permanent-phenomenon is itself a permanent phenomenon, these coextensives are mutually exclusive with functioning thing, for there is no common locus of something which is one of these four and also is a functioning thing. Subsequently, since all of these are permanent phenomena, there are three possibilities between these coextensives and permanent phenomenon. Otherwise, the phenomena coextensive with the isolate of a permanent phenomenon compare similarly to definition and definiendum as do the phenomena coextensive with the isolate of an impermanent phenomenon.

As has been seen, there is a difference between the way the four phenomena coextensive with the isolate of functioning thing, taken as a group, compare with some other phenomena and the way that each of these individually, such as one-with-functioning-thing, compare with those same phenomena. For instance, whereas the four coextensives are mutually exclusive with the isolate of functioning thing, one-with-functioning-thing and the isolate of functioning thing are mutually inclusive because they are different phenomena and whatever is the one is necessarily the other. Also, there are three possibilities between one-with-functioning-thing and functioning thing:

1   The only thing which may be posited as both is functioning thing itself, for it alone is both a functioning thing and one with functioning thing.
2   Since only functioning thing itself is one with functioning thing and it is a functioning thing too, whatever is one with functioning thing is necessarily a functioning thing. However, whatever is a functioning thing is not necessarily one with functioning thing because, for instance, a consciousness is a functioning thing but not one with functioning thing.
3   Something which is neither is uncomposed space.

Since whatever is one with functioning thing is necessarily a functioning thing, one-with-functioning-thing (or any of the other phenomena coextensive with the isolate of functioning thing) is mutually exclusive with permanent phenomenon, for there is nothing which is both. Also, since functioning thing itself is a definiendum, there are three possibilities between one-with-functioning-thing and definiendum:

1   The only thing which is both is functioning thing.
2   Since only functioning thing is one with functioning thing and it is also a definiendum, whatever is one with

functioning thing is necessarily a definiendum. However, whatever is a definiendum is not necessarily one with functioning thing, as in the case of sound.

3   Something which is neither is that which is able to perform a function.

Since whatever is one with functioning thing is necessarily a definiendum, one can see easily that one-with-functioning-thing is mutually exclusive with definition.

The differences between one-with-functioning-thing and these phenomena carry over to the comparison of the isolate of functioning thing or any of its other coextensives to these same phenomena. For instance, the isolate of functioning thing has three possibilities with functioning thing and with definiendum, and, as in the case of one-with-functioning-thing, the isolate of functioning thing is mutually exclusive with permanent phenomenon and definition.

The four phenomena coextensive with the isolate of something may be rendered for any definition or definiendum. The phenomena coextensive with the isolate of functioning thing exemplify the coextensives of the isolate of any definiendum. In order to illustrate the phenomena coextensive with the isolate of a definition, one may use that which is able to perform a function—the definition of functioning thing. Thus, the four phenomena coextensive with the isolate of that which is able to perform a function are:

1   one-with-that-which-is-able-to-perform-a-function (*don byed nus pa dang gcig*)
2   that-which-is-able-to-perform-a-function-which-is-one-with-that-which-is-able-to-perform-a-function (*don byed nus pa dang gcig tu gyur pa'i don byed nus pa*)
3   the definition of functioning thing (*dngos po'i mtshan nyid*)
4   the triply qualified substantial existent of functioning thing (*dngos po'i rdzas yod chos gsum tshang ba*).

These phenomena compare with the isolate of that which is able to perform a function in just the same way that the phenomena coextensive with the isolate of functioning thing compare with the isolate of functioning thing.

Using the phenomena coextensive with the isolate of functioning thing as the paradigm for the coextensives of a definiendum's isolate and using the phenomena coextensive with the isolate of that which is able to perform a function as the paradigm for the coextensives of a definition's isolate, Table VIII shows the differences and similarities between these two sets:

Table VIII: The Four Phenomena Coextensive With the Isolate of Functioning Thing and The Four Phenomena Coextensive With the Isolate of That Which Is Able to Perform a Function

Four phenomena coextensive with the isolate of functioning thing:	*Four phenomena coextensive with the isolate of that which is able to perform a function:*
1 one-with-functioning-thing	1 one-with-that-which-is-able-to-perform-a-function
2 functioning-thing-which-is-one-with-functioning-thing	2 that-which-is-able-to-perform-a-function-which-is-one-with-that-which-is-able-to-perform-a-function
3 the definiendum of that which is able to perform a function	3 the definition of functioning thing
4 the triply qualified imputed existent of that which is able to perform a function	4 the triply qualified substantial existent of functioning thing

Using the coextensives listed in Table VIII as patterns one can calculate the coextensives of any definiendum's isolate and any definition's isolate. The first two coextensives are just the same for either a definition or a definiendum. The first is always formulated as "one-with-that-definition" or "one-with-that-definiendum". The second is always "that-definition-which-is-one-with-that-definition" or "that-definiendum-which-is-one-with-that-definiendum".

The latter two coextensives are formulated somewhat differently for definitions and definienda. In the case of a definiendum such as functioning thing, the formula for the third coextensive is "the definiendum of that definiendum's definition", this being illustrated by "the definiendum of that which is able to perform a function". In the case of a definition such as that which is able to perform a function, the third coextensive is formulated, "the definition of that definition's definiendum", exemplified by "the definition of functioning thing". For a definiendum the fourth coextensive is "the triply qualified imputed existent of that definiendum's definition", illustrated by "the triply qualified imputed existent of that which is able to perform a function". For a definition the fourth is "the triply qualified substantial existent of that definition's definiendum", the example of which is "the triply qualified substantial existent of functioning thing". Quite simply, in the case of a definition it is necessary to supply the appropriate definiendum and in the case of a definiendum one must supply the appropriate definition.

These rules are generally said to apply similarly to all definitions and definienda, permanent and impermanent alike. However, the Shar-dzay *Collected Topics* says:

> It is not correct to say that for any definition or definiendum there are four phenomena coextensive with its isolate corresponding to the above types because there are not four coextensive with definition's isolate; because there is no definition-which-is-

one-with-definition; because whatever is one with definition is necessarily not a definition.[1]

This view is predicated on a loose interpretation of the
expression "definition-which-is-one-with-definition", for
here the author is taking it to refer to some particular definition and not to the singular generality—definition itself.
Since definition, the only thing which is one with definition,
is not a definition but a definiendum, there is nothing which
is one with definition and also is a definition. If this author's
interpretation is correct, then any definition or definiendum
which is not an exemplifier of itself will fail to have four
phenomena coextensive with its isolate. However, his interpretation of what is in English the adjectival clause "which-
is-one-with-definition" is at odds with the interpretation
given by other scholars (see pp. 430-431). By their interpretation, since only definition itself is one with definition, the
expression "definition-which-is-one-with-definition" must
refer to definition as such and not to any particular
definition.

Although one can determine four phenomena coextensive
with the isolate of any definition or definiendum, these four
cannot be postulated for any phenomenon which is neither a
definition nor a definiendum. For instance, since the two—a
pillar and a pot—are neither a definition nor a definiendum,
only the first two coextensives can be postulated and the
latter two do not exist. Thus, the phenomena coextensive
with the isolate of the two—a pillar and a pot—are just the
two:

1 one-with-the-two—a pillar and a pot (*ka bum gnyis dang
   gcig*)
2 the-two—a pillar and a pot—which-are-one-with-the-
   two—a pillar and a pot (*ka bum gnyis dang gcig tu gyur
   pa'i ka bum gnyis*).

---

[1] Dzemay Rinbochay (*dze smad rin po che*), Shar-dzay *Collected Topics* (*shar
rtse bsdus grva*), (Mundgod, India: Drepung Loseling Printing Press, n.d.),
pp. 21-22.

The rules for rendering the four coextensives remain consistent for any definition or definiendum, but positing these four in relation to a complex definition or definiendum is somewhat more challenging. For instance, among the four phenomena coextensive with the isolate of functioning thing, the third is the definiendum of that which is able to perform a function, which refers to functioning thing and is itself a definiendum. Since it is a definiendum, one can posit four phenomena which are coextensive with the isolate of the definiendum of that which is able to perform of a function (*don byed nus pa'i mtshon bya'i ldog pa dang yin khyab mnyam bzhi*):

1 one-with-the-definiendum-of-that-which-is-able-to-perform-a-function (*don byed nus pa'i mtshon bya dang gcig*)
2 the-definiendum-of-that-which-is-able-to-perform-a-function-which-is-one-with-the-definiendum-of-that-which-is-able-to-perform-a-function (*don byed nus pa'i mtshon bya dang gcig tu gyur pa'i don byed nus pa'i mtshon bya*)
3 the definiendum of the triply qualified imputed existent of that which is able to perform a function (*don byed nus pa'i btags yod chos gsum tshang ba'i mtshon bya*)
4 the triply qualified imputed existent of the triply qualified imputed existent of that which is able to perform a function (*don byed nus pa'i btags yod chos gsum tshang ba'i btags yod chos gsum tshang ba*).

Also, among the four phenomena coextensive with the isolate of functioning thing, the fourth is the triply qualified imputed existent of that which is able to perform a function, which is a definition. Thus, one can calculate the four phenomena coextensive with the isolate of the triply qualified imputed existent of that which is able to perform a function (*don byed nus pa'i btags yod chos gsum tshang ba'i ldog pa dang yin khyab mnyam bzhi*):

1 one-with-the-triply-qualified-imputed-existent-of-that-which-is-able-to-perform-a-function (*don byed nus pa'i btags yod chos gsum tshang ba dang gcig*)

2 the-triply-qualified-imputed-existent-of-that-which-is-able-to-perform-a-function-which-is-one-with-the-triply-qualified-imputed-existent-of-that-which-is-able-to-perform-a-function (*don byed nus pa'i btags yod chos gsum tshang ba dang gcig tu gyur pa'i don byed nus pa'i btags yod chos gsum tshang ba*)

3 the definition of the definiendum of that which is able to perform a function (*don byed nus pa'i mtshon bya'i mtshan nyid*)

4 the triply qualified substantial existent of the definiendum of that which is able to perform a function (*don byed nus pa'i mtshon bya'i rdzas yod chos gsum tshang ba*).

Since in both of these sets of four coextensives one phenomenon is a definition and one is a definiendum, it is possible to formulate in turn four phenomena coextensive with the isolate of any of these. In this way, the process extends endlessly. Still, one must be careful not to postulate coextensives for something which, although it appears to be a definition or a definiendum, is a non-existent. For instance, since no definitions are themselves defined, there is nothing which is the triply qualified *substantial* existent of that which is able to perform a function (*don byed nus pa'i rdzas yod chos gsum tshang ba*) and there are no phenomena coextensive with it.

REFUTATION OF MISTAKEN VIEWS CONCERNING ISOLATES (9A.2)

In the Tutor's *Collected Topics*, the first four debates in "Identifying Isolates" focus on the way that the four phenomena coextensive with the isolate of a particular definition or definiendum compare to definition and definiendum in general. The first two debates, taking the phenomena coextensive with the isolate of functioning thing as a principal of debate, are drawn almost verbatim from the Ra-dö *Collected Topics*.[1] In that text, all of the debates in the section identifying isolates focus on the comparison of the coextensives of various definitions and definienda to definition and definiendum in general. However, that text contains no explanation of the four types of isolates.

In the Tutor's *Collected Topics*, the later debates in this third chapter present the four types of isolates, explain that the isolate of functioning thing and its coextensives are not each other and are not themselves, and focus on the precise meaning of isolates. Seven of these debates, out of a total of fifteen in the chapter, are drawn, again almost verbatim, from the Go-mang *Collected Topics*.[2] This sort of free borrowing from another source is not unusual in the Buddhist philosophical tradition and is not regarded as a violation of the original author's rights. In the Go-mang *Collected Topics*, "Identifying Isolates" consists of debates focusing on only the different types of isolates, the nature of coextensives, and the meaning of isolates. It does not present the four coextensives as does the Ra-dö *Collected Topics* but only refers to some of them in debates.

Thus, "Identifying Isolates" in the Tutor's *Collected Topics*, while borrowing freely from other sources, brings together the two main branches of the topic of isolates, the nature and types of isolates and the phenomena coextensive with the isolate of a definition or a definiendum. By combining both of the main branches in a single source, the Tutor Jam-ba-gya-tso provides his readers with easier access to the topic of isolates.

Debate C.1, First Mistaken View (9a.2)

In debate C.1 the hypothetical Defender accepts that whatever is coextensive with the isolate of functioning thing is necessarily a definition. The group of phenomena coexten-

---

[1] Jam-ȳang-chok-hla-ö-ser, Ra-dö *Collected Topics*, 7b.4-8b.1.
[2] Ngak-w̄ang-dra-śhi, Go-mang *Collected Topics*, pp. 48-56.

sive with the isolate of functioning thing, like all sets of phenomena coextensive with the isolate of a definition or a
definiendum, has four possibilities with definition. Thus,
one cannot assert any statement of pervasion between the
phenomena coextensive with the isolate of functioning thing
and definition.

> If someone [a hypothetical Defender] says,
> "Whatever is coextensive with the isolate of func-
> tioning thing is necessarily a definition," [the Sūtra
> School Challenger responds to him,] "It [absurdly]
> follows that the subject, the definiendum of that
> which is able to perform a function, is [a definition]
> because of [being coextensive with the isolate of
> functioning thing]. You asserted the pervasion."
>
> If he says that the reason is not established, [the
> Sūtra School Challenger responds,] "It follows that
> the subject [the definiendum of that which is able to
> perform a function] is [coextensive with the isolate
> of functioning thing] because (1) it is different from
> the isolate of functioning thing, (2) whatever is it is
> necessarily the isolate of functioning thing, and (3)
> whatever is the isolate of functioning thing is
> necessarily it."

Notice that beginning in this chapter the implied form of the
Defender's answers will usually not be provided, as the
meaning of his answers and the format is well known by
now. Also, since the implied meaning of the Challenger's
responses will continue to be provided, one can easily know
the meaning of the Defender's answers by the way in which
the Challenger responds.

In order for something to be coextensive with the isolate
of functioning thing it must have all three of the qualities
specified in the reason. Coextensives or mutually inclusive
phenomena must be different in name only within being
mutually pervasive.

> If he says that the first part of the reason is not
> established, [the Sūtra School Challenger responds,]

"It follows that the subject [the definiendum of that which is able to perform a function] is [different from the isolate of functioning thing] because of (1) being an existent and (2) not being one with the isolate of functioning thing."

If he says that the second part of the reason is not established, [the Sūtra School Challenger responds,] "It follows that whatever is the definiendum of that which is able to perform a function is necessarily the isolate of functioning thing because whatever is that [the definiendum of that which is able to perform a function] is necessarily one with functioning thing."

The Sūtra School Challenger is justifying one pervasion with another. Whatever is a *p* is necessarily a *q* because whatever is a *p* is necessarily an *r*. Since *p* and *r* are well known as mutually inclusive, the first pervasion is established by the second.

If he says that the third part of the reason is not established, [the Sūtra School Challenger responds,] "It follows that whatever is the isolate of functioning thing is necessarily the definiendum of that which is able to perform a function because functioning thing is the definiendum of that which is able to perform a function."

The antecedent "whatever is the isolate of functioning thing" refers only to functioning thing, and since functioning thing is the definiendum of that which is able to perform a function, whatever is the isolate of functioning thing is necessarily the definiendum of that which is able to perform a function.

This consequence is the last in the line of reasoning developing out of the hypothetical Defender's denying the establishment of the reason of the basic consequence. The Sūtra School Challenger now leads the Defender back through the three parts of the reason that he had denied and then again combines the three parts into one reason. When the

Defender accepts all of these reasons, the Challenger again poses the basic consequence:

> If he accepts the basic consequence, [the Sūtra School Challenger responds,] "It follows that the subject [the definiendum of that which is able to perform a function] is not a definition because of being a definiendum."

From among the four phenomena coextensive with the isolate of functioning thing, everyone agrees that the definiendum of that which is able to perform a function is a definiendum. The Sūtra School Challenger chose this subject in order to defeat the hypothetical Defender's acceptance of the original pervasion, that whatever is coextensive with the isolate of functioning thing is necessarily a definition. He also could have chosen as his subject either one-with-functioning-thing or functioning-thing-which-is-one-with-functioning-thing. However, since whether or not these two are definienda is disputed, he chose the one coextensive which is easiest to prove as not being a definition.

> If he says that the reason is not established, [the Sūtra School Challenger responds,] "It follows that the subject [the definiendum of that which is able to perform a function] is a definiendum because of being the definiendum of the triply qualified imputed existent of that which is able to perform a function."

Definiendum is a definiendum, for it is the definiendum of the triply qualified imputed existent. Consequently, the definiendum of that which is able to perform a function is the definiendum of the triply qualified imputed existent of that which is able to perform a function.

> If he says that the reason is not established, [the Sūtra School Challenger responds,] "It follows with respect to the subject, that which is able to perform a function, that its definiendum is the definiendum of

its triply qualified imputed existent because it is a definition."

The pervasion is accurate as it is stated, for it applies only to definitions. Since only definitions have definienda, the reference to "its definiendum" in the predicate of the consequence must refer to the definiendum of some particular definition. There is nothing which is the definiendum of a definiendum, and there is nothing which is the definiendum of a phenomenon which is neither a definition nor a definiendum such as objects of knowledge of which being them is not possible. Still, for any definition, the definiendum of that definition is the definiendum of the triply qualified imputed existent of that definition. It is necessary to exclude all but definitions from the reason.

This consequence is the last in debate C.1. The two principals of this debate, the coextensives of the isolate of functioning thing and definition, have four possibilities:

1   From among the four coextensives, the only one which is both is the triply qualified imputed existent of that which is able to perform a function.
2   Something which is a definition but not coextensive with the isolate of functioning thing is that which is able to perform a function. Although coextensive with functioning thing, that which is able to perform a function is not coextensive with the isolate of functioning thing.
3   Something which is coextensive with the isolate of functioning thing but not a definition is the definiendum of that which is able to perform a function.
4   Something which is neither is functioning thing or object of knowledge.

Debate C.2, Second Mistaken View (9b.1)

In this debate the hypothetical Defender takes a stand opposite to that adopted in debate C.1 as he now accepts that whatever is coextensive with the isolate of functioning thing is necessarily a definiendum. Of course, as in its comparison with definition, there are four possibilities between the group of phenomena coextensive with the isolate of functioning thing and definiendum; thus, one cannot reckon a correct pervasion between them.

> If someone [a hypothetical Defender] says, "Whatever is coextensive with the isolate of functioning thing is necessarily a definiendum," [the Sūtra School Challenger responds to him,] "It [absurdly] follows that the subject, the triply qualified imputed existent of that which is able to perform a function, is [a definiendum] because of [being coextensive with the isolate of functioning thing]."
>
> If he says that the reason is not established, [the Sūtra School Challenger responds,] "It follows that the subject [the triply qualified imputed existent of that which is able to perform a function] is coextensive with the isolate of functioning thing because (1) it is different from the isolate of functioning thing, (2) whatever is it is necessarily the isolate of functioning thing, and (3) whatever is the isolate of functioning thing is necessarily it."
>
> If he says that the first part of the reason is not established, apply the reasoning from the above proof.

The reason here is the same as in the corresponding consequence in debate C.1. The subject is different from the isolate of functioning thing because of (1) being an existent and (2) not being one with the isolate of functioning thing.

> If he says that the second part of the reason is not established, [the Sūtra School Challenger responds,] "It follows with respect to the subject, that which is able to perform a function, that whatever is its triply qualified imputed existent is necessarily the isolate of functioning thing because functioning thing is its triply qualified imputed existent."

The Sūtra School Challenger has formulated the consequence in this way in order to take some of the wordiness out of the predicate and reason. Since functioning thing is the only thing which is the triply qualified imputed existent of that which is able to perform a function, whatever is that is necessarily the isolate of functioning thing.

> If he says that the third part of the reason is not established, [the Sūtra School Challenger responds,] "It follows with respect to the subject, functioning thing, that whatever is its isolate is necessarily the triply qualified imputed existent of that which is able to perform a function because whatever is its isolate is necessarily the definiendum of that which is able to perform a function."

Again the Sūtra School Challenger is justifying one pervasion with another. In both cases the antecedents are the same and the two consequences are mutually inclusive; thus, the pervasion stated in the predicate of the consequence is established by the pervasion stated in the reason.

> If he accepts the basic consequence, [the Sūtra School Challenger responds,] "It follows that the subject, the triply qualified imputed existent of that which is able to perform a function, is not a definiendum because of being a definition."
>
> If he says that the reason is not established, [the Sūtra School Challenger responds,] "It follows that the subject [the triply qualified imputed existent of that which is able to perform a function] is [a definition] because of being the definition of the definiendum of that which is able to perform a function."
>
> If he says that the reason is not established, [the Sūtra School Challenger responds,] "It follows with respect to the subject, that which is able to perform a function, that its triply qualified imputed existent is

the definition of its definiendum because it is a definition."

The line of reasoning presented here parallels exactly the corresponding line of reasoning presented in debate C.1. Any definition has a definiendum, that is to say, it has a triply qualified imputed existent. Thus, the triply qualified imputed existent of any particular definition is the definition of the definiendum of any particular definition. This is true for all definitions.

There are four possibilities between the two principals of debate C.2, the coextensives of the isolate of functioning thing and definiendum:

1   Something which is both is the definiendum of that which is able to perform a function.
2   Something which is a definiendum but not coextensive with the isolate of functioning thing is functioning thing which, rather than being mutually inclusive with the isolate of functioning thing, has three possibilities with the isolate of functioning thing.
3   The triply qualified imputed existent of that which is able to perform a function is coextensive with the isolate of functioning thing but is not a definiendum.
4   Something which is neither is that which is able to perform a function, which is not coextensive with the isolate of functioning thing but has three possibilities with it.

Debate C.3, Third Mistaken View (9b.6)

In debates C.3 and C.4 the author uses "that which is able to perform a function" to present the coextensives of the isolates of a definition. Again, the debates focus on the difference between these coextensives and definition and definiendum in general. These debates do not appear in either the Ra-dö *Collected Topics* or the Go-mang *Collected Topics* and may be the creation of the Tutor. In debate C.3 the hypothetical Defender accepts that whatever is coextensive with the isolate of that which is able to perform a function is necessarily a definition. Of course, this is not accurate because the phenomena coextensive with the isolate of any definiendum or any definition include only one definition and at least one which is a definiendum.

> If someone [a hypothetical Defender] says, "Whatever is coextensive with the isolate of that which is able to perform a function is necessarily a definition," [the Sūtra School Challenger responds to him,] "It [absurdly] follows that the subject, the definition of functioning thing, is [a definition] because of [being coextensive with the isolate of that which is able to perform a function]."
>
> If he says that the reason is not established, [the Sūtra School Challenger responds,] "It follows that the subject [the definition of functioning thing] is [coextensive with the isolate of that which is able to perform a function] because (1) it is different from the isolate of that which is able to perform a function, (2) whatever is it is necessarily the isolate of that which is able to perform a function, and (3) whatever is the isolate of that which is able to perform a function is necessarily it."
>
> The first part of the reason is easy. If he says that the second part of the reason is not established, [the Sūtra School Challenger responds,] "It follows with respect to the subject, functioning thing, that whatever is its definition is necessarily the isolate of that which is able to perform a function because it is the definiendum of that which is able to perform a function."

The reason is clear. Since functioning thing is the definiendum of that which is able to perform a function, whatever is the definition of functioning thing (that is, that which is able to perform a function) is necessarily the isolate of that which is able to perform a function.

> If he says that the third part of the reason is not established, [the Sūtra School Challenger responds,]

"It follows with respect to the subject, that which is able to perform a function, that whatever is its isolate is necessarily the definition of functioning thing because it is the definition of functioning thing."

Since that which is able to perform a function is the definition of functioning thing, whatever is the isolate of that which is able to perform a function is necessarily the definition of functioning thing.

If he accepts the basic consequence, [the Sūtra School Challenger responds,] "It follows that the subject, the definition of functioning thing, is not a definition because of being a definiendum."

If he says that the reason is not established, [the Sūtra School Challenger responds,] "It follows that the subject [the definition of functioning thing] is [a definiendum] because of being the definiendum of the triply qualified substantial existent of functioning thing."

The triply qualified substantial existent of functioning thing is another of the four phenomena coextensive with the isolate of that which is able to perform a function. It defines the definition of functioning thing.

If he says that the reason is not established, [the Sūtra School Challenger responds,] "It follows with respect to the subject, functioning thing, that its definition is the definiendum of its triply qualified substantial existent because it is a triply qualified imputed existent."

Functioning thing is a triply qualified imputed existent, that is, a definiendum. As a definiendum it has a definition, and the definition of functioning thing is itself a definiendum.

If he says that the reason is not established, [the Sūtra School Challenger responds,] "It follows that the subject [functioning thing] is [a triply qualified imputed existent] because of being a definiendum."

"[It follows that] there is pervasion [i.e., whatever is a definiendum is necessarily a triply qualified imputed existent] because that which is a triply qualified imputed existent is the definition of a definiendum and that which is a triply qualified substantial existent is the definition of a definition."

By now it is well known that definition is not itself a definition, and, thus, it is not a triply qualified substantial existent. However, that which is a triply qualified *substantial* existent is a definition. Conversely, that which is a triply qualified *imputed* existent is not itself, it is not a definiendum. Still, definiendum is itself a definiendum.

The two principals of debate C.3, definition and the coextensives of the isolate of that which is able to perform a function, have four possibilities:

1 The only one among the four which is both is the triply qualified substantial existent of functioning thing.
2 Something which is a definition but not coextensive with the isolate of that which is able to perform a function is that which is able to perform a function or any definition other than the triply qualified substantial existent of functioning thing.
3 Something which is coextensive with the isolate of that which is able to perform a function but is not a definition is the definition of functioning thing.
4 Something which is neither is functioning thing or sound.

Functioning thing is not coextensive with the isolate of that which is able to perform a function but has three possibilities with it:

1 The only thing which is both a functioning thing and the isolate of that which is able to perform a function is that which is able to perform a function.
2 Whatever is the isolate of that which is able to perform a function is necessarily a functioning thing, for only that which is able to perform a function is its isolate.

However, whatever is a functioning thing is not necessarily the isolate of that which is able to perform a function, as in the case of a pot.

3   Something which is neither is one-with-functioning-thing.

Debate C.4, Fourth Mistaken View (10a.5)

In this debate, the hypothetical Defender reverses his position tendered in debate C.3, now asserting that whatever is coextensive with the isolate of that which is able to perform a function is necessarily a definiendum. Again, since there are four possibilities between these two principals, one cannot determine a pervasion between them in either direction.

> If someone [a hypothetical Defender] says, "Whatever is coextensive with the isolate of that which is able to perform a function is necessarily a definiendum," [the Sūtra School Challenger responds to him,] "It [absurdly] follows that the subject, the triply qualified substantial existent of functioning thing, is [a definiendum] because of [being coextensive with the isolate of that which is able to perform a function]."
>
> If he says that the reason is not established, [the Sūtra School Challenger responds,] "It follows that the subject [the triply qualified substantial existent of functioning thing] is [coextensive with the isolate of that which is able to perform a function] because (1) it is different from the isolate of that which is able to perform a function, (2) whatever is it is necessarily the isolate of that which is able to perform a function, and (3) whatever is the isolate of that which is able to perform a function is necessarily it."

Also acceptable as a reason proving something as coextensive with the isolate of some definition or definiendum is that it is mutually inclusive with it.

The first part of the reason is easy. If he says that the second part of the reason is not established, [the Sūtra School Challenger responds,] "It follows with respect to the subject, functioning thing, that whatever is its triply qualified substantial existent is necessarily the isolate of that which is able to perform a function because it is the triply qualified imputed existent of that which is able to perform a function."

Since functioning thing is the definiendum of that which is able to perform a function, whatever is its definition or triply qualified substantial existent (that is, that which is able to perform a function) is necessarily the isolate of that which is able to perform a function.

If he says that the third part of the reason is not established, [the Sūtra School Challenger responds,] "It follows with respect to the subject, that which is able to perform a function, that whatever is its isolate is necessarily the triply qualified substantial existent of functioning thing because it is the triply qualified substantial existent of functioning thing."

If he accepts the basic consequence, [the Sūtra School Challenger responds,] "It follows that the subject [the triply qualified substantial existent of functioning thing] is not a definiendum because of being a definition."

If he says that the reason is not established, [the Sūtra School Challenger responds,] "It follows that the subject [the triply qualified substantial existent of functioning thing] is [a definition] because of being the definition of the definition of functioning thing."

If he says that the reason is not established, [the Sūtra School Challenger responds,] "It follows with respect to the subject, functioning thing, that its triply qualified substantial existent is the definition of the definition of it because it is a triply qualified imputed existent."

Functioning thing is a definiendum and, as such, it has a definition or a triply qualified substantial existent. The triply qualified substantial existent of functioning thing is the definition of its own definiendum, the definition of functioning thing.

There are four possibilities between the two principals of debate C.4, definiendum and the phenomena coextensive with the isolate of that which is able to perform a function:

1 Something which is both is the definition of functioning thing which is proven as both in debate C.3.
2 Something which is a definiendum but not coextensive with the isolate of that which is able to perform a function is functioning thing, impermanent phenomenon, permanent phenomenon, object of knowledge, and so on.
3 From among the four, the only one which is coextensive with the isolate of that which is able to perform a function and is not a definiendum is the triply qualified substantial existent of functioning thing.
4 Something which is neither is that which is able to perform a function.

That which is able to perform a function is not coextensive with its own isolate because there are three possibilities between it and its isolate:

1 Something which is both is that which is able to perform a function which, as an impermanent phenomenon, is able to perform a function and, as an established base, is its own isolate.
2 Whatever is the isolate of that which is able to perform a function is necessarily able to perform a function. However, whatever is able to perform a function is not necessarily the isolate of that which is able to perform a function. For example, any of the phenomena mutually inclusive with that which is able to perform a function or any instance of it—a pillar, a pot, specifically characterized phenomenon, functioning thing, and so on—is able

to perform a function but is not the isolate of that which is able to perform a function.

3 Something which is neither able to perform a function nor the isolate of that which is able to perform a function is one-with-that-which-is-able-to-perform-a-function, the definition of functioning thing, the triply qualified substantial existent of that which is able to perform a function, any permanent phenomenon, or any non-existent. One-with-that-which-is-able-to-perform-a-function, for instance, is not able to perform a function because of being a permanent phenomenon. It is not the isolate of that which is able to perform a function because of not being one with that which is able to perform a function.

Debate C.5, Fifth Mistaken View (10b.3)

Debate C.5 is not found in either the Ra-dö *Collected Topics* or the Go-mang *Collected Topics*. Here the author compares the phenomena coextensive with the isolate of functioning thing to permanent phenomenon. This serves to point out that, from among the four phenomena coextensive with the isolate of any *impermanent* definition or definiendum, one of them is an impermanent phenomenon.

> If someone [a hypothetical Defender] says, "Whatever is coextensive with the isolate of functioning thing is necessarily a permanent phenomenon," [the Sūtra School Challenger responds to him,] "It [absurdly] follows that the subject, functioning-thing-which-is-one-with-functioning-thing, is [a permanent phenomenon] because of [being coextensive with the isolate of functioning thing]. You asserted the pervasion."
>
> If he says that the reason is not established, [the Sūtra School Challenger responds,] "It follows that the subject [functioning-thing-which-is-one-with-functioning-thing] is [coextensive with the isolate of functioning thing] because (1) it is different from the isolate of functioning thing, (2) whatever is it is nec-

essarily the isolate of functioning thing, and (3) whatever is the isolate of functioning thing is necessarily it."

The first and second parts of the reason are easy.

The second part of the reason, that whatever is the functioning thing which is one with functioning thing is necessarily the isolate of functioning thing, is proven by the sign that whatever is the functioning thing which is one with functioning thing is necessarily one with functioning thing. Also, whatever is the functioning thing which is one with functioning thing is necessarily the isolate of functioning thing because functioning thing is functioning thing which is one with functioning thing.

> If he says that the third part of the reason is not established, [the Sūtra School Challenger responds,] "It follows that whatever is the isolate of functioning thing is necessarily the functioning thing which is one with functioning thing because (1) whatever is the isolate of functioning thing is necessarily one with functioning thing and (2) whatever is one with functioning thing is necessarily a functioning thing."

Here the Sūtra School Challenger reasons that since functioning thing, and only functioning thing, is both the isolate of functioning thing and one with functioning thing, then just that same functioning thing, and only it, is necessarily the functioning thing which is one with functioning thing.

> If he accepts the basic consequence, [the Sūtra School Challenger responds,] "It follows that the subject [functioning-thing-which-is-one-with-functioning-thing] is not a permanent phenomenon because of being an impermanent phenomenon."
>
> If he says that the reason is not established, [the Sūtra School Challenger responds,] "It follows that the subject [functioning-thing-which-is-one-with-functioning-thing] is [an impermanent phe-

nomenon] because of being a composed phenomenon."

Since functioning thing, or any impermanent definition or definiendum, is indeed an impermanent phenomenon, functioning-thing-which-is-one-with-functioning-thing is an impermanent phenomenon. In terms of whether or not it is an impermanent phenomenon, functioning-thing-which-is-one-with-functioning-thing is no different from functioning thing itself; since functioning thing is a functioning thing, functioning-thing-which-is-one-with-functioning-thing is also a functioning thing.

The two principals of debate C.5, permanent phenomenon and the phenomena coextensive with the isolate of functioning thing, have four possibilities:

1 One-with-functioning-thing, the definiendum of that which is able to perform a function, or the triply qualified imputed existent of that which is able to perform a function are both permanent and coextensive with the isolate of functioning thing.

2 Something which is a permanent phenomenon but not coextensive with the isolate of functioning thing is object of knowledge (which has three possibilities with the isolate of functioning thing).

3 The only one of the four which is coextensive with the isolate of functioning thing but is not a permanent phenomenon is functioning-thing-which-is-one-with-functioning-thing.

4 Something which is neither is an eye sense power.

Debate C.6, Sixth Mistaken View (10b.6)

In this debate, which is also found in the Go-mang *Collected Topics*,[1] the author introduces and explains the topic of the illustration-isolate (*gzhi ldog*) of a particular phenomenon. Here the hypothetical Defender accepts that whatever is an

---

[1] *Ibid.*, pp. 48-49.

illustration-isolate of functioning thing is necessarily the isolate of functioning thing. This is not at all true. The only thing which is an illustration-isolate of functioning thing is an illustration (*mtshan gzhi*) of functioning thing, and the only thing which is the isolate of functioning thing is functioning thing itself, which, like any phenomenon, is not an illustration of itself.

> If someone [a hypothetical Defender] says, "Whatever is an illustration-isolate of functioning thing is necessarily the isolate of functioning thing," [the Sūtra School Challenger responds to him,] "It [absurdly] follows that the subject, a sound, is the isolate of functioning thing because of being an illustration-isolate of functioning thing. You asserted the pervasion."
>
> If he says that the reason is not established, [the Sūtra School Challenger responds,] "It follows that the subject, a sound, is an illustration-isolate of functioning thing because of being an illustration of functioning thing."

Whatever is an illustration of functioning thing is necessarily an illustration-isolate of functioning thing. A sound is an illustration of functioning thing because of being something which serves as a basis for illustrating functioning thing by way of being able to perform a function. Although someone might have ascertained a sound by valid cognition, that person would not necessarily have ascertained functioning thing in general by valid cognition. Therefore, a sound is an illustration-isolate of functioning thing.

> If he accepts the basic consequence, [the Sūtra School Challenger responds,] "It follows that the subject, a sound, is not the isolate of functioning thing because of being different from functioning thing."

In fact, the two principals of this debate, the isolate of functioning thing and illustration-isolate of functioning thing, are mutually exclusive phenomena. There is nothing which is a common locus of these two because (1) whatever is the isolate of functioning thing is necessarily one with functioning thing and (2) whatever is an illustration-isolate of functioning thing is necessarily different from functioning thing. As is the case with any phenomenon, functioning thing is not an illustration-isolate of itself. Because they are one and the same, having ascertained functioning thing by valid cognition, there is no possibility of not having ascertained functioning thing by valid cognition.

Debate C.7, Seventh Mistaken View (lla.2)

In this debate, also found in the Go-mang *Collected Topics*,[1] the author introduces the concept of a phenomenon's meaning-isolate (*don ldog*) and explains this as referring to that phenomenon's definition.

> If someone [a hypothetical Defender] says, "Whatever is the meaning-isolate of functioning thing is necessarily the isolate of functioning thing," [the Sūtra School Challenger responds to him,] "It [absurdly] follows that the subject, that which is able to perform a function, is the isolate of functioning thing because of being the meaning-isolate of functioning thing. You asserted the pervasion."
>
> If he says that the reason is not established, [the Sūtra School Challenger responds,] "It follows that the subject, that which is able to perform a function, is the meaning-isolate of functioning thing because of being the definition of functioning thing."

Whatever is the definition of functioning thing is necessarily the meaning-isolate of functioning thing. Thus, except for

---

[1] *Ibid.*, pp. 49-50.

that which is able to perform a function, there is nothing to posit as the meaning-isolate of functioning thing. That which is able to perform a function is the meaning of the name "functioning thing".

> If he accepts the basic consequence, [the Sūtra School Challenger responds,] "It follows that the subject, that which is able to perform a function, is not the isolate of functioning thing because of not being one with functioning thing."

The two principals of debate C.7, the isolate of functioning thing and the meaning-isolate of functioning thing, are mutually exclusive. There is no common locus of these two because whatever is the isolate of functioning thing is necessarily one with functioning thing and whatever is the meaning-isolate of functioning thing is necessarily different from functioning thing. Also, whatever is the isolate of functioning thing is necessarily a definiendum and whatever is the meaning-isolate of functioning thing is necessarily a definition.

Debate C.8, Eighth Mistaken View (lla.3)

Debate C.8 does not occur in either the Ra-dö *Collected Topics* or in the Go-mang *Collected Topics*. In this debate the Tutor Jam-ba-gya-tso explains the meaning of a general-isolate (*spyi ldog*) within the context of the types of isolates and the meaning of what it is to be an illustration of something.

> If someone [a hypothetical Defender] says, "Whatever is the general-isolate of functioning thing is necessarily an illustration-isolate of functioning thing" [the Sūtra School Challenger responds to him,] "It [absurdly] follows that the subject, functioning thing, is [an illustration-isolate of functioning thing] because of [being the general-isolate of functioning thing]."

Functioning thing itself is the general-isolate of functioning thing. General-isolate and self-isolate are mutually inclusive, and thus the expression "the isolate of functioning thing" refers to the general-isolate of functioning thing or the self-isolate of functioning thing. Hence, functioning thing, and only functioning thing, is the general-isolate of functioning thing.

> If he says that the reason is not established, [the Sūtra School Challenger responds,] "It follows that the subject [functioning thing] is [the general-isolate of functioning thing] because of being the self-isolate of functioning thing."
>
> "[It follows that] there is pervasion [i.e., whatever is the self-isolate of functioning thing is necessarily the general-isolate of functioning thing] because those two are mutually inclusive."
>
> If he accepts the basic consequence, [the Sūtra School Challenger responds,] "It follows that the subject [functioning thing] is not an illustration-isolate of functioning thing because of not being an illustration of functioning thing."
>
> If he says that the reason is not established, [the Sūtra School Challenger responds,] "It follows with respect to the subject, functioning thing, that it is not an illustration of itself because once [someone] has ascertained it with valid cognition, a non-ascertainment of functioning thing with valid cognition is not possible."

In this last consequence in debate C.8 the author explains the meaning of what it is to be an illustration of something. A phenomenon which illustrates another phenomenon must merely suggest that phenomenon and cannot be its equivalent. A proper illustrator of another phenomenon is such that correctly realizing that illustration cannot entail realizing the phenomenon illustrated.

The two principals of this debate are also mutually exclusive. There is nothing which is both an illustration-isolate of functioning thing and the general-isolate of functioning thing because (1) whatever is the general-isolate of functioning thing is necessarily one with functioning thing and (2) whatever is an illustration-isolate of functioning thing is necessarily different from functioning thing. Also, a common locus is not possible because (1) whatever is an illustration-isolate of functioning thing is necessarily an illustration of functioning thing and (2) whatever is the general-isolate of functioning thing is necessarily not an illustration of functioning thing.

Debate C.9, Ninth Mistaken View (11a.5)

The focus of debates C.9 through C.13, the last five debates in the refutation of mistaken views concerning isolates, is on identifying the precise meaning of isolates. Using pot's isolate as a basis for these five debates, the hypothetical Defender accepts five mistaken views of precisely what qualifies as being pot's isolate. All five of these debates are found in the Go-mang *Collected Topics*.[1]

In debate C.9 the hypothetical Defender accepts that pot-which-is-one-with-pot (*bum pa dang gcig tu gyur pa'i bum pa*) is pot's isolate. Using this error as a basis the debate is able to explain something about the relationship between a phenomenon's isolate and the phenomena coextensive with that phenomenon's isolate. That is, even though whatever is pot's isolate is necessarily the pot which is one with pot, and vice versa, the one is not the other.

It should be noted that it is not always necessary to begin a debate with a statement of pervasion. As in debate C.9, it is also acceptable to begin with a proposed thesis.

If someone [a hypothetical Defender] says, "Pot-which-is-one-with-pot is pot's isolate," [the Sūtra School Challenger responds to him,] "It follows that

[1] *Ibid.*, pp. 50-55.

the subject, pot-which-is-one-with-pot, is not pot's
isolate because of not being one with pot."

The Challenger does not respond with a contradictory consequence but simply denies what the Defender has asserted
and gives a reason for that denial. Pot-which-is-one-with-
pot is not one with pot because, although only pot can be
posited as either of them, the two names, "pot" and "pot-
which-is-one-with-pot", are different.

> If he says that the reason is not established, [the
> Sūtra School Challenger responds,] "It follows that
> the subject, pot-which-is-one-with-pot, is not one
> with pot because of being different from pot."
>
> If he says that there is no pervasion, [the Sūtra
> School Challenger responds,] "It follows with
> respect to the subject, pot, that whatever is different
> from it is necessarily not one with it because it is
> without a self of persons."

The Challenger is making clear the absolute separation of
what is one with something from what is different from that
same thing. For any "thing" that is selfless, be it existent or
non-existent, whatever is different from it is necessarily not
one with it.

Although the one and the different are divisions of established bases and whatever is either of them is necessarily an
established base, it is suitable to refer to what is different
from a non-existent. For instance, a pot is different from the
horn or a rabbit because of being a phenomenon which is
diverse from the horn of a rabbit. However, one cannot refer
to a non-existent as different from an existent because non-
existents are not phenomena which are diverse from an existent. Thus, an existent is different from a non-existent, but a
non-existent is not different from an existent.

Also, even though one can say that an existent is different
from a non-existent, one cannot say that an existent is one
with any non-existent or that any non-existent is one with
any "thing" that is selfless, even with itself. Thus, the pervasion is true only as it is stated: If something is without a self

of persons, then whatever is different from it is necessarily not one with it. Even though the pervasion is universalized for all existents and non-existents alike, the phrase "whatever is different from it" is limited in scope to existents only.

The pervasion would not be true if it were reversed. That is, one cannot say that if something is without a self of persons, then whatever is not one with it is necessarily different from it. This assertion is inaccurate because it leads to the absurdity that the horn of a rabbit would be different from a pot because of not being one with a pot.

> If at the above point[1] where he had said that there is no pervasion he says that the reason is not established, [the Sūtra School Challenger responds,] "It follows that pot-which-is-one-with-pot is different from pot because pot-which-is-one-with-pot is a pot which is different from pot."

Pot-which-is-one-with-pot is itself a pot, and like every other phenomenon mutually inclusive with pot and every instance of pot, since it is not pot's self-isolate, it is a pot which is different from pot.

The two principals of debate C.9, pot-which-is-one-with-pot and pot's isolate, are mutually inclusive. The point to be understood is that even though they are mutually inclusive, the one is not the other.

Debate C.10, Tenth Mistaken View (IIb.2)

In debate C.10 the hypothetical Defender now accepts that another of the phenomena coextensive with pot's isolate, one-with-pot (*bum pa dang gcig*), is pot's isolate. As before, even though the two phenomena are coextensive or mutually inclusive, the one is not the other. One can say that only pot is one with pot and also pot's isolate, but that does not mean that one-with-pot is pot's isolate.

---

[1] Here the text reads *'tshams*, but should read *mtshams*, "boundary".

> Also, if someone says, "One-with-pot is pot's iso-
> late," [the Sūtra School Challenger responds to him,]
> "It follows that the subject, one-with-pot, is not pot's
> isolate because of not being one with pot."

One-with-pot is not one with pot because the two, pot and
one-with-pot, are different phenomena.

> If he says that the reason is not established, [the
> Sūtra School Challenger responds,] "It follows that
> the subject, one-with-pot, is not one with pot
> because of being different from pot."
> If he says that the reason is not established, [the
> Sūtra School Challenger responds,] "It follows that
> the subject, one-with-pot, is different from pot
> because of being a permanent phenomenon."

Whatever is a permanent phenomenon is necessarily different from pot. Since pot itself is an impermanent phenomenon, whatever is one with it—that is, pot—is necessarily an impermanent phenomenon.

> If he says that the reason is not established, [the
> Sūtra School Challenger responds,] "It follows with
> respect to the subject, pot, that one-with-it is a per-
> manent phenomenon because it is an established
> base."

For any established base, be it permanent or impermanent,
one-with-it is necessarily a permanent phenomenon.

Debate C.11, Eleventh Mistaken View (IIb.4)

In this debate the hypothetical Defender accepts that pot's
isolate is pot's isolate. That is somewhat different from
debates C.9 and C.10 in which the author showed that the
phenomena coextensive with the isolate of something
cannot be said to be the isolate of that thing. Now he is
making the point that not even pot's isolate is pot's isolate, it
is not itself. Although the Sūtra School Challenger does not

continue to use this line of reasoning, one can prove that this is not pot's isolate because of not being one with pot. Pot's isolate is not one with pot because of being different from pot.

> If someone [a hypothetical Defender] says, "Pot's isolate is pot's isolate," [the Sūtra School Challenger responds to him,] "It follows that the subject, pot's isolate, is not pot's isolate because of not being a pot."

Whatever is not a pot is necessarily not pot's isolate. Pot is itself, it is a pot. Thus, what is not a pot is not pot's isolate. Even within what is a pot, it is only pot itself—in isolation from all of its instances and all the phenomena mutually inclusive with it—that is pot's isolate. This line of reasoning is also applicable to three of the four phenomena coextensive with pot's isolate. From among the coextensives, only pot-which-is-one-with-pot is a pot.

> If he says that the reason is not established, [the Sūtra School Challenger responds,] "It follows that the subject, pot's isolate, is not a pot because of being a permanent phenomenon."
> If he says that the reason is not established, [the Sūtra School Challenger responds,] "It follows with respect to the subject, pot, that it's isolate is a permanent phenomenon because it is an established base."

For any existent, its isolate is necessarily a permanent phenomenon. Also, the illustration-isolate of any phenomenon and the meaning-isolate of any phenomenon are permanent.

For debate C.11 one cannot reckon a difference between pot's isolate and pot's isolate because, although it is not itself, it is one with itself. In order for two phenomena to be mutually exclusive or mutually inclusive or for there to be three or four possibilities between them, those phenomena must be different. Pot's isolate is not different from itself.

Debate C.12, Twelfth Mistaken View (llb.5)

In debates C.12 and C.13 the text offers two possible interpretations of precisely what the meaning of pot's isolate must be. These are both mistaken ideas presented in the form of pervasions which are defeated by contradictory consequences. In debate C.12 the hypothetical Defender accepts that whatever is reversed from not being a pot (*bum pa ma yin pa las ldog pa*) is necessarily pot's isolate. This is not accurate because any pot, such as a gold pot, is reversed from not being a pot, and a gold pot, for instance, is not pot's isolate. "Reversed from" (*las ldog pa*) means a simple single reversal, that is, "opposite from" or "turned away from". Any pot is reversed from not being a pot because of not being something that is not a pot, since it is a pot.

> If someone [a hypothetical Defender] says, "Whatever is reversed from not being a pot is necessarily pot's isolate," [the Sūtra School Challenger responds to him,] "It [absurdly] follows that the subjects, the two—a gold pot and a copper pot, are pot's isolate because of being reversed from not being pots."

Although the Sūtra School Challenger posited pots of which being them is not possible as the counterexample, any instance of pot or any phenomenon mutually inclusive with pot would have been suitable. This particular counterexample quite strongly shows the error of the Defender's position.

> "It follows that [the two—a gold pot and a copper pot—are reversed from not being pots] because of being pots."

If it is the case that any instance of a pot is reversed from not being a pot, then "reversed from not being a pot" is not suitable as the meaning of pot's isolate. For, pot's isolate focuses on pot in isolation from all of its instances.

> If he accepts the basic consequence, [the Sūtra School Challenger responds,] "It follows that the subjects, the two—a gold pot and a copper pot, are not pot's isolate because of not being reversed from [being] different from pot."

Any instance of pot is not reversed from being different from pot (*bum pa dang tha dad las mi ldog pa*) because of being different from pot. It should be noted that the pervasion of this consequence states what whatever is *not* reversed from being different from pot is necessarily *not* pot's isolate. It does not say that whatever is reversed from being different from pot is necessarily pot's isolate, this position being the subject of debate C.13. Still, the consequence is instructive since the counter-pervasion indicates that whatever is pot's isolate is necessarily reversed from being different from pot, and this does explain something about the nature of pot's isolate.

> If he says that the reason is not established, [the Sūtra School Challenger responds,] "It follows that [the two—a gold pot and a copper pot—are not reversed from being different from pot] because [the two—a gold pot and a copper pot] are different from pot; because of being mutually exclusive with [pot]."

The two—a gold pot and a copper pot—are mutually exclusive with pot. Even though they are pots, they are mutually exclusive with pot. This is because (1) they are different from pot and (2) a common locus of pot and the two—a gold pot and a copper pot—is not possible. There is nothing which is both a pot and the two—a gold pot and a copper pot—because there is nothing which is the two—a gold pot and a copper pot. Since they are objects of knowledge of which being them is not possible, something which is them does not exist.

The two principals of debate C.12, pot's isolate and what is reversed from not being a pot, have three possibilities:

1   The only thing which can be posited as both is pot. Pot is pot's isolate because of being one with pot, and it is reversed from not being a pot because of being a pot.
2   Whatever is pot's isolate is necessarily reversed from not being a pot. However, it is not the case that whatever is reversed from not being a pot is necessarily pot's isolate. A gold pot, for instance, is reversed from not being a pot but is not pot's isolate.
3   Something which is neither is any non-pot—a pillar, a consciousness, a person, a permanent phenomenon, or a non-existent.

Debate C.13, Thirteenth Mistaken View (12a.1)

In this debate, the last in the refutation of mistaken views concerning isolates, the hypothetical Defender asserts that whatever is reversed from being different from pot is necessarily pot's isolate. "Reversed from being different from pot" means "non-different from pot" and is insufficient as a description of pot's isolate because it does not exclude non-existents, such as the horn of a rabbit. Still, any instance of pot or any phenomenon mutually inclusive with it is rightly excluded because of not being reversed from being different from pot, for any of these is different from pot.

> If someone [a hypothetical Defender] says, "Whatever is reversed from [being] different from pot is necessarily pot's isolate," [the Sūtra School Challenger responds to him,] "It [absurdly] follows that the subject, the horn of a rabbit, is pot's isolate because of being reversed from [being] different from pot. You asserted the pervasion."

In debate C.12, the Sūtra School Challenger pointed out that whatever is *not* reversed from being different from pot is necessarily not pot's isolate. This does not mean, however, that whatever *is* reversed from being different from pot is necessarily pot's isolate. The error in this position is in not seeing the difference between what is one (*gcig*) and what is non-different (*tha dad ma yin pa*). It is not the case that whatever is non-different from pot is necessarily one with pot. The horn of a rabbit is reversed from being different from pot because of not being different from pot; this, in turn, is due to its not being a *phenomenon* which is diverse from pot.

> If he says that the reason is not established, [the Sūtra School Challenger responds,] "It follows that the subject, the horn of a rabbit, is reversed from [being] different from pot because of not being different from pot."
>
> If he says that the reason is not established, [the Sūtra School Challenger responds,] "It follows that the subject, the horn of a rabbit, is not different from pot because of being non-different from pot."
>
> If he says that the reason is not established, [the Sūtra School Challenger responds,] "It follows that the subject, the horn of a rabbit, is non-different from pot because of being ascertained as non-existent [*med nges*]."

The horn of a rabbit is *ascertained* (by a valid cognizer) as non-existent. This does not mean that the horn of a rabbit is ascertained by a valid cognizer, for if it were, then according to the assertions of this system it would have to be an existent. Rather, a non-existent's *being* a non-existent (*med pa yin pa*) is observed by a valid cognizer and, thus, is an existent.

> If he accepts the basic consequence, [the Sūtra School Challenger responds,] "It follows that the subject, the horn of a rabbit, is not pot's isolate because of not being reversed from not being one with pot."

Here the text explains the most precise meaning of an isolate. The counter-pervasion of this last consequence is formulated: Whatever is pot's isolate is necessarily reversed from not being one with pot (*bum pa dang gcig ma yin pa las ldog pa*). This description excludes all which is not one with pot. Any phenomenon which is other than pot itself is different from pot and not one with pot; also, any non-existent is not one with pot. Thus, only pot is reversed from what is not one with pot. Although the text never explicitly says that whatever is reversed from not being one with pot is necessarily pot's isolate, it can be deduced from the information in this consequence together with the next consequence. Also, it can be known by the power of the fact of what it includes and what it excludes.

> "It follows that [the horn of a rabbit is not reversed from not being one with pot] because [the horn of a rabbit] is something which is not one with pot; because [it] is not one with pot."

Whatever is something which is not one with pot (*bum pa dang gcig ma yin pa*) is necessarily not reversed from not being one with pot. The counter-pervasion of the first consequence indicates that whatever is reversed from not being one with pot is necessarily not something which is not one with pot, that is, is necessarily one with pot. From the former consequence we know that whatever is pot's isolate is necessarily reversed from not being one with pot, and from the first of the present two consequences we know that whatever is reversed from not being one with pot is necessarily one with pot. Since pot's isolate and one-with-pot are coextensive or mutually inclusive, what is reversed from not being one with pot, therefore, must also be mutually inclusive with pot's isolate. This does not entail that it is pot's isolate, but it is established as the precise meaning of pot's isolate.

> "It follows that [the horn of a rabbit is not one with pot] because that is non-existent."

The two principals of debate C.13, pot's isolate and what is reversed from being different from pot, have three possibilities:

1 The only thing which is both is pot. It is reversed from being different from pot because of not being different from pot, since it is one with pot.

2 Whatever is pot's isolate is necessarily reversed from being different from pot. However, it is not the case that whatever is reversed from being different from pot is necessarily pot's isolate because any non-existent is reversed from being different from pot but is not pot's isolate.

3 Any existent other than pot is neither pot's isolate nor reversed from being different from pot.

PRESENTATION OF THE AUTHOR'S OWN SYSTEM OF IDENTIFYING ISOLATES (12A.4)

This section is drawn almost word for word from the Go-mang *Collected Topics*.[1] For the first time in this text, within the presentation of the author's own system there is an opponent who says that one of the reasons is not established.

> With respect to the second, [identifying isolates in our own system:] There is something to be posited as pot's isolate because pot is pot's isolate. The two, pot's isolate and one-with-pot, are coextensive. If something is an established base, then it is necessarily its own isolate because if something is an established base, then it is necessarily one with itself.
>
> If someone says that the reason is not established, [the Sūtra School Challenger responds,] "It follows that if something is an established base, then it is necessarily one with itself because if something is an established base, it is necessarily not different from itself."

DISPELLING OBJECTIONS TO THE AUTHOR'S SYSTEM OF IDENTIFYING ISOLATES (12A.6)

This section consists of two debates, C.14 and C.15, neither of which occur in either the Ra-dö *Collected Topics* or the Go-

---

[1] Ngak-wang-dra-shi, Go-mang *Collected Topics*, p. 56.

mang *Collected Topics* sections on isolates. Both debates focus on the distinction between being one and being mutually inclusive.

Debate C.14, First Objection (12a.6)

Here, a hypothetical Challenger, outside the system presented in this text, puts forth the view that if two phenomena are mutually inclusive, then they are one. This is radically opposed to the Collected Topics tradition in which mutually inclusive phenomena must be different and cannot be one.

> Someone [a hypothetical Challenger] might say, "It follows that functioning thing and that which is able to perform a function are one because those two are mutually inclusive." [The Sūtra School Defender answers,] "There is no pervasion."

Even though it is true that functioning thing and that which is able to perform a function are mutually inclusive, this does not entail that they are one. The Sūtra School Defender might have answered here that the pervasion is opposite (*khyab pa log pa*). That is, if functioning thing and that which is able to perform a function are mutually inclusive, they are necessarily not one. Mutually inclusive phenomena are necessarily different; thus, they cannot be one.

> "[It follows that] there is no pervasion because functioning thing and what which is able to perform a function are different; because there are [cases of someone's] ascertaining that which is able to perform a function with valid cognition without ascertaining functioning thing with valid cognition; because ascertaining that which is able to perform a function with valid cognition must precede ascertaining functioning thing with valid cognition."

Since functioning thing and that which is able to perform a function are established as a definiendum and its definition, they are different. And the last two reasons above describe a requirement of the relationship between a definition and its definiendum in particular as well as between all different phenomena in general.

The author is describing something about the essential nature of different phenomena, and by contrast, about the nature of single phenomena. If it is possible to ascertain correctly some phenomenon without necessarily also ascertaining correctly this other phenomenon, then those are separate and different phenomena. This does not mean that for all different phenomena, one must know one without knowing the other but only that such is possible. For a single phenomenon, having ascertained that basis with valid cognition, there is no possibility of not having ascertained *just that same phenomenon* with valid cognition. This is tautological: Ascertaining something with valid cognition means that one has ascertained it with valid cognition. However, for different phenomena, ascertaining one with valid cognition does not *necessarily entail* ascertaining the other with valid cognition, even though it may be a definiendum or something mutually inclusive.

Also, in light of this epistemological fact that phenomena are established as different in dependence upon certification by valid cognizers, one can see why non-existents must be excluded from being different phenomena. Indeed, there are cases of ascertaining a pot with valid cognition without ascertaining the horn of a rabbit with valid cognition, but there are no cases of ascertaining the horn of a rabbit with valid cognition without ascertaining a pot with valid cognition. This is because there are no cases of ascertaining the horn of a rabbit with valid cognition. Thus, a pot is established as different from the horn of a rabbit, but the horn of a rabbit is not established as different from a pot nor from any other "thing" without a self of persons.

As these last two reasons point out, it is true that if there are cases of ascertaining one thing with valid cognition without ascertaining another with valid cognition, then those two are necessarily different. However, this does not mean that if two phenomena are different, then one must ascertain the one with valid cognition without ascertaining the other with valid cognition, only that such does occur.

If something is the definition of another phenomenon, then one must ascertain that definition with valid cognition before one ascertains that definiendum with valid cognition. In order to know what the appellation "functioning thing" means one must first be familiar with that which is able to perform a function. In order to understand matter properly, one must have become acquainted with these things which are atomically established. A baby knows that which is wet and moistening, the essential characteristic and function of water, but does not know the name "water". A cow knows what salt is but does not know the name "salt".

Debate C.15, Second Objection (12b.1)

In this debate, the last in "Identifying Isolates", the hypothetical Challenger again asserts the view that some different phenomena are one, for he claims that mutually inclusive phenomena are one. At the end of this debate, the Sūtra School disputant clearly identifies that whatever is one must be one from the point of view of both name and meaning, thus enunciating the self-identify of what is one.

> Also, someone [a hypothetical Challenger] might say, "Functioning thing, impermanent phenomenon, product, and composed phenomenon, rather than being mere enumerations of names, are one. Similarly, object of knowledge, existent, established base, and object of comprehension are also one, as is the case with the Unequalled Son of Shuddhodana, the Omniscient Sun-Friend, and the Omniscient Sugarcane One."

The unequalled Son of Shuddhodana (*mnyam med zas gtsang sras po*), the Omniscient Sun-Friend (*kun mkhyen nyi ma'i gnyen*), and the Omniscient Sugarcane One (*kun mkhyen bu ram shing pa*) are well known epithets of Shākyamuni

Buddha, the historical Buddha. This hypothetical Challenger's thought is that since functioning thing and the phenomena mutually inclusive with it all refer to exactly the same phenomena without exception, they are not merely mutually inclusive or different names for the same thing but are one. He feels that the same is true for object of knowledge and the phenomena mutually inclusive with it, citing as his reason that the many epithets of the Buddha, as is well known, all refer to only the one Buddha.

> [The Sūtra School Defender answers,] "This is not correct because the son of Shuddhodana, the Sun-Friend, and the Sugarcane One are different phenomena."
>
> If one were to say that the reason is not established, [then the Proponent of Sūtra would become Challenger and respond,] "It follows [that the sun of Shuddhodana, the Sun-Friend, and the Sugarcane One are different phenomena] because it is possible for there to be [a case of] ascertaining with valid cognition the basis to which the term 'the son of Shuddhodana' applies without ascertaining with valid cognition the bases to which the terms 'the Sun-Friend' and 'the Sugarcane One' apply."

Correctly knowing the basis of reference of the term "the son of Shuddhodana", that is, the meaning of the name, does not necessarily entail correctly knowing the meaning of the other terms. Even knowing who the son of Shuddhodana is, one might think that the Sun-Friend is another person.

> "Therefore, although the referent basis to which the terms 'the son of Shuddhodana,' 'Sun-Friend,' and 'the Sugarcane One' apply is one, they are not one because whatever is one must be one from the point of view of both name and meaning."

REMARKS

"Identifying Isolates" is the chapter on which the trainees in the Collected Topics tradition cut their teeth. It is a critical chapter that establishes some of the main motifs that figure prominently in the Collected Topics literature.

At first glance, the doctrine of self-identity presented in this system—that any existent is one with itself and different from all else—seems quite uninvolved. However, it is just this assertion that serves as the basis for the complexity of "Identifying Isolates". In debate C.13, the precise meaning of pot's isolate was identified as "that which is reversed from not being *one* with pot" (*bum pa dang gcig ma yin pa las ldog pa*). Also, the phenomena coextensive with the isolate of some phenomenon center on what is one with that phenomenon in isolation from all else. In turn, the discussion of coextensives is the most difficult point yet encountered in the Collected Topics.

The knowledge that any existent is one with itself leads one to see what is meant by the isolate of a phenomenon. The isolate of a phenomenon is just that phenomenon itself conceptually *isolated* from all that is not exactly the same as it in both name and meaning. Thus, "Identifying Isolates" zeroes in on the abstract and speaks of the phenomenon collectively and in the singular. This particular slant on phenomena then functions as a main pillar of the Collected Topics tradition. For instance, as was explained in "Established Bases", object of knowledge is a permanent phenomenon. This does not mean that each and every object of knowledge is a permanent phenomenon; rather, the meaning of this statement is that object of knowledge—from the point of view of its self-isolate—is a permanent phenomenon.

In order to reflect this particular focus on phenomena which is so prominent in the Collected Topics tradition, the translation offered here frequently employs singular nouns without definite or indefinite articles in spite of normal

English grammar. Since the articles and plural markers that do exist in Tibetan are very rarely used in the Collected Topics or any other literature, it might be suitable to add these to the translation where English grammar calls for them. However, this would usually be a corruption of the meaning. For instance, it is true enough that *a* pot is *a* pot's isolate, but the indefinite article suggests that it is some particular pot that is being referred to or it is each and every pot. However, in reference to the isolate, the focus is not on any concrete pot but on the abstract generality "pot".

As a result of this slant on the abstract, it is said in the Collected Topics tradition that many phenomena are not themselves. For instance, definition is not a definition. What this means is that definition—from the point of view of its self-isolate—is not a definition. The generality definition does not exemplify the qualities of a definition because it itself has a definition and thus is a definiendum. It must be seen clearly that saying that definition is not a definition *does not mean* that definition is not self-identical, for it is one with itself as are all phenomena.

Through juxtaposing the topics of isolates and the nature of a phenomenon's being one with itself, "Identifying Isolates" compels one to see the distinction between self-identity and self-exemplification. Every phenomenon is self-identical, but some do not exemplify themselves. Self-identity *is* a simple doctrine, but then reckoning the natures of a phenomenon from the point of view of its self-isolate— which is built from that phenomenon's self-identity—can be more challenging.

In terms of the reasoning form, the main lesson learned in "Identifying Isolates" is the difference between copulative associations and pervasions. A copulative association is expressed in a sentence of the form:

p is a q

and focuses on the nature of the "p" phenomenon from the point of view of its self-isolate. A pervasion is expressed in a sentence of the form:

Whatever is a *p* is necessarily a *q*

and does not focus on the generality "*p*" but on the concrete exemplifiers of "*p*". As a case in point, in "Identifying Isolates" it is made clear that pot's isolate (*p*) is a permanent phenomenon (*q*) but whatever is pot's isolate—that is, pot itself—is necessarily an impermanent phenomenon. The distinction between these forms was first broached in "Established Bases" where it was said that object of knowledge is a permanent phenomenon but whatever is an object of knowledge is not necessarily a permanent phenomenon. However, the claim that pot's isolate is a permanent phenomenon but whatever is pot's isolate is necessarily not a permanent phenomenon even more radically marks the difference between these logical functionals and has to be quite surprising to the student. The clear distinction between copulative associations and pervasions as well as the breadth of that distinction will be discussed in detail in the conclusion of this work.

11 Opposite-From-Being-Something and Opposite-From-Not-Being-Something

INTRODUCTION

The fourth chapter of "The Introductory Path of Reasoning" is a condensation of the type of material presented in two sections in the Ra-dö *Collected Topics* as well as in other debate manuals. In those texts, in addition to the presentation of opposite-from-being-something (*yin log*) and opposite-from-not-being-something (*min log*) there is a separate section covering the ancillary topic of what something is (*yin gyur*) and what something is not (*min gyur*). Of the eight debates in this chapter of the Tutor's *Collected Topics*, five focus on topics usually included in the presentation of opposite-from-being-something and opposite-from-not-being-something, and three are included in the ancillary topic of what something is and what something is not. The latter topic will be discussed at the beginning of debate D.4.

The topics of opposite-from-being-something and
opposite-from-not-being-something develop out of a passage in the chapter on inference for oneself (*rang don rjes
dpag, svārtha-anumāna*), in Dharmakīrti's *Commentary on
(Dignāga's) "Compendium of Valid Cognition"* which says:

> That is also reversed from others and
> Opposite from others.[1]

Also:

> The entity of that is opposite from all.[2]

And:

> By reversal from not being a tree.[3]

Here the terms "opposite" (*log*) and "reversed" (*ldog*) are
equivalent and refer to a simple turning away from, or
negation, of some phenomenon. In this context the Tibetan
word *ldog* is translated as "reversed" or "reversal" rather
than as "isolate" as was generally done in "Identifying
Isolates". This reversal, usually referred to as "opposite", is
quite different from the double reverse as presented in the
previous chapter. Still, even in the discussion of isolates the
word "reversed" (*ldog*) is sometimes used to mean simple
negation as in the phrase "reversed from not being one with
pot" (*bum pa dang gcig ma yin pa las ldog pa*).

The two functional elements in this section are "opposite-
from-being-something" and "opposite-from-not-being-
something". These units are not usually discussed by themselves but are applied to some basis such as a functioning
thing. For instance, there is opposite-from-being-a-
functioning-thing (*dngos po yin pa las log pa*) and opposite-
from-not-being-a-functioning-thing (*dngos po ma yin pa las
log pa*).

---

[1] Dharmakīrti, *Commentary on (Dignāga's) "Compendium of Valid
Cognition"*, P5709, Vol. 130, 79.2.2.
[2] *Ibid.*, 79.4.5.
[3] *Ibid.*, 80.1.3.

Opposite-from-being-a-functioning-thing is mutually inclusive with not being a functioning thing (*dngos po ma yin pa*). In ordinary Tibetan language the word "*log*" translated here as "opposite" means to turn away from or reverse. A monk who gives up his vows is said to have turned away (*log*) from monkhood. He has become a non-monk. The term has the same meaning in this context.

Opposite-from-being-a-functioning-thing is itself; that is, it is opposite from being a functioning thing and is not a functioning thing but a permanent phenomenon. Whatever is opposite from being a functioning thing is necessarily not a functioning thing, and whatever is not a functioning thing is necessarily opposite from being a functioning thing. Since opposite-from-being-a-functioning-thing includes permanent phenomena (as well as non-existents), it is a generally characterized phenomenon and must be an appearing object of a thought consciousness.

Opposite-from-not-being-a-functioning-thing is mutually inclusive with being a functioning thing (*dngos po yin pa*). Since "opposite from" (*las log pa*) is the equivalent of "non-" (*ma yin pa*), opposite-from-not-being-a-functioning-thing means non-non-functioning-thing and indicates being a functioning thing. Whatever is opposite from not being a functioning thing is necessarily a functioning thing, and whatever is a functioning thing is necessarily opposite from not being a functioning thing. Unlike the case of the isolate of functioning thing which signifies only the isolated generality, *anything* which is a functioning thing is opposite from not being a functioning thing. For instance, a pot is not the isolate of functioning thing, but since it is a functioning thing, it is opposite from not being a functioning thing.

According to the Tutor's *Collected Topics*, opposite-from-not-being-a-functioning-thing is an impermanent phenomenon. For any impermanent phenomenon, opposite-from-not-being-it is an impermanent phenomenon. If something is opposite-from-not-being-a-functioning-thing, it is a functioning thing. "By the mere establishment of a pot itself, the entity of opposite-from-not-being-a-pot is established. It

is established in the entity of a pot."[1] In the Tutor Jam-ba-
gya-tso's opinion, opposite-from-not-being-a-pot (*bum pa ma
yin pa las log pa*) is a specifically characterized phenomenon,
established by its own nature, and does not depend on
imputation by a term or a thought consciousness. It is in the
nature of any existent that being it is opposite from not
being it. Similarly, opposite-from-not-being-a-phenomenon
is the same as being that phenomenon; being opposite from
not being a functioning thing is the same as being a
functioning thing and opposite-from-not-being-a-
functioning-thing *is* itself a functioning thing.

However, according to the Go-mang *Collected Topics*,
opposite-from-not-being-a-pot is a permanent phenomenon.
That text says:

> It follows that opposite-from-not-being-a-pot is not a
> functioning thing because (1) non-non-pot is not a
> functioning thing and (2) there is no distinction (*khyad
> par*) between those two [opposite-from-not-being-a-
> pot and non-non-pot].[2]

There is no distinction between those two in the sense that
they are mutually inclusive phenomena. The assertion that
opposite-from-not-being-a-pot is a permanent phenomenon
results from the fact that it as well as non-non-pot are
mental abstractions and thereby are generally characterized.

As phenomena (*chos, dharma*), all existents bear their own
entities. They are one with themselves, and—merely by
being only what they are—they are set apart from what they
are not. For instance, a table is one with itself, and merely by
being a table is set apart from non-table. Thus, in the system
of the Tutor Jam-ba-gya-tso, through the establishment of a
table opposite-from-not-being-a-table is also established.
Indeed, opposite-from-not-being-a-table is different from
being a table, but whatever is opposite from not being a
table is a table. One is able to apprehend what is opposite

---

[1] Denma Lochö Rinbochay, oral commentary.
[2] Ngak-wang-dra-shi, Go-mang *Collected Topics*, p. 472.

from not being a table by a direct perceiver, for a table which is opposite from not being a table appears manifestly to the senses. This is an appeal to the discrimination ('*du shes, samjñā*) of the senses. The phenomena that appear to the senses do not melt and flow into each other but are distinguished as separate entities. The table that appears to the senses is set apart from the other phenomena that appear to the senses. Also, a table, any table, is opposite from not being a table. Merely by seeing a table one sees what is opposite from not being a table.

It might seem that the Collected Topics formulators are multiplying the basis of each phenomenon into infinite different phenomena. A chair appears to the senses, opposite-from-not-being-a-chair appears to the senses, opposite-from-not-being-opposite-from-not-being-a-chair appears to the senses, and so forth *ad infinitum*. However, this seems not to be the case. Rather, a chair appears to the senses, and *being* that chair is the same as being opposite from not being that chair, not being opposite from being that chair, and so on. A chair is something which is opposite from not being a chair, it is something which is opposite from not being opposite from not being a chair, and so on. This does not mean that there are infinite chairs located with each instance of a chair, but it may imply that there are infinite qualities of being a chair.

Opposite-from-not-being-a phenomenon is mutually inclusive with *being* a phenomenon. Whatever is a phenomenon is necessarily opposite from not being a phenomenon. Even though opposite-from-not-being-a-functioning-thing and being a functioning thing are mutually inclusive, the Tutor asserts opposite-from-not-being-a-functioning-thing as a functioning thing and being a functioning thing as a permanent phenomenon. Pots and pillars are produced from causes and conditions, but *being* a pot or *being* a pillar is quite a different sort of phenomenon. *Being* something is not produced by causes and conditions. *What is* something may be so produced, but *being* something is a phenomenon which is not established from its own side and must be imputed by a term or a thought consciousness.

A book is produced, abides, and disintegrates, but *being* a book (*deb yin pa*) does not waver at all. It is steady, static, and unchanging. Indeed, being a book comes into existence when the book that is its basis is produced, but it is not something that one could build in with a tool. It lasts as long as the book which is its basis, but during the course of its existence it is static. Being a book is a quality that does not change. Also, the *existence* of a book (*deb yod pa*) is a permanent phenomenon. One may produce something which is a book, but one cannot produce the existence of a book. As it ages, the pages of a book may become worn and frayed, but that quality which is the existence of a book is invariable. From the first moment of the book through to the last its existence as a book remains. Before the book was created and when it no longer exists, it is unsuitable to designate either the existence (*yod pa*) or the being (*yin pa*) of that particular book, but this does not entail that either the being or the existence of a phenomenon is created by the same causes and conditions that created that phenomenon or that during the course of the book's abiding either the being or the existence of it is something which changes.

The rules of mutual inclusion outlined in the presentation of opposite-from-being-something and opposite-from-not-being-something apply to all phenomena. Opposite-from-being-something and not being something are mutually inclusive and opposite-from-not-being-something and being something are mutually inclusive. However, it should be seen that when these are applied to a particular phenomenon, even though that phenomenon itself exists, the resultant description may not refer to any phenomenon. For instance, object of knowledge is an existent, but opposite-from-being-an-object-of-knowledge is not. Non-object of knowledge does not exist. Whatever exists is necessarily an object of knowledge. Although opposite-from-being-an-object-of-knowledge does not exist, such non-existents may be used in statements of pervasion. For instance, the Go-mang *Collected Topics* says, "Whatever is opposite from being an existent is necessarily not an existent. Whatever is not an existent is necessarily opposite from being an existent."[1]

Also, for objects of knowledge of which being them is not possible, opposite-from-not-being-any-of-them is necessarily not an existent.[2] For instance, opposite-from-not-being-the-two—a pillar and a pot—does not exist. For any established base, if something which is it does not exist, opposite-from-not-being-it also does not exist. Whatever exists is necessarily a common locus, but since something which is the two—a pillar and a pot—is not possible, whatever is a common locus is necessarily not the two—a pillar and a pot. Since whatever is a common locus is necessarily not the two—a pillar and a pot, there is nothing which is opposite from not being the two—a pillar and a pot.

Further, for any phenomenon which is not an exemplifier of itself, it is important to assert that *being* that phenomenon is what is mutually inclusive with opposite-from-not-being-that-phenomenon. One cannot say that just that phenomenon is mutually inclusive with opposite-from-not-being-it. For instance, definition is not itself, it is not a definition, because it is a definiendum. Thus definition is not mutually inclusive with opposite-from-not-being-a-definition; rather, *being* a definition is mutually inclusive with opposite-from-not-being-a-definition. This is because definition is not opposite from not being a definition. Whatever *is* a definition is necessarily opposite from not being a definition. However, since definition itself *is not* a definition, it is not opposite from not *being* itself. Thus, only *being* a definition is mutually inclusive with opposite-from-not-being-a-definition. This applies in the same way to the many phenomena which are not themselves.

---

[1] *Ibid.*, p. 48.
[2] Denma Lochö Rinbochay, oral commentary.

Usually in debating the topics of opposite-from-being-something and opposite-from-not-being-something students stack up a number of these modifiers of the same type or mix the two together. This is done only for the sake of increasing the complexity of the debate. Opposite-from-not-being a phenomenon is mutually inclusive with being that phenomenon, and if this is doubled, opposite-from-not-being-opposite-from-not-being-a-phenomenon is still mutually inclusive with being that phenomenon as well as with opposite-from-not-being-that-phenomenon. In the same way, one can stack up the modifier "opposite-from-not-being" infinitely, and it will still be mutually inclusive with being.

Opposite-from-being-a-certain-phenomenon is mutually inclusive with not being that phenomenon, but if doubled, opposite-from-being-opposite-from-being-a-phenomenon is mutually inclusive with being that phenomenon because it is twice reversed from the original. However, if three such modifiers are put together, opposite-from-being-opposite-from-being-opposite-from-being-a-certain-phenomenon is mutually inclusive with not being that phenomenon. For the modifier "opposite-from-being" the pattern is consistent. If there is an odd number of these modifiers, the result is mutually inclusive with not being. If there is an even number, the result is mutually inclusive with being.

The difficulty of reckoning the value of a phenomenon in relation to being and not being comes when the modifiers are mixed. In this event, there is no alternative but to count the value of the modifiers to determine the result. Fortunately, it is a totally binary operation, alternating between two poles; thus, there is no need to keep a running total in order to calculate the value at the end. Rather, it is possible simply to determine the value as positive or negative as the words are spoken or read, whereby the result is known immediately at the end of the expression. Further, since both phrases "opposite from being" and "opposite from not being" contain the negating particle "opposite", it is not necessary to count these. The process is this: Every time the word "being" occurs, it changes the value of the basic phenomenon from positive to negative or negative to positive, and every time the words "not being" occur, it does not change the value in either direction.

The traditional method for making this calculation is by using the thumb to count back and forth between two joints of the forefinger. In Tibetan the phenomenon which is the basis of the calculation comes first in the utterance, but in English it comes at the end. Still, there is no difference in the process. One can arbitrarily decide that the joint closest to the palm of the hand represents being and the second one out represents not being. Beginning from the section representing being, each time the words "not being" occur one does not move the thumb from where it rests, and each time the word "being" occurs one moves the thumb to the opposite joint. By this method one can keep an accurate count.

REFUTATION OF MISTAKEN VIEWS CONCERNING
OPPOSITE-FROM-BEING-SOMETHING AND OPPOSITE-
FROM-NOT-BEING-SOMETHING (12B.4)

This section consists of six debates, the first three on opposite-from-being-something (*yin log*) and opposite-from-not-being-something (*min log*) and the latter three on what something is (*yin gyur*) and what something is not (*min gyur*).

Debate D.1, First Mistaken View (12b.4)

The first debate is the most basic introduction to the terminology of this chapter. Here the hypothetical Defender asserts that whatever is opposite from being a functioning thing is necessarily opposite from being a permanent phenomenon. Opposite-from-being-a-functioning-thing is mutually inclusive with not being a functioning thing or non-functioning thing, and opposite-from-being-a-permanent-phenomenon is mutually inclusive with not being a permanent phenomenon or non-permanent phenomenon. Thus, both include non-existents, but it is not the case that whatever is opposite from being a functioning thing is necessarily opposite from being a permanent phenomenon. For instance, object of knowledge is opposite from being a functioning thing because it is not a functioning thing, but it is not opposite from being a permanent phenomenon because it is a permanent phenomenon. The text says:

> If someone [a hypothetical Defender] says, "Whatever is opposite from being a functioning thing is necessarily opposite from being a permanent phenomenon," [the Sūtra School Challenger responds to him,] "It [absurdly] follows that the subject, object of knowledge, is [opposite from being a permanent phenomenon] because of [being opposite from being a functioning thing]. You asserted the pervasion."
>
> If he says that the reason is not established, [the Sūtra School Challenger responds,] "It follows that the subject [object of knowledge] is [opposite from being a functioning thing] because of not being a functioning thing."
>
> "[It follows that] there is pervasion [i.e., whatever is not a functioning thing is necessarily opposite from being a functioning thing] because opposite-from-being-a-functioning-thing and not being a functioning thing are mutually inclusive."
>
> If he accepts the basic consequence, [the Sūtra School Challenger responds,] "It follows that the subject [object of knowledge] is not opposite from being a permanent phenomenon because of being opposite from not being a permanent phenomenon."

It is possible to move the negative particle (*ma*) and still not affect the value of the phenomenon. Here, being opposite from not being a permanent phenomenon (*rtag pa ma yin pa las log pa yin pa*) and not being opposite from being a permanent phenomenon (*rtag pa yin pa las log pa ma yin pa*) are mutually inclusive. Whatever is opposite from not being a permanent phenomenon is necessarily a permanent phenomenon and whatever is not opposite from being a permanent phenomenon is also necessarily a permanent phenomenon.

> If he says that the reason is not established, [the Sūtra School Challenger responds,] "It follows that the subject [object of knowledge] is [opposite from not being a permanent phenomenon] because of being a permanent phenomenon."
> "[It follows that] there is pervasion [i.e., whatever is a permanent phenomenon is necessarily opposite from not being a permanent phenomenon] because the two, opposite-from-not-being-a-permanent-phenomenon and permanent phenomenon, are mutually inclusive."

Here the text does not specify *being* a permanent phenomenon as mutually inclusive with opposite-from-not-being-a-permanent-phenomenon, nor is it necessary to do so. Since permanent phenomenon is itself a permanent phenomenon, it is opposite from not being a permanent phenomenon and those two are mutually inclusive as are the two, *being* a permanent phenomenon and opposite-from-not-being-a-permanent-phenomenon.

The two principals of debate D.1, opposite-from-being-a-functioning-thing and opposite-from-being-a-permanent-phenomenon, have three possibilities without their being something which is neither. These two do not compare in the same way as their bases, functioning thing and permanent phenomenon, which are mutually exclusive. The difference is that both opposite-from-being-a-functioning-thing and opposite-from-being-a-permanent-phenomenon include non-existents, due to which there is something to be posited as both:

1   The horn of a rabbit, for instance, is opposite from being a functioning thing because of not being a functioning

thing, and it is opposite from being a permanent phenomenon because of not being a permanent phenomenon.

2 Something which is opposite from being a functioning thing but is not opposite from being a permanent phenomenon is uncomposed space.

3 Any functioning thing is opposite from being a permanent phenomenon but is not opposite from being a functioning thing.

There is nothing which is neither because between the two of them all permanent and impermanent phenomena as well as all non-existents are exhausted.

Debate D.2, Second Mistaken View (13a.1)

In this debate the author shows the way in which one can stack up the modifiers in order to make the debates more difficult. The hypothetical Defender asserts that whatever is opposite from being opposite from being a functioning thing is necessarily opposite from being a functioning thing. Opposite-from-being-opposite-from-being-a-functioning-thing is mutually inclusive with being a functioning thing and, of course, is not pervaded by being opposite from being a functioning thing.

> If someone [a hypothetical Defender] says, "Whatever is opposite from being opposite from being a functioning thing is necessarily opposite from being a functioning thing," [the Sūtra School Challenger responds to him,] "It [absurdly] follows that the subject, a pot, is [opposite from being a functioning thing] because of [being opposite from being opposite from being a functioning thing]. You asserted the pervasion."

Functioning thing itself, any phenomenon mutually inclusive with functioning thing, or any instance of functioning thing is opposite from being opposite from being a functioning thing because of being a functioning thing. A pot is a non-non-functioning thing, and it is not something which is not a functioning thing because it is a functioning thing. This is not like the isolate of functioning thing which is predicated from the rule that whatever exists is necessarily one with itself. In this chapter the principle is that of being or not being. Anything which is a functioning thing is not other than a functioning thing; it is not opposite from being a functioning thing but is a functioning thing.

> If he says that the reason is not established, [the Sūtra School Challenger responds,] "It follows that the subject [a pot] is [opposite from being opposite from being a functioning thing] because of not being opposite from being a functioning thing."

The modifier "opposite from being" can always be replaced by "not being" as is done in this consequence. This helps to simplify sometimes lengthy descriptions.

> If he says that the reason is not established, [the Sūtra School Challenger responds,] "It follows that the subject [a pot] is [not opposite from being a functioning thing] because of being opposite from not being a functioning thing."
>
> If he says that the reason is not established, [the Sūtra School Challenger responds,] "It follows that the subject [a pot] is [opposite from not being a functioning thing] because of being a functioning thing."
>
> "[It follows that] there is pervasion [i.e., whatever is a functioning thing is necessarily opposite from not being a functioning thing] because those two [functioning thing and opposite-from-not-being-a-functioning-thing] are mutually inclusive."
>
> If he accepts the basic consequence, [the Sūtra School Challenger responds,] "It follows that the subject [a pot] is not opposite from being a functioning thing because it abides as something which is a functioning thing."

The two principals of debate D.2, opposite-from-being-opposite-from-being-a-functioning-thing and opposite-from-being-a-functioning-thing, are mutually exclusive. They are different and a common locus of the two is not possible. Whatever is opposite from being opposite from being a functioning thing is necessarily a functioning thing, and whatever is opposite from being a functioning thing is necessarily not a functioning thing. These two compare as do functioning thing and non-functioning thing. Something which is both could not exist.

Debate D.3, Third Mistaken View (13a.3)

In the third debate the author mixes together the modifiers "opposite from being" and "opposite from not being" to create units that are complex in their length. Still, one can rather easily decide the meaning of the two principals by counting the value of the modifiers as described above (see pp. 488-489).

Here the hypothetical Defender accepts that whatever is opposite from not being opposite from being opposite from not being opposite from being a permanent phenomenon (*rtag pa yin pa las log pa ma yin pa las log pa yin pa las log pa ma yin pa las log pa*) is necessarily opposite from being opposite from not being a permanent phenomenon (*rtag pa ma yin pa las log pa yin pa las log pa*). The first phenomenon has four modifiers and an affirmative verb, "whatever *is* ... " The first modifier is "opposite from not being;" so, according to the rules outlined above it does not change the value of the basic phenomenon. The second modifier is "opposite from being" which does change the value, in this case from positive to negative. The third modifier is "opposite from not being" which does not change the value, and the last is "opposite from being" which changes the value back from negative to positive. Thus, we are left with only the basis, permanent phenomenon.

The second phenomenon has only two modifiers and an affirmative verb. The first is "opposite from being" which changes the value to negative, and the second is "opposite from not being" which leaves the value negative. Thus, the basis of the second principal, permanent phenomenon, is merely negated. In effect, the hypothetical Defender is asserting that whatever is a permanent phenomenon is necessarily not a permanent phenomenon. Of course, it is very easy to see his error when the two principals are reduced to their simplest meanings. The difficulty is in correctly reckoning the value of the two principals, especially during the speed of debate.

> If someone [a hypothetical Defender] says, "Whatever is opposite from not being opposite from being opposite from not being opposite from being a permanent phenomenon is necessarily opposite from being opposite from not being a permanent phenomenon," [the Sūtra School Challenger responds to him,] "It [absurdly] follows that the subject, pillar's isolate, is [opposite from being opposite from not being a permanent phenomenon] because of [being opposite from not being opposite from being opposite from not being opposite from being a permanent phenomenon]. You asserted the pervasion."
>
> If he says that the reason is not established, [the Sūtra School Challenger responds,] "It follows that the subject [pillar's isolate] is [opposite from not being opposite from being opposite from not being opposite from being a permanent phenomenon] because of being opposite from being opposite from not being opposite from being a permanent phenomenon."

The Challenger has simply dropped the first modifier, "opposite from not being", which does not affect the value of the phenomenon. The two phenomena with and without this modifier are mutually inclusive.

> If he says that the reason is not established, [the Sūtra School Challenger responds,] "It follows that

the subject [pillar's isolate] is [opposite from being opposite from not being opposite from being a permanent phenomenon] because of not being opposite from not being opposite from being a permanent phenomenon."

Here the Challenger has replaced the first modifier, "opposite from being", with a negative particle to change the value from affirmative to negative. These two are again mutually inclusive.

If he says that the reason is not established, [the Sūtra School Challenger responds,] "It follows that the subject [pillar's isolate] is [not opposite from not being opposite from being a permanent phenomenon] because of being opposite from being opposite from being a permanent phenomenon."

The Challenger has removed two negative particles, changing the verb from negative to positive and changing the modifier "opposite from not being" to "opposite from being". The two negatives cancel out each other. The resultant phenomenon expressed in the reason is mutually inclusive with that expressed in the predicate.

If he says that the reason is not established, [the Sūtra School Challenger responds,] "It follows that the subject [pillar's isolate] is [opposite from being opposite from being a permanent phenomenon] because of not being opposite from being a permanent phenomenon."

If he says that the reason is not established, [the Sūtra School Challenger responds,] "It follows that the subject [pillar's isolate] is [not opposite from being a permanent phenomenon] because of being opposite from not being a permanent phenomenon."

If he says that the reason is not established, [the Sūtra School Challenger responds,] "It follows that the subject [pillar's isolate] is [opposite from not being a permanent phenomenon] because of being a permanent phenomenon."

The Challenger has laid out a line of six reasons in support of the reason of the basic consequence. The development of these reasons demonstrates an important facet of the procedure in debate. That is, the sign of a consequence or syllogism is supposed to be easier to understand than what it is proving, the predicate. These reasons reflect that rule, for each is easier than the last.

Also, it is a fine point of debate that the reasoning process should not be pressed too hard but should be allowed to proceed along orderly lines and in gradual steps. The Challenger could have validly supported the reason of the basic consequence by the reason of being a permanent phenomenon, but the Defender would not have been able to make the conceptual leap. In this line of reasoning the essential point is that the subject is a permanent phenomenon, and it is the Challenger's role to explain that to the Defender by bringing him to the point where he can understand it. This process is one of the great benefits of debate. It serves to train students to reason in an orderly and disciplined fashion. Rather than jumping to a conclusion, albeit a valid one, debaters become skillful in establishing that conclusion by carefully working through the reasoning process, moving in gradual increments. Such a disciplined process proves to be more helpful and instructive.

It must be noted that although the debating process is gradual and careful, this does not mean that it is slow. On the contrary, the debates generally move along at quite a fast pace. In reading any debate manual, it is important to remember that the text is mere notation of something which exists essentially in the oral tradition only. The debates recorded in the text would usually have to be filled out with subsequent supporting reasons or tied together through cross-application. Debate manuals do not record the debating tradition but merely suggest it by noting some of the essential points as a guide. The tradition of debate is essentially conveyed through an oral process.

> If he accepts the basic consequence, [the Sūtra School Challenger responds,] "It follows that the subject, pillar's isolate, is not opposite from being opposite from not being a permanent phenomenon because of being opposite from not being opposite from not being a permanent phenomenon."
>
> If he says that the reason is not established, [the Sūtra School Challenger responds,] "It follows that the subject [pillar's isolate] is [opposite from not being opposite from not being a permanent phenomenon] because of being opposite from not being a permanent phenomenon."

Pillar's isolate is a permanent phenomenon, and so it is opposite from not being a permanent phenomenon, due to which it is opposite from not being opposite from not being a permanent phenomenon. With the modifier "opposite from not being", one can add on as many as one likes, and the phenomenon will still be the same as with only a single such modifier.

The two principals of debate D.3, opposite-from-not-being-opposite-from-being-opposite-from-not-being-opposite-from-being-a-permanent-phenomenon and opposite-from-being-opposite-from-not-being-a-permanent-phenomenon, are mutually exclusive. A common locus of the two is not possible because whatever is opposite from not being opposite from being opposite from not being opposite from being a permanent phenomenon is necessarily a permanent phenomenon; yet, whatever is opposite from being opposite from not being a permanent phenomenon is necessarily not a permanent phenomenon.

Debate D.4, Fourth Mistaken View (13b.1)

Debate D.4 is one of the most interesting and difficult in "The Introductory Path of Reasoning". It is taken word for word from the chapter on the ancillary topic of what something is and what something is not in the Ra-dö *Collected Topics*.[1] This debate, as well as debates D.5 and D.6, serve as the presentation of what something is and what something is not in the Tutor's *Collected Topics*.

The debates in this section play on the manner of expressing something. "What something is" (*yin gyur*) may also be rendered as "which is", and "what something is not" (*min gyur*) may be rendered as "which is not". One must understand the clause as applying to something, although just what that is may be variable. In order to give some sense to the English translation, often the word "something" or the pronoun "it" is supplied in brackets when a referent is absent.

An introductory example will be helpful. The Shar-dzay *Collected Topics* says:

> If someone says, "Whatever is an object of comprehension of an omniscient consciousness which is [it] is necessarily [it]," this is not correct because a functioning thing is that.[2]

The intention of this debate is this: In the phrase "an object of comprehension of an omniscient consciousness which is [it] (*yin par gyur pa'i rnam mkhyen gyi gzhal bya*)", "it" stands in place of any suitable predicate of an *omniscient consciousness* and that consciousness itself is also an object of comprehension of such a consciousness. Object of comprehension of an omniscient consciousness is mutually inclusive with established base; thus, whatever exists is an object of comprehension of an omniscient consciousness. Here, the adjectival clause "which is [it]" modifies not "object of comprehension of an omniscient consciousness" but "an omniscient consciousness". There are many suitable predicates of an omniscient consciousness. For instance, it is a conscious-

---

[1] Jam-yang-chok-hla-ö-ser, Ra-dö *Collected Topics*, 20b.3-21a.2.

[2] Dzemay Rinbochay, Shar-dzay *Collected Topics*, pp. 25-26.

ness, it is a functioning thing, it is an established base, and so forth.

The second portion of the above statement of pervasion is literally rendered "is necessarily" (*yin pas khyab*). There is no predicate stated, but it is to be supplied in accordance with what was supplied as the predicate of "an omniscient consciousness" in the first part of the pervasion. Because the same term must be supplied in both places, the English translation reads, "is necessarily [it]".

The question that the debate poses is this: Is there anything which is a suitable predicate of an omniscient consciousness and is an object of comprehension by that consciousness which is not also necessarily a phenomenon which pervades all objects of comprehension? The Sūtra School Challenger supplies the answer that there is indeed such a phenomenon, for a functioning thing is that. This means that it is not the case that whatever is an object of comprehension of an omniscient consciousness which is a functioning thing is necessarily a functioning thing. "A functioning thing" is a suitable predicate of an omniscient consciousness because an omniscient consciousness is a functioning thing, and it is an object of comprehension of such a consciousness; yet, this does not entail that all objects of comprehension by such consciousnesses are functioning things because such consciousnesses also comprehend permanent phenomena.

There are many such counterexamples. Any phenomenon mutually inclusive with functioning thing is suitable to show the lack of pervasion. Also, consciousness and the phenomena mutually inclusive with it, direct perceiver, valid cognizer, correct consciousness, non-mistaken consciousness, and so on may be posited here. An omniscient consciousness is an awareness, but it is not the case that whatever is an object of comprehension of such a consciousness is necessarily an awareness because an omniscient consciousness comprehends forms and so forth as well.

Also, there are many predicates that could be put into this statement that would *not* show the lack of pervasion. For instance, established base and any of the phenomena mutually inclusive with it seem to support the pervasion. It is true that whatever is an object of comprehension of an omniscient consciousness which is an established base is necessarily an established base. An omniscient consciousness is an established base, and whatever is its object of comprehension is also necessarily an established base.

The next debate in the Shar-dzay *Collected Topics* is:

> Also, if someone says, "Whatever is an object of comprehension of an omniscient consciousness which is not [it] is necessarily an existent which is not [it]," this is not correct because a permanent phenomenon is that.[1]

An omniscient consciousness is not a permanent phenomenon, so a permanent phenomenon is not a predicate of an omniscient consciousness. Yet, it is not the case that whatever is an object of comprehension of an omniscient consciousness which is not a permanent phenomenon is necessarily an existent which is not a permanent phenomenon. This is because omniscient consciousnesses do comprehend permanent phenomena, those things that are not existents which are not permanent phenomena.

Something which supports the pervasion—something which is both—is "not opposite from being an object of knowledge". Whatever is an object of comprehension of an omniscient consciousness which is not opposite from being an object of knowledge is necessarily an existent which is not opposite from being an object of knowledge. An omniscient consciousness is not opposite from being an object of knowledge because of being opposite from not being an object of knowledge since it is an object of knowledge. Also, whatever is an object of comprehension of an omniscient consciousness is necessarily not opposite from being an

---

[1] *Ibid.*, p. 26.

object of knowledge because whatever exists is necessarily an object of knowledge.

Mixing the principals of these two sample debates, it is interesting to ascertain the difference between the two, object of comprehension of an omniscient consciousness which is it (*yin par gyur pa'i rnam mkhyen gyi gzhal bya*) and object of comprehension of an omniscient consciousness which is not it (*ma yin par gyur pa'i rnam mkhyen gyi gzhal bya*). There are four possibilities between them:[1]

1   Something which is both is a definiendum. A definiendum is an object of comprehension of an omniscient consciousness which is it because (1) there is an omniscient consciousness which is it (i.e., a definiendum) and (2) this (omniscient consciousness) comprehends it (i.e., a definiendum). Specifically, an omniscient consciousness is a definiendum, as it is defined as:

> a final exalted wisdom which directly realizes all phenomena (*chos thams cad mngon sum du rtogs pa'i mthar thug pa'i ye shes*).

Also, since an omniscient consciousness comprehends a definiendum, a definiendum is an object of comprehension of an omniscient consciousness which is a definiendum.

Similarly, a definiendum is an object of comprehension of an omniscient consciousness which is *not* it because (1) there is an omniscient consciousness which is not it and (2) this (consciousness) comprehends it. More specifically, an omniscient consciousness which is not a definiendum is, for instance, a final exalted wisdom which directly realizes all phenomena. Thus, a definiendum is an object of comprehension of something which is an omniscient consciousness but, in turn, is not a definiendum but a definition.

2   Something which is an object of comprehension of an omniscient consciousness which is it but is not an object

---

[1] Denma Lochö Rinbochay, oral commentary.

of comprehension of an omniscient consciousness which is not it is an object of knowledge, a functioning thing, or a consciousness. An object of knowledge is an object of comprehension of an omniscient consciousness which is it because (1) there is an omniscient consciousness which is it and (2) this (consciousness) comprehends it. However, an object of knowledge is not an object of comprehension of an omniscient consciousness which is not it because there is no omniscient consciousness which is not an object of knowledge.

3 Something which is an object of comprehension of an omniscient consciousness which is not it but is not an object of comprehension of an omniscient consciousness which is it is a permanent phenomenon, a pot, or uncomposed space. A permanent phenomenon is an object of comprehension of an omniscient consciousness which is not it because (1) there is an omniscient consciousness which is not it and (2) this (consciousness) comprehends it. There is an omniscient consciousness which is not a permanent phenomenon because whatever is an omniscient consciousness is necessarily not a permanent phenomenon. Also, this omniscient consciousness, which is not a permanent phenomenon, comprehends a permanent phenomenon. A permanent phenomenon is not an object of comprehension of an omniscient consciousness which is it because there is no omniscient consciousness which is a permanent phenomenon.

4 Something which is neither is the child of a barren woman. The child of a barren woman is not an object of comprehension of an omniscient consciousness which is it because there is no omniscient consciousness which is the child of a barren woman. Also, it is not an object of comprehension of an omniscient consciousness which is not it because of not being an object of comprehension of an omniscient consciousness.

In debate D.4 the hypothetical Defender accepts that whatever is something which a permanent phenomenon is (*yin par gyur pa'i rtag pa*) is necessarily a permanent phenomenon. However, there is no pervasion, for there are things which are suitable predicates of a permanent phenomenon but are not themselves permanent phenomena. The Sūtra School Challenger gives the counterexample of only-a-permanent-phenomenon (*rtag pa kho na*). Only-a-permanent-phenomenon is something which a permanent phenomenon is—it is a predicate of a permanent phenomenon. Each and every permanent phenomenon is only a permanent phenomenon because it is not partially a permanent phenomenon and partially a functioning thing nor is it sometimes a permanent phenomenon and sometimes a functioning thing. Permanent phenomena are *only* permanent phenomena. Thus, only-a-permanent-phenomena is something which a permanent phenomenon is. However, only-a-permanent-phenomenon is not itself a permanent phenomenon because it is a non-existent. Only-a-permanent-phenomenon (or, translated more cogently in this context, only-permanent-phenomena) does (or do) not exist because functioning things exist too.

Similarly, only-functioning-things (*dngos po kho na*) do not exist because permanent phenomena exist. Only-a-pot does not exist, only-a-consciousness does not exist, only-a-form does not exist, and so forth. However, only-objects-of-knowledge do exist, only-established-bases exist, and so on. This is because nothing other than objects of knowledge exists. For anything which is an instance or a division of objects of knowledge, only-it does not exist because other phenomena exist as well.

One result of this situation is that, mirroring the phenomena of which being them is not possible, there are non-existents of which being them does exist (or is possible). There are four possibilities between existent and that of which being it is possible (*yin pa srid pa*):

1 Something which is both is a pot. A pot is an existent and it is something of which being it is possible because, for example, a gold pot is a pot.

2 Existents which are not something of which being them is possible are, for example, the two—a definition and a definiendum. The two—a definition and a definiendum—are objects of knowledge but there is nothing which is the two—a definition and a definiendum.

3 Something which is not an existent but is something of which being it is possible is only-a-permanent-phenomenon or only-a-functioning-thing. Being only a permanent phenomenon is possible because a permanent phenomenon is only a permanent phenomenon, but only-a-permanent-phenomenon itself does not exist.

4 Something which is neither is the horn of a rabbit. The horn of a rabbit does not exist, and it is not something of which being it is possible, for there is nothing which is the horn of a rabbit.

Also, there are three possibilities between object of knowledge of which being it is possible (*yid pa srid pa'i shes bya*) and that of which being it is possible (*yin pa srid pa*):[1]

1 Something which is both is a pot, a form, or any object of knowledge of which being it is possible.

2 Whatever is an object of knowledge of which being it is possible is necessarily something of which being it is possible. However, it is not the case that whatever is something of which being it is possible is necessarily an object of knowledge of which being it is possible. For instance, a non-existent and only-a-permanent-phenomenon are "things" of which being either of them is possible but are not objects of knowledge. A non-existent is something of which being it is possible because the horn of a rabbit, for instance, is a non-existent.

---

[1] Lati Rinbochay, oral commentary.

3   Something which is neither an object of knowledge of
which being it is possible nor something of which being
it is possible is the two—a pillar and a pot—or the horn
of a rabbit.

Corresponding to this, there are three possibilities
between objects of knowledge of which being them is not
possible (*yin pa mi srid pa'i shes bya*) and that of which being
it or them is not possible (*yin pa mi srid pa*):

1   Something which is both is the two—a permanent phenomenon and a functioning thing.
2   Whatever are objects of knowledge of which being them
is not possible are necessarily something of which being
them is not possible, but whatever is (or are) something
(or things) of which being it or them is not possible is (or
are) not necessarily objects of knowledge of which being
them is not possible. For instance, a self of persons is
something of which being it is not possible, but it is not
an object of knowledge.
3   Something which is neither is a pot.

> If someone [a hypothetical Defender] says,
> "Whatever is something which a permanent phe-
> nomenon is is necessarily a permanent phe-
> nomenon," [the Sūtra School Challenger responds to
> him,] "It [absurdly] follows that the subject, only-a-
> permanent-phenomenon, is a permanent phe-
> nomenon because of being something which a per-
> manent phenomenon is."
>
> If he says that the reason is not established, [the
> Sūtra School Challenger responds,] "It follows that
> the subject [only-a-permanent-phenomenon] is
> [something which a permanent phenomenon is]
> because of being both something which something
> is and a permanent phenomenon."

This is a very interesting consequence. According to Lati
Rinbochay, this reason must be understood as "because
being it is both something which is it and a permanent phe-

nomenon" (*khyod yin pa khyod yin pa dang rtag pa gnyis ka yin pa'i phyir*). He is explaining "being it" as an unstated grammatical subject within the reason. This is in order to give sense to a reason which is difficult to understand. This reason and the whole debate plays off the manner of verbalization. If the reason is provided with a grammatical subject, it is easier to understand.

In the interpreted reason the referent of "it" is "only-a-permanent-phenomenon". The reason means that being only a permanent phenomenon (*rtag pa kho na yin pa*) is both something which is only a permanent phenomenon and a permanent phenomenon. Whatever is a permanent phenomenon is necessarily only a permanent phenomenon; thus, being only a permanent phenomenon is something which exists. Being only a permanent phenomenon exists because, for instance, uncomposed space is only a permanent phenomenon. From among the two types of existents, being only a permanent phenomenon itself is a permanent phenomenon because it is only imputed by term or thought consciousness. Since being only a permanent phenomenon is a permanent phenomenon, it is itself—it is only a permanent phenomenon. Thus, being only a permanent phenomenon is both something which is only a permanent phenomenon and a permanent phenomenon.

Although the reason may be validly interpreted as Lati Rinbochay has suggested, it is not the way that the Sūtra School Challenger has phrased the reason. The Defender must answer according to the way in which it is stated, and as it stands there is no effective answer. The pervasion is definite, for whatever is both something which something is and a permanent phenomenon is necessarily something which a permanent phenomenon is. This is because whatever is both something which something is and a permanent phenomenon is necessarily a permanent phenomenon of which being it is possible, and whatever is a permanent phenomenon of which being it is possible is necessarily a common locus of (1) something of which being it exists and (2) also being a common locus which is a phenomenon and non-momentary. A permanent phenomenon of which being it is possible is something which a permanent phenomenon is because, for instance, object of knowledge is a permanent phenomenon of which being it is possible and all permanent phenomena are objects of knowledge.

In the text the Defender answers the above consequence by saying that the reason is not established. This looks better, but as the text shows, this too is not an effective answer. It seems as though the Challenger is saying that the subject, only-a-permanent-phenomenon, is both something which something is and a permanent phenomenon. Whereas it is easy enough to see that only-a-permanent-phenomenon is something which something is, it is certainly not a permanent phenomenon. The Defender would like to deny the second part of the reason alone, but the Challenger has constructed this reason as a single unit. If he had structured the reason in two parts saying, "Because of being (1) something which something is and (2) a permanent phenomenon", then the Defender could have answered effectively that the second part of the reason—that only-a-permanent-phenomenon is a permanent phenomenon—is not established. Indeed, in one sense only-permanent-phenomena (more sensibly phrased in this context) are permanent phenomena because functioning things and non-existents are not permanent phenomena, but only-a-permanent-phenomenon is a non-existent (and not a permanent phenomenon) because functioning things also exist. In any case, the Sūtra School Challenger has taken care not to divide the reason into two parts and thus allow this possible response. The Defender is left with only the option of denying the reason as a unit. This is the line that the text follows:

> If he says that the reason [that only-a-permanent-phenomenon is both something which something is and a permanent phenomenon] is not established, [the Sūtra School Challenger responds,] "It follows that [something] is both something which is only a

permanent phenomenon and a permanent phenomenon because of being a permanent phenomenon."

This is the most crucial consequence in the debate. There is a
difference between what the hypothetical Defender thinks
he is denying and the way in which the Sūtra School Challenger responds. The Defender, thinking correctly that only-
a-permanent-phenomenon is not a permanent phenomenon,
appropriately denies the reason, that only-a-permanent
phenomenon is both something which something is and a
permanent phenomenon. The Challenger responds on a
different note saying that something, unspecified here, is
both something which is only a permanent phenomenon
and a permanent phenomenon. The Challenger has very
cleverly removed the words "the subject" (*chos can*) from the
consequence and melded what was the subject, only-a-
permanent-phenomenon, into the predicate of the consequence. He has thereby radically altered the grammar of the
sentence. This move is what makes the entire debate possible. Otherwise, it seems that the former reason is
indefensible.

In general, the words "the subject" serve to specify the
basis of debate by separating it off. It is acceptable, however,
for the Challenger to remove the words "the subject" from a
consequence because the sentence will still make sense, and
in general it does not alter the grammar. For instance, if the
Defender says that the reason—that the color of a white
religious conch is a color—is not established, the Challenger
may respond to him, "It follows that the color of a white
religious conch is a color because of being white." In this
example the response is easy enough to understand and the
fundamental grammar of the sentence has not altered. "The
color of a white religious conch" is a subject in the
Defender's answer and it remains such in the Challenger's
response.

In the present consequence, when the Challenger
removed the words "the subject" from the response and

melded "only-a-permanent-phenomenon" into the predicate, he made possible a second, and quite different, interpretation of the grammar. In the Defender's answer "only-a-permanent-phenomenon" is the subject nominative of the predicate "is both something which something is and a permanent phenomenon". In the Challenger's response, as usual, this same interpretation of the grammar is possible, but it is evident from the subsequent consequences and from the favorability of another interpretation that the Challenger intends "only-a-permanent-phenomenon" to now be melded in with the predicate and be a part of that predicate. This is made possible by the fact that the old predicate had an open verb of being (*yin pa*), here translated as "something which something is", without any referent. By adding in the former subject, only-a-permanent-phenomenon, the Challenger produces a reference to "something which is only a permanent phenomenon". By this second interpretation, there is no grammatical subject of the predicate of the consequence and no logical subject of the consequence. "Something" unspecified is both something which is only a permanent phenomenon and a permanent phenomenon. Any permanent phenomenon qualifies as this, for whatever is a permanent phenomenon is necessarily only a permanent phenomenon.

Again, Lati Rinbochay points out that this consequence is to be understood as meaning that *being* only a permanent phenomenon is something which is only a permanent phenomenon and a permanent phenomenon (*rtag pa kho na yin pa rtag pa kho na yin pa dang rtag pa yin pa*). Still, the Defender must respond to what has been stated. He is thinking, according to the original interpretation of the grammar, that the Sūtra School Challenger is saying that only a permanent phenomenon is a permanent phenomenon; so, of course, he denies the establishment of the reason.

> If he says that the reason [that something is a permanent phenomenon] is not established, [the Sūtra School Challenger responds,] "It follows that

> [something] is a permanent phenomenon because of
> (1) being an existent and (2) not being a functioning
> thing."

The grammatical subject "something" is supplied in the English translation in order to give sense to the sentences; there is no corresponding word in the Tibetan original. The Defender would still hear this as applying to only-a-permanent-phenomenon, but here there is no subject at all nor even something which appears to be a subject. It is not that the Defender is slow to catch on, but that what the Challenger is reported to say here is a standard sort of abbreviation used in debate and thereby goes unnoticed.

Again there is no effective answer against this consequence. There is pervasion, for whatever (1) is an existent and (2) is not a functioning thing is necessarily a permanent phenomenon. Also, the Defender cannot successfully deny the reason. If he denies either the first part—that something is an existent—or the second part—that something is not a functioning thing, he may be held to the position that something is not an existent or that something is a functioning thing. Since the reason does not apply back to any subject, the Challenger can use the Defender's answers against him to posit unwanted consequences. This is precisely the pattern that the debate follows.

> The first part of the reason is easy. If he says that the
> second part of the reason is not established, [the
> Sūtra School Challenger responds,] "It follows that
> it is a functioning thing because of being a
> functioning thing."

When the hypothetical Defender denies that something is not a functioning thing, a logical consequence is that, according to his view, it is a functioning thing. It is not necessary for the Challenger always to prove the reasons that the Defender denies; he can give that denial back to the Defender in the form of a consequence, and then draw out the consequences of his opponent's position. Here the Challenger has provided a grammatical subject "it" (*khyod*) in his response. Now the Defender is on the skids. He has asserted that some unspecified thing is a functioning thing by denying that it is not a functioning thing. Thus, he cannot question either the pervasion or the establishment of the reason. He accepts the consequence.

> If he accepts [that it is a functioning thing, the Sūtra School Challenger responds] "It follows that there is a cause of it because it is a functioning thing."

If something is a functioning thing, then there necessarily is a cause of it. This is a consequence in accordance with the hypothetical Defender's position that it, the unspecified subject, is a functioning thing. The reason justifying the consequence is precisely what the Defender has just accepted, that it is a functioning thing.

> If he accepts [that there is a cause of it, the Sūtra School Challenger responds,] "It follows that it is produced from its cause because there is a cause of it."

Here "cause" refers to the necessary causes for something. If there is a cause of it, it is necessarily produced from its cause. Again, this consequence is in accordance with the Defender's position, and the reason is just what he has accepted, that there is a cause of it.

> If he accepts [that it is produced from its cause, the Sūtra School Challenger responds,] "It follows that it is the effect of its cause because it is produced from its cause."
>
> If he accepts [that it is the effect of its cause, the Sūtra School Challenger responds,] "It follows that it is related with its cause as that arisen from it because you accepted [that it is produced from its cause]."

The first chapter in "The Middling Path of Reasoning" is a presentation of mutually exclusive phenomena (*'gal ba, virodha*) and related phenomena (*'brel ba, saṃbandha*). There it is explained that the two types of related phenomena are (1) those related as that arisen from it (*de byung 'brel, tadutpatti-saṃbandha*) as an effect is related to its cause and (2) those related as the same essence (*bdag gcig 'brel, tādātmya-saṃbandha*) as a pot is related to functioning thing. Thus, in the last consequence the Sūtra School Challenger points out that, in accordance with the hypothetical Defender's acceptance that some unspecified subject is produced from its cause, it must be related with its cause as that arisen from it. Here the Challenger is still giving consequences that are in accordance with the Defender's position and justifying them with what he has accepted. In the last consequence the reason is simply, "Because you accepted it" (*'dod pa'i phyir*). This is a very common procedure; rather than spelling out what the Defender accepted, the Challenger simply refers to it.

> If he accepts [that it is related with its cause as that arisen from it, the Sūtra School Challenger responds,] "It follows that if there is no cause of it, it must not exist because it is related with its cause as that arisen from it."
>
> If he accepts [that if there is no cause of it, it must not exist, the Sūtra School Challenger responds,] "It [absurdly] follows with respect to the subject, object of knowledge, that it does not exist because there is no cause of it."

Now the ax has fallen. The Challenger has finally taken the hypothetical Defender's mistaken acceptance of qualities, apart from any basis for those qualities, and applied that acceptance to a opposing subject, object of knowledge. In the former consequence, it is true for any *impermanent* phenomenon that if there is no cause of it, then it must not exist because any impermanent phenomenon is related with its cause as that arisen from it. However, this does not apply to *permanent* phenomena such as object of knowledge, as they are not related causally to anything because they do not have any causes. Thus, the Challenger applies the hypothetical Defender's acceptance of a general rule to a basis of debate opposing his views. If what he accepted were true, then it would absurdly follow that no permanent phenomenon exists because there is no cause of a permanent phenomenon.

The procedure in this portion of debate D.4 is no different from the way in which most of the debates in this manual begin. A hypothetical Defender accepts a mistaken pervasion, and the Sūtra School Challenger flings back an unwanted consequence. In this case, however, the Challenger has led his opponent on quite a ways before pointing out his error. In an earlier reason, when the Defender denied the second portion of the reason—that something is not a functioning thing—he implicitly accepted that it is a functioning thing. At that point the Challenger could have thrown back the absurd consequence that uncomposed space is a composed phenomenon because of being a functioning thing, but instead he led his opponent on through several consequences.

> If he says that the reason is not established, [the Sūtra School Challenger responds,] "It follows with respect to the subject [object of knowledge] that [there is no cause of it] because it is a permanent phenomenon."
>
> If he accepts the basic consequence, [the Sūtra School Challenger responds,] "It [absurdly] follows that the subject, only-a-permanent-phenomenon, is an existent because of being a permanent phenomenon."

Usually in the debates in this manual when the Defender accepts the basic consequence, the Challenger moves to explain that he cannot accept that by giving a consequence proving the opposing view. However, whenever the Defender accepts something which is not accurate, the Challenger has the option of countering that view with an absurd consequence. Here the Challenger counters his opponent's acceptance of the basic consequence with another contradictory consequence. If he accepts that only-a-permanent-phenomenon is a permanent phenomenon, then it absurdly follows that only-a-permanent-phenomenon is an existent. This procedure may more closely reflect the normal strategy in debate. Rather than proving the opposite, the debaters tend to rely on the potency of contradictory consequences to influence the decisions of the opponent.

> If he accepts [that only-a-permanent-phenomenon is an existent, the Sūtra School Challenger responds,] "It follows that there is not only-a-permanent-phenomenon because functioning things exist."

If functioning things exist, then it could not be the case that only-a-permanent-phenomenon exists.

> If he says that the reason is not established, [the Sūtra School Challenger responds,] "It follows that functioning things exist because of being selfless."

This last consequence in debate D.4 is an interesting case of a reason with a verb of being (*yin pa*) proving a predicate with a verb of existence (*yod pa*). This is a consequence that one can know is accurate because there is nothing to harm it—that is, there is nothing that one can posit that will show it to be incorrect. The pervasion is that if something is selfless, then functioning things necessarily exist. There is no need to state a subject with this consequence because any existent or non-existent satisfies the requirement of the reason, being selfless, but none of them can show that functioning things do not exist. That functioning things exist is manifestly obvious.

There are at least two major points to be understood in debate D.4. One is that only-a-permanent-phenomenon is not an existent, only-a-functioning-thing is not an existent, only-a-pot is not an existent, and so on. This is important because one might feel to assert that only-a-permanent-phenomenon is, for instance, a generally characterized phenomena, whereas such cannot be held in debate.

The second major point is that one can alter the meaning of a consequence by manipulating the terms within that consequence. In general, this is a point that is easily understood. However, the trick played in the Tibetan original of debate D.4 cannot be translated as smoothly into English. This is because the verb in a Tibetan sentence comes at the end, often preceded by both a subject and a predicate in that order. Thus, just where the subject of a sentence ends and the predicate begins is not clearly demarcated by a verb as in an English sentence. By removing the words "the subject" (*chos can*) which frequently serve to set off the grammatical, as well as logical, subject of a consequence, the Challenger was able to alter the basic structure of the sentence to defeat his opponent. This second point is not as easily communicated in English; still, one must note that there is very little about the Collected Topics tradition of debate that is bound inextricably to either the cultures or languages of Eastern peoples.

The two principals of debate D.4, permanent phenomenon and something which a permanent phenomenon is (*yin par gyur pa'i rtag pa*), have four possibilities:

1   Something which is both is object of knowledge, established base, permanent phenomenon, uncomposed space, and so on. For instance, object of knowledge is a permanent phenomenon, and it is something which a permanent phenomenon is because of being both something which something is and a permanent phenomenon. Any permanent phenomenon is an object of knowledge.

2   Any permanent phenomena of which being them is not possible are permanent phenomena but are not something which a permanent phenomenon is. For instance, the two—a definition and a definiendum—are permanent phenomena because of being phenomena which are only imputed by a term or a thought consciousness and are not established as specifically characterized phenom-

ena. The two—a definition and a definiendum—are not something which a permanent phenomenon is because they are not both something which something is and a permanent phenomenon. This is because a common locus of being the two—a definition and a definiendum—and also being a permanent phenomenon does not exist. This, in turn, is because there is nothing which is the two—a definition and a definiendum. Whatever exists is necessarily not the two—a definition and a definiendum.

3 Only-a-permanent-phenomenon, only-a-generally-characterized-phenomenon, only-an-uncomposed-phenomenon, and so forth are not permanent phenomena but are "things" which a permanent phenomenon is. Only-a-permanent-phenomenon is something which a permanent phenomenon is because of being both something which something is and a permanent phenomenon. This is supported in the same way as in debate D.4. However, only-a-permanent-phenomenon is not a permanent phenomenon because of being a nonexistent.

4 Something which is neither is a functioning thing, a pot, the horn of a rabbit, and so on. A functioning thing, for instance, is not something which a permanent phenomenon is because of not being both something which something is and a permanent phenomenon. No permanent phenomenon is a functioning thing, and no functioning thing is a permanent phenomenon.

Debate D.5, Fifth Mistaken View (13b.6)

Debate D.5, like debate D.4, is drawn word for word from the section on the ancillary topic of what something is and what something is not in the Ra-dö *Collected Topics*.[1] Here the principals of debate are permanent phenomenon and something which a permanent phenomenon is not (*ma yin*

---

[1] Jam-ỹang-chok-hla-ö-ser, Ra-dö *Collected Topics*, 21a.2-5.

par gyur pa'i rtag pa). From understanding that there are four possibilities between permanent phenomenon and something which a permanent phenomenon is, one can understand that there are also four possibilities between the two principals of this debate. Thus, one cannot render a correct pervasion between them.

> If someone [a hypothetical Defender] says, "Whatever is something which a permanent phenomenon is not is necessarily a permanent phenomenon," [the Sūtra School Challenger responds to him] "It [absurdly] follows that the subject, a pillar, is [a permanent phenomenon] because of [being something which a permanent phenomenon is not]."
>
> If he says that the reason is not established, [the Sūtra School Challenger responds,] "It follows that the subject, a pillar, is [something which a permanent phenomenon is not] because of being both something which something is not and a permanent phenomenon."

This reason parallels exactly the corresponding one in debate D.4. Here it looks as though the Sūtra School Challenger is saying that a pillar is something which something is not and a permanent phenomenon. Obviously, a pillar is something which something is not because, for instance, a pot is not a pillar, but a pillar is not a permanent phenomenon. Even so, this reason may be supported in the same way that the corresponding one in debate D.4 was supported.

This reason too may be interpreted viably according to the way Lati Rinbochay suggested for the corresponding one in debate D.4. That is, if this reason is taken to mean "because being a pillar is both something which is not a pillar and a permanent phenomenon" *(ka ba yin pa ka ba ma yin pa dang rtag pa gnyis ka yin pa'i phyir),* this is sensible. *Being* a pillar is a permanent phenomenon because it is only imputed by a thought consciousness. *Pillars* are produced from causes and conditions, *being* a pillar is not. Since being a pillar is a permanent phenomenon, it is something which is not a pillar.

> If he says that the reason is not established, [the Sūtra School Challenger responds,] "It follows that [something] is both something which is not a pillar and is a permanent phenomenon because of being a common locus of something which is not a pillar and is a permanent phenomenon."

The strategy is just the same as before. The words "the subject" were taken out and the former subject, a pillar, was melded into the predicate of the consequence. Here an unspecified subject is justified as both something which is not a pillar and is a permanent phenomenon by the sign of being a common locus of something which is not a pillar and is a permanent phenomenon. Again, *being* a pillar is suitable as the unspecified subject, but any permanent phenomenon is something which is not a pillar and is a permanent phenomenon.

> If he says that the reason is not established, [the Sūtra School Challenger responds,] "It follows that [something is a common locus of something which is not a pillar and is a permanent phenomenon] because of being a permanent phenomenon."

Whatever is a permanent phenomenon is necessarily such a common locus. This debate could go on just as debate D.4 did. If the hypothetical Defender says that the reason is not established, the Challenger would be able to respond that it follows that something is a permanent phenomenon because of (1) being an existent and (2) not being a functioning thing. The debate might proceed from here in the same way. However, since that pattern was demonstrated in debate D.4, there is no need to reproduce it here; rather, the text moves to the hypothetical Defender's acceptance of the basic consequence.

> If he accepts the basic consequence, [the Sūtra School Challenger reports,] "It follows that the sub-

ject, a pillar, is not a permanent phenomenon because of being an impermanent phenomenon." The reason is easy.

As mentioned above, there are four possibilities between the two principals of debate D.5, permanent phenomenon and something which a permanent phenomenon is not (*ma yin par gyur pa'i rtag pa*):

1   Any permanent phenomenon of which being it is not possible is both something which a permanent phenomenon is not and also a permanent phenomenon. For instance, the two—a definition and a definiendum—are permanent phenomena because both definition and definiendum are individually permanent phenomena. Also, the two—a definition and a definiendum—are something which a permanent phenomenon is not because of not being both something which is not something and a permanent phenomenon since there is nothing which is a common locus of the two—a definition and a definiendum—and is also a permanent phenomenon. This, in turn, is because whatever exists is necessarily not the two—a definition and a definiendum.

2   Something which is not something which a permanent phenomenon is not but is a permanent phenomenon is object of knowledge. Object of knowledge is not something which a permanent phenomenon is not because of not being both something which something is not and a permanent phenomenon; this is because whatever exists is necessarily an object of knowledge.

3   Many subjects are not permanent phenomenon and also are not "things" which a permanent phenomenon is not—a pillar, the horn of a rabbit, a composed phenomenon, and so forth. This is proven in debate D.5.

4   Something which is neither something which a permanent phenomenon is not and also is not a permanent phenomenon is only-a-permanent-phenomenon. It is not something which a permanent phenomenon is not because whatever is a permanent phenomenon is neces-

sarily only a permanent phenomenon. Yet, only-a-permanent-phenomenon is not a permanent phenomenon.

Debate D.6, Sixth Mistaken View (14a.2)

In this debate, which does not appear in the Ra-dö *Collected Topics*, the hypothetical Defender accepts that whatever is selfless is necessarily not both suitable as an object of an awareness which is [it] and suitable as an object of an awareness which is not [it] (*yin par gyur pa'i blo'i yul du bya rung dang ma yin par gyur pa'i blo'i yul du bya rung*). This debate is similar to the sample ones above quoted from the Shar-dzay *Collected Topics* (see pp. 499-503). As in those debates, here the word "it" is supplied in brackets in place of the unspecified predicate, this being a predicate of "an awareness" and not necessarily a predicate of "that which is suitable as an object of an awareness", which is how the hypothetical Defender understands the unspecified predicate. Awarenesses share many qualities—they are objects of knowledge, established bases, functioning things, consciousnesses, knowers, and so on. The Defender is thinking that there is no quality which one awareness of an object could have and another awareness of the same object would not have. Could there be anything which is simultaneously both an object of an awareness which is it and is an object of an awareness which is not it?

> If someone [a hypothetical Defender] says, "Whatever is selfless is necessarily not both suitable as an object of an awareness which is [it] and suitable as an object of an awareness which is not [it]," [the Sūtra School Challenger responds to him,] "It [absurdly] follows that the subject, a definiendum, is [not both suitable as an object of an awareness which is it and suitable as an object of an awareness which is not it] because of [being selfless]."

Whatever exists is necessarily suitable as an object of an awareness (*blo, buddhi*) because whatever exists is necessarily an object of knowledge and that which is suitable as an object of an awareness is the definition of an object of knowledge. Thus, a definiendum is suitable as an object of an awareness. Moreover, a definiendum, or any existent, is suitable as an object of an awareness which is a definiendum because an *awareness* itself is a definiendum and whatever exists is suitable as an object of an awareness. Also, a definiendum is suitable as an object of an awareness which is not a definiendum because whatever exists may be said to be suitable as an object of a *knower* (*rig pa, saṃvedana*) and, since a knower is the definition of an awareness, it is not a definiendum.

> The reason is easy. If he accepts [the basic consequence, the Sūtra School Challenger responds,] "It follows that the subject, a definiendum, is both suitable as an object of an awareness which is [it] and suitable as an object of an awareness which is not [it] because of (1) being the first and (2) also being the second."

The above reason, that a definiendum is selfless, is easy because any existent or non-existent is selfless. Here the text says simply, "if he accepts", and does not need to specify that the hypothetical Defender is accepting the basic consequence because there is no line of reasoning supporting the establishment of the reason of the basic consequence. Rather, the text goes directly to the branch of the debate developing out of the Defender's accepting the basic consequence.

> If he says that the first part of the reason is not established, [the Sūtra School Challenger responds,] "It follows that [a definiendum] is suitable as an object of an awareness which is a definiendum because of (1) being suitable as an object of an awareness and (2) an awareness is a definiendum."

If he says that the second part of the above reason is not established, [the Sūtra School Challenger responds,] "It follows that [a definiendum] is suitable as an object of an awareness which is not a definiendum because of being suitable as an object of an awareness which is a definition."

"It follows that it is so because of (1) being suitable as an object of a knower and (2) a knower is the definition of an awareness."

The Sūtra School Challenger also might have given the reason, "because of (1) being suitable as an object of the clear and knowing (*gsal zhing rig pa*) and (2) the clear and knowing is the definition of a consciousness (*shes pa, jñāna*)". Awareness, knower, consciousness, and the clear and knowing are all mutually inclusive. Thus, whatever exists is necessarily suitable as an object of an awareness, a knower, a consciousness, or the clear and knowing.

The two principals of debate D.6, the selfless and what is not both suitable as an object of an awareness which is it and suitable as an object of an awareness which is not it, have three possibilities without there being something which is neither:

1 Something which is both is a functioning thing, which is selfless because of being an existent. It is not both suitable as an object of an awareness which is a functioning thing and suitable as an object of an awareness which is not a functioning thing because of not being suitable as an object of an awareness which is not a functioning thing, for there is no awareness which is not a functioning thing.

2 Whatever is not both suitable as an object of an awareness which is it and suitable as an object of an awareness which is not it is necessarily selfless. However, it is not the case that whatever is selfless is necessarily not both suitable as an object of an awareness which is it and suitable as an object of an awareness which is not it. For instance, a definition or a definiendum is selfless but

either is also both suitable as an object of an awareness which is it and suitable as an object of an awareness which is not it.

3   There is nothing which is neither because there is nothing that one can posit which is not selfless.

Perhaps more interesting than the comparison of the two principals of debate D.6 is that of the two, suitable as an object of an awareness which is it and suitable as an object of an awareness which is not it, which have four possibilities:

1   Something which is both is a definition, a definiendum, or a thought consciousness. A thought consciousness is suitable as an object of an awareness which is it because whatever exists is suitable as an object of a thought consciousness, since whatever exists is necessarily a hidden phenomenon. Also, a thought consciousness is suitable as an object of an awareness which is not a thought consciousness because of being suitable as an object of an awareness which is a direct perceiver, for a thought consciousness is an impermanent phenomenon. A thought consciousness, as a consciousness, is an impermanent phenomenon, and impermanent phenomena are the appearing objects of direct perceivers.

2   Something which is suitable as an object of an awareness which is it but is not suitable as an object of an awareness which is not it is a functioning thing or a consciousness. A functioning thing is suitable as an object of an awareness which is a functioning thing because (1) there is an awareness which is a functioning thing and (2) this (awareness) realizes a functioning thing (*dngos po yin par gyur pa'i blo yod pa gang zhig 'di dngos po rtogs pa'i phyir*). However, nothing is suitable as an object of an awareness which is not a functioning thing because such an awareness does not exist.

3   Something which is suitable as an object of an awareness which is not it but is not suitable as an object of an awareness which is it is matter, a form, a permanent

phenomenon, or a non-associated compositional factor. For instance, a form is suitable as an object of an awareness which is not it because (1) there is an awareness which is not it and (2) this (awareness) realizes it. There is an awareness which is not a form because whatever is an awareness is necessarily not a form, and this awareness which is not a form realizes form. Thus, form is suitable as an object of an awareness which is not a form. However, a form is not suitable as an object of an awareness which is a form because there is no awareness which is a form.

4   Something which is neither is a non-existent. A non-existent is not suitable as an object of an awareness which is a non-existent because there is no awareness which is non-existent. A non-existent is also not suitable as an object of an awareness which is not a non-existent because a non-existent is not suitable as an object of an awareness.

PRESENTATION OF THE AUTHOR'S OWN SYSTEM OF OPPOSITE-FROM-BEING-SOMETHING AND OPPOSITE-FROM-NOT-BEING-SOMETHING (14A.5)

With respect to the second, [opposite-from-being-something and opposite-from-not-being-something] in our own system: The two, opposite-from-not-being-something and being something, are mutually inclusive. The two, opposite-from-being-something and not being something, are mutually inclusive. Even though one may stack up [the modifiers] "opposite-from-not-being", it is mutually inclusive with a single "opposite-from-not-being". An even number of [the modifiers] "opposite-from-being" is mutually inclusive with "opposite-from-not-being". If something has an odd number of [the modifiers] "opposite-from-being", it is mutually inclusive with a single "opposite-from-being".

DISPELLING OBJECTIONS TO THE AUTHOR'S SYSTEM OF
OPPOSITE-FROM-BEING-SOMETHING AND OPPOSITE-
FROM-NOT-BEING-SOMETHING (14B.1)

Debate D.7, First Objection (14b.1)

In this debate a hypothetical Challenger assails the author's
assertion that opposite-from-being-a-functioning-thing
(*dngos po ma yin pa las log pa*) is an impermanent phenomenon, a position which the Tutor holds in contrast to the
Go-mang *Collected Topics* (see p. 484).

> Someone [a hypothetical Challenger] might say, "It
> follows that opposite-from-not-being-a-functioning-
> thing is a permanent phenomenon because (1)
> opposite-from-not-being-a-functioning-thing does
> exist and (2) opposite-from-not-being-something is a
> permanent phenomenon." [To this the Sūtra School
> Defender responds,] "There is no pervasion."

It is true that opposite-from-not-being-a-functioning-thing
does exist and that opposite-from-not-being-something,
considered alone, is a permanent phenomenon. Still, this
does not necessarily entail that opposite-from-not-being-a-
functioning-thing is a permanent phenomenon. In the
Tutor's system, it is not a permanent phenomenon because
it is not merely imputed by a name or a thought but is an
object established from its own side.

> "[It follows that] the reason is established because
> the two, opposite-from-being-something and
> opposite-from-not-being-something, individually
> are permanent phenomena."

These two must be permanent phenomena because,
divorced from any basis, they are mere expressions of
names or mere imputations of thought consciousnesses. In
relation to a basis which is a permanent phenomenon, these

are permanent phenomena. Also, being, in general, is a permanent phenomenon because it is a mental abstraction and is not something that is produced. Similarly, existence is a permanent phenomenon because, although phenomena may come into existence and go out of existence, their existence is not something that is produced. Impermanent phenomena arise, abide, and disintegrate, but their existence does not fluctuate along with them. Indeed, there was a time before the cup existed and there will be a time after which it no longer exists, but so long as the cup remains, its existence exists without disintegrating.

Debate D.8, Second Objection (14b.2)

This last debate in the presentation of opposite-from-being-something and opposite-from-not-being-something has a hypothetical opponent challenging the author's view that being non-non-something (*ma yin pa ma yin pa*) and being something (*yin pa*) are mutually inclusive. The opponent feels that nothing could possibly both be non-non-something and also be something. He is claiming that, for instance, being a pot is not the same as being a non-non-pot.

> Also, someone [a hypothetical Challenger] might say, "It follows that the two, being non-non-something and being something, are not mutually inclusive because if something both is non-non-something and [also] is something, then anything would be possible." [To this the Sūtra School Defender responds, "The reason is not established."]
> "[It follows that] the reason [that if something both is non-non-something and is something, then anything would be possible] is not established because an object of knowledge is both a non-non-[object of knowledge] and [an object of knowledge]."

Being any object of knowledge of which being it is possible is mutually inclusive with being non-non-that object of knowledge. For example, if this rule is applied to a pot, being a pot is mutually inclusive with being a non-non-pot. This is an appeal to the simple equivalence between being something and being non-non-something. For objects of knowledge of which being them is not possible, such as the two—a gold pot and a copper pot, being them does not exist. Objects of knowledge of which being them does not exist are defined as objects of knowledge with respect to which being any of them does not exist. Thus, one cannot say that being the two—a gold pot and a copper pot—is mutually inclusive with being non-non-the two—a gold pot and a copper pot—because, as both of these "beings" are non-existents, they are not different phenomena. Still, for any object of knowledge of which being it is possible, this rule holds. Being it is mutually inclusive with being non-non-it.

> "It follows that [an object of knowledge is both a non-non-object of knowledge and an object of knowledge] because of (1) being a non-non-object of knowledge and (2) being an object of knowledge."

In the former consequence "an object of knowledge" served as the subject of the reason clause, "because an object of knowledge is both a non-non-object of knowledge and an object of knowledge". In the present supporting consequence, "an object of knowledge" still serves as the logical and grammatical subject of the predicate and reason. An object of knowledge *is* a non-non-object of knowledge and it is an object of knowledge.

> "Both reasons are individually established because of being an existent."

An object of knowledge is a non-non-object of knowledge because of being an existent, and an object of knowledge is an object of knowledge because of being an existent. Whatever exists is necessarily a non-non-object of knowledge, and whatever exists is necessarily an object of knowledge.

Even objects of knowledge of which being them is not possible are non-non-objects of knowledge and also are objects of knowledge because of being existents. *Being* the two—a pillar and a pot—does not exist, but the two—a pillar and a pot—do exist as non-non-objects of knowledge and as objects of knowledge.

REMARKS

To a great extent, "Opposite-From-Being-Something and Opposite-From-Not-Being-Something" has the least content of any chapter in "The Introductory Path of Reasoning". All of the debates in this chapter are verbal games. The first three debates, addressing the topics of opposite-from-being-something (*yin log*) and opposite-from-not-being-something (*min log*) proper, play on the simple combination of positive and negative modifiers. By carefully counting the modifiers, one can easily understand any such debate. Being something is the same as being opposite from not being that thing, not being something is the same as being opposite from being that thing, and so forth. The complexity of these debates is only in the length of their components. "Opposite-From-Being-Something and Opposite-From-Not-Being-Something" is renowned as "a ge-shay's shame".[1] Even though such a learned scholar has long since passed through the Collected Topics and has studied the vast and the profound, it is possible for a novice who is presently skilled in the debates using these modifiers to confuse and defeat his elder, if he loses count.

The debates on what something is (*yin gyur*) and what something is not (*min gyur*) too are verbal games. Rather than playing on lengthy configurations of positive and negative modifiers, these debates pose misleading questions such as, "Is anything suitable as an object of an awareness which is it?" The debates in this section communicate helpful information about the range of possible

---

[1] Lati Rinbochay, oral commentary.

interpretations of a phrase, a very important theme in debate, as well as about the nature of being something. For instance, debate D.6 points out that an *awareness*, which is itself a definiendum, may also ascertain a definiendum and that an awareness such as a *knower*, which is not itself a definiendum, may also ascertain a definiendum; yet, both an awareness and a knower are awarenesses. By putting tension on phrases such as through describing a thing which simultaneously is something and comprehends that same thing which it is, these debates coax the mind to a more complex level.

Thus, the main import of "Opposite-From-Being-Something and Opposite-From-Not-Being-Something" is communicated as a subliminal message. This chapter is not a rigorous and straightforward explanation of the nature of being according to the Collected Topics tradition, but all of the components introduced in this chapter focus in one way or another on the nature of being.

Finally, the fourth chapter has value as a contrast to the information presented in "Identifying Isolates". In that chapter, it was explained that, for example, pot itself is pot's isolate and that none of the other things which are pots are pot's isolate. This contrasts with what is said in this chapter—that *anything* which is a pot (a gold pot, non-non-pot, and so forth) is opposite from not being a pot. Through this contrast, "Opposite-From-Being-Something and Opposite-From-Not-Being-Something" marks the distinction between being something—in the sense of exemplifying a certain quality—and being one with something—in the sense of being precisely equivalent with that thing. Consequently, this chapter counter-balances and thereby supports the study of "Identifying Isolates".

12 The Introductory Presentation of Causes and Effects

INTRODUCTION

Buddha is revered as the one who discovered the causes and effects of the processes of suffering and liberation. In teaching the four noble truths Buddha identified the nature of cyclic existence, an effect, as only suffering and identified the causes of suffering as contaminated actions and afflictions—desire, hatred, and, the root of these, ignorance. Since suffering and cyclic existence are conditioned phenomena which arise in dependence on their causes and conditions, they are not merely adventitious or causeless and they do not arise due to the wish of some deity. As effects, when the causes of suffering and cyclic existence are removed, sufferings too will be ended.

Buddha also identified that there is a path, a cause, leading to the state of freedom from suffering and cyclic existence, this state of release being an effect. The path which causes one to achieve liberation is the wisdom directly realizing selflessness. This wisdom consciousness is the actual antidote to ignorance, the chief cause of suffering. It is a cause of release from the fever of cyclic existence, like a medicine which cures one of an ordinary illness.

The four noble truths are the essence of Buddha's doctrine and the source of all monastic studies.[1] Buddha identified the causes and effects to be abandoned, contaminated actions and afflictions being the causes and suffering being the effects. He taught the causes and effects to be adopted, the paths leading to liberation being the causes and the path of liberation being the effect. For this reason, the study of causes and effects is of quintessential importance in Buddhism.

In traditional monastic training, this study begins with "The Introductory Presentation of Causes and Effects" (*rgyu 'bras chung ngu*) in "The Introductory Path of Reasoning". Here the students learn the definitions and divisions of causes (*rgyu, hetu* or *kāraṇa*) and effects ('*bras bu, phala*) in a study that focuses on the time of arising, relation, and nature of these. In the Tutor's *Collected Topics*, this chapter also incorporates several debates focusing on the various types of sameness (*gcig, ekatva*) and difference (*tha dad, nānātva*) of phenomena. Beyond the study of causes and effects presented in "The Introductory Path of Reasoning", the Tutor's *Collected Topics* also includes "The Greater Presentation of Causes and Effects" (*rgyu 'bras che ba*), the fourth chapter in "The Middling Path of Reasoning", an extensive presentation of the topic.

Because of the importance of causes and effects in Buddhist doctrine, there are many passages in Buddhist literature which broach the topic. Some of the passages quoted in the Ra-dö *Collected Topics* at the beginning of "The Introductory Presentation of Causes and Effects" are the following. In the chapter on inference for oneself in Dharmakīrti's *Commentary on (Dignāga's) "Compendium of Valid Cognition"* it says:

---

[1] Geshé Rabten, *The Life and Teaching of Geshé Rabten, A Tibetan Lama's Search for Truth*, p. 14.

> As much as the nature of causes do not exist, so much
> so they do not arise.
> Effects are a reason [showing the presence of causes].[1]

Also, from that same source:

> ... is what is inferred as producing an effect from a
> collection of causes.[2]

Also:

> An effect of fire is smoke.[3]

And:

> From ascertaining the nature of causes, one ascertains
> the nature of effects.[4]

The presentation of causes and effects develops from these
and other passages.

The three—functioning thing, cause, and effect—are
mutually inclusive. Whatever is any of these is necessarily
both of the others; thus any impermanent phenomenon is
both a cause and an effect. For this reason, impermanent
phenomena are called "composed phenomena" (*'dus byas,
saṃskṛta*) because they are composed after the aggregation
of their causes and they are called "products" (*byas pa, kṛta*)
because they are effects produced from their causes. The
definition of a cause (*rgyu, hetu* or *kāraṇa*) is:

> a producer (*skyed byed, janaka*)

and the definition of an effect (*'bras bu, phala*) is:

> the produced (*bskyed bya, janya*).

Effects are objects produced from causes, their producers.
An example of any of the three—a functioning thing, a

---

[1] Dharmakīrti, *Commentary on (Dignāga's) "Compendium of Valid
Cognition"*, P5709, Vol. 130, 78.2.8.
[2] *Ibid.*, 78.3.3.
[3] *Ibid.*, 78.5.3.
[4] *Ibid.*, 82.4.4.

cause, or an effect—is a pot. A pot is a functioning thing because of being able to perform a function, chiefly the function of producing effects. It is a cause because of being a producer, for it produces the pot of the next moment, which is its own continuation, or, if broken, it produces the shards of a pot. A pot is an effect because of being that produced from its causes and conditions (*rkyen, pratyaya*)—clay, the pot of the former moment, and so forth. A cause is alternatively defined as:

a helper (*phan 'dogs byed*),

and an effect is alternatively defined as:

the object helped (*phan gdags bya*).

A cause is a helper in that it "helps" by producing effects, and an effect is the object helped because it is helped by its causes.

   These definitions and definienda may be added onto any impermanent basis. For instance, the definition of a cause of functioning thing (*dngos po'i rgyu*) is:

a producer of functioning thing (*dngos po'i skyed byed*).

An illustration is a pot which is a cause of functioning thing (*dngos po'i rgyur gyur pa'i bum pa*), a prior arising of functioning thing (*dngos po'i snga logs su byung ba*), or a substantial cause of functioning thing (*dngos po'i nyer len*). Even though *a pot which is a cause of functioning thing* is a cause of functioning thing, one cannot say that *a pot* is a cause of functioning thing. This is because a pot is not a different substantial entity (*rdzas tha dad*) from functioning thing but is the same substantial entity (*rdzas gcig, eka-dravya*) as functioning thing. A pot and functioning thing are the same substantial entity because they (1) appear to a direct perceiver and (2) do not appear separately.[1] A pot *is* a functioning thing and when a pot appears to a direct perceiver, its ability to perform a function also appears to a

---

[1] Lati Rinbochay, oral commentary.

direct perceiver. It is an instance of functioning thing (*dngos po'i bye brag*) and whatever is an instance of functioning thing is necessarily not a cause of functioning thing. Rather, one must specify that a pot *which is a cause of* functioning thing is a cause of functioning thing.

Within the context of this discussion, "functioning thing" is stated in the singular and without an article as in the phrases "a pot which is a cause of *functioning thing*", "a prior arising of *functioning thing*", "a different substantial entity from *functioning thing*", and "the same substantial entity as *functioning thing*". This form of expression, although at odds with normal English, must be used in order to communicate accurately the intention of the Collected Topics formulators without involving false implications. Other forms of expression would not be suitable. For example, it would not be suitable to refer to functioning thing in the plural as in the phrase "a pot which is a cause of *functioning things*" because this falsely suggests that there might be a pot which is a cause of each and every functioning thing, whereas such does not exist.

Also, if in this context "functioning thing" were supplied with an indefinite article "a", this too would be misleading, for "a pot which is a cause of *a functioning thing*" is suitable as a description of any pot. This is because each and every pot is a cause of *some* functioning thing—its own continuation of the next moment, shards, etc. Also, if one referred to a pot which is a cause of a functioning thing, since the phrase describes every pot, such a pot would be the same substantial entity as functioning thing and, thus, could not be a cause of functioning thing. However, these possible translations do not represent what is intended by such descriptions within the Collected Topics tradition. Rather, these phrases are meant to describe a pot which is a cause of the singular generality, functioning thing; something which is the same substantial entity as the singular generality, functioning thing; and so forth. Thus, within this context functioning thing is referred to in the singular and without an article in order to connote the singular generality—

functioning thing, understood from the point of view of its self-isolate. Still, as is seen in the translation and annotations, within certain other contexts it is suitable to refer to a cause of a functioning thing when the discussion focuses on issues that apply not only to functioning thing itself but to each and every functioning thing.

The definition of an effect of functioning thing (*dngos po'i 'bras bu*) is:

> that produced by functioning thing (*dngos po'i bskyed bya*).

An instance is a subsequent arising of functioning thing (*dngos po'i phyi logs su byung ba*), a pillar which is a subsequent arising of functioning thing (*dngos po'i phyi logs su byung ba'i ka ba*), or a pillar which is an effect of functioning thing (*dngos po'i 'bras bu su gyur pa'i ka ba*). Here again, one cannot say that *a pillar* is an effect of functioning thing because if it were, then a pillar and functioning thing would have to be different substantial entities. One must qualify the subject as *a pillar which is an effect of functioning thing.* There is a pillar which is an effect of functioning thing, and it is a different substantial entity from functioning thing because, although they both appear to direct perceivers, they appear separately. A pillar which is an effect of functioning thing does not and could not exist in the same moment as does functioning thing, its cause. Therefore, a pillar which is an effect of functioning thing *must* appear to a direct perceiver as separate from functioning thing. A pillar, on the other hand, exists at the same time as functioning thing, and does not appear as separate in the sense that a pillar's ability to perform a function *appears*, whether it is perceived or not, together with the pillar.

Although cause and effect in general are mutually inclusive, if these are applied to a specific basis, they are mutually exclusive. For instance, a particular pot's cause and its effect are mutually exclusive. Each of these is named in relation to the pot, which is on one hand the effect of the cause of a pot (*bum pa'i rgyu'i 'bras bu*) and on the other the cause of the effect of a pot (*bum pa'i bras bu'i rgyu*). The three—the cause of a pot, a pot, and the effect of a pot—exist sequentially. Once one has arisen, the earlier ones are no longer present and the later ones are not yet arisen. This is not to say that a pot's cause is necessarily not a pot, but that when a pot, as such, exists, then its causes are no longer present and its effects are not yet arisen. There is no time when the cause of a pot and its arising (*byung ba*), a pot, exist together. Nor is there a time when a pot and its effect exist together. Since a pot's cause and its effect do not exist simultaneously and there is nothing that one can posit which is both, they are mutually exclusive. A pot is not both because it is the effect of its cause and the cause of its effect; it is neither its own cause nor its own effect. This is true for any functioning thing.

Although a pot's cause and its effect, a pot, do not exist simultaneously, one cannot say in general that pot's cause and *pot* are mutually exclusive. Rather, there are four possibilities between these two:

1 Something which is both a cause of pot and a pot is a gold pot which is a cause of pot. A gold pot which is a cause of pot is a pot which existed in a former moment, and, because it is a producer of pot, it is a cause of the present pot. It is a pot because of being a bulbous flat-based phenomenon able to perform the function of holding water.
2 Something which is a pot but is not a cause of pot is a gold pot. A gold pot is not pot's cause because of not being a different substantial entity from pot.
3 Something which is a cause of pot but is not a pot is the clay which serves as a cause of a clay pot (*rdza bum gyi rgyur gyur ba'i 'jim pa*). Clay is not a pot because it is unable to perform the functions of a pot.
4 Something which is neither a pot nor pot's cause is a pillar, functioning thing, a cause of functioning thing, and so forth.

Similarly, the difference between pot and pot's effect is four possibilities:

1 Something which is both is a pot which is an effect of pot (*bum pa'i 'bras bu su gyur pa'i bum pa*).
2 Something which is a pot but is not an effect of pot is a gold pot or pot itself.
3 Something which is an effect of pot but is not a pot is an eye consciousness in the continuum of a person apprehending a pot. This is not to say that a pot is the only cause of such a consciousness but that it is one cause.
4 Something which is neither is the clay which is a cause of a pot.

Although a particular functioning thing such as pot, sound, and so forth may have four possibilities with its cause and with its effect, there are three possibilities between functioning thing itself and its cause and between it and its effect:

1 Something which is both a functioning thing and a cause of functioning thing is a prior arising of functioning thing, a functioning thing which is a cause of functioning thing, or a pillar which is a cause of functioning thing.
2 Whatever is a cause of functioning thing is necessarily a functioning thing. However, it is not the case that whatever is a functioning thing is necessarily a cause of functioning thing. For instance, an effect of functioning thing is a functioning thing but not a cause of functioning thing.
3 Something which is neither a functioning thing nor a cause of functioning thing is functioning thing's being, the existence of functioning thing, or opposite-from-being-a-functioning-thing.

Functioning thing also has three possibilities with functioning thing's effect:

1 Something which is both is a functioning thing which is an effect of functioning thing.
2 Whatever is an effect of functioning thing is necessarily a functioning thing, but whatever is a functioning thing is not necessarily an effect of functioning thing because functioning thing itself is a functioning thing but not an effect of functioning thing.
3 Something which is neither is a permanent phenomenon.

Any phenomenon mutually inclusive with functioning thing has three possibilities with its cause and with its effect. From among the instances of functioning thing, mostly those of which being them is possible—pot, sound, and so on—have four possibilities with their causes and with their effects. However, there are exceptions. For instance, functioning-thing-which-is-one-with-functioning-thing and the cause of functioning-thing-which-is-one-with-functioning-thing, do not have four possibilities but are mutually exclusive even though functioning-thing-which-is-one-with-functioning-thing is a functioning thing of which being it is possible.[1] This is because whatever is the functioning thing which is one with functioning thing is necessarily one with functioning thing, but whatever is a cause of functioning-thing-which-is-one-with-functioning-thing is necessarily different from functioning thing. Similarly, pillar-which-is-one-with-pillar and the cause of pillar-which-is-one-with-pillar are mutually exclusive, and so on for each functioning thing.

If two things are functioning things of which being them is *not* possible, then they and their cause are mutually exclusive. For instance, the two—a pillar and a pot—are mutually exclusive with the cause of the two—a pillar and a pot. As functioning things, there is a cause of the two—a pillar and a pot, but there is nothing which is both such a cause and also is the two—a pillar and a pot—because

---

[1] *Ibid.*

something which is the two—a pillar and a pot—does not exist. Similarly, the two—a pillar and a pot—are mutually exclusive with their effect.

DIRECT AND INDIRECT CAUSES AND EFFECTS

Causes may be divided into two types: direct causes (*dngos rgyu, sākṣhāt-kāraṇa*) and indirect causes (*brgyud rgyu, paramparya-kāraṇa*). The definition of a direct cause of functioning thing (*dngos po'i dngos rgyu*) is:

> a direct producer of functioning thing (*dngos po'i dngos su skyed byed*).

An illustration is a prior arising of functioning thing (*dngos po'i snga logs su byung pa*). The definition of an indirect cause of functioning thing (*dngos po'i brgyud rgyu*) is:

> an indirect producer of functioning thing (*dngos po'i brgyud nas skyed byed*).

An illustration is a prior arising of functioning thing's prior arising (*dngos po'i snga logs su byung ba'i snga logs su byung pa*). This is the functioning thing of two moments earlier which is a cause of functioning thing of the present. It is an indirect cause of functioning thing because, since it is separated from the present functioning thing by functioning thing's direct cause, it does not join functioning thing in the chronological sequence. Another illustration of an indirect cause of functioning thing is the prior arising of the prior arising of functioning thing's prior arising (*dngos po'i snga logs su byung ba'i snga logs su byung ba'i snga logs su byung ba*). Any prior arising of functioning thing which was two or more moments earlier is an indirect cause of functioning thing. In general, functioning thing's prior arising refers to any cause of functioning thing, both direct and indirect, because each of those causes arose prior to functioning thing; however, technically it refers to functioning thing's direct cause only.

Corresponding to this division of causes, effects too may be divided into two types: direct effects (*dngos 'bras, sākṣhāt-phala*) and indirect effects (*brgyud 'bras, paramparya-phala*). The definition of a direct effect of functioning thing (*dngos po'i dngos 'bras*) is:

> that produced directly by functioning thing (*dngos po'i dngos su bskyed bya*).

An illustration is a subsequent arising of functioning thing (*dngos po'i phyi logs su byung pa*). The definition of an indirect effect of functioning thing (*dngos po'i brgyud 'bras*) is:

> that produced indirectly by functioning thing (*dngos po'i brgyud nas bskyed bya*).

An illustration is a subsequent arising of functioning thing's subsequent arising (*dngos po'i phyi logs su byung ba'i phyi logs su byung ba*). As before, any subsequent arising of functioning thing which is not its direct effect is its indirect effect. The definitions and illustrations of direct and indirect causes and direct and indirect effects may be applied to all functioning things in the same way.

In general, direct cause and indirect cause are mutually inclusive, and, moreover, these two are mutually inclusive with cause. Whatever is a cause is necessarily both a direct cause and an indirect cause. Whatever is a direct cause is also necessarily an indirect cause. Any impermanent phenomenon is both a direct cause and an indirect cause. Also, the three—effect, direct effect, and indirect effect—are mutually inclusive. However, as in the case of cause and effect, when direct causes and direct effects are reckoned for a particular impermanent phenomenon or when direct effects and indirect effects are analyzed with a view to a particular phenomenon, they are mutually exclusive.

For instance, a common locus of functioning thing's direct cause and its indirect cause is not possible because whatever is functioning thing's direct cause is necessarily not its indirect cause and whatever is its indirect cause is necessarily not its direct cause. Still, in general whatever is a cause is necessarily both a direct cause and an indirect cause. Indeed, functioning thing's direct cause is also an indirect cause because it is the indirect cause of functioning thing's subsequent arising. And functioning thing's indirect cause is also a direct cause because it is the direct cause of functioning thing's direct cause. However, when direct and indirect causes are associated with a particular phenomenon, they are identified in relation to their effect such that there is no possibility of something's being both a direct and an indirect cause of that same effect because those causes could not exist simultaneously. When functioning thing's direct cause has arisen, its indirect cause has ceased. And when its indirect cause is present, its direct cause has not yet been produced. This situation also holds true for direct effects and indirect effects.

One of the complexities that comes in the presentation of causes and effects is in the descriptions of phenomena as causes and effects. As was suggested above, every impermanent phenomenon may be described in infinitely various ways in relation to its prior arisings and its subsequent arisings. For instance, a pot is the direct cause of a pot's subsequent arising, the indirect cause of a pot's subsequent arising's subsequent arising, a pot's prior arising's prior arising's subsequent arising's subsequent arising, the direct effect of a pot's prior arising, the indirect effect of a pot's prior arising's prior arising, a pot's subsequent arising's subsequent arising's prior arising's prior arising, and so on *ad infinitum*. The Ra-dö *Collected Topics* explains:

> Briefly, if something is a composed phenomenon, its prior arising is necessarily its direct cause, and although one may add on two or more, its prior arising's prior arising is necessarily its indirect cause. Similarly, if something is a composed phenomenon, its subsequent arising is necessarily its direct effect, and although one may add on two or more, its subsequent arising's subsequent arising is necessarily its indirect effect. If something is a composed phe-

nomenon, the time of a pair such as its prior arising's subsequent arising is necessarily simultaneous with it. If there is one prior arising more, then it is necessarily its cause. If there is one subsequent arising more, it is necessarily its effect.[1]

There are three possibilities between functioning thing and its direct cause, its indirect cause, its direct effect, and its indirect effect. For instance, for functioning thing and its direct cause:

1 Something which is both is a prior arising of functioning thing.
2 Whatever is a direct cause of functioning thing, or any of the other causes and effects of functioning thing, is necessarily a functioning thing. However, it is not the case that whatever is a functioning thing is necessarily a direct cause of functioning thing. For example, a pot, a person, functioning thing's prior arising's prior arising, a subsequent arising of functioning thing, or that which is simultaneous with functioning thing are all functioning things which are not direct causes of functioning thing.
3 Something which is neither a functioning thing nor a direct cause of functioning thing is any permanent phenomenon or any non-existent.

Functioning thing's comparison to its indirect cause, direct effect, and indirect effect may be understood from this example.

As before, although functioning thing itself has three possibilities with its cause and its effect, many of the instances of functioning thing have four possibilities with their direct and indirect causes as well as with their direct and indirect effects. For instance, there are four possibilities between tree and indirect cause of a tree:

1 Something which is both is a tree which is a tree's prior arising's prior arising. The main function performed by

---

[1] Jam-ȳang-chok-hla-ö-ser, Ra-dö *Collected Topics*, 27a.3-7.

a tree is the production of the effect which is its own continuation. The tree of the present moment is produced from the tree of the last moment and is the continuation of the substantial entity of that prior tree.

2   Something which is a tree but is not an indirect cause of a tree is a tree's prior arising, which is its direct cause.

3   Something which is a tree's indirect cause but is not a tree is an acorn which is a cause of a tree; this is an indirect cause of a tree because of being the indirect cause of an oak tree.

4   Something which is neither is a subsequent arising of a leaf.

SUBSTANTIAL CAUSES AND COOPERATIVE CONDITIONS

In "The Introductory Presentation of Causes and Effects", causes are also divided into substantial causes (*nyer len, upādāna*) and cooperative conditions (*lhan cig byed rkyen, sahakāri-pratyaya*). The definition of a substantial cause of functioning thing (*dngos po'i nyer len*) is:

> that which is a main producer of functioning thing as a continuation of its own substantial entity (*dngos po rang gi rdzas rgyun du gtso bor skyed byed*).

An illustration is a product which is functioning thing's cause (*dngos po'i rgyur gyur pa'i byas pa*). The definition of a cooperative condition of functioning thing (*dngos po'i lhan cig byed rkyen*) is:

> that which is a main producer of functioning thing as a substantial entity which is not a continuation of its own substantial entity (*dngos po rang gi rdzas rgyun ma yin par rdzas su gtso bor skyed byed*).

An illustration is a person who is a cause of functioning thing (*dngos po'i rgyur gyur pa'i gang zag*).

A substantial cause is the very substance out of which a functioning thing is produced. "It is a cause which is suitable to assume the entity of its effect."[1] The substantial cause of a clay pot is the clay which is a clay pot's cause, for clay is a main producer of a clay pot as a continuation of its own substantial entity. The substantial cause of a tree is a tree which is the prior arising of a tree or an acorn which is a cause of a tree. The tree grows out of its seed, which is a main producer of a tree as a continuation of its own substantial entity. The substantial cause of a consciousness is a former moment of a consciousness which serves as a cause of a consciousness. The substantial cause of functioning thing must be a functioning thing which is a cause of functioning thing, a product which is a cause of functioning thing, or any phenomenon mutually inclusive with functioning thing qualified as being a cause of functioning thing. A pillar which is a cause of functioning thing is not a substantial cause of functioning thing because functioning thing itself is not the continuation of the substantial entity of a pillar. A pillar which is a cause of functioning thing must be a cooperative condition of functioning thing.

A cooperative condition is something which accompanies and assists the substantial cause. "It is not suitable to assume the entity of its effect, but is a cause which helps, or benefits, that effect."[2] A cooperative condition of a clay pot is, for example, a person who produces a clay pot. Such a person is a main producer of a clay pot as a substantial entity which is not a continuation of his or her own substantial entity. A person molds the clay into a pot, but a pot is not a continuation of the person's substantial entity. Also, a cooperative condition of an eye consciousness apprehending blue is, for instance, the color blue or the eye sense power. An external color or shape and the eye sense power accompany and assist the substantial cause of an eye consciousness, a former moment of consciousness, to produce together an eye consciousness apprehending a visible form.

---

[1] Denma Lochö Rinbochay, oral commentary.
[2] *Ibid.*

Lati Rinbochay explains that in terms of the person, the substantial cause of one's own human body is the semen and blood (*khu khrag, rasa-rakta*) of the father and mother.[1] The father's semen and the mother's blood, or egg, form together to produce the zygote, the basis out of which one's own human body has developed. A cooperative condition of one's human body is an accumulated action of a former lifetime which impelled the body of this lifetime. In order to be reborn as a human it is necessary to have accumulated an action of ethics (*tshul khrims, shīla*) in a former lifetime. This is the meaning of the passage in Nāgārjuna's *Precious Garland of Advice for the King* (*rājaparikathā-ratnamālā*) which says: "From giving, resources [arise]; from ethics, a happy [migration arises]."[2] By accumulating an action of giving (*sbyin pa, dāna*) one is able to gain resources whereas by accumulating an action of ethics, one is able to gain rebirth in a happy migration (*bde 'gro, sugati*) as a human, demigod, or god. The substantial causes of one's human mind of this lifetime is the mind of a former lifetime in one's own continuum. The substantial cause of the mind of a former lifetime is the mind of a still earlier lifetime. A cooperative condition of the mind of this lifetime is an action of a former lifetime or one's father and mother. "Buddha said, 'Look at your present body to determine what you did in the past. Look at your present mind to determine what will come in the future.' "[3] In the Buddhist view, one's body, resources, environment, and so forth are arisen through past actions, and what these will be in the future will arise due to present actions, these actions being engendered in the mind.

In general, cooperative condition is mutually inclusive with cause, direct cause, indirect cause, functioning thing,

---

[1] Lati Rinbochay, oral commentary.

[2] Nāgārjuna, *The Precious Garland of Advice for the King*, in Nagarjuna and Kaysang Gyatso, the Seventh Dalai Lama, *The Precious Garland* and *The Song of the Four Mindfulnesses*, stanza 438, p. 83.

[3] *Meditations of a Tibetan Tantric Abbot: Kensur Lekden*, trans. and ed. by Jeffrey Hopkins (Dharamsala, India: Library of Tibetan Works and Archives, 1974), pp. 39-40.

effect, direct effect, and indirect effect. However, as shown in debate E.9, substantial cause is not mutually inclusive with cause and so on. This is because it is not the case that whatever is a cause is necessarily a substantial cause. For instance, a flame in its final moment is a cause because of being a functioning thing; it is a cooperative condition of smoke. However, a flame in its last moment is not a substantial cause because the continuation of its substantial entity is about to be severed. It does not produce a flame of a later moment. Thus, rather than being mutually inclusive, there are three possibilities between substantial cause and cause, cooperative condition, and so forth.

The nature of functioning things as impermanent phenomena is clear. If wood is burned, its nature of coarse impermanence is quickly revealed. A pot may easily be broken, showing its coarse impermanence. Reflecting this nature of caused phenomena, the Collected Topics logicians assert that whatever is a cause is not necessarily a substantial cause, for the continuum of an impermanent phenomena may be severed. If substantial cause were mutually inclusive with cause, this would imply that, once produced, a phenomenon would continue to abide in the same type and its continuum would not end.

Every impermanent phenomenon is a cooperative condition because, though its substantial continuum may cease, it nonetheless does have an effect on an impermanent phenomenon of a different substantial continuum. The division of causes into substantial causes and cooperative conditions focuses on the interdependence of functioning things and shows the limits of what it means to assert all impermanent phenomena as causes.

Reckoned in relation to a particular impermanent phenomenon, the substantial causes and cooperative conditions of that phenomenon are mutually exclusive. For instance, the substantial causes of a book are paper and ink, whereas the cooperative conditions are the author, the typesetter, the presses, the person who delivers the paper to the presses, and so forth. There can be nothing which is both a book's substantial cause and its cooperative condition.

Lati Rinbochay points out that the direct causes of a functioning thing may be divided into its direct substantial causes (*dngos po'i dngos kyi nyer len*) and its direct cooperative conditions (*dngos po'i dngos kyi lhan cig byed rkyen*). Similarly, the indirect causes of a functioning thing may be divided into its indirect substantial causes (*dngos po'i brgyud kyi nyer len*) and its indirect cooperative conditions (*dngos po'i brgyud kyi lhan cig byed rkyen*). Once this is the case, the substantial causes of a functioning thing may be divided into its direct substantial causes and its indirect substantial causes. The cooperative conditions of a functioning thing may be divided into its direct cooperative conditions and its indirect cooperative conditions. These divisions may be applied similarly to any impermanent phenomenon.

Because there are these divisions, one can understand that there are four possibilities between a functioning thing's substantial cause and its direct cause, between its substantial cause and its indirect cause, between its cooperative condition and its direct cause, and between its cooperative condition and its indirect cause.

Denma Lochö Rinbochay gives the example of the comparison of a clay pot's substantial cause and its direct cause:[1]

1 Something which is both is the clay which is the cause of a clay pot (*rdza bum gyi rgyur gyur pa'i 'jim pa*). This is a clay pot's direct cause because of being a direct producer of a clay pot. It is a clay pot's substantial cause because of being a main producer of a clay pot as a continuation of its own substantial entity.

2 Something which is a clay pot's direct cause but is not its substantial cause is a person who makes a clay pot (*rdza bum bzo ba po'i gang zag*). Such a person is a direct producer of a clay pot, but not a clay pot's substantial cause because of not being suitable to assume the entity of a clay pot.

---

[1] Denma Lochö Rinbochay, oral commentary.

3 Something which is a clay pot's substantial cause but not its direct cause is the dry clay which is a cause of a clay pot (*rdza bum gyi rgyur gyur pa'i sa skam po*). A clay pot is the continuation of the substantial entity of the dry clay which is its cause, but dry clay is not a direct producer of a clay pot because water must be added to the clay before it can be molded into a pot.

4 Something which is neither is a gold pot.

Also, there are four possibilities between a clay pot's substantial cause and its indirect cause:[1]

1 Something which is both is the dry clay which is a cause of a clay pot.

2 Something which is a clay pot's substantial cause but is not its indirect cause is the clay which is a cause of a clay pot.

3 Something which is a clay pot's indirect cause but is not its substantial cause is a pickax used to dig the clay which is a cause of a clay pot (*rdza bum gyi rgyur pa'i sa sko byed kyi 'jor*).

4 Something which is neither is the hand of a person who makes a clay pot (*rdza bum gyi bzo ba po'i lag pa*) or a person who makes a clay pot, both of which are direct cooperative conditions of a clay pot.

REFUTATION OF MISTAKEN VIEWS CONCERNING [TOPICS OF] "THE INTRODUCTORY PRESENTATION OF CAUSES AND EFFECTS" (14B.4)

This first section of "The Introductory Presentation of Causes and Effects" consists of thirteen debates, ten focusing on causes and effects proper and three focusing on the various types of sameness and difference. Several of these debates are paraphrasings of debates found in the Ra-dö *Collected Topics* and the Go-mang *Collected Topics*.

---

[1] *Ibid.*

Debate E.1, First Mistaken View (14b.4)

In the first debate the hypothetical Defender accepts that whatever is an established base is necessarily either a cause or an effect. This debate primarily serves to make clear in the beginning that only impermanent phenomena are causes and effects and permanent phenomena are not.

> If someone [a hypothetical Defender] says, "Whatever is an established base is necessarily either a cause or an effect," [the Sūtra School Challenger responds to him,] "It [absurdly] follows that the subject, object of knowledge, is [either a cause or an effect] because of [being an established base]."
>
> If he says that the reason is not established, [the Sūtra School Challenger responds,] "It follows that the subject [object of knowledge] is [an established base] because of being established by a valid cognizer."
>
> If he accepts the basic consequence, [the Sūtra School Challenger responds,] "It follows that the subject [object of knowledge] is neither a cause nor an effect because of not being a functioning thing."
>
> If he says that the reason is not established, [the Sūtra School Challenger responds,] "It follows that the subject [object of knowledge] is [not a functioning thing] because of being a permanent phenomenon."

There are three possibilities between the two principals of debate E.1, established base and either a cause or an effect:

1 Something which is both is a pot, a consciousness, a moment, or any other functioning thing.
2 Whatever is either a cause or an effect is necessarily an established base, but whatever is an established base is not necessarily either a cause or an effect. This is because

any permanent phenomenon is an established base but is neither a cause nor an effect.

3 Something which is neither is a non-existent.

Debate E.2, Second Mistaken View (14b.5)

In the second debate, which is modeled on a debate in the Ra-dö *Collected Topics*,[1] the hypothetical Defender accepts that whatever is a cause is necessarily not an effect. On first glance, this seems a reasonable view. One might think that cause and effect are mutually exclusive. However, within the Collected Topics presentation of causes and effects, since cause and effect are mutually inclusive, whatever is either of them is necessarily both.

The Sūtra School Challenger uses the counterexample of a functioning thing to refute the Defender's acceptance that whatever is a cause is necessarily not an effect, for any functioning thing is both a cause and an effect. "A functioning thing" is the predominant subject in the debates of "The Introductory Presentation of Causes and Effects". *Within the contexts of these debates*, it is suitable to translate *"dngos po"* as "a functioning thing", supplying an indefinite article "a", because the points raised in these debates apply equally to each and every functioning thing and are not limited to the singular, functioning thing, as such. As in this debate, *each and every* functioning thing is both a cause and an effect; thus, it is suitable to render the subject as "a functioning thing" in order to show that it is not the case that whatever is a cause is necessarily not an effect. There is evidence that the subject is always referred to from the point of view of its self-isolate, as the singular functioning thing and so forth; however, if, within the context of the particular debate, what is being said applies to each and every case of the subject and not to just the singular entity, then, in order to show the general application, the subject is supplied with an indefi-

---

[1] Jam-ÿang-chok-hla-ö-ser, Ra-dö *Collected Topics*, 23b.5-24a.2.

nite article. This procedure is followed throughout the translation.

> If someone [a hypothetical Defender] says, "Whatever is a cause is necessarily not an effect," [the Sūtra School Challenger responds to him,] "It [absurdly] follows that the subject, a functioning thing, is [not an effect] because of [being a cause]. You asserted the pervasion."
>
> If he says that the reason is not established, [the Sūtra School Challenger responds,] "It follows that the subject [a functioning thing] is [a cause] because there is an effect of it."
>
> If he says that the reason is not established, [the Sūtra School Challenger responds,] "It follows with respect to the subject [a functioning thing] that [there is an effect of it] because a functioning thing's subsequent arising is an effect of it."

Of course, a functioning thing's subsequent arising's subsequent arising is also an effect of a functioning thing because it is its indirect effect, but the Sūtra School Challenger needs only mention one effect of a functioning thing in order to show that it has an effect.

> If he says that the reason is not established, [the Sūtra School Challenger responds,] "It follows with respect to the subject [a functioning thing] that its subsequent arising is an effect of it because it is a composed phenomenon."
>
> If he accepts the basic consequence, [the Sūtra School Challenger responds,] "It follows that the subject [a functioning thing] is an effect because there is a cause of it."
>
> If he says that the reason is not established, [the Sūtra School Challenger responds,] "It follows with respect to the subject [a functioning thing] that [there is a cause of it] because its prior arising is a cause of it."

As before, the Sūtra School Challenger also might have said that its prior arising's prior arising is a cause of a functioning thing because of being its indirect cause. In any case, there is a cause of a functioning thing, and a functioning thing is an effect.

> If he says that the reason is not established, [the Sūtra School Challenger responds,] "It follows with respect to the subject [a functioning thing] that [its prior arising is a cause of it] because it is a functioning thing."

The two principals of this debate, cause and what is not an effect or non-effect, are mutually exclusive. In general, cause and effect are mutually inclusive; thus, whatever is a cause is necessarily an effect and whatever is not an effect is necessarily not a cause. A common locus of a cause and a non-effect is not possible.

Debate E.3, Third Mistaken View (15a.2)

In this debate, the hypothetical Defender asserts that whatever is a direct cause is necessarily not an indirect cause. Again, at first glance this seems a sensible view. However, it is only within the context of a particular impermanent phenomenon's causes that the direct cause of that phenomenon is necessarily not its indirect cause. Like cause and effect in general, direct cause and indirect cause are mutually inclusive, and they are both mutually inclusive with cause, effect, and functioning thing.

> If someone [a hypothetical Defender] says, "Whatever is a direct cause is necessarily not an indirect cause," [the Sūtra School Challenger responds to him,] "It [absurdly] follows that the subject, a functioning thing, is [not an indirect cause] because of [being a direct cause]."

> If he says that the reason is not established, [the
> Sūtra School Challenger responds,] "It follows that
> the subject [a functioning thing] is [a direct cause]
> because of being a direct cause of a functioning
> thing's subsequent arising."

In this debate the Tutor Jam-b̄a-gya-tso is showing how one
can work the description of an impermanent phenomenon
to show that any of them are causes, effects, direct causes,
indirect causes, and so on.

> If he says that the reason is not established, [the
> Sūtra School Challenger responds,] "It follows with
> respect to the subject [a functioning thing] that it is a
> direct cause of its subsequent arising because it is a
> functioning thing."
>
> If he accepts the basic consequence, [the Sūtra
> School Challenger responds,] "It follows that the
> subject [a functioning thing] is an indirect cause
> because of being an indirect cause of a functioning
> thing's subsequent arising's subsequent arising."
>
> If he says that the reason is not established, [the
> Sūtra School Challenger responds,] "It follows with
> respect to the subject [a functioning thing] that it is
> an indirect cause of its subsequent arising's subse-
> quent arising because it is a composed phe-
> nomenon."

The two principals of this debate, direct cause and what is
not an indirect cause, are mutually exclusive. Since direct
cause and indirect cause on their own are mutually inclusive, direct cause and what is not an indirect cause must be
mutually exclusive. A common locus which is a direct cause
but is not an indirect cause is not possible because whatever
is a direct cause is necessarily an indirect cause and whatever is not an indirect cause is necessarily not a direct cause.

Debate E.4, Fourth Mistaken View (15a.4)

In the fourth debate the hypothetical Defender asserts that whatever is a direct effect is necessarily not an indirect effect. This debate is not substantially different from the last two debates. Direct effect and indirect effect are mutually inclusive with each other and each is mutually inclusive with cause, effect, and functioning thing. Whatever is a direct effect is necessarily an indirect effect.

> If someone [a hypothetical Defender] says, "Whatever is a direct effect is necessarily not an indirect effect," [the Sūtra School Challenger responds to him,] "It [absurdly] follows that the subject, a functioning thing, is [not an indirect effect] because of [being a direct effect]."
>
> If he says that the reason is not established, [the Sūtra School Challenger responds,] "It follows that the subject [a functioning thing] is [a direct effect] because of being a direct effect of a functioning thing's prior arising."
>
> If he says that the reason is not established, [the Sūtra School Challenger responds,] "It follows with respect to the subject [a functioning thing] that it is a direct effect of its prior arising because it is a product."
>
> If he accepts the basic consequence, [the Sūtra School Challenger responds,] "It follows that the subject [a functioning thing] is an indirect effect because of being an indirect effect of a functioning thing's prior arising's prior arising."
>
> If he says that the reason is not established, [the Sūtra School Challenger responds,] "It follows with respect to the subject [a functioning thing] that it is an indirect effect of its prior arising's prior arising because it is a composed phenomenon."

Since the two, direct effect and indirect effect, are mutually inclusive, the two principals of debate E.4, direct effect and what is not an indirect effect, are mutually exclusive.

Debate E.5, Fifth Mistaken View (15a.6)

In this debate, modeled after a debate in the Ra-dö *Collected Topics*,[1] the hypothetical Defender accepts that whatever is a cause of functioning thing is necessarily a direct cause of functioning thing. Of course, this is not true because an indirect cause of functioning thing is a cause of it but not its direct cause.

> If someone [a hypothetical Defender] says, "Whatever is a cause of functioning thing is necessarily a direct cause of functioning thing," [the Sūtra School Challenger responds to him,] "It [absurdly] follows that the subject, functioning thing's prior arising's prior arising, is [a direct cause of functioning thing] because of being [a cause of functioning thing]. You asserted the pervasion."

Within the context of this debate, it is necessary to translate the subject as "functioning thing" rather than "a functioning thing". If the above pervasion were rendered as, "Whatever is a cause of a functioning thing is necessarily a direct cause of a functioning thing," then the hypothetical Defender would be correct to accept it. This is because whatever is a cause of a functioning thing is a direct cause of that cause's own direct effect, even though the functioning thing of which that is a cause and the functioning thing which is its direct effect may be different. In other words, any cause is a cause of a functioning thing and also is a direct cause of a functioning thing; however, those functioning things which it causes may be different. Also, if the subject were "a functioning thing" rather than "functioning thing", then the hypothetical Defender would be correct to accept the conse-

---

[1] *Ibid.*, 24a.2-5.

quence that a functioning thing's prior arising's prior arising is a direct cause of a functioning thing, for a functioning thing's prior arising's prior arising is a direct cause of that functioning thing's prior arising. Thus, in this debate the subject is stated as "functioning thing" in order to specify the causal sequence for a particular phenomenon, thereby emphasizing the particular rather than the general application.

> If he says that the reason is not established, [the Sūtra School Challenger responds,] "It follows that the subject [functioning thing's prior arising's prior arising] is [a cause of functioning thing] because of being a prior arising of functioning thing."

Here the Sūtra School Challenger is calling functioning thing's prior arising's prior arising, which is an indirect cause, by the name of what is a direct cause, a prior arising of functioning thing. This is the general use of the term "prior arising" to refer to any cause. Whatever is a prior arising of functioning thing is necessarily a cause of functioning thing. Even an indirect cause is a prior arising.

> If he accepts the basic consequence, [the Sūtra School Challenger responds,] "It follows that the subject [functioning thing's prior arising's prior arising] is not a direct cause of functioning thing because of being an indirect cause of functioning thing."
> If he says that the reason is not established, [the Sūtra School Challenger responds,] "It follows that the subject [functioning thing's prior arising's prior arising] is [an indirect cause of functioning thing] because functioning thing is its indirect effect."

Functioning thing is the indirect effect of its own prior arising's prior arising. Functioning thing's prior arising is the direct effect of functioning thing's prior arising's prior arising, and functioning thing itself is a direct effect of its prior arising.

If he says that the reason is not established, [the Sūtra School Challenger responds,] "It follows that functioning thing is an indirect effect of its own prior arising's prior arising because functioning things [*dngos po rnams*] must be posited as the indirect effects of their own prior arising's prior arising and as the direct effects of their own prior arising, and [moreover] a functioning thing's prior arising's prior arising must be posited as [that functioning thing's] indirect cause and its prior arising must be posited as its direct cause."

The two principals of debate E.5, cause of functioning thing and direct cause of functioning thing, have three possibilities:

1   Something which is both is a ruby which is a prior arising of functioning thing (*dngos po'i snga logs su byung ba'i pad ma rā ga*) which is both a cause of functioning thing and a direct cause of functioning thing because of being a prior arising of functioning thing.

2   Whatever is a direct cause of functioning thing is necessarily a cause of functioning thing. However, whatever is a cause of functioning thing is not necessarily a direct cause of functioning thing. For instance, a white flower which is a prior arising of functioning thing's prior arising (*dngos po'i snga logs su byung ba'i snga logs su byung ba'i me tog dkar po*) is a cause of functioning thing but not a direct cause of functioning thing because of being an indirect cause of functioning thing.

3   Something which is neither is a subsequent arising of functioning thing, which is an effect of functioning thing and not a cause of it.

Like functioning thing itself, there are three possibilities between cause of functioning thing and any of the subdivisions of the causes of functioning thing. That is, cause of functioning thing has three possibilities with direct cause of functioning thing (as is shown above), indirect cause of functioning thing, substantial cause of functioning thing, and cooperative condition of functioning thing. This probably holds true when applied to any instance of functioning thing as well. For instance, a table's cause has three possibilities with a table's direct cause, a table's indirect cause, a table's substantial cause, and a table's cooperative condition. This seems to hold true as well for functioning things of which being them is not possible and for functioning-thing-which-is-one-with-functioning-thing.

The corresponding effects compare in the same way. For instance, there are three possibilities between effect of functioning thing and direct effect of functioning thing:

1 Something which is both is the subsequent arising of functioning thing.
2 Whatever is a direct effect of functioning thing is necessarily an effect of functioning thing, but whatever is an effect of functioning thing is not necessarily a direct effect of functioning thing. For example, the subsequent arising of functioning thing's subsequent arising is an effect of functioning thing but not its direct effect because of being its indirect effect.
3 Something which is neither is a prior arising of functioning thing.

The difference between functioning thing's effect and its indirect effect also may be understood from this example.

Debate E.6, Sixth Mistaken View (15b.4)

Debate E.6 revolves around the meaning of the term "direct effect" (*dngos 'bras*) but is mainly a lesson in interpreting grammar. Here the hypothetical Defender accepts that whatever is a direct effect of functioning thing is necessarily an effect of what is produced directly from a functioning thing (*dngos po las dngos su skyes pa'i 'bras bu*). One could understand the Tibetan as "an effect *which is* produced directly from a functioning thing", but the Sūtra School Challenger presses the preferred reading of "an effect *of what is* produced directly from a functioning thing". Thus, this debate is essentially a play on Tibetan grammar, teaching a preferred reading of an ambiguous genitive. At the same time, it posits and analyzes explanations of the term "direct effect". (Here, "a functioning thing" refers either to the same specific functioning thing or to functioning thing collectively.)

> If someone [a hypothetical Defender who intends to say, "Whatever is a direct effect of functioning thing is necessarily an effect which is produced directly from a functioning thing," instead] says, "Whatever is a direct effect of a functioning thing is necessarily an effect of what is produced directly from a functioning thing," [the Sūtra School Challenger responds to him,] "It [absurdly] follows that the subject, a subsequent arising of a functioning thing, is [an effect of what is produced directly from a functioning thing] because of [being a direct effect of a functioning thing]. You asserted the pervasion."
>
> If he says that the reason is not established, [the Sūtra School Challenger responds,] "It follows with respect to the subject, a functioning thing, that its subsequent arising is its direct effect because it is an impermanent phenomenon."

Indeed, a subsequent arising of a functioning thing is a direct effect of that functioning thing, but it cannot be said to be an effect of what is produced directly from that functioning thing. "What is produced directly from a functioning thing" must refer to a direct effect of that functioning thing, its subsequent arising; thus, an effect of what is produced directly from that functioning thing would then be an *indirect* effect of that functioning thing.

> If he accepts the basic consequence, [the Sūtra School Challenger responds,] "It follows that the subject, a subsequent arising of a functioning thing, is not an effect of what is produced directly from a functioning thing because of arising simultaneously

with what is produced directly from a functioning thing."

A subsequent arising of a functioning thing, its direct effect, arises simultaneously with what is produced directly from that functioning thing; thus, a direct effect of a functioning thing is something which is produced directly from that functioning thing and, thereby, is not an effect of what is produced directly from that functioning thing.

> If he says that the reason is not established, [the Sūtra School Challenger responds,] "It follows that the subject [a subsequent arising of a functioning thing does arise simultaneously with what is produced directly from a functioning thing] because of being produced simultaneously with the direct effect of a functioning thing."

The Challenger is making quite explicit that a subsequent arising of a functioning thing arises simultaneously with what is produced directly from that functioning thing and with the direct effects of that functioning thing. This is by way of showing that a subsequent arising of a functioning thing cannot be *an effect* of what is produced directly from that functioning thing because of being produced simultaneously with what is produced directly from that functioning thing.

> "It follows that [a subsequent arising of a functioning thing is produced simultaneously with the direct effect of a functioning thing] because, once the subsequent arising of a functioning thing is established, there is no time when a direct effect of a functioning thing is not also produced, and once a direct effect of a functioning thing is established, there is no time when the subsequent arising of a functioning thing is not also produced."

A direct effect of a functioning thing and, as it is interpreted here, an effect of what is produced directly from a functioning thing are mutually exclusive. A common locus is not

possible because (1) whatever is an effect of what is produced directly from a functioning thing is necessarily its
indirect effect and (2) whatever is a functioning thing's indirect effect is necessarily not its direct effect.

Debate E.7, Seventh Mistaken View (16a.1)

In debate E.7, which is modeled after a debate in the Go-
mang *Collected Topics*,[1] the Defender asserts that whatever is
a pot's cause is necessarily a pot's substantial cause. This is,
of course, not true because a pot's causes also include its
cooperative conditions such as a being who serves as a
cause of a pot (*bum pa'i rgyur gyur pa'i skyes bu*). Pots do not
arise spontaneously from clay but are fashioned into pots
only with human effort.

> If someone [a hypothetical Defender] says,
> "Whatever is a pot's cause is necessarily a pot's
> substantial cause," [the Sūtra School Challenger
> responds to him,] "It [absurdly] follows that the
> subject, a being who serves as a cause of a pot, is a
> pot's substantial cause because of being a pot's
> cause. You asserted the pervasion."

A being who serves as a cause of a pot is an indirect and
even a direct cooperative condition of a pot. Immediately
preceding the arising of a pot, the person is in contact with
the materials out of which the pot is constructed; yet, a pot
is not created as a continuation of the substantial entity of a
person.

> If he says that the reason is not established, [the
> Sūtra School Challenger responds,] "It follows that
> the subject [a being who serves as a cause of a pot] is
> [a pot's cause] because of being a pot's cooperative
> condition."
> If he says that the reason is not established, [the
> Sūtra School Challenger responds,] "It follows that

---

[1] Ngak-ẃang-ḋra-s̄hi, Go-mang *Collected Topics*, pp. 78-79.

the subject [a being who serves as a cause of a pot] is [a pot's cooperative condition] because of being a main producer of a pot, his cooperative effect, which is not a continuation of his own substantial entity."

The Sūtra School Challenger specifies a pot as a cooperative effect of a being who serves as a cause of a pot. Although the text does not present a division of effects into substantial effects (*nyer 'bras*) and cooperative effects (*lhan cig byed 'bras*), such a division is probably suitable. The definition of a substantial effect of functioning thing (*dngos po'i nyer 'bras*) might be posited as:

that which is a main object produced by functioning thing as a continuation of [functioning thing's] own substantial entity (*dngos po rang gi rdzas rgyun du gtso bor bskyed bya*).

An example is a product which is an effect of functioning thing. The definition of a cooperative effect of functioning thing (*dngos po'i lhan cig byed 'bras*) might be posited as:

that which is a main object produced by functioning thing as a substantial entity which is not a continuation of [functioning thing's] own substantial entity (*dngos po rang gi rdzas rgyun ma yin par rdzas su gtso bor bskyed bya*).

An example is a pot which is an effect of functioning thing. Still, it must be analyzed why the texts do not posit these definitions, though they do refer to substantial and cooperative effects.

If he accepts the basic consequence, [the Sūtra School Challenger responds,] "It follows that the subject, a being who serves as a cause of a pot, is not a pot's substantial cause because of not being a main producer of a pot as a continuation of his own substantial entity."

If he says that the reason is not established, [the Sūtra School Challenger responds,] "It follows that

> the subject [a being who serves as a cause of a pot] is
> [not a main producer of a pot as a continuation of
> his own substantial entity] because there is no pot
> which is a subsequent continuation of his
> substantial entity."

The Sūtra School Challenger is indicating something about
the nature of substantial causes. They produce effects which
are continuations of their own substantial entities. There is
no pot which is a continuation of a person's substantial
entity. Even if a pot were produced from the flesh and bones
of a person, this would not be a continuation of the substantial entity of a person because flesh and bones and the pots
that they might produce are matter but a person is a non-
associated compositional factor.

> If he says that the reason is not established, [the
> Sūtra School Challenger responds,] "It follows with
> respect to the subject [a being who serves as a cause
> of a pot that there is no pot which is a subsequent
> continuation of his substantial entity] because he is a
> person."

There are three possibilities between the two principals of
debate E.7, a pot's cause and a pot's substantial cause:

1   Something which is both is the clay which is a cause of a
    clay pot.
2   Whatever is a pot's substantial cause is necessarily a
    pot's cause. However, whatever is a pot's cause is not
    necessarily a pot's substantial cause. For instance, a
    being who serves as a cause of a pot, the hand of a per-
    son who serves as a cause of a pot, or a potter's wheel
    which serves as a cause of a pot are all cooperative
    conditions of a pot and a pot's causes but not a pot's
    substantial causes.
3   Something which is neither is a pot of the present
    moment or a pot's effect.

Debate E.8, Eighth Mistaken View (16a.3)

In debate E.8 the hypothetical Defender takes a stance opposite to that in debate E.7, now asserting that whatever is a pot's cause is necessarily a pot's cooperative condition. The Sūtra School Challenger posits the counter-example of the clay that serves as a cause of a pot. A clay pot is a continuation of the substantial entity of the clay that serves as a cause of a pot.

> If someone [a hypothetical Defender] says, "Whatever is a pot's cause is necessarily a pot's cooperative condition," [the Sūtra School Challenger responds to him,] "It [absurdly] follows that the subject, the clay that serves as a cause of a pot, is [a pot's cooperative condition] because of [being a pot's cause]. You asserted the pervasion."
>
> If he says that the reason is not established, [the Sūtra School Challenger responds,] "It follows that the subject [the clay that serves as a cause of a pot] is [a pot's cause] because a pot is its effect."
>
> If he says that the reason is not established [the Sūtra School Challenger responds,] "It follows with respect to the subject, a pot, that it is an effect of the clay that serves as its own cause because there is clay that serves as its own cause."

The Challenger has changed the subject from the clay that serves as a cause of a pot to a pot. In his answer to the former consequence the Defender said that the reason, that a pot is an effect of the clay that serves as its own cause, is not established. The Challenger simply took what was the grammatical subject of the former reason, a pot, and made it the grammatical and logical subject of the present consequence.

> If he accepts the basic consequence, [the Sūtra
> School Challenger responds,] "It follows that the
> subject [the clay that serves as a cause of a pot] is
> not a pot's cooperative condition because of being a
> pot's substantial cause."

The clay that serves as a cause of a pot is a pot's substantial
cause because of being a main producer of a pot as a continuation of its own substantial entity.

There are three possibilities between the two, a pot's
cause and a pot's cooperative condition:

1   Something which is both is a person who serves as a
    cause of a pot.
2   Whatever is a pot's cooperative condition is necessarily a
    pot's cause. However, it is not the case that whatever is a
    pot's cause is necessarily a pot's cooperative condition
    because, for instance, the clay that serves as a cause of a
    pot is a pot's cause but not a pot's cooperative condition.
3   Something which is neither is a pot's effect or a clay pot.

There are three possibilities between a pot's cause and any
of the particular types of a pot's causes.

Debate E.9, Ninth Mistaken View (16a.5)

In this debate, which is modeled after a debate in the Go-
mang *Collected Topics*,[1] the hypothetical Defender asserts
that whatever is a cause is necessarily a substantial cause.
Any of the other types of causes—cooperative conditions,
direct causes, and indirect causes—are mutually inclusive
with cause. However, substantial cause is not. There is a
time when the substantial entity of many functioning things
comes to an end.

Indeed, all functioning things must have a substantial
cause, but this does not mean that all causes are substantial
causes. Some impermanent phenomena do not produce a

---

[1] *Ibid.*, pp. 77-78.

continuation of their own substantial entities. The Sūtra School Challenger posits the counterexample of the flame of a butter lamp in its final moment. The Tibetans commonly use butter as the fuel in offering lamps. In its final moment a flame does not produce a flame of the next moment. Its continuum is severed; therefore, it is not a substantial cause.

> If someone [a hypothetical Defender] says, "Whatever is a cause is necessarily a substantial cause," [the Sūtra School Challenger responds to him,] "It [absurdly] follows that the subject, the flame of a butter lamp in its final moment, is [a substantial cause] because of [being a cause]. You asserted the pervasion."
>
> If he says that the reason is not established, [the Sūtra School Challenger responds,] "It follows that the subject [the flame of a butter lamp in its final moment] is [a cause] because of being a functioning thing."

The flame of a butter lamp in its final moment may serve as a cooperative condition for the smoke that arises when the flame is extinguished, or an eye consciousness seeing that flame, and so on.

> If he accepts the basic consequence, [the Sūtra School Challenger responds,] "It follows that the subject, the flame of a butter lamp in its final moment, is not a substantial cause because of not being a main producer of its own substantial effect as a subsequent continuation of its own substantial entity."

There is no substantial effect of a flame in its final moment, and because a flame in its final moment is not a main producer of its own substantial effect as a subsequent continuation of its own substantial entity, it is not a substantial cause.

> If he says that the reason is not established, [the Sūtra School Challenger responds,] "It follows that the subject [the flame of a butter lamp in its final

moment] is [not a main producer of its own substantial effect as a subsequent continuation of its
own substantial entity] because a subsequent continuation of its own substantial entity does not
exist."

If he says that the reason is not established, [the
Sūtra School Challenger responds,] "It follows with
respect to the subject [the flame of a butter lamp in
its final moment] that [a subsequent continuation of
its own substantial entity does not exist] because it
is a functioning thing with respect to which the continuation of its own substantial entity is about to be
severed [*rdzas rgyun chad kha ma'i dngos po*]."

The flame of a butter lamp in its final moment is not a functioning thing with respect to which a continuation of its own
substantial entity is already severed—it is about to be
severed.

There are three possibilities between the two principals of
debate E.9, cause and substantial cause:

1   Something which is both is the clay which is a cause of a
    clay pot, a functioning thing which is a cause of
    functioning thing, a seed which is a cause of a sprout,
    and so forth.
2   Whatever is a substantial cause is necessarily a cause.
    However, whatever is a cause is not necessarily a sub-
    stantial cause. For instance, the flame of a butter lamp in
    its final moment, lightening in its final moment, the final
    moment of a snowflake, and so forth are all causes but
    not substantial causes.
3   Something which is neither is a functioning thing's
    isolate.

Debate E.10, Tenth Mistaken View (16b.1)

In debates E.10, E.11, and E.12 the Tutor Jam-ba-gya-tso
introduces briefly the topic of the various types of sameness
and difference. All three of these debates are modeled after

debates that appear in the Go-mang *Collected Topics*.[1] This latter text includes a separate chapter on the topic of one (*gcig, ekatva*) and different (*tha dad, nānātva*).[2]

Technically, whatever is one is necessarily one from the point of view of both name and meaning. Only a pot is one with a pot. This is the most rigorous type of oneness that could possibly be presented. It means that only a pot is *exactly the same as* a pot. This is one way of showing the sameness or difference between phenomena. In the case of what is properly qualified as one, the phenomenon is totally self-reflexive; that is, it is one with itself alone.

However, even though two phenomena may not be *exactly* the same as each other, they may be the same in some sense. For instance, a gold pot is the same as a copper pot in the sense that they are both pots. Someone noticing a gold pot and a copper pot might naturally think, "This and that are alike." A gold pot and a copper pot are not exactly the same, but they are entities of the *same type* (*rigs gcig pa, eka-jāti*). Also, product and impermanent phenomenon are mutually inclusive, but they are not one because they have different names. They are the *same entity* (*ngo bo gcig pa, eka-rūpatā*) in that whatever is the one is necessarily the other; however, since they are reversed from different bases of reversal (*log sa tha dad las ldog pa*)—i.e., non-one-with-product and non-one-with-impermanent-phenomenon—they are different isolates. Thus, product's isolate is mutually exclusive with impermanent phenomenon's isolate, but product and impermanent phenomenon are mutually inclusive and the same entity.

All phenomena which are not the same from the point of view of name or meaning are different. Every existent except for a pot is different from a pot. Still, within being different some phenomena are totally unrelated (*mi 'brel ba*) and others share some relationship. For instance, a pot is different from a pillar, and they are unrelated. They do not

---

[1] *Ibid.,* pp. 60-1, 64-6.
[2] *Ibid.,* pp. 56-75.

refer to the same entities, and a person noticing a pillar and a pot would not think that they were alike. On the other hand, a cause of a functioning thing and that functioning thing which is its effect are different and mutually exclusive, but they are related (*'brel ba*) causally, for that particular functioning thing is arisen from its cause.

Seeing that all phenomena which are the same in one sense or another are not rigorously one with each other (that is, not *exactly* the same as each other), the Go-mang *Collected Topics* identifies several types of sameness and difference.[1] According to that text, there are three types of sameness:

1   the same self-isolate (*rang ldog gcig pa*)
2   the same entity (*ngo bo gcig pa, eka-rūpatā*)
3   the same type (*rigs gcig pa, eka-jāti*).[2]

The definition of phenomena which are the same self-isolate is:

> phenomena which are not diverse self-isolates (*rang ldog so so ba ma yin pa'i chos*).[3]

An illustration is the two, product and product, for they are not phenomena which are diverse self-isolates. Product is the self-isolate of product, and product is the self-isolate of product. In the strictest sense, whatever phenomena are one are necessarily the same self-isolate. The definition of a phenomenon which is the same self-isolate as existent (*yod pa dang rang ldog gcig pa*) is:

> a phenomenon the self-isolate of which is not diverse from existent (*yod pa dang rang ldog so so ba ma yin pa'i chos*).[4]

---

[1] The source for this explanation of the various types of sameness and difference is Ngak-w̄ang-d̄ra-s̄hi, Go-mang *Collected Topics*, pp. 66-72.

[2] Ngak-w̄ang-d̄ra-s̄hi, Go-mang *Collected Topics*, p. 66.

[3] *Ibid.*

[4] *Ibid.*, pp. 66-67.

The only thing that one may posit as a phenomenon which is the same self-isolate as existent is existent itself. This may be applied to all phenomena similarly.

The definition of phenomena which are the same entity is:

> phenomena which are not diverse entities (*ngo bo so so ba ma yin pa'i chos*).[1]

The three—phenomena which are the same entity (*ngo bo gcig pa, eka-rūpatā*), phenomena which are the same nature (*rang bzhin gcig pa, eka-prakṛtika*), and phenomena which are the same essence (*bdag nyid gcig pa, eka-ātman*)—are mutually inclusive.[2] The definition of a phenomenon which is the same entity as object of knowledge (*shes bya dang ngo bo gcig pa*) is:

> a phenomenon the entity of which is not diverse from object of knowledge (*shes bya dang ngo bo so so ba ma yin pa'i chos*).[3]

An example is an existent. Existents are the same entity as objects of knowledge. Also, a functioning thing is the same entity as object of knowledge. This does not mean that whatever is an object of knowledge is necessarily a functioning thing but that a functioning thing is a phenomenon the entity of which is not diverse from object of knowledge. Functioning things are objects of knowledge, and if there were no objects of knowledge, there would be no functioning things. Thus, a phenomenon need not be mutually inclusive with object of knowledge in order to be the same entity as it; rather: "Whatever is an object of knowledge is necessarily a phenomenon which is the same essence [or the same entity] as object of knowledge."[4]

Impermanent phenomena which are the same entity are also referred to as being the same substantial entity (*rdzas*

---

[1] *Ibid.*, p. 67.
[2] *Ibid.*
[3] *Ibid.*
[4] *Ibid.*, p. 129.

gcig, eka-dravya). The definition of phenomena which are the same substantial entity is:

> phenomena which are produced as what is not diverse in terms of a substantial entity (*rdzas kyi sgo nas so so ba ma yin par skye ba'i chos*).[1]

An illustration is the two, product and impermanent phenomenon. Product and impermanent phenomenon are functioning things that cannot be found separately—their entities are the same. They may appear separately for a thought consciousness, but one cannot find a product which is not an impermanent phenomenon, nor an impermanent phenomenon which is not a product.

Lati Rinbochay posits the definition of phenomena which are the same substantial entity as:

> those which (1) appear to a direct perceiver and (2) do not appear separately (*mngon sum la snang ba gang zhig so so bar mi snang ba*).[2]

It is not suitable to posit this definition merely as:

> those which do not appear separately to a direct perceiver (*mngon sum la so so bar mi snang ba*)

because the horn of a rabbit and a permanent phenomenon do not appear separately to a direct perceiver but they are not the same substantial entity. Phenomena which are the same substantial entity must be established as substantial entities (*rdzas su grub pa*), that is, as functioning things. Except for composed phenomena there are no phenomena which are the same substantial entity.

Phenomena which are the same substantial entity and phenomena which are the same entity are of two types:

1   those that have greater and lesser pervasions (*khyab che chung yod mkhan*)

---

[1] *Ibid.*, p. 67.
[2] Lati Rinbochay, oral commentary.

2   those that do not have greater and lesser pervasions (*khyab che chung med mkhan*).[1]

Mutually inclusive phenomena do not have greater and lesser pervasions; they are equivalent in terms of what they pervade. For example, product and impermanent phenomenon are the same substantial entity and the same entity and do not have greater and lesser pervasions because they range over all the same phenomena. Also, existent and object of knowledge are the same entity (though not the same substantial entity because they are permanent) and do not have greater and lesser pervasions. On the other hand, a pot and functioning thing are the same substantial entity and the same entity, but they do have greater and lesser pervasions. There are three possibilities between these two. All pots are functioning things, but not all functioning things are pots. Also, object of knowledge and permanent phenomenon are the same entity and have greater and lesser pervasions because all permanent phenomena are objects of knowledge, but not all objects of knowledge are permanent phenomena.

In saying that a pot and functioning thing are the same substantial entity and that they do not appear separately to a direct perceiver, this does not mean that if a functioning thing appears, then a pot will appear. Rather, if a pot appears, it will appear as a functioning thing. The nature of a pot as something able to perform a function appears to a direct perceiver together with the pot. One cannot find a pot and a functioning thing apart. One can find a functioning thing which is not a pot, but one cannot find a pot which is not a functioning thing. If there were no functioning things, there would be no pots. They are phenomena which are the same entity and the same substantial entity.

Similarly, a functioning thing is the same entity as object of knowledge, though they are not the same substantial entity. Not all objects of knowledge are functioning things, and one can find an object of knowledge which is not a

---

[1] *Ibid.*

functioning thing, but one cannot find a functioning thing which is not an object of knowledge. If there were no objects of knowledge, there would be no functioning things.

Even phenomena which are mutually exclusive may be the same entity or the same substantial entity. For instance, the two—a pillar and a pot—are mutually exclusive with object of knowledge, functioning thing, and so forth, but the two—a pillar and a pot—are nonetheless phenomena which are the same entity as object of knowledge and functioning thing. Like all objects of knowledge of which being them is not possible, the two—a pillar and a pot—are mutually exclusive with all other phenomena because there is no common locus of the two. There is nothing which, on the one hand, is the two—a pillar and a pot—and, on the other, is also an object of knowledge because there is nothing which is the two—a pillar and a pot. Still, the two—a pillar and a pot—are objects of knowledge and the same entity as object of knowledge because the entity of the two—a pillar and a pot—is not diverse from object of knowledge. Similarly, the two—a pillar and a pot—are the same substantial entity as functioning thing because their entity is produced as non-diverse from functioning thing.

It is an uncommon (*thun mong ma yin pa*) or unshared assertion of the Buddhists that the self and the five aggregates are the same entity.[1] The aggregates are the bases of designation (*gdags gzhi*) of the self. That is, one says, "I saw so and so," in dependence upon having seen some of the aggregates of that person. Yet, the aggregates and the self are different self-isolates and mutually exclusive phenomena. There is nothing which is both the self and the aggregates. The non-Buddhists say not only are the self and the aggregates mutually exclusive, but their entities are also mutually exclusive. The Buddhists say that there is indeed a sense and an appearance of a self that exists separately from the aggregates, but such a self does not exist. One strongly identifies oneself with the aggregates. If one's hand is cut,

---

[1] Kensur Jambel Shenpen, oral commentary.

one will feel that one's self has been harmed. In fact, one cannot harm the self except by harming the aggregates. There is no way to understand the emptiness of the person without understanding this: The self and the aggregates are mutually exclusive, but they are the same entity.

Not only are some mutually exclusive phenomena the same entity, but also some phenomena which are not mutually exclusive are different entities. For instance, there are three possibilities between functioning thing and functioning thing's cause but they are different entities and different substantial entities. They are different substantial entities because, even though they appear to direct perceivers, they appear separately. Since they do not exist simultaneously, they must appear separately. When applied to a specific basis, the causes and effects of that particular impermanent phenomenon are not the same entity. One of the purposes for including the study of sameness and difference in "The Introductory Presentation of Causes and Effects" is to indicate the characteristic of causes and effects as different substantial entities.

The third division of sameness is phenomena which are the same type (*rigs gcig pa, eka-jāti*). The definition of phenomena which are the same type is:

> phenomena which are not diverse types (*rigs so so ba ma yin pa'i chos*).[1]

According to the Go-mang text, phenomena which are the same type may be divided into the two:

1　phenomena which are the same isolate type (*ldog pa rigs gcig pa*)
2　phenomena which are the same type of substantial entity (*rdzas rigs gcig pa*).[2]

Phenomena which are the same isolate type may be divided, in turn, into the two:

---

[1] Ngak- wang-dra-shi, Go-mang *Collected Topics*, p. 67.
[2] *Ibid.*, pp. 67-68.

1 positive phenomena which are the same isolate type (*sgrub par gyur pa'i ldog pa rigs gcig pa*)
2 negative phenomena which are the same isolate type (*dgag par gyur pa'i ldog pa rigs gcig pa*).[1]

The definition of positive phenomena which are the same isolate type is:

> phenomena naturally able to produce an awareness [in a person] thinking, "This and that are alike," upon merely being seen by whosoever directs the mind [toward them] (*gang zag gang dang gang gi yid gtad pas mthong tsam nyid nas 'di dang 'di 'dra'o snyam pa'i blo ngang gis skyed nus pa'i chos*).[2]

For example, a gold pot and a copper pot are naturally able to produce an awareness in a person thinking, "This and that are alike," upon merely being seen by whosoever directs the mind toward them. Thought constantly proceeds by association and discrimination, and two phenomena of the same type are able to produce a thought consciousness which discriminates that type and associates them. A gold pot and a copper pot are positive phenomena because in order to associate them conceptually it is not necessary to eliminate explicitly any object of negation (*dgag bya, prati-ṣhedhya*). Positive phenomena which are the same isolate type are of three kinds:

1 consciousnesses which are the same isolate type (*shes par gyur pa'i ldog pa rigs gcig pa*)
2 forms which are the same isolate type (*gzugs su gyur pa'i ldog pa rigs gcig pa*)
3 non-associated compositional factors which are the same isolate type (*ldan min 'du byed du gyur pa'i ldog pa rigs gcig pa*).[3]

---

[1] *Ibid.*, p. 68.
[2] *Ibid.*
[3] *Ibid.*

An example of consciousnesses which are the same isolate type is the two, Devadatta's (*lhas sbyin*) eye consciousness and Yajñadatta's (*mchod sbyin*) eye consciousness. An example of forms which are the same isolate type is the two, a sandalwood pillar and a juniper pillar (*tsan dan gyi kva ba dang shug pa'i kva ba gnyis*).[1] An example of non-associated compositional factors which are the same isolate type is the two, the productness of a sound and the productness of a pot (*sgra'i byas pa dang bum pa'i byas pa gnyis*).[2] These pairs of phenomena are such that they are naturally able to produce an awareness which associates them upon merely observing them. This does not mean that they necessarily would produce such a consciousness but that they are able to do so. The definition of negative phenomena which are the same isolate type is:

> different non-affirming negatives which merely eliminate the same type of object of negation (*dgag bya rigs gcig bkag tsam gyi tha dad pa'i med dgag*).[3]

Negative phenomena are such that in order to know them one must explicitly eliminate an object of negation. For instance, in order to understand non-cow one must explicitly eliminate cow, the object of negation. The definition specifies these as "non-affirming negatives". Within negative phenomena there are affirming negatives (*ma yin dgag, paryudāsa-pratiṣhedha*) that imply another phenomenon in their place and non-affirming negatives (*med dgag, prasajya-pratiṣhedha*) which do not imply any positive phenomenon or affirming negative in their place. An example of the first type is coffee without sugar. Here sugar is the object of negation and coffee is what is implied. An example of the second type is selflessness. A substantially existent self is the

---

[1] The Go-mang *Collected Topics* spells the Tibetan word for pillar as *kva ba* rather than *ka ba*, which is the spelling given in the Tutor's *Collected Topics*.
[2] These examples are from Ngak-wang-dra-shi, Go-mang *Collected Topics*, pp. 68-69.
[3] *Ibid.*, p. 69.

object of negation, and nothing is implied in place of it. The topic of positive and negative phenomena is presented in detail in "The Greater Path of Reasoning". Negative phenomena which are the same isolate type are non-affirming negatives which have the same object of negation. An illustration is the two, the personal selflessness of a pot and the personal selflessness of a pillar (*bum pa gang zag gi bdag med dang kva ba gang zag gi bdag med gnyis*).[1] These are both nonaffirming negatives because they do not imply anything in their place, and they have the same object of negation, a personal self.

The remaining phenomena of the same type are those that are the same type of substantial entity (*rdzas rigs gcig pa*). The definition of phenomena which are the same type of substantial entity is:

> different composed phenomena which are produced from their own same direct substantial cause (*rang gi dngos kyi nyer len gcig las skyes pa'i tha dad pa'i 'dus byas*).[2]

If divided, there are three:

1 forms which are the same type of substantial entity (*gzugs su gyur pa'i rdzas rigs gcig pa*)
2 consciousnesses which are the same type of substantial entity (*shes par gyur pa'i rdzas rigs gcig pa*)
3 non-associated compositional factors which are the same type of substantial entity (*ldan min 'du byed du gyur pa'i rdzas rigs gcig pa*).[3]

An example of forms which are the same type of substantial entity is the two, a white clay pot and a blue clay pot which are produced from the same clay which is their substantial cause (*rang gi nyer len 'jim pa gcig las skye ba'i rdza bum dkar po dang rdza bum sngon po gnyis*). An example of conscious-

---

[1] This example is from Ngak-w̄ang-d̄ra-s̄hi, Go-mang *Collected Topics*, p. 69.
[2] *Ibid.*
[3] *Ibid.*, pp. 69-70.

nesses which are the same type of substantial entity is the two, different perceivers which are produced from their own same direct substantial cause (*rang gi dngos kyi nyer len gcig las skyes pa'i rnam shes tha dad pa gnyis po*). An example of non-associated compositional factors which are the same type of substantial entity is the two, the productness of sound and the impermanence of sound which are produced from their own same substantial cause (*rang gi nyer len gcig las skyes pa'i sgra'i byas pa dang sgra'i mi rtag pa gnyis*).[1]

All phenomena are the same type in that they are all objects of knowledge, but it is not the case that, for instance, a pillar and a pot can produce naturally an awareness thinking, "This and that are alike," upon merely being seen by whosoever directs the mind toward them. One would not naturally associate them as objects of knowledge or even as impermanent phenomena. Indeed, some persons who observe a pillar and a pot do associate them as objects of knowledge, but these objects are not able to induce that association naturally in whosoever turns the mind toward them. For instance, a person untrained in philosophy would not naturally discriminate a pillar and a pot as the same in terms of being objects of knowledge.

Phenomena which are not one or the same in some sense are different. The definition of phenomena which are different is:

> phenomena which are diverse (*so so ba'i chos*).

According to the Go-mang *Collected Topics*, there are three kinds of phenomena which are different:

1 those which are different self-isolates (*rang ldog tha dad pa*)
2 those which are different entities (*ngo bo tha dad pa*)
3 those which are different types (*rigs tha dad pa*).[2]

---

[1] These examples are from Ngak-ŵang-dra-śhi, Go-mang *Collected Topics*, p. 70.
[2] *Ibid.*

The definition of phenomena which are different self-isolates is:

> phenomena which are diverse self-isolates (*rang ldog so so ba'i chos*).[1]

An illustration is the two, a pillar and a pot. The definition of a phenomenon which is a different self-isolate from object of knowledge (*shes bya dang rang ldog tha dad pa*) is:

> a phenomenon which is a diverse self-isolate from object of knowledge (*shes bya dang rang ldog so so ba'i chos*).[2]

An illustration is a pillar. This may be applied in the same way to all phenomena. In the strictest sense, all phenomena which are different are different self-isolates.

The definition of phenomena which are different entities is:

> phenomena which are diverse entities (*ngo bo so so ba'i chos*).[3]

The three—different entities, different essences, and different natures—are mutually inclusive. An illustration is the two, permanent phenomenon and impermanent phenomenon. Phenomena which are different entities cannot be found together. There is nothing which is both a permanent phenomenon and an impermanent phenomenon. However, it is not the case that all phenomena which are mutually exclusive are also different entities. For instance, the self and the aggregates are mutually exclusive but they are the same entity. There is nothing which is both the self and the aggregates, but they cannot be found separately. If the self appears to a direct perceiver, it does not appear separately from the aggregates.

The definition of phenomena which are different types is:

---

[1] *Ibid.*

[2] *Ibid.*, p. 71.

[3] *Ibid.*

phenomena which are diverse types (*rigs so so ba'i chos*).[1]

Phenomena which are different types (*rigs tha dad pa*), phenomena which are discordant types (*rigs mi mthun pa'i chos*), phenomena which are dissimilar types (*rigs mi 'dra ba'i chos*), and phenomena which are not the same type (*rigs mi gcig pa'i chos*) are mutually inclusive.[2] If phenomena which are dissimilar types are divided, there are two:

1 phenomena which are dissimilar isolate types (*ldog pa rigs mi 'dra ba*)
2 phenomena which are dissimilar types of substantial entities (*rdzas rigs mi 'dra ba*).[3]

An example of phenomena which are dissimilar isolate types is the two, a horse and an ox. An example of phenomena which are dissimilar types of substantial entities is the two, consciousness and matter.[4] A horse and an ox are probably also suitable as dissimilar types of substantial entities because they are not different composed phenomena produced from their own same direct substantial cause, but they are different isolate types because they are not naturally able to produce an awareness thinking, "This and that are alike," merely upon being seen by whosoever directs the mind toward them.

Although phenomena which are different types are divided into those which are different isolate types and those which are different types of substantial entities, it is not the case that whatever phenomena are included by the divisions are necessarily different types. For instance, a gold pot and a copper pot are different types of substantial entities but are not different types. A gold pot and a copper pot are different types of substantial entities because of being

---

[1] *Ibid.*
[2] *Ibid.*
[3] *Ibid.*
[4] These examples are from Ngak-ŵang-dra-shi, Go-mang *Collected Topics*, pp. 71-72.

different composed phenomena which are produced from their own diverse direct substantial causes, for a gold pot is produced from gold but not copper and a copper pot is produced from copper but not gold. Nonetheless, even though a gold pot and a copper pot are different types of substantial entities, they are not phenomena which are different types because they are the same type. This is because they are the same isolate types, for they are positive phenomena which are the same isolate types due to being phenomena naturally able to produce an awareness thinking, "This and that are alike," upon merely being seen by whosoever directs the mind toward them.[1]

Table IX shows the various types of sameness and difference described in the Go-mang *Collected Topics* with an example of each:

---

[1] *Ibid.*, pp. 72-73.

Table IX: Sameness and Difference

I Sameness

A. the same self-isolate (*rang ldog gcig pa*), e.g., product and product

B. the same entity (*ngo bo gcig pa, eka-rūpatā*), e.g., functioning thing and object of knowledge

C. the same type (*rigs gcig pa, eka-jāti*)

  1 the same isolate type (*ldog pa rigs gcig pa*)

    a. positive phenomena which are the same isolate type (*sgrub par gyur pa'i ldog pa rigs gcig pa*)

      1 consciousnesses which are the same isolate type (*sgrub par gyur pa'i ldog pa rigs gcig pa*), e.g., Devadatta's eye consciousness and Yajñadatta's eye consciousness

      2 forms which are the same isolate type (*gzugs su gyur pa'i ldog pa rigs gcig pa*), e.g., a sandalwood pillar and a juniper pillar

      3 non-associated compositional factors which are the same isolate type (*ldan min 'du byed du gyur pa'i ldog pa rigs gcig pa*), e.g., the productness of a sound and the productness of a pot

    b. negative phenomena which are the same isolate type (*dgag par gyur pa'i ldog pa rigs gcig pa*), e.g., the personal selflessness of a pot and the personal selflessness of a pillar

  2 the same type of substantial entity (*rdzas rigs gcig pa*)

    a. forms which are the same type of substantial entity (*gzugs su gyur pa'i rdzas rigs gcig pa*), e.g., a white clay pot and a blue clay pot which are produced from the same clay which is their substantial cause

(Table IX: Sameness and Difference cont.)

b. consciousnesses which are the same type of substantial entity (*shes par gyur pa'i rdzas rigs gcig pa*), e.g., different perceivers which are produced from their own same direct substantial cause

c. non-associated compositional factors which are the same type of substantial entity (*ldan min 'du byed du gyur pa'i rdzas rigs gcig pa*), e.g., the productness of sound and the impermanence of sound which are produced from their own same substantial cause

II Difference

A. different self-isolates (*rang ldog tha dad pa*), e.g., a pillar and a pot
B. different entities (*ngo bo tha dad pa*), e.g., a permanent phenomenon and an impermanent phenomenon
C. different types (*rigs tha dad pa*)
    1 different isolate types (*ldog pa rigs tha dad pa*), e.g., a horse and an ox
    2 different types of substantial entities (*rdzas rigs tha dad pa*), e.g., consciousness and matter.

In debate E.10, which is modeled after a debate in the Go-mang *Collected Topics*,[1] the hypothetical Defender accepts that whatever phenomena are the same in terms of establishment and abiding (*grub bde gcig, eka-yogakṣhema*) are necessarily the same substantial entity in terms of establishment and abiding (*grub bde rdzas gcig*). Phenomena which are the same in terms of establishment and abiding are those which are established simultaneously, abide simultaneously, and disintegrate simultaneously. They may be mutually exclusive phenomena such as the color and shape of a form, but if they are established, abide, and disintegrate simultaneously, then they are the same in that sense. However, phenomena which are the same *substantial entity* in terms of establishment and abiding must be the same substantial entity (that is, impermanent phenomena which are the same entity) as well as being established simultaneously, abiding simultaneously, and disintegrating simultaneously.

It is not the case that whatever phenomena are the same in terms of establishment and abiding are necessarily the same substantial entity in terms of establishment and abiding. There are phenomena which are established, abide, and disintegrate simultaneously which are not the same substantial entity—for instance, the color of sandalwood and the odor of sandalwood. Because they are both part of the same mass, they are established, abide, and disintegrate simultaneously, but they are not the same substantial entity because of not being different composed phenomena which are produced from their own same direct substantial cause. The direct substantial cause of the color of sandalwood is the prior arising of the color of sandalwood, and the direct substantial cause of the odor of sandalwood is the prior arising of the odor of sandalwood. The color and odor of sandalwood are found together, but they are different substantial entities which appear separately to direct perceivers.

---

[1] *Ibid.*, pp. 64-65.

If someone [a hypothetical Defender] says, "Whatever phenomena are the same in terms of establishment and abiding are necessarily the same substantial entity in terms of establishment and abiding," [the Sūtra School Challenger responds to him,] "It [absurdly] follows that the subjects, the two—the color of sandalwood and the odor of sandalwood, are [the same substantial entity in terms of establishment and abiding] because of [being the same in terms of establishment and abiding]. You asserted the pervasion."

If he says that the reason is not established, [the Sūtra School Challenger responds,] "It follows that the subjects [the two—the color of sandalwood and the odor of sandalwood] are [the same in terms of establishment and abiding] because those two are established simultaneously, abide simultaneously, and disintegrate simultaneously."

"[It follows that] there is pervasion [i.e., if those two are established simultaneously, abide simultaneously, and disintegrate simultaneously, then they are necessarily the same in terms of establishment and abiding] because that is the meaning of being the same in terms of establishment and abiding."

A phenomenon and its cause or its effect necessarily are not the same in terms of establishment and abiding. A pot and a pot's cause are not established simultaneously, do not abide simultaneously, and do not disintegrate simultaneously.

If he accepts the basic consequences, [the Sūtra School Challenger responds,] "It follows that the subjects, the two—the odor of sandalwood and the color of sandalwood, are not the same substantial entity in terms of establishment and abiding because of not being the same substantial entity."

The counter-pervasion of this consequence is that whatever phenomena are the same substantial entity in terms of establishment and abiding are necessarily the same substantial entity. There are three possibilities between these two:

1   Things which are both the same substantial entity in terms of establishment and abiding and also the same substantial entity are the two—product and impermanent phenomenon. These two are the same substantial entity because of being phenomena which are produced as non-diverse entities since they (1) appear to a direct perceiver and (2) do not appear separately. They are the same substantial entity in terms of establishment and abiding because (1) they are the same substantial entity and (2) they are established simultaneously, abide simultaneously, and disintegrate simultaneously.

2   It is not the case that whatever phenomena are the same substantial entity are necessarily the same substantial entity in terms of establishment and abiding. A pot, for instance, is the same substantial entity as functioning thing, but it is not the same substantial entity as functioning thing in terms of establishment and abiding. Functioning thing and a pot are not established together, do not abide together, and do not disintegrate together.

3   Something which is neither is a pot. A pot is neither the same substantial entity nor the same substantial entity in terms of establishment and abiding because of not being different, due to being just one thing. Also, the two—a pillar and a pot—are neither because of being different substantial entities.

> If he says that the reason is not established, [the Sūtra School Challenger responds,] "It follows that the subjects, the two—the odor of sandalwood and the color of sandalwood, are not the same substantial entity because of being phenomena which are produced as diverse entities."

The entity of sandalwood's color is mutually exclusive with the entity of sandalwood's odor. There is nothing which is both. The Go-mang *Collected Topics* explains, "If something is a mass which is composed of the eight substantial

particles, then the two—its color and its odor—are
necessarily different substantial entities."[1] Any composite
material phenomenon is a mass composed of the eight
substantial particles. Also, that same text says, "If something
is a mass composed of the eight substantial particles, then
the two—its color and its odor—are necessarily established
simultaneously, abide simultaneously, and disintegrate
simultaneously."[2] The color and odor of a material
phenomenon are the same in terms of establishment and
abiding but are necessarily different substantial entities.

There are three possibilities between the two principals of
debate E.10, phenomena which are the same in terms of
establishment and abiding and phenomena which are the
same substantial entity in terms of establishment and
abiding:

1   Product and impermanent phenomenon are both. These
    two are the same in terms of establishment and abiding
    because they are established simultaneously, abide
    simultaneously, and disintegrate simultaneously. They
    are also the same substantial entity because of being
    phenomena which are produced as what is not diverse
    in terms of a substantial entity. Also, they are (1) phe-
    nomena which appear to a direct perceiver and (2) do
    not appear separately. One cannot find a product sepa-
    rate from an impermanent phenomenon. Thus, product
    and impermanent phenomenon are the same substantial
    entity in terms of establishment and abiding.
2   Whatever phenomena are the same substantial entity in
    terms of establishment and abiding are necessarily the
    same in terms of establishment and abiding. This is so
    because phenomena which are the same substantial
    entity in terms of establishment and abiding must be the
    same in terms of establishment and abiding as well as
    being the same substantial entity. However, it is not the
    case that whatever phenomena are the same in terms of

---

[1] *Ibid.*, p. 65.
[2] *Ibid.*, p. 64.

establishment and abiding are necessarily the same substantial entity in terms of establishment and abiding. For instance, the color of sandalwood and the odor of sandalwood are the same in terms of establishment and abiding but are not the same substantial entity in terms of establishment and abiding.

3 An example of a pair which is neither is the odor of sandalwood and a cause of the odor of sandalwood. These two are not established simultaneously, do not abide simultaneously, and do not disintegrate simultaneously because once the odor of sandalwood is established, there is no time when the causes of the odor of sandalwood also exist.

Debate E.11, Eleventh Mistaken View (16b.4)

In debate E.11, which is also modeled after a debate in the Go-mang *Collected Topics*,[1] the hypothetical Defender asserts that whatever phenomena are the same type of substantial entity (*rdzas rigs gcig pa*) are necessarily the same substantial entity (*rdzas gcig pa, eka-dravya*). Phenomena which are the same type of substantial entity are different composed phenomena which are produced from their own same direct substantial cause. These are one of the two kinds of phenomena of the same type: the same isolate type and the same type of substantial entity. However, phenomena which are the same substantial entity must be merely composed phenomena which are the same entity and need not be the same type. An example is the two—a large and a small barley grain produced from one barley head which is their substantial cause (*nyer len nas rdog gcig las skyes pa'i nas 'bru che chung gnyis*). These two grains are the same type of substantial entity because they are produced from the same substantial cause, but they are not the same substantial entity because they are not the same entity. They are

---

[1] *Ibid.*, pp. 65-66.

different phenomena which appear separately to direct perceivers.

There are many subjects that the Sūtra School Challenger could posit. For instance, the two—a large and a small apple produced from one tree which is their substantial cause—or the two—a blue pot and a brown pot produced from the same clay which is their substantial cause—are the same types of substantial entities, but they are not the same substantial entities. As explained by Kensur Jambel Shenpen, with any of these subjects one could take one away and not harm the other. One could eat one apple and leave the other. This shows that they are different substantial entities.[1]

> If someone [a hypothetical Defender] says, "Whatever phenomena are the same type of substantial entity are necessarily the same substantial entity," [the Sūtra School Challenger responds to him,] "It [absurdly] follows that the subjects, the two—a large and a small barley grain produced from one barley head which is their substantial cause, are the same substantial entity because of being the same type of substantial entity. You asserted the pervasion."
>
> If he says that the reason is not established, [the Sūtra School Challenger responds,] "It follows that the subjects [the two—a large and a small barley grain produced from one barley head which is their substantial cause] are [the same type of substantial entity] because of being different composed phenomena which are produced from their own same substantial cause."

In the definition of phenomena which are the same type of substantial entity given in the Go-mang *Collected Topics* they are specified as being produced from the same *direct* substantial cause. Here the Tutor Jam-ba-gya-tso does not include the specification of their substantial cause as neces-

---

[1] Kensur Jambel Shenpen, oral commentary.

sarily being a *direct* one. Thus, two clay pots made from the same dry clay, which is an indirect substantial cause, but not made from the same moist clay, which is a direct substantial cause, would then be included as phenomena which are the same type of substantial entity according to the Tutor's interpretation but would be excluded by the Go-mang explanation.

> "[It follows that] there is pervasion [i.e., whatever are different composed phenomena which are produced from their own same substantial cause are necessarily the same type of substantial entity] because the meaning of being phenomena which are the same or are not the same type of substantial entity must refer to their substantial cause as being the same or not the same; because there is a way of explaining the meaning of phenomena which are the same or are not the same type of substantial entity."
>
> If he accepts the basic consequence [the Sūtra School Challenger responds,] "It follows that the subjects, those two [a large and a small barley grain produced from one barley head which is their substantial cause], are not the same substantial entity because of not being phenomena which are produced as the same substantial entity; because of being different entities."

The Go-mang *Collected Topics* goes on to justify these two grains as different entities because of being objects which are mutually unrelated to each other and factually other (*phan tshun 'brel med don gzhan*).[1] Lati Rinbochay explains that phenomena which are different substantial entities are of two types, those that have a relation (*'brel ba yod mkhan*) and those that do not have a relation (*'brel ba med mkhan*). An example of different substantial phenomena which have a relation is a functioning thing and its cause, which have a

---

[1] Ngak-ŵang-d̄ra-s̄hi, Go-mang *Collected Topics*, p. 66.

causal relationship. A functioning thing is produced from its causes. Also, a functioning thing and its effects are different composed phenomena which have a causal relation. An example of different substantial entities which do not have a relation is two different persons, a pillar and a pot, or an eye consciousness and an odor. Any two phenomena which are mutually unrelated are necessarily different entities, but whatever phenomena are different entities are not necessarily mutually unrelated.[1]

There are four possibilities between the two principals of debate E.11, phenomena which are the same type of substantial entity and phenomena which are the same substantial entity:

1 Product and impermanent phenomenon are both the same substantial entity (because of being phenomena which are produced as the same entity) and the same type of substantial entity (because of being different composed phenomena which are produced from their own substantial cause). One can posit the substantial cause of product as a functioning thing which is a cause of product, and this also serves as a substantial cause of impermanent phenomenon.

2 An example of phenomena which are the same type of substantial entity but not the same substantial entity is a large apple and a small apple which are produced from the same branch of an apple tree which is their substantial cause.

3 Examples of phenomena which are the same substantial entity but not the same type of substantial entity are molasses and the visible form of molasses, or the self and the five aggregates, and so forth. These are phenomena which are produced as the same entity and appear inseparably to direct perceivers, but they are not produced from their own same substantial cause. For instance, the substantial cause of molasses is the molasses which is a cause of molasses. Whether

---

[1] Lati Rinbochay, oral commentary.

molasses is considered a taste-source or a tangible-object-source (as water because it is wet and moistening) the molasses of the former moment which is its substantial cause is the same; that is, it is either a taste-source or a tangible object-source. The visible form of molasses, however, is only the color and shape of molasses; thus, its substantial cause is a prior arising of the visible form of molasses and is not the same as the substantial cause of molasses. Still, molasses and the visible form of molasses are phenomena which are produced as the same entity. They are absolutely concomitant and appear inseparably to direct perceivers, but they are not produced from the same substantial cause.

4 Something which is neither is any singular phenomenon such as a pot, any two phenomena including at least one permanent phenomenon such as a pot and uncomposed space, a pillar and a pot, a positive phenomenon and a negative phenomenon, and so forth.

Debate E.12, Twelfth Mistaken View (16b.6)

Debate E.12, which is also modeled after a debate in the Go-mang *Collected Topics*,[1] is the final debate focusing on the various types of sameness and difference. Here the hypothetical Defender asserts that whatever phenomena are the same type (*rigs gcig pa, eka-jāti*) are necessarily the same essence (*bdag nyid gcig pa, eka-ātman*). Sameness is of three types: the same self-isolate, the same entity, and the same type. Phenomena which are the same essence are mutually inclusive with phenomena which are the same entity but not with phenomena which are the same type. Although these three categories are not mutually exclusive, whatever is the one is not necessarily the other. It is not the case that whatever phenomena are the same type are necessarily the same essence. The Sūtra School Challenger posits the counter-

---

[1] Ngak-w̄ang-d̄ra-s̄hi, Go-mang *Collected Topics*, pp. 60-61.

example of the two—a white horse and a black horse (*rta dkar nag gnyis*). These two are the same type because they are the same isolate type. However, they are not the same essence because they are not the same entity, for they are diverse entities.

> If someone [a hypothetical Defender] says, "Whatever phenomena are the same type are necessarily the same essence," [the Sūtra School Challenger responds to him,] "It [absurdly] follows that the subjects, the two—a white horse and a black horse, are the same essence because of being the same type. You asserted the pervasion."
>
> If he says that the reason is not established, [the Sūtra School Challenger responds,] "It follows that the subjects [the two—a white horse and a black horse] are [the same type] because of being the same isolate type."
>
> If he says that the reason is not established, [the Sūtra School Challenger responds,] "It follows that the subjects [the two—a white horse and a black horse] are [the same isolate type] because of being phenomena naturally able to produce an awareness thinking, 'This and that are alike,' upon merely being seen by whosoever directs the mind toward them."
>
> "[It follows that] there is pervasion [i.e., whatever phenomena are naturally able to produce an awareness thinking, 'This and that are alike,' upon merely being seen by whosoever directs the mind toward them are necessarily the same isolate type] because there is a meaning of being the same isolate type."

A white horse and a black horse are the same in the sense that they are able to induce a thought consciousness that associates them as horses. Thought consciousnesses proceed by a discrimination of types and a subsequent association of those types. Anyone seeing a white horse and a black horse might think that they are alike in being horses. Phenomena which are the same isolate type are defined as being the same in some respect for thought consciousnesses, but they are necessarily different phenomena and, probably, necessarily mutually exclusive.

> If he accepts the basic consequence, [the Sūtra School Challenger responds,] "It follows that the subjects [the two—a white horse and a black horse] are not the same essence because of being different entities; because of being mutually unrelated to each other and factually other."

Phenomena which are the same essence are mutually inclusive with phenomena which are the same entity. Whatever phenomena are different entities are necessarily not the same essence, and whatever objects are mutually unrelated to each other are necessarily different entities. Phenomena which are related to each other are related either causally or as phenomena which are the same essence. Therefore, whatever objects are mutually unrelated are necessarily not the same essence, and whatever phenomena are not the same essence are necessarily different entities.

There are four possibilities between the two principals of debate E.12, phenomena which are the same type and phenomena which are the same essence:

1   A pair which is both is the two—product and impermanent phenomenon. These are the same type because of being the same type of substantial entity. They are the same essence because of being the same substantial entity.

2   Things which are the same type but not the same essence are the two—a white horse and a black horse, the two—a large apple and a small apple produced from different substantial causes, and so forth.

3   An example of phenomena which are the same essence but are not the same type is the two—object of knowledge and impermanent phenomenon. These two are the same essence because of being phenomena the entities of which are not diverse. The entity of impermanent phe-

nomenon is not separate from the entity of object of knowledge. However, object of knowledge and impermanent phenomenon are not the same type because of being diverse types. To consider individually the divisions of phenomena which are the same type, these two are not the same type of substantial entity because of not being composed phenomena. Also, they are not the same isolate type, for they are neither positive phenomena which are the same isolate type nor negative phenomena which are the same isolate type. They are not negative phenomena which are the same isolate type because of not being negative phenomena. And they are not positive phenomena which are the same isolate type because they are not naturally able to produce an awareness thinking, "This and that are alike," upon merely being seen by whosoever directs the mind toward them.

4   Things which are neither are a pillar and a pot, a pot, and so forth.

Debate E.13, Thirteenth Mistaken View (17a.3)

In debate E.13, the last in this first section of the refutation of mistaken views with respect to causes and effects, the text leaves the consideration of the various types of sameness and difference to return to the general topic of causes and effects. Here the hypothetical Defender asserts that whatever is an effect of functioning thing's substantial cause is necessarily a substantial effect of functioning thing. This debate turns on a misinterpretation of the sequence of arising. Functioning thing's substantial effects are phenomena which arise *subsequently* to the arising of functioning thing itself, but the effects of functioning thing's substantial cause arise simultaneously with functioning thing and continue after that. Thus, the Sūtra School Challenger flings back the consequence that functioning thing would be a substantial effect of functioning thing (that is, of itself) because it is an effect of the substantial cause of functioning thing.

> If someone [a hypothetical Defender] says, "Whatever is an effect of functioning thing's substantial cause is necessarily a substantial effect of functioning thing," [the Sūtra School Challenger responds to him,] "It [absurdly] follows that the subject, functioning thing, is a substantial effect of functioning thing because of being an effect of functioning thing's substantial cause. You asserted the pervasion."
>
> If he says that the reason is not established, [the Sūtra School Challenger responds,] "It follows that the subject [functioning thing] is an effect of its own substantial cause because its substantial cause is a cause of it."

Functioning thing's substantial cause is a cause of functioning thing. It is not the only cause, but it is a cause and perhaps the most important one. The substance that makes up a composed phenomenon is a necessary but not sufficient condition for that phenomenon.

> If he accepts the basic consequence, [the Sūtra School Challenger responds,] "It follows that the subject [functioning thing] is not a substantial effect of functioning thing because of not being an effect of functioning thing."
>
> If he says that the reason is not established, [the Sūtra School Challenger responds,] "It follows with respect to the subject [functioning thing] that it is not its own effect because of being selfless."

No product is its own effect. A cause and its own effect cannot exist simultaneously. This is true for anything selfless. Of course, only functioning things have causes and effects, but permanent phenomena and non-existents too are not their own effects.

There are three possibilities between the two principals of debate E.13, effect of functioning thing's substantial cause and substantial effect of functioning thing:

1   Something which is both is a direct substantial effect of functioning thing. It is a substantial effect of functioning thing because of being a main object produced by functioning thing as a continuation of its substantial entity. A direct substantial effect of functioning thing is also an effect of functioning thing's substantial cause because of being an indirect effect of functioning thing's substantial cause.

2   Whatever is a substantial effect of functioning thing is necessarily an effect of functioning thing's substantial cause. This is because whatever is a substantial effect of functioning thing is necessarily an indirect effect of functioning thing's substantial cause. However, it is not the case that whatever is an effect of functioning thing's substantial cause is necessarily a substantial effect of functioning thing. This is because functioning thing, and only functioning thing itself, is an effect of functioning thing's substantial cause, but it is not a substantial effect of functioning thing.

3   Something which is neither is a substantial cause of functioning thing, which is neither an effect of itself nor an effect of its effect because it is selfless.

PRESENTATION OF THE AUTHOR'S OWN SYSTEM IN "THE INTRODUCTORY PRESENTATION OF CAUSES AND EFFECTS" (17A.5)

> Second, in our own system: There is a definition of a cause because a producer is the definition of a cause. The three—cause, effect, and functioning thing—are mutually inclusive. There is a definition of a cause of functioning thing because a producer of functioning thing is the definition of a cause of functioning thing; because if something is a

functioning thing, then its producer is necessarily the definition of its cause.

If the causes of functioning thing are divided, there are two because there are the two, the direct causes of functioning thing and the indirect causes of functioning thing. There is a definition of a direct cause of functioning thing because a direct producer of functioning thing is the definition of a direct cause of functioning thing. There is an illustration because a prior arising of functioning thing is a direct cause of functioning thing. There is a definition of an indirect cause of functioning thing because an indirect producer of functioning thing is the definition of an indirect cause of functioning thing. There is an illustration because a prior arising of functioning thing's prior arising is an indirect cause of functioning thing. Extend the reasoning in that way to the direct and indirect causes of all functioning things.

If the causes of functioning thing are divided in another way, there are two because there are the two, the substantial causes of functioning thing and the cooperative conditions of functioning thing. There is a definition of a substantial cause of functioning thing because a main producer of functioning thing as a continuation of its own substantial entity is the definition of a substantial cause of functioning thing. There is an illustration because a product which is a cause of functioning thing is a substantial cause of functioning thing. There is a definition of a cooperative condition of functioning thing because a main producer of functioning thing as a substantial entity which is not a continuation of its own substantial entity is the definition of a cooperative condition of functioning thing. There is an illustration because a person who is a cause of functioning thing is a cooperative condition of functioning thing.

600 Debate in Tibetan Buddhism

There is a definition of an effect because the produced is the definition of an effect. There is a definition of an effect of functioning thing because that
produced by functioning thing is the definition of an
effect of functioning thing. There is an illustration
because a subsequent arising of functioning thing is
an effect of functioning thing.

If the effects of functioning thing are divided,
there are two because there are the two, the direct
effects of functioning thing and the indirect effects
of functioning thing. There is a definition of a direct
effect of functioning thing because that produced
directly by functioning thing is the definition of a
direct effect of functioning thing. There is an illustration because a subsequent arising of functioning
thing is a direct effect of functioning thing. There is
a definition of an indirect effect of functioning thing
because that produced indirectly by functioning
thing is the definition of an indirect effect of functioning thing. There is an illustration because a subsequent arising of functioning thing's subsequent
arising is an indirect effect of functioning thing.
Extend the reasoning in that way to the direct and
indirect effects of other functioning things.

DISPELLING OBJECTIONS TO "THE INTRODUCTORY
PRESENTATION OF CAUSES AND EFFECTS" (18A.1)

This third and final section in the Tutor's introductory presentation of causes and effects consists of five debates, all of
which focus on the nature of causes and effects and do not
directly address the topic of the various types of sameness
and difference.

Debate E.14, First Objection (18a.1)

In this debate the hypothetical Challenger poses the consequence that there is no substantial cause of a functioning

thing because the prior arising of a functioning thing is not a substantial cause of a functioning thing. In fact, the reason is established. One cannot say that a functioning thing's prior arising is its substantial cause because its prior arising has two aspects, that of a substantial cause and that of a cooperative condition.

> Someone [a hypothetical Challenger] might say, "It follows that there is no substantial cause of a functioning thing because the prior arising of a functioning thing is not [its substantial cause]."

The correct answer to this consequence is that there is no pervasion. Even though it is true that the prior arising of a functioning thing is not its substantial cause, this does not necessarily entail that there is no substantial cause of a functioning thing. Rather, a functioning thing which is a cause of functioning thing is a substantial cause of functioning thing, but the prior arising of a functioning thing includes both its substantial causes and its cooperative conditions.

> If [another] says that the reason is not established, [the hypothetical Challenger will respond,] "It follows that the subject, the prior arising of a functioning thing, is not a substantial cause of a functioning thing because it is not definite to become a functioning thing [*khyod dngos por 'gyur nges ma yin pa'i phyir*]."

This reasoning does not obtain if applied to functioning thing itself. It is probably true for a particular instance of functioning thing that whatever is its substantial cause is definite to become *a* functioning thing.

> If [another] says that the reason is not established, [the hypothetical Challenger will respond], "It follows that the subject, the prior arising of a functioning thing, is not definite to become a functioning thing because of having become a functioning thing [*dngos po'i gyur zin pa'i phyir*]."

The prior arising of a functioning thing is something that has become a functioning thing because it is a functioning thing. In relation to the most general category of functioning things, its causes have become functioning things and they are also definite to become other functioning things. This is not necessarily the case for particular instances of functioning thing such as a pot. A pot's prior arising is something that is definite to become a pot, but it is not necessarily something that has become a pot because, for instance, clay may be a prior arising of a pot but it is not itself a pot.

> [To this the Sūtra School Defender responds,] "There is no pervasion [i.e., although it is true that the prior arising of a functioning thing has become a functioning thing, this does not entail that it is not definite to become a functioning thing]."

Any cause has become a functioning thing and also is definite to become a functioning thing.

> If someone [a hypothetical Defender] were to say that the reason [of the last consequence] is not established, [then the Sūtra School Challenger responds,] "It follows that the subject, the prior arising of a functioning thing, has become a functioning thing because of being a functioning thing."

Whatever is a functioning thing necessarily has become a functioning thing. This does not mean merely that whatever is a functioning thing is a functioning thing, but, more importantly, points out something about the nature of being a functioning thing and the process of becoming a functioning thing. Functioning things have become functioning things; they are newly arising effects.

Debate E.15, Second Objection (18a.3)

In this debate the hypothetical Challenger applies some of the information about causes and effects to the difficult case of functioning things of which being them is not possible. If, for instance, the two—a pillar and a pot—are functioning things, or even, *a* functioning thing, then their causes must exist, their effects must exist, and so on.

> Someone [a hypothetical Challenger] might say, "It follows with respect to the subjects, the two—a pillar and a pot, that their substantial cause exists because they are a functioning thing. You asserted the pervasion."

The author asserted the pervasion of this consequence in his general presentation of causes and effects. Also, the reason, that the two—a pillar and a pot—are a functioning thing, is established. The proper answer to this consequence is to accept it, the answer which a hypothetical Defender now gives.

> If [another] accepts the consequence, [the hypothetical Challenger responds,] "It follows with respect to the subjects, the two—a pillar and a pot, that there is something which is definite to become them because their substantial cause exists. You asserted the reason."
>
> If [another] accepts the consequence, [the hypothetical Challenger responds,] "It follows with respect to the subjects, the two—a pillar and a pot, that there is something which is them because there is something which is definite to become them."

The proper response to this consequence is that the reason is not established. There is nothing which is definite to become the two—a pillar and a pot. If there were something which is definite to become the two—a pillar and a pot, then there would soon be something which is the two—a pillar and a pot, as the pervasion of this consequence indicates.

However, the pervasion of this consequence is also faulty. It is not the case that if there is something which is definite to become it or them, then something which is it or them necessarily exists. This is because, for instance, as regards a particular functioning thing of the next moment, there is something which is definite to become it, but there is nothing which is it.

Also, one cannot accept the above consequence, that there is something which is the two—a pillar and a pot—because such is not possible. For consequences that lack both the establishment of the reason and the pervasion, one answers that the reason is not established because to deny the pervasion without first challenging the establishment of the reason implies acceptance of the reason. Here, the text does not provide any response to the consequence, but addresses an earlier consequence that the Sūtra School Defender would have answered differently.

> [To this the Sūtra School Defender responds,] "Earlier there was no pervasion [i.e., if their substantial cause exists, then something which is definite to become them does not necessarily exist]."

Even though it is true that there is a substantial cause of the two—a pillar and a pot, this does not necessitate that there is something which is definite to become the two—a pillar and a pot. That their substantial cause exists only means that there are substantial causes of each, it does not suggest that one thing becomes both of them. The debate revolves around Tibetan grammar which usually does not make distinctions of singular and plural; the student is being taught how to give a preferred reading in a particular context.

Here the text does not indicate specifically which of the "earlier" consequences this answer is intended to address. There are three consequences before this answer. With the first one the hypothetical Challenger correctly points out that the pervasion is in accord with the author's own system, thus one cannot effectively deny the pervasion now and still maintain the system of causes and effects as presented above. With the second consequence the hypothetical Challenger pointed out that the Sūtra School Defender had asserted the reason, but this is not a discordant circumstance for denying the pervasion. Also, as explained above, the proper answer to the third consequence is that the reason is not established. Thus the "earlier" consequence referred to here must be the second one.

The answer to the earlier consequence represents the effective end of debate E.15, but as an ancillary debate the Tutor Jam-ba-gya-tso spells out one underlying assumption of his system of causes and effects that gave rise to this debate, and relevant to that assumption, offers another possible debate.

> With respect to the position that whatever is a functioning thing is necessarily an effect of a cause of itself, someone [a hypothetical Challenger] might say, "It [absurdly] follows with respect to the subject, a cause of itself, that [it is an effect of the cause of itself] because of [being a functioning thing]."

It is an assertion of the Sūtra School that whatever is a functioning thing is necessarily an effect of its own cause, and this assertion was relevant to the hypothetical Challenger's consequence stated above that there is a substantial cause of the two—a pillar and a pot—because they are a functioning thing. Here the hypothetical Challenger is stating an absurd consequence based on this basic Sūtra School position. The assertion is stated in general, and his debate plays off the manner of expressing the general rule.

> [To this the Sūtra School Defender responds,] "The reason [that a cause of itself is a functioning thing] is not established because there is no cause of itself; because itself is a permanent phenomenon."

A cause of itself (*rang gi rgyu*) does not exist because "itself" (*rang*) in general is a permanent phenomenon. "Itself" is a permanent phenomenon because it is a mere abstraction. Outside the context of a specific usage, it does not refer to any particular thing but may refer to anything—an impermanent phenomenon, a permanent phenomenon, or even a non-existent. Thus, on its own its meaning is indefinite and abstract. Also, "it" (*khyod*), another pronoun frequently used in debate, is in general a permanent phenomenon for the same reasons.

Similarly, in general the subject (*chos can*), the predicate (*bsgrub bya'i chos* or *gsal ba*), and the sign (*rtags*) are also permanent because they are abstractions that may be any phenomenon, permanent and impermanent alike, as well as non-existents.

Although "itself" is in general a permanent phenomenon, the pervasion, whatever is a functioning thing is necessarily an effect of a cause of itself, is accurate as it is stated, for there is no viable counterexample. Whatever has the quality of being a functioning thing is pervaded by being an effect of a cause of itself. A cause of itself does not qualify because of not being a functioning thing since it is a non-existent. Permanent phenomena are uncaused; therefore, the cause of a permanent phenomenon does not exist.

Debate E.16, Third Objection (18a.5)

In this debate the hypothetical Challenger poses the absurd consequence that a pot is cause and effect because of being both a cause and an effect. A pot, like any functioning thing, is both a cause and an effect. It is a cause because of being a prior arising of a pot of the next moment. It is an effect because of being an effect of its own cause. Still, this does not necessarily imply that a pot is cause and effect, that is, in a relation of cause and effect like a seed and its sprout, because in order for things to be cause and effect they must be plural whereas a pot is only singular. For instance, a pot and a pot's effect are cause and effect because a pot is a cause of its own effect and its effect is an effect of the pot.

> Someone [a hypothetical Challenger] might say, "It follows that the subject, a pot, is cause and effect because of being both a cause and an effect." [To this the Sūtra School Defender responds,] "There is no pervasion."
>
> If someone were to accept the consequence, [then the Sūtra School Proponent would become

Challenger and respond,] "It follows that the subject, a pot, is not cause and effect because of not being different; because of being one."

Debate E.17, Fourth Objection (18a.6)

Debate E.17 develops out of the difference between functioning thing and what is not a permanent phenomenon. Here the hypothetical Challenger reasons that since whatever is a cause is necessarily a cause of a non-permanent phenomenon, then it absurdly follows that there is a cause of non-permanent phenomenon. Non-permanent phenomenon (*rtag pa ma yin pa*) cannot have a cause because it itself is a permanent phenomenon. Something which is not a permanent phenomenon may be any functioning thing or any non-existent; it is a category which does not include any permanent phenomena whatsoever. It is mutually exclusive with permanent phenomenon, but it is nonetheless a permanent phenomenon because, as an abstraction, non-permanent phenomenon can be the appearing object of only a thought consciousness.

> Someone [a hypothetical Challenger] might say, "It [absurdly] follows that there is a cause of non-permanent phenomenon because whatever is a cause is necessarily a cause of [a] non-permanent phenomenon."

It is indeed true that whatever is a cause is necessarily a cause of a non-permanent phenomenon because only functioning things are caused phenomena and all functioning things are not permanent phenomena. However, one can interpret this phrase (*rtag pa ma yin pa'i rgyu*) to mean "a cause of non-permanent phenomenon" and in this sense it cannot be true that a cause is a cause of non-permanent phenomenon because non-permanent phenomenon is itself an uncaused phenomenon. Similarly, in one sense it is true that whatever is a cause is necessarily a cause of an object of knowledge because all caused phenomena are objects of knowledge. However, one cannot say that whatever is a cause is necessarily a cause of object of knowledge because object of knowledge, as a permanent phenomenon, has no cause. This difference is easily communicated by the presence and absence of the article "a" in English, but in Tibetan the tendency not to use articles such as *zhig* requires that students learn to distinguish the proper reading by context.

> [To this the Sūtra School Defender responds,] "That is not correct because whatever is a cause is necessarily not a cause of non-permanent phenomenon."

Here the Sūtra School Defender's answer that the Challenger's reasoning "is not correct" has the force of answering that the reason is not established, for he justifies his denial with a reason that is the opposite of the Challenger's reason. Whatever is a cause is necessarily not a cause of non-permanent phenomenon because the latter does not exist. The Sūtra School Defender chooses to interpret the phrase to mean "a cause of non-permanent phenomenon", dropping the understood article, and a cause of non-permanent phenomenon does not exist even though a cause is necessarily a cause of *a* non-permanent phenomenon.

> "It follows that [whatever is a cause is necessarily not a cause of non-permanent phenomenon] because whatever is an established base is necessarily not a cause of non-permanent phenomenon."

Since whatever is an established base is not a cause of non-permanent phenomenon, the Sūtra School Proponent is showing that a cause of non-permanent phenomenon does not exist.

> "It follows that [whatever is an established base is necessarily not a cause of non-permanent phenomenon] because with regard to all established bases non-permanent phenomenon is not an effect."

This last reason is an unusual formulation of a statement of pervasion because the predicate portion of the pervasion contains both a grammatical subject and predicate whereas the first part does not. Thus, the first part, normally translated as "whatever is an established base", is here rendered "with regard to all established bases". In either case, this initial phrase serves to define the quantity of the statement, that is, to identify the limits of what is pervaded. This pervasion has the sense that from among all existents, non-permanent phenomenon is not found to be an effect. It is not being said that with regard to all established bases whatever is a non-permanent phenomenon is necessarily not an effect because any functioning thing is a non-permanent phenomenon which is an effect.

> "It follows that [with regard to all established bases non-permanent phenomenon is not an effect] because with regard to all established bases non-permanent phenomenon is not a functioning thing."

Since effects are functioning things and non-permanent phenomenon is not a functioning thing, it is also not an effect. There is no cause of non-permanent phenomenon.

Debate E.18, Fifth Objection (18b.2)

In debate E.18, the last in "The Introductory Presentation of Causes and Effects", a hypothetical Challenger tries to show that there is a common locus which is a cause of functioning thing and an effect of functioning thing; he is probably thinking that an impermanent phenomenon is a cause of *a* functioning thing and an effect of another functioning thing. However, this does not mean that there is something which is both a cause of functioning thing and an effect of functioning thing because once functioning thing's effects have arisen, its causes are no longer present and, on the other hand, at the time when functioning thing's causes exist, its effects are not yet arisen. This is a verbal debate, based on the manner of expressing objects and plays on the position of the words within the expression.

> Also, someone [a hypothetical Challenger] might say, "It follows that there is a common locus which is a cause of functioning thing and an effect of functioning thing because there is an effect of a functioning thing which is a cause of functioning thing." [To this the Sūtra School Defender responds,] "There is no pervasion."

As the text goes on to prove, in support of the Sūtra School Defender's answer that there is no pervasion, there is indeed an effect of a functioning thing which is a cause of functioning thing. Still, this does not necessarily entail that there is a common locus which is a cause of functioning thing and also its effect. An effect of a functioning thing which is a cause of functioning thing is, for instance, functioning thing itself. A functioning thing which is a cause of functioning thing exists prior to functioning thing itself, and its effect exists simultaneously with functioning thing itself. This is a convoluted way of expressing functioning thing in terms of its cause and its effect. Any functioning thing is both a cause and an effect, but this does not mean that a functioning thing is a common locus of its causes and its effects.

> [If another says that the reason is not established, then the Sūtra School Challenger responds,] "It follows that there is an effect of a functioning thing which is a cause of functioning thing because a functioning thing which is a cause of functioning thing is a cause."

Since a functioning thing which is a cause of functioning is a cause, its effect exists.

> "It follows that [a functioning thing which is a cause of functioning thing is a cause] because that [functioning thing which is a cause of functioning thing] is a functioning thing."

"Furthermore, it follows that there is an effect of a functioning thing which is a cause of functioning thing because functioning thing is an effect of a functioning thing which is a cause of functioning thing; because that [functioning thing] is a subsequent arising of a functioning thing which is a cause of functioning thing."

Generally, the term "furthermore" (*gzhan yang*) serves to introduce another line of reasoning arising from the same point of debate. A functioning thing which is a cause of functioning thing must exist prior to functioning thing itself although it need not exist in the immediately preceding moment. It is identified as a cause of functioning thing, and functioning thing itself is its effect or subsequent arising.

If someone says that the reason [that functioning thing is a subsequent arising of a functioning thing which is a cause of functioning thing] is not established, [the Sūtra School Challenger responds,] "It follows with respect to the subject, functioning thing, that it is a subsequent arising of a functioning thing which is a cause of it because it is a composed phenomenon."

Functioning thing, or even, *a* functioning thing, is a composed phenomenon, and if something is a composed phenomenon, it is necessarily a subsequent arising, or effect, of a functioning thing which served as its cause. Functioning things do not exist causelessly. They are inevitably the effects of other functioning things which existed prior to them and served as their causes.

With respect to what was said, someone [a hypothetical Challenger] might say, "It follows with respect to the subject, functioning thing, that there is no effect of it [i.e., a functioning thing] which is a cause of it [i.e., functioning thing] because there is nothing which is its cause and its effect."

Here the consequence is stated in the generalized form with the pronoun "it", but because the subject is "functioning thing" it bears the same force as the above statements. When the Sūtra School Defender answered the Challenger's original consequence that there is no pervasion, he implicitly accepted the establishment of the reason, that there is an effect of a functioning thing which is a cause of functioning thing. Then, becoming the Challenger, the Sūtra School Proponent further supported this position against the denial of another Defender. Thus, when the new Challenger now asserts that there is no such effect of a functioning thing which is a cause of functioning thing, the Sūtra School Defender again moves to deny that position.

> [To this the Sūtra School Defender responds,] "There is no pervasion [i.e., even though it is true that there is nothing which is its cause and its effect, this does not necessarily imply that there is no effect of it which is a cause of it."

When stated in the generalized form, it seems obvious that there could be no effect of something which is a cause of something, and, indeed, if the relative pronoun "which" is taken as referring to *"effect"* thus meaning "effect which is a cause of something", then such could not exist. Such an effect could not exist because as a cause of something it would have to occur prior to that which it causes and, absurdly, prior to that of which it is an effect. The supposed sequence is that there is some phenomenon which produces an effect which is also a cause of just that some phenomenon which produced it. This position is ridiculous by any reckoning of the nature of cause and effect.

Nevertheless, here the Sūtra School Proponent is defending that there is an effect of something which is a cause of something, but this is not understood in the sense outlined above. Rather, in the preferred interpretation, the relative pronoun "which" refers, not to "an effect" as in "an effect which", but to *"something"*, thus meaning "something which is a cause of something". In this sense something which is a cause of some [other] thing is the same as its effect in the sense that both share the quality of being the same type of composed phenomena—pots, pillars, consciousnesses, functioning things, and so on. Once something is identified as a cause of some [other] thing, there must certainly be an effect of it. In this sense, an effect of something which is a cause of something may be understood.

> [One cannot accept that there is no effect of it which is a cause of it, for] "It follows with respect to the subject, functioning thing, that there is an effect of it which is a cause of it because (1) there is something [i.e., a functioning thing] which is a cause of it [i.e., functioning thing] and (2) that [functioning thing which is a cause of functioning thing] is not a permanent phenomenon."

Here the Sūtra School Challenger is showing that there is an effect of a functioning thing which is a cause of functioning thing merely by showing that there is a functioning thing which is a cause of functioning thing. Once something is a cause, its effect will exist. Also, if something is a functioning thing, it will necessarily produce an effect. Thus, the reason that (1) there is something which is a cause of it and (2) that cause is not a permanent phenomenon implies that there necessarily exists an effect of that thing which is a cause of it.

Moreover, that there is an effect of a functioning thing which is a cause of functioning thing is not limited to merely the singular class of functioning things, for it is also true of pots and so forth. For instance, there is an effect of a pot which is a cause of a pot. With respect to a pot the continuum of which exists in two consecutive moments, the pot that exists in the second moment has as its substantial cause the pot that existed in the first moment. The pot which existed in the first moment is a pot which is a cause of a pot. Its effect is a pot. Thus, there is a pot which is an effect of a pot which is a cause of a pot.

REMARKS

"The Introductory Presentation of Causes and Effects" forces consideration of some of the major themes in the Collected Topics tradition. Several of the debates in this chapter teach the student to discriminate between references to functioning thing in general and functioning thing collectively. This information, which is communicated in English as an article game (that is, does the referent take an indefinite article or not) leads the student to consider closely just what is being referred to as the subject. Is the subject a (specific but unspecified) functioning thing, functioning things in general, or the collective functioning thing? If it is the collective functioning thing, what does this represent? These questions will be taken up in detail in the conclusion (see pp. 773ff).

Relevant to the consideration of the nature of the subject, in "The Introductory Presentation of Causes and Effects" the Collected Topics logicians are forced to put forth some incredible assertions. For instance, in the presentation of the author's own system the text posits "a product which is a cause of functioning thing" as a substantial cause of functioning thing and "a person who is a cause of functioning thing" as a cooperative condition of functioning thing. These assertions point up what is almost an obsession in the Collected Topics tradition with positing collective phenomena, however vague they may be, and trying to posit their causes, effects, and so forth even if they are difficult to imagine. The difficulty here is this: Why is it that a person is a cooperative condition of functioning thing but a product is a substantial cause of functioning thing? Is it not the case that a person or a pot or a pillar equally contribute to the substantial entity of functioning thing as well as does any product? This question leads one to wonder whether the substantial cause referred to here is *a* product which is a cause of functioning thing or *product* which is a cause of functioning thing. Clearly, being a product is more predominantly associated with being a functioning thing than is being a person.

This emphasis on positing collective subjects has the pedagogical function of forcing students to analyze the referent closely. In turn, this sort of analysis matures the student for the study of the Middle Way School through suggesting the distinction between the functionality of phenomena and the ultimate findability of those phenomena, for the Proponents of the Middle Way assert that phenomena exist and perform functions but under analysis cannot be found to be ultimately existent.

A second major quandary in this chapter is that even though a pot which is a cause of functioning thing is a pot and also is a functioning thing, it is not the same substantial entity as functioning thing. Is it not reasonable that every functioning thing is the same substantial entity as functioning thing? Yet, this is denied in the Collected Topics tradition. Their denial of this borders on the absurd. They reason that since a cause of functioning thing exists prior to functioning thing, it is not simultaneous with its effect and thus cannot be the same substantial entity. Still, it is a functioning thing and thus would seem to be the same entity as functioning thing, as is the relation between an instance and a generality. However, a cause of functioning thing, though a functioning thing itself, is not an instance of functioning thing. We are being introduced to the counterintuitive.

Although the previous chapters broach these issues of the article game and the nature of the referent, this chapter forcefully brings them into the open. However, it would be misleading to suggest that the only purpose of "The Introductory Presentation of Causes and Effects" is to treat these topics. Rather, the study of causes and effects, traditionally begun with this chapter in "The Introductory Path of Reasoning", serves to reduce one's inflated sense of a permanent self by causing one to view all functioning things, including one's own mind and body, as dependent phenomena produced from causes and conditions. Once one's mind and body are caused phenomena, when those causes which gave rise to this body and mind are exhausted, then this body and mind will separate. Seeing the dependent nature of a human life, Buddhist practitioners are inspired to make effort toward the practices which produce happiness. Lati Rinbochay compares effort to a horse which carries a rider toward happiness, and knowledge of impermanence, made firm by the study of causes and effects, to a rider's whip which enables the rider to hasten on the horse of effort toward the happiness of enlightenment.

13 Generalities and Instances

INTRODUCTION

Effects are related to their causes as that arisen from them;
instances and their generalities are related as the same
essence. The followers of Dignāga and Dharmakīrti assert
only two types of relations: phenomena related as the same
essence (*bdag gcig 'brel, tādātmya-saṃbandha*) and phenomena
related as that arisen from that (*de byung 'brel, tadutpatti-
saṃbandha*). For example, a clay pot is related to its substantial cause, clay, as that arisen from it. It is the effect of the
clay. And, a clay pot is related to its generalities, such as
functioning thing, as the same essence.

Causes and their effects are not related as the same
essence, and the one is neither an instance nor a generality
of the other. This is one way in which generalities and
instances are distinguished from causes and effects. For, the
process for establishing a phenomenon as an instance of its
generality involves establishing it as related with that generality as the same essence, and this excludes the cause-
effect relationship.

The definition of a generality (*spyi, sāmānya*) is:

> a phenomenon that encompasses its manifestations (*rang gi gsal ba la rjes su 'gro ba'i chos, *svavyakti-anvaya-dharma*).

A generality must be an existent, and it may be either a permanent or an impermanent phenomenon. An example is object of knowledge, which encompasses its manifestations (that is to say, its instances) in the sense that each and every object of knowledge is of the same type—each is suitable as an object of an awareness. The instances of object of knowledge are its manifestations, for they manifest the quality of an object of knowledge. The term "manifestation" (*gsal ba, vyakti*) is taken from a non-Buddhist tradition.[1] The Ra-dö *Collected Topics* says:

> At the time of debating, the definition of a generality [should be posited as] a phenomenon which has manifestations (*gsal ldan gyi chos*).[2]

The Shar-dzay *Collected Topics* puts the definition as:

> a pervader (*khyab byed*).[3]

A generality is a pervader of its manifestations; it encompasses and accompanies them. For instance, wherever a manifestation of functioning thing exists, there functioning thing necessarily exists.

An instance (*bye brag, visheṣa*) is defined as:

> a phenomenon which has a type engaging it as a pervader (*khyab byed du 'jug pa'i rang gi rigs yod pa can gyi chos*)

or, as in the Shar-dzay *Collected Topics*, as:

> the pervaded (*khyab bya*).[4]

---

[1] According to Jeffrey Hopkins, this is in Den-dar-hla-ram-ba's *Beginnings of a Presentation of Generally and Specifically Characterized Phenomena*.
[2] Jam-ȳang-chok-hla-ö-ser, Ra-dö *Collected Topics*, 34a.3.
[3] Dzemay Rinbochay, Shar-dzay *Collected Topics*, p. 31.
[4] *Ibid.*

An example is a functioning thing, as it is an instance of object of knowledge, a type that pervades all functioning things.

The followers of the system of reasoning founded by Dignāga and Dharmakīrti argue that there is no generality as a separate entity from its instances and that a generality and its instances are the same essence. However, some non-Buddhists say that there is a generality above and beyond its instances and that it is a different essence from its instances. In his *Commentary on (Dignāga's) "Compendium of Valid Cognition"* Dharmakīrti refutes the notion that there could be a generality which exists as a separate entity from its instances.[1]

For example, every man, woman, and child is an instance of the generality, human, which pervades every human. Some non-Buddhists assert that this generality is a different entity from the instances of humans that it pervades. The Buddhists deny this, saying that the generality and its instances are not different entities. Even though it certainly seems as if there is some general person who is separate and apart from all of its various manifestations, the Buddhists say that when one investigates to find what this is, it cannot be found. Still, the two, a human who is an instance of human and the human which is a generality, are mutually exclusive. There is no common locus of these two, but even so they are not different entities; they are the same entity. Because all the instances are men, women, and children and the human generality is said by some non-Buddhists to be a different entity from its instances, as a functioning thing the generality would also be a different substantial entity from its instances. Since it is a functioning thing, it would be an object of a direct perceiver and would be perceived as a different substantial entity from its instances, but such is not seen.

---

[1] This section on the refutation of a generality which is a separate entity from its instances is from Kensur Jambel Shenpen, oral commentary.

There is also a refutation of a difference of entity of a generality and its instances done in terms of gross objects. For instance, within a table there are many subtle particles, and one has a sense of the gross and subtle as separate. To thought, it appears that, on the one hand, there is the gross table and, on the other, there are all of the subtle particles. Still, these are not different entities, for they are the same entity. If indeed they were separate entities, then just as one can separate one table from another, so one should be able to put all of the subtle particles in one place and still have the gross table. A gross table and its subtle or minute particles can be separated out for the appearance and determining factors of thought consciousnesses in the sense that it is possible to talk and think about the subtle particles apart from the gross table. However, if they were indeed different entities, they would have to be simultaneous, different entities, for a gross table and the subtle particles that compose it cannot exist in different times but must exist together in time. If they were simultaneous, different entities, then one ought to be able to separate them for they would be unrelated, as they would not be causally related because of being simultaneous and they would not be related as the same essence because of being different entities. If they were unrelated different entities, one should be able to remove the subtle particles and still have the table or lift off the table and still have the subtle particles. One can separate the gross from the subtle in terms of what appears to thought, but in fact the two—the gross table and the subtle particles of the table—are undifferentiably mixed together. They are different for thought, but they are not different entities.

In this way, generalities also are not separate entities from their instances. Since they are not causally related, if they were also separate entities they would be totally unrelated phenomena, but obviously they are not. Rather, a generality is designated to the basis of its instances. Apart from men, women, and children there are no humans. In order to understand the non-inherent existence (*rang bzhin gyis ma grub pa*) of all phenomena as presented in the Middle Way Consequence School (*dbu ma thal 'gyur pa, prāsaṅgika-mādhyamika*) an understanding of this sort of topic is an essential beginning.[1]

THE THREE CHARACTERISTICS QUALIFYING A PHENOMENON AS AN INSTANCE OF A CERTAIN GENERALITY

Even though it is true that an instance of a phenomenon must be the same essence as that phenomenon, it is not the case that whatever phenomena are related as the same essence are necessarily a generality and its instance. Rather, the process for establishing a phenomenon as an instance of its generality involves the establishment of three necessary qualities. According to the Ra-dö *Collected Topics*:

> The definition of something's being an instance of that phenomenon (*rang nyid chos de bye brag yin pa*) is that which is observed as a common locus such that (1) it is that phenomenon, (2) it is related with that phenomenon as the same essence, and (3) many common locuses of not being it [that is, the instance] and also being that phenomenon are established (*rang nyid chos de yin rang nyid chos de dang bdag gcig tu 'brel rang nyid ma yin zhing chos de yang yin pa'i gzhi mthun du ma grub pa yang yin pa'i gzhi mthun du dmigs pa de*).[2]

For instance, a horse is an instance of a person because of being observed as a common locus such that (1) it is a person, (2) it is related with person as the same essence, and (3) many common locuses of not being it (that is, a horse) and also being a person are established. If all three of these qualities are complete, the phenomenon is established as an instance of that generality. If any one of the three is not fulfilled, the phenomenon does not qualify as an instance of

---

[1] Kensur Jambel Shenpen, oral commentary, trans. by Elizabeth Napper.
[2] Jam-yang-chok-hla-ö-ser, Ra-dö *Collected Topics*, 34a.4-5.

that other phenomenon. It is important to examine each of the three requirements in turn as well as to consider the interplay between them.

First Requirement: An Instance Demonstrates the Quality of Its Generality

The first characteristic qualifying a phenomenon as an instance of a certain generality is that it must have the quality of that phenomenon which is its generality. A horse is a person. This is because it is a being who is imputed in dependence upon any of the five aggregates. This first quality of an instance is the least restrictive and the most apparent. It is obvious that an instance of some phenomenon must be that phenomenon. Otherwise, one might say that a pot is an instance of permanent phenomenon.

The first requirement is the most obvious; in any system of philosophy it must be the case that an instance embodies the quality of a phenomenon which is its generality. It must be that phenomenon as a wooden chair is a chair. A phenomenon which is not a certain thing cannot be an instance of that thing. Still, despite its obvious importance, the first requirement alone is not sufficient.

Second Requirement: An Instance Is Related With Its Generality as the Same Essence

The second characteristic qualifying a phenomenon as an instance of a certain generality is that it must be related with its generality as the same essence. For instance, a horse is related with person as the same essence because, according to the reasoning given in the Tutor's *Collected Topics*:

> (1) it is the same essence as person, (2) it is different from person, and (3) if persons did not exist, then it [that is, a horse] too would not exist (*gang zag dang*

> *bdag nyid gcig yin pa gang zhig gang zag dang tha dad*
> *kyang yin gang zag med na khyod med dgos pa'i phyir).*[1]

A horse is the same essence as person because of being the
same nature (*rang bzhin gcig pa*) as person. Person and
horses are the same substantial entity. Of course, it is not the
case that whatever is a person is necessarily a horse, but
whatever is a horse is necessarily a person. One cannot find
the two of them apart. If there is a horse, there is a person.
Secondly, a horse is different from person in the sense that it
is not exactly the same as person in both name and meaning.
Finally, if persons did not exist, then horses too would not
exist. At a place where there are no persons there are no
horses. To use Western vocabulary, horses are a proper sub-
set of all persons, and they are related with persons in the
sense that they are included within them.

Third Requirement: There Are Many Common Locuses of Not Being That Particular Instance and Also Being That Generality

The third requirement of an instance assures that there are
other phenomena which have the quality of that generality.
For example, there are many common locuses of not being a
horse and also being a person because (1) a cow is such a
common locus and (2) a human is such a common locus and
(3) those two (a cow and a human) are established as
mutually different. It is clear that neither a cow nor a human
is a horse and that both a cow and a human are persons
because they are beings who are imputed in dependence on
any of the five aggregates. Also, a cow and a human are
established as *mutually* different because a cow is different
from a human and a human is different from a cow.

---

[1] Pur-bu-jok Jam-ba-gya-tso, "The Introductory Path of Reasoning" of the
Tutor's *Collected Topics*, 19a.2-3.

What Each Requirement Excludes

The mere requirement that an instance must embody the quality of its generality is by itself too broad, for it would allow the possibility of some non-generalities to have "instances". For example, there are non-existents such as only-a-permanent-phenomenon (*rtag pa kho na*) for which, although they themselves do not exist, there are phenomena which are them. For instance, uncomposed space is only a permanent phenomenon, and if merely being something qualified a phenomenon as an instance of it, then uncomposed space would be an instance of only-a-permanent-phenomenon and only-a-permanent-phenomenon would be a generality. Since all generalities are objects of knowledge, only-a-permanent-phenomenon would then absurdly be an existent. If only-a-permanent-phenomenon existed, then functioning things would not exist.

Since an instance must be that phenomenon which is its generality, some phenomena such as objects of knowledge of which being them is not possible cannot qualify as generalities, for there is nothing which demonstrates the being of any of them. For example, even though the two—a pillar and a pot—exist, there is nothing which is such an object of knowledge. Thus, the two—a pillar and a pot, along with all objects of knowledge of which being them is not possible, are not generalities.

Nonetheless, objects of knowledge of which being them is not possible are instances, for this first requirement of an instance does not prevent the two—a pillar and a pot—from being an instance. Rather, these two are a functioning thing and an instance of functioning thing, they are an object of knowledge and an instance of object of knowledge, and so on.

The second requirement of instances, that they are related with their generalities as the same essence, serves to eliminate non-existents, unrelated phenomena, and phenomena which are causally related. A non-existent cannot be an instance of any generality because it cannot be related with anything as the same essence, for it is not a phenomenon. Some non-existents fulfill the first and third requirements of an instance, but the second prevents them from being instances of anything. For example, on the one hand the horn of a rabbit is selfless and many common locuses of not being the horn of a rabbit and also being selfless are established; however, since the horn of a rabbit is not related with the selfless as the same essence, it is not an instance of the selfless. No non-existent can be related with any phenomenon because whatever is related must be an existent, for it must be a different *phenomenon* from that to which it is related. Clearly, a non-existent cannot be an instance because of not being a phenomenon which has a type engaging it as a pervader—the definition of an instance—for it is not a phenomenon.

Also, the second requirement of an instance prevents non-existents not only from being instances but also from being generalities. Again, the first and third requirements may be satisfied, but the second cannot be complete. In the case of a non-existent of which being it is possible (*yin pa srid pa'i med pa*), such as only-a-permanent-phenomenon, there is something which is it, for uncomposed space is only a permanent phenomenon. Also, there are many phenomena which are not uncomposed space but are only permanent phenomena. Thus, the first and third requirements of an instance are complete. Yet, uncomposed space is not related with only-a-permanent-phenomenon as the same essence because even though only-a-permanent-phenomenon does not exist, uncomposed space still exists.

In the case of a non-existent of which being it is not possible (*yin pa mi srid pa'i med pa*), none of the three requirements of an instance are met. For instance, a child of a barren woman is not a generality because (1) there is nothing which is the child of a barren woman, (2) there is nothing which is related with the child of a barren woman as the same essence, and (3) there is no common locus which is not anything but is the child of a barren woman. In this case, none of the three requirements are established, but even if only one were not established, that would effectively prevent something from being an instance or a generality.

Because instances are characterized as being related with their generalities as the same essence, unrelated phenomena and causally related phenomena cannot be established as a generality and its instance. For example, a gold pot and a copper pot are unrelated phenomena because they are neither related as the same essence nor causally related. They are not related as the same essence because if gold pots did not exist, a copper pot might still exist and even if copper pots did not exist, a gold pot might exist. They are not causally related because neither is the cause or effect of the other. Thus, a gold pot is neither an instance nor a generality of a copper pot because they are unrelated phenomena. Of course, in this case the first requirement also would not be met, for a gold pot is not a copper pot and a copper pot is not a gold pot.

Also, a cause of functioning thing is not an instance of functioning thing even though it is a functioning thing and many common locuses of not being a cause of functioning thing and also being a functioning thing are established. This is because a cause of functioning thing is not related with functioning thing as the same essence, for it is not the same essence as functioning thing. Functioning thing and its cause are impermanent phenomena which appear separately to direct perception. They are different substantial entities and different essences but are causally related. Therefore, they are not a generality and its instance.

The third requirement of instances prevents their being a generality with fewer than three existents which are that phenomenon. There must be the instance in question and "many", meaning at least two other phenomena, which embody the quality of that generality. For example, sound is not an instance of sound's isolate because, even though sound is sound's isolate and sound is related with its isolate as the same essence, other than sound itself there is nothing which one can posit as sound's isolate. This is also true for anything coextensive with the isolate of some phenomenon. One-with-sound (a phenomenon coextensive with sound's isolate) is not a generality of sound because, even though sound is one with sound and it is related with one-with-sound as the same essence, there is no common locus which is not sound and also is one with sound. Also, the definiendum of an object of hearing is not a generality of sound, nor is the triply qualified imputed existent of an object of hearing, and so forth.

In addition, because of the third requirement, mutually inclusive phenomena cannot be a generality and its instance. For example, impermanent phenomenon is a functioning thing and it is related to functioning thing as the same essence, but there is nothing which is not an impermanent phenomenon and also is a functioning thing; thus, impermanent phenomenon is not an instance of functioning thing.

Similarly, object of knowledge is not an instance of existent. It is an existent and it is related to existent as the same essence, but other than objects of knowledge there are no existents. Because of the third requirement, established base and the phenomena mutually inclusive with it cannot be an instance of anything, for there is no common locus which is not an existent. Someone might suggest that object of knowledge is an instance because it is an instance of the selfless. This is so, he may reason, because (1) object of knowledge is selfless, (2) it is related with the selfless as the same essence, and (3) many common locuses of not being an object of knowledge and also being selfless are established. It is true that object of knowledge, like any existent or nonexistent, is selfless. Also, it is related with the selfless as the same essence because (1) it is the same essence as the selfless, (2) it is different from the selfless, and (3) if the selfless did not exist, then objects of knowledge also would not exist. However, the third part of the reason—that there are many common locuses of not being an object of knowledge and also being selfless—is not established. An opponent might insist that there are many such common locuses because the horn of rabbit is such and also the child of a barren woman is such, and those two are mutually different. This position, however, is mistaken because the horn of a rabbit and the child of a barren woman are not established by a valid cognizer. The third requirement involves that "many common locuses must be *established*", and this means that they must be established (as existing) by valid cognition. Thus, non-existents are not common locuses because whatever is a common locus must be an established base. Though the horn of a rabbit is not an object of knowledge and also is selfless, it is not a common locus of these two. A non-existent is not a locus of any qualities. Further, the horn of a rabbit and the child of a barren woman are not mutually different because neither is different from the other, for neither is a phenomenon. Moreover, the horn of a rabbit and the child of a barren woman are not many (*du ma*) because if things are many, they must be existents. Whatever is either one or many must exist. A non-existent is neither one nor many because of not being a phenomenon.[1]

Thus, it is concluded that object of knowledge and the phenomena mutually inclusive with it are not instances of any generality, not even the selfless. However, this does not mean that the selfless is not a generality, for it has many instances—functioning thing, permanent phenomenon, definition, definiendum, and so forth; it only means that the selfless is not a generality of object of knowledge. Since object of knowledge is a generality but not an instance, it is only a generality (*spyi kho na*). Any of the phenomena mutually inclusive with object of knowledge and the selfless as well are only generalities.

Also, phenomena such as different-from-functioning-thing are only generalities. Different-from-functioning-thing is a generality, for there are instances of it such as a permanent phenomenon and a pot. For example, a permanent phenomenon is an instance of different-from-functioning-thing because (1) it is different from functioning thing, (2) it

---

[1] Denma Lochö Rinbochay, oral commentary.

is related with different-from-functioning-thing as the same essence, and (3) there are many common locuses of not being a permanent phenomena and also being different from functioning thing. However, different-from-functioning-thing is not an instance of any phenomenon, even object of knowledge or the selfless. It is an object of knowledge, and it is related with object of knowledge as the same essence, but many common locuses of not being different from functioning thing and also being objects of knowledge are not established. There is only functioning thing itself which is not different from functioning thing and also is an object of knowledge. Thus, different-from-functioning-thing and similar phenomena are not instances of anything.

Only-a-generality, like only-a-permanent-phenomenon, is a non-existent of which being it is possible. Only-a-generality does not exist because it is not the case that only generalities exist since instances exist, but there are phenomena which are only generalities, such as object of knowledge.

Similarly, there are phenomena which are only instances but only-an-instance does not exist because it is not the case that only instances exist since there are generalities. For example, the two—a pillar and a pot—are only an instance. Objects of knowledge of which being them is not possible are instances of, for example, object of knowledge, but since there is nothing which is any particular object of knowledge of which being them is not possible, they are not generalities. Also, isolates and the phenomena coextensive with isolates are instances which are not generalities.

THE DIVISIONS OF GENERALITIES

Objects of knowledge are exhaustively divided into generalities and instances. There is nothing which is not one or the other. However, unlike the division of established bases into permanent and impermanent phenomena such that there is nothing which is both, there are phenomena which are both instances and generalities. Functioning thing, for example, is an instance of object of knowledge and a generality of form. Some phenomena are only generalities and some are only instances, but whatever exists is necessarily one or the other or both. Generality and instance are both permanent phenomena, for they are merely imputed to their bases. Of course, one cannot say that whatever is a generality or an instance is necessarily a permanent phenomenon, but generality as such and instance as such are permanent phenomena like one and different.

Generalities are terminologically divided into the three:

1 type-generalities (*rigs spyi, jāti-sāmānya*)
2 meaning-generalities (*don spyi, artha-sāmānya*)
3 collection-generalities (*tshogs spyi, sāmagrī-sāmānya*).

A terminological division (*sgras brjod rigs kyi sgo nas dbye ba*) here indicates that some of the divisions of generalities are not necessarily generalities and are only called such. Indeed, the Go-mang *Collected Topics* says that whatever is a generality is necessarily a type-generality, and the two, generality and type-generality, are mutually inclusive.[1] Moreover, some meaning-generalities and some collection-generalities are not generalities, as will be explained below.

The definition of a type-generality is:

> a phenomenon which encompasses the many which have its type (*rang gi rigs can du ma la rjes su 'gro ba'i chos*).

This definition incorporates elements from both the definition of a generality and the definition of an instance. A generality is a phenomenon which encompasses its manifestations, and an instance is a phenomenon which has a type engaging it as a pervader. A type-generality encompasses the many phenomena which have its type. The "many phenomena which have its type" are its instances, and the way

---

[1] Ngak-ŵang-dra-ŝhi, Go-mang *Collected Topics*, p. 152.

in which a type-generality, or any generality, "encompasses" its instances is as a pervader. A generality engages its instances as a pervader. For example, all objects of knowledge share the quality of being suitable as objects of an awareness. All phenomena, permanent and impermanent, are *included within the type* of things which are objects of knowledge. Instances of one generality share certain qualities. The generality encompasses its instances.

The Tutor's *Collected Topics* does not give a definition of a meaning-generality as such, but when applied to a particular case such as pot one can posit a definition. The definition of the meaning-generality of pot (*bum pa'i don spyi*), as in the Tutor's *Collected Topics*, is:

> that imputed factor which, although it is not a pot, appears to the thought apprehending a pot as a pot (*bum 'dzin rtog pa la bum pa ma yin bzhin du bum pa lta bur snang ba'i sgro btags kyi cha*).

A meaning-generality is a mental construction of an image like a pot which mistakenly seems to be a pot to a thought consciousness, insofar as one understands a pot by the appearance of something which is not a pot. It is not a pot because it cannot perform the functions of a pot—holding water and so forth. An illustration of a meaning-generality of pot is an appearance (to a thought consciousness in its second moment of apprehending a pot) of opposite-from-not-being-pot-of-the-second-moment.

Meaning-generality is a generality because it has instances. An instance of meaning-generality is a meaning-generality of pot. A meaning-generality of pot is also a generality because it has as its instances the meaning-generalities of pot which exist in the mental continuums of many persons or the many moments of a meaning-generality of pot in one person's continuum. However, whatever is a meaning-generality is not necessarily a generality because the two—the meaning generality of pot that exists in one person's continuum and the meaning-generality of pot that exists in another person's continuum—are meaning-generalities, but since there is nothing which is the two of them, they are not a generality.

The definition of a collection-generality is:

> a gross form which is a composite of its many parts
> (*rang gi cha shes du ma 'dus pa'i gzugs rags pa*)

These are only material phenomena. A gross form is not merely what is readily perceivable, but is a form that is a composite of material particles and is not a subtle form such as a single material particle. Such a particle is a collection of the various *potencies* of earth, water, and so forth, but it is an extremely subtle material phenomenon and not a gross one. Illustrations of a collection-generality are a pot, a pillar, and so on. Such material phenomena are gross forms which are composites of their many parts, the various particles that make them up. Any composite matter is a collection-generality. Even the two—a pillar and a pot—are a collection-generality because of being gross forms which are composites of their many parts. Since the two together are considered a collection-generality, whatever is a collection-generality is not necessarily a generality because material phenomena of which being them is not possible cannot be generalities since there is nothing which can satisfy the first requirement of an instance of any of them. The reason for calling a collection-generality a "generality" is not that each and every one of them is a generality but because they are gross compositions of their many parts.

REFUTATION OF MISTAKEN VIEWS CONCERNING GENERALITIES AND INSTANCES (18B.5)

In the Tutor's *Collected Topics*, the first section in the presentation of generalities and instances consists of eight debates. Several of the debates in this and the other sections are modeled after debates in the Go-mang and Ra-dö *Collected Topics*. This subject matter is very fertile for debate because the various components of establishing a phenomenon as an instance of its generality can each serve as a source for debate, and also, as in some of the later debates, by combining the qualifiers describing a phenomenon one can create quite difficult debates. For instance, rather than debating about merely a generality of a pot, one might debate on the generality of a generality-of-a-pot.

Debate F.1, First Mistaken View (18b.6)

Debate F.1 is closely modeled after a debate in the Go-mang *Collected Topics*.[1] Here the hypothetical Defender asserts that whatever is a generality is necessarily not an instance. Of course, such is not the case in this system. The Sūtra School Challenger posits the counterexample of functioning thing, something which is both a generality and an instance. This debate is provided for the sake of showing that even though established bases are divided completely between generalities and instances, it is not the case that these two are mutually exclusive. Something which is one may also be the other.

> If someone [a hypothetical Defender] says, "Whatever is a generality is necessarily not an instance," [the Sūtra School Challenger responds to him,] "It [absurdly] follows that the subject, functioning thing, is not an instance because of being a generality. You asserted the pervasion."
>
> If he says that the reason is not established, [the Sūtra School Challenger responds,] "It follows that the subject, functioning thing, is a generality because there are instances of it."

This is the standard reason for justifying a subject as a generality—because there are instances of it. If there are instances of something, then it is necessarily a generality. Being a generality depends on having instances. If a phenomenon's instances go out of existence, then it can no longer remain as a generality. When dinosaurs ceased to

---

[1] *Ibid.*, pp. 127-130.

exist, then dinosaur as a generality also ceased to exist. According to the Buddhist view, beyond the mere abolition of the actual dinosaurs nothing further is required for the dissolution of dinosaur as a generality. There can be no generality apart from its instances in the sense of being a separate entity from them.

> If he says that the reason is not established, [the Sūtra School Challenger responds,] "It follows with respect to the subject, functioning thing, that there are instances of it because a pot is [an instance of functioning thing]."

In order to prove that there are instances of some generality, it is sufficient to posit only one instance. If a pot is an instance of functioning thing, then there is an instance of functioning thing. In proving a pot as such one does not also establish other phenomena as instances of functioning thing, but one must establish that there are "many" other phenomena which are functioning things. And once there are many things that are functioning things, there are likely other instances. There is no counterexample to this position. If something has one instance, it necessarily has many.

> If he says that the reason is not established, [the Sūtra School Challenger responds,] "It follows with respect to the subject, a pot, that it is an instance of functioning thing because (1) it is a functioning thing, (2) it is related with functioning thing as the same essence, and (3) many common locuses of not being it and also being a functioning thing are established."

The usual mode of procedure in "Generalities and Instances" involves establishing a phenomenon as an instance by this three-part reason. Here the Challenger has taken what was the grammatical subject of the reason, a pot, and made it the logical subject, the basis of debate, in order to establish it as an instance of functioning thing. This procedure of switching the subject may not be strictly necessary, for one could justify functioning thing as a generality of a pot, "because (1) a pot is it, (2) a pot is related with it as the same essence, and (3) many common locuses of not being a pot and also being it are established". Lati Rinbochay confirmed that theoretically there is nothing wrong with this reason, but the consequence is always run the other way—justifying the subject as an instance of some phenomenon.[1]

Here the hypothetical Defender does not deny the first part of the reason, that a pot is a functioning thing. This is not a point that one would wish to contest, but it should be noted that any or all parts of this reason are "open" to opposition by the Defender. In many cases, this first foot of the reason would be a source of inquiry.

> If he says that the second part of the reason is not established, [the Sūtra School Challenger responds,] "It follows that the subject, a pot, is related with functioning thing as the same essence because of (1) being the same essence as functioning thing, (2) also being different from functioning thing, and (3) if functioning things did not exist, then it [too] would not exist."

The Go-mang *Collected Topics* gives a different reason in support of this same consequence. That text says:

> It follows that the subject, a pot, is related with functioning thing as the same essence because of (1) being different from functioning thing within being the same essence, and (2) if functioning things did not exist, then it [too] would not exist (*dngos po dang bdag nyid gcig gi sgo nas tha dad dngos po med na khyod med dgos pa'i phyir*).[2]

(This same type of reasoning is used in the Ra-dö *Collected Topics*.)[3] The second part of this reason is just the same as the

---

[1] Lati Rinbochay, oral commentary.
[2] Ngak-wang-dra-shi, Go-mang *Collected Topics*, p. 128.
[3] See Jam-yang-chok-hla-ö-ser, Ra-dö *Collected Topics*, 27b.4.

third part of the reason given in the Tutor's *Collected Topics*, and the first part, though somewhat different, expresses just the same qualities of a pot's relation to functioning thing as the first two parts of the reason given in the Tutor's text. Being different from functioning thing within being the same essence is mutually inclusive with being (1) the same essence as functioning thing and (2) also different from functioning thing. In the Tutor's *Collected Topics* the need for separating these two qualities is indefinite, but this approach does give the student easier access to the points. Also, the Go-mang text, in the Challenger's justification for this first part of the reason, treats these two components separately.

Any phenomenon which is related with functioning thing as the same essence is necessarily different from functioning thing. Only functioning thing is a phenomenon which is not different from functioning thing and, since no phenomenon is related with itself as the same essence, whatever is related with functioning thing as the same essence is necessarily different from functioning thing.

The Ra-dö *Collected Topics* offers, in at least one case, another type of reason in support of an instance's being related with its generality as the same essence. Here the generality is existent and its instance is related with it as the same essence "because of (1) being related with existent and (2) not being related with existent as being arisen from it (*yod pa dang 'brel ba gang zhig yod pa dang de byung 'brel ma yin pa'i phyir*)".[1] Since, according to the Collected Topics logicians, there are only two types of relations, if phenomena are related and they are not causally related, then they must be related as the same essence.

Denma Lochö Rinbochay gave still another reason in support of an instance's being related with its generality as the same essence. For example, a consciousness is related with functioning thing as the same essence "because (1) it is different from functioning thing within being the same essence

---

[1] *Ibid.*, 28b.4.

and (2) by the power of the vanishing of functioning thing it [too] must vanish (*khyod dngos po dang bdag nyid gcig pa'i sgo nas tha dad gang zhig dngos po ldog stobs kyis khyod ldog dgos pa'i phyir)*".[1] This means that what is not a functioning thing is also not a consciousness or any other instance of functioning thing. Functioning things include consciousnesses, and except among functioning things there are no consciousnesses.

> If he says that the first part [of the last reason] is not established, [the Sūtra School Challenger responds,] "It follows that the subject, a pot, is the same essence as functioning thing because of being the same nature as functioning thing."

Whatever is the same nature as functioning thing is necessarily the same essence as functioning thing. Same essence and same nature are mutually inclusive.

> If he says that the second part of the reason is not established, [the Sūtra School Challenger responds,] "It follows that the subject, a pot, is different from functioning thing because of being a form."

Whatever is a form is necessarily a functioning thing, but, nonetheless, whatever is a form is necessarily different from functioning thing. Functioning thing is not a form.

> If he says that the third part of the reason is not established, [the Sūtra School Challenger responds,] "It follows with respect to the subject, a pot, that if functioning things did not exist, then it [too] would not exist because if functioning things did not exist, then anything would be possible."

The reason rendered here, "because if functioning things did not exist, then anything would be possible (*dngos bo med na gang dran dran yin dgos pa'i phyir)*", literally means, "because if functioning things did not exist, then whatever one thinks

---

[1] Denma Lochö Rinbochay, oral commentary.

must be". The force of this reason is that it is inconceivable that functioning things might not exist. This seems a rather weak reason. At what point does it break down? Indeed, it is inconceivable that there would be no functioning things, that there might be no matter, or no consciousnesses, but is it inconceivable that there would be no pots, or no cars, or no dinosaurs? Many scholars abandon this reasoning in favor of the reason given by Lochö Rinbochay, that by the power of the vanishing of functioning thing any instance of functioning thing too must vanish. Nevertheless, the basic assertion—if functioning things did not exist, then pots too would not exist—is well founded.

There is an alternate reasoning in support of this last point which is not a mere appeal to the necessity for the existence of functioning things. This reasoning is indicated in the Ra-dö *Collected Topics* where the Sūtra School Challenger proves that if pots did not exist, then a gold pot which is an effect of a functioning thing would not exist "because if a gold pot which is an effect of a functioning thing exists, then a pot must exist".[1] Here the Challenger has changed the value of the two qualities and reversed the pervasion. That is, the pervasion, "if p does not exist, then q too would not exist," implies the counter-pervasion "if q exists, then p too would exist." Applied to the case at hand—if functioning things did not exist, then a pot too would not exist—implies that if a pot exists, then a functioning thing too must exist. Rather than rigorously proving the basic assertion by bringing in more information, this reasoning is showing an implication of that assertion which is often easier to understand. At a place where there is no functioning thing there is no pot because if there is a pot, then there must be a functioning thing. The reasoning applies both generally—if functioning things did not exist, pots too would not exist—and specifically—wherever a functioning thing does not exist a pot too must not exist.

---

[1] Jam-ȳang-chok-hla-ö-ser, Ra-dö *Collected Topics*, 29b.7-30a.1.

If he says that the third part of the reason above is not established, [the Sūtra School Challenger responds,] "It follows with respect to the subject, a pot, that many common locuses of not being it and also being a functioning thing are established because a sandalwood pillar is such and also a juniper pillar is such."

It should be noted here that, as opposed to the standard procedure in the Ra-dö *Collected Topics*, the text does not specify that the two common locuses are established as mutually different. The Tutor's *Collected Topics* is following the lead of its source for this debate, the Go-mang *Collected Topics*, which gives the reason just as it is here. If the two common locuses posited to justify the third part of the reason are established as mutually different, then they must be two *existents* which are not the same. However, since *many* common locuses must be posited, then they must be multiple and different, and since they both must be *common locuses*, then, according to Lochö Rinbochay, they must be established bases. The need for including the specification that the two common locuses are established as mutually different is indefinite.

The reason of the last consequence, that a sandalwood pillar is such and also a juniper pillar is such, means that a sandalwood pillar is a common locus of not being a pot and also being a functioning thing and that a juniper pillar is also the same sort of common locus. In justifying the former reason, that many such common locuses are established, the Challenger must posit at least two phenomena which have the requisite qualities. His reasoning may fail in either or both of two ways: (1) by positing only one such common locus or (2) by positing something which is not such a common locus. For instance, if he tried to prove that many common locuses of not being a pot and also being a functioning thing are established because a clay pot is such and also a child of a barren woman is such, his reasoning would fail in both ways. A clay pot is not a common locus of not being a pot and also being a functioning thing because of being a pot. Also, a child of a barren woman is not such a common locus because of not being a functioning thing. Moreover, as a non-existent, it is not a common locus of any sort.

In debating the topics of generalities and instances, very often the debaters will follow out this reasoning—testing to see whether or not the phenomena posited are indeed such common locuses. The Challenger might say:

> It follows that the subject, a sandalwood pillar, is a common locus of not being a pot and also being a functioning thing because of (1) not being a pot and (2) also being a functioning thing. The first part of the reason is established because of being a pillar. The second part of the reason is established because of being a form.

In debating these topics it is important to follow the basic procedure, carefully working one's way through the line of reasoning, in order to avoid confusion. Functioning thing is a generality of a pot because a pot is an instance of functioning thing. A pot is an instance of functioning thing because of such and such. Each of these three things are established because of such and such. By debating in this way the Challenger more easily avoids faulty reasoning and better allows the Defender to understand any possible errors or to exonerate his position.

> If he accepts the basic consequence, [the Sūtra School Challenger responds,] "It follows that the subject, functioning thing, is an instance because of being an instance of object of knowledge."
>
> If he says that the reason is not established, [the Sūtra School Challenger responds,] "It follows that the subject, functioning thing, is an instance of object of knowledge because (1) it is an object of knowledge, (2) it is related with object of knowledge as the same essence, and (3) many common locuses

of not being it and also being an object of knowledge are established."

The Go-mang *Collected Topics*, the source for this debate, goes on to justify each of the three parts of this reason as was done before. In the Tutor's *Collected Topics* this consequence is the last of the debate. The procedure for establishing functioning thing as an instance of object of knowledge is just the same as in the case of establishing a pot as an instance of functioning thing. One can easily apply the reasoning as before.

There are four possibilities between the two principals of debate F.1, generality and non-instance:

1 Something which is both is object of knowledge or any of the phenomena mutually inclusive with it, the selfless, different-from-functioning-thing, and so on. All of these phenomena are only generalities; they are generalities which are not instances.

2 Something which is a generality and is not a non-instance is anything which is both a generality and an instance—functioning thing, permanent phenomenon, definition, definiendum, generality, instance, and so forth.

    Generality itself is a generality because there are instances of it. For example, functioning thing is an instance of generality, permanent phenomenon is an instance of generality, definition is an instance of generality, and so forth. These phenomena are generalities, they are related with generality as the same essence, and there are other phenomena which are also generalities. Moreover, generality is also an instance because it is an instance of object of knowledge.

    Similarly, instance is both a generality and an instance. It is a generality because there are instances of it, for functioning thing is an instance of instance, permanent phenomenon is an instance of instance, and so forth. These phenomena are instances because of being instances of object of knowledge, established base, and so on. Functioning thing, permanent phenomenon, and so forth are related with instance as the same essence because of (1) being different from instance within being the same essence and (2) if instances did not exist, they too would not exist. There are also other phenomena which are instances. Further, instance is itself—it is an instance—because of being an instance of object of knowledge.

3   Something which is a non-instance and is not a generality is any non-existent, such as the horn of a rabbit. Only non-existents are neither instances nor generalities, for whatever is an established base is necessarily either a generality or an instance.

4   Something which is only an instance, such as the isolate of functioning thing or the two—definition and definiendum, is neither a generality nor an instance. The isolate of functioning thing is only an instance because of being an instance which is not a generality. It is an instance because of being an instance of permanent phenomenon. It is not a generality because other than functioning thing itself there is nothing which is also the isolate of functioning thing.

From this information and the information in debate F.1, one can easily infer that there are also four possibilities between generality and instance:

1   Functioning thing, generality, pot, and so on are both.
2   Object of knowledge, the selfless, different-from-pot, and so on are generalities but not instances.
3   Something which is an instance but is not a generality is the two—a functioning thing and a permanent phenomenon—or pillar's isolate.
4   Something which is neither is the horn of a rabbit.

Debate F.2, Second Mistaken Position (19a.6)

In this debate, also modeled after a debate in the Go-mang *Collected Topics*,[1] the hypothetical Defender asserts that whatever is a generality of functioning thing is necessarily a generality of that which is able to perform a function. This position is very appealing because of the special relationship between functioning thing and that which is able to perform a function. There is nothing which is the one that is not also the other as well and, for the most part, whatever the one is the other also is. However, the Sūtra School Challenger correctly points out that there is a difference because definiendum, for instance, is a generality of functioning thing but it is not a generality of that which is able to perform a function.

> If someone [a hypothetical Defender] says, "Whatever is a generality of functioning thing is necessarily a generality of that which is able to perform a function," [the Sūtra School Challenger responds to him,] "It [absurdly] follows that the subject, definiendum, is a generality of that which is able to perform a function because of being a generality of functioning thing. You asserted the pervasion."
>
> If he says that the reason is not established, [the Sūtra School Challenger responds,] "It follows with respect to the subject, definiendum, that it is a generality of functioning thing because functioning thing is an instance of it."
>
> If he says that the reason is not established, [the Sūtra School Challenger responds,] "It follows that the subject, functioning thing, is an instance of definiendum because (1) it is a definiendum, (2) it is related with definiendum as the same essence, and

---

[1] Ngak-w̄ang-d̄ra-s̄hi, Go-mang *Collected Topics*, pp. 130-132.

> (3) many common locuses of not being it and also being a definiendum are established."

The Go-mang *Collected Topics* goes on to justify each of the three parts of this reason. One can understand the procedure from the former debate. Functioning thing is a definiendum because its definition exists. It is related with definiendum as the same essence because (1) it is different from definiendum within being the same essence and (2) by the power of the vanishing of definiendum functioning thing too vanishes. If definienda did not exist, functioning thing too would not exist. Thirdly, there are many phenomena which are not functioning things but are definienda; for example, object of knowledge is such a common locus and existent is also such a common locus.

> If he accepts the basic consequence [that definiendum is a generality of that which is able to perform a function, the Sūtra School Challenger responds,] "It follows with respect to the subject, that which is able to perform a function, that it is not an instance of definiendum because of being a definition; because of being the definition of a functioning thing."

Here the text departs from the usual form of response to the Defender's accepting the basic consequence and in so doing the Challenger's response skips one step in the sequence of reasoning. The consequence that is not provided here but is implied is, "It follows that the subject, definiendum, is not a generality of that which is able to perform a function because that which is able to perform a function is not an instance of it." The Challenger's response provided in the text effectively moves to support the reason of this implied consequence.

At this same point in the debate, the Go-mang *Collected Topics* takes another approach by positing an unwanted consequence of the hypothetical Defender's mistaken acceptance of definiendum as a generality of that which is able to perform a function. That text says:

[The Sūtra School Challenger responds,] "It [absurdly] follows with respect to the subject, that which is able to perform a function, that (1) it is a definiendum, (2) it is related with definiendum as the same essence, and (3) many common locuses of not being it and also being a definiendum are established because it is an instance of definiendum. You asserted the reason."

If he accepts the consequence, [the Sūtra School Challenger responds,] "It follows with respect to the subject, that which is able to perform a function, that it is a definiendum because (1) it is a definiendum, (2) it is related with definiendum as the same essence, and (3) many common locuses of not being it and also being a definiendum are established. You asserted the reason."

If he accepts the consequence, [the Sūtra School Challenger responds,] "It follows that the subject, that which is able to perform a function, is not a definition because of being a definiendum. You asserted the reason."

"You cannot accept [that that which is able to perform a function is not a definition] because of being a definition."

"It follows that it is so because of being the definition of a functioning thing."[1]

The essential points of the reasoning presented in the Gomang *Collected Topics* are reproduced in the Tutor's *Collected Topics*.

There are four possibilities between the two principals of debate F.2, generality-of-that-which-is-able-to-perform-a-function and generality-of-functioning-thing:

1 Something which is both is the selfless, object of knowledge, one, non-permanent phenomenon, non-matter, or different-from-consciousness.

---

[1] *Ibid.*, pp. 131-132.

2   Something which is a generality of functioning thing but is not a generality of that which is able to perform a function is definiendum or different-from-that-which-is-able-to-perform-a-function.
3   Something which is a generality of that which is able to perform a function but is not a generality of functioning thing is definition or different-from-functioning-thing.
4   Something which is neither is a pot, an eye consciousness, the flower of a dry tree, one-with-functioning-thing, different, or permanent phenomenon.

Debate F.3, Third Mistaken View (19b.3)

Debate F.3, which is also drawn from the Go-mang *Collected Topics*,[1] is in the same vein as debate F.2. Here the hypothetical Defender accepts that whatever is a generality of functioning thing is necessarily a generality of impermanent phenomenon. The Sūtra School Challenger posits the correct counterexample of different-from-impermanent-phenomenon, for it is a generality of functioning thing but not a generality of impermanent phenomenon. Again, two quite similar phenomena which one might think would have all the same generalities are shown to be different in that respect. Debates F.2 and F.3 suggest that no two different phenomena could have exactly the same generalities.

> If someone [a hypothetical Defender] says, "Whatever is a generality of functioning thing is necessarily a generality of impermanent phenomenon," [the Sūtra School Challenger responds,] "It [absurdly] follows that the subject, different-from-impermanent-phenomenon, is a generality of impermanent phenomenon because of being a generality of functioning thing. You asserted the pervasion."
>
> If he says that the reason is not established, [the Sūtra School Challenger responds,] "It follows with

---

[1] *Ibid.*, pp. 132-134.

respect to the subject, different-from-impermanent-phenomenon, that it is a generality of functioning thing because functioning thing is an instance of it."

The Go-mang *Collected Topics* proceeds to justify this reason:

If he says that the reason is not established, [the Sūtra School Challenger responds,] "It follows with respect to the subject, functioning thing, that it is an instance of different-from-impermanent-phenomenon because (1) it is different from impermanent phenomenon, (2) it is related with different-from-impermanent-phenomenon as the same essence, and (3) many common locuses of not being it and also being different from impermanent phenomenon are established."

If he says that the first part of the reason is not established, [the Sūtra School Challenger responds,] "It follows that the subject, functioning thing, is different from impermanent phenomenon because of (1) being an existent and (2) not being one with impermanent phenomenon."

If he says that the second part of the reason is not established, [the Sūtra School Challenger responds,] "It follows that the subject, functioning thing, is related with different-from-impermanent-phenomenon as the same essence because of (1) being different from different-from-impermanent-phenomenon within being the same essence and (2) if different-from-impermanent-phenomenon did not exist, then it too would not exist."

If he says that the third part of the reason is not established, [the Sūtra School Challenger responds,] "It follows with respect to the subject, functioning thing, that many common locuses of not being it and also being different from impermanent phenomenon are established because definition is such and definiendum is also such."[1]

---

[1] *Ibid.*, p. 133.

Again the Tutor's *Collected Topics* has supplied only the essential points of the debate and relies on the student to ascertain the implications and justifications. The Tutor's text continues:

> If he accepts the basic consequence, [the Sūtra School Challenger responds,] "It follows that the subject, different-from-impermanent-phenomenon, is not a generality of impermanent phenomenon because impermanent phenomenon is not an instance of it."
>
> If he says that the reason is not established, [the Sūtra School Challenger responds,] "It follows that the subject, impermanent phenomenon, is not an instance of different-from-impermanent-phe- nomenon because of not being different from impermanent phenomenon."

Once impermanent phenomenon is not different from impermanent phenomenon, it cannot be an instance of different-from-impermanent-phenomenon because it does not meet the first requirement of an instance of different- from-impermanent-phenomenon.

> If he says that the reason is not established, [the Sūtra School Challenger responds,] "It follows with respect to the subject, impermanent phenomenon, that it is not different from itself because it is with- out a self of persons."

Nothing, be it existent or non-existent, is different from itself.

There are four possibilities between the two principals of debate F.3, generality-of-functioning-thing and generality- of-impermanent-phenomenon:

1 Something which is both is established base or any of the phenomena mutually inclusive with it, the selfless, definiendum, one, non-different, generality, or instance.

2   Something which is a generality of functioning thing but is not a generality of impermanent phenomenon is different-from-impermanent-phenomenon or non-one-with-impermanent-phenomenon.

3   Something which is a generality of impermanent phenomenon but is not a generality of functioning thing is different-from-functioning-thing or non-one-with-functioning-thing.

4   Something which is neither is a cause of the two—a functioning thing and an impermanent phenomenon, the two—high and low, the two—form and consciousness, generally characterized phenomenon, different, pot, functioning thing, product, and so forth.

Debate F.4, Fourth Mistaken View (19b.6)

Debate F.4 is also drawn from the Go-mang *Collected Topics*.[1] In this debate the text presents information about generality as an instance and instance as a generality. As mentioned above (see pp. 641-642), both generality and instance are both generalities and instances. Here the hypothetical Defender mistakenly asserts that there is no common locus of generality-of-generality (*spyi'i spyi*) and instance-of-instance (*bye brag gi bye brag*). Such is not the case, the Sūtra School Challenger points out, because permanent phenomenon is both a generality of generality and an instance of instance. The Challenger could not have chosen any generality of generality such as object of knowledge because object of knowledge is not an instance of anything. Nor could he have chosen an impermanent phenomenon such as functioning thing which although it is an instance of instance it is not a generality of generality, for whatever is a generality of generality is necessarily a permanent phenomenon.

If someone [a hypothetical Defender] says, "There is no common locus of being a generality of generality

---

[1] *Ibid.*, pp. 134-136.

and also being an instance of instance," [the Sūtra School Challenger responds to him,] "It follows that there is [a common locus of being a generality of generality and also being an instance of instance] because permanent phenomenon is such."

If he says that the reason is not established, [the Sūtra School Challenger responds,] "It follows with respect to the subject, permanent phenomenon, that it is a common locus of being a generality of generality and also being an instance of instance because (1) it is a generality of generality and (2) it is an instance of instance."

If he says that the first part of the reason is not established, [the Sūtra School Challenger responds,] "It follows with respect to the subject, permanent phenomenon, that it is a generality of generality because generality is an instance of it."

Generality is a permanent phenomenon because of being a generally characterized phenomenon, merely imputed by terms or thought consciousnesses. It is not the case that whatever is a generality is necessarily a permanent phenomenon, but generality—from the point of view of its self-isolate—is a permanent phenomenon. Generality is related with permanent phenomenon as the same essence. If permanent phenomena did not exist, then generality also would not exist. Also, there are many common locuses of being a permanent phenomenon but not being a generality, for the two—a permanent phenomenon and a functioning thing—are such a common locus and also the two—a definition and a definiendum—are such a common locus. As permanent phenomena of which being them is not possible, these are only instances and not generalities. Thus, for these reasons, generality is an instance of permanent phenomenon.

If he says that the second part of the reason is not established, [the Sūtra School Challenger responds,] "It follows that the subject, permanent phenomenon, is an instance of instance because (1) it is an instance, (2) it is related with instance as the same essence, and (3) many common locuses of not being it and also being an instance are established."

Permanent phenomenon is an instance because of being an instance of object of knowledge. However, one cannot say that it is an instance of instance because of being an instance of object of knowledge or because of being an instance, for there is no pervasion. It is not the case that whatever is an instance of object of knowledge or whatever is an instance is necessarily an instance of instance. Instance itself is an instance and an instance of object of knowledge, but it is not an instance of instance. Nothing is an instance of itself.

There are four possibilities between the two, generality-of-generality and instance-of-instance:

1   Something which is both is permanent phenomenon or any of the phenomena mutually inclusive with it, one, non-different, object of knowledge of which being it is possible, positive phenomenon, non-product, and so forth.

For example, one is an instance of instance because (1) it is an instance, (2) it is related with instance as the same essence, and (3) many common locuses of not being it and also being an instance are established. One is an instance because of being an instance of object of knowledge, of permanent phenomenon, and so forth. There are many phenomena which are not one but are instances because any objects of knowledge of which being them is not possible are an instance of object of knowledge but not one because of being different.

One is a generality of generality because generality is an instance of it. Generality is an instance of one because (1) it is one, (2) it is related with one as the same essence, and (3) many common locuses of not being a generality and also being one are established. The third part of the reason is established because the isolate of any phenomenon is one but cannot be a generality. For example, the isolate of functioning thing is one but not a generality because, other than functioning thing, there is nothing which is the isolate of functioning thing. Also, such phenomena as one-with-functioning-thing, the definiendum of that which is able to perform a function, and the triply qualified imputed existent of that which is able to perform a function are individually one but not generalities. Whatever is one is not necessarily a generality.

2 Something which is a generality of generality but is not an instance of instance is object of knowledge or any of the phenomena mutually inclusive with it, the selfless, different-from-functioning-thing, instance, different-from-instance, and so forth.

Object of knowledge, the phenomena mutually inclusive with it, and the selfless are generalities of generality because generality is included within the type of object of knowledge and the selfless. However, they are not instances of instance because they are not instances of any phenomenon.

Different-from-functioning-thing is a generality of both generality and instance, but it is not an instance of instance because other than functioning thing there is no common locus of not being different from functioning thing and also being an instance.

Both instance and different-from-instance are generalities of generality, but they are not instances of instance. Generality is an instance, and it is different from instance. It is related with instance and with different-from-instance as the same essence. Also, there are many phenomena which are not generalities but are instances and different from instance. This is because any objects of knowledge which being them is not possible are not a generality but are an instance and different from instance. Thus, generality is an instance of instance and an instance of different-from-instance.

However, instance is not an instance of instance because (1) it is not related with instance as the same essence and (2) there is nothing which is a common locus of not being an instance and also being an instance. No phenomenon can be an instance of itself. Also, different-from-instance is not an instance of instance because it does not fulfill any of the three qualities of an instance of instance.

3   Something which is an instance of instance but is not a generality of generality is generality, non-generality, definition, definiendum, negative phenomenon, objects of knowledge of which being them is not possible, different, non-permanent phenomenon, functioning thing, the two—a pillar and a pot, a pot, and so forth.

Generality is an instance of instance because (1) it is an instance, (2) it is related with instance as the same essence, and (3) there are many phenomena which are not generalities but are instances, such as objects of knowledge of which being them is not possible and isolates of phenomena. However, generality is not a generality of itself because of being without a self of persons. Nothing can be a generality of itself.

Moreover, non-generality is also an instance of instance but not a generality of generality. It is an instance because of being an instance of object of knowledge. It is related with instance as the same essence. And there are many phenomena which are not non-generalities but are instances, for functioning thing is such a common locus and also permanent phenomenon is such a common locus. However, non-generality is not a generality of generality because generality is not an instance of it, since generality is not a non-generality.

Both definition and definiendum are instances of instance but not generalities of generality. They both are instances, they are related with instance as the same essence, and there are many phenomena (such as the two—a pillar and a pot) which are neither of them but are instances. Definition is not a generality of generality because generality is not an instance of it, since generality is not a definition. Generality is also not an instance of definiendum because, although it is a definiendum and it is related with definiendum as the same essence, it seems that there are no phenomena which are definienda but not generalities. Whatever is a definiendum is necessarily a generality because definienda are established in dependence on their illustrations, some of these illustrations doubling as instances as well. Definienda have instances and are generalities.

4 Something which is neither is any non-existent, different-from-generality, non-instance, and so forth.

Different-from-generality is not an instance of instance because there are not many common loci of not being different from generality and also being an instance, since only generality is both not different from generality and also an instance. Also, different-from-generality is not a generality of generality because generality is not an instance of it, since generality is not different from itself.

Non-instance is not an instance of instance because it is not an instance. Also, non-instance is not a generality of generality because generality is not a non-instance.

In the same vein as reckoning the difference between instance-of-instance and generality-of-generality, it is also helpful to consider the difference between generality-of-instance (*bye brag gi spyi*) and instance-of-generality (*spyi'i bye brag*). There are four possibilities between these two as well:

1 Something which is both a generality of instance and an instance of generality is permanent phenomenon and the phenomena mutually inclusive with it, definiendum, one, positive phenomenon, and so on.

Definiendum is a generality of instance because instance is an instance of it, since (1) instance is a definiendum, (2) it is related with definiendum as the same essence, and (3) many common loci of not being an instance and also being a definiendum are established. There are many phenomena which are not instances but are definienda such as object of knowledge, established base, the selfless, and so on.

Also, definiendum is an instance of generality because (1) it is a generality, (2) it is related with generality as the same essence, and (3) there are many phenomena which are not definienda but are generalities. Definitions such as that which is able to perform a function, the momentary, and suitable as an object of an awareness are not definienda but are generalities.

One is a generality of instance because instance is an instance of it. Instance is one, it is related with one as the same essence, and there are many phenomena which are not instances but are one, since object of knowledge and the phenomena mutually inclusive with it are individually one and they are not instances. Also, one is an instance of generality because it is a generality, it is related with generality as the same essence, and there are many phenomena which are not one but are generalities. For example, the two—an object of knowledge and an existent—are different, but they are a generality. This is because they are a generality of functioning thing, permanent phenomenon, definition, and so forth. For example, functioning thing is both an object of knowledge and an existent, it is related with those two as the same essence, and there are many phenomena which are not functioning things and also are the two—an object of knowledge and an existent.

2 Something which is a generality of instance but is not an instance of generality is object of knowledge and any of the phenomena mutually inclusive with it, the selfless, generality, different-from-generality, object of knowledge of which being it is possible, different-from-permanent-phenomenon, different-from-functioning-thing, and so forth.

Generality is a generality of instance because instance is an instance of it. Instance is a generality, it is related with generality as the same essence, and there are many phenomena which are generalities but not instances.

However, generality is not an instance of itself just because it exists—in other words, nothing is an instance of itself. Also, different-from-generality is a generality of instance. Instance is different from generality. There are also many phenomena which are not instances but are different from generality, for object of knowledge and the phenomena mutually inclusive with it are such phenomena. However, different-from-generality is not an instance of generality because there is only one phenomenon which is not different from generality but is a generality.

Also, object of knowledge of which being it is possible is a generality of instance, for instance is an instance of it. Instance is an object of knowledge of which being it is possible, and there are many phenomena which are objects of knowledge of which being them is possible but are not instances, since object of knowledge and so forth are such phenomena. However, object of knowledge of which being it is possible is not an instance of generality, for there are no phenomena which are not objects of knowledge of which being them is possible but are generalities. Whatever is a generality is necessarily an object of knowledge of which being it is possible or objects of knowledge of which being them is possible.

3 Something which is an instance of generality but is not a generality of instance is definition, instance, objects of knowledge of which being them is not possible, non-generality, different, negative phenomenon, functioning thing and the phenomena mutually inclusive with it, a pot, and so forth.

Whereas definiendum is something which is both a generality of instance and an instance of generality, definition is an instance of generality but not a generality of instance. Definition is not a generality of instance because instance is not an instance of it, for instance is not a definition. Furthermore, whereas generality is a generality of instance but not an instance of generality, instance is the opposite—an instance of generality but not a generality of instance.

Similarly, whereas object of knowledge of which being it *is* possible is a generality of instance but not an instance of generality, objects of knowledge of which being them is *not* possible is the opposite. Instance is not an instance of object of knowledge of which being it is not possible because of being an object of knowledge of which being it is possible. However, objects of knowledge of which being them is not possible are an instance of generality because they are a generality, they are related with generality as the same essence, and there are many phenomena which are not objects of knowledge of which being them is not possible but are generalities. Any generality is an object of knowledge of which being it is possible or objects of knowledge of which being them is possible. Even objects of knowledge of which being them is not possible is an object of knowledge of which being it is possible, for it is an existent and there are phenomena which are it. There are phenomena which are objects of knowledge of which being them is not possible because, for example, the two—a pillar and a pot—are that and the two—long and short—are that.

Non-generality is an instance of generality because it is a generality, it is related with generality as the same essence, and there are many phenomena which are not non-generalities and are generalities. Non-generality is a generality because there are instances of it, for the two—a definition and a definiendum—are an instance of non-generality. Also, pot's isolate is an instance of non-generality because it is a non-generality, it is related with non-generality as the same essence, and there are many phenomena which are not pot's isolate but are non-generalities. Any phenomenon which is only an instance is a non-generality. Thus, non-generality is a generality. Also, there are many phenomena which are not non-generalities and are generalities because whatever is a generality is necessarily a common locus of not being a non-generality and being a generality. Even non-generality itself is such a common locus, for it is not itself—it is not a non-generality—because of being a generality. Thus, non-generality is an instance of generality. However, non-generality is not a generality of instance, for instance is not a non-generality.

4   Something which is neither a generality of instance nor an instance of generality is any non-existent, different-from-instance, non-instance, the two—a pillar and a pot, and so on.

Non-instance is not a generality of instance because instance is not an instance of it, for instance is not a non-instance. Also, non-instance is not an instance of generality because non-instance is not a generality. This is because there are no instances of non-instance. The only things which are non-instances are non-existents, the selfless, object of knowledge and the phenomena mutually inclusive with it, and such phenomena as different-from-functioning-thing. None of these are instances of anything, not even of non-instance, for there is no phenomenon which is, for example, not an object of knowledge and also is a non-instance.

Having considered the difference between instance-of-instance and generality-of-generality and the difference between generality-of-instance and instance-of-generality, it is also instructive to ascertain the limits of pervasion between other constructions of these two, instance and generality. The Shar-dzay *Collected Topics* says:

> Similarly, the four possibilities between generality-of-generality and instance-of-generality, the four possibilities between generality-of-instance and instance-of-instance, the four possibilities between generality-of-generality and generality-of-instance, and the four possibilities between instance-of-generality and instance-of-instance must be known.[1]

---

[1] Dzemay Rinbochay, Shar-dzay *Collected Topics*, pp. 33-34.

Using the former two as examples one can easily ascertain the differences between the phenomena suggested by the Šhar-dzay *Collected Topics*.

Debate F.5, Fifth Mistaken View (20a.2)

In this debate the text turns away from the abstraction of instance and generality in association with each other and focuses on the generalities and instances of permanent phenomenon. Here the Defender mistakenly asserts that whatever is a generality of permanent phenomenon is necessarily not an instance of permanent phenomenon. He has not understood the great interplay between generalities and instances. He may be thinking that a generality of permanent phenomenon could only be those broader phenomena such as established base within which permanent phenomena are included. The Sūtra School Challenger shows that such is not the case by positing the counterexample of generality which is both an instance and a generality of permanent phenomenon.

> If someone [a hypothetical Defender] says, "Whatever is a generality of permanent phenomenon is necessarily not an instance of permanent phenomenon," [the Sūtra School Challenger responds to him,] "It [absurdly] follows that the subject, generality, is [not an instance of permanent phenomenon] because of [being a generality of permanent phenomenon]."
>
> "It follows that [generality is a generality of permanent phenomenon] because permanent phenomenon is an instance of it."
>
> "It follows that [permanent phenomenon is an instance of generality] because (1) permanent phenomenon is a generality, (2) permanent phenomenon is related with generality as the same essence, and (3) many common loci of not being

> a permanent phenomenon and also being a general-
> ity are established."

Permanent phenomenon is a generality because its instances
exist. This is so because uncomposed space is an instance of
permanent phenomenon and also definition is an instance of
permanent phenomenon. Permanent phenomenon is related
with generality as the same essence because they are different, the same essence, and if generalities did not exist, then
permanent phenomena also would not exist. Finally, there
are many phenomena which are generalities but are not
permanent phenomena, for bread is such a phenomenon
and also milk is such a phenomenon.

> If he accepts the basic consequence, [the Sūtra
> School Challenger responds,] "It follows that the
> subject, generality, is an instance of permanent phe-
> nomenon because (1) it is a permanent
> phenomenon, (2) it is related with permanent
> phenomenon as the same essence, and (3) many
> common locuses of not being it and also being a
> permanent phenomenon are established."

Generality is a permanent phenomenon, a mere abstraction
based on its instances. It is related with permanent phenomenon as the same essence because it is different from
permanent phenomenon within being the same essence and
by the power of the vanishing of permanent phenomena,
generality also would vanish. Finally, there are many common locuses of being a permanent phenomenon but not
being a generality because the two—a definition and a
definiendum—are such a common locus and also the two—
one and different—are such a common locus.

There are four possibilities between the two principals of
debate F.5, generality-of-permanent-phenomenon and non-
instance-of-permanent-phenomenon:

1   Something which is both a generality of permanent phe-
    nomenon and not an instance of permanent
    phenomenon is object of knowledge and any of the phe-

nomena mutually inclusive with it, the selfless, different-from-product, different-from-generally-characterized-phenomenon, non-matter, non-consciousness, and so forth.

2 Something which is a generality of permanent phenomenon but not a non-instance of permanent phenomenon (that is to say, both a generality and an instance of permanent phenomenon) is generality, instance, one, definiendum, object of knowledge of which being it is possible, positive phenomenon, and so forth.

All of these are examples of permanent phenomena which are things which permanent phenomenon is. For example, one is a permanent phenomenon (and also an instance of permanent phenomenon), and permanent phenomenon is one and an instance of one. Similarly, definiendum is a permanent phenomenon (and also an instance of permanent phenomenon), and permanent phenomenon is a definiendum and an instance of definiendum. The same holds true of the others.

3 Something which is a non-instance of permanent phenomenon and not a generality of permanent phenomenon (that is to say, neither an instance nor a generality of permanent phenomenon) is functioning thing as well as any of the phenomena mutually inclusive with it, any of the instances of functioning thing, permanent phenomenon and any of the phenomena mutually inclusive with it, non-thing, or any non-existent.

Any functioning thing is not an instance of permanent phenomenon because of not being a permanent phenomenon, and any functioning thing is not a generality of permanent phenomenon because whatever is a generality of permanent phenomenon is necessarily a permanent phenomenon. Permanent phenomenon itself, of course, is not an instance or generality of itself. Also, the phenomena mutually inclusive with permanent phenomenon cannot be instances or generalities of perma-

662   *Debate in Tibetan Buddhism*

nent phenomenon because of the third quality of instances.

Like functioning thing, non-thing is also a non-instance of permanent phenomenon. Even though non-thing is a permanent phenomenon and it is related with permanent phenomenon as the same essence, since there are no common locuses of not being a non-thing and also being a permanent phenomenon, non-thing is not an instance of permanent phenomenon. Something which is both a functioning thing and a permanent phenomenon could not exist. Also, non-thing is not a generality of permanent phenomenon, for permanent phenomenon is not an instance of it. This is because there are no *phenomena* which are not permanent phenomena and also are non-things.

4   Something which is neither a non-instance of permanent phenomenon nor a generality of permanent phenomenon (that is, something which is an instance but not a generality of permanent phenomenon) is definition, different, objects of knowledge of which being them is not possible, negative phenomenon, non-permanent phenomenon, non-generality, non-instance, and so forth.

These are all things which are permanent phenomena but which permanent phenomenon is not. For example, different is a permanent phenomenon (and also an instance of permanent phenomenon), but, since permanent phenomenon is not different, different is not a generality of permanent phenomenon. Also, non-permanent phenomenon is a permanent phenomenon because of being a phenomenon which is merely imputed (and it is also an instance of permanent phenomenon), but, since permanent phenomenon is not a non-permanent phenomenon, permanent phenomenon is not an instance of non-permanent phenomenon.

Having ascertained the four possibilities between generality-of-permanent-phenomenon and non-instance-of-permanent-phenomenon, one can understand easily that there are four possibilities between generality-of-permanent-phenomenon and instance-of-permanent-phenomenon.

Evolving from this study of the limits of pervasion between the generalities and instances of permanent phenomenon the Ra-dö *Collected Topics* presents a somewhat more complicated debate which investigates the nature of generality-of-permanent-phenomenon itself as a generality and as an instance.[1] In this debate the two principals are (1) generality-of-generality-of-permanent-phenomenon (*rtag pa'i spyi'i spyi*) and (2) instance-of-generality-of-permanent-phenomenon (*rtag pa'i spyi'i bye brag*). Denma Lochö Rinbochay explains that there are four possibilities between these two:[2]

1 Something which is both an instance of generality-of-permanent-phenomenon and a generality of generality-of-permanent-phenomenon is definiendum, one, instance, or positive phenomenon.

The procedure is just the same here as before. In all cases, an instance must have the three qualities of an instance. For example, definiendum is an instance of generality-of-permanent-phenomenon because (1) it is a generality of permanent phenomenon, (2) it is related with generality-of-permanent-phenomenon as the same essence, and (3) there are many phenomena which are not definienda but are generalities of permanent phenomenon. Also, definiendum is a generality of generality-of-permanent-phenomenon, for generality-of-permanent-phenomenon is an instance of it. This is because generality-of-permanent-phenomenon is a definiendum (since it is the definiendum of a phenomenon which encompasses its manifestations, permanent phenomena), it is related with definiendum as the same essence, and there are many phenomena which are

[1] See Jam-ÿang-chok-hla-ö-ser, Ra-dö *Collected Topics*, 30a.5ff.
[2] Denma Lochö Rinbochay, oral commentary.

not generalities of permanent phenomena but are definienda, such as functioning thing, permanent phenomenon, and definition.

Also, positive phenomenon is both a generality and an instance of generality-of-permanent-phenomenon. It is an instance of generality-of-permanent-phenomenon because it is a generality of permanent phenomenon, it is related with generality-of-permanent-phenomenon as the same essence, and there are many phenomena which are not positive phenomena but are generalities of permanent phenomenon. The third part of the reason is established because opposite-from-not-being-an-object-of-knowledge is a common locus of not being a positive phenomenon and being a generality of permanent phenomenon and also non-matter is such a common locus. Positive phenomenon is also a generality of generality-of-permanent-phenomenon because generality-of-permanent-phenomenon is an instance of it, for generality-of-permanent-phenomenon fulfills the three qualities of an instance of positive phenomenon.

2   There are many phenomena which are generalities of generality-of-permanent-phenomenon but are not instances of generality-of-permanent-phenomenon, for the selfless, object of knowledge and the phenomena mutually inclusive with it, permanent phenomenon and the phenomena mutually inclusive with it, different-from-functioning-thing, non-thing, generality, object of knowledge of which being it is possible, non-matter, non-consciousness, and so forth are such common locuses.

The selfless, object of knowledge and the phenomena mutually inclusive with it, and different-from-functioning-thing are generalities of generality-of-permanent-phenomenon, but since they are only generalities they are not instances of generality-of-permanent-phenomenon or any other phenomenon.

Permanent phenomenon, or any of the phenomena mutually inclusive with it, is a generality of generality-of-permanent-phenomenon, for generality-of-permanent-phenomenon is an instance of permanent phenomenon. This is because generality-of-permanent-phenomenon is a permanent phenomenon, it is related with permanent phenomenon as the same essence, and there are many phenomena such as uncomposed space and conventional truth which are not generalities of permanent phenomenon but are permanent phenomena. However, permanent phenomenon is not an instance of generality-of-permanent-phenomenon because of not being a generality of permanent phenomenon.

3   Although many phenomena are generalities but not instances of generality-of-permanent-phenomenon, examples of phenomena which are instances of generality-of-permanent-phenomenon but not generalities of generality-of-permanent-phenomenon are very rare. Denma Lochö Rinbochay posited one example, definiendum-which-is-different-from-generality-of-permanent-phenomenon (*rtag pa'i spyi dang tha dad du gyur pa'i mtshon bya*).[1]

This subject is an instance of generality-of-permanent-phenomenon because it is a generality of permanent phenomenon, it is related with generality-of-permanent-phenomenon as the same essence, and there are many phenomena which are not it and also are generalities of permanent phenomenon. The first part of the reason, that definiendum-which-is-different-from-generality-of-permanent-phenomenon is a generality of permanent phenomenon, is established because permanent phenomenon is an instance of it. This is because permanent phenomenon is a definiendum which is different from generality-of-permanent-phenomenon, it is related with definiendum-which-is-different-from-generality-of-permanent-phenomenon as the same essence, and there are many phenomena such as a pot and a form which are not permanent phenomena but are

---

[1] *Ibid.*

definienda which are different from generality-of-permanent-phenomenon. Thus, definiendum-which-is-different-from-generality-of-permanent-phenomenon is a generality of permanent phenomenon. Also, the third part of the reason, that there are many phenomena which are not definienda which are different from generality-of-permanent-phenomenon but are generalities of permanent phenomenon, is established because suitable as an object of an awareness is such a common locus and also established by a valid cognizer is such a common locus. Each of these phenomena are generalities of permanent phenomenon but they are not definienda which are different from generality-of-permanent-phenomenon because of being definitions. Consequently, it is established that definiendum-which-is-different-from-generality-of-permanent-phenomenon is an instance of generality-of-permanent-phenomenon.

However, definiendum-which-is-different-from-generality-of-permanent-phenomenon is not a generality of generality-of-permanent-phenomenon because generality-of-permanent-phenomenon is not an instance of it. This is because generality-of-permanent-phenomenon is not a definiendum which is different from generality-of-permanent-phenomenon, for it is not different from itself.

4   Something which is neither a generality of generality-of-permanent-phenomenon nor an instance of generality-of-permanent-phenomenon is any non-existent, functioning thing as well as its instances and the phenomena mutually inclusive with it, different, definition, negative phenomenon, or object of knowledge of which being it is possible.

For example, definition is not an instance of generality-of-permanent-phenomenon because it is not a generality of permanent phenomenon, for permanent phenomenon is not a definition. Also, definition is not a generality of generality-of-permanent-phenomenon because generality-of-permanent-phenomenon is not a definition, for it is a definiendum.

Debate F.6, Sixth Mistaken View (20a.4)

In this debate, the focus switches from the generalities and instances of permanent phenomena to those of functioning thing. This is quite a different case, for the generalities and instances of functioning thing do not compare as do the generalities and instances of permanent phenomenon.

Whereas there are four possibilities between generality-of-permanent-phenomena and instance-of-permanent-phenomenon, the two, generality-of-functioning-thing and instance-of-functioning-thing, are mutually exclusive. All generalities of functioning thing are permanent phenomena, for they are only such things as the selfless, object of knowledge and the phenomena mutually inclusive with it, definiendum, object of knowledge of which being it is possible, non-cow, different-from-impermanent-phenomenon, and so forth. On the other hand, whatever is an instance of functioning thing is necessarily a functioning thing, for it must meet the first requirement of an instance—being a functioning thing.

Even so, both generality-of-functioning-thing and instance-of-functioning-thing are permanent phenomena. All instances of functioning thing are impermanent phenomena, but instance-of-functioning-thing, from the point of view of its self-isolate, is a permanent phenomenon because it is only mentally imputed. Each instance of functioning thing is *an* instance of functioning thing but none is the collective instance of functioning thing as such. The same is true for the instance of any generality, be it permanent or impermanent.

In this debate, the Defender mistakenly asserts that it is not the case that whatever is a generality of functioning thing is necessarily not an instance of functioning thing. He is thinking that there is at least one thing which is both an instance and a generality of functioning thing.

> If someone [a hypothetical Defender] says,
> "Whatever is a generality of functioning thing is not
> necessarily not an instance of functioning thing,"
> [the Sūtra School Challenger responds to him,]
> "That is not correct because there is nothing which
> is both a generality of functioning thing and an
> instance of functioning thing."

In saying that what the hypothetical Defender has asserted
is not correct, the Challenger is opposing the Defender's
position and countering that whatever is a generality of
functioning thing is necessarily not an instance of functioning thing. This is because there is nothing which is both.
They are mutually exclusive.

> "It follows that [there is nothing which is both a
> generality of functioning thing and an instance of
> functioning thing] because there is no permanent
> phenomenon which is such [a common locus] and
> also there is no impermanent phenomenon which is
> such [a common locus]."

If there is neither a permanent phenomenon nor an impermanent phenomenon which is a common locus of such and
such, then that common locus does not exist.

> "It follows that the first part of the reason [i.e., that
> there is no permanent phenomenon which is a
> common locus of being a generality of functioning
> thing and an instance of functioning thing is estab-
> lished] because whatever is a permanent phe-
> nomenon is necessarily not an instance of function-
> ing thing; because whatever is a permanent phe-
> nomenon is necessarily not a functioning thing."

Whatever is an instance of functioning thing must be a
functioning thing, and since no permanent phenomenon is a
functioning thing, no permanent phenomenon can be an
instance of functioning thing.

"The second part of the reason above [i.e., that there is no impermanent phenomenon which is a common locus of being a generality of functioning thing and an instance of functioning thing] is established because if there were a functioning thing which is a generality of functioning thing, then anything would be possible."[1]

If functioning thing were an instance of any other functioning thing, such as specifically characterized phenomenon, then it would have to be the case that there would be phenomena which are specifically characterized phenomena but not functioning things. Such a common locus is not possible. Whatever is a generality of functioning thing is necessarily a permanent phenomenon.

The two, generality-of-functioning-thing and instance-of-functioning-thing, are mutually exclusive because (1) whatever is a generality of functioning thing is necessarily a permanent phenomenon and (2) whatever is an instance of functioning thing is necessarily a functioning thing. However, there are three possibilities between the two principals of debate F.6, generality-of-functioning-thing and non-instance-of-functioning-thing:

1 Something which is both a generality of functioning thing and a non-instance of functioning thing is the self-less, object of knowledge or any of the phenomena mutually inclusive with it, definiendum, one, generality, instance, object of knowledge of which being it is possible, positive phenomenon, different-from-product, non-form, and so forth.

2 Whatever is a generality of functioning thing is necessarily a non-instance of functioning thing. However, it is not the case that whatever is a non-instance of functioning thing is necessarily a generality of functioning thing. There are things which are neither generalities nor instances of functioning thing. For example, permanent

---

[1] Here *yin* is translated as *yod*.

phenomenon and the phenomena mutually inclusive with it, definition, different, non-generality, non-instance, objects of knowledge of which being them is not possible, negative phenomenon, the isolate of functioning thing, or any non-existent are things which are neither generalities nor instances of functioning thing.

3   Something which is neither a generality of functioning thing nor a non-instance of functioning thing (that is to say, is an instance) is form, consciousness, non-associated compositional factor, a pot, the two—a pillar and a pot, and so forth.

Debate F.7, Seventh Mistaken View (20a.6)

In this debate a hypothetical Challenger states a possible qualm concerning an assertion made implicitly in the previous debate, that whatever is a functioning thing is necessarily not a generality of functioning thing. This debate is a totally verbal argument and depends on the structure of Tibetan grammar to be plausible. In a Tibetan sentence the verb comes at the end and is preceded by the subject and the predicate of the sentence in that order. For example, in the utterance, "Jefferson an American is", the subject "Jefferson" is stated first, the predicate "an American" is stated in the middle, and the verb "is" comes at the end. In this debate the subject is sound-impermanent-phenomenon (*sgra mi rtag pa*). This is a subject and predicate without a verb. However, when this construction is plugged into the formula for determining whether or not something is an instance of it, it is supplied with a verb and comes to have the sense of, "Sound is an impermanent phenomenon."

In this way, sound-impermanent-phenomenon is suitable as a generality of many phenomena. Debate F.7 presents the argument that functioning thing is an instance of sound-impermanent-phenomenon. This is so, the text argues, because functioning thing fulfills the three qualities of an instance of sound-impermanent-phenomenon.

There is nothing that one can state, be it permanent or impermanent, which negates sound-impermanent-phenomenon. This is because, when one states them together in a sentence with a copulative verb, it is still true that sound is an impermanent phenomenon. This construction is similar to a powerless subject (*chos can nus med*) such as in the consequence, "It follows with respect to the subject, the horn of a rabbit, that sound is an impermanent phenomenon" (*ri bong rva chos can sgra mi rtag pa yin par thal*). In Tibetan, this consequence might appear to say that the horn of a rabbit is impermanent sound. Such a position is, of course, ridiculous, and the Defender is inclined to ask why it is so. To this the Challenger might respond, "With respect to the subject, the horn of a rabbit, sound is an impermanent phenomenon because sound is a product." Thus, this debate is occurring on two levels, one interpretation is plausible if one takes "impermanence" as a quality of sound and another interpretation is plausible according to the Challenger's intention that "impermanent phenomenon" is a predicate nominative and appositive to sound as in the expression, "Sound is an impermanent phenomenon."

It is only the structure of a Tibetan sentence that makes this deceit possible. This debate cannot be effectively translated into English. It may be reproduced only after a fashion and at best may serve as a guide to those interested in the Tibetan original.

> If, in reference to our statement that whatever is a functioning thing is necessarily not a generality of functioning thing, someone [a hypothetical Challenger] says, "It follows that the subject, sound-impermanent-phenomenon, is [not a generality of functioning thing] because of [being a functioning thing]," [the Sūtra School Defender responds to him,] "The reason is not established."

This debate is in the same style as those in the third section of each chapter, dispelling objections to the author's own

presentation. In accordance with the explanation of generalities and instances given here, the Sūtra School Defender
gives an answer to this possible qualm.

He answers that the reason, that sound-impermanent-
phenomenon is a functioning thing, is not established.
Sound-impermanent-phenomenon must be a permanent
phenomenon because (1) it is a generality and (2) it is not a
functioning thing. Perhaps it is from the point of view of
sound's *being* an impermanent phenomenon that the text
implies this. As explained in the presentation of opposites,
being anything is a permanent phenomenon, for it is an
abstraction and something that does not change moment by
moment. Sound disintegrates moment by moment, but
sound's *being* an impermanent phenomenon does not vary
or change. The Go-mang *Collected Topics* takes a different
approach on this point, as that text says: "It follows with
respect to the subject, sound, that its impermanence is a
functioning thing because it is a functioning thing."[1] The
Go-mang author takes this subject as a quality and the qualified, the impermanence of sound.

> [If another accepts that sound-impermanent-
> phenomenon is not a generality of functioning
> thing, then the Proponent of the Sūtra School, as
> Challenger, responds,] "One cannot accept it
> because sound-impermanent-phenomenon is a
> generality of functioning thing; because functioning
> thing is an instance of sound-impermanent-
> phenomenon."
>
> "It follows that [functioning thing is an instance of
> sound-impermanent-phenomenon] because (1)
> functioning thing/sound is an impermanent phe-
> nomenon, (2) functioning thing/sound is related
> with impermanent phenomenon as the same
> essence, and (3) many common loci of not being
> a functioning thing and also sound is an imperma-
> nent phenomenon are established."

---

[1] Ngak-wang-dra-shi, Go-mang *Collected Topics*, p. 39.

In the first part of the reason "functioning thing" appears in the position of a grammatical subject, but since it does not figure into the sentence it is set off by a slash. No matter what the meaning of "functioning thing/sound is an impermanent phenomenon", "functioning thing" does not change the fact that sound is an impermanent phenomenon. Thus, the subject really has no bearing on the predicate, "Sound is an impermanent phenomenon." It is irrelevant and does not affect the matter.

Just what is meant by saying that functioning thing/sound is related with impermanent phenomenon as the same essence is unclear. It must be intended that if sound's being an impermanent phenomenon did not exist, then functioning thing too would not exist. This point is unclear.

The third part of the reason, that many common locuses of not being a functioning thing and also sound is an impermanent phenomenon, means that no matter what one may state as a subject, it will not alter the fact that sound is an impermanent phenomenon. Permanent phenomenon/sound is an impermanent phenomenon. Object of knowledge/sound is an impermanent phenomenon. The so called "subject nominative"— functioning thing, permanent phenomenon, object of knowledge, or whatever—does not figure into the truth value of the sentence. It is superfluous, since the sentence still has a subject and predicate.

It should be noted that, according to the Go-mang interpretation of this subject as the *impermanence* of sound, only one of the three qualities of a phenomenon's being an instance of the impermanence of sound would be established for functioning thing. The impermanence of sound is a non-associated compositional factor, for it is itself an impermanent phenomenon but not matter and not consciousness.[1] Thus, one cannot say that functioning thing is an instance of the impermanence of sound, as no generality

_____

[1] See Ngak-w̄ang-d̄ra-s̄hi, Go-mang *Collected Topics*, p. 39.

of functioning thing is an impermanent phenomenon. Two of the three qualities of an instance of the impermanence of sound are not established for functioning thing because (1) it is not the impermanence of sound and (2) there are no phenomena which are not functioning things but are the impermanence of sound.

One can no more say that functioning thing is the impermanence of sound than one can say that it is a person or that it is matter. Also, according to the Go-mang interpretation, there is no common locus of not being a functioning thing but being the impermanence of sound. The impermanence of sound is a functioning thing and whatever is it is necessarily a functioning thing. However, functioning thing is the same essence as the impermanence of sound, as it is a non-associated compositional factor. Being the same essence is a mutual relationship; if p is the same essence as q, then q is the same essence as p. The Go-mang understanding of this phrase which they interpret to mean "the impermanence of sound" seems more reasonable than the interpretation given in the Tutor's *Collected Topics*.

> "The latter reason[1] [that many common locuses of not being a functioning thing and also sound is an impermanent phenomenon are established] follows because object of knowledge is such and also permanent phenomenon is such."
>
> "It follows that it is so because with respect to whatever is selfless sound is necessarily an impermanent phenomenon."

There is nothing which one can posit that will affect whether or not sound is an impermanent phenomenon. This is because whatever one puts into the so called subject nominative position will not figure into the grammar of the sentence. This is true for any existent or non-existent. As a consequence of this pervasion, it follows with respect to the subject, the child of a barren woman, that sound is an

---

[1] Here the text mistakenly reads *rtag* for *rtags*.

impermanent phenomenon because of being selfless. According to the system presented here, this consequence is to be accepted, for no matter what one may state before it sound is an impermanent phenomenon.

Debate F.8, Eighth Mistaken View (20b.3)

Debate F.8 is the last in the first section, refuting mistaken views concerning generalities and instances. In this debate the hypothetical Defender mistakenly asserts that whatever is an instance of awareness (*blo, buddhi*) is necessarily an instance of functioning thing. On first consideration this seems reasonable as awareness is an instance of functioning thing and whatever is an awareness is necessarily a functioning thing. However, the Sūtra School Challenger counters this view by pointing out that an awareness which is a cause of functioning thing (*dngos po'i rgyur gyur pa'i blo*) is an awareness and an instance of awareness, but such an awareness is not an instance of functioning thing because of being a cause of functioning thing. An awareness which is a cause of functioning thing must be a cooperative condition of functioning thing, something which existed prior to functioning thing and contributed to its arising in the sense that it helped to produce it.

> If someone [a hypothetical Defender] says, "Whatever is an instance of awareness is necessarily an instance of functioning thing," [the Sūtra School Challenger responds to him,] "It [absurdly] follows that the subjects, the two—a prime cognizer and a subsequent cognizer—which are a cause of functioning thing,[1] are [an instance of functioning thing] because of being [an instance of awareness]. You asserted the pervasion."

The two—a prime cognizer and a subsequent cognizer—which are a cause of functioning thing (*dngos po'i rgyur gyur*

---

[1] Here the text mistakenly spells *bcad shes* as *bcad bshes*.

pa'i tshad ma dang bcad shes gnyis) are objects of knowledge of which being them is not possible, and as such they are only an instance. As the text explains, they are an instance of awareness because of fulfilling the three qualities of an instance of awareness. Still, there is no special reason for positing objects of knowledge of which being them is not possible as a counterexample to break down the pointedness of the mistaken pervasion. Either alone would have been sufficient. For example, a prime cognizer which is a cause of functioning thing is an instance of awareness but not an instance of functioning thing. However, by positing this subject the text provides an opportunity for instruction on the difference between prime cognizers and subsequent cognizers, a topic which is investigated in detail in the presentation of "Awareness and Knowledge" (*blo rig*), an internal division of "The Greater Path of Reasoning".

A prime cognizer (*tshad ma, pramāṇa*), which has normally been translated as a valid cognizer in this work, is defined as:

> a new and incontrovertible knower (*gsar du mi slu ba'i rig pa*).

It is an *incontrovertible* consciousness in the sense that it is a valid and reliable knower. "'Incontrovertible' means that this cognizer has eliminated superimpositions with regard to its object—it has obtained or got at its object of distinguishment (*bcad don thob pa*)."[1] A prime cognizer is a *new* consciousness in the sense that it is the first moment in a stream of consciousness realizing an object. "'New' means that the object of the consciousness is being met with, or comprehended, for the first time."[2] Only direct perceivers and inferential cognizers may be prime cognizers and, within these, only the first moment of each is a prime cognizer.

---

[1] Lati Rinbochay, *Mind in Tibetan Buddhism*, p. 52.
[2] *Ibid.*

"Later moments within the same continuum—i.e., knowing the same object and without interruption by a consciousness knowing another object—are still direct perceivers (or inferential cognizers) but, no longer prime cognizers, are now subsequent cognizers."[1] The definition of a
subsequent cognizer (*bcad shes* or *dpyad shes*, *parichchhinna-
jñāna*) is:

> a knower which realizes that which has already been
> realized.[2]

This is a consciousness which arises subsequently to a prime
cognizer that has already realized an object, and continues
to realize that object incontrovertibly. Prime cognizers are
only the first moment of a direct perceiver or inferential
cognizer. Subsequent cognizers are induced by and continue
over later moments after a prime cognizer. In order to mark
this distinction as made in particular by the Sūtra School
Following Reasoning, in this debate *tshad ma* is translated as
"prime cognizer" rather than "valid cognizer", for
subsequent cognizers are "valid" but not "prime".

> If he says that the reason is not established, [the
> Sūtra School Challenger responds,] "It follows that
> the subjects [the two—a prime cognizer and a sub-
> sequent cognizer—which are a cause of functioning
> thing] are [an instance of awareness] because (1)
> they are an awareness [or awarenesses] (2) they are
> related with awareness as the same essence, and (3)
> many common loci of not being them and also
> being an awareness are established."
> The first and second parts of the reason are easy.
> If he says that the third part of the reason is not
> established, [the Sūtra School Challenger responds,]
> "It follows that many such common loci are
> established because (1) an exalted knower of all
> aspects is such, (2) a prime cognizer also is such, and

---

[1] *Ibid.*, p. 32.
[2] *Ibid.*, p. 85.

(3) these two [an exalted knower of all aspects and a prime cognizer] are established as mutually different."

An exalted knower of all aspects (*rnam mkhyen, sarvā-kāra-jñāna*) is the omniscient consciousness of a Buddha, the best of all consciousnesses. Although such a consciousness is necessarily a prime cognizer, it is established as mutually different from a prime cognizer because they are consciousnesses which are not exactly the same. Both an exalted knower of all aspects and a prime cognizer are awarenesses, but neither of them is the two—a prime cognizer and a subsequent cognizer—which are a cause of functioning thing.

If he accepts the basic consequence, [the Sūtra School Challenger responds,] "It follows that the subjects [the two—a prime cognizer and a subsequent cognizer—which are a cause of functioning thing] are not an instance of functioning thing because of not being related with functioning thing as the same essence."

If he says that the reason is not established, [the Sūtra School Challenger responds,] "It follows that the subjects [the two—a prime cognizer and a subsequent cognizer—which are a cause of functioning thing] are [not related with functioning thing as the same essence] because of being a cause of functioning thing." The reason is easy.

These subjects are not related with functioning thing as the same essence because of being causally related with functioning thing, for functioning thing is arisen from them. They are not the same essence as functioning thing because they do not exist simultaneously with it. Also, it is not the case that if functioning thing does not exist, then its causes too must not exist. This is because, even though the functioning thing which is their effect may not yet exist, its causes may exist. In fact, at a place where functioning thing's causes exist, the functioning thing which is their effect necessarily does *not* exist. And if the functioning thing which is their effect exists, the causes of it necessarily do *not* exist. The causes of functioning thing, despite being functioning things, are not the same essence as functioning thing.

There are four possibilities between the two principals of debate F.8, instance-of-awareness and instance-of-functioning-thing:

1 Something which is both is a prime cognizer, a subsequent cognizer, an eye consciousness, an ear consciousness, and so forth.
2 Something which is an instance of awareness but not an instance of functioning thing is an awareness which is a cause or effect of functioning thing—such as a prime cognizer which is a cause of functioning thing or an eye consciousness which is a cause of functioning thing.
3 Something which is an instance of functioning thing but not an instance of awareness is matter, a non-associated compositional factor, a pot, a pillar, a person, and so forth.
4 Something which is neither is a material cause or effect of functioning thing, a permanent phenomenon, one, different, and so forth.

PRESENTATION OF THE AUTHOR'S OWN SYSTEM OF GENERALITIES AND INSTANCES (20B.6)

> Second, in our own system: There is a definition of a generality because a phenomenon which encompasses its manifestations is the definition of a generality. If generalities are divided terminologically, there are three because there are the three: type-generalities, meaning-generalities, and collection-generalities.
> There is a definition of a type-generality because a phenomenon which encompasses the many which have its type is the definition of a type-generality.

There is an illustration because object of knowledge is a type-generality.

There is a definition of the meaning-generality of pot because that imputed factor which, although it is not a pot, appears to the thought consciousness apprehending a pot as a pot is the definition of the meaning-generality of pot. There is an illustration because an appearance (to a thought consciousness in its second moment of apprehending a pot) of opposite-from-not-being-pot-of-the-second-moment is an illustration of the meaning-generality of pot.

There is a definition of a collection-generality because a gross form which is a composite of its many parts is the definition of a collection-generality. There are illustrations because a pot and a pillar are collection-generalities.

There is a common locus of being a collection-generality and a type-generality because a pot is such a common locus. There is a common locus of not being a collection-generality and being a type-generality because object of knowledge is such a common locus. There is a common locus of not being a type-generality and being a collection-generality because the two—a pillar and a pot—are such a common locus. There is a common locus of not being a type-generality and not being a collection-generality because the two—a permanent phenomenon and a functioning thing—are such a common locus.

There is a definition of an instance because a phenomenon which has a type engaging it as a pervader is the definition of its being an instance.

The presentation of the author's own system of generalities and instances found in the Tutor's *Collected Topics* is modeled after the same section in the Go-mang *Collected Topics*.[1]

---

[1] Ngak-ẁang-ḏra-śhi, Go-mang *Collected Topics*, pp. 151-153.

DISPELLING OBJECTIONS TO THE AUTHOR'S SYSTEM OF
GENERALITIES AND INSTANCES (21A.5)

This third and final section in "Generalities and Instances"
consists of seven debates.

Debate F.9, First Objection (21a.6)

In this debate the hypothetical Challenger's qualm develops
from the discussion of the difference between generality and
collection-generality that has just been presented in the previous section. Whatever is a collection-generality is not necessarily a generality, for any gross form which is a composite of its many parts is a collection-generality but not necessarily a generality.

> Someone [a hypothetical Challenger] might say, "It
> follows that the subjects, the two—a pillar and a pot,
> are a generality because of being a collection-gen-
> erality." [To this the Sūtra School Defender
> answers,] "There is no pervasion."

It is true that the two—a pillar and a pot—are a collection-
generality, but that does not entail that they are a generality.

> [If another says that the reason, that the two—a
> pillar and a pot—are a collection-generality, is not
> established, then the Proponent of the Sūtra School,
> as Challenger, responds to him, "It follows that] the
> reason is established because of being a mass com-
> posed of the eight particle substances."

The two—a pillar and a pot—are matter and a gross form
composed of their many parts; thus, they are a collection-
generality.

> If he accepts the consequence [that the two—a pillar
> and a pot—are a generality, the Sūtra School Chal-
> lenger responds,] "It follows that the subjects [the

two—a pillar and a pot—are not a generality because there are no instances of them."

If he says that the reason is not established, [the Sūtra School Challenger responds,] "It follows with respect to the subjects [the two—a pillar and a pot—that there are no instances of them] because they are objects of knowledge of which being [them] is not possible."

Just as in the case of type-generality and collection-generality, there are four possibilities between generality and collection-generality:

1 Something which is both is matter, pot, pillar, tree, and so on.
2 Something which is a generality but not a collection-generality is permanent phenomenon, functioning thing, object of knowledge, definition, definiendum, and so forth.
3 Something which is a collection-generality but not a generality is the two—a gold pot and a copper pot, the two—red and white, the two—round and square, and so on.
4 Something which is neither is the two—a permanent phenomenon and a functioning thing, the two—a definition and a definiendum, and so on.

Debate F.10, Second Objection (21b.1)

In this debate a hypothetical Challenger raises a qualm that object of knowledge is not a generality because it is not a generality of that which is object of knowledge (*shes bya yin pa*). His qualm seems ridiculous, for no generality is a generality of that which is object of knowledge since object of knowledge (or that which is object of knowledge) is not an instance of anything. However, the Challenger is playing on the ambiguity of the Tibetan in *shes bya yin pa'i spyi*, which could be read as "a generality of that which is *an* object of knowledge". For object of knowledge to be a generality, its instances must be objects of knowledge; thus, object of knowledge is a generality of that which is *an* object of knowledge. The Challenger is saying that if object of knowledge is a generality, it must be a generality of that which is an object of knowledge and yet it cannot be, since it is not a generality of that which is object of knowledge (or, alternatively, being object of knowledge). The debate revolves around an ambiguity in Tibetan and thus essentially cannot be rendered in English.

> Also, someone [a hypothetical Challenger] might say, "It follows that object of knowledge is not a generality because it is not a generality of that which is object of knowledge." [The Sūtra School Defender responds,] "There is no pervasion."

Although it is true that object of knowledge is not a generality of that which is object of knowledge, this does not necessarily imply that it is not a generality.

> If [another says that the reason is not established, then the Proponent of the Sūtra School, as Challenger, responds,] "It follows that it is not a generality of that which is object of knowledge because there is no generality of that which is object of knowledge."
>
> If he says that the reason is not established, [the Sūtra School Challenger responds,] "It follows that [there is no generality of that which is object of knowledge because (1) there is no generality of object of knowledge and (2) the two, object of knowledge and that which is object knowledge, are mutually inclusive."

Whatever is an object of knowledge is necessarily something which is an object of knowledge and whatever is something which is an object of knowledge is necessarily an object of knowledge.

> If someone were to accept the above consequence, [the Sūtra School Challenger responds,] "It follows

that the subject, object of knowledge, is a generality because of being a phenomenon which encompasses its manifestations."

If he says the reason is not established, [the Sūtra School Challenger responds,] "It follows that the subject [object of knowledge] is [a phenomenon which encompasses its manifestations] because of being a phenomenon which encompasses the many that have its type."

If he says that the reason is not established, [the Sūtra School Challenger responds,] "It follows that the subject [object of knowledge] is [a phenomenon which encompasses the many that have its type] because of encompassing the many that have its type."

It is interesting to note that whatever encompasses the many that have its type is necessarily a *phenomenon* which encompasses the many that have its type. The pervasion seems to imply that whatever encompasses others in this way is necessarily a *phenomenon*, an existent. For example, only-a-permanent-phenomenon, although it is not a phenomenon, seems to encompass the many that have its type, for there are many phenomena which are only permanent phenomena. Still, it is fair to assume that the way in which a generality "encompasses" its manifestations is not merely by having instances which are that generality but also by having instances which are the same essence and so on. In this regard, only-a-permanent-phenomenon fails to encompass the phenomena which are only permanent phenomena. If interpreted in this way, it is the case that whatever encompasses the many that have its type is necessarily a *phenomenon* which encompasses in that way.

If he says that the reason is not established, [the Sūtra School Challenger responds,] "It follows that the subject [object of knowledge, encompasses the many which have its type] because all permanent phenomena and functioning things are included within its type."

Instances, which have the type of their generality, are included (*gtogs pa*) in the type of that generality. A generality includes phenomena of various types. It is not possible to have a generality with only one instance or with no instances at all. There is no generality which is a separate entity from its instances, the *many* which have its type.

Debate F.11, Third Objection (21b.4)

Debate F.11 is another verbal qualm based on Tibetan grammar. In Tibetan the nominative case, unlike the other seven grammatical cases, is not marked by a case ending; thus, one understands by context what is in the nominative case and what is not. In this debate the play is on two possible ways of reading the initial consequence, one by interpreting a subject in the nominative case and another by inserting an unstated subject and taking the rest as a unified predicate.

By taking object of knowledge as a subject in the nominative case, the consequence may be interpreted to mean:

Object of knowledge is a generality of that-which-is-not.

In this way, "that which is not" (*ma yin pa*) is an incomplete phrase of negation. Alternatively, this same consequence may be understood to mean:

[Something] is a generality of non-object of knowledge.

This second reading involves taking object of knowledge not as a subject nominative but as a noun modified by "non-" or "that which is not" and as a portion of a genitive phrase (rendered in English as a prepositional phrase) in the predicate, "generality of non-object of knowledge".

The first reading is the preferred understanding, but the hypothetical Challenger intends the second reading, for his qualm, that there might be a generality of non-object of knowledge, is an unwanted consequence. Non-object of knowledge is a non-existent and since whatever is it is necessarily a non-existent, nothing which is a non-object of knowledge can be an instance. Again, this debate cannot be effectively translated into English but may be reproduced as a serviceable guide to those interested in the Tibetan original.

> Also, someone [a hypothetical Challenger] might say, "It [absurdly] follows that [something] is a generality of non-object of knowledge because that-which-is-not is an instance of object of knowledge." [To this the Sūtra School Defender answers,] "There is no pervasion."

It is true that that-which-is-not is an instance of object of knowledge and that object of knowledge is a generality of that-which-is-not because that-which-is-not is a permanent phenomenon and an object of knowledge, it is related with object of knowledge as the same essence, and there are many phenomena which are objects of knowledge and are not that-which-is-not. Still, this does not imply that anything is a generality of non-object of knowledge.

> If someone [a hypothetical Defender] accepts the consequence [that something is a generality of non-object of knowledge, then the Proponent of the Sūtra School, as Challenger, responds,] "It follows that [whatever exists] is not a generality of non-object of knowledge because if something were a generality of non-object of knowledge, then anything would be possible."

One cannot interpret this last consequence to mean that object of knowledge is not a generality of that-which-is-not because in answering that there is no pervasion to the former consequence the Sūtra School Defender implicitly accepted the establishment of the reason, that that-which-is-not is an instance of object of knowledge. Thus, object of knowledge is a generality of that-which-is-not.

Debate F.12, Fourth Objection (21b.5)

In this debate the text once again focuses on the comparison of generality and instance. Here the hypothetical Challenger contends that there is an instance of non-instance. The Sūtra School Defender cannot accept this because non-instance is not a generality. There are no instances of it. There are phenomena which are only generalities (that is, generalities which are not instances) such as the selfless, object of knowledge and the phenomena mutually inclusive with it, and different-from-functioning-thing. However, none of these phenomena can be an instance, not even of non-instance. For example, object of knowledge is not an instance of non-instance because it does not satisfy the third quality of an instance. There is no phenomenon which is not an object of knowledge but is a non-instance. Thus, there are no instances of non-instance. In another way, it is very easy to see that there could not be an instance of non-instance because if something were an instance of non-instance, according to the first requirement of an instance, it would have to be a non-instance and, absurdly, not an instance of non-instance.

> Also, someone [a hypothetical Challenger] might say, "It [absurdly] follows that there is an instance of non-instance because there is a generality of non-generality." [To this the Sūtra School Defender answers,] "There is no pervasion."

Although it is true that there is a generality of non-generality, this does not imply that there is an instance of non-instance.

> [If another says that the reason—that there is a generality of non-generality—is not established, then the Proponent of the Sūtra School, as Challenger, responds, "It follows that] the reason is established

because object of knowledge is a generality of non-generality."

If he says that the reason is not established, [the Sūtra School Challenger responds,] "It follows that the subject, object of knowledge, is a generality of non-generality because non-generality is an instance of it."

Phenomena which are non-generalities are only instances, instances which are not generalities, such as objects of knowledge of which being them is not possible, the isolate of functioning thing, one-with-functioning-thing, and so forth. Further, non-generality itself is not a non-generality, for it is a generality because there are instances of it. For example, one-with-pillar is an instance of non-generality because (1) it is a non-generality, (2) it is related with non-generality as the same essence, and (3) many common locuses of not being one with pillar and also being non-generalities are established. The third part of the reason is established because the two—a permanent phenomenon and a functioning thing—are such a common locus and also pot's isolate is such a common locus. Also, non-generality is an instance, for it is an instance of object of knowledge and the phenomena mutually inclusive with it, permanent phenomenon, negative phenomenon, and so on.

Debate F.13, Fifth Objection (21b.6)

Debate F.13 is a very short argument developed from the last debate. Here a hypothetical Challenger reckons that object of knowledge could not be a generality of non-generality (*spyi ma yin pa*) because it is a generality of that which is a generality (*spyi yin pa*). There is no pervasion. It is true that object of knowledge is a generality of that which is a generality, but this does not necessitate that it is not a generality of non-generality. Many opposites are subsumed under object of knowledge—functioning thing and non-thing, one and different, positive phenomenon and negative phenomenon, and so forth.

Also, someone [a hypothetical Challenger] might say, "It follows that the subject, object of knowledge, is not a generality of non-generality because of being a generality of that which is a generality." [To this the Sūtra School Defender answers,] "There is no pervasion."

"The reason is established because that which is a generality is an instance of it."

Debate F.14, Sixth Objection (21b.6)

In this debate the text once again brings up the subject of sound-impermanent-phenomenon (*sgra mi rtag pa*). As before, this debate cannot be effectively translated because it depends on the grammatical structure of the Tibetan language. In debate F.7 the text implies that sound-impermanent-phenomenon is a permanent phenomenon and establishes it as a generality of functioning thing. Here a hypothetical Challenger raises the qualm that sound-impermanent-phenomenon is not a generality of permanent phenomenon because of being a generality of functioning thing. According to this reasoning, object of knowledge would not be a generality of permanent phenomenon because of being a generality of functioning thing.

The qualm is insignificant, but the debate does serve to show that according to the Proponents of the Sūtra School, as interpreted in the Tutor's *Collected Topics*, sound-impermanent-phenomenon is a generality of both permanent and impermanent phenomena. However, according to the system of the Go-mang *Collected Topics*, *sgra mi rtag pa*, understood as the impermanence of sound, is not a generality of any permanent phenomenon nor even of functioning thing because of being a non-associated compositional factor.

Also, someone [a hypothetical Challenger] might say, "It follows that permanent phenomenon is not an instance of sound-impermanent-phenomenon because functioning thing is an instance of sound-impermanent-phenomenon." [To this the Sūtra School Defender answers,] "There is no pervasion."

[This is so, for] "It follows that permanent phenomenon is an instance of sound-impermanent-phenomenon because sound-impermanent-phenomenon is a phenomenon which encompasses its manifestations, permanent phenomena."

"It follows that [sound-impermanent-phenomenon is a phenomenon which encompasses its manifestations, permanent phenomena] because among the manifestations of [sound-impermanent-phenomenon] there are permanent phenomena; because among the manifestations of that there are both permanent phenomena and functioning things."

In this debate, as in debate F.7, the text seems to bow to the force of Tibetan grammar which allows anything to be sound-impermanent-phenomenon. There is nothing that one can state which will change or even affect the proposition that sound is an impermanent phenomenon.

Debate F.15, Seventh Objection (22a.2)

Debate F.15, the last in "Generalities and Instances", is modeled after a debate in the Ra-dö *Collected Topics*.[1] To some extent this debate also depends on the Tibetan language in order to be effective, but it does not rely on the structure or possible differences of interpretations so much as that the same Tibetan word "*yod pa*" is used in one context as a noun, "existent", and in another context as a verb of possession, "has" or "have". The definition of an instance is:

a phenomenon which has a type engaging it as a pervader (*khyab byed du 'jug pa'i rang gi rigs yod pa can gyi chos*)

---

[1] Jam-ȳang-chok-hla-ö-ser, Ra-dö *Collected Topics*, 34a.5-6.

Part of this definition, "which has a type" (*rigs yod pa can*), involves the verbal form of existent, *yod pa*. Here a hypothetical Challenger uses this ambiguity of meaning to assert that existent is an instance because there is an existent engaging it as a pervader rather than admitting the usual interpretation of the word as meaning *"has* a pervader engaging it"*. There are phenomena such as object of knowledge which pervade existent, of course, but existent cannot be a phenomenon which has a type that engages it as a pervader, for that pervading generality could not have any other instances which are not also existent.

> Someone [a hypothetical Challenger] might say, "It follows that the subject, existent, is an instance because of being a phenomenon which has a type engaging it as a pervader."
> "It follows that it is so because there is an existent which engages it as a pervader."
> [To this the Sūtra School Defender answers,] "There is no pervasion [i.e., even though it is true that there is an existent which engages it as a pervader, this does not entail that it is a phenomenon which has a type engaging it as a pervader] because there is a purpose for the statement, 'has a type,' as a part of the definition."

The Ra-dö *Collected Topics* adds to this:

> If it were not like that, it would follow with respect to the subject, the horn of a rabbit, that it has a type because there is an existent. The pervasion is parallel.[1]

In the second consequence in this debate the hypothetical Challenger claimed:

> It follows that the subject, existent, is a phenomenon which has a type engaging it as a pervader because there is an existent which engages it as a pervader.

---

[1] *Ibid.*, 34a.5.

The above passage from the Ra-dö *Collected Topics* claims that the pervasion—if there is an existent, then it necessarily has a type—is parallel to the pervasion in the earlier consequence—if there is an existent which engages it as a pervader, then it is necessarily a phenomenon which has a type engaging it as a pervader.

REMARKS

This sixth chapter in the Tutor's *Collected Topics* is considerably more complex and difficult than the preceding chapters. The text presents the nature of generalities and instances, identifying what it means to say that pot is an instance of functioning thing, that object of knowledge is a generality of functioning thing, and so forth. Another important approach to the nature of generalities and instances presented here is the study of generalities as instances and instances as generalities. Also, generalities are discussed through the terminological division into type-generalities, collection-generalities, and meaning-generalities.

In many ways the division of established bases into generalities and instances is the most fascinating and complex. Rather than being a division of stark contrast as in the case of permanent phenomena and functioning things, there is great interplay and mixture between generalities and instances. This complexity tremendously increases the material for debate.

Also, more than any chapter before it, "Generalities and Instances" depends on a good understanding of the previous material. In order to understand phenomena which are only generalities it is necessary to have an acquaintance with the material in "Established Bases". In order to understand phenomena which are only instances one must be familiar with objects of knowledge of which being them is not possible, isolates, and the phenomena coextensive with an isolate. Also, because they must be related as the same essence, generalities and instances are distinguished from particular causes and their effects. The Collected Topics study and all of traditional Ge-luk-ba education depend on such cumulative build-up of knowledge beginning with an understanding of these essential introductory topics.

"Generalities and Instances" serves to shed light on the nature of what is meant by the collective entity so prevalently referred to in this system. For example, a pot is an instance of *functioning thing*, and functioning thing in turn is a generality of a pot. In this translation system it is not said that a pot is an instance of *a* functioning thing because supplying "functioning thing" with the indefinite article "a" suggests that a pot is its instance simply because it is a functioning thing and does not capture the full range of what is required to be such an instance. Since an instance of something must be the same essence as that thing, it would be misleading to suggest that a pot is the same essence as *a* functioning thing, for this assertion is open to the absurdity that a pot is the same essence as a pillar because a pot is the same essence as a functioning thing and a pillar is a functioning thing. Rather, in order to express the collective functioning thing, here the singular term without an article is preferred, and "*a* functioning thing" is preserved for either specific cases or general applications. Thus, the collective functioning thing refers to that generality which encompasses its instances, the many that have its type—pots, pillars, persons, consciousnesses, and so forth.

14 *Substantial And Isolate Phenomena*

INTRODUCTION

The seventh chapter of the Tutor's *Collected Topics*, the last in "The Introductory Path of Reasoning", serves as an effective summary of the material presented in previous chapters by organizing it into a coherent and orderly system. In this chapter phenomena are differentiated mainly (1) on the basis of whether or not they are themselves in the sense of exemplifying themselves and (2) on the basis of whether non-that phenomenon is or is not that phenomenon. This classification emphasizes two of the main themes of the Collected Topics system—that some phenomena are themselves and others are not and that for some phenomena non-it is nonetheless it. These points have been critical to understanding the chapters that have gone before and are essential for the coherence and consistency of the system of Buddhist reasoning presented here. Thus, in order to understand this final chapter with any facility it is necessary to have a firm grasp of the topics explained in previous chapters.

696 Debate in Tibetan Buddhism

The presentation of substantial phenomena (*rdzas chos,* *dravya-dharma*) and isolate phenomena (*ldog chos,* *vyatireka-dharma*) given in the Tutor's *Collected Topics* is not accepted by Go-mang College. In the Go-mang system, substantial phenomenon is taken as mutually inclusive with functioning thing and isolate phenomenon is taken as mutually inclusive with permanent phenomenon. However, this does not hold in the system explained here, for some functioning things are asserted as isolate phenomena and some permanent phenomena are asserted as substantial phenomena. This is because in the Tutor's *Collected Topics* version of substantial and isolate phenomena, objects are classified in accordance with whether or not they are themselves and whether non-that object is or is not that object, not merely according to whether they are functioning things or permanent phenomena.

The system of substantial and isolate phenomena provided in the Tutor's *Collected Topics* is reported in the Go-mang text to have been formulated by the twelfth century Ga-dam-ba (*bka' gdams pa*) scholar Cha-ba-chö-ğyi-šeng-gay (*cha pa chos kyi seng ge,* 1109-1169),[1] author of the first Collected Topics text.[2] According to Lati Rinbochay, some nuns in the vicinity of Šang-bu invited Cha-ba-chö-ğyi-šeng-gay to instruct them on the topic of logic and epistemology. Since he had heard that they were very sharp, he set forth his system of substantial and isolate phenomena. When he had finished, he asked for questions, but because they were confused, they had nothing to say.[3]

The substantial and isolate phenomena explained in this chapter are essentially of eight types, one type of substantial phenomenon and seven types of isolate phenomena. Isolate phenomena and further distinguished as the first three iso-

---

[1] The dates for Cha-ba-chö-ğyi-šeng-gay are from L.W.J. Van de Kuijp, p. 355.

[2] Ngak-wang-dra-shi in the Go-mang *Collected Topics* refers to the organization of substantial and isolate phenomena as presented in the Tutor's *Collected Topics* as Cha-ba's system (*cha pa'i lugs*).

[3] Lati Rinbochay, oral commentary.

late phenomena (*ldog chos dang po gsum*) and the latter four similitudes (*phyi ma rjes mthun bzhi*). Each of these eight phenomena is mutually exclusive with all of the others. Nothing can be a common locus of any two of these, not even a phenomenon and its similitude. The eight substantial and isolate phenomena together with their definitions and some illustrations are listed in Table X:

Table X: Substantial and Isolate Phenomena[1]

1 substantial phenomenon (*rdzas chos*)

that which is a common locus such that:
1 it is an established base
2 it is itself
3 non-it is not it
4 its isolate is not mutually exclusive with substantial phenomenon

Illustrations: object of knowledge, functioning thing, consciousness, a pot, a pillar and so forth

2 isolate-phenomenon-which-is-itself (*rang yin pa'i ldog chos*)

that which is a common locus such that:
1 it is an established base
2 it is itself
3 non-it is it
4 its isolate is not mutually exclusive with isolate-phenomenon-which-is-itself

Illustrations: definiendum, permanent phenomenon, one, generality, instance, that which is without a self of persons, non-the-two—a pillar and a pot, mutually-different-from-object-of-knowledge, non-thing, different-from-pot, and so on

---

[1] Some of the illustrations are from Dzeṁay Rinbochay, Śhar-dzay *Collected Topics*, pp. 37-38.

3 isolate-phenomenon-which-is-not-itself (*rang ma yin pa'i ldog chos*)

that which is a common locus such that:

1 it is an established base
2 it is not itself
3 not-it is not it
4 its isolate is not mutually exclusive with isolate-phenomenon-which-is-not-itself

Illustrations: definition, different, the mutually exclusive, objects of knowledge of which being them is not possible, one-with-pot, the two—a pillar and a pot, the isolate of functioning thing, substantial phenomenon, isolate-phenomenon-which-is-itself

4 isolate-phenomenon-of-the-third-type (*ldog chos phung sum tsam po ba*)

that which is a common locus such that:

1 it is an established base
2 it is not itself
3 non-it is it
4 its isolate is not mutually exclusive with isolate-phenomenon-of-the-third-type

Illustrations: negative phenomenon, generality-of-functioning-thing, instance-of-generality-of-pot etc.

5 similitude-of-substantial-phenomenon (*rdzas chos kyi rjes mthun*)

that which is a common locus such that:

1 it is an established base
2 it is itself
3 non-it is not it
4 its isolate is not mutually exclusive with the similitude of substantial phenomenon

Illustrations: functioning-thing-which-is-an-isolate-phenomenon, that which is mutually exclusive with substantial phenomenon, and so on

6 similitude-of-isolate-phenomenon-which-is-itself (*rang yin pa'i ldog chos kyi rjes mthun*)

that which is a common locus such that:
1 it is an established base
2 it is itself
3 non-it is it
4 its isolate is not mutually exclusive with similitude-of-isolate-phenomenon-which-is-itself

Illustration: non-isolate-phenomenon-which-is-itself

7 similitude-of-isolate-phenomenon-which-is-not-itself (*rang ma yin pa'i ldog chos kyi rjes mthun*)

that which is a common locus such that:
1 it is an established base
2 it is not itself
3 not-it is not it
4 its isolate is not mutually exclusive with similitude-of-isolate-phenomenon-which-is-not-itself

Illustration: isolate-phenomenon-which-is-not-itself

8 similitude-of-isolate-phenomenon-of-the-third-type (*ldog chos phung sum tsam po ba'i rjes mthun*)

that which is a common locus such that:
1 it is an established base
2 it is not itself
3 non-it is it
4 its isolate is not mutually exclusive with similitude-of-isolate-phenomenon-of-the-third-type

Illustration: isolate-phenomenon-of-the-third-type

THE FOUR REQUIREMENTS

Something is established as an illustration of any one of these eight phenomena if and only if it is a common locus of all four prerequisite qualities of that substantial or isolate phenomenon. For instance, a pot is established as a substantial phenomenon because of being a common locus such that (1) it is an established base, (2) it is itself, (3) non-it is not it, and (4) its isolate is not mutually exclusive with substantial phenomenon. First, a pot is an established base because it is a functioning thing. Second, a pot is itself—it is a pot— because it is a bulbous flat-based phenomenon able to perform the function of holding water. Third, non-pot is not a pot because non-pot is a permanent phenomenon and, consequently, unable to perform the functions of a pot. Fourth, a pot's isolate is not mutually exclusive with substantial phenomenon because there is a common locus of these two, since a pot is a common locus of being a pot's isolate and also being a substantial phenomenon. The procedure for establishing something as any of these phenomena is just the same.

The First Requirement

The first requirement of every substantial and isolate phenomenon is that it must be an established base. This requirement merely serves to eliminate non-existents, any of which would satisfy the second and third requirements for two of these eight phenomena. For instance, non-existent is itself, for it is not an existent. Also, non-non-existent is not a non-existent but an existent. In this way non-existent completes the second and third requirements of a substantial phenomenon, but it is not a substantial phenomenon because of not being an established base. Moreover, no non-existent could satisfy the fourth requirement of any substantial or isolate phenomenon. This is because there cannot be an isolate of any non-existent, for nothing is reversed from not being one with a non-existent. Nothing is one with a non-existent.

As a second example, only-a-permanent-phenomenon (*rtag pa kho na*) satisfies the second and third requirements of an isolate phenomenon of the third type. Only-a-permanent-phenomenon is not only a permanent phenomenon because it is a non-existent. Non-only-a-permanent-phenomenon is only a permanent phenomenon because non-only-a-permanent-phenomenon is a permanent phenomenon. However, since only-a-permanent-phenomenon is not an established base, it is not an isolate phenomenon of any type.

The Second Requirement

The second requirement of any substantial or isolate phenomenon centers on whether the object is or is not itself. For instance, a pot is a pot, but definition is not a definition. This means that a pot is an exemplifier of itself (for it is able to perform the functions of a pot) but definition is not an exemplifier of itself (for it is a definiendum and not a definition). In this requirement the focus is on the object itself—the singular collective entity—understood from the point of view of its self-isolate. For some phenomena, it itself shares the same qualities as its many instances. Each and every pot is a bulbous flat-based phenomenon able to perform the functions of holding water, and so too pot, understood collectively, is taken to be a bulbous flat-based phenomenon able to perform the functions of holding water. However, other phenomena, when understood from the point of view of their self-isolates, do not share the same qualities as their instances. For example, each and every definition is a definition—a triply qualified substantial existent, but definition itself is not a definition (for it is not a triply qualified substantial existent because it is a triply qualified *imputed* existent).

The Third Requirement

The third requirement of any substantial or isolate phenomenon centers on whether non-that object is or or is not that object in the sense of demonstrating the qualities of that object. For instance, non-pot is not a pot because non-pot is a permanent phenomenon and thus not able to perform the functions of a pot. On the other hand, non-generality (*spyi ma yin pa*) is a generality because it has instances such as the isolate of sound and the two—a pillar and a pot. In the third requirement, one considers the nature of non-that object collectively rather than generally. That is, even though each and every non-generality is not a generality, non-generality itself is a generality.

The Fourth Requirement

In general the fourth requirement functions to eliminate mutually exclusive cases and also serves to assure that substantial phenomenon and each of the seven types of isolate phenomena are mutually exclusive with each of the others. This requirement—that the isolate of an illustration of substantial phenomenon or some isolate phenomenon must not be mutually exclusive with that phenomenon it illustrates— means that the *example itself* has the quality of being a substantial phenomenon or that type of isolate phenomenon. For instance, functioning thing is a substantial phenomenon. This means that there must be a common locus of the two, the isolate of functioning thing and substantial phenomenon. There is such a common locus, for functioning thing—and only functioning thing—is both the isolate of functioning thing and a substantial phenomenon. Thus, the isolate of functioning thing is not mutually exclusive with substantial phenomenon. This does not mean that the isolate of functioning thing itself is a substantial phenomenon, for it is not. This means that the isolate of functioning thing is not mutually exclusive with substantial phenomenon. Since only an object itself is its own isolate, if its isolate is not mutually exclusive with substantial phenomenon or some isolate phenomenon, then this means that that object *itself* is that substantial or isolate phenomenon which it illustrates.

It must be noted carefully that the fourth requirement is not that the object itself is not mutually exclusive with the substantial or isolate phenomenon which it is, but that the *isolate* of that object is not mutually exclusive with the substantial of isolate phenomenon which it is. Thus, the question is not whether or not that object is mutually exclusive with the substantial or isolate phenomenon it illustrates, but whether or not it itself *is* that substantial or isolate phenomenon. This fourth requirement functions to allow cases in which, even though the object itself is mutually exclusive with the substantial or isolate phenomenon it illustrates, it nonetheless is that substantial or isolate phenomenon. This is similar to the case of definition and definiendum, for definition is a definiendum even though it is mutually exclusive with definiendum. The two, definition and definiendum, are mutually exclusive because there is nothing which is a common locus of the two; however, the two, definition's isolate and definiendum, are not mutually exclusive because there is a common locus of the two, for definition is both definition's isolate and a definiendum.

In just this same way, there are some isolate phenomena which are nonetheless mutually exclusive with the phenomena they illustrate. For instance, one-with-pot is an isolate phenomenon which is not itself, yet it is mutually exclusive with isolate-phenomenon-which-is-not-itself. There is nothing which is both one with pot and an isolate phenomenon which is not itself because (1) whatever is one with pot is necessarily not an isolate phenomenon which is not itself and (2) whatever is an isolate phenomenon which is not itself is necessarily not one with pot. The only thing which is one with pot is pot, and pot is a substantial phenomenon; therefore, there is nothing which is both one with pot and also is an isolate phenomenon which is not itself. Thus, one-with-pot is mutually exclusive with isolate-phenomenon-which-is-not-itself.

Nonetheless, one-with-pot is an isolate phenomenon which is not itself because of being a common locus such that (1) it is an established base, (2) it is not itself, (3) non-it is not it, and also (4) its isolate is not mutually exclusive with isolate-phenomenon-which-is-not-itself. First, one-with-pot is an established base because of being a permanent phenomenon. Second, one-with-pot is not one with pot because it is different from pot. Third, non-one-with-pot is also not one with pot because of being different from pot. Fourth, the isolate of one-with-pot is not mutually exclusive with isolate-phenomenon-which-is-not-itself because there is a common locus, for one-with-pot is both the isolate of one-with-pot and an isolate phenomenon which is not itself. Thus, one-with-pot is an isolate phenomenon which is not itself even though it is mutually exclusive with that phenomenon. If the fourth requirement did not specify that it is the object's *isolate* which is not mutually exclusive with the substantial or isolate phenomenon it illustrates, then one-with-pot would not be able to qualify as an isolate phenomenon which is not itself and, further, it would not qualify as any of these eight phenomena and could not be included in the presentation of substantial and isolate phenomena. There are many such cases.

Also, the specification of the *isolate* in the fourth requirement functions to allow some phenomena which are not themselves to be included in the presentation of substantial and isolate phenomena. For instance, one-with-pot is not one with pot and, from this point of view, if the fourth requirement were that one-with-pot must not be mutually exclusive with isolate-phenomenon-which-is-not-itself then there could be no common locus. Something which is both one with pot and an isolate phenomenon which is not itself does not exist.

Thus, the purpose for specifying the isolate in the fourth requirement is to affirm an object as *being* that substantial or isolate phenomenon which it is. However, the two main purposes for the fourth requirement are: (1) to eliminate mutually exclusive cases which, although they satisfy the first three requirements of a phenomenon, do not satisfy the fourth and (2) to assure that substantial phenomenon and each of the many types of isolate phenomena are mutually exclusive with the others.

The first three requirements of a substantial phenomenon are just the same as the first three requirements of similitude-of-substantial-phenomenon and the first three requirements of each of the first three types of isolate phenomena are just the same as the first three requirements of their similitudes. In this sense the latter four isolate phenomena are "similitudes" of the first four phenomena. However, since there is the fourth requirement, no particular illustration can be both a phenomenon and its similitude. Working together with the other three requirements, the fourth makes definite that nothing can be more than one of these eight types of phenomena.

Despite its functional purpose in the definitions of the substantial and isolate phenomena, the fourth requirement is nonetheless an odd sort of logical necessity. It requires that the reasoning establishing something as a substantial or isolate phenomenon must be looped back into that very reasoning process. For instance, in order to establish that functioning thing is a substantial phenomenon one must show that the isolate of functioning thing is not mutually exclusive with substantial phenomenon. In order to do this one must show that there is a common locus of the isolate of functioning thing and substantial phenomenon, meaning that one must show that functioning thing itself *is* a substantial phenomenon. Thus, in order to establish functioning thing as a substantial phenomenon, one must effectively beg the question and show that functioning thing is a substantial phenomenon. It would seem that in order to prove the fourth requirement one would have to have already established all four requirements. Thus, in those cases in which the object at hand actually is not mutually exclusive with the substantial or isolate phenomenon which it is, the fourth requirement does not add any support to the reasoning establishing that object as such. However, in those cases in which some object satisfies the first three requirements but not the fourth, the fourth requirement prevents that object from being both a phenomenon and its similitude. In so doing, the fourth requirement does not beg the question. Consequently, one can see that the *effective* purpose of the fourth requirement is elimination of mutually exclusive examples, not affirmation of satisfactory ones.

THE NECESSITY FOR POSITING THE SIMILITUDES

The Ra-dö *Collected Topics* explains that substantial phenomenon and any of the first three isolate phenomena are mutually exclusive with their similitudes because whatever is a substantial phenomenon or any of the first three isolate phenomena is necessarily something which abides as an actual substantial phenomenon or as one of the first three isolate phenomena. However, "Whatever is a similitude of [substantial phenomenon or one of the types of isolate phenomena] is necessarily a phenomenon which is a mere similitude of that."[1] The similitudes merely correspond to the first four phenomena, but they are mutually exclusive with them.

The second and third defining characteristics of substantial and isolate phenomena are the ones that best serve to distinguish them. There are only two variables here: (1) an object is or is not itself and (2) non-that object is or is not that object. These two variables are exhausted in four alternative combinations. In this regard, a substantial phenomenon and an isolate phenomenon of the third type are opposites. Whatever is a substantial phenomenon must be a common locus such that (1) it is itself and (2) non-it is not it, but whatever is an isolate phenomenon of the third type must

---

[1] Jam-ȳang-chok-hla-ö-ser, Ra-dö *Collected Topics*, 36a.4-5.

be a common locus such that (1) it is not itself and (2) non-it is it. In this same way, an isolate phenomenon which is itself and an isolate phenomenon which is not itself are opposites. Whatever is an isolate phenomenon which is itself is necessarily a common locus such that (1) it is itself and (2) non-it is it, but whatever is an isolate phenomenon which is not itself is necessarily a common locus such that (1) it is not itself and (2) non-it is not it. The four alternative combinations of these two variables are exhausted between the four—substantial phenomenon and the first three isolate phenomena.

Since all possible combinations of these two variables are taken up by these four phenomena, it may appear that there is no necessity for positing the four similitudes. However, since these four phenomena are each characterized by not merely two but *four* defining qualities, it is not the case that whatever is an established base is necessarily one of these four.

Similitude-of-Substantial-Phenomenon

For instance, consider the case of functioning-thing-which-is-an-isolate-phenomenon (*ldog chos su gyur pa'i dngos po*). "Functioning-thing-which-is-an-isolate-phenomenon" is a general expression referring to such phenomena as (1) the two—a pillar and a pot (which is an isolate phenomenon which is not itself), (2) pot-which-is-one-with-pot (which is also an isolate phenomenon which is not itself), and so forth. Such objects are functioning things and they are isolate phenomena.

The Ra-dö *Collected Topics* carefully shows that functioning-thing-which-is-an-isolate-phenomenon cannot be a substantial phenomenon and it also cannot be any of the first three isolate phenomena.[1] In accordance with the reasoning presented in that text, if someone says that functioning-thing-which-is-an-isolate-phenomenon is a sub-

---

[1] See Jam-ȳang-chok-hla-ö-ser, Ra-dö *Collected Topics*, 34b.5-35a.7.

stantial phenomenon, then it would have to be a common locus such that (1) it is an established base, (2) it is itself, (3) non-it is not it, and (4) its isolate is not mutually exclusive with substantial phenomenon, for this is the definition of a substantial phenomenon. If one accepts that functioning-thing-which-is-an-isolate-phenomenon is an object which is itself, then it would be a functioning thing which is an isolate phenomenon and could not be a substantial phenomenon because substantial phenomenon and isolate phenomenon are mutually exclusive. Thus, if one accepts that functioning-thing-which-is-an-isolate-phenomenon is a substantial phenomenon, then it absurdly results that it cannot be an isolate phenomenon because it is a substantial phenomenon; yet, it cannot be a substantial phenomenon, for it cannot be itself. By this reasoning the Ra-dö *Collected Topics* establishes that functioning-thing-which-is-an-isolate-phenomenon cannot be a substantial phenomenon.

Further, Denma Lochö Rinbochay points out that if one were to say that it is a substantial phenomenon, then according to the fourth requirement of such a phenomenon its isolate could not be mutually exclusive with substantial phenomenon. If the isolate of functioning-thing-which-is-an-isolate-phenomenon were not mutually exclusive with substantial phenomenon, then since functioning-thing-which-is-an-isolate-phenomenon is the only thing which is its isolate it would have to be a substantial phenomenon. Again, if it were a substantial phenomenon, then it could not be an isolate phenomenon because of being a substantial phenomenon. Since such absurdities arise, one must conclude that functioning-thing-which-is-an-isolate-phenomenon is not a substantial phenomenon.[1]

Within the context of analyzing whether or not functioning-thing-which-is-an-isolate-phenomenon is a substantial phenomenon, it is shown that it cannot be itself. However, this does not imply in general that functioning-thing-which-is-an-isolate-phenomenon is not itself. On the

---

[1] Denma Lochö Rinbochay, oral commentary.

contrary, since it is not a substantial phenomenon, functioning-thing-which-is-an-isolate-phenomenon must be an isolate phenomenon, and if it is an isolate phenomenon then it is itself. Functioning-thing-which-is-an-isolate-phenomenon can only be itself if it is an isolate phenomenon.

Since functioning-thing-which-is-an-isolate-phenomenon is an object which is itself, one might suspect that it is an isolate phenomenon which is itself. If it is an isolate phenomenon which is itself, then it must be a common locus such that (1) it is an established base, (2) it is itself, (3) non-it is it, and (4) its isolate is not mutually exclusive with isolate-phenomenon-which-is-itself, for this is the definition of an isolate phenomenon which it itself. According to the third requirement of such an isolate phenomenon, non-thing-which-is-an-isolate-phenomenon must be a functioning thing which is an isolate phenomenon. However, non-thing-which-is-an-isolate-phenomenon is a permanent phenomenon; thus, it is not a functioning thing of any sort. There is no functioning thing for which non-it is it because with respect to any functioning thing non-it is necessarily not a functioning thing. Thus, it is concluded that functioning-thing-which-is-an-isolate-phenomenon is not an isolate phenomenon which it itself.

Next one might suspect that functioning-thing-which-is-an-isolate phenomenon is an isolate phenomenon which is not itself. If this were the case, then it would have to be a common locus such that (1) it is an established base, (2) it is not itself, (3) non-it is not it, and (4) its isolate is not mutually exclusive with isolate-phenomenon-which-is-not-itself. However, one cannot accept that functioning-thing-which-is-an-isolate-phenomenon is not itself because (1) it is an isolate phenomenon (for it is a phenomenon which is not a substantial phenomenon) and (2) it is a functioning thing. Since it is a phenomenon which is itself, functioning-thing-which-is-an-isolate-phenomenon is not an isolate phenomenon which is not itself.

If one considers that functioning-thing-which-is-an-isolate-phenomenon might be an isolate phenomenon of the third type, then one encounters the same problem as when accepting that it is an isolate phenomenon which is itself—that non-it would have to be it. Whatever is an isolate phenomenon of the third type is necessarily a common locus such that (1) it is an established base, (2) it is not itself, (3) non-it is it, and (4) its isolate is not mutually exclusive with isolate-phenomenon-of-the-third-type. Since non-thing-which-is-an-isolate-phenomenon is not a functioning thing which is an isolate phenomenon, functioning-thing-which-is-an-isolate-phenomenon is not an isolate phenomenon of the third type. Moreover, if it were an isolate phenomenon of the third type, then according to the second requirement of such an isolate phenomenon it would not be itself. If functioning-thing-which-is-an-isolate-phenomenon were not itself, then it would have to be a substantial phenomenon and it could not be an isolate phenomenon of the third type. Since these absurdities arise, it is concluded that functioning-thing-which-is-an-isolate-phenomenon is neither a substantial phenomenon nor any of the first three isolate phenomena.

Functioning-thing-which-is-an-isolate-phenomenon is asserted to be a similitude of substantial phenomenon. This is because it is a common locus such that (1) it is an established base, (2) it is itself, (3) non-it is not it, and (4) its isolate is not mutually exclusive with similitude-of-substantial-phenomenon. First, functioning-thing-which-is-an-isolate-phenomenon is an established base because it is a functioning thing. Second, functioning-thing-which-is-an-isolate-phenomenon is a functioning thing which is an isolate phenomenon. This is established by the fact that it is a functioning thing which cannot be a substantial phenomenon. Third, non-thing-which-is-an-isolate-phenomenon is not a functioning thing which is an isolate phenomenon because it is a permanent phenomenon. Fourth, the isolate of functioning-thing-which-is-an-isolate-phenomenon is not mutually exclusive with similitude-of-substantial-phenomenon. This does not say that its isolate is not mutually exclusive with substantial phenomenon but that it is not mutually exclusive with *similitude*-of-substantial-phenomenon. There is a common locus of the two, the isolate of functioning-thing-which-is-an-isolate-phenomenon and similitude-of-substantial-phenomenon, because functioning-thing-which-is-an-isolate-phenomenon is both its own isolate and a similitude of substantial phenomenon. Thus, it is established that functioning-thing-which-is-an-isolate-phenomenon is a similitude of substantial phenomenon. Since there are such phenomena which are neither substantial phenomena nor any of the first three isolate phenomena, the similitudes must be posited.

The first three defining qualities of a substantial phenomenon are the same as those of similitude-of-substantial-phenomenon. However, the fourth requirement serves to prevent there being something which is both a substantial phenomenon and a similitude of substantial phenomenon. There is nothing which is both a substantial phenomenon and an isolate phenomenon of any type, nor is there anything which is two different types of isolate phenomena.

Similitude-of-Isolate-Phenomenon-Which-Is-Itself

The necessity for positing the first similitude, similitude-of-substantial-phenomenon, is established by the reasoning on the nature of functioning-thing-which-is-an-isolate-phenomenon. However, the necessity for positing the second and third similitudes is not as readily apparent. One of the most interesting aspects of the topic of substantial and isolate phenomena comes when the reasoning for establishing these phenomena is focused onto the phenomena themselves. Is substantial phenomenon itself included as one of these eight phenomena? If so, which one is it? Where is isolate-phenomenon-which-is-not-itself included?

The necessity for positing similitude-of-isolate-phenomenon-which-is-itself develops out of the consideration of the nature of isolate-phenomenon-which-is-itself.[1] In investigating the nature of a phenomenon as a substantial phenomenon or an isolate phenomenon, the first main variable to be considered is whether or not that phenomenon is itself. For the case of isolate-phenomenon-which-is-itself, the process for ascertaining whether or not something is it is clear, for there is a definition which serves as a guide. If one assumes that isolate-phenomenon-which-is-itself is itself, then it would follow that isolate-phenomenon-which-is-itself is a common locus such that (1) it is an established base, (2) it is itself, (3) non-it is it, and (4) its isolate is not mutually exclusive with isolate-phenomenon-which-is-itself. First, it is clear that isolate-phenomenon-which-is-itself is an established base, for it is a generality. Second, whether or not isolate-phenomenon-which-is-itself satisfies the second requirement, that it is itself, is the issue at hand and must be set aside for the moment.

The key for ascertaining whether or not it is itself lies in the analysis of the third requirement. If one supposes that isolate-phenomenon-which-is-itself is an isolate phenomenon which is itself, then according to the third requirement of such a phenomenon it follows that non-isolate-phenomenon-which-is-itself is also an isolate phenomenon which is itself. From this consequence, it absurdly follows that if non-isolate-phenomenon-which-is-itself is an isolate phenomenon which is itself, then it must be itself, for this is the second requirement of an isolate phenomenon which is itself. That is, if non-isolate-phenomenon-which-is-itself is an isolate phenomenon which is itself, then non-isolate-phenomenon-which-is-itself must be a non-isolate phenomenon which is itself. This is explicitly contradictory. Thus, non-isolate-phenomenon-which-is-itself cannot be an isolate phenomenon which is itself and, consequently, isolate-phenomenon-which-is-itself cannot be an isolate phenomenon which is itself. In this way it is established that isolate-phenomenon-which-is-itself is not an isolate phe-

---

[1] See Jam-ȳang-chok-hla-ö-ser, Ra-dö *Collected Topics*, 36a.1-38a.5.

nomenon which is itself. That is, isolate-phenomenon-which-is-itself is a phenomenon which is not itself. From among the eight—substantial phenomenon and the seven types of isolate phenomena—there are only four which include phenomena which are not themselves: (1) isolate-phenomenon-which-is-not-itself, (2) isolate-phenomenon-of-the-third-type, (3) similitude-of-isolate-phenomenon-which-is-not-itself, and (4) similitude-of-isolate-phenomenon-of-the-third-type.

The second main variable to be ascertained when investigating the nature of an object as a substantial or isolate phenomenon is whether non-that object is or is not that object. This question is functionally no different from the first except that here one is not analyzing whether or not the object is itself but whether or not non-that object is itself. It has been established that the object being investigated, isolate-phenomenon-which-is-itself, is a phenomenon which is not itself and, thereby, that it is one of the four types of isolate phenomena identified above. For two of these phenomena non-it must be it and for the remaining two non-it must not be it. Thus, by establishing whether non-isolate-phenomenon-which-is-itself is or is not an isolate phenomenon which is itself, two of these four possibilities may be eliminated. In fact, it has already been shown that non-isolate-phenomenon-which-is-itself is not an isolate phenomenon which is itself, for if it were an isolate phenomenon which is itself, then it absurdly results that it would not be an isolate phenomenon which is itself. Thus, non-isolate-phenomenon-which-is-itself is a phenomenon that is itself—it is not an isolate phenomenon which is itself—and with respect to the basis, isolate-phenomenon-which-is-itself, non-it is not it.

It is established for isolate-phenomenon-which-is-itself that (1) it is not itself and (2) non-it is not it. From among the eight substantial and isolate phenomena only two include objects that have both of these qualities. Thus, isolate-phenomenon-which-is-itself must be either an isolate phenomenon which is not itself or a similitude of isolate-phenomenon-which-is-not-itself. It must be one or the other, but it cannot be both. There is no special reason for considering it a similitude of isolate-phenomenon-which-is-not-itself, and according to the Shar-dzay *Collected Topics* it is an isolate phenomenon which is not itself.[1] Whereas it is true that the eight substantial and isolate phenomena are mutually exclusive, this does not imply that the one cannot be the other. As in the case of definition and definiendum, although they are mutually exclusive, definition is a definiendum. It is possible for a phenomenon mutually exclusive with another to nonetheless be that phenomenon. Thus, it is concluded that isolate-phenomenon-which-is-itself is an isolate phenomenon which is not itself.

As mentioned above, analysis of isolate-phenomenon-which-is-itself leads one to understand the necessity for positing similitude-of-isolate-phenomenon-which-is-itself. However, it has been established that isolate-phenomenon-which-is-itself is an isolate phenomenon which is not itself; thus, from the point of view of this basis there is no clear reason for positing its similitude. Still, evolving from this investigation of isolate-phenomenon-which-is-itself there is an analysis of the nature of non-isolate-phenomenon-which-is-itself. It has already been proven that non-isolate phenomenon-which-is-itself is not an isolate phenomenon which is itself; therefore, with respect to the basis, non-isolate-phenomenon-which-is-itself, it is an object which is itself.

Secondly, the question arises, "Is non-non-isolate-phenomenon-which-is-itself an isolate phenomenon which is itself or is it a non-isolate phenomenon which is itself?" Non-non-isolate-phenomenon-which-is-itself is mutually inclusive with isolate-phenomenon-which-is-itself; therefore, if non-non-isolate-phenomenon-which-is-itself is not a non-isolate phenomenon which is itself, then it is an isolate phenomenon which is itself. If non-non-isolate-phenomenon-which-is-itself is an isolate phenomenon

---

[1] Dzemay Rinbochay, Shar-dzay *Collected Topics*, p. 37.

which is itself, then, according to the second requirement of isolate phenomena which are themselves, non-non-isolate-phenomenon-which-is-itself would be a non-non-isolate phenomenon which is itself. This is to say that isolate-phenomenon-which-is-itself would then be an isolate phenomenon which is itself. However, it has already been shown that isolate-phenomenon-which-is-itself is an isolate phenomenon which is *not* itself. (The reason for this is that non-isolate-phenomenon-which-is-itself is not an isolate phenomenon which is itself, for if it were such a phenomenon, then it would not be such a phenomenon.) Because this absurdity arises from the assumption that non-non-isolate-phenomenon-which-is-itself is not a non-isolate phenomenon which is itself, is is established that non-non-isolate-phenomenon-which-is-itself is a non-isolate phenomenon which is itself. Therefore, with respect to the basis, non-isolate-phenomenon-which-is-itself, it is concluded that non-it is it.

In conjunction with the first variable, it is established that non-isolate-phenomenon-which-is-itself is a common locus such that (1) it is itself and (2) non-it is it. From among the eight substantial and isolate phenomena only two include phenomena which are such common locuses. They are isolate-phenomenon-which-is-itself and similitude-of-isolate-phenomenon-which-is-itself. Non-isolate-phe-nomenon-which-is-itself must be one of these two. If one searches to find whether or not it is an isolate phenomenon which is itself, it is shown not to be because it fails to satisfy the four requirements of an isolate phenomenon which is itself. First, if non-isolate-phenomenon-which-is-itself were an isolate phenomenon which is itself, then according to the second requirement it would be a non-isolate phenomenon which is itself. This consequence is explicitly contradictory with the assumption that non-isolate-phenomenon-which-is-itself is an isolate phenomenon which is itself.

It should be noted that within the context of deciding whether or not non-isolate-phenomenon-which-is-itself is or is not an isolate phenomenon which is itself it is explicitly contradictory to say that it is itself, for then it would not be itself; however, this does not necessitate that in general one can conclude that non-isolate-phenomenon-which-is-itself is not itself. Rather, the very fact that it cannot be an isolate phenomenon which is itself shows that it is itself, it is a non-isolate phenomenon which is itself. In other words, since manifest absurdities arise out of the assumption that non-isolate-phenomenon-which-is-itself is an isolate phenomenon which is itself, that alone shows that it cannot be an isolate phenomenon which is itself.

The only remaining alternative is that non-isolate-phenomenon-which-is-itself is a similitude of isolate-phenomenon-which-is-itself, and according to the Collected Topics texts this is so. By this reasoning, the necessity for positing similitude-of-isolate-phenomenon-which-is-itself is established. There is nothing else which non-isolate-phenomenon-which-is-itself could be except a similitude of isolate-phenomenon-which-is-itself.

Moreover, according to both Lati Rinbochay and Denma Lochö Rinbochay other than this one case, non-isolate-phenomenon-which-is-itself, there is nothing else which can be posited as a similitude of isolate-phenomenon-which-is-itself. It *may* be suitable to say that permanent-phenomenon-that-is-not-an-isolate-phenomenon-which-is-itself (*rang yin pa'i ldog chos ma yin par gyur pa'i rtag pa*) is a similitude of isolate-phenomenon-which-is-itself and that object-of-knowledge-that-is-not-an-isolate-phenomenon-which-is-itself (*rang yin pa'i ldog chos ma yin par gyur pa'i shes bya*) is also a similitude of isolate-phenomenon-which-is-itself, but these are only alternative descriptions of what has already been posited, non-isolate-phenomenon-which-is-itself. Non-isolate-phenomenon-which-is-itself is a permanent phenomenon that is not an isolate phenomenon which is itself and, of course, it is also an object of knowledge that is not an isolate phenomenon which is itself. These qualifications do not delimit the nature of non-isolate-phenomenon-which-is-itself, but merely further specify it. Still, the point that there is nothing other than non-isolate-phenomenon-which-is-itself that one can posit as a similitude of isolate-phenomenon-which-is-itself is well taken, for even if any of these alternative descriptions are similitudes of isolate-phenomenon-which-is-itself, still they must be non-isolate phenomena which are themselves.

If there is nothing other than non-isolate-phenomenon-which-is-itself that one can posit as a similitude of isolate-phenomenon-which-is-itself, then it is an illustration of similitude-of-isolate-phenomenon-which-is-itself but it is not an instance of it. This is because the third requirement of an instance of similitude-of-isolate-phenomenon-which-is-itself is not complete, for there is nothing which is not a non-isolate-phenomenon-which-is-itself but is a similitude of isolate-phenomenon-which-is-itself. Any of these phenomena with added specification, such as object-of-knowledge-that-is-not-an-isolate-phenomenon-which-is-itself, must be a non-isolate phenomenon which is itself. Thus, there is only one illustration of similitude-of-isolate-phenomenon-which-is-itself and the similitude is not a generality. The similitudes are rare. There are many objects which are substantial phenomena or one of the first three isolate phenomena, but objects which are any of the similitudes are hard to find.

Similitude-of-Isolate-Phenomenon-Which-Is-Not-Itself

The necessity for positing similitude-of-isolate-phenomenon-which-is-not-itself is established by similar, but perhaps less difficult, reasoning. Again, this investigation must begin with an analysis of the nature of the basis of the similitude, isolate-phenomenon-which-is-not-itself. First, in considering whether this phenomenon is itself or not, one can easily see that it is manifestly obvious that it cannot be itself. Whatever is an isolate phenomenon which is not itself must be a common locus such that (1) it is an established base, (2) it is not itself, (3) non-it is not it, and (4) its isolate is not mutually exclusive with isolate-phenomenon-which-is-not-itself. According to the second requirement if isolate-phenomenon-which-is-not-itself were itself, then it would have to be such that it is not itself. Such an absurdity is not possible. Thus, it is concluded that isolate-phenomenon-which-is-not-itself is a phenomenon which is not itself.

Second, in order to know the nature of isolate-phenomenon-which-is-not-itself, one must ascertain whether non-it is it or not. If non-isolate-phenomenon-which-is-not-itself is an isolate phenomenon which is not itself, then according to the second requirement it must not be a non-isolate phenomenon which is not itself (that is to say, it must be an isolate phenomenon which is not itself). Whether this is true or not is the question under consideration and will be decided by this argument. It may be taken as an assumption at this point. According to the third requirement if non-isolate-phenomenon-which-is-not-itself is an isolate phenomenon which is not itself, then non-non-isolate-phenomenon-which-is-not-itself must not be a non-isolate phenomenon which is not itself. Following the rules for mutual inclusion outlined in the eleventh chapter, the presentation of opposite-from-being-something and opposite-from-not-being-something, this would mean that isolate-phenomenon-which-is-not-itself would have to be an isolate phenomenon which is not itself. Such is not possible because, as was shown above, if it were itself then it could not be itself.

Thus, non-isolate-phenomenon-which-is-not-itself is not an isolate phenomenon which is not itself, for it cannot satisfy the third requirement of such a phenomenon. Therefore, with respect to the basis under consideration, isolate-phenomenon-which-is-not-itself, non-it is not it. Consolidating this information with what was found in regard to the first variable, it is proven that isolate-phenomenon-which-is-not-itself is a common locus such that (1) it is not itself and (2) non-it is not it.

From among the seven types of isolate phenomena, only two, isolate-phenomenon-which-is-not-itself and similitude-of-isolate-phenomenon-which-is-not-itself, have phenomena which are such common locuses. It has previously been shown that isolate-phenomenon-which-is-not-itself cannot be an isolate phenomenon which is not itself. Therefore, it is indicated that it is a similitude of isolate-phenomenon-which-is-not-itself.

Beyond the middle two requirements of such a phenomenon, which have already been established for isolate-phenomenon-which-is-not-itself, it also is an established base and its isolate is not mutually exclusive with similitude-of-isolate-phenomenon-which-is-not-itself. Consequently, it is concluded that isolate-phenomenon-which-is-not-itself is a similitude of isolate-phenomenon-which-is-not-itself.

As in the case of similitude-of-isolate-phenomenon-which-is-itself, this is the only illustration of similitude-of-isolate-phenomenon-which-is-not-itself. Again, this implies that isolate-phenomenon-which-is-not-itself is an illustration but not an instance of similitude-of-isolate-phenomenon-which-is-not-itself and that this similitude is not a generality.

At this point one can understand clearly a reason for specifying in the fourth requirement of these phenomena that it is the *isolate* of the illustration that is not mutually exclusive with that substantial or isolate phenomenon. This serves to set the object in isolation from all of its instances and all the phenomena mutually inclusive with it. For example, in the last case it is *only* isolate-phenomenon-which-is-not-itself, rather than any of its instances, that is a similitude of isolate-phenomenon-which-is-not-itself. If the fourth requirement did not specify that it is the *isolate* of isolate-phenomenon-which-is-not-itself that is not mutually exclusive with its similitude, then the fourth requirement could not be established, for there is nothing which is both an isolate phenomenon which is not itself and a similitude of isolate-phenomenon-which-is-not-itself. This is because only isolate-phenomenon-which-is-not-itself is its similitude and nothing which is an isolate phenomenon which is not itself is also a similitude of isolate-phenomenon-which-is-not-itself. The point of the fourth requirement is not that the object at hand is not mutually exclusive with the substantial or isolate phenomenon it is but that it *is* that phenomenon. Isolate-phenomenon-which-is-not-itself is mutually exclusive with similitude-of-isolate-phenomenon-which-is-not-itself; nevertheless, isolate-phenomenon-which-is-not-itself *is* a similitude of isolate-phenomenon-which-is-not-itself.

Similitude-of-Isolate-Phenomenon-of-the-Third Type

Up to this point the necessity for positing the first three similitudes has been shown. The necessity for positing the fourth, similitude-of-isolate-phenomenon-of-the-third-type, is not so clearly required by logical necessity as in the cases of the first three similitudes. As before, the investigation into the necessity for positing the similitude must begin with an analysis of the nature of the basis for that similitude. Just as in the previous case of isolate-phenomenon-which-is-not-itself, one can easily understand that isolate-phenomenon-of-the-third-type cannot be itself. Whatever is an isolate phenomenon of the third type is necessarily a common locus such that (1) it is an established base, (2) it is not itself, (3) non-it is it, and (4) its isolate is not mutually exclusive with isolate-phenomenon-of-the-third-type. Thus, if isolate-phenomenon-of-the-third-type were itself, then, according to the second requirement of such a phenomenon, it must not be itself. This is a manifestly absurd consequence; therefore, with respect to the basis, isolate-phenomenon-of-the-third-type, it is established that it is not itself.

Once isolate-phenomenon-of-the-third-type is not itself, in order to ascertain whether or not it is included among the remaining seven substantial and isolate phenomena one must discriminate the second variable, whether non-it is or is not it. Thus, if non-isolate-phenomenon-of-the-third-type is an isolate phenomenon of the third type, then it must be a common locus such that (1) it is an established base, (2) it is not itself, (3) non-it is it, and (4) its isolate is not mutually exclusive with isolate-phenomenon-of-the-third-type. First, non-isolate-phenomenon-of-the-third-type is an established base because of being a permanent phenomenon.

Second, if non-isolate-phenomenon-of-the-third-type is an isolate phenomenon of the third type, then it must not be itself. This means that it must be an isolate phenomenon of the third type. This consequence is consistent with the assumption being considered in this investigation. Still, for the moment, whether non-isolate-phenomenon-of-the-third-type is or is not itself must be tabled, as there is not sufficient evidence on the basis of which to decide.

Third, if non-isolate-phenomenon-of-the-third-type is an isolate phenomenon of the third type, then non-non-isolate-phenomenon-of-the-third-type must be a non-isolate phenomenon of the third type. This means that isolate-phenomenon-of-the-third-type, which is mutually inclusive with non-non-isolate-phenomenon-of-the-third-type, must not be an isolate phenomenon of the third type. This has already been established, for if isolate-phenomenon-of-the-third-type were itself, then it would have to not be itself. The assumption that non-isolate-phenomenon-of-the-third-type is an isolate phenomenon of the third type is consistent with and supportive of the logical necessity that isolate-phenomenon-of-the-third-type cannot be itself.

Fourth, if non-isolate-phenomenon-of-the-third-type is an isolate phenomenon of the third type, then the isolate of non-isolate-phenomenon-of-the-third-type must not be mutually exclusive with isolate-phenomenon-of-the-third-type. It must be emphasized again that the fourth requirement is not that the illustration is not mutually exclusive with that substantial or isolate phenomenon it illustrates. If this were the requirement, then non-isolate-phenomenon-of-the-third-type could not be mutually exclusive with isolate-phenomenon-of-the-third-type. There would have to be a common locus of the two, non-isolate-phenomenon-of-the-third-type and isolate-phenomenon-of-the-third-type. However, such is not possible as these two are explicit contradictories like product and non-product. Rather, the fourth requirement is that the *isolate* of the object must not be mutually exclusive with that substantial or isolate phenomenon. There must be a common locus of the two, the *isolate* of the object and that substantial or isolate phenomenon. For the case at hand, there must be a common locus of the two, the isolate of non-isolate-phenomenon-of-the-third-type and isolate-phenomenon-of-the-third-type. The only thing which is the isolate of non-isolate-phenomenon-of-the-third-type is non-isolate-phenomenon-of-the-third-type, and if it is also an isolate phenomenon of the third type, then there is a common locus of these two.

There is no fault in asserting non-isolate-phenomenon-of-the-third-type as an isolate phenomenon of the third type, for it is able to satisfy the four requirements of such a phenomenon without entailing any logical absurdities; however, there is also no convincing evidence in the sense of logical necessity that non-isolate-phenomenon-of-the-third-type must be an isolate phenomenon of the third type. The main result of considering non-isolate-phenomenon-of-the-third-type to be an isolate phenomenon of the third type is that it accords with and further confirms the already established necessity that isolate-phenomenon-of-the-third-type cannot be itself.

Still, one cannot single-pointedly hold that non-isolate-phenomenon-of-the-third-type is an isolate phenomenon of the third type, for it may be taken as an isolate phenomenon which is itself. This is because non-isolate-phenomenon-of-the-third-type can be said to fulfill the four qualities of an isolate phenomenon which is itself. It is an established base. If it is not an isolate phenomenon of the third type, then it is itself (that is to say, non-isolate-phenomenon-of-the-third-type is a non-isolate phenomenon of the third type). If it is an isolate phenomenon which is itself, then non-non-isolate-phenomenon-of-the-third-type must be a non-isolate phenomenon of the third type. This is established by the necessity for isolate-phenomenon-of-the-third-type to be something which is not itself. Finally, if it is an isolate phenomenon which is itself, then its isolate must not be mutually exclusive with isolate-phenomenon-which-is-itself. One can say that this fourth requirement is established without entailing any logical faults.

724 *Debate in Tibetan Buddhism*

Now if one takes non-isolate-phenomenon-of-the-third-type to be an isolate phenomenon which is itself, then this affects one's decision on the nature of isolate-phenomenon-of-the-third-type. The Go-mang *Collected Topics* says that isolate-phenomenon-of-the-third-type is an isolate phenomenon which is not itself.[1] The claim is that isolate-phenomenon-of-the-third-type is a common locus such that (1) it is an established base, (2) it is not itself, (3) not-it is not it, and (4) its isolate is not mutually exclusive with isolate-phenomenon-which-is-not-itself. Clearly, isolate-phenomenon-of-the-third-type is something which is not itself, and if non-isolate-phenomenon-of-the-third-type is an isolate phenomenon which is itself, then non-it is not it. Also, one can claim that the isolate of isolate-phenomenon-of-the-third-type is not mutually exclusive with isolate-phenomenon-which-is-not-itself. Thus, one can assert isolate-phenomenon-of-the-third-type as an isolate phenomenon which is not itself and one can assert equally as well that non-isolate-phenomenon-of-the-third-type is an isolate phenomenon which is itself. There is no logical fault in these assertions, but again there is no convincing evidence.

The source of this indecisiveness concerning the nature of isolate-phenomenon-of-the-third-type is that the only result of the analysis of its own nature and the nature of non-it is the convincing necessity that it cannot be itself. This means that isolate-phenomenon-of-the-third-type must be one of the types of isolate phenomena for which the object is not itself. Further, from among these four types of isolate phenomena it cannot be an isolate phenomenon of the third type. Also, the necessity that isolate-phenomenon-of-the-third-type must not be itself entails that non-isolate-phenomenon-of-the-third-type must be an isolate phenomena such that non-it is it, and it is generally taken to be either an isolate phenomenon of the third type or an isolate phenomenon which is itself.

---

[1] Ngak-ŵang-d̄ra-s̄hi, Go-mang *Collected Topics*, p. 200.

If non-isolate-phenomenon-of-the-third-type is an isolate phenomenon which is itself, then isolate-phenomenon-of-the-third-type must be an isolate phenomenon which is not itself. However, if non-isolate-phenomenon-of-the-third-type is an isolate phenomenon of the third type, then isolate-phenomenon-of-the-third-type must be a similitude of isolate-phenomenon-of-the-third-type. It is the system of the Tutor's *Collected Topics* and the more prevalent assertion that the latter is true, that isolate-phenomenon-of-the-third-type is a similitude of isolate-phenomenon-of-the-third-type. Isolate-phenomenon-of-the-third-type does satisfy the four qualities of a similitude of isolate-phenomenon-of-the-third-type, for it is a common locus such that (1) it is an established base, (2) it is not itself, (3) non-it is it, and (4) its isolate is not mutually exclusive with similitude-of-isolate-phenomenon-of-the-third-type. Isolate-phenomenon-of-the-third-type is demonstrably not itself by logical necessity and also, in accordance with this assumption, because of being a similitude of isolate-phenomenon-of-the-third-type. One may say that non-it is it and also that its isolate is not mutually exclusive with similitude-of-isolate-phenomenon-of-the-third-type. There is no substantial argument against the assertion that isolate-phenomenon-of-the-third-type is a similitude of isolate-phenomenon-of-the-third-type.

On the other hand, if one asserts that isolate-phenomenon-of-the-third-type is an isolate phenomenon which is not itself, then one may levy the criticism that then there would be no similitude-of-isolate-phenomenon-of-the-third-type.[1] As in the cases of similitude-of-isolate-phenomenon-which-is-itself and similitude-of-isolate-phenomenon-which-is-not-itself, there is only one thing that one can posit as a similitude of isolate-phenomenon-of-the-third-type. If isolate-phenomenon-of-the-third-type is not its similitude, then there is nothing that one can posit which is that similitude. If there is nothing to be posited, then similitude-of-isolate-phenomenon-of-the-third-type must

---

[1] Denma Lochö Rinbochay, oral commentary.

not exist. Since there is no similitude-of-isolate-phenomenon-of-the-third-type, there cannot be four similitudes. If there are not four similitudes, then there are not the seven isolate phenomena. However, since the books refer to the first three isolate phenomena and the latter four similitudes, most scholars conclude that isolate-phenomenon-of-the-third-type must be asserted as a similitude of isolate-phenomenon-of-the-third-type.

Other than this line of reasoning there is nothing to defeat the view that isolate-phenomenon-of-the-third-type is an isolate phenomenon which is not itself. Thus, positing similitude-of-isolate-phenomenon-of-the-third-type is not so strictly ruled by logical necessity as in the cases of similitude-of-isolate-phenomenon-which-is-itself and similitude-of-isolate-phenomenon-which-is-not-itself.

The Similitudes of the Similitudes

The necessity for positing each of the four similitudes generally depends on the nature of the bases of those various similitudes. Since a study of the bases leads to this necessity, one is led to wonder whether the similitudes themselves are included as any of the seven types of isolate phenomena and, if they are, which each of them might be. It has been indicated that none of the similitudes are themselves, for illustrations of the similitudes are very rare and a similitude was not given as an illustration of any of them. In the case of the first similitude, functioning-thing-which-is-an-isolate-phenomenon or that which is mutually exclusive with substantial phenomenon (*rdzas chos dang 'gal ba*) are similitudes of substantial phenomenon. In the cases of the latter three similitudes, there is only one illustration to be posited for each of them. Thus, it appears that none of the similitudes are themselves. Further, since the similitudes are not substantial phenomena or any of the first three isolate phenomena, it is clear that none of them are included by the eight substantial and isolate phenomena.

In fact, an investigation of the nature of the similitudes leads one to understand that it is necessary to posit similitudes of the similitudes. For example, consider similitude-of-isolate-phenomenon-which-is-not-itself. First, one can easily understand that like its basis, isolate-phenomenon-which-is-not-itself, this similitude cannot be itself. This is so because whatever is a similitude of isolate-phenomenon-which-is-not-itself must be such that it is not itself. Thus, if similitude-of-isolate-phenomenon-which-is-not-itself were itself, then it could not be itself. Because such absurdities arise, similitude-of-isolate-phenomenon-which-is-not-itself is an object which is not itself.

Also, as in the case of isolate-phenomenon-which-is-not-itself, non-it is not it, for non-it cannot satisfy the four requirements of being it. This is because non-similitude-of-isolate-phenomenon-which-is-not-itself does not fulfill the third requirement of a similitude of isolate-phenomenon-which-is-not-itself. If non-similitude-of-isolate-phenomenon-which-is-not-itself were a similitude of isolate-phenomenon-which-is-not-itself, then according to the third requirement non-non-similitude-of-isolate-phenomenon-which-is-not-itself would have to not be a non-similitude-of-isolate-phenomenon-which-is-not-itself. According to the rules of mutual inclusion laid out in the eleventh chapter, the presentation of opposite-from-being-something and opposite-from-not-being-something, this implies that similitude-of-isolate-phenomenon-which-is-not-itself would have to be a similitude of isolate-phenomenon-which-is-not-itself. It has already been established that such is not possible, for if this similitude were itself, then it could not be itself.

Thus, with respect to the basis, similitude-of-isolate-phenomenon-which-is-not-itself, it is a common locus such that (1) it is not itself and (2) non-it is not it. From among the seven types of isolate phenomena, only two, isolate-phenomenon-which-is-not-itself and similitude-of-isolate-phenomenon-which-is-not-itself, include phenomena which are such common locuses. It has already been proven that similitude-of-isolate-phenomenon-which-is-not-itself cannot be itself; thus, if it were to be included among the seven types of isolate phenomena, it would have to be an isolate phenomenon which is not itself. However, it seems that no one asserts any of the similitudes as a substantial phenomenon or any of the first three isolate phenomena. Presumably, there is no reason of logical necessity that a similitude could not be its basis, but the Ra-dö *Collected Topics* says, "Whatever is a similitude of [substantial phenomenon or some isolate phenomenon] is necessarily a phenomenon which is a mere similitude of [substantial phenomenon or some isolate phenomenon]."[1] The similitudes are phenomena posited out of logical necessity that merely correspond to their bases in the sense that the first three requirements are the same for the basis and the similitude; however, the similitude is merely concordant with that phenomenon which is its basis and is not that phenomenon.

This means that similitude-of-isolate-phenomenon-which-is-not-itself is not asserted to be an isolate phenomenon which is not itself. Rather, it is a similitude of similitude-of-isolate-phenomenon-which-is-not-itself (*rang ma yin pa'i ldog chos kyi rjes mthun gyi rjes mthun*). Further, just as isolate-phenomenon-which-is-not-itself is the only thing to be posited as a similitude of isolate-phenomenon-which-is-not-itself, so is similitude-of-isolate-phenomenon-which-is-not-itself the only thing to be posited as a similitude of similitude-of-isolate-phenomenon-which-is-not-itself.

Following the reasonings outlined above in proving the necessity for positing the similitudes, one can posit the similitudes of the similitudes. Moreover, once one posits these one may further postulate similitudes of the similitudes of the similitudes and so on. There is no limit to the similitudes that can be posited. The Lo-šel-ling *Collected Topics* says, "The similitudes of the similitudes and so forth are limitless."[2] Thus, some objects of knowledge are neither

---

[1] Jam-ȳang-chok-hla-ö-ser, Ra-dö *Collected Topics*, 36a.5.
[2] Jam-b̄el-trin-lay-yön-dan-gya-tso, Lo-šel-ling *Collected Topics*, p. 13.

substantial phenomena nor any of the *seven* types of isolate phenomena. In the system of substantial and isolate phenomena formulated by Cha-ba-chö-ḡyi-ṡeng-gay, whatever is an established base is necessarily a substantial phenomenon or an isolate phenomenon, but whatever is an established base is not necessarily a substantial phenomenon or one of the *seven* types of isolate phenomena.

Debate G.1, First Mistaken View (22a.3)

Unlike the previous six chapters, the presentation of substantial and isolate phenomena in the Tutor's *Collected Topics* is not subdivided into the three sections of refutation of mistaken views, presentation of the author's system, and dispelling objections to the author's system. Rather, here there is only one long debate which serves to present the definitions of substantial phenomenon and each of the seven isolate phenomena and also shows the procedure for debating these topics. At the end of this debate there are some notes positing illustrations for each of the seven types of isolate phenomena. This final chapter is the shortest and perhaps the most difficult in "The Introductory Path of Reasoning".

> If someone [a hypothetical Defender] says, "Whatever is a substantial phenomenon is necessarily an isolate phenomenon," [the Sūtra School Challenger responds to him,] "It [absurdly] follows that the subject, a pot, is [an isolate phenomenon] because of [being a substantial phenomenon]. You asserted the pervasion."

Since the two, substantial phenomenon and isolate phenomenon, are mutually exclusive, whatever is a substantial phenomenon is necessarily *not* an isolate phenomenon and vice versa.

> If he says that the reason is not established, [the Sūtra School Challenger responds,] "It follows that the subject [a pot] is [a substantial phenomenon] because (1) it is an established base, (2) it is itself, (3)

non-it is not it, and (4) its isolate is not mutually
exclusive with substantial phenomenon."
"[It follows that] the first part of the reason [that a
pot is an established base] is established because of
being an existent."
If he says that the second part of the reason is not
established, [the Sūtra School Challenger responds,]
"It follows that a pot is a pot because a pot exists."

Although this consequence may be valid as it applies to a
pot it certainly cannot be applied across the board. For
instance, it is not suitable to say that the two—a gold pot
and a copper pot—are the two—a gold pot and a copper
pot—because the two—a gold pot and a copper pot—exist.
This argument lacks pervasion. Although it is true that the
two—a gold pot and a copper pot—do exist, this does not
imply that the two—a gold pot and a copper pot—are the
two—a gold pot and a copper pot. Nothing is the two—a
gold pot and a copper pot. As regards the consequence
stated in the text, there is pervasion. It is true that a pot
exists, and if a pot exists, then a pot is a pot. However, particularly within the context of the presentation of substantial
and isolate phenomena, this reasoning seems unconvincing.
Denma Lochö Rinbochay consistently used another reason
in support of such theses, saying, for instance, that a pot is a
pot because there is a valid cognizer which realizes a pot as
a pot (*bum pa bum pa yin par rtogs pa'i tshad ma yod pa'i
phyir*).[1] Valid cognizers are by definition incontrovertible
consciousnesses; they cannot be mistaken. Thus, if there is a
valid cognizer which realizes a pot as a pot, then a pot is a
pot. Since whatever exists is necessarily observed by a valid
cognizer, the pervasion works the other way as well, for if a
pot is a pot, then there is a valid cognizer which realizes a
pot as a pot. The factor of a pot's being a pot is an object of
knowledge and is realized by a valid cognizer.

---

[1] Denma Lochö Rinbochay, oral commentary.

> If he says that the third part of the reason is not
> established, [the Sūtra School Challenger responds,]
> "It follows that non-pot is not a pot because non-pot
> is a permanent phenomenon."

With respect to any functioning thing, non-it is not it
because non-it is necessarily a permanent phenomenon. This
means that no functioning thing may be an isolate phenomenon which is itself or an isolate phenomenon of the
third type. A permanent phenomenon cannot perform the
functions of a thing. Here again Denma Lochö Rinbochay
used an alternative reason, that there is no valid cognizer
which realizes non-pot as a pot (*bum pa ma yin pa bum pa yin
par rtogs pa'i tshad ma med pa'i phyir*).[1] If there were such a
valid cognizer, then it would have to be true that non-pot is
a pot; however, since whatever exists is observed by valid
cognizers and there is no valid cognizer realizing non-pot as
a pot, one can conclude that the factor of non-pot's being a
pot is not to be found among existents.

> If he says that the fourth part of the reason is not
> established, [the Sūtra School Challenger responds,]
> "It follows that a pot's isolate is not mutually exclu-
> sive with substantial phenomenon because there is a
> common locus of being a pot's isolate and a sub-
> stantial phenomenon."
>   If he says that the reason is not established, [the
> Sūtra School Challenger responds,] "It follows that
> [there is a common locus of being a pot's isolate and
> a substantial phenomenon] because a pot is such."

A pot is a pot's isolate and it is also a substantial phenomenon. Whatever is a substantial phenomenon must satisfy these four qualities.

Objects which are substantial phenomena include object
of knowledge and any of the phenomena mutually inclusive
with it, functioning thing and any of the phenomena mutu-

---

[1] *Ibid.*

ally inclusive with it, uncomposed space, form, a color, a pot, a pillar, and so forth. There are four possibilities between substantial phenomenon and permanent phenomenon and between substantial phenomenon and functioning thing. There are three possibilities between substantial phenomenon and generality:

1   Something which is both a substantial phenomenon and a generality is object of knowledge or functioning thing.
2   Whatever is a substantial phenomenon is necessarily a generality, but whatever is a generality is not necessarily a substantial phenomenon. For instance, permanent phenomenon is a generality, but it is not a substantial phenomenon because of being an isolate phenomenon which is itself.
3   Something which is neither is the two—a pillar and a pot.

There are four possibilities between substantial phenomenon and instance:

1   Something which is both is a functioning thing or a consciousness.
2   Something which is a substantial phenomenon but not an instance is object of knowledge.
3   Something which is an instance but not a substantial phenomenon is the two—a permanent phenomenon and a functioning thing, the isolate of functioning thing, permanent phenomenon, and so on.
4   Something which is neither is different-from-sound, the horn of a rabbit, and so forth.

There are three possibilities between substantial phenomenon and the isolate of functioning thing:

1   Something which is both is functioning thing.
2   Whatever is the isolate of functioning thing is necessarily a substantial phenomenon, but whatever is a substantial phenomenon is not necessarily the isolate of functioning thing. For example, a cause is a substantial

phenomenon but it is not the isolate of functioning thing.

3   Something which is neither is permanent phenomenon.

The two, substantial phenomenon and the phenomena coextensive with the isolate of functioning thing, are mutually exclusive, for (1) they are different and (2) a common locus of the two is not possible. Whereas whatever is a substantial phenomenon is necessarily itself, whatever is a phenomenon coextensive with the isolate of functioning thing is necessarily not itself. For instance, one-with-functioning-thing is not itself—it is not one with functioning thing—because of being different from functioning thing.

There are three possibilities between substantial phenomenon and object of knowledge of which being it is possible:

1   Something which is both is object of knowledge or food.
2   Whatever is a substantial phenomenon is necessarily an object of knowledge of which being it is possible. However, it is not the case that whatever is an object of knowledge of which being it is possible is necessarily a substantial phenomenon, for permanent phenomenon is an object of knowledge of which being it is possible but not a substantial phenomenon.
3   Something which is neither is the two—a gold pot and a copper pot.

Since there are three possibilities between substantial phenomenon and object of knowledge of which being it is possible, one can understand easily that the two, substantial phenomenon and objects of knowledge of which being them is not possible, are mutually exclusive.

There are four possibilities between substantial phenomenon and one:

1   Something which is both is phenomenon.
2   Something which is a substantial phenomenon but not one is the two—a product and an impermanent phenomenon.

3   Something which is one but not a substantial phenomenon is one itself, which is an isolate phenomenon
which is itself.

4   Something which is neither is the two—a permanent
phenomenon and a functioning thing, the two—a
definition and a definiendum, and so on.

There are also four possibilities between the two, substantial
phenomenon and different, which one can understand by
adjusting the above examples.

There are four possibilities between substantial phenomenon and color:

1   Something which is both is red.
2   Something which is a substantial phenomenon but not a
color is matter.
3   Something which is a color but not a substantial phenomenon is the two—red and white.
4   Something which is neither is different.

Substantial phenomenon itself is generally asserted to be an
isolate phenomenon which is not itself although there is no
logical necessity that it must be such an isolate phenomenon.[1] If it is an isolate phenomenon which is not itself,
then according to the second requirement of such a phenomenon it must not be itself. If substantial phenomenon is
an isolate phenomenon, then it is indeed not itself. Also, if
substantial phenomenon is an isolate phenomenon which is
not itself, then according to the third requirement non-it
must not be it. It is established by logical necessity that non-
substantial phenomenon is not a substantial phenomenon
for if it were, then it would have to be itself (that is to say, it
would have to be a non-substantial phenomenon).

However, there is no logical necessity that a substantial
phenomenon is not itself. If it is not itself, then it must be an
isolate phenomenon which is not itself, but if it is itself then
it must be a substantial phenomenon and non-it must not be
it. There is no fault in asserting substantial phenomenon as a

---

[1] For instance, see Dzemay Rinbochay, Shar-dzay *Collected Topics*, p. 37.

substantial phenomenon. Some say that substantial phenomenon is an isolate phenomenon because definition is a definiendum, but this argument is unconvincing. According to this reasoning, one could assert that impermanent phenomenon is a permanent phenomenon because definition is a definiendum. Still, it is suitable to consider substantial phenomenon as an isolate phenomenon. It is mutually exclusive with isolate phenomenon, but even so substantial phenomenon itself may be an isolate phenomenon. The argument cited above merely indicates that there is a precedent for such comparisons. Definition is mutually exclusive with definiendum, but definition itself is a definiendum. Also, the isolate of functioning thing is mutually exclusive with permanent phenomenon, but the isolate of functioning thing is itself a permanent phenomenon. If substantial phenomenon is an isolate phenomenon, then neither substantial phenomenon nor any of the many types of isolate phenomena would be a phenomenon which is itself.

Up to this point in the text, it has been established that a pot is a substantial phenomenon. In order to defeat the hypothetical Defender's assertion that whatever is a substantial phenomenon is necessarily an isolate phenomenon the Sūtra School Challenger must now show that a pot is not any type of isolate phenomenon.

> If he accepts the basic consequence, [the Sūtra School Challenger responds,] "It follows that the subject [a pot] is not an isolate phenomenon because of (1) not being any of the first three isolate phenomena and (2) not being any of the four similitudes."

If, according to the passage in the Lo-śel-ling *Collected Topics*, the similitudes are limitless, then there is no pervasion in this last consequence. It is not the case that whatever (1) is not any of the first three isolate phenomena and (2) is not any of the four similitudes is necessarily not an isolate phenomenon.

An analysis of the nature of isolate phenomenon reveals that it must be an isolate phenomenon which is itself. Isolate phenomenon cannot be a substantial phenomenon, for if if were, then according to the second requirement of a substantial phenomenon it would have to be itself. If isolate phenomenon were an isolate phenomenon, then it could not be a substantial phenomenon. Thus, isolate phenomenon is an isolate phenomenon. There is no reason to think that it would be any of the similitudes, and, from among the first three isolate phenomena, the only one which includes phenomena which are themselves is isolate-phenomenon-which-is-itself.

If isolate phenomenon is an isolate phenomenon which is itself, then non-it must be an isolate phenomenon. If non-isolate phenomenon is an isolate phenomenon, then it is not itself. Since isolate phenomenon must be an isolate phenomenon, then non-non-isolate phenomenon must not be a non-isolate phenomenon. Then with respect to the basis, non-isolate phenomenon, it is not itself and non-it is not it; thus, it is an isolate phenomenon which is not itself. By this reasoning, one may conclude that isolate phenomenon is an isolate phenomenon which is itself, for it is itself and non-it is also it.

There are four possibilities between isolate phenomenon and functioning thing, between it and permanent phenomenon, between it and generality, between it and instance (something which is an isolate phenomenon but not an instance is different-from-permanent-phenomenon), between it and one, between it and different, between it and object of knowledge of which being it is possible, and between it and color. There are three possibilities between isolate phenomenon and objects of knowledge of which being them is not possible, for whatever are objects of knowledge of which being them is not possible are necessarily isolate phenomena. Isolate phenomenon is mutually exclusive with the isolate of functioning thing. There are three possibilities between isolate phenomenon and the phenomena coextensive with the isolate of functioning thing, for whatever is a phenomenon coextensive with the isolate of functioning thing is necessarily an isolate phenomenon.

> If he says that the first part of the reason is not established, [the Sūtra School Challenger responds,] "It follows that the subject [a pot] is [not any of the first three isolate phenomena] because of (1) not being an isolate phenomenon which is itself, (2) not being an isolate phenomenon which is not itself, and (3) also not being an isolate phenomenon of the third type."
>
> If he says that the first part of the reason [that a pot is not an isolate phenomenon which is itself] is not established, [the Sūtra School Challenger responds,] "It [absurdly] follows with respect to the subject [a pot] that non-it is it because it is an isolate phenomenon which is itself. You asserted the reason."
>
> "[It follows that] there is pervasion because that which is a common locus such that (1) it is an established base, (2) it is itself, (3) non-it is it, and also (4) its isolate is not mutually exclusive with isolate-phenomenon-which-is-itself is the definition of its being an isolate phenomenon which is itself."
>
> If he accepts the consequence [that non-pot is a pot, the Sūtra School Challenger responds,] "It follows that non-pot is not a pot because non-pot is not a functioning thing."

Since non-pot is not a pot, a pot is not an isolate phenomenon which is itself. No functioning thing is an isolate phenomenon which is itself because (1) with respect to whatever is an isolate phenomenon which is itself, non-it is necessarily it and (2) with respect to whatever is a functioning thing, non-it is necessarily not it. There is no functioning thing for which non-it is it because with respect to any functioning thing non-it is necessarily a permanent phenomenon. Thus, the two, functioning thing and isolate-phenomenon-which-is-itself, are mutually exclusive. So there are three possibilities between the two, permanent phenomenon and isolate-phenomenon-which-is-itself, for whatever is an isolate phenomenon which is itself is necessarily a permanent phenomenon.

Isolate-phenomenon-which-is-itself includes among its illustrations the selfless, permanent phenomenon and any of the phenomena mutually inclusive with it, definiendum, one, object of knowledge of which being it is possible, generality, instance, non-the-two—a pillar and a pot, mutually-different-from-object-of-knowledge, non-thing, and different-from-pot. For instance, the selfless is selfless, and the non-selfless (which is a non-existent) is also selfless, for the selfless includes all existents and non-existents alike. Also, definiendum is a definiendum because it is the definiendum of the triply qualified imputed existent, and non-definiendum is also a definiendum because its definition is that which is not a triply qualified imputed existent. Further, generality is a generality, and non-generality is also a generality, for its instances include the isolate of functioning thing, pot's isolate, the two—a pillar and a pot, and so forth. Similarly, instance is an instance, and also non-instance is an instance (although not a generality), for it is an instance of object of knowledge.

There are three possibilities between the two, generality and isolate-phenomenon-which-is-itself:

1 Something which is both is the selfless or permanent phenomenon.
2 Whatever is an isolate phenomenon which is itself is necessarily a generality, but whatever is a generality is not necessarily an isolate phenomenon which is itself. For instance, substantial phenomenon and functioning thing are generalities, but they are not isolate phenomena which are themselves.
3 Something which is neither is the two—a pillar and a pot—which are an isolate phenomenon which is not itself and also are only an instance.

There are four possibilities between isolate-phenomenon-which-is-itself and instance:

1 Something which is both is permanent phenomenon, one, instance, generality, and so on.
2 Something which is an isolate phenomenon which is itself but is not an instance is the selfless.
3 Something which is an instance but not an isolate phenomenon which is itself is substantial phenomenon, functioning thing, and so on.
4 Something which is neither is object of knowledge.

There are four possibilities between isolate-phenomenon-which-is-itself and definition:

1 Something which is both is that which is a common locus of a phenomenon and the non-momentary, a phenomenon which encompasses its manifestations, and so forth.
2 Something which is an isolate phenomenon which is itself and is not a definition is permanent phenomenon, generally characterized phenomenon, one, and so forth.
3 Something which is a definition but is not an isolate phenomenon which is itself is that which is established by a valid cognizer, the momentary, and so on.
4 Something which is neither is a pot, uncomposed space, and so on.

Since there are four possibilities between isolate-phenomenon-which-is-itself and definition, one can easily understand that there are also four possibilities between isolate-phenomenon-which-is-itself and definiendum.

Isolate-phenomenon-which-is-itself is mutually exclusive with objects of knowledge of which being them is not possible, for whatever are objects of knowledge of which being them is not possible are necessarily isolate phenomena which are not themselves. Consequently, there are three possibilities between isolate-phenomenon-which-is-itself and object of knowledge of which being it is possible.

There are four possibilities between isolate-phenomenon-which-is-itself and different:

1   Something which is both is the two—a permanent phenomenon and a generally characterized phenomenon.
2   Something which is an isolate phenomenon which is itself but is not different is definiendum.
3   Something which is different but is not an isolate phenomenon which is itself is the two—a product and an impermanent phenomenon.
4   Something which is neither is different, which is an isolate phenomenon which is not itself.

There are also four possibilities between the two, isolate-phenomenon-which-is-itself and one. One can understand the comparison of these two by re-applying the illustrations given above.

As was noted above, there are three possibilities between isolate-phenomenon-which-is-itself and permanent phenomenon, and there are also three possibilities between isolate-phenomenon-which-is-itself and the isolate of permanent phenomenon. The only thing which is both is permanent phenomenon, and then whatever is the isolate of permanent phenomenon is necessarily an isolate phenomenon which is itself. Because all isolate phenomena which are themselves are permanent phenomena, one may also reckon three possibilities between it and only-a-permanent-phenomenon:

1   Something which is both is definiendum, which is only a permanent phenomenon because of being a permanent phenomenon. Whatever is a permanent phenomenon is necessarily only a permanent phenomenon.
2   Whatever is an isolate phenomenon which is itself is necessarily only a permanent phenomenon, but whatever is only a permanent phenomenon is not necessarily an isolate phenomenon which is itself. For example, the two—a permanent phenomenon and a functioning thing—or object of knowledge are only permanent phe-

nomena, but they are not isolate phenomena which are themselves.

3   Something which is neither is color or only-a-permanent-phenomenon (which is a non-existent).

Now returning to the debate, the Sūtra School Challenger is to the point of showing that a pot is not an isolate phenomenon which is not itself.

> If he says that the second part of the reason [that a pot is not an isolate phenomenon which is not itself] is not established, [the Sūtra School Challenger responds,] "It [absurdly] follows with respect to the subject, a pot, that it is not itself because it is an isolate phenomenon which is not itself. You asserted the reason."
>
> "[It follows that] there is pervasion because that which is a common locus such that (1) it is an established base, (2) it is not itself, (3) non-it is not it, and also (4) its isolate is not mutually exclusive with isolate-phenomenon-which-is-not-itself is the definition of its being an isolate phenomenon which is not itself."
>
> If he accepts the consequence [that a pot is not itself, the Sūtra School Challenger responds,] "It follows that a pot is a pot because a pot exists."

If a pot is itself, then a pot cannot be an isolate phenomenon which is not itself.

Isolate-phenomenon-which-is-not-itself includes among its instances definition, different, that which is mutually exclusive, objects of knowledge of which being them is not possible, one-with-pot, pot's isolate, and the two—a pillar and a pot. For example, definition is not a definition because it is a definiendum of the triply qualified substantial existent, and non-definition is not a definition because it is the definiendum of what which is not a triply qualified substantial existent. Also, different is not different because it is one, for it is a singular phenomenon. Non-different is also not different, for it too is singular. Similarly that which is mutually exclusive is not mutually exclusive any more than a pot is mutually exclusive or a functioning thing is mutually exclusive, for each of these is only one and things which are mutually exclusive must be different. For the same reason, that which is not mutually exclusive is not mutually exclusive.

Also, objects of knowledge of which being them is not possible (referred to collectively) is not itself for two separate and sufficient reasons: (1) it is not different, for it is one and (2) being such exists, for there are things which are objects of knowledge of which being them is not possible. Objects of knowledge of which being them is not possible (collectively) is an object of knowledge of which being it *is* possible because of (1) being an object of knowledge and (2) being such exists. There are things which are objects of knowledge of which being them is not possible such as the two—a pillar and a pot, the two—a definition and a definiendum, and so forth. Non-objects of knowledge of which being them is not possible is also not an object of knowledge of which being it is not possible because (1) it is not different and (2) being it exists.

Any particular case of objects of knowledge of which being them is not possible is also an isolate phenomenon which is not itself. For instance, the two—a permanent phenomenon and a functioning thing—are not the two—a permanent phenomenon and functioning thing, for nothing is such. For this same reason, non-the-two—a permanent phenomenon and a functioning thing—is also not the two—a permanent phenomenon and a functioning thing. This applies in the same way to all objects of knowledge of which being them is not possible.

The isolate of any phenomenon as well as any of the phenomena coextensive with that isolate are also isolate phenomena which are not themselves. Pot's isolate is not pot's isolate because only pot is pot's isolate or, more cogently, because pot's isolate is not one with pot. Non-pot's isolate is not pot's isolate for the same reason—it is not one with pot. Also, the phenomena coextensive with pot's isolate are not themselves. For instance, the definiendum of a bulbous flat-based phenomenon which is able to perform the function of holding water is not itself, for only pot is the definiendum of that definition. Moreover, non-the definiendum of a bulbous flat-based phenomenon which is able to perform the function of holding water is not the definiendum of that definition. It is the same for all self-isolates and the phenomena coextensive with those isolates; they are isolate phenomena which are not themselves.

There are four possibilities between isolate-phenomenon-which-is-not-itself and functioning thing, between it and permanent phenomenon, between it and one, between it and different, and between it and generality. There are three possibilities between isolate-phenomenon-which-is-not-itself and instance, for whatever is an isolate phenomenon which is not itself is necessarily an instance. There are four possibilities between isolate-phenomenon-which-is-not-itself and object of knowledge of which being it is possible, but there are three possibilities between it and objects of knowledge of which being them is not possible (collectively understood) because whatever are objects of knowledge of which being them is not possible are necessarily an isolate phenomenon which is not itself.

At this point in the debate the Sūtra School Challenger must show that a pot is not an isolate phenomenon of the third type. This isolate phenomenon is so called for the sake of brevity. The first two types of isolate phenomena, isolate-phenomenon-which-is-itself and isolate-phenomenon-which-is-not-itself, are given descriptive names. In the first case the objects which are such isolate phenomena are themselves, and in the second case the objects which are such isolate phenomena are not themselves. In the case of isolate-phenomenon-of-the-third-type, any object which is such an isolate phenomenon is a common locus such that (1) it is not itself and (2) non-it is it. If isolate-phenomenon-of-the-third-type had been given a descriptive name as were the first two, it would have to be called "isolate-phenomenon-which-is-not-itself-and-also-non-it-is-it" in order to distinguish it from the others. Thus, for the sake of a briefer name, it is called merely "isolate-phenomenon-of-the-third-type".

> If he says that the third part of the reason [that a pot is not an isolate phenomenon of the third type] is not established, [the Sūtra School Challenger responds,] "It [absurdly] follows with respect to the subject, a pot, that non-it is it because it is an isolate phenomenon of the third type. You asserted the reason."
>
> "[It follows that] there is pervasion because that which is a common locus such that (1) it is an established base, (2) it is not itself, (3) non-it is it, and (4) its isolate is not mutually exclusive with isolate-phenomenon-of-the-third-type is the definition of an isolate phenomenon of the third type."
>
> If he accepts the consequence [that non-pot is a pot, the Sūtra School Challenger responds,] "It follows that non-pot is not a pot because non-pot is not a pot."

This consequence is not at all effective. The reason, as a mere repetition of the predicate of the consequence, does not in the least help one to understand that non-pot is not a pot. A better reason was given earlier: "Non-pot is not a pot because non-pot is a permanent phenomenon." Also, one might more effectively say, "Non-pot is not a pot because there is no valid cognizer which realizes non-pot as a pot."

Isolate-phenomenon-of-the-third type has relatively less variety among its instances than do some of the other types of isolate phenomena. Its instances include negative phenomenon, generality-of-functioning-thing (or generality-of-any-phenomenon), and instance-of-generality-of-functioning-thing (or instance-of-generality-of-any-phenomenon).

For example, negative phenomenon is not a negative phenomenon, for it is a positive phenomenon. In order to understand negative phenomenon it is not necessarily to eliminate any object of negation. Whatever is a negative phenomenon is necessarily something understood only after the elimination of some object of negation, but negative phenomenon itself is understood in the manner of a positive phenomenon. However, non-negative phenomenon is a negative phenomenon because in order to understand it one must eliminate an object of negation, i.e., negative phenomenon itself. Thus, negative phenomenon is a common locus such that (1) it is not itself and (2) non-it is it.

Also, generality-of-functioning-thing is an isolate phenomenon of the third type. Generality-of-functioning-thing is not a generality of functioning thing because functioning thing is not an instance of it. Functioning thing is not an instance of generality-of-functioning-thing because functioning thing is not a generality of functioning thing. No phenomenon is a generality of itself.

However, non-generality-of-functioning thing is a generality of functioning thing because functioning thing is an instance of it. Functioning thing is an instance of non-generality-of-functioning-thing because (1) it is a non-generality of functioning thing, (2) it is related with non-generality-of-functioning-thing as the same essence, and (3) many common locuses of not being a functioning thing and also being a non-generality of functioning thing are established. Functioning thing is a non-generality of functioning thing because it is not a generality of functioning thing. Thus, with respect to the basis, generality-of-functioning-thing, it is an object which is not itself and non-it is it. The same holds true for the generality of any phenomenon: It is not itself and non-it is it.

Further, instance-of-generality-of-functioning-thing is an isolate phenomenon of the third type. Instance-of-generality-of-functioning-thing is not an instance of generality-of-functioning-thing because it does not fulfill the first requirement of an instance of generality-of-functioning-thing. It is not a generality of functioning thing. If instance-of-generality-of-functioning-thing were a generality of functioning thing, then functioning thing would have to be an instance of instance-of-generality-of-functioning-thing. Then functioning thing would have to be a generality of itself.

Since it is not, functioning thing is not an instance of generality-of-functioning-thing and instance-of-generality-of-functioning-thing is not an instance of generality-of-functioning-thing.

Nevertheless, non-instance-of-generality-of-functioning-thing is an instance of generality-of-functioning-thing because (1) it is a generality of functioning thing, (2) it is related with generality-of-functioning-thing as the same essence, and (3) many common locuses of not being it and also being a generality of functioning thing are established. Non-instance-of-generality-of-functioning-thing is a generality of functioning thing because functioning thing is an instance of it. Functioning thing is a non-instance of generality-of-functioning-thing because it is not an instance of generality-of-functioning-thing, for it is not a generality of itself. Functioning thing is related with non-instance-of-generality-of-functioning-thing as the same essence. Since functioning thing is a non-instance of generality-of-functioning-thing, if there were no non-instances of generality-of-functioning-thing, then functioning thing too would not exist. Finally, there are many common locuses of not being a non-instance of generality-of-functioning-thing and also being a generality of functioning thing because definiendum and also positive phenomenon are such common locuses. For instance, positive phenomenon is a generality of functioning thing and it is also an instance of generality-of-functioning-thing. Positive phenomenon is an instance of generality-of-functioning-thing because (1) it is a generality of functioning thing, (2) it is related with generality-of-functioning-thing as the same essence, and (3) there are many common locuses of not being a positive phenomenon and also being a generality of functioning thing (such as opposite-from-not-being-an-object-of-knowledge and non-cow).

Thus, non-instance-of-generality-of-functioning-thing is an instance of generality-of-functioning-thing and with respect to the basis, instance-of-generality-of-functioning-thing, it is an object such that (1) it is not itself and (2) non-it is it. Both of these factors of the nature of instance-of-generality-of-functioning-thing arise out of the necessity that functioning thing cannot be its own generality. This is equally true for any phenomenon: It cannot be its own generality.

Isolate-phenomenon-of-the-third-type is mutually exclusive with functioning thing because (1) with respect to whatever is an isolate phenomenon of the third type non-it is necessarily it and (2) with respect to whatever is a functioning thing non-it is necessarily not it. Then there are three possibilities between isolate-phenomenon-of-the-third-type and permanent phenomenon, for whatever is an isolate phenomenon of the third type is necessarily a permanent phenomenon. There are three possibilities between isolate-phenomenon-of-the-third-type and generality:

1 Something which is both is negative phenomenon or generality-of-functioning-thing. Generality-of-functioning-thing is a generality (although not a generality of functioning thing) because of being a generality of one, definiendum, and positive phenomenon.

2 Whatever is an isolate phenomenon of the third type is necessarily a generality; however, it is not the case that whatever is a generality is necessarily an isolate phenomenon of the third type. For example, object of knowledge is a generality but not an isolate phenomenon of the third type.

3 Something which is neither is the isolate of functioning thing or one-with-pot.

Similarly, there are three possibilities between isolate-phenomenon-of-the-third-type and instance, for whatever is an isolate phenomenon of the third type is necessarily an instance.

To this point in the debate, the Sūtra School Challenger has shown that a pot is a substantial phenomenon and is not any of the first three types of isolate phenomena. He must now prove that it is none of the similitudes.

If he says that the second part of the main reason above [i.e., that a pot is not any of the four similitudes] is not established, [the Sūtra School Challenger responds,] "It follows that the subject, a pot, is not any of the four similitudes because of (1) not being a similitude of isolate-phenomenon-which-is-itself, (2) not being a similitude of isolate-phenomenon-which-is-not-itself, (3) not being a similitude of isolate-phenomenon-of-the-third-type, and (4) also not being a similitude of substantial phenomenon."

If he says that the first part of the reason [that a pot is not a similitude of isolate-phenomenon-which-is-itself] is not established, [the Sūtra School Challenger responds,] "It [absurdly] follows with respect to the subject, a pot, that non-it is it because it is a similitude of isolate-phenomenon-which-is-itself. You asserted the reason."

"[It follows that] there is pervasion because that which is a common locus such that (1) it is an established base, (2) it is itself, (3) non-it is it, and also (4) its isolate is not mutually exclusive with similitude-of-isolate-phenomenon-which-is-itself is the definition of its being a similitude of isolate-phenomenon-which-is-itself."

If he accepts the consequence, [that non-pot is a pot], that has been refuted above (see p. 737).

The only thing which one can posit as a similitude of isolate-phenomenon-which-is-itself is non-isolate-phenomenon-which-is-itself (see pp. 712-718). Since this unique illustration is a permanent phenomenon, similitude-of-isolate-phenomenon-which-is-itself is mutually exclusive with functioning thing. There are three possibilities between it and permanent phenomenon, for whatever is a similitude of isolate-phenomenon-which-is-itself is necessarily a permanent phenomenon.

Similarly, there are three possibilities between it and generality, for whatever is a similitude of isolate-phenomenon-which-is-itself is necessarily a generality. Non-isolate-phenomenon-which-is-itself is a generality because there are instances of it such as substantial phenomenon, permanent phenomenon, functioning thing, and so on. There are also three possibilities between similitude-of-isolate-phenomenon-which-is-itself and instance, for whatever is a similitude of isolate-phenomenon-which-is-itself is necessarily an instance. Non-isolate-phenomenon-which-is-itself is an instance of object of knowledge and also of permanent phenomenon.

Similitude-of-isolate-phenomenon-which-is-itself has three possibilities with one, for whatever is it is necessarily one. Consequently, this similitude is mutually exclusive with different. Similarly, there are three possibilities between this similitude and object of knowledge of which being it is possible, for whatever is it is necessarily an object of knowledge of which being it is possible. Thus, it is mutually exclusive with objects of knowledge of which being them is not possible.

Finally, this similitude also has three possibilities with definiendum, for whatever is it is necessarily a definiendum. Non-isolate-phenomenon-which-is-itself is a definiendum because it is the definiendum of what which is *not* a common locus such that (1) it is an established base, (2) it is itself, (3) non-it is it, and (4) its isolate is not mutually exclusive with isolate-phenomenon-which-is-itself.

Returning to the debate, the Sūtra School Challenger will now show that a pot is not a similitude of isolate-phenomenon-which-is-not-itself.

> If he says that the second part of the reason [that a pot is not a similitude of isolate-phenomenon-which-is-not-itself] is not established, [the Sūtra School Challenger responds,] "It [absurdly] follows with respect to the subject, a pot, that it is not itself

because it is a similitude of isolate-phenomenon-which-is-not-itself. You asserted the reason."

"[It follows that] there is pervasion because that which is a common locus such that (1) it is an established base, (2) it is not itself, (3) non-it is not it, and also (4) its isolate is not mutually exclusive with similitude-of-isolate-phenomenon-which-is-not-itself is the definition of its being a similitude of isolate-phenomenon-which-is-not-itself."

If he accepts the consequence [that a pot is not itself], that has been refuted above (see p. 741).

Similar to the case of similitude-of-isolate-phenomenon-which-is-itself there is only one illustration of this similitude—isolate-phenomenon-which-is-itself. Again this illustration is a permanent phenomenon, so similitude-of-isolate-phenomenon-which-is-not-itself is mutually exclusive with functioning thing and has three possibilities with permanent phenomenon, for whatever is this similitude is necessarily a permanent phenomenon. There are three possibilities between it and generality, for whatever is it is necessarily a generality. Isolate-phenomenon-which-is-not-itself is a generality of definition, objects of knowledge of which being them is not possible, pot's isolate, and so on. Also, there are three possibilities between this similitude and instance, for whatever is it is necessarily an instance. This is because isolate-phenomenon-which-is-itself is an instance of object of knowledge, permanent phenomenon, definiendum, and so forth. There are three possibilities between this similitude and object of knowledge of which being it is possible, and it is mutually exclusive with objects of knowledge of which being them is not possible. Finally, there are three possibilities between it and one, and it is mutually exclusive with different.

The Sūtra School Challenger will now address the Defender's suspicion that a pot might be a similitude of isolate-phenomenon-of-the-third-type.

If he says that the third part of the reason [that a pot is not a similitude of isolate-phenomenon-of-the-third-type] is not established, [the Sūtra School Challenger responds,] "It [absurdly] follows with respect to the subject, a pot, that it is not itself because it is a similitude of isolate-phenomenon-of-the-third-type."

"[It follows that] there is pervasion because that which is a common locus such that (1) it is an established base, (2) it is not itself, (3) non-it is it, and also (4) its isolate is not mutually exclusive with similitude-of-isolate-phenomenon-of-the-third-type is the definition of its being a similitude of isolate-phenomenon-of-the-third-type."

If he accepts [that a pot is not itself], that has been refuted above (see p. 741).

Only isolate-phenomenon-of-the-third-type is an illustration of similitude-of-isolate-phenomenon-of-the-third-type. Since this is a permanent phenomenon, once again, this similitude is mutually exclusive with functioning thing and has three possibilities with permanent phenomenon, for whatever is a similitude of isolate-phenomenon-of-the-third-type is necessarily a permanent phenomenon. There are three possibilities between this similitude and generality. Isolate-phenomenon-of-the-third-type is a generality, for its instances include negative phenomenon, pot's generality, and so on. There are also three possibilities between this similitude and instance, for whatever is it is necessarily an instance. Its illustration is an instance of object of knowledge and of definiendum. There are three possibilities between similitude-of-isolate-phenomenon-of-the-third-type and object of knowledge of which being it is possible and between it and one.

In his argument that a pot is not an isolate phenomenon, the only remaining point for the Sūtra School Challenger to prove is that it is not a similitude of substantial phenomenon. This is certainly the most likely possibility, for a pot does satisfy the first three qualities of this similitude whereas for all of the other isolate phenomena it satisfied no more than two of the requirements. The hypothetical Defender may feel that since a pot satisfies the first three requirements of this similitude it must likely satisfy the fourth as well.

> If he says that the fourth part of the reason [that a pot is not a similitude of substantial phenomenon] is not established, [the Sūtra School Challenger responds,] "It [absurdly] follows with respect to the subject, a pot, that its isolate is not mutually exclusive with similitude-of-substantial-phenomenon because it is a similitude of substantial phenomenon. You asserted the reason."
>
> "[It follows that] there is pervasion because that which is a common locus such that (1) it is an established base, (2) it is itself, (3) non-it is not it, and also (4) its isolate is not mutually exclusive with similitude-of-substantial-phenomenon is the definition of its being a similitude of substantial phenomenon."

If a pot were a similitude of substantial phenomenon, then it would have to be the case that its isolate is not mutually exclusive with similitude-of-substantial-phenomenon. The fault of this is less obvious than the fault accrued by the assertion of a pot as any of the other isolate phenomena. However, since substantial phenomenon and any of the various types of isolate phenomena are asserted as mutually exclusive, this consequence is equally effective in defeating the idea that a pot might be an isolate phenomenon of some type.

> Furthermore, "It follows that the subject, a pot, is not a similitude of substantial phenomenon because of actually abiding as a substantial phenomenon."
>
> If he says that the reason is not established, [the Sūtra School Challenger responds,] "It follows with respect to the subject [a pot] that [it actually abides

as a substantial phenomenon] because [it] is a substantial phenomenon."

If he says that there is no pervasion, [the Sūtra
School Challenger responds,] "It follows with
respect to the subject, a substantial phenomenon,
that whatever is it necessarily actually abides as it
because it is selfless."

Phenomena naturally, actually abide as themselves; they are
one with themselves and are not different from themselves.
Whatever is a substantial phenomenon necessarily actually
abides as a substantial phenomenon. It is the nature of the
illustrations of substantial phenomenon that they are substantial phenomena and that they are not similitudes of
substantial phenomenon. The functional assumption here is
that substantial phenomenon is mutually exclusive with its
similitude, for there is nothing which is a common locus of
these two.

On this same point of the mutual exclusion of a phenomenon and its similitude, the Ra-dö *Collected Topics* says,
"It follows that the two, isolate-phenomenon-which-is-itself
and the similitude-of-that, are mutually exclusive because
(1) whatever is an isolate phenomenon which is itself necessarily actually abides as an isolate phenomenon which is
itself and (2) whatever is a similitude of that is necessarily a
phenomenon which is merely a similitude of that"[1] The
similitudes correspond to their bases in the sense that the
first three requirements of each are the same, but it is a mere
similitude. In the case of substantial phenomenon it is not its
similitude, and in every case the similitude is mutually
exclusive with its basis. Whatever is one of them is necessarily not the other.

Unlike the other three similitudes, similitude-of-
substantial-phenomenon is not limited to only one illustration. The phenomena which are similitudes of substantial
phenomenon are exemplified by two types: (1) functioning-
thing-which-is-an-isolate-phenomenon and (2) that which is

---

[1] Jam-ȳang-chok-hla-ö-ser, Ra-dö *Collected Topics*, 36a.4-5.

mutually exclusive with substantial phenomenon. It has already been established that functioning-thing-which-is-an-isolate-phenomenon is a similitude of substantial phenomenon (see pp. 708-712). Furthermore, one can also say that impermanent-phenomenon-which-is-an-isolate-phenomenon, consciousness-which-is-an-isolate-phenomenon, pillar-which-is-an-isolate-phenomenon, and so forth are similitudes of substantial phenomenon. Consciousness-which-is-an-isolate-phenomenon is like consciousness-which-is-one-with-consciousness. It is a consciousness because of being an awareness just as functioning-thing-which-is-one-with-functioning-thing is a functioning thing. It is an isolate phenomenon because of being an isolate phenomenon which is not itself. However, one cannot posit permanent-phenomenon-which-is-an-isolate-phenomenon as a similitude of substantial phenomenon because it does not fulfill the third quality of such a similitude, for non-permanent-phenomenon-which-is-an-isolate-phenomenon is a permanent phenomenon which is an isolate phenomenon.

The second main example cf a similitude of substantial phenomenon is that which is mutually exclusive with substantial phenomenon (*rdzas chos dang 'gal ba*). This subject is itself (that is, that which is mutually exclusive with substantial phenomenon is mutually exclusive with substantial phenomenon), for the two, that which is mutually exclusive with substantial phenomenon and substantial phenomenon, are (1) different and (2) a common locus is not possible. There is nothing which is both a substantial phenomenon and also mutually exclusive with substantial phenomenon, for (1) whatever is a substantial phenomenon is necessarily not mutually exclusive with substantial phenomenon and (2) whatever is mutually exclusive with substantial phenomenon is necessarily not a substantial phenomenon.

Also, that which is not mutually exclusive with substantial phenomenon is not mutually exclusive with substantial phenomenon because there is a common locus of the two, that which is not mutually exclusive with substantial phenomenon and substantial phenomenon, for a pot is such a common locus. A pot is a substantial phenomenon and it is also not mutually exclusive with substantial phenomenon. Whatever is a substantial phenomenon is necessarily a common locus of these two.

Therefore, with respect to the basis, that which is mutually exclusive with substantial phenomenon, (1) it is itself and (2) non-it is not it. However, one cannot say that that which is mutually exclusive with substantial phenomenon is a substantial phenomenon because the isolate of that which is mutually exclusive with substantial phenomenon is not mutually exclusive with substantial phenomenon. Rather, that which is mutually exclusive with substantial phenomenon is mutually exclusive with substantial phenomenon. This is the same as the first main variable—it is itself. Thus, one may conclude that that which is mutually exclusive with substantial phenomenon is a similitude of substantial phenomenon.

Also unlike the other three similitudes, similitude-of-substantial-phenomenon is a generality, for there are instances of it. For example, functioning-thing-which-is-an-isolate-phenomenon is an instance of similitude-of-substantial-phenomenon because (1) it is a similitude of substantial phenomenon, (2) it is related with similitude-of-substantial-phenomenon as the same essence, and (3) many common locuses of not being it and also being a similitude of substantial phenomenon are established. There are many common locuses because that which is mutually exclusive with substantial phenomenon is such a common locus and also phenomenon-which-does-not-have-a-common-locus-with-substantial-phenomenon is such a common locus, and these two are established as mutually different.

For instance, that which is mutually exclusive with substantial phenomenon is not a functioning thing which is an isolate phenomenon because of being a permanent phenomenon which is an isolate phenomenon, and it is also a similitude of substantial phenomenon. These two examples, that which is mutually exclusive with substantial phe-

nomenon and phenomenon-which-does-not-have-a-common-locus-with-substantial-phenomenon, are mutually
different in the sense of not being exactly the same, but they
are not substantively different. It is not necessary that the
examples in this position be substantively different, that
there be something which is the one and not the other. It is
only necessary that they be different in name or meaning.
Thus, functioning-thing-which-is-an-isolate-phenomenon is
established as an instance of similitude-of-substantial-
phenomenon and this similitude is established as a
generality.

There are four possibilities between similitude-of-
substantial-phenomenon and permanent phenomenon:

1   Something which is both is that which is mutually
    exclusive with substantial phenomenon or phenomenon-
    which-does-not-have-a-common-locus-with-substantial-
    phenomenon.
2   Something which is a similitude of substantial phe-
    nomenon but is not a permanent phenomenon is
    functioning-thing-which-is-an-isolate-phenomenon,
    product-which-is-an-isolate-phenomenon, pot-which-is-
    not-a-substantial-phenomenon, and so on.
3   Something which is a permanent phenomenon but not a
    similitude of substantial phenomenon is permanent
    phenomenon or uncomposed space.
4   Something which is neither is a pot, the two—a gold pot
    and a copper pot, pot-which-is-one-with-pot, and so on.

There are also four possibilities between similitude-of-
substantial-phenomenon and functioning thing. By re-
applying the examples given in the last case one can easily
understand the phenomena which exemplify the four possibilities between this similitude and functioning thing.

There are three possibilities between similitude-of-
substantial-phenomenon and generality:

1   Something which is both is functioning-thing-which-is-
    an-isolate-phenomenon. This is a generality because its
    instances include pot-which-is-one-with-pot, the two—

matter and consciousness, and so on. Also, that which is mutually exclusive with substantial phenomenon is a generality for its instances include the two—matter and consciousness, isolate-phenomenon-which-is-itself, the isolate of permanent phenomenon, and so on.

2   Whatever is a similitude of substantial phenomenon is necessarily a generality, but whatever is a generality is not necessarily a similitude of substantial phenomenon. For example, object of knowledge is a generality but not a similitude of substantial phenomenon.

3   Something which is neither is pot's isolate.

There are also three possibilities between similitude-of-substantial-phenomenon and instance, for whatever is a similitude of substantial phenomenon is necessarily an instance. Both functioning-thing-which-is-an-isolate-phenomenon and that which is mutually exclusive with substantial phenomenon are instances of object of knowledge, generality, instance, one, object of knowledge of which being it is possible, and so forth.

The remainder of this chapter consists of some notes listing illustrations of the seven types of isolate phenomena. These notes are written in a style similar to those sections in which the author's own presentation is made.

> Hence, there are isolate phenomena which are themselves because definiendum, permanent phenomenon, generality, instance, and so forth are such phenomena.
>
> There are isolate phenomena which are not themselves because definition, different, one-with-pot, the two—a pillar and a pot, and all phenomena of which being them is not possible are such phenomena.
>
> There are isolate phenomena of the third type because instance-of-generality-of-functioning-thing, generality-of-functioning-thing, and so forth are such phenomena.

There is a similitude of substantial phenomenon because functioning-thing-which-is-an-isolate-phenomenon is such a phenomenon.

There is a similitude of isolate-phenomenon-which-is-itself because non-isolate-phenomenon-which-is-itself is such a phenomenon.

There is a similitude of isolate-phenomenon-which-is-not-itself because isolate-phenomenon-which-is-not-itself is such a phenomenon.

There is a similitude of isolate-phenomenon-of-the-third-type because isolate-phenomenon-of-the-third-type is such a phenomenon.

Toward the spread of virtue and goodness.

"The Introductory Path of Reasoning" closes with a final expression of auspiciousness. The author requests that his efforts be dedicated "toward the spread of virtue and goodness (*dge legs 'phel*)".

As mentioned above (see p. 696), the presentation of substantial and isolate phenomena given in the Tutor's *Collected Topics* is the system formulated by Cha-b̄a-chö-ḡyi-s̄eng-gay. Although beneficial as a summary organization of many of the main points that have come before, it is not universally accepted as the definitive presentation of substantial and isolate phenomena in the Sūtra School Following Reasoning. In the Go-mang *Collected Topics*, after presenting the system of substantial and isolate phenomena formulated by Cha-b̄a-chö-ḡyi-s̄eng-gay, the text presents the more usual interpretation of substantial and isolate phenomena in this system of tenets.[1] It is important to be aware of this interpretation of substantial and isolate phenomena, as it aids one in understanding the two truths in the system of the Sūtra School Following Reasoning.

According to this interpretation, substantial phenomenon is mutually inclusive with functioning thing and isolate phenomenon is mutually inclusive with permanent phenomenon. The Go-mang *Collected Topics* says:

---

[1] See Ngak-w̄ang-d̄ra-s̄hi, Go-mang *Collected Topics*, pp. 214-227.

There is a definition of a substantial phenomenon because:

> a functioning thing which is able to perform a function ultimately and which is an object established from its own side without being merely imputed by a thought consciousness

is the definition of a substantial phenomenon. The three—substantial phenomenon, substantial existent (*rdzas yod*), and functioning thing—are mutually inclusive.[1]

That portion of the definition specifying: "and which is an object established from its own side without being merely imputed by a thought consciousness", does not function to discriminate substantial phenomena from some other type of functioning things which are able to perform a function ultimately but are not objects established from their own side. Rather, that specification merely serves to describe more completely the nature of substantial phenomena. There are no functioning things which are not objects established from their own side without being merely imputed by thought consciousnesses. Permanent phenomena do depend on imputation by thought consciousnesses, but functioning things truly, substantially exist without depending on any imputation by thought consciousnesses. The Go-mang *Collected Topics* continues:

> There is an illustration of a substantial phenomenon because form is such. With respect to the subject, form, there is a reason for calling it "a substantial phenomenon" because, since it is a common locus of being substantial and also being a phenomenon, it is so called. With respect to the subject, form, there is a reason for calling it "a substantial existent" because, since it exists substantially, it is so called.[2]

---

[1] *Ibid.*, pp. 222-223.
[2] *Ibid.*, p. 223.

Whatever is a substantial phenomenon is necessarily both substantial (*rdzas*) and a phenomenon. "The substantial" is also mutually inclusive with functioning thing, and since whatever is a functioning thing is necessarily a phenomenon, then whatever is substantial is also necessarily a substantial phenomenon. The text continues:

> If substantial existents are divided terminologically, there are four because there are the four:
>
> 1   substantial existent in the sense of being established by reasoning (*rigs pas grub pa'i rdzas yod*)
> 2   substantial existent in the sense of being statically unchanging (*brtan par mi 'gyur ba'i rdzas yod*)
> 3   substantial existent in the sense of being able to perform a function (*don byed nus pa'i rdzas yod*)
> 4   substantial existent in the sense of being self-sufficiently apprehensible (*rang skya 'dzin thub pa'i rdzas yod*).[1]

This is a *terminological* division (*sgras brjod rigs kyi sgo nas dbye ba*) of substantial existents rather than an actual division because whatever is an actual substantial existent is necessarily an impermanent phenomenon, but some of the phenomena included by the divisions of substantial existents given here are not impermanent phenomena and are not actual substantial existents. The text explains:

> The two, substantial existent in the sense of being established by reasoning and existent, are mutually inclusive.[2]

A substantial existent in the sense of being established by reasoning is a phenomenon established by reasoning and established by a valid cognizer. Whatever exists is established by a valid cognizer and whatever exists is also a substantial existent in the sense of being established by reason-

---

[1] *Ibid.*
[2] *Ibid.*

ing. This characteristic of phenomena corresponds to the nature of phenomena as objects of knowledge and hidden phenomena. As objects of knowledge, whatever exists is necessarily suitable as an object of an awareness; however, from among existents, the permanent phenomena are suitable as appearing objects of only conceptual awarenesses. All phenomena, permanent and impermanent alike, are *suitable* as objects of conceptual knowers; for this reason, all existents are hidden phenomena, objects realized in a hidden manner by the *thought* consciousnesses apprehending them. Since whatever exists is both established by a valid cognizer and also suitable as an object of a thought consciousness, whatever exists is suitable as an object of an inferential valid cognizer, a conceptual knower incontrovertibly realizing an object. Indeed, impermanent phenomena may be apprehended by direct valid cognizers, but they are also *suitable* as objects of inferential valid cognizers. Since inferential valid cognizers are produced by a process of reasoning, it is from this point of view that whatever exists is necessarily a substantial existent in the sense of being established by reasoning.

According to this interpretation of substantial and isolate phenomena, whatever is a substantial existent is necessarily a functioning thing. Since substantial existent in the sense of being established by reasoning is mutually inclusive with existent, there are three possibilities between substantial existent and substantial existent in the sense of being established by reasoning. This is because whatever is a substantial phenomenon is necessarily a substantial phenomenon in the sense of being established by reasoning, but whatever is a substantial phenomenon in the sense of being established by reasoning is not necessarily a substantial phenomenon. For instance, uncomposed space is a substantial phenomenon in the sense of being established by reasoning, but it is not a substantial phenomenon. The text continues:

> The two, substantial existent in the sense of being statically unchanging and permanent phenomenon, are mutually inclusive.[1]

Permanent phenomena are unchanging, though not necessarily everlasting, phenomena. Substantial existent and substantial existent in the sense of being statically unchanging are mutually exclusive, just as are functioning thing and permanent phenomenon. There is nothing which on the one hand is a substantial existent and on the other hand is a substantial existent in the sense of being statically unchanging. The text continues:

> The two, substantial existent in the sense of being able to perform a function and functioning thing, are mutually inclusive.[2]

Whatever is a substantial phenomenon is necessarily a substantial phenomenon in the sense of being able to perform a function. The text continues:

> There is a definition of a substantial existent in the sense of being self-sufficiently apprehensible because:
>
> > a phenomenon with respect to which the ascertainment of it by a valid cognizer does not need to depend on the ascertainment by a valid cognizer of another phenomenon which is not its entity (*rang nyid tshad mas nges pa rang gi ngo bor ma gyur pa'i chos gzhan tshad mas nges pa la ltos mi dgos pa'i chos*)
>
> is the definition of a substantial existent in the sense of being self-sufficiently apprehensible. There are illustrations because the five external sources [visible objects, sounds, odors, tastes, and tangible objects]

---

[1] *Ibid.*
[2] *Ibid.*

and all consciousnesses are substantial existents in the sense of being self-sufficiently apprehensible.[1]

The five internal sense powers—eye sense power, ear sense power, and so forth—as well as all non-associated compositional factors, including persons, are substantial existents but are not substantial existents in the sense of being self-sufficiently apprehensible. Substantial existents which are self-sufficiently apprehensible are so called because from their own sides they are adequate to be perceived. In the sense that one does not need to first apprehend some other phenomenon before one can apprehend a substantial phenomenon of this type, they are self-sufficiently apprehensible.

As non-associated compositional factors, all persons are substantial existents in the sense of being able to perform a function but not substantial existents in the sense of being self-sufficiently apprehensible. Rather, according to the Go-mang *Collected Topics* persons are "imputed existents in the sense of not being self-sufficiently apprehensible".[2] This means that persons are imputed existents in this sense even though they are also substantial existents in the sense of being able to perform a function. Persons are imputed because in order to ascertain a person by a valid cognition one must first ascertain by valid cognition the aggregates of that person. This reflects the definition of a person as a being who is imputed in dependence on any of the five aggregates. For instance, with respect to a human, one can ascertain a human by valid cognition only after having ascertained by valid cognition some phenomenon other than the person—the mind, body, voice, or such. Apprehending the body and/or mind of a person leads one to an apprehension of the person. If persons were substantial phenomena in the sense of being self-sufficiently apprehensible, then they would appear to the mind

---

[1] *Ibid.*, pp. 223-224.
[2] *Ibid.*, p. 218.

apprehending them without depending on the appearance of some other phenomenon.

In the Lesser Vehicle systems of tenets the presentation of selflessness is restricted to persons. In both the Great Exposition School and the Sūtra School the coarse selflessness of persons is identified as the person's lack of being a permanent, partless, independent self and the subtle selflessness of persons is identified as the lack of being a self-sufficient person.[1] A person is not self-sufficient because of not being substantially existent, for the person depends on mind and body just as one leg of a tripod depends on the other two. There is a false appearance of a person as self-sufficient that is being negated by the Proponents of the Sūtra School. A passage in *Tantra in Tibet* identifies this false appearance:

> Here a yogi cognises that a person does not substantially exist or exist as a self-sufficient entity in the sense of being the controller of mind and body. The mind and body falsely seem to depend on the person whereas the person does not seem to depend on mind and body. The person seems like a master, and the mind and body his subjects.[2]

The Proponents of the Sūtra School assert this misconception of the person as the root ignorance which leads one into contaminated actions and binds one in the suffering of cyclic existence.

The person is not a self-sufficient substantial entity in the sense of being "a lord of the mansion" who controls the slaves of mind and body. In Go-mang, the expression "self-sufficient substantial existent" is used only in reference to persons, for the suspicion of there being a person who is such a substantial existent occurs with respect to persons only. No one would suspect that a table might be a self-sufficient substantial entity in the sense of controlling its parts.

---

[1] Tsong-ka-pa, *Tantra in Tibet*, p. 180.
[2] *Ibid.*, p. 181.

Moreover, here the Go-mang *Collected Topics* is pointing out that the person is also not a substantial existent in the sense of being self-sufficiently apprehensible because in order to ascertain the person by valid cognition one must first ascertain other phenomena by valid cognition. Not only persons but also all non-associated compositional factors lack this sort of substantial existence. For instance, in order to ascertain the impermanence of a pot by valid cognition one must first ascertain the pot by valid cognition.

Still, other phenomena—the five external sources and all consciousnesses—are asserted to be substantial existents in the sense of being self-sufficiently apprehensible. For instance, sound is a substantial existent in the sense of being self-sufficiently apprehensible because of being a phenomenon ascertained by valid cognition without depending on the ascertainment of another phenomenon by valid cognition. Sound is self-sufficient for its apprehension. Within the context of speaking of sound as a definiendum or as an object illustrated it is held that in order to ascertain sound by valid cognition one must first ascertain by valid cognition its definition, an object of hearing, or an illustration of sound such as an object of hearing which is a drum beat. However, this does not negate the assertion of sound as self-sufficiently apprehensible because the definition and illustrations of sound are the same entity as sound. In order to ascertain sound by valid cognition one need not first validly ascertain any phenomenon which is a *different* entity.

There are three possibilities between the two, substantial existent in the sense of being able to perform a function and substantial existent in the sense of being self-sufficiently apprehensible:

1 Something which is both is any external form or any consciousness—sound, color, a valid cognizer, and so on.
2 Whatever is a substantial existent in the sense of being self-sufficiently apprehensible is necessarily a substantial existent in the sense of being able to perform

a function but whatever is a substantial existent in the sense of being able to perform a function is not necessarily a substantial existent in the sense of being self-sufficiently apprehensible. Any non-associated compositional factor—a person, time, functioning thing (collectively), and so on—is a substantial existent in the sense of being able to perform a function but not a substantial existent in the sense of being self-sufficiently apprehensible.

3   Something which is neither is any permanent phenomenon or any non-existent.

The Go-mang *Collected Topics* continues:

> There is a definition of an imputed existent [*btags yod*] because:
>
> > a phenomenon which is an object established merely through imputation by a thought consciousness without being an entity whose mode of subsistence is established from its own side (*yul rang gi ngos nas grub pa'i gnas lugs kyi ngo bo ma yin par rtog pas btags tsam du grub pa'i chos*)
>
> is the definition of an imputed existent. The three— imputed existent, isolate phenomenon, and permanent phenomenon—are mutually inclusive.[1]

An imputed existent is merely imputed by a thought consciousness and is not established from its own side because in order to ascertain an imputed existent by valid cognition one must generate a thought consciousness apprehending a meaning-generality which serves as a representation of that object. One cannot apprehend an imputed existent directly. Such a phenomenon depends on imputation by a thought consciousness in order to be known; therefore, they are called "imputed existents". The text continues:

----

[1] Ngak-wang-dra-shi, Go-mang *Collected Topics*, p. 224.

If imputed existents are divided terminologically, there are three because there are the three:

1 imaginary (*kun btags*)
2 non-associated compositional factor (*ldan min 'du byed*)
3 thoroughly established phenomenon (*yongs grub*).[1]

Similar to the case of substantial existents, imputed existents are divided terminologically. Some of the divisions of imputed existents include things which are other than permanent phenomena.

For instance, from the point of view of expression, non-associated compositional factors are included as a division of imputed existents, but such phenomena are not actual imputed existents because they are impermanent phenomena and substantial existents in the sense of being able to perform functions. However, non-associated compositional factors are imputed in the sense of not being self-sufficiently apprehensible because of being phenomena which must be ascertained only after the ascertainment of another phenomenon which is not its entity.[2] Still, this does not qualify non-associated compositional factors as actual imputed existents, for they are not *merely* imputed. Rather, after having ascertained by valid cognition some other phenomenon which is not its entity, one may directly ascertain a non-associated compositional factor.

Also, the imaginary includes not only permanent phenomena (other than selflessnesses) but also all non-existents as well. There are existent imaginaries such as uncomposed space and non-existent imaginaries such as the horn of a rabbit or a self-sufficient phenomenon. The Go-mang *Collected Topics* says:

There is a mode of positing an imaginary in relation to each and every phenomenon because the establish-

---

[1] *Ibid.*
[2] *Ibid.*, pp. 218-219.

ment of form as a self-sufficient substantial existent is
an imaginary in relation to form, the establishment of
an exalted knower of all aspects as a self-sufficient
substantial existent is an imaginary in relation to an
exalted knower of all aspects, and the reasoning for all
phenomena is similar.[1]

Form which is a self-sufficient substantial existent does not
exist; therefore, the establishment of form as such an entity
is only imputed, it is a non-existent imaginary. This is true
for every phenomenon—the establishment of it as a self-
sufficient substantial existent is a non-existent imaginary.
No phenomenon is a self-sufficient substantial existent.
Indeed, form is self-sufficiently apprehensible in the sense
that in order to ascertain it by valid cognition one need not
ascertain by valid cognition any other phenomenon which is
a different entity from it. However, form is not self-
sufficient. Hypothetically, a self-sufficient impermanent
phenomenon would be one that did not depend on its
causes and conditions, for being self-sufficient implies a
non-dependence on any other phenomenon. Since form and
all impermanent phenomena are products, produced from
their causes and conditions, they must depend on other
phenomena and are not self-sufficient substantial existents.

Further, permanent phenomena are not self-sufficient
substantial existents. Although they do not depend on production from causes and conditions, permanent phenomena
do depend on imputation by thought consciousnesses. They
are neither self-sufficient nor self-sufficiently apprehensible.
Permanent phenomena, with the exception of thoroughly
established phenomena, are included as existent imaginaries. They are imaginary in the sense that they are *merely*
imputed, but they are nonetheless existents because they are
observed by valid cognizers.

The most important non-existent imaginary is a self-
sufficient person. Like all phenomena, persons do not exist
self-sufficiently; however, it is the Sūtra School assertion

---

[1] *Ibid.*, p. 413.

that through the ordinary conception of themselves as self-sufficient persons sentient beings are drawn into contaminated actions and suffering. A self-sufficient person does not exist and as a non-existent it cannot be destroyed or overcome. However, the *conception* of a self-sufficient person does exist and, as an impermanent phenomenon created from causes and conditions, when those causes and conditions are exhausted the conception too will cease to arise.

In the Sūtra School presentation of the path structure, the conception of a self-sufficient person is the main object of abandonment (*spang bya*), for it is the root ignorance that binds one in cyclic existence. The actual antidote to this root ignorance is the wisdom realizing the person's lack of being a self-sufficient entity. To the end of developing this wisdom, the main object of meditation (*sgom bya*), according to the Proponents of the Sūtra School, is the person's lack of being a self-sufficient entity. Placing emphasis on this point of doctrine the Go-mang *Collected Topics* points out that a person who is a self-sufficient substantial existent is a non-existent imaginary.

The remaining division of imputed existents, thoroughly established phenomena, are actual imputed existents. Emphasizing the main object of meditation of the Proponents of the Sūtra School, the Go-mang *Collected Topics* says:

> There is a mode of positing a thoroughly established phenomenon in relation to each and every phenomenon because the non-establishment of an exalted knower of all aspects as a self of persons is a thoroughly established phenomenon in relation to an exalted knower of all aspects and, accordingly, the reasoning for all phenomena is similar.[1]

A self of persons does not exist. No phenomenon, neither a person nor any other phenomenon, is a self of persons in the sense that no phenomenon is a self-sufficient person. The Proponents of the Sūtra School assert a selflessness of per-

---

[1] *Ibid.*

sons which is a person's lack of being a self-sufficient substantial existent, but they do not assert a selflessness of phenomena other than persons. However, the assertion that
persons are not self-sufficient implies that other phenomena
are not objects of use of such a person. Still, in the Sūtra
School the main object of meditation is the person's non-
establishment as a self of persons, the person's lack of being
self-sufficient. Moreover, as the passage from the Go-mang
Collected Topics says, "The reasoning for all phenomena is
similar." No phenomenon is established as a self of persons.
A person's non-establishment as a self of persons is a thoroughly established phenomenon. Selflessnesses are actual
imputed existents in that they are permanent phenomena
and must be imputed by a thought consciousness, but by
calling them "thoroughly established phenomena" the Go-
mang *Collected Topics* emphasizes the importance of selflessnesses as objects of inference and as objects of meditation.

REMARKS

The Go-mang *Collected Topics* generously provides not only
the system of substantial and isolate phenomena formulated
by Cha-ba-chö-ĝyi-šeng-gay but also an alternative interpretation of substantial and imputed existents. Within explaining the topics and issues involved in the study of substantial
and imputed existents, the Go-mang text furnishes the student with an introduction and brief explication of selflessness in the Sūtra School system. This topic is dealt with in
detail in later portions of the program of monastic training.

Cha-ba-chö-ĝyi-šeng-gay's system of substantial and isolate phenomena is a cogent and valuable summation of
many of the important issues presented in the Collected
Topics literature. Without a firm grasp of the material
explained in the previous chapters one cannot understand
the various classes of phenomena in terms of whether they
are or are not themselves, etc. The general application of an
object (that is, what it pervades and what pervades it—its
comparison to other objects) is irrelevant in the analysis of

an object as a substantial or isolate phenomenon. Rather, in "Substantial and Isolate Phenomena" the analysis centers on the nature of the object itself, understood from the point of view of its self-isolate. Discriminating objects on the basis of whether or not they are themselves and on the basis of whether non-it is or is not it, the student is forced to categorize the objects presented in previous chapters. In so doing, the student makes firm his understanding of these objects and learns that an object may be said to exist in any of several different contexts.

Part Three
Conclusion

15 Conclusion

One of the main lessons of reasoning learned in "The Introductory Path of Reasoning" is the difference between copulative associations and pervasions. For instance, one learns very early on that object of knowledge is a permanent phenomenon, but that it is not the case that whatever is an object of knowledge is necessarily a permanent phenomenon. A copulative association is expressed in a sentence of the form:

   p is a q,

whereas a pervasion is expressed in a sentence of the form:

   Whatever is a p is necessarily a q.

In this system of reasoning, what is being distinguished is not copulative *statements* and *statements* of pervasion, but the *actual* copulative association between two phenomena represented by the letters "p" and "q" and the corresponding pervasion. What is of primary importance to the Collected Topics logicians is whether p actually is or is not a q and whether or not whatever is a p is necessarily a q, not just the manner of expressing these states of being of actual phenomena.

Of course, the emphasis in this form of Buddhist reasoning on the *qualities* of phenomena has important implications for the manner of expressing those phenomena. The verbal indication, the term or terms that express a certain phenomenon, identifies and limits the topic under discussion not only in the sense of clearly establishing the boundaries of pervasion of that phenomenon but also in the sense of denoting a phenomenon having its own unique entity. Every phenomenon is unique in the sense that it alone is one with itself. No matter how a phenomenon is expressed, only it is one with it. This is one angle on the expression of phenomena in copulative sentences. Another is that a phenomenon, in its own specific nature, may have a nature different from everything which illustrates that phenomenon. For instance, different, in its own specific nature, is one; yet, whatever phenomena are different are necessarily not one.

This situation implies that the manner of expressing a subject has a profound impact on the conclusions that one may be able to draw. For instance, it is said in this system of reasoning that permanent phenomenon and impermanent phenomenon are mutually exclusive. According to the way mutually exclusive phenomena are defined, this implies that there is nothing which is both a permanent phenomenon and an impermanent phenomenon. This is thoroughly established, for there is nothing among all existents that is on the one hand a permanent phenomenon and on the other an impermanent one. However, this does not mean that an impermanent phenomenon cannot have the quality of a phenomenon which is itself, when considered alone, a permanent phenomenon. For instance, it is commonly said that a pot is an object of knowledge. A pot itself is an impermanent phenomenon, but object of knowledge is a permanent phenomenon; yet, a pot is said to be an object of knowledge in the sense of being suitable as an object of an awareness. Thus, a pot exemplifies another phenomenon which is itself a permanent phenomenon, but a pot is not a permanent phenomenon.

Similarly, a pillar is an impermanent phenomenon, and a pillar is a pillar's isolate. Since a pillar's isolate is a permanent phenomenon, does this imply that a pillar is a permanent phenomenon? It might seem as though a pillar is on the one hand an impermanent phenomenon because of being created from causes and conditions and on the other hand a permanent phenomenon because of being a pillar's isolate. However, such is not the case. Saying that a pillar is a pillar's isolate does not imply that a pillar is a permanent phenomenon. In terms of verbalization, it means that the term expressing a pillar is suitable to be used as the subject nominative in a copulative sentence which has a term expressing a permanent phenomenon (i.e., a pillar's isolate) as the predicate nominative.

With respect to the manner of existence, this association means that an impermanent phenomenon may exist as and demonstrate the quality of something else which is itself a permanent phenomenon. Saying that a pillar is a pillar's isolate is from one point of view an ontological statement, for it declares that a pillar exists as itself and does not mix with other phenomena. It intends only that a pillar is exactly the same as a pillar in all respects. From another point of view, this association is epistemological, for within the framework of this system of reasoning it implies a difference between the way in which one can understand a pillar and the way in which one can understand a pillar's isolate. A pillar is an appearing object of a direct perceiver (that is, a directly perceiving consciousness) whereas a pillar's isolate is an appearing object of a thought consciousness. One can feel the hardness and obstructiveness of a pillar, but a pillar's isolate, as the abstraction non-non-one with a pillar, must be observed conceptually. Thus, in what sense is it that a pillar is a pillar's isolate? It is in the ontological sense, in the sense that a pillar exists as reversed from non-one with a pillar.

Reconciling the apparent contradiction between saying that a phenomenon is impermanent yet demonstrates a quality of another phenomenon which, on its own, is a permanent phenomenon is essential for understanding this system of reasoning. In order to make this reconciliation one must understand the different contexts in which it may be said that *p* is a *q*. This involves a firm grasp of the difference between copulative associations and pervasions.

COPULATIVE ASSOCIATIONS

Now the question arises: "In this system of reasoning what is the meaning of saying that *p* is a *q*?" For instance, it is said:

> Pot is a generality,

and it is also said:

> Pot is an impermanent phenomenon.

In these two cases, it appears that the *p*-term, the grammatical subject, "pot", is used in radically different ways.

In the first case, "Pot is a generality," "pot" is used as an *abstract singular term*.[1] It is abstract in that it refers to an abstract entity, and it is singular in that it refers to only one thing. That is, it refers to pots *collectively*, to pot considered alone. In this sense, "pot" is not used to refer to each and every pot, for it is not the case that every pot is a generality. For instance, a single pot held in one's hand is not a generality of many pots. What is intended in this sentence is that pot alone, the singular phenomenon, is a generality. This use of "pot" as an abstract singular term is comparable to the use of the phrase "the triangle" in the sentence:

> The triangle is the principal figure of Euclidian geometry.

Here "the triangle" serves as an abstract singular term, referring to the triangle as such, not to each and every triangle.

---

[1] The system of classification used in this section is drawn from John Stuart Mill, *A System of Logic, Ratiocinative and Inductive* (New York: Harper & Brothers, 1874), especially the section on names and propositions, pp. 32-34.

In the second case above, "Pot is an impermanent phenomenon," on first consideration it appears that "pot" is being used exclusively as a *concrete general term*. Such a term is concrete because the range of things it applies to are concrete entities, and it is general because it refers to many things, *each and every* pot. This is comparable to the use of the phrase "the triangle" in the sentence:

The triangle is a three-sided figure.

Here "the triangle" is used to refer to each and every triangle, explaining something about the nature of every triangle. However, these cases are not strictly comparable, for it seems that the use of the term "pot" in the sentence, "Pot is an impermanent phenomenon," as used in the Collected Topics tradition, is not exclusively used as a concrete general term. Rather, it appears that in this sentence "pot" functions simultaneously as an abstract singular term and as a concrete general term. It functions as an abstract singular term in that it says that pot, as such, is an impermanent phenomenon. At the same time, it seems to function also as a concrete general term, referring to each and every pot as in the proposition that all pots are impermanent phenomena.

Another approach to this issue of the meaning of the grammatical subject in a copulative structure as used in the Collected Topics system is the reckoning of *predication*, that is, looking at what is said in the grammatical predicate about the subject. In this regard, there is a distinction made between *collective predication* and *distributive predication*. Collective predication means that the predicate is applied to the subject collectively; that is, the predicate says something about the subject collectively, considered alone in its own specific nature and apart from the many things which exemplify it. This is clearly the case in the examples:

Pot is a generality

and

The triangle is the principal figure of Euclidian geometry.

In each of these cases the predicate says something about the subject considered alone; it is applied to the subject collectively. Also, in each of these cases the subject functions as an abstract singular term, denoting the subject as such. Often for cases in which the subject is used as an abstract singular term, the predication is said to be collective.

Distributive predication means that the predicate is applied to the subject distributively; that is, the predicate says something about the subject distributively, about each and every occurrence of the subject. For instance, in the sentences:

Pot is an impermanent phenomenon

and

The triangle is a three-sided figure

it appears that the predication is distributive. Each and every pot is an impermanent phenomenon and each and every triangle is a three-sided figure. Also, in each of these cases the subject may be said to be serving as a concrete general term, referring to each and every occurrence of that subject. Thus, in many cases in which the subject functions as a concrete general term, the predication is said to be distributive.

In the Collected Topics system, the predication of an *acceptable* copulative sentence may never be exclusively distributive. For instance, there is the sentence, fallacious according to the rules of this system:

Definition is a triply qualified substantial existent.

Here, if the predication is interpreted as distributive, the sentence says that each and every definition is a triply qualified substantial existent. Although this is true, in debate one cannot interpret this sentence as having exclusively distributive predication and, thus, one cannot accept it. If the predication is taken as collective, the sentence indicates that definition on its own, taken as an abstract singular term, is a triply qualified substantial existent. This is not true and, thus, is unacceptable, for definition itself is a triply qualified *imputed* existent, a definiendum. Thus, in this system it is not suitable to accept a copulative sentence that must be interpreted as having exclusively distributive predication in order to be accurate. On the other hand, it is suitable to accept a sentence that must be interpreted as having exclusively collective predication.

Thus, it would seem that in this system there are two types of copulative sentences. Clearly, a sentence may have exclusively collective predication and may have a subject which is used as an abstract singular term only. For instance, this is the case in each of the following sentences:

Pot is a generality

and

Pot is one with pot

and

Object of knowledge is a permanent phenomenon.

In none of these sentences may the subject be interpreted as a concrete general term, for it is not the case that each and every pot is a generality, nor that each and every pot is one with pot, nor that each and every object of knowledge is a permanent phenomenon.

Also, it seems that in the Collected Topics tradition a copulative sentence may simultaneously have both collective and distributive predication; that is, have a subject which simultaneously serves as a singular and a general term. For instance, this appears to the case in each of the following sentences:

Pot is an impermanent phenomenon

and

Pot is an object of knowledge

and

Object of knowledge is an existent.

In each of these cases the subject may be understood as an abstract singular term .Pot, itself, is an impermanent phenomenon. Pot, considered alone, is an object of knowledge. Object of knowledge, the singular generality, is an existent. Also, in each of these sentences the subject may be understood as a concrete general term, for every pot is an impermanent phenomenon, every pot is an object of knowledge, and every object of knowledge is an existent. Thus, it appears that each of these sentences succumbs to the fallacy of *equivocation*, for the subjects simultaneously serve as abstract singular terms and as concrete general terms; hence, they are ambiguous and open to misinterpretation.

Clearly, within the normal flow of debate as practiced in the Collected Topics tradition, the predication may appear to change. An example will make this clear. For instance, in the consequence:

> It follows that the subject, pot, is an object of knowledge because of being an impermanent phenomenon,

the (grammatical and logical) subject is used as a concrete and general term (or simultaneously as an abstract singular term and a concrete general term) in relation to both the predicate of the consequence and the reason. Each and every pot is an object of knowledge and each and every pot is an impermanent phenomenon.

Now if a hypothetical Defender says that the reason of this consequence, that pot is an impermanent phenomenon, is not established, the Challenger may say to him:

> It follows that the subject, pot, is an impermanent phenomenon because of being one with pot.

Here the subject clearly seems to equivocate. For, in relation to the predicate of the consequence, "pot" is used as a concrete general term (or, perhaps, simultaneously as both an abstract singular term and as a concrete general term). However, in relation to the reason, "pot" can only be interpreted as an abstract singular term, for only pot, considered alone, is one with pot.

This apparent equivocation gives rise to much debate in the Collected Topics tradition. The Defender may be thinking that he is debating on the nature of a pot, any pot, when suddenly the Challenger switches the predication from distributive to collective to make it clear that the subject is only pot, considered alone as an abstract singular. Many debates revolve around the possibility of such misinterpretation in an attempt to teach the student how to interpret terms properly by context.

In a more careful system of logic there would be a notation to mark the use of the subject as an abstract singular term and the use of it in a way that might be interpreted as a concrete general term. In the Collected Topics system no such notation is made. Still, the Collected Topics logicians are clearly aware of the difference between collective and distributive predication. It would seem that the difference between this system and one that would make a notation for term usage is not so much a difference of doctrine as a difference of methodology. It is like the difference between two paths to the top of a mountain.[1] One approach is a to build a cable car up the side of the mountain for quickest and easiest ascent. By this method the less fit may be able to reach the top of the mountain. Another approach is to leave each to their own power so that everyone who reaches the top of the mountain arrives by his or her own wit and strength. These two approaches reflect different purposes. The guide service will prefer the cable car, but the method of the self-powered produces better mountain-climbers, training students to be wary of details and appearances at every point.

However, there is an interpretation of this last consequence that circumvents the fallacy of equivocation. The problem is that *in relation to the predicate of the consequence* it may be said that "pot" functions both as an abstract singular term and as a concrete general term because pot itself is an impermanent phenomenon and also each and every pot is

---

[1] This analogy was suggested by Prof. James Cargile of the University of Virginia's Department of Philosophy.

an impermanent phenomenon, but *in relation to the reason* such a dual interpretation is not possible because only the abstract singular, pot, is one with pot. However, if this sentence is interpreted as only collectively predicated, then there is no equivocation since the abstract singular, pot, is both an impermanent phenomenon and one with pot. Thus, in order to avoid the fallacy of equivocation the Collected Topics logicians must give priority, if not exclusive acceptance, to the interpretation of the subject in copulative structures as a singular term and as a subject in a sentence having collective predication. The evidence that this is the case is that subjects may be used in a context in which they may be interpreted only as singular terms but never occur in a context in which they may be interpreted only as general terms. Thus, it appears that in the interest of consistency and clarity the subject must be taken as a singular term, even though it may in some contexts reasonably be understood as a general term.

An example of the strength and priority of collective predication in this system is demonstrated in the thesis:

The subject, definition, is a definiendum.

Obviously, here the subject must be taken as an abstract singular term, but this is more than just another example. In this case, *no* definition is a definiendum. It is only the abstract singular, definition, that is a definiendum. This is unlike the case of pot's being a generality, for some pots are generalities and some are not, whereas pot, on its own, certainly is a generality. In any line of reasoning, the interpretation of a subject as an abstract singular term may come into play at any time. For those cases in which the subject appears to function simultaneously as both an abstract singular term and as a concrete general term, the interpretation as a concrete general term is only coincidental and is not the intention of the argument.

Thus, it must be concluded that in all cases the subject in this form of reasoning must be taken as a singular term because of the faults incurred through equivocation and because of the practical priority given to collective predication. Hence, the sentence, "Pot is an impermanent phenomenon," *does not mean* each and every pot is an impermanent phenomenon (though that is true) but must be taken to mean that pot, considered alone, is an impermanent phenomenon. In no case is there fault in taking the subject to be singular, and this is the intention of the system.

However, this is not to say that all subjects in this form of reasoning must be taken as abstract singular terms, for they are not. For instance, the subject may be taken as a *concrete singular term* as in the syllogisms:

> The subject, Shākyamuni Buddha, is not a sentient being because of being a Buddha

and

> The subject, this page, is a product because of being produced from causes and conditions

and

> The subject, the White House, is an impermanent phenomenon because of being a product.

The subjects in these syllogisms are concrete terms because they refer to concrete entities, and they are singular because each applies to only one thing. Thus, the subjects used in the Collected Topics forms of arguments may be either abstract or concrete, but they are always singular.

Now the obvious question is, what about dual or multiple subjects such as the two—a pillar and a pot? These cases seem to pose no special problem to the rule of collective predication. Clearly, such subjects may be used in copulative sentences having collective predication. For instance, there is the thesis:

> The subjects, the two—a pillar and a pot, are one with the two—a pillar and a pot.

Here the predication is applied to the subject collectively, it says something about the subjects considered as a unit. Only

786 Debate in Tibetan Buddhism

the two—a pillar and a pot—taken together are one with the two—a pillar and a pot. It is difficult to say that dual or multiple subjects are used as *singular* terms; however, in a sentence having collective predication, they are logically (though not grammatically) singular, for they are taken together (not as one, for they are separate and different) as a single set.

If the *p*-term, the subject, is always a singular term in this system of reasoning, what does this imply about the *q*-term, the predicate separate from the verb? In sentences such as:

Pot is a generality

and

Uncomposed space is a permanent phenomenon,

the predicates are grammatically singular, but are used as *abstract general terms*. They are abstract terms because the range of things they refer to—generalities and permanent phenomena—are abstract entities, and they are general terms because each applies to a number of things. In the first case it is being said that pot is one among many generalities, and in the second case it is being said that uncomposed space is one among many permanent phenomena. More striking is the example:

Object of knowledge is an existent.

Even though there are no existents which are not objects of knowledge (that is, objects of knowledge are not just some portion from among all existents), this sentence claims that object of knowledge is *an* existent. Here "object of knowledge" clearly is being taken collectively, as an abstract singular term. In this sense, there are many objects of knowledge other than the abstract singular, object of knowledge, for it is just one existent among many.

In sentences having a dual or multiple subject the *q*-term or predicate is not usually grammatically singular. For example, there is the thesis:

The subjects, the two—a pillar and a pot, are objects of knowledge of which being [them] is not possible.

Here the predicate is plural, but this case is essentially similar to the cases in which the subject is grammatically singular in that the predicate, here as in all cases, is an instantiation. That is, the predicate claims that the subject is an exemplification of something. For instance, in the sentences:

Pot is *a* generality

and

Object of knowledge is *an* existent

and

The two—a pillar and a pot—are [a case of] objects of knowledge of which being [them] is not possible,

the claim is that pot demonstrates the nature of a generality, that object of knowledge has the quality of being an existent, and so forth. Whether or not there are phenomena other than pot which are generalities or phenomena other than object of knowledge which are existents is irrelevant to this claim. That is, it is not being said that pot is an *instance* of generality (though that is true), or that object of knowledge is an *instance* of existent (for it is not). Rather, it is only being said, for example, that pot demonstrates the characteristics of a generality and is a generality.

The remaining portion of a copulative sentence, "*p* is a *q*," is the copula, the verb "is" or "are". In this system of reasoning, "is" never means "is identical to". For, in the Collected Topics tradition, the meaning of "is identical to" is that a phenomenon is exactly the same in both name and meaning as itself. Thus, only a pot *is identical to* a pot. Rather, in this system, the copula *always* means:

has the quality of being

or

has the nature of being.

Thus, the assertion that pot is an object of knowledge means that pot has the quality of being an object of knowledge in the sense that it is suitable as an object of an awareness and thereby demonstrates the nature of an object of knowledge. Similarly, pot is said to be an impermanent phenomenon because it has the nature of being momentary.

Moreover, as in the presentation of substantial and isolate phenomena, it is said that pot is *a* pot. This does not mean that pot is self-identical. If that were the case, then all phenomena would be substantial phenomena, for all phenomena are one with themselves. This statement means that the abstract singular, pot, has the quality of being a pot—it is a bulbous, flat-based phenomenon able to perform the function of holding water—and that it demonstrates the nature of being a pot. It is from this point of view that it is said that definition is not a definition. Of course, definition is definition, for it is self-identical, one with itself. However, definition is not *a* definition, for it does not have the quality of being a definition. All phenomena are self-identical, but they are not necessarily themselves in the sense of being exemplifiers of themselves.

One result of the nature of copulative sentences in this system is that they cannot be used reliably to bear the relation of transitivity. A relation is transitive if whenever x has a certain relation to y and y has the same relation to z, then x has the same relation to z. An example of such a transitive relation is "being an ancestor of". If x is an ancestor of y and y is an ancestor of z, then x too is an ancestor of z. Transitivity cannot always be communicated by the type of copulative sentences used in the Collected Topics system. For instance, a pot is a pot's isolate and a pot's isolate is a permanent phenomenon; however, a pot is not a permanent phenomenon. Still, the fact that these sentences cannot bear transitivity does not mean that the Collected Topics logicians reject the principle of transitivity. Rather, it is evidence that the copulative structure in this system is not one of equivalence, for equivalence between three things entails transitivity between them. Being something does not mean equalling that thing. More correctly, being something means having the basic quality of that thing. As will be explained below, within this system of reasoning transitivity is handled by pervasions.

At this point the evidence suggests that in the Collected Topics tradition the meaning of a copulative sentence is that some phenomenon p has the quality of being phenomenon q, that within this sentence the term "p" is used as a singular term (in a sentence with collective predication), and that phenomenon p is an instantiation of phenomenon q. For instance, the assertion that pot is an impermanent phenomenon means that pot has the quality of being an impermanent phenomenon, that "pot" is used here as a singular term, and that pot is an instantiation of impermanent phenomena.

The pressing question that remains is, "What is the nature of the abstract singular pot that is the subject of this assertion?" Of course, many things have been said about the nature of this subject—it is an object of knowledge, it is an impermanent phenomenon, it is matter, it is able to perform the function of holding water, it is a pot. "Pot" in this sentence does not refer to each and every pot, and in a sense neither does it refer to the collection of all pots as a gross gathering of all pots in existence. Also, here "pot" does not refer to the *idea* of a pot, for an idea, as a mental abstraction, is an appearing object of a thought consciousness and a permanent phenomenon. Rather, in this type of sentence, "pot" refers to pot as such, taken not as a whole, but as the singular generality.

The qualities of a phenomenon as a singular entity may be distinct from the qualities of the illustrations of that phenomenon. For instance, pot is a generality of a gold pot, but an illustration of pot such as a bulbous, flat-based phenomenon which is made from gold and is able to perform the function of holding water is not a generality of a gold pot.

PERVASIONS

If, in this system of reasoning, the predication of a copulative sentence is always collective, being applied to the subject as a singular term, then how is distributive information
about phenomena communicated? It is by pervasions, which
assert something about each and every occurrence of a phenomenon. In a statement of pervasion, a sentence of the
form:

Whatever is a p is necessarily a q,

the pervasion says something about each and every occurrence of the p-phenomenon (though not necessarily about
each and every occurrence of the q-phenomenon). For
instance, in a pervasion such as:

Whatever is a functioning thing is necessarily an
impermanent phenomenon,

it may be understood that *all* functioning things are *all*
impermanent phenomena, for the comparative extensions of
the two phenomena are just the same; that is, they are mutually inclusive. However, in a pervasion such as:

Whatever is a functioning thing is necessarily an
object of knowledge,

the statement may be understood as *all* functioning things
are *some* objects of knowledge, for the extension of functioning things is lesser than that of objects of knowledge. In no
case may a proper pervasion say something about some of
the p-phenomena but not all. Thus, any correct statement of
pervasion says something about each and every occurrence
of the p-phenomenon.

Because of the distributive nature of pervasions, a statement of pervasion implies copulative sentences; however, it
is not a copulative sentence and does not have the same
value as a copulative sentence. For instance, the statement of
pervasion:

Whatever is a pot is necessarily a functioning thing

implies that a gold pot is a functioning thing, that a copper pot is a functioning thing, that a clay pot is a functioning thing, and so forth. The emphasis of the first part of the pervasion, "whatever is a pot ... ", is not just on pot itself (though, in this case, it does apply to the abstract singular pot) but on all things which are pots. Here the word "whatever" stands in place of the points of emphasis—for a gold pot, a copper pot, a clay pot, and so on, including pot itself. It is also suitable to translate statements of pervasion into the form of English conditional sentences. For instance, the claim that whatever is a pot is necessarily a functioning thing may be rendered into the form:

If something is a pot, then it is necessarily a functioning thing.

In this form, the word "something" stands in place of the points of emphasis. The intention of this pervasion is not just the nature of pot itself (though that is included because pot, considered alone, is a pot) but anything which is suitable to be used correctly as a subject in a copulative sentence ending, "is a pot". A gold pot *is a pot*, a copper pot *is a pot*, a clay pot *is a pot*, and so forth. The pervasion implies: since a gold pot, a copper pot, and so forth are pots, they are functioning things.

Because the objects intended by a pervasion are not just the phenomenon stated in the first part of the sentence but those things which are that phenomenon, pervasions are not the equivalent of copulative sentences. They imply copulative sentences but are not themselves copulative sentences. This nature of pervasions and the universal quantification they entail enable the Tibetan logicians to handle with pervasions some forms of reasoning that cannot be handled reliably by copulative sentences. For instance, the relation of transitivity—whenever a first thing has a certain relation to a second, the second to a third, and the first has that same relation to the third—holds for *any* phenomena so stated within a series of three correct pervasions. For instance, whatever is a pot is necessarily an impermanent phenomenon and whatever is an impermanent phenomenon is necessarily an object of knowledge; therefore, whatever is a pot is necessarily an object of knowledge. This type of transitivity holds true for any three phenomena so stated within correct pervasions regardless of their relative comparisons; they need not be mutually inclusive.

Since pervasions imply copulative sentences having subjects drawn from the phenomena over which the pervasion is quantified, this sequence of reasoning also works for phenomena which are not themselves. For instance, in saying that whatever is the definiendum of that which is able to perform a function is necessarily the isolate of functioning thing, the object of implication is functioning thing itself, for functioning thing is the only thing which is the definiendum of that which is able to perform a function. This pervasion implies that since functioning thing is that, it is also the isolate of functioning thing.

In the same way, there is the sequence of reasoning: whatever is the definiendum of that which is able to perform a function is necessarily the isolate of functioning thing and whatever is the isolate of functioning thing is necessarily one with functioning thing; therefore, whatever is the definiendum of that which is able to perform a function is necessarily one with functioning thing. This transitive sequence implies that, since functioning thing is the definiendum of that which is able to perform a function, it is the isolate of functioning thing and, since it is the isolate of functioning thing, it is one with functioning thing. As a statement of pervasion, the first sentence implies that *anything at all* which is the definiendum of that which is able to perform a function is necessarily the isolate of functioning thing. This is the *distributive potency* of pervasions. It is irrelevant that functioning thing is the only phenomenon which is the definiendum of that which is able to perform a function.

Statements of pervasion imply copulative sentences precisely because they are universally quantified. In saying that whatever is a pot is necessarily a functioning thing, this means that a gold pot is a functioning thing, a copper pot is a functioning thing, and so on. The copulative associations that may be predicated from a pervasion draw their subjects from among the phenomena specified in the first part of the pervasion. Of course, statements of pervasion do not merely imply copulative sentences, for they manifestly reveal information about the relative extensions of the two principals that comprise its components. Saying that whatever is a pot is necessarily a functioning thing makes the point that pots are pervaded by being functioning things. *All* pots are functioning things. In a correct pervasion the extensions of the two phenomena may be equal or the extension of the first phenomenon may be lesser.

In this translation system, the word "necessarily" in statements of pervasion is an interpretive translation, for the Tibetan term used, *"khyab"*, and its Sanskrit antecedent, *"vyāpti"*, more literally mean "pervades". However, the Tibetan term indicating necessity (*dgos*) is used interchangeably in these statements with the term meaning "pervades". Thus, the interpretive use of the word "necessarily" does not go against the Tibetan understanding. Moreover, in his commentary on *The Wheel of Reasons* (*hetu-chakra, phyogs chos 'khor lo*), Den-dar-hla-ram-ba explains that the association of pervasion between the sign and the predicate to be proven "is objectively established, and is not established by one's mere wish. ... If pervasion were established through one's mere wish, then even contradictory signs would become correct provers."[1] The correct pervasion of the reason by the predicate to be proven is a necessary association of those two phenomena. It is objectively established, from the side

---

[1] Ḍen-dar-hla-ram-ba (*bstan dar lha ram pa*), *Precious Lamp Illuminating the Treatise "Wheel of Properties of the Subject" Formulated by Dignāga* (*phyogs glang gis mdzad pa'i phyogs chos 'khor lo zhes pa'i bstan bcos gsal bar byed pa'i rin chen sgron me*), Collected Works of Bstan-dar Lha-ram of A-lag-sha, Vol. 1 (New Delhi: Lama Guru Deva, 1971), 143.5-6.

of the objects, and is not built up out of one's subjective interpretation or imagination. Pervasion is a necessary association of two related phenomena and predicated from the natures of those phenomena.

Also, the interpretive use of the word "necessarily" in translating pervasions is in accordance with the concepts of necessity familiar to Western scholarship. In Aristotle's system of reasoning, a proposition is necessary if it is true at all times. This is the chronological understanding of necessity. The way that pervasion is understood in this system of reasoning satisfies the chronological requirement of necessity, for an association of pervasion is understood to be true at all times. For instance, whatever is a product is necessarily an impermanent phenomenon, and there is no time when something is a product but not an impermanent phenomenon.

In the understanding of Gottfried Wilhelm Liebniz, the seventeenth and eighteenth century German philosopher and mathematician, a proposition is necessary if its negation is not possible. Again the concept of pervasion agrees with this interpretation of necessity, for the negation of a pervasion is not possible. For example, if the proposition, "Whatever is a product is an impermanent phenomenon," is negated to form the proposition, "It is not the case that whatever is a product is an impermanent phenomenon," then one is forced to support this negation by demonstrating something which is a product but is not an impermanent phenomenon. In the system of ontology presented in the Collected Topics texts, such a thing is radically impossible. More generally, the negation of any correct pervasion is not possible. Thus, the concept of pervasion tendered in this system of reasoning is understood as a *necessary* association of the sign and the predicate, and it is suitable to use the interpretive term "necessarily" to communicate this association.

The Collected Topics system focuses on the qualities of phenomena and on the comparative associations of those phenomena. Through the use of both copulative sentences and statements of pervasion, this system is intentional, for it analyzes the essential defining characteristics of phenomena, and it is also extensional, for it investigates the quantitative extensions of phenomena on their own and in comparison to each other.

THE ALLIANCE OF COPULATIVE ASSOCIATIONS AND PERVASIONS IN THE COLLECTED TOPICS TRADITION

The purpose of this section is to demonstrate the way in which copulative sentences and statements of pervasion are allied in this system to communicate information about phenomena both as singulars, considered alone, and as universals, applying to their instantiations. This will be accomplished by a study of the variety of ways in which it may be said that *p* is a *q* and that *p* is not a *q*.[1] The information presented in this section is drawn entirely from "The Introductory Path of Reasoning" and, though this data is well understood by the debaters within the tradition, this way of organizing the material is not found within the system.

THE CONTEXTS IN WHICH P IS A Q

According to the information found in this system, *p* is a *q* within one of four different contexts. These various ways in which one phenomenon is another are discriminated by the comparative pervasion or lack of it that exists between those same two phenomena. The four contexts are:

1 *p* is a *q*, and whatever is a *p* is necessarily a *q*.
2 *p* is a *q*, but whatever is a *p* is not necessarily a *q*.
3 *p* is a *q*, but except for *p* itself, whatever is a *p* is necessarily not a *q*.
4 *p* is a *q*, but whatever is a *p* is necessarily not a *q*.

---

[1] This organization of the variety of contexts in which it may be said that *p* is a *q* and that *p* is not a *q* was first formulated by Professors Jeffrey Hopkins and Donald Lopez.

These contexts relate to the information that was given in the chapter on subjects (pp. 75-98). They demonstrate the difference between copulative associations and pervasions by showing that the mere fact that there is a copulative association, p is a q, does not serve to identify anything about the comparative boundaries of pervasion between p and q.

Context 1: p *is a* q, *and Whatever Is a* p *Is Necessarily a* q

This is the most normal context in the sense that it is what one would most expect. However, one cannot say that it is the most normal context in terms of prevalence, for such is indeterminate.

This case may be subdivided into two types: (1) those that are mutually inclusive and (2) those that have three possibilities.

Context 1, Variety 1: Mutually Inclusive Phenomena

An example of the first type is product (p) and impermanent phenomenon (q). Product is an impermanent phenomenon and since product and impermanent phenomenon are mutually inclusive, whatever is a product is necessarily an impermanent phenomenon (and whatever is an impermanent phenomenon is necessarily a product).

It may be helpful in considering these four different contexts to represent them diagrammatically, by use of Euler diagrams, invented by the eighteenth-century Swiss mathematician Leonhard Euler. These show the comparison of two things by (a) setting a smaller circle inside a larger one, showing two circles (b) equally extensive with each other, (c) totally apart from each other, or (d) overlapping with each other. The procedure here will be to represent diagrammatically: (1) that p is a q, (2) the comparative boundaries of pervasion between p and q, and (3) then to combine these two factors into a single diagram.

Thus, the fact that product (*p*) is an impermanent phenomenon (*q*) is represented in Figure 1 by placing the letter "*p*" representing product, as such, within a circle W*q* representing whatever is an impermanent phenomenon or all impermanent phenomena.

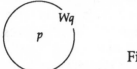

Figure 1

This diagram is meant to show that *p*, product, is a *q*, an impermanent phenomenon. This means that product as such is one among many different impermanent phenomena. In this figure the letter "*p*" represents product in isolation from all else that is not exactly the same as product in both name and meaning. The notation "W*q*" marks the circle, the extension of which is all impermanent phenomena. Since product and impermanent phenomenon are mutually inclusive, there is nothing which is one but not the other; however, product, from the point of view of its self-isolate, is only one among many different things which are impermanent phenomena. Figure 1 demonstrates only that "product" is suitable to be used as a subject in a copulative sentence ending with the predicate, "is an impermanent phenomenon". That is, product is an impermanent phenomenon.

It may be noted ancillarily, although it is not cogent to this discussion, that *q* is also a *p*, impermanent phenomenon is also a product. This is shown in Figure 2.

Figure 2

Here "W*p*" marks the circle defining the extension or boundaries of pervasion of products. That is, all products are encompassed within the perimeters of the circle W*p*, whatever is a product. Since impermanent phenomenon is a product, the letter "*q*" representing impermanent phenomenon, as such, is placed within the perimeters of circle *Wp*.

In comparing the relative boundaries of pervasion of product and impermanent phenomenon, the extension of each of these is precisely the same. This fact is represented in Figure 3. Here the circles are marked "*Wp*", representing whatever is a *p* or whatever is a product, and "*Wq*", representing whatever is a *q* or whatever is an impermanent phenomenon. As mutually inclusive phenomena, their extensions or comparative boundaries of pervasion are just the same, for whatever is the one is necessarily the other. Thus, Figure 3 shows two circles marking the same space.[1]

Wp   *Wq*

Figure 3

Although Figure 3 shows that whatever is a product is necessarily an impermanent phenomenon and that whatever is an impermanent phenomenon is necessarily a product, it does not show anything about whether or not *p* is a *q* nor about whether or not *q* is a *p*. These are shown by Figures 1 and 2. Figure 1 shows that product (*p*) is an impermanent phenomenon (*q*) and Figure 2 shows that impermanent phenomenon is a product. However, Figures 1 and 2 do not show anything about the comparative boundaries of pervasion of product and impermanent phenomenon. The information represented in these three figures may be combined into a fourth which shows both the comparative pervasions of the two and that *p* is a *q* and *q* is a *p*. The letters "*p*" and "*q*" are placed within the intersection of *Wp*, whatever is a *p*, and *Wq*, whatever is a *q*, to show that *p*, product, is both a

---

[1] These charts do not illustrate a difference between saying that whatever is a *p* is a *q* and whatever is a *p* is *necessarily* a *q*. There is no special notation to mark necessity. (See pp. 793-794 on necessity.)

product and an impermanent phenomenon and to show that q, impermanent phenomenon, is also both a product and an impermanent phenomenon.

Figure 4

In figure 4, everything which is a product is represented within circle Wp. Similarly, everything which is an impermanent phenomenon is represented within the perimeters of circle Wq. Thus, all products and impermanent phenomena are to be found in the circles Wp and Wq and, since there are no products which are not also impermanent phenomena and no impermanent phenomena which are not also products, the two circles encompass exactly the same extension. In this way a single diagram shows that product (p) is an impermanent phenomenon and impermanent phenomenon (q) is a product as well as that whatever is a product (Wp) is necessarily an impermanent phenomenon and whatever is an impermanent phenomenon (Wq) is necessarily a product.

In summary the four figures are shown together in Chart 1:

Chart 1

p is a *q*.
Context 1: *p* is a *q*, and whatever is a *p* is necessarily a *q*.
First Variety: mutually inclusive phenomena
p represents product.
q represents impermanent phenomenon.
Wp represents whatever is a product.
Wq represents whatever is an impermanent phenomenon.
Product is an impermanent phenomenon, and whatever is a product is necessarily an impermanent phenomenon.

1 *p* is a *q*. Product is an impermanent phenomenon.

2 *q* is a *p*. Impermanent phenomenon is a product.

3 Whatever is a *p* is necessarily a *q*. Whatever is a product is necessarily an impermanent phenomenon, such as a pot. (Whatever is an *q* is necessarily a *p*. Whatever is an impermanent phenomenon is necessarily a product.)

4 All of the above.

This first variety is just as one might expect. Product itself is an impermanent phenomenon, and each and every product is an impermanent phenomenon. However, as was shown earlier, this is not always the case, for a phenomenon considered alone in its own specific nature (as it is referred to in a copulative sentence) may have a nature different from the phenomenon or phenomena which exemplify it.

In the case of product and impermanent phenomenon, the copulative association goes both ways, for not only is product an impermanent phenomenon but also impermanent phenomenon is a product. Even so, it should be noted that this is not the case for all mutually inclusive phenomena. For instance, definiendum and the triply qualified imputed existent are mutually inclusive because they have the relationship of a definiendum and its definition; however, the copulative association is only uni-directional. Definiendum is a triply qualified imputed existent, but the triply qualified imputed existent is not a definiendum because it is a definition. Still, *all* cases of mutually inclusive phenomena such that *p* is a *q* are included within the first of these four contexts, but the order of *p* and *q* must be specified.

Context 1, Variety 2: Phenomena Having Three Possibilities

The second variety, phenomena that have three possibilities, of the first context, in which *p* is a *q* and whatever is a *p* is necessarily a *q*, is exemplified by pot (*p*) and functioning thing (*q*). Pot itself is a functioning thing, and whatever is a pot is necessarily a functioning thing. Here again the order must be specified. Pot is a functioning thing, but functioning thing is not a pot. Also, in this variety the pervasion is uni-directional, for whatever is a pot is necessarily a functioning thing but whatever is a functioning thing is not necessarily a pot. For example, a consciousness or a chair is a functioning thing but not a pot.

As before, these facts may be represented with Euler diagrams. Figure 1 shows the fact that pot (*p*) is a functioning thing. This is shown by placing the letter "*p*" within the circle *Wq*, whatever is a functioning thing, indicating that pot is within the extension of functioning things, it is included among functioning things.

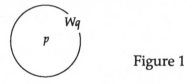

Figure 1

In the next figure the comparative extensions of pot and functioning thing are shown. Here the circle *Wp* represents whatever is a pot or all pots and the circle *Wq* represents whatever is a functioning thing or all functioning things. The circle *Wp* is drawn inside of circle *Wq* to show that the extension of pots is lesser than the extension of functioning things. This shows that whatever is a pot (*Wp*) is necessarily a functioning thing, but whatever is a functioning thing (*Wq*) is not necessarily a pot.

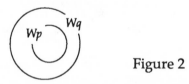

Figure 2

The information represented in these two figures may be shown together in a combined figure. Figure 3 shows that pot (*p*) is both a functioning thing and a pot, that whatever is a pot (*Wp*) is necessarily a functioning thing but whatever is a functioning thing (*Wq*) is not necessarily a pot. In addition, the information that functioning thing (*q*) is a functioning thing but not a pot is shown by.placing the letter "*q*" within the circle *Wq*, indicating that functioning thing itself is within the extension of functioning things, but outside the circle *Wp*, indicating that functioning thing itself is not within the extension of pots.

Figure 3

Variety 2 of Context 1 is still what one would normally expect. Pot itself is a functioning thing and each and every pot is a functioning thing. However, the veneer is beginning to crack. The fact that pots have a lesser extension than functioning things shows that pots and functioning things are in no sense equivalent. This is not like saying that Thomas Jefferson was the third President of the United States or that all products are all impermanent phenomena. This is saying that all pots are some functioning things and indicates that saying that p is a q, that pot is a functioning thing, does not mean that pot and functioning thing are equivalent.

Chart 2 shows all of the figures for this variety together with the essential information:

Chart 2

p is a *q*.
Context 1: *p* is a *q*, and whatever is a *p* is necessarily a *q*.
Second Variety: phenomena having three possibilities
p represents pot.
q represents functioning thing.
Wp represents whatever is a pot.
Wq represents whatever is a functioning thing.
Pot is a functioning thing, and whatever is a pot is necessarily a functioning thing.

1 *p* is a *q*. Pot is a functioning thing.

2 Whatever is a *p* is necessarily a *q*. Whatever is a pot is necessarily a functioning thing, such as a gold pot. (Whatever is a *q* is not necessarily a *p*. Whatever is a functioning thing is not necessarily a pot, such as a consciousness.)

3 All of the above. (Also, *p* is itself and *q* is a *q* but not a *p*. Pot is a pot and functioning thing is a functioning thing but not a pot.)

Context 2: p *Is a* q, *but Whatever Is a* p *Is Not Necessarily a* q

This context may be divided into two varieties: (1) those that have three possibilities and (2) those that have four possibilities. No mutually inclusive phenomena are included here because, for this group, it is specified that whatever is a *p* is not necessarily a *q* and for all mutually inclusive phenomena whatever is a *p* is necessarily a *q*. Further, although it is true for all mutually exclusive phenomena that whatever is a *p* is not necessarily a *q*, they are all included within another context because for them there is contradictory pervasion such that whatever is a *p* is necessarily not a *q*, the pervasion that characterizes the fourth context within this system of classification. Thus, to avoid duplication, mutually exclusive phenomena are not included here.

Context 2, Variety 1: *Phenomena Having Three Possibilities*

This case is demonstrated by object of knowledge (*p*) and permanent phenomenon (*q*). Object of knowledge itself is a permanent phenomenon, but whatever is an object of knowledge is not necessarily a permanent phenomenon. Object of knowledge, from the point of view of its self-isolate (that is, not considering its illustrations and so forth) is a permanent phenomenon. Figure 1 shows this copulative association, for object of knowledge (*p*) is shown within circle *Wq* representing whatever is a permanent phenomenon or the extension of all permanent phenomena.

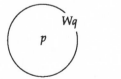

Figure 1

Now since objects of knowledge are of two types, permanent phenomena and impermanent phenomena, whatever is an object of knowledge is not necessarily a permanent phenomenon. For instance, a color or a table is an object of knowledge but not a permanent phenomenon. Figure 2 shows the comparative extensions by representing circle *Wq*, whatever is a permanent phenomenon, as a smaller circle within circle *Wp*, whatever is an object of knowledge.

Figure 2

If one suspects that the meaning of saying that *p* is a *q* is that each and every *p* is a *q*, then it is quite surprising to learn, as this case illustrates, that even though *p* itself may be a *q* this does not mean that all *p*'s are *q*'s. Object of knowledge itself is a permanent phenomenon, but some objects of knowledge are not permanent phenomena. This rather surprising situation arises because "object of knowledge", within the copulative sentence, is used as an abstract singular term and a subject within a sentence having collective predication whereas the pervasion refers to object of knowledge distributively, claiming that some objects of knowledge are not permanent phenomena.

The information from the first two figures is shown together in Figure 3. Also, Figure 3 shows not only that object of knowledge (*p*) is a permanent phenomenon but also that it is an object of knowledge and that permanent phenomenon (*q*) too is both a permanent phenomenon and an object of knowledge.

Figure 3

Chart 3 shows the three figures together with the explanatory information:

Chart 3

p is a *q*.
Context 2: *p* is a *q*, but whatever is a *p* is not necessarily a *q*.
First Variety: phenomena having three possibilities
p represents object of knowledge.
q represents permanent phenomenon.
Wp represents whatever is an object of knowledge.
Wq represents whatever is a permanent phenomenon.
Object of knowledge is a permanent phenomenon, but whatever is an object of knowledge is not necessarily a permanent phenomenon.

1 *p* is a *q*. Object of knowledge is a permanent phenomenon.

2 Whatever is a *p* is not necessarily a *q*. Whatever is an object of knowledge is not necessarily a permanent phenomenon, such as a color. (Whatever is a *q* is necessarily a *p*. Whatever is a permanent phenomenon is necessarily an object of knowledge.)

3 All of the above. (Also, *p* is a *p* and *q* is both a *q* and a *p*. Object of knowledge is an object of knowledge and permanent phenomenon is both a permanent phenomenon and an object of knowledge.)

Context 2, Variety 2: Phenomena Having Four Possibilities

This case is exemplified by impermanent phenomenon (*p*) and different-from-functioning-thing (*q*). Impermanent phenomenon itself is different from functioning thing, but whatever is an impermanent phenomenon is not necessarily different from functioning thing. This is so because functioning thing, and only functioning thing, is an impermanent phenomenon but not different from functioning thing. Figure 1 shows that impermanent phenomenon is different from functioning thing, for *p* (impermanent phenomenon) appears within the enclosure of circle *Wq*, whatever is different from functioning thing.

   Figure 1

Since there are four possibilities between impermanent phenomenon and different-from-functioning-thing, Figure 2 shows the circle *Wp*, whatever is an impermanent phenomenon, and the circle *Wq*, whatever is different from functioning thing, overlapping. The circles do not have exactly the same extensions as do mutually inclusive phenomena, so the one is not concomitant with the other. No pervasion may be predicated between impermanent phenomenon and different-from-functioning-thing; so one circle is not drawn within the other. Also, since there is a common locus of these two phenomena—impermanent phenomenon itself or a pot, a pencil, etc.—the two circles are not completely separate but overlap. Functioning thing alone is in the portion of circle *Wp* outside circle *Wq*. Figure 2 shows the comparative extensions of whatever is an impermanent phenomenon (*Wp*) and whatever is different from functioning thing (*Wq*).

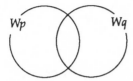

Figure 2

This variety includes all cases for which it may be said that *p* is a *q* and that there are four possibilities between *p* and *q*. This is not to say that all sets of phenomena having four possibilities are included here. For instance, even though blue and the color of cloth have four possibilities, since it cannot be said that blue is the color of cloth or that the color of cloth is blue, they are not included here (or anywhere within the contexts in which it may be said that *p* is a *q*).

The next figure shows the information from the last two figures combined. This case is similar to the last variety in that whereas the phenomenon itself is one thing, it is not the case that everything which is that phenomenon has that same quality. Here impermanent phenomenon (*p*) is different from functioning thing, but, from among impermanent phenomena, only functioning thing itself is not different from functioning thing. Figure 3 shows that impermanent phenomenon is itself, it is an impermanent phenomenon, and that it is also different from functioning thing, for the letter "*p*" appears within the intersection of circle *Wp*, whatever is an impermanent phenomenon, and *Wq*, whatever is different from functioning thing. This figure also shows that different-from-functioning-thing (*q*) is different from functioning thing but not an impermanent phenomenon, for the letter "*q*", representing different-from-functioning-thing, appears within circle *Wq* but outside circle *Wp*.

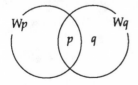

Figure 3

Chart 4 shows these three figures together:

Chart 4

p is a *q*.
Context 2: *p* is a *q*, but whatever is a *p* is not necessarily a *q*.
Second Variety: phenomena having four possibilities
p represents impermanent phenomenon.
q represents different-from-functioning-thing.
Wp represents whatever is an impermanent phenomenon.
Wq represents whatever is different from functioning thing.
Impermanent phenomenon is different from functioning thing, but whatever is an impermanent phenomenon is not necessarily different from functioning thing.

1 *p* is a *q*. Impermanent phenomenon is different from functioning thing.

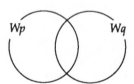

2 Whatever is a *p* is not necessarily a *q*. Whatever is an impermanent phenomenon is not necessarily different from functioning thing, for functioning thing is an impermanent phenomenon but not different from functioning thing. (Whatever is a *q* is not necessarily a *p*. Whatever is different from functioning thing is not necessarily an impermanent phenomenon, such as uncomposed space.)

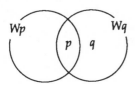

3 All of the above. (Also, *p* is a *p* and *q* is a *q* but not a *p*. Impermanent phenomenon is an impermanent phenomenon and different-from-functioning-thing is different from functioning thing but not an impermanent phenomenon.)

Context 3: p Is a q, but Except For p Itself, Whatever Is a p Is Necessarily Not a q

There is only one type within this context, phenomena having three possibilities. This case is similar to the last one, for it too is an association in which *p* itself is a *q*, but whatever is a *p* is not necessarily a *q*. However, this context is different in that, except for *p* itself, whatever is a *p* is necessarily not a *q*. This case is exemplified by pot (*p*) and pot's isolate (*q*). Pot is pot's isolate, but except for pot itself, whatever is a pot is necessarily not pot's isolate. For example, a gold pot is a pot, but it is not pot's isolate because it is not one with pot. Figure 1 shows the copulative association between pot and pot's isolate, for *p*, pot, is shown within circle *Wq*, whatever is pot's isolate.

Figure 1

It should be understood that pot (*p*) is the only thing within circle *Wq*, for pot is the only thing which is pot's isolate. Since pot is a pot, *p* is a *p*, whatever is pot's isolate (that is, pot itself) is also a pot. However, whatever is a pot is not necessarily pot's isolate. Everything except pot itself, isolated from all of its instances and illustrations, is not pot's isolate. A gold pot, a copper pot, a clay pot, pot's definition, the phenomena mutually inclusive with pot, and so forth

are not pot's isolate. Thus, whatever is pot's isolate is
necessarily a pot, but whatever is a pot is not necessarily
pot's isolate. Figure 2 shows this situation, for the circle *Wq*,
whatever is pot's isolate, is shown within the greater circle
Wp, whatever is a pot.

Figure 2

At this point it is clear that this context applies only to phenomena in the *p* slot which are themselves. Since *p* is a *p*, pot
is a pot, the circle *Wq*, whatever is pot's isolate—meaning
pot itself, may be shown within the confines of circle *Wp*,
whatever is a pot. If pot were not a pot, if *p* were not a *p*, the
circle *Wq* would have to be shown completely outside of
circle *Wp*.

Here again, for one who thinks that the meaning of saying
that *p* is a *q* is that all *p*'s are *q*'s, this case is quite illuminating. Here, even though *p* is a *q*, except for *p* itself, nothing
which is a *p* is also a *q*. This is like the well-known example
of organization membership. The United States of America
(*p*) is a member of the United Nations (*q*), but the individual
states that comprise the United States are not members of
the United Nations. Thus, *p* itself, the United States of
America, is a *q*, but none of the individual members of *p* are
also members of *q*, the United Nations. In the same way, pot
is pot's isolate, but except for pot itself none of the things
which are pots are also pot's isolate. Conversely, for those
who think that if *p* itself is a *q* then it is unlikely that the
individual members of *p* would also be *q*'s, the first context,
in which *p* itself is a *q* and each and every *p* is also a *q*,
would be illuminating.

The information from the last two figures is combined
into Figure 3. Also, this figure shows that pot (*p*) is a pot, for
p is within both circles *Wq*, whatever is pot's isolate, and
Wp, whatever is a pot. However, since pot's isolate (*q*) is

neither a pot nor pot's isolate, it is shown outside of both circle *Wp* and circle *Wq*.

Figure 3

Chart 5 shows these three figures together:

Chart 5

p is a *q*.
Context 3: *p* is a *q*, but except for *p* itself, whatever is a *p* is not necessarily a *q*.
p represents pot.
q represents pot's isolate.
Wp represents whatever is a pot.
Wq represents whatever is pot's isolate.
Pot is pot's isolate, but except for pot itself, whatever is a pot is necessarily not pot's isolate.

1 *p* is a *q*. Pot is pot's isolate.

2 Whatever is a *p* is not necessarily a *q*. Whatever is a pot is not necessarily pot's isolate, such as a gold pot. (Whatever is a *q* is necessarily a *p*. Whatever is pot's isolate is necessarily a pot.)

3 All of the above. (Also, *p* is a *p* and *q* is neither a *p* nor a *q*. Pot is a pot and pot's isolate is neither a pot nor a pot's isolate.)

Note: This figure is the same as Figure 3 of Context 2, Variety 1, but here *p* alone is within the *Wq* circle.

Context 4: p *Is a* q, *but Whatever Is a* p *Is Necessarily Not a* q

Context 4 is exactly the opposite of what one might normally expect, for *p* is a *q* but nothing which is a *p* is a *q*. For one who thinks that the meaning of *p*'s being a *q* is that each and every *p* is a *q*, this context in which *p* is a *q* would be quite surprising. Within the Collected Topics tradition, the fact that *p* is a *q* does not imply anything about the comparative pervasions that exist between *p* and *q*.

This context too has only one type, mutually exclusive phenomena. If whatever is a *p* is necessarily not a *q*, then it follows that whatever is a *q* is necessarily not a *p*. Once this is the case, there can be no common locus of the two, *p* and *q*. If there is no common locus of the two, *p* and *q*, and those two are two different phenomena, then they are necessarily mutually exclusive. Even though *p* and *q* may be mutually exclusive, some phenomenon *p* may be a *q* in the copulative sense. For instance, definition (*p*) is a definiendum (*q*), but there is no common locus of definition and definiendum because even definition itself is not a definition. Rather, definition itself is a definiendum, for there is a definition of definition. Figure 1 shows this copulative association, for definition (*p*) is placed within circle *Wq* representing whatever is a definiendum or the extension of definienda.

Figure 1

In representing the comparative extensions of definition and definiendum or any mutually exclusive phenomena, the circles are completely separate. Since there is nothing which is both, the circles do not overlap, they do not coincide as for phenomena having exactly the same extension, and one circle is not included within the other. In this case the lack of pervasion, whatever is a definition is necessarily not a

definiendum, may be understood to mean that no definitions are definienda. The comparative extensions of definition (*p*) and definiendum (*q*) are shown in Figure 2 where
circle *Wp*, whatever is a definition, is completely separate
from circle *Wq*, whatever is a definiendum.

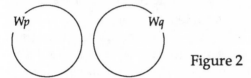

Figure 2

Figure 3 combines the information represented in Figures 1
and 2. This figure shows that definition (*p*) is a definiendum,
that whatever is a definition (*Wp*) is necessarily not a
definiendum, that whatever is a definiendum (*Wq*) is necessarily not a definition, and that definiendum (*q*) is a
definiendum.

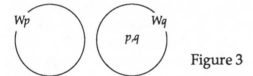

Figure 3

Chart 6 shows these three figures together with the essential
information:

Chart 6

p is a *q*.
Context 4: *p* is a *q*, but whatever is a *p* is necessarily not a *q*.
p represents definition.
q represents definiendum.
Wp represents whatever is a definition.
Wq represents whatever is a definiendum.
Definition is a definiendum, but whatever is a definition is necessarily not a definiendum.

1 *p* is a *q*. Definition is a definiendum.

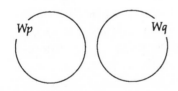

2 Whatever is a *p* is necessarily not a *q*. Whatever is a definition is necessarily not a definiendum, such as that which is able to perform a function. (Whatever is a *q* is necessarily not a *p*. Whatever is a definiendum is necessarily not a definition, such as functioning thing.)

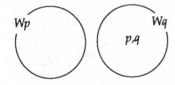

3 All of the above. (Also, *q* is a *q*. Definiendum is a definiendum.)

In summary, in the Collected Topics system it may be said that p is a q within any of four contexts:

1 p is a q, and whatever is a p is necessarily a q.
2 p is a q, but whatever is a p is not necessarily a q.
3 p is a q, but except for p itself, whatever is a p is necessarily not a q.
4 p is a q, but whatever is a p is necessarily not a q.

Only in the first context may it be said that the fact that p is a q indicates that p is equivalent to q in the sense that p is a q, q is a p, and whatever is a p is necessarily a q and vice versa. Nevertheless, it cannot be said that p is whatever q is. As in our example above of product and impermanent phenomenon, even though impermanent phenomenon is the definiendum of the momentary, product is not the definiendum of the momentary but of the created. Within the first context it is only for mutually inclusive phenomena that even this limited "equivalence" may be predicated, for it is not true of the remaining variety within that context, phenomena having three possibilities. Also, from among mutually inclusive phenomena, "equivalence" may be predicated only for those such that not only is it the case that p is a q but also it is true that q is a p. For instance, product and impermanent phenomenon are such mutually inclusive phenomena, whereas definition and the triply qualified substantial existent are not. Thus, only for a very few cases may it be said that p is the equivalent of q. And even for these cases it must be stressed that this sort of "equivalence" does not imply identity, the relationship that a phenomenon bears only to itself.

Thus, the "equivalence" that may be predicated between p and q must be interpreted in a restricted sense. For instance, as mutually inclusive phenomena, product and impermanent phenomenon are different phenomena from the point of view of name but not meaning, and they are the same entity but different isolates. They are equivalent in meaning but they are not *exactly* the same. In the truest sense of equivalence, only p is equivalent to p in that only p is one with *p*. Any phenomenon is exactly the same as itself from the point of view of both name and meaning.

Thus, it is apparent that being something is not, at least not in all senses, the same as being the equivalent of something. Reasoning in this system of logic and epistemology is not equational but copulative and associative.

THE CONTEXTS IN WHICH P IS NOT A Q

Similar to the four contexts in which it may be said that *p* is a *q*, there are three contexts in which it may be said that *p* is not a *q*. As before, these contexts are distinguished by the comparative pervasions or lack of pervasion that exist between those same two phenomena. The three contexts are:

1   *p* is not a *q*, and whatever is a *p* is necessarily not a *q*.
2   *p* is not a *q*, but it is not the case that whatever is a *p* is necessarily not a *q*.
3   *p* is not a *q*, but whatever is a *p* is necessarily a *q*.

These contexts in which *p* is not a *q* also serve to demonstrate the difference between copulative associations and pervasions in this system by showing that the phenomenon *p* itself may have a nature quite different from the natures of the individual things that are *p*'s. As before, these may be demonstrated by Euler diagrams.

Context 1: p Is Not a q, and Whatever Is a p Is Necessarily Not a q

This first context might seem to be the most "normal". Once *p* is not a *q*, naturally one is lead to expect that each and every thing which is a *p* also would not be a *q*. In fact, this is just the case here; it is true for this context only.

Only mutually exclusive phenomena are included within this context. Since it is specified in this context that whatever is a *p* is necessarily not a *q*, according to the method for converting a forward pervasion into a counter-pervasion this implies that whatever is a *q* is necessarily not a *p*. Whatever is the one is necessarily not the other. Thus, there can be no common locus of *p* and *q*, due to which only mutually exclusive phenomena are included here.

This context is exemplified by permanent phenomenon (*p*) and functioning thing (*q*). Permanent phenomenon is not a functioning thing, and whatever is a permanent phenomenon is necessarily not a functioning thing. Figure 1 represents the fact that permanent phenomenon is not a functioning thing, for the letter "*p*", representing permanent phenomenon, appears outside the sphere of the circle W*q*, whatever is a functioning thing.

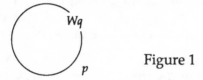

Figure 1

The next figure shows the comparative extensions of permanent phenomena and functioning things. Since they are mutually exclusive and have no common locus, the circles W*p*, whatever is a permanent phenomenon, and W*q*, whatever is a functioning thing, are not concomitant, the one is not included within the other, and they do not overlap. Rather, the two circles are completely separate, showing that nothing is both a permanent phenomenon and a functioning thing.

Figure 2

Figure three combines the information from the first two figures showing that permanent phenomenon (*p*) is not a functioning thing, that whatever is a permanent phenomenon (W*p*) is necessarily not a functioning thing, and that whatever is a functioning thing (W*q*) is necessarily not a permanent phenomenon. This figure also shows that permanent phenomenon (p) is a permanent phenomenon and that functioning thing (q) is a functioning thing.

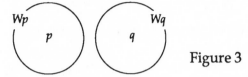

Figure 3

This first context is just what one might normally expect. If p itself is not a q, then one might be lead to believe that this also implies that whatever is a p is necessarily not a q. However, as the latter two contexts will show, this is not always the case.

Chart 7 shows the three figures for this context together and provides the essential information:

Chart 7

p is not a q.
Context 1: p is not a q, and whatever is a p is necessarily not
a q.
p represents permanent phenomenon.
q represents functioning thing.
Wp represents whatever is a permanent phenomenon.
Wq represents whatever is a functioning thing.
Permanent phenomenon is not a functioning thing, and
whatever is a permanent phenomenon is necessarily not a
functioning thing.

1 p is not a q. Permanent phenomenon is not a functioning
thing.

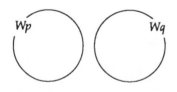

2 Whatever is a p is necessarily
not a q. Whatever is a permanent phenomenon is necessarily not a functioning thing,
such as uncomposed space.
(Whatever is a q is necessarily
not a p. Whatever is a functioning thing is necessarily
not a permanent pheno-
menon, such as a pencil.)

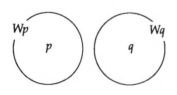

3 All of the above. (Also, p is a p
and q is a q. Permanent phenomenon is a permanent phenomenon and functioning
thing is a functioning thing.)

Context 2: p *Is Not a* q, *but It Is Not the Case That Whatever Is a* p *Is Necessarily Not a* q

In this context, even though *p* itself is not a *q* some of the things that are *p*'s are *q*'s and some are not. This context shows that the fact that *p* is not a *q* does not mean that each and every *p* is not a *q*. There are two varieties within this context: (1) phenomena having three possibilities and (2) phenomena having four possibilities.

Context 2, Variety 1: Phenomena Having Three Possibilities

This case is exemplified by object of knowledge (*p*) and functioning thing (*q*). Object of knowledge is not a functioning thing because of being a permanent phenomenon. However, it is not the case that whatever is an object of knowledge is necessarily not a functioning thing. Some objects of knowledge such as a pot are functioning things, and some such as uncomposed space are not.

Figure 1 shows that object of knowledge is not a functioning thing. Here object of knowledge (*p*) appears outside of circle *Wq*, whatever is a functioning thing.

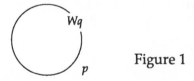

Figure 1

Figure 2 shows the comparative extensions of object of knowledge and functioning thing. The circle *Wq*, whatever is a functioning thing, is wholly included within the circle *Wp*, whatever is an object of knowledge. This shows that each and every functioning thing is an object of knowledge, but some objects of knowledge are not functioning things.

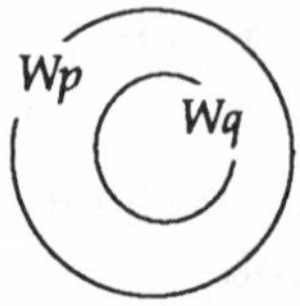

Figure 2

The information from the last two figures is combined together in Figure 3 which shows that object of knowledge (*p*) is not a functioning thing, that whatever is a functioning thing (*Wq*) is necessarily an object of knowledge, and that it is not the case that whatever is an object of knowledge (*Wp*) is necessarily not a functioning thing. This figure also shows that whatever is an object of knowledge is not necessarily a functioning thing, that object of knowledge is an object of knowledge but not a functioning thing, and that functioning thing (*q*) is both a functioning thing and an object of knowledge.

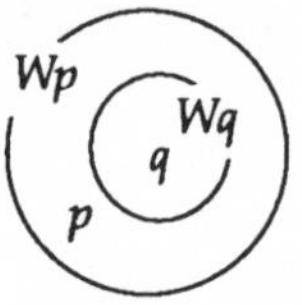

Figure 3

These three figures are shown together in Chart 8:

Chart 8

p is not a *q*.
Context 2: *p* is not a *q*, but it is not the case that whatever is a *p* is necessarily not a *q*.
First Variety: phenomena having three possibilities
p represents object of knowledge.
q represents functioning thing.
Wp represents whatever is an object of knowledge.
Wq represents whatever is a functioning thing.
Object of knowledge is not a functioning thing, but it is not the case that whatever is an object of knowledge is necessarily not a functioning thing.

1 *p* is not a *q*. Object of knowledge is not a functioning thing.

2 It is not the case that whatever is a *p* is necessarily not a *q*. It is not the case that whatever is an object of knowledge is necessarily not a functioning thing, such as a pot. (Also, whatever is a *p* is not necessarily a *q*. Whatever is an object of knowledge is not necessarily a functioning thing, such as uncomposed space.) (Whatever is a *q* is necessarily a *p*. Whatever is a functioning thing is necessarily an object of knowledge.)

3 All of the above. (Also, *p* is a *p* but not a *q* and *q* is both a *q* and a *p*. Object of knowledge is an object of knowledge but not a functioning thing and functioning thing is both a functioning thing and an object of knowledge.)

Context 2, Variety 2: Phenomena Having Four Possibilities

This type is exemplified by functioning thing (*p*) and different-from-functioning-thing (*q*). Functioning thing is not different from functioning thing because it is one with functioning thing, but it is not the case that whatever is a functioning thing is necessarily not different from functioning thing. This means that some functioning things are different from functioning thing. For instance, a pot is a functioning thing and also different from functioning thing.

Figure 1 shows that functioning thing is not different from functioning thing by representing functioning thing (*p*) outside the extension of circle *Wq*, whatever is different from functioning thing.

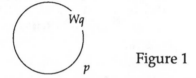

Figure 1

Since there are four possibilities between functioning thing and different-from-functioning-thing, the comparative extensions of these two phenomena are represented by two overlapping circles. Figure 2 illustrates the comparative extensions of *Wp*, whatever is a functioning thing, and *Wq*, whatever is different from functioning thing.

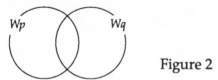

Figure 2

Every area of the two circles has at least one illustration. In the left-hand side of circle *Wp* within the sphere of functioning thing but outside the sphere of different-from-functioning-thing there is functioning thing alone, for it alone is a functioning thing but not different from functioning thing. Within the intersection of the two circles there are functioning things which are different from functioning thing such as a pot, a pillar, a person, and so on. In the right-hand side of circle Wq, within the sphere of different-from-functioning-thing and outside the sphere of functioning thing, are all permanent phenomena, for they are all different from functioning thing and none are functioning things.

Figure 3 combines the information shown in the previous two figures and also shows that functioning thing (p) is a functioning thing but not different from functioning thing and that different-from-functioning-thing (q) is different from functioning thing but not a functioning thing.

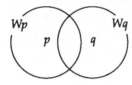

Figure 3

These three figures are shown together with the essential information in Chart 9:

Chart 9

p is not a q.
Context 2: p is not a q, but it is not the case that whatever is a p is necessarily not a q.
Second Variety: phenomena having four possibilities
p represents functioning thing.
q represents different-from-functioning-thing.
Wp represents whatever is a functioning thing.
Wq represents whatever is different from functioning thing.
Functioning thing is not different from functioning thing, but it is not the case that whatever is a functioning thing is necessarily not different from functioning thing.

1 p is not a q. Functioning thing is not different from functioning thing.

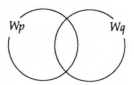

2 It is not the case that whatever is a p is necessarily not a q. It is not the case that whatever is a functioning thing is necessarily not different from functioning thing, such as a pillar. (It is not the case that whatever is a q is necessarily not a p. It is not the case that whatever is different from functioning thing is necessarily not a functioning thing, such as a pillar.)

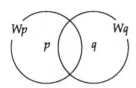

3 All of the above. (Also, *p* is a *p* but not a *q* and *q* is a *q* but not a *p*. Functioning thing is a functioning thing but not different from functioning thing and different-from-functioning-thing is different from functioning thing but not a functioning thing.)

Context 3: p *Is Not a* q, *but Whatever Is a* p *Is Necessarily a* q

In this context, although *p* itself is not a *q*, anything which is a *p* is a *q*. This situation is just the opposite of what one might normally expect. For one who thinks that the meaning of saying that *p* is not a *q* is that each and every *p* is not a *q*, it is surprising to learn that even though *p* itself is not a *q*, each and every *p* is a *q*. Obviously, this context applies only to *p* phenomena which are not themselves in the sense of not being exemplifiers of themselves, as definition does not exemplify the quality of being a definition. There are two varieties within this context: (1) phenomena having three possibilities and (2) mutually inclusive phenomena.

Context 3, Variety 1: Phenomena Having Three Possibilities

An example of this type is pot's isolate (*p*) and pot (*q*). Pot's isolate is not a pot because of being a permanent phenomenon; yet, whatever is pot's isolate is necessarily a pot. This is so because pot itself is the only thing which is pot's isolate and pot is a pot.

Figure 1 shows that pot's isolate (*p*) is not a pot, for it is represented outside the extension of circle *Wq*, whatever is a pot.

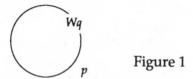

Figure 1

Figure 2 shows the comparative extensions of pot's isolate and pot. Here the circle *Wp*, whatever is pot's isolate, is drawn smaller and included within the circle *Wq*, whatever is a pot. Again, since the only thing which is pot's isolate is pot itself and pot is a pot, everything which is pot's isolate is also a pot. Figure 2 illustrates this situation.

Figure 2

Figure 3 brings together the information illustrated in the last two figures and also shows that pot's isolate (*p*) is neither pot's isolate nor a pot and that pot (*q*) is both pot's isolate and a pot.

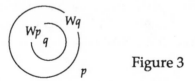

Figure 3

Chart 10 shows these three figures with the essential information:

Chart 10

p is not a *q*.
Context 3: *p* is not a *q*, but whatever is a *p* is necessarily a *q*.
Variety 1: phenomena having three possibilities
p represents pot's isolate.
q represents pot.
Wp represents whatever is pot's isolate.
Wq represents whatever is a pot.
Pot's isolate is not a pot, but whatever is pot's isolate is nec-
essarily a pot.

1 *p* is not a *q*. Pot's isolate is not a
  pot.

2 Whatever is a *p* is necessarily a
  q. Whatever is pot's isolate is
  necessarily a pot. (Whatever is
  a *q* is not necessarily a *p*. Whatever is a pot is not necessarily
  pot's isolate, such as a copper
  pot.)

3 All of the above. (Also, *p* is
  neither a *p* nor a *q* and *q* is both
  a *p* and a *q*. Pot's isolate is neither pot's isolate nor a pot and
  pot is both pot's isolate and a
  pot.)

Context 3, Variety 2: Mutually Inclusive Phenomena

An example of this case is definition (*p*) and the triply qualified substantial existent (*q*), the definition of definition.
Definition itself is not a triply qualified substantial existent
because it is not a definition but a definiendum; yet, whatever is a definition is necessarily a triply qualified substantial existent. Because definition and the triply qualified
substantial existent are a definiendum and its definition
respectively, the eight approaches of pervasion exist
between them, and so they are mutually inclusive. Still,
definition itself, from the point of view of its self-isolate, is
not a triply qualified *substantial* existent but a triply
qualified *imputed* existent (that is, a definiendum). The fact
that definition (*p*) is not a triply qualified substantial existent
is shown in Figure 1, for definition is represented outside
the enclosure of circle *Wq*, whatever is a triply qualified
substantial existent.

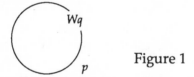

Figure 1

The next figure shows the comparative extensions of definition and the triply qualified substantial existent. As mutually inclusive phenomena, these two include all the same
phenomena. Whatever is the one is necessarily the other.
Thus, circle *Wp*, whatever is a definition, and circle *Wq*,
whatever is a triply qualified substantial existent, are precisely concomitant.

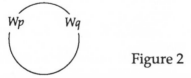

Figure 2

This context is exactly the opposite of what one might
expect. If one were unaware that the subject in a copulative

sentence is always used as a singular term and that the *p*-term in a statement of pervasion is always a general term, then one might be quite surprised to learn that definition is not a triply qualified substantial existent but each and every definition is.

Figure 3 combines the information from the last two figures showing that definition (*p*) is not a triply qualified substantial existent, that whatever is a definition (*Wp*) is necessarily a triply qualified substantial existent, and that whatever is a triply qualified substantial existent (*Wq*) is necessarily a definition. This figure also shows that definition is neither a definition nor a triply qualified substantial existent and that the triply qualified substantial existent (*q*) is both a definition and a triply qualified substantial existent.

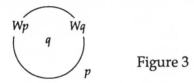   Figure 3

Chart 11 shows these three figures together:

Chart 11

p is not a *q*.
Context 3: *p* is not a *q*, but whatever is a *p* is necessarily a *q*.
Variety 2: mutually inclusive phenomena
p represents definition.
q represents the triply qualified substantial existent.
Wp represents whatever is a definition.
Wq represents whatever is a triply qualified substantial existent.
Definition is not a triply qualified substantial existent, but whatever is a definition is necessarily a triply qualified substantial existent.

1 *p* is not a *q*. Definition is not a triply qualified substantial existent.

2 Whatever is a *p* is necessarily a *q*. Whatever is a definition is necessarily a triply qualified substantial existent, such as that which is able to perform a function. (Whatever is a *q* is necessarily a *p*. Whatever is a triply qualified substantial existent is necessarily a definition.)

3 All of the above. (Also, *p* is neither a *p* nor a *q* and *q* is both a *p* and a *q*. Definition is neither a definition nor a triply quali- fied substantial existent and the triply qualified substantial existent is both a definition and a triply qualified substantial existent.)

To review, there are three contexts in which it may be said that *p* is not a *q*:

1   *p* is not a *q*, and whatever is a *p* is necessarily not a *q*.
2   *p* is not a *q*, but it is not the case that whatever is a *p* is necessarily not a *q*.
3   *p* is not a *q*, but whatever is a *p* is necessarily a *q*.

Similar to the different contexts in which one may say that *p* is a *q*, the fact that *p* is not a *q* does not clearly imply any- thing about the comparative extensions of the two phenom- ena, *p* and *q*. There are mutually exclusive phenomena for which *p* is not a *q*. There are phenomena having three pos- sibilities and those having four possibilities for which *p* is not a *q*. There are even mutually inclusive phenomena for which *p* is not a *q*. Given that *p* is not a *q*, one usually is not able to deduce anything about the comparative pervasions that exist between *p* and *q*.

    The fact that *p* is not a *q* does not mean that all *p*'s are not *q*'s. It means that *p*, considered alone from the point of view of its self-isolate, does not have the quality of being a *q*. This does not imply anything about the comparative extensions of *p* and *q*, for a statement of pervasion gives information about each and every *p* whereas a copulative statement says something about *p* itself, understood as a singular. The three different contexts in which it may be said that *p* is not a *q* and the four different contexts in which it may be said that *p* is a *q* indicate strikingly the difference between copulative associations and pervasions.

The difference between these two results from a difference between the thing itself, taken not as a whole but as the singular generality, and the illustrations of that thing. The qualities of a phenomenon as a singular entity may be distinct from the qualities of the illustrations of that phenomenon. For instance, object of knowledge is a generality of matter, consciousness, and so forth, but an illustration of object of knowledge such as a pot is not a generality of matter, consciousness, and so forth. Understanding the difference between copulative associations and pervasions is one of the first main essentials communicated by "The Introductory Path of Reasoning".

COMPARISON OF THE SYLLOGISMS USED IN THE COLLECTED TOPICS AND ARISTOTELIAN SYSTEMS OF REASONING

The comparison of Buddhist and Western systems of philosophy is a field of tremendous potential. The present work, by and large, has not undertaken to make comparisons though some notations on form are provided; many fruitful areas of comparison remain untouched. For instance, the theory of definitions and definienda presented in this system is an approach quite at odds with standard theories in the West. Also, the presentations of form, the process of direct perception, causes and effects, generalities and instances, negation, and meaning-generalities are subjects of great interest which are worthy of comparison. The approach of the present work has been to provide basic information from the Ge-luk-ba tradition of reasoning. In many ways, the enterprise of comparative work is the most difficult of all, for it presumes expertise in all areas under consideration.

As a start, some general notes on the Collected Topics system may prove helpful. First, this system uses a form of syllogism which is a single sentence including both premises and the conclusion. This single-sentence form of argument is an *enthymeme,* an argument containing one or more suppressed premises. In the Collected Topics form of syllogism, for instance:

The subject, sound, is an impermanent phenomenon because of being a product,

the property of the subject, sound is a product, and the conclusion, sound is an impermanent phenomenon, are openly stated. However, the pervasion, whatever is a product is necessarily an impermanent phenomenon, is suppressed. It is not openly stated but must be reckoned from one's knowledge of the argument form.

Second, since in the Collected Topics system formal logic is inextricably tied with epistemological concerns, an argument is not determined to be valid merely by its form. Rather, a valid argument requires that the premises and the conclusion must be validly ascertained by the person for whom the argument is valid.

Third, a correct syllogism, as described in the Collected Topics tradition, requires the capacity and readiness to make a correct inference on the part of the person for whom the argument is valid. A syllogism is not valid for one such as a Buddha who has already made the inference and no longer seeks to know the thesis. Nor is a syllogism valid for one who is incapable of understanding. The validity of a syllogism is not merely formal but is linked to the person who is ready to make an inference in dependence on that syllogism.

Clearly, the categorical or Aristotelian logic is not the focus of modern Western logic. Still, a brief comparison of the Collected Topics and Aristotelian systems, similar in that they are both rooted in antiquity, may prove instructive. For this purpose the presentation of Aristotelian logic is as represented in the scholastic tradition. It is difficult to know what Aristotle's actual thought was on a number of points, but his system as preserved by medieval Christian logicians is well known.

Many syllogisms found in this system may be roughly correlated to the categorical syllogisms of Aristotelian logic. The units, premises, and conclusion of the Collected Topics form of syllogism correspond to the terms, premises, and conclusion of one type of valid categorical syllogism. However, whereas this correlation may hold for certain Tibetan syllogisms, it cannot be said in general that the Collected Topics form of syllogism corresponds to the categorical syllogism.

Some syllogisms which are valid according to the rules of the Collected Topics tradition may not be translated successfully into the form of a valid categorical syllogism. In every such case, this is due to the well known difficulty in categorical logic of handling the singular case. This is because the Aristotelian system deals with four categories only. These four are the two universally quantified sentences:

All A's are B's[1]

and

No A's are B's

and the two particular sentences:

Some A's are B's

and

Some A's are not B's.

Since the subject in a Tibetan syllogism is an abstract or concrete singular term, many syllogisms found in this system

---

[1] In this section on the comparison of the Collected Topics and Aristotelian forms of syllogisms, the letters "A" are "B" are used rather than "p" are "q" as have been used elsewhere in this book. This variation is made in deference to the symbols normally used to demonstrate categorical logic and is not meant to indicate that the Collected Topics logic compares more closely to Aristotle's logic than it does to other Western systems, such as the propositional logic.

may not be re-formed straightforwardly into a valid categorical syllogism. Those syllogisms that may be translated into the categorical form are only those that may be read ambiguously as universally quantified or singular. By the same token, there are many valid categorical syllogisms that cannot be reproduced in the form of a valid syllogism as used in the Collected Topics system. This is because the Collected Topics system is unable to handle particular sentences, of the form, "Some *A*'s are *B*'s" or "Some *A*'s are not *B*'s," within the syllogistic structure (although it can through statements of pervasion).

A comparison of the argument forms found in these two systems will illustrate the points of similarity and difference between them. First, a syllogism which may be shown to be equally valid in either system is expressed first in the Collected Topics form:

> The subject, sound, is an impermanent phenomenon because of being a product.

This sample syllogism may be successfully re-formulated as a categorical syllogism of Aristotelian logic:

> All products are impermanent phenomena.
> All sounds are products.
> _____
> Therefore, all sounds are impermanent phenomena.

Here the pervasion, whatever is a product is necessarily an impermanent phenomenon, is re-expressed as the major premise, all products are impermanent phenomena. The property of the subject, sound is an impermanent phenomenon, is expressed as the minor premise, all sounds are products. The thesis/conclusion, sound is an impermanent phenomenon, is expressed as the conclusion, all sounds are impermanent phenomena. The subject, which in this case is *sound*, corresponds to the minor term, the term that occurs as the subject of the conclusion in a categorical syllogism of Aristotelian logic. The predicate or quality to be proven, which is *impermanent phenomenon* in this sample syllogism, corresponds to the major term, the term which is the predi-

cate of the conclusion in the categorical syllogism. The sign
or reason in the Collected Topics syllogism, *product*, corresponds to the middle term in the Aristotelian syllogism, the
term that occurs in both premises but not in the conclusion.

However, as mentioned in the chapter on subjects (pp. 75-
98) and above in this conclusion (p. 785) the quantification
of a subject in the Tibetan form of syllogism is singular.
Thus, in converting the above syllogism to the categorical
form the quantifier "all" is added as in the conclusion, "All
sounds are impermanent phenomena." This quantifier does
not appear in the Collected Topics formulation. Although it
is admissible to say that all sounds are impermanent phenomena in so far as it is in accordance with the assertions of
this system, such quantification is a superimposition onto
the subject drawn from knowledge of Sūtra School metaphysics. As described earlier, the subject, sound, is stated in
the singular with neither a universal nor a particular quantifier.

Still, it is suitable to apply the quantifier "all" to the subject in such syllogisms. In no case may the subject be said to
be quantified by the universal negative "no" or by a particular "some". Thus, in those cases for which it is suitable to
say that the subject can be quantified as a universal or
particular sentence, it is always quantified as a universal
affirmative.

This means that in these cases the property of the subject,
corresponding to the minor premise, and the conclusion can
both be interpreted as universal affirmative sentences, sentences of the form "All *A*'s are *B*'s." Further, since the pervasion, corresponding to the major premise, always has the
import of a universal affirmative sentence, all Collected
Topics syllogisms that can accept the overlay of quantification correspond to the Barbara-mood categorical syllogism.

The mood of a categorical syllogism refers to the types
and sequence of sentences used in that argument. A
Barbara-mood syllogism has three universal affirmative sentences, both premises and the conclusion being of the form,
"All *A*'s are *B*'s." The universal affirmative sentence is rep-

resented by the letter "A". Thus, the mood of a syllogism having three universal affirmative sentences may be represented as "AAA". For the sake of easy recollection, medieval Christian logicians designated the various moods of valid syllogisms with names having the same corresponding vowels. "Barbara" is a name having three "a's", and thus a categorical syllogism having an "AAA" mood was designated by the name "Barbara".

All Collected Topics syllogisms that can accept the overlay of universal quantification may be converted to the Barbara-mood categorical syllogism. Consequently, any categorical syllogism of the Barbara-mood or any categorical syllogism which can be converted to the Barbara-mood may be represented by the Collected Topics form of syllogism. For instance, there is the famous syllogism used to exemplify the Aristotelian system of logic:

> All men are mortal.
> Socrates is a man.
> _____
> Therefore, Socrates is mortal.

This Barbara-mood Aristotelian syllogism may be converted into the Collected Topics form of syllogism including both what is to be proven and the proof in one sentence:

> The subject, Socrates, is mortal because of being a man.

The major premise, all men are mortal, is understood as the pervasion, whoever is a man is necessarily mortal.[1] The minor premise, Socrates is a man, corresponds to the property of the subject which is in the same formulation, Socrates is a man. The conclusion of the Aristotelian formulation,

_____

[1] It is interesting that in the Great Vehicle interpretation the pervasion of this syllogism (that is, the major premise, "All men are mortal") is not established. This means that the followers of the Great Vehicle assert there are men who are not mortal. For instance, Shākyamuni Buddha was a human, not a human migrator (see "Established Bases" pp. 367-368), and not mortal. Still, the example serves adequately to demonstrate the comparison of the syllogistic forms.

Socrates is mortal, is formulated just the same in the converted thesis/conclusion, Socrates is mortal.

The formulation used in debate in the Ge-luk-ba colleges is perhaps not so much of a syllogism in the sense of an argument consisting of a series of premises leading to a conclusion.[1] Rather, this formula is a condensation which implies a series of premises and a conclusion. One understands the property of the subject, the forward pervasion, the counter-pervasion, and the conclusion from a single-sentence argument. The property of the subject is: Socrates is a man. The forward pervasion is: whoever is a man is necessarily mortal. The counter-pervasion is: whatever is not mortal is necessarily not a man. The counter-pervasion corresponds to the contrapositive, all non-mortals are non-men, in the Aristotelian form. Having ascertained these three "premises" one then understands the conclusion, Socrates is a mortal. Thus, the single-sentence form:

The subject, Socrates, is mortal because of being a man

implies the series:

Socrates is a man.
Whoever is a man is necessarily mortal.
Whatever is not a mortal is necessarily not a man.
Socrates is mortal.

These premises and the conclusion represent the "syllogism" that is understood and implied by the single sentence Tibetan form.[2] The single-sentence syllogism is a form like an ordinary language argument and is very adaptable to the flow of debate, for by replacing even one term a debater effectively alters at least two of the implied sentences.

It was mentioned above that all syllogisms in this system that can accept the overlay of quantification may be con-

---

[1] Suggested by Tom Tillemans.
[2] See Jeffrey Hopkins, *Meditation on Emptiness*, pp. 729-733, on proof statements and also Katherine Rogers, "Tibetan Logic", pp. 178-192.

verted into Barbara-mood categorical syllogisms. However, this does not mean that this form of syllogism is incapable of handling universal negative sentences, propositions of the form, "No *A*'s are *B*'s." For instance, the information that no functioning things are permanent phenomena is communicated by the pervasion, whatever is a functioning thing is necessarily not a permanent phenomenon. This pervasion is properly converted to the universal affirmative categorical sentence, all functioning things are non-permanent phenomena, which then may be obverted to the universal negative, no functioning things are permanent phenomena. Since the premises and the conclusion that are implied by the Collected Topics form of syllogism must be converted as universal affirmative sentences, it is from this point of view that the convertible syllogisms are all of the Barbara-mood.

Still, the Collected Topics form is able to handle syllogisms of other moods, although it is limited to those having only universally quantified sentences. From among the valid types of categorical syllogisms three moods contain only universally quantified sentences. These are Barbara—AAA, Celarent—EAE, and Camestres—AEE. Here the letter "E" represents the universal negative sentence of the form, "No *A*'s are *B*'s." The Collected Topics syllogism is able to convey the argument of valid Celarent-mood and Camestres-mood categorical syllogisms. For instance, the Celarent-mood syllogism:

> No functioning things are permanent phenomena.
> All sounds are functioning things.
> ———————————————————
> Therefore, no sounds are permanent phenomena.

may be expressed by the syllogism:

> The subject, sound, is not a permanent phenomenon because of being a functioning thing.

Here the major premise, no functioning things are permanent phenomena, is represented by the pervasion, whatever is a functioning thing is necessarily not a permanent phenomenon. This pervasion has the sense of a universal affirmative sentence, all functioning things are non-permanent phenomena, which may be obverted into a universal negative sentence, no functioning things are permanent phenomena. Similarly, the conclusion has the sense of a universal affirmative, all sounds are non-impermanent phenomena, which may be obverted to the form, no sounds are permanent phenomena. In this way the syllogism as stated in the popular form of debate in Tibet communicates the information of a Celarent-mood categorical syllogism.

Also, this type of syllogism is able to convey the argument of a valid Camestres-mood categorical syllogism. For instance, the categorical syllogism:

> All permanent phenomena are generally characterized phenomena.
> No sounds are generally characterized phenomena.
> Therefore, no sounds are permanent phenomena.

may be expressed by the syllogism:

> The subject, sound, is not a permanent phenomenon because of not being a generally characterized phenomenon.

Here the major premise, all permanent phenomena are generally characterized phenomena, is conveyed by the counter-pervasion, whatever is a permanent phenomenon is necessarily a generally characterized phenomenon. The forward pervasion, whatever is not a generally characterized phenomenon is necessarily not a permanent phenomenon, may be expressed by the universal affirmative, all non-generally characterized phenomena are non-permanent phenomena, which has as its contrapositive the universal affirmative, all permanent phenomena are generally characterized phenomena. This contrapositive appears as the major premise in the Camestres-mood sample syllogism above. The property of the subject which is formulated here, sound is not a generally characterized phenomenon, has the sense of the universal affirmative, all sounds are non-generally characterized phenomena. This sentence may be obverted to the universal negative, no sounds are generally characterized phenomena, the proposition that appears as the minor premise in the categorical syllogism. By the same process, the conclusion, sound is not a permanent phenomenon, may be reformulated in the universal negative, no sounds are permanent phenomena, which is the conclusion of the categorical syllogism. Thus, the debate form of syllogism as found in Tibet is able to convey the argument of any valid categorical syllogism having only universally quantified sentences.

It must be noted again that converting these syllogisms to the categorical forms with quantifiers added onto the logical functionals is an overlay predicated from knowledge of the metaphysics of this system. Thus, this process of conversion is as if done by mirrors, for although it appears to be solidly established it is contingently predicated. Moreover, conversion is limited from both sides to only some examples.

Some valid categorical syllogisms may not be successfully converted to this form of syllogism. Any syllogism having a premise or a conclusion which is quantified as a particular may not be expressed by such a syllogism. That is, any categorical sentence of the form, "Some *A*'s are *B*'s," or of the form, "Some *A*'s are not *B*'s," cannot be expressed within the framework of this type of syllogism. For instance, the valid Disamis-mood categorical syllogism:

> Some impermanent phenomena are sounds.
> All impermanent phenomena are products.
> _____
> Therefore, some products are sounds.

is a valid argument which cannot be communicated within the confines of the syllogistic form used for debate in Tibet. This is so because the logical functionals are either understood only in a singular sense or expressible as universally quantified. In no case is any part of this sort of Tibetan syllogism quantified as a particular. For instance, the pervasion of a syllogism is formulated, "Whatever is that reason is necessarily that predicate." The information that some *A*'s are not *B*'s is expressed by the form, "Whatever is an *A* is *not* necessarily a *B*." The information that some *A*'s are *B*'s must be conveyed by two statements, "Whatever is a *B* is necessarily an *A*, but whatever is an *A* is not necessarily a *B*." The former statement affirms that all *B*'s are *A*'s and the latter refines this to say that some *A*'s are not *B*'s. Thus, the argument presented in the above Disamis-mood categorical syllogism is communicated by a series of sentences:

> Whatever is a sound is necessarily an impermanent phenomenon.
> Whatever is an impermanent phenomenon is not necessarily a sound.
> Whatever is an impermanent phenomenon is necessarily a product.
> _____
> Therefore, whatever is a sound is necessarily a product, but whatever is a product is not necessarily a sound.

However, no debate takes this form. Still, this information would be communicated in the process of analyzing the comparative differences between phenomena. The fact that this type of syllogism is not able to express many types of valid categorical syllogisms does not mean that information such as some *A*'s are *B*'s and some are not is not a point of emphasis in this system, for it is. The information is communicated not by the syllogistic form, but by a standardized form for examining comparative difference (see pp. 133-165).

On the other hand, some valid Tibetan syllogisms cannot be accurately converted to categorical syllogisms by straightforwardly translating the forms of the sentences. For all cases in which this is true, the subject can be understood only in its own specific nature, neither universally nor particularly quantified although it is singular. As an example there is the syllogism which is valid in this system of reasoning:

> The subject, definition, is a definiendum because of being a triply qualified imputed existent.

This syllogism has a sign which is the three modes. The property of the subject, (roughly formulated) definition is a triply qualified imputed existent, is established because definition is the triply qualified imputed existent (that is, the definiendum) of the triply qualified substantial existent (the definition of definition). The forward pervasion, (roughly formulated) whatever is a triply qualified imputed existent is necessarily a definiendum, is established because the triply qualified imputed existent is the definition of definiendum. Once these two are established, the conclusion, definition is a definiendum, must be established.

However, this syllogism cannot be communicated in the strict categorical form because of quantification problems. If converted into the form of a Barbara-mood syllogism, this argument would be expressed:

All triply qualified imputed existents are
definiendums.
All definitions are triply qualified imputed existents.
Therefore, all definitions are definiendums.

The overlay of quantification onto this subject results in absurdity. The pervasion, whatever is a triply qualified imputed existent is necessarily a definiendum, is accurately expressed as the major premise, all triply qualified imputed existents are definiendums. However, both propositions in which the subject is involved cannot be universally quantified successfully. The property of the subject, definition is a triply qualified imputed existent, is mistakenly expressed as the minor premise, all definitions are triply qualified imputed existents. Such is not the case because no definition is a triply qualified *imputed* existent, for every definition is a triply qualified *substantial* existent. Similarly, the conclusion, definition is a definiendum, is falsely expressed as the universal affirmative, all definitions are definiendums. Of course, no definitions are definiendums; they are only mutually exclusive.

Further, it is also unsuitable to change the quantification of the minor premise and conclusion to yield particular sentences. It is equally untrue, according to this system, to say that some definitions are triply qualified imputed existents or to say that some definitions are definiendums. Thus, it must be concluded that the categorical form is unable to express accurately the sense of the Tibetan Buddhist syllogism cited above. There are many such examples of syllogisms used in Tibetan debate which cannot be converted to categorical syllogisms.

In the above syllogism, Aristotelian logic is unable to express the particular slant on the subject, definition, that is the intention. This is because definition, in the sense in which it is used here, defies quantification except as the singular collective entity. The quantitative approach to reasoning is built up out of an assessment of relative pervasion or the lack of pervasion. Indeed, if something is true of all examples of such and such, then it is true of any one example of such and such. However, this does not say anything about such and such itself, considered alone. For example, it is true that all definitions are triply qualified substantial existents, and this implies that the momentary, as the definition of impermanent phenomenon, is a triply qualified substantial existent. However, this does not reveal the nature of definition, on its own. The categorical approach to reasoning is able to express all forms of pervasion or lack of pervasion, but it is unable to express all forms of copulative associations just as they are.

The reason why some sentences used in the Tibetan system of debate cannot be converted into the form of a categorical sentence is because the subject is singular, quantified neither as a universal nor a particular. The inability to handle the singular case is a well known weakness of categorical logic. In Western logic, one way of resolving this problem is to insert a phrase which renders the singular sentence suitable to be translated into a categorical sentence. Thus a sentence such as, "Definition is a definiendum," may be translated into the sentence, "All things identical to definition are definienda." This sentence is in proper categorical form and accurately maintains the sense of the original sentence. Since there is only one thing identical to definition (that is, definition itself), it follows that if the original sentence is accurate then the categorical sentence too is accurate.

APPLICATIONS

In the traditional monastic setting, debate is only for the sake of helping one toward liberation. Logic and epistemology are not studied as mere scholasticism but as vitally important tools to assist one on the path to liberation. Further, debate is not merely for the sake of sharpening one's intellect so that later when one is ready to investigate the profound topics one will then be prepared. Rather, debate is a lively study of those profound topics right from the beginning. This system of education involves applying immediately all the information that one has with all the skill that one has gained. The application of debate is both immediate and profound. It is immediate in the sense that the knowledge and skill learned in the morning is brought to the debating courtyard and exercised in the afternoon. It is profound in that the main subject of debate is the two truths, conventional truths (*kun rdzob bden pa, samvrti-satya*) and ultimate truths (*don dam bden pa, paramārtha-satya*).

According to the Ge-luk-ba interpretation of the Sūtra School Following Reasoning, conventional truth is mutually inclusive with permanent phenomenon and ultimate truth is mutually inclusive with impermanent phenomenon. The two truths are distinguished in terms of the consciousnesses to which they appear, conventional truths being the appearing objects of thought consciousnesses and ultimate truths being the appearing objects of direct perceivers.

By calling them "ultimate truths" the Proponents of the Sūtra School Following Reasoning are indicating impermanent phenomena as endowed with a special nature. Impermanent phenomena are objects of an ultimate mind, a mind which is not at all mistaken with regard to what appears to it. An impermanent phenomenon appears to a direct perceiver together with all of its specific characteristics of impermanence and so forth without being mixed with phenomena of other places, times, and natures. It fully appears in all of its presence and freshness.

In calling permanent phenomena "conventional truths" the Proponents of the Sūtra School Following Reasoning are indicating something about the epistemological disadvantages involved in realizing permanent phenomena. A conventional truth must be known by a conventional mind, a thought consciousness apprehending a meaning-generality which merely represents the actual object of ascertainment. Such a mind perceives an object which is mixed with other phenomena of different places, times, and natures; thus, it is mistaken with respect to its appearing object.

This presentation indicts the thought process as necessarily mistaken. Consequently, the process of reasoning is brought into question, for reasoning is necessarily conceptual. Still, the Ge-luk-bas assert reasoning as necessary although they recognize that it alone is not sufficient to establish one in liberation (see Chapter 1, pp. 13-21). In the traditional setting the main application of debate is in the process of acquiring an understanding of the two truths, not only as presented in the Sūtra School Following Reasoning but also in all of the Buddhist systems of tenets.

Debate also has useful application in contemporary non-monastic Buddhist studies. Not only do all of the debate manuals use basic reasoning forms as a method of presenting the doctrine, but also a significant part of the Tibetan commentarial tradition incorporates this debate style as the principal means of explaining philosophy. Thus, in order to understand the various philosophical stances in Tibetan studies it is essential to apprehend the procedure in debate. The study of the practice and theory of introductory debate serves to open a little wider the door to the vast literature on Buddhist reasoning as well as other branches of philosophical studies.

If one is to understand the Ge-luk-b̄a presentation of phenomena, the paths, and the fruits of the paths, one must have a certain basic measure of facility with the reasoning forms. Debate is the traditional means for students to learn the general and specific points of Buddhist doctrine, and the vast majority of the Ge-luk-b̄as' philosophical literature is couched in the language of debate. Of course, it is not necessary for modern scholars in Buddhist studies to learn doctrine strictly by traditional means, but in order to understand the commentarial exegesis some familiarity with debate is required.

In the title of his text Pur-bu-jok Jam-b̄a-gya-tso refers to "The Introductory Path of Reasoning" as a "magical key to the path of reasoning". In the Ge-luk-b̄a perspective, one may approach the doors to the many philosophical topics, but if one lacks the "magical key" one will not be able to enter them to gain understanding. Lacking the essential familiarity with introductory forms of reasoning inevitably results in misinterpretations of the points of doctrine set forth in the texts.

An example will serve to illustrate. In his classic *Buddhist Logic* F. Th. Stcherbatsky identifies "the Universal" as "*spyii-mtshan ñid* or *sāmānya-lakṣaṇa*",[1] which is here translated as "generally characterized phenomenon". Stcherbatsky explains, "It is clear that every thing possessing general features is included in the category of general essences or Universals."[2] In this understanding, generally characterized phenomenon or "every thing possessing general features", is pervaded by generality, "general essences or Universals". According to the Ge-luk-b̄a interpretation, as presented in "The Introductory Path of Reasoning", such is not the case. Stcherbatsky's interpretation implies that the two, generally characterized phenomenon and generality, are either mutually inclusive or have three possibilities, for one is pervaded

---

[1] F. Th. Stcherbatsky, *Buddhist Logic* (New York: Dover Publications, Inc., 1962), Vol. 2, p. 398, note 4.
[2] *Ibid.*

by the other. He indicates that whatever is a generally characterized phenomenon is necessarily a generality. According to the Ge-luk-ba perspective, Stcherbatsky has not taken into account that there are generally characterized phenomena which are not generalities. For instance, one-with-permanent-phenomenon is a generally characterized phenomenon, but it is not a generality because there are no instances of it. There is only one thing which is one with permanent phenomenon—permanent phenomenon itself—and in order for something to be a generality there must be many things which are it. A generality must have many instances. If Stcherbatsky's understanding is that according to the texts on valid cognition there can be a generality which has only one instance, then this is quite a serious error, at least in the Ge-luk-ba perspective. According to "The Introductory Path of Reasoning", there are four possibilities between generally characterized phenomenon and generality:

1 Something which is both is permanent phenomenon or object of knowledge.
2 Something which is a generally characterized phenomenon but not a generality is one-with-pot, the two—definition and definiendum, or the definiendum of that which is able to perform a function.
3 Something which is a generality but not a generally characterized phenomenon is functioning thing, pot, and so forth.
4 Something which is neither is functioning-thing-which-is-one-with-functioning-thing or the two—a pillar and a pot.

As in any case of four possibilities, no pervasion can be predicated between the two principals. It is clear that Stcherbatsky's interpretation is at odds with the Ge-luk-ba understanding.

A second example is more closely related to the issues raised in this chapter. In his *Presuppositions of India's Philosophies*, Karl H. Potter identifies the association between the subject (*chos can, dharmin*) and the predicate to be proven (*bsgrub bya'i chos, sādhya-dharma*) as a case of pervasion. He explains: "*p* [that is, the *pakṣha* or subject] is asserted to be pervaded by *s* [that is, the *sādhya* or what is to be proven], which is to say that it is asserted that *s* pervades *p*."[1] This interpretation is totally at odds with the Ge-luk-ba understanding of the reasoning form. Professor Potter diagrams the association between the subject (*p*) and the predicate to be proven (*s*) in his Figure 1:[2]

 Figure 1

Using the language of class logic, he describes the nature of pervasion:

> Pervasion (*vyāpti*) is the relation of class-inclusion. To say that class A pervades class B is to say that all members of B are members of A. ... To say that class A is pervaded by class B is to say that all members of A are members of B.[3]

This interpretation is plausible, though non-traditional, as it applies to some theses such as "Sound is an impermanent phenomenon." According to his interpretation this means that sound is pervaded by impermanent phenomenon or, in another way, that impermanent phenomenon pervades sound. Fitting this into his own description of the meaning of pervasion, to say that the class of impermanent phenomena pervades the class of sounds is to say that all members of [the class of] sounds are members of [the class of] impermanent phenomena. For this case, the results are in accordance with the assertions of the Collected Topics tradition.

---

[1] Karl H. Potter, *Presuppositions of India's Philosophies* (Englewood Cliffs, N.J.: Prentice-Hall, Inc., 1963), p. 65.
[2] *Ibid.*, p. 61.
[3] *Ibid.*, p. 65.

However, for many theses Professor Potter's interpretation of the association between the subject and the predicate is misguided. For example, the thesis "Object of knowledge is a permanent phenomenon" cannot be interpreted just as he says. According to his method, this sentence means that permanent phenomenon pervades object of knowledge and to say that the class of permanent phenomena pervades the class of objects of knowledge is to say that all members of [the class of] objects of knowledge are members of [the class of] permanent phenomena. If every member of the class of objects of knowledge were also a member of the class of permanent phenomena, then a pot, which is a member of the class of objects of knowledge, would also be a member of the class of permanent phenomena. If a pot were a permanent phenomenon, then it would not be able to perform the function of holding water. Since this interpretation leads to absurdities, it is clearly mistaken from the viewpoint of the Collected Topics tradition.

In the above passage, Professor Potter identifies pervasion as "the relation of class-inclusion". In class logic there is an important distinction made between *membership* and *inclusion*. The class *p* is a *member* of *q* if *p* belongs to the class of *q's*; that is, *p* itself is counted among the things which comprise the class *q*. The class *p* is *included* in *q* if every member of *p* is also a member of *q*. According to this distinction, the class of objects of knowledge is a member of the class of permanent phenomena, for the class of objects of knowledge itself is a permanent phenomenon. This does not imply anything about the individual members of the class of objects of knowledge, only about the class as a whole. On the other hand, the class of objects of knowledge is not included in the class of permanent phenomena because the class of objects of knowledge includes impermanent phenomena. This means that it is not the case that each and every member of the class of objects of knowledge is also a member of the class of permanent phenomena. Thus, the class of objects of knowledge is a member of the class of permanent phenomena, but it is not included in the class of permanent phenomena. This means that the interpretation of a subject/predicate relation as one of pervasion and pervasion as the relation of *class-inclusion* fails in this and many instances.

Still, there is one possible interpretation of Professor Potter's position that is plausible. In his main example, he identifies the subject as a unit class, a class with exactly one member. If this identification is carried over to the example of object of knowledge, then the unit class of object of knowledge is both a member of and included in the class of permanent phenomena. It is unclear whether or not he means to identify every subject as a unit class, but, if he does, his interpretation is more defensible. However, given that he identifies the subject-predicate association as that of pervasion or class-inclusion and explains that *p*'s being pervaded by *q* means that all members of *p* are members of *q*, he clearly implies that the subject class may have many members and that each and every one of these members is also a member of the predicate-class. If this is his intention, it sharply disagrees with the Ge-luk-bas' understanding of the form of reasoning. In any case, Professor Potter's explanation of the thesis as meaning that the subject is pervaded by the predicate is totally at odds with this tradition and is fundamentally misguided.

It is in such ways that a study of the Collected Topics helps to explain and clarify the interrelationships of the units of syllogistic forms. In the study of "The Introductory Path of Reasoning" the student learns the essential procedure of debate as well as much of the introductory philosophy. The procedure involves knowing both how to defeat mistaken positions and how to establish correct ones. However, according to Lati Rinbochay, if one is skilled in debate, even though someone says something that is correct, one can, through skill in drawing out issues, involve that person in contradictions. If the opponent says that something is such and such, then one can push him into accepting that it is not. And if the opponent says that it is not such and such, one can push him the other way, into accepting that it is such and such. This does not mean that there is no correct position in debate but that a skillful debater is able to raise many qualms to any position. Debate serves to increase the agility, clarity, and creativeness of one's mind, supplying a critical attitude for investigating assertions.

The other side of debate is in establishing the irrefutable. Anyone may be able to raise qualms against a position, but if the position is well founded, one who is skilled in debate will be able to resolve those apparent qualms. This is the more difficult of the two branches of debate. In introductory debate one learns how to ask the questions to draw out the implications of an assertion. However, this procedure is not adequate, for it is merely an investigative tool and will not assuredly lead one to an established conclusion. The more important position is that of the Defender, who asserts and holds a position. If, as some scholars say, debate is for the sake of establishing the truth, it is in the role as the Defender that one learns to hold the irrefutable.

Both the Challenger and the Defender must bring a critical attitude to the debating courtyard. The Challenger questions the Defender's assertions and conclusions, and the Defender must constantly assess the value of the Challenger's reasoning. However, in the Challenger's role, merely asking questions and raising qualms, one does not need to know the answers. The Defender must know the answers and must be able to uphold a correct position.

Evidence for the priority of the Defender's role is that when a student is tested in the intermediate and final examinations in the Ge-shay program, he must assume the role of Defender to demonstrate his learning. The student must be able to dispel objections by reconciling apparent inconsistencies and elucidating a cogent interpretation of a point of doctrine. Thus, debate is by no means a mere rote learning of accepted assertions. Imaginative thought is applauded. Many issues are left unresolved although the student equipped with the path of reasoning is often able to reach his own reasoned conclusion.

The Ge-luk-ba claim is that through lack of analysis and investigation into the mode of existence of phenomena sentient beings are drawn into suffering within cyclic existence. The valid establishment of just what does exist and in just what manner those phenomena do exist becomes of quintessential importance. Debate is a prime means for establishing the scope and nature of phenomena. By sharpening the intellect, one is eventually able to cognize selflessness with inference. Through repeated familiarization with this inferential realization, one is gradually able to realize selflessness by means of direct perception. In this process reasoning is essential in the beginning and the middle, but eventually it is no longer necessary. For this system, debate is rigorous conceptuality for the sake of eventually transcending conceptuality.

Glossary
Bibliography
Index
Tibetan Text

Glossary

Note: Sanskrit terms marked with an asterisk are reconstructions from the Tibetan and may have not occurred in Sanskrit literature.

English	Tibetan	Sanskrit
action/karma	las	karma
affirming negative	ma yin dgag	paryudāsa-pratiṣhedha
affliction	nyon mongs	klesha
aggregate	phung po	skandha
Amitābha	'od dpag med	amitābha
Amitāyus	tshe dpag med	amitāyus
Amoghasiddhi	don yod grub pa	amoghasiddhi
animal	dud 'gro	tiryañch
animals living in the depths	dud 'gro bying na gnas pa	

English	*Tibetan*	*Sanskrit*
animals scattered [about the surface]	dud 'gro kha 'thor ba	
appearance factor	snang ngor	
appearing object	snang yul	*pratibhāsa-viṣhaya
appearing object of a direct perceiver	mngon sum gyi snang yul	
appearing object of a thought consciousness	rtog pa'i snang yul	
apprehended object	bzung yul	grāhya-viṣhaya
arising	byung ba	
ascertainment factor	nges ngor	
ascertainment factor of a direct perceiver	mngon sum gyi nges ngor	
astringent	bska ba	kaṣhāya
attractive	phya legs pa	
awareness	blo	buddhi
awareness to which an object appears but is not ascertained	snang la ma nges pa	*aniyata-pratibhāsa
basis of debate	rtsod gzhi	
basis of designation	gdags gzhi	
basis of inference	dpag gzhi	
basis of relation	ltos gzhi	
being	yin pa	

English	*Tibetan*	*Sanskrit*
being/person	skyes bu	
being a pot	bum pa yin pa	
bitter	kha ba	tikta
blue	sngon po	nīla
Bodhisattva Superior	byang sems kyi 'phags pa	bodhisattva-ārya
Bodhisattva Vehicle	byang sems kyi theg pa	bodhisattva-yāna
body consciousness	lus shes	kāya-jñāna
body sense power	lus kyi dbang po	kāya-indriya
boundaries of pervasion	khyab mtha'	
Buddha Superior	sangs rgyas 'phags pa	buddha-ārya
cause	rgyu	hetu/kāraṇa
cause of a pot	bum pa'i rgyu	
Challenger	rigs lam pa	
child of a barren woman	mo gsham gyi bu	
clear form	gzugs dvang pa	rūpa-prasāda
cloud	sprin	abhra
coarse	rags pa	sthūla
coarse impermanence	rags pa'i mi rtag pa	*sthūla-anitya
coextensive	yin khyab mnyam	
cold	grang ba	shīta
cold hell-being	grang dmyal ba	

English	*Tibetan*	*Sanskrit*
Collected Topics	bsdus grva	
collection-generality	tshogs spyi	sāmagrī-sāmānya
collective engager	sgrub 'jug	*vidhi-pravṛtti
color	kha dog	varṇa
color-form	kha dog gi gzugs	
combined reason	sdoms rtags	
common being	so so'i skye bo	pṛthak-jana
common being having the basis of a demigod	lha ma yin pa'i rten can gyi so so'i skye bo	
common being having the basis of a god	lha'i rten can gyi so so'i skye bo	
common being having the basis of a hell-being	dmyal ba'i rten can gyi so so'i skye bo	
common being having the basis of a human	mi'i rten can gyi so so'i skye bo	
common being having the basis of a hungry ghost	yi dvags kyi rten can gyi so so'i skye bo	
common being having the basis of an animal	dud 'gro'i rten can gyi so so'i skye bo	
common locus	gzhi mthun pa	samāna-adhikaraṇa
composed phenomenon	'dus byas	saṃskṛta
compositional factor	'du byed	saṃskāra
concentration	bsam gtan	dhyāna

English	*Tibetan*	*Sanskrit*
condition	rkyen	pratyaya
consciousness	shes pa	jñāna/vijñāna
consciousnesses which are the same isolate type	shes par gyur pa'i ldog pa rigs gcig pa	
consciousnesses which are the same type of substantial entity	shes par gyur pa'i rdzas rigs gcig pa	
consequence/ contradictory consequence	thal 'gyur	prasaṅga
Consequence School/ Consequentialist	thal 'gyur pa	prāsaṅgika
contaminated	zag bcas	sāsrava
contradictory reason	'gal ba'i gtan tshigs	viruddha-hetu
conventional awareness	blo kun rdzob pa	
conventional truth	kun rdzob bden ba	saṃvṛti-satya
cooperative condition	lhan cig byed rkyen	sahakāri-pratyaya
cooperative effect	lhan cig byed 'bras	
correct consequence	thal 'gyur yang dag	samyak-prasaṅga
correct sign/correct logical sign	rtags yang dag	*samyak-liṅga
correctly assuming consciousness	yid dpyod	*manaḥ-parīkṣha
counter-pervasion	ldog khyab	vyatireka-vyāpti
counterfeit consequence	thal 'gyur ltar snang	prasaṅga-abhāsa

English	Tibetan	Sanskrit
counterfeit direct perceiver	mngon sum ltar snang	pratyakṣa-ābhāsa
counterfeit sign	rtags ltar snang	liṅga-ābhāsa
cyclic existence	'khor ba	saṃsāra
darkness	mun pa	andhakāra
debating courtyard	chos ra	
Defender	dam bca' ba	
definiendum	mtshon bya	lakṣhya
definition	mtshan nyid	lakṣhana
definition which eliminates discordant types	rigs mi mthun sel ba'i mtshan nyid	
definition which eliminates wrong ideas	log rtag sel ba'i mtshan nyid	
demigod	lha ma yin	asura
demonstrable form	bstan yod kyi gzugs	
Desire Realm	'dod khams	kāma-dhātu
determined object	zhen yul	*adhyavasāya-viṣhaya
determinative knower	zhen rig	*adhyavasāya-saṃvedana
different/different phenomena/ difference	tha dad	nānātva
different entities	ngo bo tha dad pa	
different-from-pot	bum pa dang tha dad	

English	Tibetan	Sanskrit
different self-isolates	rang ldog tha dad pa	
different substantial entities	rdzas tha dad pa	
different types	rigs tha dad pa	
direct cause	dngos rgyu	sākṣhāt-kāraṇa
direct cooperative condition	dngos kyi lhan cig byed rkyen	
direct effect	dngos 'bras	sākṣhāt-phala
direct perceiver/ direct perception	mngon sum	pratyakṣha
direct substantial cause	dngos kyi nyer len	
direct valid cognizer/direct prime cognizer	mngon sum tshad ma	pratyakṣha-pramāṇa
discrimination	'du shes	samjñā
dispelling objections	rtsod pa spong ba	
dissimilar class	mi mthun phyogs	vipakṣha
dissimilar isolate types	ldog pa rigs mi 'dra ba	
dissimilar types of substantial entities	rdzas rigs mi 'dra ba	
distinction	khyab par	
distraction	rnam par g.yeng ba	
doctrine	chos	dharma
doubt tending to the factual	don 'gyur gyi the tshom	
doubt tending to the non-factual	don mi 'gyur gyi the tshom	

English	*Tibetan*	*Sanskrit*
dust	brdul	rajaḥ
ear consciousness	rna shes	shrotra-jñāna
ear sense power	rna ba'i dbang po	shrotra-indriya
earth	sa	pṛthivī
effect	'bras bu	phala
effect of a pot	bum pa'i 'bras bu	
eight good luck symbols	bkra shis rtags brgyad	
element	'byung ba	bhūta
eliminative engager	sel 'jug	*apoha-pravṛtti
emptiness	stong pa nyid	shūnyatā
entity	ngo bo	vastu
equal doubt	cha mnyam pa'i the tshom	
equal fragrant odor	zhim pa'i dri mnyam pa	sama-sugandha
equal odor	dri mnyam pa	sama-gandha
equal unfragrant odor	mi zhim pa'i dri mnyam pa	sama-durgandha
established base	gzhi grub	*vastu-siddha
establishment from its own side	rang ngos nas grub pa	*svarūpa-siddhi
ethics	tshul khrims	shīla
exalted knower of all aspects	rnam mkhyen	sarvā-kāra-jñāna
existence from its own side	rang ngos nas grub pa	*svarūpa-siddhi

English	*Tibetan*	*Sanskrit*
existent/existence	yod pa	sat
expressive sound	brjod byed kyi sgra	
external form	phyi'i gzugs	bahirdhā-rūpa
external matter	phyi'i bem po	bahirdhā-kanthā
external object	phyi'i don	*bahirdhā-artha
eye	mig	
eye consciousness	mig shes	*chakṣhur-jñāna
eye-constituent	mig gi khams	
eye sense power	mig gi dbang po	chakṣhur-indriya
eye sense power which is a basis	rten bcas kyi mig dbang	
eye sense power which is like a basis	rten mtshungs kyi mig dbang	
fallacy of a pervasion that is too extensive	khyab che ba'i skyon	
fallacy of non-occurrence	mi srid pa'i skyon	
fallacy of non-pervasion	ma khyab pa'i skyon	
feeling	tshor ba	vedanā
fire	me	teja
first three isolate phenomena	ldog chos dang po gsum	
flower of a dead tree	shing skam po'i me tog	
Foe Destroyer	dgra bcom pa	arhan

English	*Tibetan*	*Sanskrit*
Followers of Reasoning	rigs pa'i rje su 'brang pa	*nyāya-anusārin
Followers of Scripture	lung gi rje su 'brang pa	*agama-anusārin
form/visible form	gzugs	rūpa
form aggregate	gzugs kyi phung po	rūpa-skandha
form-constituent	gzugs kyi khams	
form for the mental consciousness	chos kyi skye mched pa'i gzugs	dharma-āyatana-rūpa
Form Realm	gzugs khams	rūpa-dhātu
form-source	gzugs kyi skye mched	rūpa-āyatana
Formless Realm	gzugs med khams	ārūpya-dhātu
forms which are the same isolate type	gzugs su gyur pa'i ldog pa rigs gcig pa	
forms which are the same type of substantial entity	gzugs su gyur pa'i rdzas rigs gcig pa	
forward pervasion	rjes khyab	anvaya-vyāpti
four possibilities	mu bzhi	
fragrant manufactured odor	zhim pa'i sbyar byung gi dri	sāmyogika-sugandha
fragrant natural odor	zhim pa'i lhan skyes kyi dri	sahaja-sugandha
fragrant odor	dri zhim pa	sugandha
functioning thing/ thing	dngos po	bhāva
furthermore	gzhan yang	

English	Tibetan	Sanskrit
ge-shay	dge bshes	kalyāna-mitra
general-isolate	spyi ldog	
generality	spyi	sāmānya
generally character-ized phenomenon	spyi mtshan	sāmānya-lakshana
giving	sbyin pa	dāna
god of the Desire Realm	'dod khams kyi lha	kāma-dhātu-deva
god of the Form Realm	gzugs khams kyi lha	rūpa-dhātu-deva
god of the Formless Realm	gzugs med khams kyi lha	ārūpya-dhātu-deva
good qualities	yon tan	guna
Great Exposition School	bye brag smra ba	vaibhāshika
Great Prayer Festival	mon lam chen mo	
Great Vehicle	theg pa chen po	mahāyāna
happy migration	bde 'gro	sugati
Hearer Superior	nyan thos kyi 'phags pa	shrāvaka-ārya
Hearer Vehicle	nyan thos kyi theg pa	shrāvaka-yāna
hearing	thos pa	shruta
heaviness	lci ba	gurutva
hell-being	dmyal ba	nāraka
helper	phan 'dogs byed	

English	*Tibetan*	*Sanskrit*
hidden phenomenon	lkog gyur	parokṣha
high	mtho ba	unnata
horn of a rabbit	ri bong rva	
horse	rta	ashva
hot hell-being	tsha dmyal ba	
human	mi	manuṣhya
humans of the eight subcontinents	gling phran brgyad kyi mi	
humans of the four continents	gling bzhi'i mi	
hunger	bkres pa	bubhūkṣhā
hungry ghost	yi dvags	preta
hungry ghost having both external and internal obstructions	sgrib pa phyi nang gnyis ka yod pa'i yi dvags	
hungry ghost having external obstructions	sgrib pa phyi na yod pa'i yi dvags	
hungry ghost having internal obstructions	sgrib pa nang na yod pa'i yi dvags	
ignorance	ma rig pa	avidyā
illumination	snang ba	āloka
illustration	mtshan gzhi	
illustration-isolate	gzhi ldog	
illustrator	mtshon byed	

English	Tibetan	Sanskrit
imaginary	kun btags	parikalpita
impermanent phenomenon	mi rtag pa	anitya
imputed existent/ imputedly existent	btags yod/btags su yod pa	prajñapti-sat
incontrovertible	mi slu ba	avisaṃvādin
indefinite reason	ma nges pa'i gtan tshigs	anaikāntika-hetu
indirect cause	brgyud rgyu	*pāramparya-kāraṇa
indirect cooperative condition	brgyud kyi lhan cig byed rkyen	
indirect effect	brgyud 'bras	paramparya-phala
indirect substantial cause	brgyud kyi nyer len	
inference by the power of the fact	dngos stobs rjes dpag	*vastu-bala-anumāna
inference for oneself	rang don rjes dpag	svārtha-anumāna
inference through belief	yid ches rjes dpag	*āpta-anumāna
inferential cog-nizer/inferential cognition	rjes dpag	anumāna
inferential valid cognizer	rjes dpag tshad ma	anumāna-pramāṇa
instance	bye brag	visheṣha
instance of pot	bum pa'i bye brag	
internal matter	nang gi bem po	ādhyātmika-kanthā
isolate	ldog pa	*vyatireka
isolate phenomenon	ldog chos	*vyatireka-dharma

English	*Tibetan*	*Sanskrit*
isolate-phenomenon-of-the-third-type	ldog chos phung sum tsam po ba	
isolate-phenomenon-which-is-itself	rang yin pa'i ldog chos	
isolate-phenomenon-which-is-not-itself	rang ma yin pa'i ldog chos	
jealousy	phrag dog	irṣhyā
knower	rig pa	saṃvedana
knowledge	chos mngon pa	abhidharma
lack of being a permanent, partless, independent self	rtag gcig rang dbang can bdag gis stong pa	
lack of being a substantially existent self in the sense of being self-sufficient	rang rkya thub pa'i rdzas yod bdag gis stong pa	
lama	bla ma	guru
Land of Happiness	bde ba can	sukhā-vatī
Land of Jambu	'dzam bu gling	jambu-dvīpa
latter four similitudes	phyi ma rjes mthun bzhi	
lesser hell-being	nyi tshe'i dmyal ba	
Lesser Vehicle	theg dman pa	hīnayāna

English	*Tibetan*	*Sanskrit*
level	phya le ba	shāta
lightness	yang ba	laghutva
long	ring ba	dīrgha
low	dma' ba	avanata

Manjughosha	'jam dbyangs	mañjughoṣha
Manjushrī	'jam dpal	mañjushrī
manifest phenomenon	mngon gyur	abhimukhī
manifestation	gsal ba	vyakti
manufactured	sbyar byung	sāṃyogika
manufactured primary color	sbyar byung gi rtsa ba'i kha dog	sāṃyogika-mūla-varṇa
many	du ma	
matter	bem po	kanthā
meaning	don	artha
meaning-generality	don spyi	artha-sāmānya
meaning-isolate	don ldog	
meditating	sgom pa	bhāvana
mental consciousness	yid shes	mano-jñāna
mental direct perceiver	yid kyi mngon sum	mānasa-pratyakṣha
method	thabs	upāya
Middle Way School	dbu ma pa	mādhyamika
migrator	'gro ba	gati
mind of enlightenment	byang chub kyi sems	bodhichitta

English	*Tibetan*	*Sanskrit*
Mind Only School	sems tsam pa	chittamātra
miserliness	ser sna	mātsarya
mist	kung sna	mahikā
mistaken consciousness	'khrul shes	bhrānti-jñāna
mode of statement	'god tshul	
momentary	skad cig ma	kṣhanika
mud	'jim pa	
mutually different	phan tshun tha dad	
mutually exclusive/ mutually exclusive phenomena	'gal ba	virodha
mutually inclusive/ mutually inclusive phenomena	don gcig	ekārtha

name	ming	
natural	lhan skyes	sahaja
natural primary color	lhan skyes kyi rtsa ba'i kha dog	sahaja-mūla-varṇa
nature	rang bzhin	
negative phenomena which are the same isolate type	dgag par gyur pa'i ldog pa rigs gcig pa	
negative phenomenon	dgag pa	pratiṣhedha
neighboring hell-being	nye 'khor ba'i dmyal ba	
nominal expression	ming gi brjod pa	

English	*Tibetan*	*Sanskrit*
non-	ma yin pa	
non-affirming negative	med dgag	prasajya-pratiṣhedha
non-associated compositional factor	ldan min 'du byed	viprayukta-saṃskara
non-associated compositional factor which has life	srog dang ldan pa'i ldan min 'du byed	
non-associated compositional factor which is a person	gang zag yin par gyur pa'i ldan min 'du byed	pudgala-viprayukta-saṃskāra
non-associated compositional factor which is not a person	gang zag ma yin par gyur pa'i ldan min 'du byed	apudgala-viprayukta-saṃskāra
non-associated compositional factors which are the same isolate type	ldan min 'du byed du gyur pa'i ldog pa rigs gcig pa	
non-associated compositional factors which are the same type of substantial entity	ldan min 'du byed du gyur pa'i rdzas rigs gcig pa	
non-conceptual consciousness	rtog med kyi shes pa	nirvikalpaka-jñāna
non-conceptual mental consciousness	rtog med yid shes	nirvikalpaka-mano-jñāna
non-existent	med pa	asat
non-level	phya le ba ma yin pa	vishāta
non-mistaken	ma 'khrul pa	abhrānta

English	Tibetan	Sanskrit
non-product	ma byas pa	akṛta
non-revelatory form	rnam par rig byed ma yin pa'i gzugs	avijñapti-rūpa
non-thing	dngos med	abhāva
nose consciousness	sna shes	ghrāṇa-jñāna
nose sense power	sna'i dbang po	ghrāṇa-indriya
not being a pot	bum pa ma yin pa	
number	grangs	saṃkhyā

object	yul	viṣaya
object helped	phan gdags bya	
object of abandonment	spang bya	
object of comprehension	gzhal bya	prameya
object of comprehension of an omniscient consciousness	rnam mkhyen gyi gzhal bya	sarvākārā-jñāna-prameya
object of engagement	'jug yul	*pravṛtti-viṣaya
object of hearing	nyan bya	
object of knowledge	shes bya	jñeya
object of meditation	sgom bya	
object of negation	dgag bya	pratiṣhedhya
object-source	yul gyi skye mched	viṣaya-āyatana

English	Tibetan	Sanskrit
object[s] of knowledge of which being [it or them] is possible	yin pa srid pa'i shes bya	
objects of knowledge of which being [them] is not possible	yin pa mi srid pa'i shes bya	
observed by valid cognition	tshad mas dmigs pa	*pramāṇa-ālaṃbīta
observed-object-condition	dmigs rkyen	ālambana-pratyaya
odor	dri	gandha
odor-constituent	dri'i khams	gandha-dhātu
odor-source	dri'i skye mched	gandha-āyatana
one/singular phenomenon	gcig	ekatva
one-with-pot	bum pa dang gcig	
only-a-permanent-phenomenon	rtag pa kho na	
opposite	log	
opposite from	las log pa	
opposite-from-being-something	yin log	
opposite-from-being-a-pot	bum pa yin pa las log pa	
opposite-from-not-being-something	min log	
opposite-from-not-being-a-pot	bum pa ma yin pa las log pa	

English	*Tibetan*	*Sanskrit*
order	go rim	anukrama
our own system	rang lugs	
path	lam	mārga
path of accumulation	tshogs lam	sambhāra-mārga
path of meditation	sgom lam	bhāvanā-mārga
path of no more learning	mi slob lam	ahaikṣa-mārga
path of preparation	sbyor lam	prayoga-mārga
path of reasoning	rigs lam	
path of seeing	mthong lam	darshana-mārga
permanent phenomenon	rtag pa	nitya
permanent phenomenon which is occasional	res 'ga' ba'i rtag pa	
permanent phenomenon which is stable in time	dus brtan pa'i rtag pa	
person	gang zag	pudgala/puruṣha
pervaded	khyab bya	
pervader	khyab byed	
pervasion of being	yin khyab	
pervasion of existence	yod khyab	
phenomena which are different types	rigs tha dad pa	

English	*Tibetan*	*Sanskrit*
phenomena which are discordant types	rigs mi mthun pa'i chos	
phenomena which are dissimilar types	rigs mi 'dra ba'i chos	
phenomena which are not the same type	rigs mi gcig pa'i chos	
phenomenon	chos	dharma
phenomenon-source	chos kyi skye mched	dharma-āyatana
phenomenon which has a basis of negation	dgag gzhi can gyi chos	
phenomenon which is a non-thing	dngos med kyi chos	abhāva-dharma
physical sense power	dbang po gzugs can pa	
pillar	ka ba	
place	yul	
pleasant articulate sound caused by elements conjoined with consciousness	zin pa'i 'byung ba las gyur pa'i sems can du ston pa'i sgra snyan pa	upātta-mahābhūta-hetuka-sattvākhya-yasha-shabda
pleasant articulate sound caused by elements not conjoined with consciousness	ma zin pa'i 'byung ba las gyur pa'i sems can du ston pa'i sgra snyan pa	anupātta-mahābhūta-hetuka-sattvākhya-yasha-shabda

English	*Tibetan*	*Sanskrit*
pleasant inarticulate sound caused by elements conjoined with consciousness	zin pa'i 'byung ba las gyur pa'i sems can du mi ston pa'i sgra snyan pa	upātta-mahābhūta-hetuka-asattvākhya-yasha-shabda
pleasant inarticulate sound caused by elements not conjoined with consciousness	ma zin pa'i 'byung ba las gyur pa'i sems can du mi ston pa'i sgra snyan pa	anupātta-mahābhūta-hetuka-asattvākhya-yasha-shabda
positive phenomena which are the same isolate type	sgrub par gyur pa'i ldog pa rigs gcig pa	
positive phenomenon	sgrub pa	vidhi
pot	bum pa	ghaṭa/kumbha
pot's isolate	bum pa'i ldog pa	
pot-which-is-one-with-pot	bum pa dang gcig tu gyur pa'i bum pa	
powerless subject	chos can nus med	
predicate	bsgrub bya'i chos/gsal ba	
predicate to be negated	dgag bya'i chos	*pratiṣhedhya-dharma
predicate to be proven	bsgrub bya'i chos	sādhya-dharma
presentation of our own system	rang lugs bzhag pa	
primary color	rtsa ba'i kha dog	mūla-varṇa
prior arising	snga logs su byung ba	

English	Tibetan	Sanskrit
prior arising of pot	bum pa'i snga logs su byung ba	
produced	bskyed bya	janya
producer	skyed byed	janaka
product/produced phenomenon	byas pa	kṛta
proof	sgrub byed	sādhana
property of the subject	phyogs chos	pakṣha-dharma
Proponents of a Person	gang zag yod par smra ba	pudgala-vādin
protector	mgon po	
proven	bsgrub bya	
pungent	tsha ba	kaṭuka
reason	gtan tshigs	hetu
red	dmar po	lohita
refined gold	gser btso ma	
refutation of mistaken views	'khrul ba dgag pa	
refutation of others' systems	gzhan lugs dgag pa	
related/related phenomena	'brel ba	sambandha
related as that arisen from that	de byung 'brel	tadutpatti-sambandha
related as the same essence	bdag gcig 'brel	tādātmya-sambandha
religious conch	chos dung	

English	*Tibetan*	*Sanskrit*
reversed	ldog	
roughness	rtsub pa	karkashatva
round	zlum po	parimaṇḍala
ruby	pad ma'i ra ga	padma-rakta
salty	lan tshva ba	lavaṇa
same entity	ngo bo gcig pa	eka-rūpatā
same essence	bdag nyid gcig pa	eka-ātman
same in terms of establishment and abiding	grub bde gcig	eka-yogakṣhema
same isolate type	ldog pa rigs gcig pa	
same nature	rang bzhin gcig pa	eka-prakṛtika
same self-isolate	rang ldog gcig pa	
same substantial entity	rdzas gcig pa	eka-dravya
same substantial entity in terms of establishment and abiding	grub bde rdzas gcig	
same type	rigs gcig pa	eka-jāti
same type of substantial entity	rdzas rigs gcig pa	
sapphire	in dra ni la	indranīla
Sarasvatī	dbyang can ma	sarasvatī
secondary color	yan lag gi kha dog	aṅga-varṇa
self	bdag	ātman
self-isolate	rang ldog	

English	*Tibetan*	*Sanskrit*
self-knower	rang rig	svasaṃvedana
self-sufficient	rang rkya ba	
selfless	bdag med	nairātmya
selflessness of persons	gang zag gi bdag med	pudgala-nairātmya
selflessness of phenomena	chos kyi bdag med	dharma-nairātmya
sense consciousness	dbang shes	indriya-jñāna
sense direct perceiver	dbang po'i mngon sum	indriya-pratyakṣha
sense power	dbang po	indriya
sentient being	sems can	sattva
shadow	grib ma	chhāyā
shape	dbyibs	saṃsthāna
shape-form	dbyibs kyi gzugs	
short	thung ba	hrasva
sign/reason	rtags	liṅga
similar class	mthun phyogs	sapakṣha
similitude-of-isolate-phenomenon-of-the-third-type	ldog chos phung sum tsam po ba'i rjes mthun	
similitude-of-isolate-phenomenon-which-is-itself	rang yin pa'i ldog chos kyi rjes mthun	
similitude-of-isolate-phenomenon-which-is-not-itself	rang ma yin pa'i ldog chos kyi rjes mthun	
similitude-of-substantial-phenomenon	rdzas chos kyi rjes mthun	

English	*Tibetan*	*Sanskrit*
slightly hidden phenomenon	cung zad lkog gyur	kimchid-parokṣha
smoke	du ba	dhūma
smoothness	'jam pa	shlakṣhṇatva
Solitary Realizer Superior	rang sangs rgyas kyi 'phags pa	pratyeka-buddha-ārya
Solitary Realizer Vehicle	rang sangs rgyas kyi theg pa	pratyeka-buddha-yāna
something which a permanent phenomenon is	yin par gyur pa'i rtag pa	
something which a permanent phenomenon is not	ma yin par gyur pa'i rtag pa	
sound	sgra	shabda
sound-constituent	sgra'i khams	shabda-dhātu
sound-imperma-nent-phenomenon	sgra mi rtag pa	
sound-source	sgra'i skye mched	shabda-āyatana
sound which indi-cates meaning to a sentient being	sems can la ston pa'i sgra	
sour	skyur ba	āmla
source	skye mched	āyatana
space	nam mkha'	ākāsha
spatially partless particles	rdul phran phyogs kyi cha med	
specifically characterized phenomenon	rang mtshan	svalakṣhaṇa
square	lham pa	vṛtta

English	*Tibetan*	*Sanskrit*
subject/logical subject	chos can	dharmin
subject/object-possessor	yul can	viṣhayin
subsequent arising	phyi logs su byung ba	
subsequent arising of pot	bum pa'i phyi logs su byung ba	
subsequent cognizer	bcad shes/dpyad shes	*parichchhinna-jñāna
substantial cause	nyer len/nyer len gyi rgyu	upadāna/upādāna-kāraṇa
substantial effect	nyer 'bras	
substantial entity	rdzas rgyun	dravya
substantial existent/substantially existent	rdzas yod/rdzas su yod pa	dravya-sat
substantial existent in the sense of being able to perform a function	don byed nus pa'i rdzas yod	
substantial existent in the sense of being established by reasoning	rigs pas grub pa'i rdzas yod	
substantial existent in the sense of being self-sufficiently apprehensible	rang skya 'dzin thub pa'i rdzas yod	
substantial existent in the sense of being statically unchanging	brtan par mi 'gyur pa'i rdzas yod	

English	*Tibetan*	*Sanskrit*
substantial phenomenon	rdzas chos	dravya-dharma
subtle	phra ba	sūkṣhma
subtle impermanence	phra ba'i mi rtag pa	*sūkṣhma-anitya
sunlight	nyi ma'i 'od ser	ātapa
Superior	'phags pa	ārya
Superior Body	lus 'phags po	videha
Superior's path	'phags pa'i lam	ārya-marga
Sūtra School	mdo sde pa	sautrāntika
sweet	mngar ba	madhura
syllogism	sbyor ba	prayoga
tangible object	reg bya	spraṣhṭavya
tangible object arisen from the elements	'byung 'gyur gyi reg bya	bhautika-spraṣhṭavya
tangible object which is an element	'byung bar gyur pa'i reg bya	bhūta-spraṣhṭavya
taste	ro	rasa
temporally partless moments	skad cig cha med	
terminological division	sgras brjod rigs kyi sgo nas dbye ba	
that [or those] of which being it [or them] is not possible	yin pa mi srid pa	

English	*Tibetan*	*Sanskrit*
that [or those] of which being it [or them] is possible	yin pa srid pa	
that which is able to perform a function	don byed nus pa	artha-kriyā-shakti/artha-kriyā-sāmarthya
that which is to be negated	dgag bya	pratiṣhedhya
that which is to be proven	bsgrub bya	sādhya
the two—a pillar and a pot	ka bum gnyis	
thesis	dam bca'	pratijñā
thinking	bsam pa	chintā
thirst	skom pa	pipāsā
thoroughly established phenomenon	yongs grub	pariniṣhpanna
thought/thought consciousness/conceptual consciousness	rtog pa	kalpanā
three modes	tshul gsum	
three possibilities	mu gsum	
three scriptural collections	sde snod gsum	tripiṭaka
three spheres	'khor gsum	
time	dus	kāla
tongue consciousness	lce shes	jihvā-jñāna
tongue sense power	lce'i dbang po	jihvā-indriya

English	*Tibetan*	*Sanskrit*
true cessations	'gog bden	nirodha-satya
true origins	kun 'byung bden pa	samudaya-satya
true paths	lam bden	mārga-satya
true sufferings	sdug bsngal bden pa	duḥkha-satya
truly established	bden par grub pa	satya-siddha
truth for a conventional [mind]/ truth for an obscured [mind]	kun rdzob bden pa	samvṛti-satya
tutor	yongs 'dzin	
type-generality	rigs spyi	jāti-sāmānya
ultimate awareness	blo don dam pa	
ultimate truth	don dam bden pa	paramārtha-satya
unattractive	phya legs pa ma yin pa	
uncommon/ unshared	thun mong ma yin pa	
uncommon empowering condition	thun mong ma yin pa'i bdag rkyen	asādhārana-adhipati-pratyaya
uncomposed	'dus ma byas	asaṃskṛta
uncomposed phenomenon	'dus ma byas kyi chos	asaṃskṛta-dharma
uncomposed space	'dus ma byas kyi nam mkha'	asaṃskṛta-akasha
unembodied emanation	sprul pa'i gang zag	

English	*Tibetan*	*Sanskrit*
unequal fragrant odor	zhim pa'i dri mi mnyam pa	visama-sugandha
unequal odor	dri mi mnyam pa	visama-gandha
unequal unfragrant odor	mi zhim pa'i dri mi mnyam pa	visama-durgandha
unfragrant manu-factured odor	mi zhim pa'i sbyar byung gi dri	sāṃyogika-durgandha
unfragrant natural odor	mi zhim pa'i lhan skyes kyi dri	sahaja-durgandha
unfragrant odor	dri mi zhim pa	durgandha
unpleasant articulate sound caused by elements conjoined with consciousness	zin pa'i 'byung ba las gyur pa'i sems can du ston pa'i sgra mi snyan pa	upātta-mahābhūta-hetuka-sattvākhya-ayasha-shabda
unpleasant articulate sound caused by elements not conjoined with consciousness	ma zin pa'i 'byung ba las gyur pa'i sems can du ston pa'i sgra mi snyan pa	anupātta-mahābhūta-hetuka-sattvākhya-ayasha-shabda
unpleasant inarticulate sound caused by elements conjoined with consciousness	zin pa'i 'byung ba las gyur pa'i sems can du mi ston pa'i sgra mi snyan pa	upātta-mahābhūta-hetuka-asattvākhya-ayasha-shabda
unpleasant inarticulate sound caused by elements not conjoined with consciousness	ma zin pa'i 'byung ba las gyur pa'i sems can du mi ston pa'i sgra mi snyan pa	anupātta-mahābhūta-hetuka-asattvākhya-ayasha-shabda
Unpleasant Sound	sgra mi snyan	kuru
unrelated/unre-lated phenomena	mi 'brel ba	asaṃbandha

English	Tibetan	Sanskrit
unwanted consequence	mi 'dod pa'i thal 'gyur	
Using Oxen	ba gling spyod	godānīya
valid cognition/ prime cognition	tshad ma	pramāṇa
valid cognizer/ prime cognizer	tshad ma	pramāṇa
valid consequence	thal 'gyur yang dag	
vehicle	theg pa	yāna
very hidden phenomenon	shin tu lkog gyur	atyartha-parokṣha
water	chu	ap
what something is	yin gyur	
what something is not	min gyur	
white	dkar po	avadāta
wind	rlung	vāyu
wisdom	shes rab	prajñā
wrong consciousness	log shes	viparyaya-jñāna
wrong view	log rtog	mithyā-saṃkalpa
yellow	ser po	pīta
yogic direct perceiver/yogic direct perception	rnal 'byor mngon sum	yogi-pratyakṣha

Bibliography *of works cited*

Note: The abbreviation P is used for citations in *Tibetan Tripiṭaka* (Tokyo-Kyoto: Tibetan Tripitaka Research Foundation, 1956)

1 *Works in Tibetan*

Ḇel-den-chö-jay (dpal ldan chos rje)/a.k.a. Ngak-w̄ang-ḇel-den (ngag dbang dpal ldan)

> *Explanation of the Meaning of Conventional and Ultimate in the Four Tenet Systems*
>
>> grub mtha' bzhi'i lugs kyi kun rdzob dang don dam pa'i don rnam par bshad pa
>> New Delhi: Lama Guru Deva, 1972

Ḇel-jor-hlün-drup (dpal 'byor lhun grub)

> *Commentary on the Difficult Points in (Ḏzong-ka-ḇa's) "The Essence of the Good Explanations", Lamp for the Teaching*
>
>> legs bshad snying po'i dka' 'grel bstan pa'i sgron me
>> Delhi: Rong tha mchog sprul, 1969

Ḏak-tsang (stag tshang lo tsā ba shes rab rin chen)

> *Ocean of Good Explanations, Explanation of "Freedom From Extremes Through Understanding All Tenets"*

grub mtha' kun shes nas mtha' bral grub pa zhes
bya ba'i bstan bcos rnam par bshad pa legs bshad
kyi rgya mtsho
Thim-phu: Kun-bzang-stobs-rgyal, 1976

Den-dar-hla-ram-ba (bstan dar lha ram pa)
*Notes Helping with the Difficult Points in Signs and Reasoning,
Clear Sunlight of New Explanation*
rtags rigs kyi dka' ba'i gnas la phan pa'i zin bris gsar
bshad nyi ma'i 'od zer
Collected Works of Bstan-dar Lha-ram of A-lag-sha,
Vol. 1
New Delhi: Lama Guru Deva, 1971

*Precious Lamp Illuminating the Treatise "Wheel of Properties of
the Subject" Formulated by Dignāga*
phyogs glang gis mdzad pa'i phyogs chos 'khor lo
zhes pa'i bstan bcos gsal bar byed pa'i rin chen
sgron me
Also: Collected gzung 'bum of Bstan-dar Lha-ram of
A-lag-sha, Vol. 1
New Delhi: Lama Guru Deva, 1971

*Beginnings of a Presentation of Generally and Specifically
Characterized Phenomena*
rang mtshan spyi mtshan gyi rnam gzhag rtsom
'phrol
Also: Collected Works of Bstan-dar Lha-ram of A-
lag-sha, Vol. 1
New Delhi: Lama Guru Deva, 1971

Dharmakīrti (chos kyi grags pa)
Seven Treatises on Valid Cognition
Analysis of Relations
saṁbandhaparīkṣhāvṛtti
'brel pa brtag pa'i rab tu byed pa
P5713, Vol. 130

Ascertainment of Valid Cognition
pramāṇavinishchaya
tshad ma rnam par nges pa
P5710, Vol. 130

Commentary on (Dignāga's) "Compendium of Valid Cognition"
pramāṇavarttikakārikā
tshad ma rnam 'grel gyi tshig le'ur byas pa
P5709, Vol. 130

Drop of Reasoning
nyāyabinduprakaraṇa
rigs pa'i thigs pa zhes bya ba'i rab tu byed pa
P5711, Vol. 130

Drop of Reasons
hetubindunāmaprakaraṇa
gtan tshigs kyi thigs pa zhes bya ba'i rab tu byed pa
P5712, Vol. 130

Proof of Other Continuums
saṁtānāntarasiddhināmaprakaraṇa
rgyud bzhan grub pa zhes bya ba'i rab tu byed pa
P5716, Vol. 130

Reasoning for Debate
vādanyāyanāmaprakaraṇa
rtsod pa'i rigs pa zhes bya ba'i rab tu byed pa
P5715, Vol. 130

Dzeṁay Rinbochay (dze smad rin po che)
Ṣhar-dzay *Collected Topics*
shar rtse bsdus grva
Mundgod, India: Drepung Loseling Printing Press,
n.d.

Gen-dün-drup-ba (dge 'dun grub pa)
*Commentary on (Vasubandhu's) "Treasury of Knowledge",
Illuminating the Path to Liberation*
dam pa'i chos mngon pa'i mdzod kyi rnam par
bshad pa thar lam gsal byed
Sarnath, India: Pleasure of Elegant Sayings Press,
1973

Jam-bel-trin-lay-yön-dan-gya-tso ('jam dpal 'phin las yon tan rgya
mtsho)
Lo-ṣel-ling *Collected Topics*
blo gsal gling bsdus grva
Mundgod, India: Drepung Loseling Press, 1978

Jam-ȳang-chok-hla-ö-ser ('jam dbyangs phyogs lha 'ad zer)
Ra-dö *Collected Topics*
    rva stod bsdus grva
    Dharamsala, India: Damchoe Sangpo, Library of
    Tibetan Works and Archives, 1980

Jang-ḡya (lcang skya)
*Presentation of Tenets/Clear Expositions of the Presentations of
Tenets, Beautiful Ornament for the Meru of the Subduer's
Teaching*
    grub pa'i mtha'i rnam par bzhag pa gsal bar bshad
    pa thub bstan lhun po'i mdzes rgyan
    Sarnath, India: Pleasure of Elegant Sayings Press,
    1970

Losang Gyatso (blo zang rgya mtsho)
*Compendium of the Important Points in the Presentation of Types
of Awarenesses, [an Internal Division of] the Greater Path of
Reasoning*
    rigs lam che ba blo rigs kyi rnam gshag nye mkho
    kun btus
    Dharamsala, India: Shes rig par khang, 1974

Mi-nyak Ge-shay Tsul-trim-ñam-gyel (mi nyag dge bshes tshul
khrims rnam rgyal)
*The Presentation of Signs and Reasonings, A Mirror
Illuminating All Phenomena*
    rtags rigs kyi rnam bzhag chos kun gsal ba'i me long
    In: *The First Magical Key Opening a Hundred Doors to
    the Path of Reasoning*
    rigs lam sgo brgya 'byed pa'i 'phrul gyi lde mig
    dang po
    Mundgod, India: Drepung Loseling Library, 1979

Ngak-̄wang-dra-shi (ngag dbang bkra shis)
Go-mang *Collected Topics*
    sgo mang bsdus grva
    n.p.,n.d.

Pur-bu-jok Jam-ba-gya-tso (phur bu lcog byams pa rgya mtsho)
"The Greater Path of Reasoning"
  rigs lam che ba
  In: *The Presentation of Collected Topics Revealing the*
    Meaning of the Texts on Valid Cognition, the Magical
    Key to the Path of Reasoning
  tshad ma'i gzhung don 'byed pa'i bsdus grva'i rnam
    bzhag rigs lam 'phrul gyi lde mig
  Buxa, India: n.p., 1965

"The Introductory Path of Reasoning"
  rigs lam chung ngu
  In: *The Presentation of Collected Topics Revealing the*
    Meaning of the Texts on Valid Cognition, the Magical
    Key to the Path of Reasoning
  tshad ma'i gzhung don 'byed pa'i bsdus grva'i rnam
    bzhag rigs lam 'phrul gyi lde mig
  Buxa, India: n.p., 1965

"The Middling Path of Reasoning"
  rigs lam 'bring
  In: *The Presentation of Collected Topics Revealing the*
    Meaning of the Texts on Valid Cognition, the Magical
    Key to the Path of Reasoning
  tshad ma'i gzhung don 'byed pa'i bsdus grva'i rnam
    bzhag rigs lam 'phrul gyi lde mig
  Buxa, India: n.p., 1965

Shāntirakṣhita (zhi ba 'tsho)
  Ornament to the Middle Way
  madhyamakālaṁkarakārikā
  dbu ma rgyan gyi tshig le'ur byas pa
  P5284, Vol.101

Vasubandhu (dbyig gnyen)
  Treasury of Knowledge
  abhidharmakoshakārikā
  chos mngon pa'i mdzod kyi bshad pa
  P5590, Vol. 115

2 *Other Works*

Anacker, Stefan. "Vasubandhu: Three Aspects". Ph.D. dissertation, University of Wisconsin, 1970.

Conze, Edward. *Buddhist Scriptures*. Harmondsworth, Middlesex, England: Penguin, 1973.

Dalai Lama. "Spiritual Contributions to Social Progress", *The Wall Street Journal* (October 29, 1981).

Dhargyey, Geshey Ngawang. *Tibetan Tradition of Mental Development*. Dharamsala, Library of Tibetan Works & Archives, 1974.

Downs, Hugh R. *Rhythms of a Himalayan Village*. San Francisco: Harper & Row, 1980.

Gyatso, Tenzin: The Fourteenth Dalai Lama. *The Buddhism of Tibet and The Key to the Middle Way*, The Wisdom of Tibet Series 1, trans. by Jeffrey Hopkins and Lati Rimpoche. New York: Harper & Row, 1975.

Hattori, Masaaki. *Dignāga, On Perception, being the Pratyakṣapariccheda of Dignāga's 'Pramāṇasamuccaya' from the Sanskrit Fragments and the Tibetan Versions*. Cambridge, Massachusetts: Harvard University Press, 1968.

Hopkins, Jeffrey. *Meditation on Emptiness*. London: Wisdom Publications, 1983.

Khetsun Sangbo Rinbochay. *Tantric Practice in Nying-Ma*. London: Rider, 1982.

Klein, Anne C. *Knowledge and Liberation: Tibetan Buddhist Epistemology in Support of Transformative Religious Experience*. Ithaca, New York: Snow Lion Publications, 1986.

Lati Rinbochay. *Mind in Tibetan Buddhism*, trans., ed., with an introduction by Elizabeth Napper. Valois, New York: Gabriel Press, 1980.

Lati Rinbochay, Denma Lochö Rinbochay, Leah Zahler, and Jeffrey Hopkins. *Meditative States in Tibetan Buddhism* London: Wisdom Publications, 1983.

Lauf, Detlef Ingo. *Tibetan Sacred Art, The Heritage of Tantra.* Berkeley: Shambala, 1976.

Lekden, Kensur Ngawang. *Meditations of a Tibetan Tantric Abbot: Kensur Lekden,* trans. and ed. by Jeffrey Hopkins. Dharamsala, India: Library of Tibetan Works and Archives, 1974.

Lodrö, Geshe G. *Geschichte der Kloster-Universität Drepung.* Weisbaden, West Germany: Franz Steiner Verlag GmbH, 1974.

Maitreya, Ārya. *The Sublime Science (Uttaratantra)* trans. by E. Obermiller. In: "The Sublime Science of the Great Vehicle to Salvation, being a Manual of Buddhist Monism". *Acta Orientalia,* vol. IX (1931).

Mates, Benson. *Elementary Logic.* New York: Oxford University Press, 1972.

Mill, John Stuart. *A System of Logic, Ratiocinative and Inductive.* New York: Harper & Brothers, 1874.

Nāgārjuna. *Nāgārjuna's Letter to King Gautamīputra,* trans. by Ven. Lozang Jamspal, Ven. Ngawang Samten Chophel, and Peter Della Santina. Delhi: Motilal Banarsidass, 1978.

_____. *The Precious Garland of Advice for the King (rāja-parikathā-ratnamālā),* in Nagarjuna and Kaysang Gyatso, the Seventh Dalai Lama, *The Precious Garland and The Song of the Four Mindfulnesses,* The Wisdom of Tibet Series 2, trans. by Jeffrey Hopkins and Lati Rimpoche with Anne Klein. New York: Harper & Row, 1975.

Potter, Karl H. *Presuppositions of India's Philosophies.* Englewood Cliffs, N.J.: Prentice-Hall, Inc., 1963.

Rabten, Geshe. *The Life and Teaching of Geshé Rabten, A Tibetan Lama's Search for Truth,* trans. and ed. by B. Alan Wallace (Gelong Jhampa Kelsang). London: George Allen & Unwin, 1980.

Rogers, Katherine. "Tibetan Logic: A Translation, with Commentary, of Pur-bu-jok Jam-ba-gya-tso's *The Topic of Signs and Reasonings from the 'Great Path of Reasoning' in The Magic Key to the Path of Reasoning, Explanation of the Collected Topics Revealing the Meaning of the Texts on Valid Cognition".* M.A. thesis, University of Virginia, 1980.

Sierksma, K. "Rtsod-pa: The Monachal Disputation in Tibet". *Indo-Iranian Journal*, Vol. 8 (1964).

Sopa, Geshe Lhundup. *Lectures on Tibetan Religious Culture*. University of Wisconsin, unpublished manuscript, 1972.

Sopa, Geshe Lhundup and Hopkins, Jeffrey. *Practice and Theory of Tibetan Buddhism*. New York: Grove Press, Inc., 1976.

Stcherbatsky, F. Th. *Buddhist Logic*. New York: Dover Publications, Inc., 1962.

Tsong-ka-pa. *Tantra in Tibet, The Great Exposition of Secret Mantra*, trans. and ed. by Jeffrey Hopkins. London: George Allen & Unwin, 1977.

Van de Kuijp, L.W.J. "Phya-Pa Chos Kyi Seng-Ge's Impact on Tibetan Epistemological Theory". *Journal of Indian Philosophy*, vol.5 (1978).

Wittgenstein, Ludwig. *Remarks on Colour*, ed. by G.E.M. Anscombe, trans. by Linda L. McAlister and Margarete Schättle. Berkeley, California: University of California Press, 1978.

Index

A

Abhidharmakoshakārikā (see
Treasury of Knowledge)
abstract general term
  in the Collected Topics logic 786
  meaning of name 786
abstract singular term (see also
singular collective entity), 164
  and collective predication 780
  in the Collected Topics logic
  778-789
  meaning of name 778
afflictions 6, 10
aggregates, five 363
  as appropriated 396
  as contaminated 396
  as the same entity as the self 574
Ajitamitra 188
Amitābha 203, 223
Amitāyus 78, 223
Amoghasiddhi 78, 235
annotations in this text 172
  arrangement of xx
  formatting in translation of 169

from the oral tradition xxii
sources of xix-xxvii
use of hyphens in 77n.1
use of masculine pronouns in xx
appearance factor 314, 404
  of a direct perceiver compared
  to the ascertainment factor of a
  direct perceiver 405
appearing object 14, 286
apprehended object 286
  and what is being
  comprehended 296
argument
  forms of 33, 54
  soundness and validity of 50-51
  validity of 33
Aristotle
  categorical syllogism of
  compared to the Collected
  Topics syllogism 836-849
  on necessity 794
Aronson, Harvey xxvii
ascertainment factor 404
  of a direct perceiver compared
  to the appearance factor of a
  direct perceiver 405

Ashvaghoṣha
   cited 4
Avalokiteshvara 27
awareness 82, 675
   defined 355
   phenomena mutually inclusive
   with 271, 523
   regarding the definition of 357-
   359
"Awareness and Knowledge" xiv,
xvii
   alternatively titled "Types of
   Awarenesses" 355n.3
awareness to which an object
appears but is not ascertained 292
awareness, ultimate 278

B

Bacon, Kimberly xxvii
basic consequence 108, 110, 116,
122, 125, 131
basis of debate 36
basis of inference 36
basis of relation 39, 42, 47
being
   and existence 88-89, 94, 334, 340,
   470
   and opposite-from-not-being-
   something 483-486
   as a permanent quality of
   phenomena 485-486
   as mutually inclusive with non-
   non-being 527-529
   meaning of the copula 787-788
   something which is a non-
   existent 504
   something's being itself 85-86,
   234, 339, 695, 702-703, 778-789
   something's not being itself 234,
   339, 349, 426, 465, 478, 487, 695,
   702-703, 778-789
Bel-den-chö-jay
   as the source of the Ge-luk-ba
   response to Dak-tsang on the

two truths 313
   cited 200
   date of birth of 313
blue
   compared to the color of cotton
   cloth 154-159
body consciousness
   defined 361
body sense power
   defined 219
boundaries of pervasion 133
bsDus grva (see Collected Topics)
Buddha
   appeal to reasoning by 178-183
   as a doctor 5
   as a man but not mortal 841n.1
   as a Superior 366
   as a teacher of causes and effects
   277, 531
   as a Valid Teacher 178-183
   as both a being and person but
   not of cyclic existence 366n.2
   as free of thought 20
   as free of wrong
   consciousnesses 15
   as the source of the Collected
   Topics xvii
   cited 3, 18, 178, 188, 546
   cross-functionality of
   consciousnesses in 218
   epithets of 475
   on mind and rebirth 546
   reason for reverence for 18
Buddhahood 27

C

Cargile, James xxvii
categorical logic
   syllogism of compared to the
   Collected Topics syllogism 836-
   849
cause 80, 170
   and effect as the primary
   focuses of debate 12, 532

and effect in the Tutor's *Collected Topics* 532

as a different substantial entity from its effect 575, 615

as a functioning thing 276-277

as mutually inclusive with direct cause and indirect cause 541-542

as neither a generality nor an instance of its effect 615, 617, 626, 675-679

as temporally separate from its effect 537, 609-613, 678

compared to substantial cause 547, 566-568

compared to what is not an effect 551-553

defined 273, 533

defined alternatively 534

divided into direct and indirect causes 540

divided into substantial causes and cooperative conditions 277, 544

phenomena mutually inclusive with 272-279

used in complex descriptions of things 542

Cha-ba-chö-ġyi-šeng-gay 170

as the formulator of a system of substantial and isolate phenomena 696

dates of xviii

Challenger 28-32, 100

as first to speak in debate 102

as non-Proponent of Sūtra in dispelling objections 172

as Proponent of Sūtra in refutation of mistaken views 171

as the easier position 31, 130

assertions of in debate 55

exclaims, "Finished!" 125

physical movements by 29, 125n.3

role of in comparing phenomena 133, 137, 141, 143n.1, 147

use of counterexamples by 105, 511

warns, "You asserted the pervasion." 110

warns, "You asserted the reason." 255

characteristics, uncommon 298-299

Chatterjee, A.K. xxiv

Chittamātra (see Mind Only School)

class logic 853

and the distinction between membership and inclusion 854

clear internal form 218

cloud color

compared to secondary color 242

which is a secondary color 196

coextensives with an isolate 422-440

as isolate phenomena which are not themselves 742

as not being a generality of the thing which is it 626

enumeration of 428

method for establishing 423-424

of "complex" definitions and definienda 439-440

of phenomena other than definitions and definienda 438

reason for name 422

table of 436

Collected Topics

as a literary genre xiv

as an ordered part of a sequence of study 693

as formalization of normal disputation 106

as preliminary for later study xv, 22, 130, 171, 851

as the first class in the ge-shay degree program 21-23
comparison of with Western thought xxi-xxii, xxiv, 775-857
"Established Bases" as the most important chapter in 267
first text xviii
flow of consequences in 131
form of syllogism used in 49, 836
meaning of name xviii
philosophical grounding of xix, 5
presentation of colors in 185
scope of this study of xiii-xxiii, 836
sources of xvii
syllogism of compared to a Western form 836-849, 852-855
textual form of debates 99, 121, 126-131, 225, 231, 236-237, 239, 253-254, 319, 320, 344-345, 353-354, 387-391, 497, 513, 604, 608, 611, 644, 672
textual style 193, 249, 263-264, 324, 441
collection-generality 630
compared to generality 681-682
compared to type-generality 680
defined 632
collective engager
and eliminative engagers 297-300
color 101, 185, 194-197
compared to primary color 235-238
compared to red 143-148
compared to shape 199
defined 62, 194
defined alternatively 70
divided into twelve 194
divided into two 194
illustration of defined 71
purpose for study of 185-187, 264-265

color-form 79, 244
compared to form 246-248
Commentary on (Dignāga's) "Compendium of Valid Cognition" xviii
on a generality which is a separate entity from its instances 619
on Buddha as a Valid Teacher 183
on causes and effects 532
on isolates 416
on mind 355
on opposites 482
on the enumeration of valid cognizers 296
on the two truths and specifically and generally characterized phenomena 305
on visible forms 193
Commentary on (Vasubandhu's) "Treasury of Knowledge"
on odors 206
on particle substances in atoms 205n.3
on secondary colors 196
on shapes 199
on sound 204n.1
common being 367-373
and intermediate state beings 368n.1
and the causes of being reborn in a happy migration 546
defined 364
demigods 371
eighteen types of hell-beings 369
six types of having the basis of a migrator 367
three types of hungry ghosts 369
twenty-seven types of gods 372
common locus 123, 138, 159
two types of animals 370
as including all existents 336

as necessarily an existent 628
comparison of phenomena 133-165
  as the form for relaying the information that "some are ... " and "some are not ... " 846
  chart of 134
  nature of the principals in 163-165
compassion
  as symbolized in the monk's clothing 26
Compendium of Valid Cognition xviii
  on counterfeit direct perceivers 291
composed phenomenon
  defined 273
  phenomena mutually inclusive with 272-279
  reason for name 276, 533
composite phenomenon
  as conventional truths according to Ḍak-tsang's interpretation 309-311
  as not being a separate entity from its subtle particles 620
conceptual consciousness
  fault of 14
concrete general term
  and distributive predication 780
  in the Collected Topics logic 778-789
  meaning of name 779
concrete singular term
  in the Collected Topics logic 785
  meaning of name 785
consciousness 82, 355-362
  compared to specifically characterized phenomenon 382-386
  defined 355
  defined alternatively 355
  divided into two 297, 359

phenomena mutually inclusive with 271, 523
  regarding the definition of 355-357
consequence 33, 54-60
  as an outflow of the opponent's assertion 104
  as essential in Tibetan debate 105
  contrasted to syllogisms 55-56, 109-110
  divided into two 56
  efficacy of 54-55, 58, 59, 110
  epistemological requirement for 56, 58-59
  example of 55, 57, 59
  flow from one to the next 116, 119, 123, 124, 131, 353, 387-391
  in refutation of mistaken views 171
  possible verbal faults of 228-230, 324-325, 402-404, 508-514, 518
  procedure for formulating 56-59, 228-230, 236, 320-321, 324-325, 344-345, 353-354, 447, 513, 515, 634
  reliance on counterexamples for 106
  stretching the limits of 506-516, 518
  thesis implied by 57
  translation of 55, 229
  with a two-part reason 239-242, 402-404, 507-514
Consequence School
  reliance on consequences in 33, 54-55
contaminated 5
contradictory reason 43
conventional awareness 286, 316
conventional truth 283
  and ultimate truths 284-317, 849-850

compared to permanent phenomenon according to Ḍaktsang's interpretation 312
criteria for according to Bel-den-chö-jay 315
defined 282
defined according to Ḍaktsang's interpretation 308
identified in relation to an conventional awareness 316
phenomena mutually inclusive with 279-284
cooperative condition 80, 277, 544-549
as mutually exclusive with the substantial causes of a basis 547
identified for a clay pot 545
phenomena mutually inclusive with 546
cooperative condition (of functioning thing)
defined 544
divided into two 548
nature of 614
cooperative effect (of functioning thing)
proposed definition of 563
copulative association
and pervasion 425-426, 478, 775-836
contexts of 795-836
meaning of 775-789
statements of 775-789
copulative statement 39, 40
and statements of pervasion 775
and translation of statements of pervasion 45
as implied by pervasions 790-793
as unable to bear the relation of transitivity 788
as used in the proof of an object of knowledge of which being it is possible 328

as used in the proof of objects of knowledge of which being them is not possible 332, 339
in relation to being and existence 88
nature of the copulas in 787-788
nature of the predicates in 786-787
nature of the subjects in 778-789
subjects of 93
correct consequence 56, 109, 110, 118
correct sign 38-49
defined 38
divided into two 44
example of 38
correct sign (in the proof of sound as an impermanent phenomenon by the sign, product)
defined 38
correctly assuming consciousness 14, 15
counter-pervasion 38, 47-49, 53
formulated 48
in relation to forward pervasion 49
counter-pervasion (in the proof of sound as an impermanent phenomenon)
defined 48
counterexample 105, 106
counterfeit consequence 56, 58, 60
counterfeit sign 38
creator deity
refuted 9-10
cyclic existence 3, 11
and liberation 17
and wisdom 29
as an effect 531
as only suffering 4
nature of 368-373
source of 6
three realms of 372

D

Ḍak-tsang
  as the source for the Śa-ḡya-ba
    interpretation of the Sūtra
    School Following Reasoning 305
  date of birth of 305
  on composite phenomena as
    conventional truths 309-311
Dalai Lama, Fourteenth
  on learning and practice 8
Dalai Lama, Thirteenth xiii
debate 15, 21
  actual session of 28-32
  and normal disputation 106,
    117, 842
  as critical analysis 31, 130
  as providing suppleness of
    mind 22
  as religious practice 6-8, 24, 849
  as the style in texts explaining
    philosophy 850
  disputants in 28, 100, 130
  etiquette of 111, 142, 254
  examinations in 31
  flow of consequences in 116,
    119, 123, 124, 131, 353, 387-391
  for establishing the differences
    between phenomena 133-165
  for refuting mistaken views 130
  interpretation of grammar in 83,
    399, 430, 506, 509-510, 518, 521,
    529, 559, 604, 607, 609, 612, 670-
    675, 683, 685-687, 689-690, 691
  involving a two-part reason 239-
    242, 402-404, 507-514
  meaning of clapping in 30
  opening statement in 28, 103
  physical movements in 29-30,
    125n.3
  procedure in 21, 56-60, 99-131,
    133, 225, 228-230, 239-242, 324-
    325, 344-345, 353-354, 387-391,
    402-404, 462, 497-498, 507-514,
    604, 640

purpose for 5, 6, 13, 60, 121, 185-
    187, 849-857
  related to the three trainings 7
  review of consequences in 120-
    122, 225, 240-242, 389-391
  stylistic points in 228-230, 236,
    320-321, 324-326, 344-345, 353-
    354, 402-404, 497, 513, 515
  three approaches of 6, 9-13, 171,
    855
  traditional setting for 24-32
Debate A.1 57-60, 100-129
  comparing the principals of 143-
    148, 163-165
  implied form of 126-129
  textual form of 101-102, 222-223
debating courtyard 28
Defender 28-32, 100
  alternative answers to the
    Challenger's first question
    104n.1
  answers of 103, 107-108, 110-
    116, 131, 137, 239-242, 403-404,
    507-514, 608
  answers to a two-part reason
    239-242, 403-404
  answers, "I accept it." 111, 121,
    514
  answers, "The combined reason
    is not established." 241, 403-404
  answers, "The pervasion is
    opposite." 113, 254
  answers, "The reason is not
    established." 112
  answers, "There is no
    pervasion." 112
  answers, "Why?" 107
  as making assertions through
    answers 102, 511
  as non-Proponent of Sūtra in
    refutation of mistaken views 171
  as Proponent of Sūtra in
    dispelling objections 172
  as the more difficult position 31,
    130, 856

assertions of in debate 58-59, 60
inability to respond to a correct
consequence 109
role of in comparing
phenomena 133, 137, 141, 142,
147, 161
table of answers of 115
definiendum 61-74, 83, 97
and its definition as positive or
negative phenomena 356-357
as being permanent by its
nature 413
as having all four isolates 420
as mutually exclusive with
definition 63, 815-817
as necessarily a generality as
well 654
as the name 62
compared to definition 160-161
compared to one-with-
functioning-thing 434
compared to the four
coextensives of the isolate of
functioning thing 432, 445-448
compared to the four
coextensives of the isolate of
that which is able to perform a
function 452-454
defined 69
establishing the relationship
with the definition of each 66-68
four phenomena coextensive
with the isolate of any 436-437
three qualities of 69-70
definiendum of that which is able
to perform a function 83, 423, 442
as a definiendum 429
as permanent 429
four phenomena coextensive
with the isolate of 439
definition 61-74
and its definiendum as positive
or negative phenomena 356-357
as a meaning-isolate 419

as being permanent by its
nature 413
as mutually exclusive with
definiendum 63, 815-817
as the focus of the philosophy
61, 63
as the object 62
compared to definiendum 160-
161
compared to functioning thing
338
compared to the four
coextensives of the isolate of
functioning thing 432, 441-445
compared to the four
coextensives of the isolate of
that which is able to perform a
function 448-451
defined 68
divided into two 72-74
each compared to its
definiendum 61-62
establishing the relationship
with the definiendum of each
66-68
fallacy of a pervasion that is too
extensive in 64
fallacy of non-occurrence in 65,
72
fallacy of non-pervasion in 64
four phenomena coextensive
with the isolate of any 436-437
identifying nature and function
211, 274
primacy of 67, 473-475, 765
quantification of 85-86
three possible faults of 63-66
three qualities of 68-69
which eliminates discordant
types 72-74
which eliminates wrong ideas
72-74
definition of functioning thing 84,
97

Ḏen-dar-hla-ram-ba
  on the nature of pervasion 793
Denma Lochö Rinbochay xxiv
  on being related as the same
  essence 636
  on direct and substantial causes
  548
  on functioning-thing-which-is-
  an-isolate-phenomenon 709
  on generality-of-permanent-
  phenomenon 663, 665
  on generating wisdom 173
  on isolates 416, 422
  on similitude-of-isolate-
  phenomenon-which-is-itself 717
  on the meaning of path 365
  on the opening statement in
  debate 29
  on the proof of something as
  itself 730, 731
  on the proposed definition of
  non-existent 72
  on the three possible faults of a
  definition 64
determinative knower 285
determined object 285
dharma
  as medicine 5
Dharmakīrti xviii, 13
  as a source for the Collected
  Topics 34, 177
  cited 193
  dates of xviii
  Seven Treatises on Valid
  Cognition by xx
different/different phenomena/
difference 61, 95, 119, 134
  and being different from a non-
  existent 463
  and mutually different
  phenomena 350-351
  and objects of knowledge of
  which being them is not
  possible 335-339

  and objects of knowledge of
  which being them is possible
  335-339
  and one 346-350, 463-464, 469-
  472, 474
  and the definition of something
  which is different from sound
  348
  as being permanent by nature
  411-413
  as explained in the Go-mang
  Collected Topics 568-584
  as itself being one 349
  ascertaining one without
  ascertaining the other 473-476
  defined 346
  divided into three 579
  divided into two 159
  table of 583
  types of in debate 134-165, 347
different entities
  defined 580
  phenomena mutually inclusive
  with 580
different-from-functioning-thing
652
  as only a generality 628
  compared to functioning thing
  348, 826-829
  compared to non-thing 349
different-from-pot
  as being permanent by its
  nature 411-413
  definition of something which is
  412
different self-isolate (from object
of knowledge)
  defined 580
different self-isolates
  defined 580
different substantial entities 534
  divided into two 591
  proven 536
different types
  defined 580

phenomena mutually inclusive
with 581
Dignāga xviii, xxii
as a source for the Collected
Topics 34, 177
dates of xvii
direct cause 80, 540-544
as mutually inclusive with
cause and indirect cause 541-542
compared to what is not an
indirect cause 553-554
direct cause (of a clay pot)
compared to substantial cause
of a clay pot 548
direct cause (of functioning thing)
as mutually exclusive with its
indirect cause 541
compared to functioning thing
543
compared to functioning thing's
cause 556-558
defined 540
divided into two 548
direct effect 540-544
as mutually inclusive with effect
and indirect effect 541
compared to what is not an
indirect effect 555-556
direct effect (of functioning thing)
as mutually exclusive with its
indirect effect 542
compared to functioning thing's
effect 559
compared to the effect of what
is produced directly from
functioning thing 559-562
defined 541
direct perceiver/direct perception
17, 20
and other non-conceptual
consciousnesses 291-292
appearing object of 286, 420-422
as a collective engager 297-300
as an impermanent phe-
nomenon perceiving other

impermanent phenomena 292
as an ultimate awareness 278
as correct 290
as establishing phenomena 270
as inducing conceptions 293-294
as non-conceptual 293-294
as non-mistaken 290
as not mixing place, time, and
nature 302-304
as not superimposing
characteristics 299
as superior to thought 286
as the sole perceiver of
specifically characterized
phenomena 290-294
defined 290
development of 13-19
development of from inferential
cognition 17-18, 294
divided into two 292
reason for name 290
what appears to and what is
ascertained by 291, 404-407
direct valid cognizer/direct prime
cognizer 72-73, 178, 180
defined 72
Discipline 22, 23
dispelling objections 9, 172, 252-
253
role of Proponent of Sūtra in
172, 254
dissimilar class 43, 47, 52
in relation to the sign 48
dissimilar class (in the proof of
sound as an impermanent
phenomenon)
defined 47
dissimilar types
divided into two 581
division (of phenomena) 263
as sometimes including things
outside what is divided 581, 630
terminological 630, 760
doubt
equal 14, 15

tending to the factual 14, 15
tending to the non-factual 14, 15
Dre-b̄ung Monastic University
xxiii, xxv, xxvi, 35, 307
Dreyfus, Georges xxvii
Dzemay Rinbochay xix
Ḏzong-ka-b̄a xxvi
and Mañjushrī 175

E

ear consciousness
defined 360
ear sense power
defined 219
earth
defined 211
manifest as stability 212
effect 80, 170
as a different substantial entity
from its cause 575
as a functioning thing 276-277
as mutually inclusive with
direct effect and indirect effect
541
as neither a generality nor an
instance of its cause 615, 617,
626, 675-679
as temporally separate from its
cause 536, 537, 609-613, 678
as the main function of
functioning things 272
defined 273, 533
defined alternatively 534
divided into direct and indirect
effects 541
divided into substantial and
cooperative effects 563
phenomena mutually inclusive
with 272-279
used in complex descriptions of
things 542
effort 12, 26
eight approaches of pervasion 66-
67, 138

elements, four 79, 202, 211-215
and all other forms 216
as mutually exclusive with what
is arisen from the elements 255-
258
eliminative engager
and collective engagers 297-300
empowering condition 362
emptiness 268
entity
as what all phenomena bear 271
epistemology 170
equivalence 62
and exemplification 787-789
and self-identity 818
established
meaning of 628
established base 227, 269-317
as being permanent itself but
including impermanent
phenomena 318-321
as not being an instance 627
as permanent by its nature 318
compared to either a cause or an
effect 550-551
compared to permanent
phenomenon 318-321
defined 269
divided into one and different
346-350, 463
divided into permanent
phenomena and functioning
things 272
phenomena mutually inclusive
with 269-272, 388
table of phenomena mutually
inclusive with 270
those suitable to appear to
direct perceivers and those
which must appear to thought
consciousnesses 295-296
Euler, Leonhard
diagrams of 134, 796

existence
    and being 88-89, 94, 334, 340,
    470
    and establishment 406
    as a permanent quality of
    phenomena 486
    as predominating in sets
    including both existents and
    non-existents 330
existent 82, 95, 269, 270-317, 760
    as never being a self-sufficient
    substantial existent 768
    as not being an instance 627
    as predominating in sets
    including both existents and
    non-existents 330
    as selfless 269
    compared to functioning thing
    322-326
    compared to non-thing 326
    compared to that of which being
    it is possible 504
    defined 269
    phenomena mutually inclusive
    with 269-272
external form 187, 192-217
    divided into five 192
    phenomena mutually inclusive
    with 192
external matter
    defined 189
external object 188
eye consciousness 217
    defined 360
    substantial cause and
    cooperative condition of 545
    when mistaken and wrong 291
eye sense power
    defined 218
    divided into two 218
    phenomena mutually inclusive
    with 218

F

fire
    defined 211
    manifest as heat 213
Foe Destroyer
    four types of 367n.1
form 170, 187-265
    as a collection-generality 632
    as an observed-object-condition
    for consciousness 361
    as appropriated 396
    as contaminated 396
    as mutually inclusive with
    matter 189
    classification of an individual
    220
    compared to color-form 246-248
    compared to shape-form 244-
    246
    defined 189
    divided into eleven 188
    divided into ten 191
    divided into three 190
form for the mental consciousness
188
    defined 191
form-source 79, 192, 247
    defined 192
    divided into twenty 194
    divided into two 194
    phenomena mutually inclusive
    with 193
forward pervasion 38, 41-47, 53
    formulated 45
    in relation to counter-pervasion
    49
forward pervasion (in the proof of
sound as an impermanent
phenomenon)
    defined 42
four noble truths 4, 25
    true cessations 4
    true origins 4

true paths 5
true sufferings 4
four possibilities
  chart of 158
  paradigm for establishing 153-159
  without there being something which is neither 162-163
four seals 181
functioning thing 10, 77
  also referred to as "thing" 77n.2
  as an effect of its own cause 605-606
  as itself being a non-associated compositional factor 373
  as mutually inclusive with substantial phenomenon 758-770
  compared to definition 338
  compared to different-from-functioning-thing 348, 826-829
  compared to existent 322-326
  compared to functioning thing's cause 538
  compared to functioning thing's effect 538
  compared to its direct and indirect causes and effects 543
  compared to one-with-functioning-thing 434
  compared to the four coextensives of the isolate of functioning thing 431
  compared to the isolate of that which is able to perform a function 451
  compared to the phenomena mutually inclusive with it 427
  defined 272
  divided into the five aggregates 363
  divided into three 354-376
  general-isolate of 460-462
  general-isolate of compared to the illustration-isolate of 462

  illustration of 457-459, 460-462
  illustration-isolate of 457-459, 460-462
  meaning-isolate of 459-460
  opposite-from-being-a- compared to opposite-from-being-a-permanent-phenomenon 489-492
  phenomena mutually inclusive with 272-279, 384, 391
  table of divisions of 375-376
  table of phenomena mutually inclusive with 273
  translated as non-thing in the negative 323n.1
functioning thing, cause of
  as not being an instance of functioning thing 615, 626
  compared to functioning thing 538
  compared to functioning thing's direct cause 556-558
  compared to functioning thing's effect 609-613
  compared to various types of its causes 558
  defined 534
functioning thing, effect of
  compared to functioning thing 538
  compared to functioning thing's cause 609-613
  compared to functioning thing's direct effect 559
  defined 536
functioning thing, isolate of
  compared to illustration-isolate of functioning thing 459
  compared to meaning-isolate of functioning thing 460
  compared to the phenomena coextensive with the isolate of functioning thing 426
  compared to various phenomena 435

enumeration of the phenomena coextensive with 428

four phenomena coextensive with compared to definiendum 432, 445-448

four phenomena coextensive with compared to definition 432, 441-445

four phenomena coextensive with compared to functioning thing 431

four phenomena coextensive with compared to permanent phenomenon 431, 455-457

phenomena coextensive with 423

functioning-thing-which-is-an-isolate-phenomenon 708

proven to be a similitude of substantial phenomenon 708-712

functioning-thing-which-is-one-with-functioning-thing 423, 455

as mutually exclusive with its cause 539

denied to be a definiendum 430

proposed definition of 430

qualified as impermanent 428

G

Gan-den Monastic University xiii, xxiii, xxv, xxvi

Garland of the Life Tales
on learning 4

Ge-den-chö-ling Nunnery xxi

Ge-luk-ba xix, xx, xxvii, 75
and reasoning 13
education in 21, 24
on ordinary mental direct perception 293
on the efficacy of debate 15
on the essentials for direct perception of selflessness 17

on the limits of reasoning 16, 18

on the necessity for reasoning 20

on the two truths in the Sūtra School Following Reasoning 304-317

reliance on consequences in 55

Gen-dün-drup-ba 196, 199

general-isolate 417, 460-462
as mutually inclusive with self-isolate 417
as what is referred to as an isolate 420
of functioning thing compared to the illustration-isolate of functioning thing 462

generality 87, 170, 233
as a generality of instance 656
as a permanent phenomenon 630
as an instance of instance 652, 653
as an instance of permanent phenomenon 650
as itself a generality and an instance 641, 649-659
as not being a separate entity from its instances 619-621
as not being mutually exclusive with instance 629
as related with its instances as the same essence 617
as the pervader 618
compared to collection-generality 681-682
compared to generally characterized phenomenon 852
compared to instance 633-642
compared to non-instance 641
defined 83, 618
defined alternatively 618
divided into three 630
proof of something as a 633-635
regarding the definition of 684

generality-of-functioning-thing
as an isolate phenomenon of the
third type 745
compared to generality-of-
impermanent-phenomenon 646-
649
compared to generality-of-that-
which-is-able-to-perform-a-
function 643-646
compared to non-instance-of-
functioning-thing 667-670
generality-of-permanent-
phenomenon
compared to non-instance-of-
permanent-phenomenon 659-
663
defined 664
generality-of- compared to
instance-of- 663-667
generally characterized
phenomenon 284, 386-392
and specifically characterized
phenomena 284-304
as defined by Gön-chok-jik-
may-w̄ang-b̄o 307
as perceived with a mixture of
place, time, and nature 300-301
compared to generality 852
compared to hidden
phenomenon 386-392
defined 282
phenomena mutually inclusive
with 279-284
reason for name 287, 300
Geshay Belden Drakba xxiv
ge-s̄hay degree 8, 31
final examination for 23
hla-ram-b̄a retainer class for 22-
24
ka-ram-b̄a retainer class for 22-
24
program of studies for 21-24
rankings of 23
Ge-s̄hay D̄ra-s̄hi Bum xxv
Ge-s̄hay Ḡa-ȳang xxv

Geshay Jamb̄el Thardö xxiii
Geshe Lobsang Tharchin xxiii
on debate 8-13
Geshé Rabten xxiv
on studying colors 185
on the monk's clothing 24-28
Go-mang *Collected Topics* xix
as a source for "Generalities and
Instances" 633, 643, 646, 649, 681
as a source for "Identifying
Isolates" 441, 457, 459, 462, 472
as a source for "The
Introductory Presentation of
Causes and Effects" 562, 566,
568, 585, 589, 593
on being related as the same
essence 635
on Cha-ba's system of
substantial and isolate
phenomena 696
on different entities 591
on five types of functioning
things 363
on form-sources 193
on generality and type-
generality 630
on isolate-phenomenon-of-the-
third-type 724
on opposite-from-being-an-
existent 486
on opposite-from-not-being-a-
pot 484
on persons as imputed existents
763
on sameness and difference 568-
584
on shapes 199
on sound-impermanent-
phenomenon 672, 674, 690
on substantial and isolate
phenomena 758-770
on the color and odor of a
composed phenomenon 587
on the comparison of color and
shape 199

on the establishment of many common locuses 639
on the eye sense power 218
Go-mang *Types of Awarenesses*
on a knower of an object 357
on the definition of a consciousness 355
Gön-chok-jik-may-wang-bo
dates of 306
Great Exposition School xix
on being permanent 280
on forms 191
on momentary disintegration 276
on partless particles and partless moments 311
on permanent phenomena as functional 283
on permanent phenomena as ultimate truths 313
on shapes 200
on the selflessness of persons 268, 764
on the two truths 309
Great Prayer Festival 23, 75
Great Vehicle
and the mind of enlightenment 30
motivation in 29
on Buddha as a man but not mortal 841n.1
on direct perception of selflessness 16
on the types of selflessness 268
philosophical systems in xix
practice of 365
"The Greater Path of Reasoning" xiv, xv, 22, 56, 172
topics in xvi
Groner, Paul xxvii
guru 176

H

Hartt, Julian xxvii
hidden phenomenon 269, 271, 295-317, 386-394, 761
compared to generally characterized phenomenon 386-392
defined 269
phenomena mutually inclusive with 269-272
Hinayāna (see Lesser Vehicle)
Hopkins, Jeffrey xxiii, xxvii
horn of a rabbit 77

I

ignorance 3, 4, 764
as illness 5
as not inherent in the mind 6
as the conception of a substantially existent self 15, 768
as the "foe" 24
compared to the nose-ring of a bull 5
final transcendence of 17
its antidote identified 17, 294
reasoning against 13
subtle 5
illustration 68, 70-72, 418-419, 457-459, 460-462
defined 70, 418
primacy of 71
illustration-isolate 417, 418-419, 457-459, 460-462
of functioning thing compared to the general-isolate of functioning thing 462
imaginary 767
as a division of imputed existents 767-769
existent variety 768
non-existent variety 768

posited in relation to every phenomenon 767

impermanence, coarse 275, 547

impermanence, subtle 275
  as not ascertained by ordinary direct perception 292
  development of a consciousness realizing 294, 302

impermanent phenomenon 77
  and direct perception of selflessness 16, 280, 358
  and its uncommon characteristics 298-299
  and permanent phenomena 284-304
  and subtle impermanence 274
  as a caused phenomenon 10
  compared to ultimate truth according to Ḍak-tsang's interpretation 312
  defined 78, 273
  phenomena mutually inclusive with 272-279
  span of its momentary existence identified 275

imputed existent 69, 200

imputed existent (in the Go-mang system)
  defined 766
  divided into three 767
  phenomena mutually inclusive with 766
  reason for name 766

incontrovertible 15, 19
  reason for name 676

indefinite reason 44

indirect cause 80, 540-544
  as mutually inclusive with cause and direct cause 541-542

indirect cause (of a clay pot)
  compared to substantial cause of a clay pot 549

indirect cause (of a tree)
  compared to tree 543

indirect cause (of functioning thing)
  as mutually exclusive with its direct cause 541
  defined 540
  divided into two 548

indirect effect 540-544
  as mutually inclusive with effect and direct effect 541

indirect effect (of functioning thing)
  as mutually exclusive with its direct effect 542
  defined 541

inferential cognizer/inferential cognition 14
  and syllogisms and consequences 33
  as dependent on a sign 20
  as establishing phenomena 270
  as incontrovertible 15
  as mistaken but not wrong 289
  through belief 179, 182
  through the power of the fact 178, 181
  transformed into direct perception 17, 19, 294

instance 71, 170, 233
  as a generality of generality 652, 653
  as a permanent phenomenon 630
  as an instance of generality 656
  as being one of many instances of a generality 623, 639-640
  as exemplifying its generality 622
  as itself a generality and an instance 641, 649-659
  as not being mutually exclusive with generality 629
  as related with its generality as the same essence 617, 622, 635-638

as the pervaded 618
compared to generality 633-642
defined 618
defined alternatively 618
proof of something as an 634-640
regarding the definition of 691
three requirements for 621-629
internal form 217-220
internal matter
defined 190
"The Introductory Path of Reasoning" xiv, xv, xxi, 22
alternate translations of title xiv n.1
auspicious final expression of 758
designation of debates in 84, 222
expression of worship in 177-183
formatting of translation of 169, 222
introduction 169-183
line citations for Tibetan text of 222
obeisance in 173-177
summary of chapters in 169
three subsections of each chapter in 171-173
topics in xvi
isolate (see also coextensives with an isolate, pot's isolate, and functioning thing, isolate of), 226-227, 411
and meaning-generalities 421
as a factor in the definition of substantial and isolate phenomena 703-707
as a fundamental quality of phenomena 416-417
as an isolate phenomenon which is not itself 742
as being permanent by its nature 414
as not being a generality of the

thing which is it 626
correctly identified 414, 470-471
divided into four 417
mistakenly identified 462-472
nature of 414-417, 477
phenomena coextensive with 422-440
phenomena mutually inclusive with 422-440
purpose for study of 420-422
reason for translation term 414
isolate phenomenon 170
and substantial phenomena 695-771
and substantial phenomenon, table of 698
as an established base 701
as exemplifying or not exemplifying itself 702
as itself being an isolate phenomenon which is itself 736
as mutually inclusive with permanent phenomenon 758
compared to substantial phenomenon 729-757
compared to various phenomena 736
divided into seven 696
divided into two types 696
each as mutually exclusive with every other isolate phenomenon and with substantial phenomenon 703
four requirements for 701-707
phenomena mutually inclusive with 766
regarding non-it as exemplifying or not exemplifying it 703
the first three 696, 735-747
the fourth requirement for 703-707
the latter four similitudes 696, 747-757

isolate-phenomenon-of-the-third-type 743-747
  as not being itself 721-726
  asserted to be a similitude of isolate-phenomenon-of-the-third-type 725-726
  compared to various phenomena 747
  defined 699
  non-it taken to be an isolate phenomenon of the third type 721-723, 725
  non-it taken to be an isolate phenomenon which is itself 723-724, 725
  reason for name 743
  taken to be an isolate phenomenon which is not itself 724, 725
isolate-phenomenon-which-is-itself 737-741
  as itself being an isolate phenomenon which is not itself 712-715
  compared to various phenomena 737-741
  defined 698
  non-it proven to be a similitude of isolate-phenomenon-which-is-itself 715-718
isolate-phenomenon-which-is-not-itself 741-743
  as itself being a similitude of isolate-phenomenon-which-is-not-itself 718-721
  compared to various phenomena 743
  defined 699

J

Jam-b̄el-trin-lay-yön-d̄en-gya-tso xix
Jam-ȳang-chok-hla-ö-ser xix

Jang-ḡya Rol-b̄ay-dor-jay
  cited 191

K

Kajiyama, Yuichi xxv
Kāshyapa Chapter Sūtra
  on the necessity for analysis 18
Kensur Jamb̄el Shenpen xxvi
  on different substantial entities 590
Kensur Ngawang Lekden xxiii
  on the span of a moment 275n.2
Kensur Yeshay Tupd̄en xxv, xxvi
  on animals living in the depths 370n.1
  on isolates and meaning-generalities 421
  on shape itself as level or non-level 260n.1
  on something's being permanent by its nature 411
  on the comparison of phenomena 162-163
  on the existence of sets including both existents and non-existents 331
  on the meaning of "valid cognizer" 19n.2
  on the prayer to Mañjushri 174n.2
  on the purpose for studying isolates 420
  on visible forms 193
Klein, Anne xxvii
knower
  phenomena mutually inclusive with 271
Knowledge 173

L

lama 176-177
  etymologies of 176
  importance of 18

Lati Rinbochay xxiii, xxv
  on a layman's
  misunderstanding of debate 75
  on different substantial entities
  591
  on direct and indirect causes
  548
  on effort and knowledge of
  impermanence 616
  on illustrations 419
  on learning 4
  on Mañjushrī 173
  on phenomena which are the
  same substantial entity 572
  on primary colors 195
  on shapes 198
  on similitude-of-isolate-
  phenomenon-which-is-itself 717
  on skill in debate 855
  on Superiors 368
  on the causes of a human body
  546
  on the clapping in debate 30n.1
  on the comparison of
  phenomena 162-163
  on the origin of Cha-ba's system
  of substantial and isolate
  phenomena 696
  on the primacy of a definition
  67
  on the proof of something as a
  generality 635
  on the role of the lama 176
  on what something is and what
  something is not 506, 510, 518
learning 4
  "in a box" 28
  insufficiency of 8
Lesser Vehicle
  on direct perception of
  selflessness 16
  on the selflessness of persons
  268, 764
  on the selflessness of
  phenomena 269

philosophical systems in xix
  practices of 365
liberation 3, 11
  as an effect 531
  as requiring understanding of
  selflessness 267
  as the goal of debate 6, 849
  necessity of reasoning for 13-21
Liebniz, Gottfried Wilhelm
  on necessity 794
Lochö Rinbochay (see Denma
Lochö Rinbochay)
Losang Gyatso 130n.1
  on the meaning of knower 359
Lo-śel-ling *Collected Topics* xix
  on external forms 191
  on secondary colors 196
  on shapes 199
  on the enumeration of valid
  cognizers 296
  on the purpose for studying
  isolates 420
  on the similitudes 728

M

Madhyamakālaṁkarakārikā (see
Ornament to the Middle Way)
Mādhyamika (see Middle Way
School)
Magee, William xxvi
Mahāyāna (see Great Vehicle)
manifest phenomenon 179, 180,
278, 295, 392-394
  defined 273
  phenomena mutually inclusive
  with 272-279
manifestation 83
  reason for name 618
Mañjughoṣha 79
Mañjushrī xiii, 27, 173-176
  seed syllable of 28, 103
matter 170, 211-217
  as a collection-generality 632

as mutually inclusive with form 189
as not being a separate entity from its subtle particles 620
defined 189, 354
divided into two 189
potencies of 205, 211, 216
maturation of consciousness 13-21
meaning
and name 419, 775-789
meaning-generality 287-290, 630, 766
(of pot) defined 422, 631
and isolates 421
as a generality 631
as having place, time, and nature mixed 300
as like a mirror image 291
meaning-isolate 417, 419, 459-460
memorization 24, 28
mental consciousness 20
as depending on a mental sense power 360, 361
defined 359
mental direct perceiver 293-294
method 30, 174
Middle Way 22, 23
Middle Way School xx, 621
on non-findability of objects 340
"The Middling Path of Reasoning" xiv, xv, 22, 68, 172
topics in xvi
Mill, John Stuart 778n.1
Mimaki, Katsumi xxv
mind
as a caused phenomenon 277
causes of 546
nature of 6
mind of enlightenment 30
Mind Only School xx
Mi-nyak Ge-shay Tsul-trim-ñam-gyel 35
mistaken consciousness
defined 289

mixture of place, time, and nature 300-304
non-mixture of nature 303
non-mixture of place 303
non-mixture of time 303
mode of proof 42
mode of statement 40
monastic life
education xxii, xxvii, 4, 6-8, 21-32, 263-265
monk's clothing 24-28
Mount Meru 198, 371
Murti, T.R.V. xxv
mutually exclusive phenomena 124, 512
as objects of knowledge of which being them is not possible 336-337, 338
as ordinary objects 340
as still perhaps being the same entity 574-575
for which the one is the other 704-705
paradigm for establishing 159-162
mutually inclusive phenomena 61, 67
and one/sameness 473-476
as being the same entity but different isolates 415
paradigm for establishing 138-142
when mutually pervasive but the one is not the other 425-426
mutually pervasive 61

N

Nāgārjuna 188
cited 182
Nagatomi, Prof. M.
on the meaning of the term *pramāṇa* 19n.2
Naiyāyikas 73

name
and meaning 419, 775-789
Nam-gyal College xiv
naming 288
Napper, Elizabeth xxvii
nature 300
negation 170
negative phenomenon 577
as an isolate phenomenon of the
third type 744
cognized together with a
positive phenomenon 358
divided into two 577
in relation to definitions and
definienda 356-357
Ngak-w̄ang-d̄ra-s̄hi xix
Ngakwang Lekden xxv
Ngak-w̄ang Nyi-ma xxv
non-associated compositional
factor 362-374, 763
as a division of imputed
existents 767
defined variously 362
divided into two 363
reason for name 363
non-associated compositional
factor which is a person 363-373
phenomena mutually inclusive
with 364
non-associated compositional
factor which is not a person 373-
374
non-conceptual consciousness 291
non-cow
as an example of a permanent
phenomenon 280
non-existent 91
as being neither one nor
different 348
as itself being something of
which being it is possible 505
as neither a substantial nor
isolate phenomenon 701
as not being a generality 625
as not being an instance 624

as not being different from
anything 350, 463, 469-472, 474
as occurring in some objects of
knowledge of which being them
is not possible 333-334
as occurring in some objects of
knowledge of which being them
is possible 329-331
as predominated over by
existence in sets including both
existents and non-existents 330
as selfless 269
of which being it is possible 504
proposed definition of 72
non-generality
as an instance of generality 657
as an instance of instance 653
non-instance 654, 658
as not being a generality 687
compared to generality 641
non-permanent phenomenon
as a permanent phenomenon
and uncaused 607
non-produced phenomenon
defined 282
phenomena mutually inclusive
with 279-284
non-product
defined 323
phenomena mutually inclusive
with 325
non-revelatory form 188
example of 191
non-thing
as the translation term rather
than non-functioning thing
323n.1
compared to different-from-
functioning-thing 349
compared to existent 326
compared to permanent
phenomenon 326
compared to phenomenon 377-
379
defined 323

phenomena mutually inclusive
with 325
nose consciousness
defined 361
nose sense power
defined 219

O

object 269-317
defined 269
divided into two 272
phenomena mutually inclusive
with 269-272
object of comprehension 269-317
defined 269
divided into three 179
phenomena mutually inclusive
with 269-272
related to the two valid
cognizers 296-297
object of comprehension of an
omniscient consciousness 269-317,
499-503
defined 269
phenomena mutually inclusive
with 269-272
which is it 499
which is it compared to which is
not it 502
which is not it 501
object of engagement 14, 285
object of knowledge 82, 95, 269,
271-317
as a generality of non-generality
689
as non-level 258-261
as not being an instance 627
as only a generality 628
as permanent 259
compared to non-impermanent
phenomenon 148-153
compared to objects of
knowledge of which being them
is possible 343-352

defined 269
divided into generalities and
instances 629
divided into objects of
knowledge of which being them
is possible and objects of
knowledge of which being them
is not possible 327
phenomena mutually inclusive
with 269-272
object of knowledge of which
being it is possible 327-328
compared to that of which being
it is possible 505
defined 327
proposed definition of 398-402
object-possessor 272
objects of consciousnesses, four
285-287
objects of knowledge of which
being [them] is not possible 81,
331-344, 382-385
addition of pronoun "them"
327n.1
and different phenomena 335-
339
as a class, being permanent 341
as including only mutually
exclusive phenomena 336-337,
338
as including sets having both
existents and non-existents 333-
334
as instances 624
as itself being a generality 657
as itself being an object of
knowledge of which being it is
possible 657, 742
as lacking a common locus 336
as mutually exclusive with their
cause 539
as not being generalities 624
compared to that of which being
it or them is not possible 506
defined 331

defined more generally 333
examples of included among functioning things, form, etc. 341
phenomena coextensive with the isolate of 438
proposed definition of 398-402
purpose for study of 339-341
objects of knowledge of which being [them] is possible 327-331
addition of pronoun "them" 327n.1
and different phenomena 335-339
as a class, being permanent 341
as including mutually inclusive phenomena and phenomena having three or four possibilities 337-339
as including sets having both existents and non-existents 329-331
compared to object of knowledge 343-352
defined 329
defined more generally 331
examples of included among functioning things, form, etc. 341
proposed definition of 398-402
observed-object-condition
and the sense consciousnesses 361
obstructions, two 367n.1
odor 206-208
divided into four 206-208
divided into two 207
phenomena mutually inclusive with 206
odor-source
defined 206
omniscient consciousness 678
defined 502
one/singular phenomenon/ same/sameness 95, 119, 134

and different phenomena 346-350, 463-464, 469-472, 474
and mutually inclusive phenomena 473-476
and self-exemplification 478
and the definition of something which is one with sound 348
as a generality of generality 651
as a generality of instance 655
as an instance of generality 655
as an instance of instance 651
as being permanent by its nature 412-413
as explained in the Go-mang *Collected Topics* 568-584
as forming the basis for isolates 414-417, 477
as necessarily an object of knowledge of which being it is possible 328
as self-identity 569
defined 346
divided into three 570
in relation to isolates 226, 569
table of 583
one-with-functioning-thing 423
as permanent 429
compared to definiendum 434
compared to functioning thing 434
denied to be a definiendum 430
proposed definition of 429
one-with-pot 84, 704-705
as being permanent by its nature 412-413
as not being pot's isolate 464-465
defined 412
only-a-generality 628
as a non-existent of which being it is possible 629
only-a-permanent-phenomenon 77, 89, 91
as included in sets of which being them is possible 329-330

as not being a generality 624, 625

as the subject in debate D.4 504-515

ontology 170

opposite

meaning of 482-483

opposite-from-being-something 481-498, 525-530

and counting mixed modifiers 488

as a modifier in describing "complex" phenomena 488-489, 492-498

as a modifier in describing non-existents 486-487

as a permanent phenomenon 483

as applied in contrast to functioning thing and permanent phenomenon 489-492

as applied to a particular basis 482

as mutually inclusive with not being something 483

phenomena mutually inclusive with 488, 525

opposite-from-not-being-something 481-498, 525-530

and counting mixed modifiers 488

as a modifier in describing "complex" phenomena 488-489, 492-498

as a modifier in describing non-existents 486-487

as applied to a particular basis 482

as mutually inclusive with being something 483-486

as mutually inclusive with being that thing which is not itself 487

distinguished from isolates 483, 530

interpreted as impermanent for impermanent bases 483-486, 526

interpreted as permanent for impermanent bases 484, 526

phenomena mutually inclusive with 488, 490, 525

oral tradition xxii, 199

and the annotations in this text 173

as prompted by the text 264

as the main repository of the debating tradition 497

on definitions and definienda 61, 66

on the procedure in debate 100, 121

Ornament to the Middle Way

on consciousness 355

P

Padmasambhava

on cyclic existence 4

Paṇchen Sö-nam-drak-ba

dates of 356

particular-form sentence 136, 839

as expressed in statements of pervasion 845

as not expressed in the Collected Topics syllogism 845

partless particles and moments

as ultimate truths 311

path

as a cause 531

five types of in each of the three vehicles 365-367

in "The Introductory Path of Reasoning" xv

meaning of name 365

path of reasoning xiv-xvi

perception

three causes of 217

Perfection of Wisdom 22, 23, 174
permanent phenomenon 83, 95, 96, 762
    a phenomenon's being permanent by its nature 318, 411-414
    and impermanent phenomena 284-304
    as including abstracts that may refer to anything 605
    as including phenomena having both permanent and impermanent instances 259, 318, 411
    as including phenomena having only impermanent instances 667
    as mutually inclusive with isolate phenomenon 758-770
    as non-functional 9, 283
    as non-momentary, not eternal 280
    as not directly realized 16
    as the object of a thought consciousness only 280
    as uncaused 283
    compared to conventional truth according to Ḍak-tsang's interpretation 312
    compared to established base 318-321
    compared to non-thing 326
    compared to something which a permanent phenomenon is 504-517
    compared to something which a permanent phenomenon is not 517-521
    compared to the four coextensives of the isolate of functioning thing 431, 455-457
    defined 279
    divided into two 281, 342
    four phenomena coextensive with the isolate of 433
    opposite-from-being-a- compared to opposite-from-

being-a-functioning-thing 489-492
    phenomena mutually inclusive with 279-284, 384, 391
    table of phenomena mutually inclusive with 282
person
    and the causes of a human body 546
    as a non-associated compositional factor 363-373
    as imputed existents 763
    as not being a self-sufficient substantial existent 764, 768
    as not being self-sufficiently apprehensible 763-765
    as not denied by selflessness 364
    as selfless 5, 13-19, 268, 764
    defined 363
    divided into two 364
    phenomena mutually inclusive with 364
    selflessness of identified as a thoroughly established phenomenon 769
pervaded 45, 109
pervader 45, 109
pervasion 41-49, 104, 106, 837, 839
    and copulative associations 46, 425-426, 478, 775-836
    and distributive predication 790-795
    applying a Defender's pervasion to a consequence 108
    as a necessary association of two phenomena 793-794
    as able to bear the relation of transitivity 791
    as able to relay the information that "some are ... " and "some are not ... " 845
    as associative 46-47, 425-426, 478, 775, 790-836
    as implying copulative statements 790-793

as implying establishment of the
reason 113
relation of two types of 49
translation of statements of 45-
47, 609, 791, 793-794
phenomenon 82, 269, 271-317
compared to non-thing 377-379
compared to what is not a
phenomenon that has a basis of
negation 379-382
defined 269
establishment of xv
final nature of 3
phenomena mutually inclusive
with 269-272
phenomenon-source 192
phenomenon that has a basis of
negation 379-382
phenomenon which is a non-thing
defined 282
phenomena mutually inclusive
with 279-284
positive phenomenon 576
cognized together with a
negative phenomenon 358
in relation to definitions and
definienda 356-357
possibility 142, 152
pot 79
as a cause and an effect 533
as an example of a substantial
phenomenon 701, 729-731
as an object of knowledge of
which being it is possible 327
as the same substantial entity as
functioning thing 573
compared to pot's cause 537
compared to pot's effect 538
compared to the two—a gold
pot and a copper pot 468
defined 274
four isolates of 417
illustration of defined 418
meaning-generality of defined
422

regarding the definition of 380
pot's cause
as mutually exclusive with pot's
effect 536
compared to pot 537
compared to pot's cooperative
condition 565-566
compared to pot's substantial
cause 562-564
pot's effect
compared to pot 538
pot's isolate 84
as a permanent phenomenon
414
as not being a pot 415, 829-831
as not being itself 465-466
compared to what is reversed
from being different from pot
469-472
compared to what is reversed
from not being a pot 467-469
correctly identified 414, 470-471
mistakenly identified 462-472
pot-which-is-one-with-pot 79, 93
as not being pot's isolate 462-
464
Potter, Karl H. 852
Pramāṇavarttikakārikā (see
*Commentary on (Dignāga's)
"Compendium of Valid Cognition"*)
Prāsaṅgika (see Consequence
School)
Precious Garland 188
*Precious Garland of Advice for the
King*
on giving 182
on giving and ethics 546
Precious Garland of Tenets
on specifically and generally
characterized phenomena 306
predicate to be negated 37, 52
predicate to be proven 35, 37, 52,
839
as a permanent phenomenon
606

in relation to the sign 41, 45, 48
predication
  and the abstract singular term
  780
  and the concrete general term
  780
  collective 779
  distributive 779, 790-795
  in the Collected Topics logic
  778-789
premises 49-50
presentation of our own system 9,
172, 248-252
*Presentation of Signs and
Reasonings, A Mirror Illuminating
All Phenomena* 35
Presentation of the Two Truths
  on shapes 200
primary color 194, 232
  compared to color 235-238
  defined 195
  divided into four 195
  divided into two 195
prime cognizer (see valid
cognizer/valid cognition)
prior arising 80, 540
  as neither a substantial cause
  nor a cooperative condition 600-
  602
  as referring to any cause 557
  in relation to other causes and
  effects 542
product 276
  defined 273
  phenomena mutually inclusive
  with 272-279
  reason for name 533
proof 34, 45
  phenomena mutually inclusive
  with 37
property of the subject 38, 39-41,
52, 837, 839
  formulated 39

property of the subject (in the
proof of sound as an impermanent
phenomenon)
  defined 39
Protector 175
proven 45
Pur-bu-jok Jam-ba-gya-tso 169
  as the source for this
  interpretation of the Sūtra
  School Following Reasoning 304
  dates of xiii
  obeisance by 177
  referred to as the "Tutor" xiii

Q

quantification 85-88
  absence of particular 86, 839
  and use of articles in the
  translation 88, 92, 164, 245-246,
  382n.2, 477, 535, 551, 556, 608,
  614, 693
  appearance of universal 86, 778-
  789, 840, 842-845
  singular 86-88, 163-165, 477, 614,
  778-789

R

Ra-dö *Collected Topics* xix
  and the source quotes on causes
  and effects 532
  as a source for "Generalities and
  Instances" 691
  as a source for "Identifying
  Isolates" 440
  as a source for "Opposite-From-
  Being-Something and Opposite-
  From-Not-Being-Something"
  481, 498, 517
  as a source for "The
  Introductory Presentation of
  Causes and Effects" 551, 556
  on a phenomenon and its
  similitude 753

on being related as the same
essence 635, 636, 638
on functioning-thing-which-is-
an-isolate-phenomenon 708-712
on generality-of-permanent-
phenomenon 663
on one-with-it as neither a
definition nor definiendum 430
on prior arisings and
subsequent arisings 542
on the definition of an instance
692
on the definition of generality
618
on the establishment of many
common locuses 639
on the proof of something as an
instance 621
on the similitudes 707, 728
reason 34, 840
phenomena mutually inclusive
with 37
rather than "sign" as a
translation of *rtags* 101n.1
reasoning xiii, xiv, xv
and obvious experience 62
as necessary but not sufficient
16-21
as necessary for liberation 13-21
as religious practice 20
compared to the analysis of
gold 178-183
in Ge-luk-ba xix
purpose for 3-32, 294
refuge 27
refutation of mistaken views 9-13,
171, 222
role of Proponent of Sūtra in 171
related phenomena 569
divided into two 512, 617
related as that arisen from that
617
related as the same essence 617,
635-638

religion
compatibility with reasoning 20
reversed from
meaning of 467, 482
Rogers, Katherine xvii n.2
round form 79

S

Śa-ġya-ba
on the two truths in the Sūtra
School Following Reasoning
304-317
Śa-ġya Paṇḍita
cited 63
Samdong Rinbochay 178n.2
same/sameness (see one/singular
phenomenon/same/sameness)
same entity 80, 95, 569
defined 571
divided into two 572
phenomena mutually inclusive
with 571
proven 571
same entity (as object of
knowledge)
defined 571
same essence 571, 623
compared to same type 593-596
same in terms of establishment
and abiding 585
compared to same substantial
entity in terms of establishment
and abiding 585-589
same isolate type 575
divided into two 575
same isolate type, negative phenomena which are the
defined 577
same isolate type, positive phenomena which are the
defined 576
divided into three 576
same nature 571

same self-isolate
    defined 570
same self-isolate (as existent)
    defined 570
same substantial entity 81
    compared to same substantial
    entity in terms of establishment
    and abiding 586
    compared to same type of
    substantial entity 589-593
    defined 572
    defined alternatively 572
    divided into two 572
    proven 534, 573
same substantial entity in terms of
establishment and abiding 585
    compared to same in terms of
    establishment and abiding 585-
    589
    compared to same substantial
    entity 586
same type 81, 95, 569
    and natural association 579
    compared to same essence 593-
    596
    defined 575
    divided into two 575
same type of substantial entity 81,
575
    compared to same substantial
    entity 589-593
    defined 578
    divided into three 578
    regarding the definition of 590
Sanskrit citations ix-xi
Sarvāstivādin
    monk's vows 24
Sautrāntika (see Sūtra School)
School of Dialectics xxvii
secondary color 194
    compared to cloud color 242
    compared to the eight types of
    secondary color 238-243
    defined 195
    divided into eight 196, 243

self
    as mutually inclusive with non-
    associated compositional factor
    which is a person 364
    as the same entity as the five
    aggregates 574
    as what is negated in
    selflessness 267
    lack of being permanent 12
self-exemplification 85-86, 234, 339
    and non-exemplification of self
    234, 339, 349, 426, 465, 478, 487
    and non-exemplification of self
    as one basis for substantial and
    isolate phenomena 695, 702-703,
    707
    and self-identity 347, 478, 787-
    789
self-isolate (see also singular
collective entity), 417, 536, 551,
702, 771, 835
    as mutually inclusive with
    general-isolate 417
    as the singular collective nature
    of phenomena 477-479
    as what is referred to as an
    isolate 420
self-knower 20
selfless
    as including existents and non-
    existents but not being existent
    and non-existent 333
    as the broadest category 267-269
    compared to what is not both
    suitable as an object of an
    awareness which is it and
    suitable as an object of an
    awareness which is not it 521-
    524
selflessness 5, 15, 17
    and the two types of selflessness
    of persons 268, 764
    as a non-affirming negative 577
    as a permanent phenomenon
    281

as an emptiness of self 267
as not denying persons 364
as realized by yogic direct
perceivers 294, 358
development of a consciousness
realizing 13-19
direct perception of 16-18, 280,
358
divided into two 268
in regard to self and the
aggregates as the same entity
574
in the various Buddhist systems
268-269, 574
of persons identified as a
thoroughly established
phenomenon 769
realization of as essential for
Superiors 366
self-sufficient person 5, 14
as a non-existent imaginary 768
lack of a 764
meaning of "self-sufficient" 768
sense consciousness 20, 188
defined 359
divided into five 360
order of the five types 220
sense direct perceiver
divided into five 292
sense power 188, 190, 763
as an uncommon empowering
condition 360, 361
divided into five 217-220
sentient being 3
as a patient 5
Śe-ra Monastic University xiii,
xxiii, xxv, xxvi
Shāntirakṣhita
cited 355
shape 197-200
compared to color 199
compared to level or non-level
form 261
compared to level or non-level
shape 262

compared to the level or non-
level 258-261
defined 198
divided into eight 197
shape-form 79, 244
compared to form 244-246
Shar-dzay *Collected Topics* xix
on isolate-phenomenon-which-
is-itself 715
on sounds 202
on the coextensives of an isolate
437
on the comparisons of
generality and instance as
generalities and instances 658
on what something is and what
something is not 499, 501
sign 20, 35, 52, 840
as a permanent phenomenon
606
as easier to understand than the
predicate 497
divided into two 38
in relation to the dissimilar class
48
in relation to the predicate to be
proven 41, 45, 48
in relation to the similar class
44-45
in relation to the subject 39
phenomena mutually inclusive
with 37
two-part 239-242, 402-404
"Signs and Reasonings" xiv, xvii,
35
similar class 42, 43, 52
in relation to the sign 44-45
similar class (in the proof of sound
as an impermanent phenomenon)
defined 42
similitude
as having limitless varieties 728,
735

as mutually exclusive with
substantial phenomenon and
the first three isolate
phenomena 707
    necessity for positing 707-729
    of a similitude 726-729
    reason for name 706
similitude-of-isolate-
phenomenon-of-the-third-type
721-726, 750-751
    compared to various
    phenomena 751
    defined 700
similitude-of-isolate-
phenomenon-which-is-itself 712-
718, 748-749
    compared to various
    phenomena 748-749
    defined 700
similitude-of-isolate-
phenomenon-which-is-not-itself
718-721, 749-750
    as a similitude of similitude-of-
    isolate-phenomenon-which-is-
    not-itself 727-728
    compared to various
    phenomena 750
    defined 700
similitude-of-substantial-
phenomenon 708-712, 751-757
    compared to various
    phenomena 756
    defined 699
singular collective entity (see also
abstract singular term, self-isolate,
and singular generality), 164, 848
    as the nature of generalities 693
    as the nature of isolates 414-417,
    477
    as the nature of the principals in
    a comparison of phenomena
    163-165
    as the nature of the subjects of
    debate 85-88, 535, 614

as what is considered in
deciding substantial and isolate
phenomena 702-703
    established base considered as a
    318
    nature of 789
singular generality (see also
singular collective entity), 79, 92,
411, 535, 789
singular phenomenon (see
one/singular phenomenon/
same/sameness)
slightly hidden phenomenon 179,
181
sound 12, 200-206
    articulate 203
    as matter 205
    as self-sufficiently
    apprehensible 765
    caused by elements conjoined
    with consciousness 202
    defined 65, 200
    divided into eight 201-205
    divided into two 202
    phenomena mutually inclusive
    with 200
    pleasant 204
sound-impermanent-phenomenon
82, 95, 670-675, 689
sound-source
    defined 200
space
    as an element 214
    uncomposed 279
Sparham, Gareth xxvii
specifically characterized
phenomenon 278
    and generally characterized
    phenomena 284-304
    as defined by Gön-chok-jik-
    may-w̄ang-bo 307
    as perceived without a mixture
    of place, time, and nature 299

compared to consciousness 382-386
defined 273
phenomena mutually inclusive with 272-279
reason for name 299
Stcherbatsky, F. Th. 851
subject 35, 52, 839
  as a permanent phenomenon 606
  nature of 778-789
  powerless subject 671
  two requirements for 36
subjects of debate 75-98
  eight categories of 88-98
  fifty-three 76-84
  nature of 778-789
  quantification of 85-88, 163-165, 245-246, 382n.2, 477, 535, 551, 556, 614
  translation of 88, 92
subsequent arising 80, 541
  in relation to other causes and effects 542
subsequent cognizer
  defined 677
substantial cause 80, 273, 277, 544-549
  as mutually exclusive with the cooperative conditions of a basis 547
  compared to cause 547, 566-568
  identified for a clay pot 544
substantial cause (of a clay pot) 565
  compared to direct cause of a clay pot 548
  compared to indirect cause of a clay pot 549
substantial cause (of functioning thing)
  defined 544
  divided into two 548
  nature of 614

substantial effect (of functioning thing)
  compared to the effect of functioning thing's substantial cause 596-598
  proposed definition of 563
substantial entity 81, 572
substantial existent 68, 200
substantial existent (in the Go-mang system)
  compared to substantial existent in the sense of being established by reasoning 761
  divided into four 760
  phenomena mutually inclusive with 759
  reason for name 759
substantial existent in the sense of being able to perform a function 760
  as mutually inclusive with functioning thing 762
  compared to substantial existent in the sense of being self-sufficiently apprehensible 765
substantial existent in the sense of being established by reasoning 760
  as mutually inclusive with existent 760
  compared to substantial existent 761
substantial existent in the sense of being self-sufficiently apprehensible 760
  compared to substantial existent in the sense of being able to perform a function 765
  defined 762
  reason for name 763
substantial existent in the sense of being statically unchanging 760
  as mutually inclusive with permanent phenomenon 762

substantial phenomenon 170, 729-735
  and isolate phenomena 695-771
  and isolate phenomena, table of 698
  as an established base 701
  as exemplifying itself 702
  as itself being a substantial phenomenon 734
  as itself being an isolate phenomenon which is not itself 734
  as mutually exclusive with every isolate phenomenon 703
  as mutually inclusive with functioning thing 758
  compared to isolate phenomenon 729-757
  compared to various phenomena 732-734
  defined 698
  four requirements for 701-707
  regarding non-it as not exemplifying it 703
  the fourth requirement for 703-707
substantial phenomenon (in the Go-mang system)
  defined 758
  phenomena mutually inclusive with 759
  reason for name 759
substantially existent person 5, 14, 17
  lack of a 764
suffering 4, 25
  as an effect 531
  freedom from 5-21
  source of 3-5
suitable as an object of an awareness 270
  which is it compared to which is not it 524
Superior 294, 365-367
  divided into four 366

having the basis of a migrator 368
Sūtra School xix
  Challenger's role as a proponent of 100n.1
  divided into two xx
  main object of abandonment of 769
  main object of meditation of 769
  on destroying ignorance 17, 768
  on direct perception of selflessness 280, 358
  on forms 191
  on momentary disintegration 276
  on shapes 200
  on the selflessness of persons 268, 764
  on the selflessness of phenomena 269, 769
  on the uncommon characteristics of impermanent phenomena 298
Sūtra School Following Reasoning
  as the philosophical grounding for the Collected Topics 185
  on conventional truths as permanent phenomena 283
  on direct perceivers and other non-conceptual consciousnesses 291-292
  on direct perception of selflessness 16-17
  on matter 205
  on non-revelatory form 188n.3
  on overcoming ignorance 14, 768
  on permanent and impermanent phenomena 284-304
  on products 43
  on substantial and isolate phenomena 758-770
  on subtle ignorance 5

on the necessity for syllogisms 33
on the two truths 304-317
on ultimate truths as impermanent phenomena 278
on valid cognizers/prime cognizers 677
reason for name xx
Sūtra School Following Scripture xx
syllogism 33-53
  as an enthymeme 836
  Collected Topics form of and the "Barbara" categorical syllogism 840, 842
  Collected Topics form of compared to a Western form 836-849, 852-855
  contrasted to consequences 55-56, 109-110
  elements of 35-37
  epistemological requirement for 36-37, 40-41, 43, 48, 49, 51, 837
  example of 34
  form of 49-50, 836
  ontological requirement for 41, 43, 45, 48, 49
  soundness and validity of 50-51
  table of components of a 52
  translation of 229
  use of in comparing phenomena 141
  use of in the presentation of our own system 251
  validity of 36, 40-41, 49-51

T

tangible object 210-217
  defined 210
  divided into eleven 210
  divided into two 210
tangible objects arisen from the elements 215
  compared to forms arisen from

the elements 257
  divided into seven 210
tangible objects which are elements 79, 210-215
  divided into four 210
tantra 213
taste 208-210
  and the elements 209
  defined 208
  divided into six 208
  table of 210
Tharpa Choeling Centre xxiv
that which is able to perform a function 78
  compared to the isolate of that which is able to perform a function 454
  four phenomena coextensive with the isolate of 435
  four phenomena coextensive with the isolate of compared to definiendum 452-454
  four phenomena coextensive with the isolate of compared to definition 448-451
  the isolate of compared to functioning thing 451
that which is to be negated 37, 52
that which is to be proven 37, 52
the two—a pillar and a pot 81, 94
  as functioning things, matter, etc. 385
  as having a substantial cause 602-604
  as objects of knowledge of which being them is not possible 336
  as one with themselves 347
  as the same entity as object of knowledge 574
  phenomena coextensive with the isolate of 438
thesis 34, 37, 839
thing (see functioning thing)

thoroughly established
phenomenon 767
   as a division of imputed
   existents 769
   posited in relation to every
   phenomenon 769
thought consciousness 84
   appearing object of 286-290, 420-
   422
   as a determinative knower 285
   as a mistaken consciousness
   287-290
   as an eliminative engager 297-
   300
   as an obscured mind 284
   as getting at its object of
   engagement 289
   as inferior to direct perceivers
   286
   as mixing place, time, and
   nature 300-301
   as perceiving phenomena in a
   general way by elimination 299-
   301
   as the apprehender of hidden
   phenomena 271
   three modes 38-49
three poisons 25
three possibilities
   chart of first type 147
   chart of second type 152
   paradigms for establishing 142-
   153
   two types 143-153
   without there being something
   which is neither 162-163
three scriptural collections
   as symbolized in the monk's
   clothing 26
three spheres 58
three trainings 7, 26
Tibet 61
Tibetan citations ix-xi
   system of phonetics for ix
Tibetan medicine 214-215

tongue consciousness
   defined 361
tongue sense power
   defined 219
translation
   format of 100
   use of hyphens in 77n.1
   use of masculine pronouns in xx
Treasury of Knowledge xviii, 22, 23
   on common beings 367
   on form-sources 194
   on forms 187, 188, 191
   on odors 206
   on secondary colors 196
   on shapes 197, 200
   on tangible objects 210
   on the two truths 308
*Treasury of Reasoning about Valid
Cognition*
   on the three possible faults of a
   definition 63
triply qualified imputed existent
of that which is able to perform a
function 84, 423, 446
   as a definition 429
   as permanent 429
   four phenomena coextensive
   with the isolate of 439
triply qualified substantial
existent of functioning thing 84
Tutor (see Pur-bu-jok Jam-ba-gya-
tso)
Tutor's *Collected Topics*
   and the first Collected Topics
   text xviii
   as the source for the Ge-luk-ba
   interpretation of the Sūtra
   School Following Reasoning 305
   designation of debates in 84, 222
   expression of worship in 177-
   183
   formatting of translation of 169,
   222
   full title of xiii
   introduction 169-183

layout and sources of "Colors— White, Red, and So Forth" in 185, 187, 193, 222, 248, 252
layout and sources of "Established Bases" in 296, 305, 317, 394, 398
layout and sources of "Generalities and Instances" in 632, 633, 643, 646, 649, 681, 691
layout and sources of "Identifying Isolates" in 416, 440-441, 448, 455, 457, 459, 460, 462, 472
layout and sources of "Opposite-From-Being-Something and Opposite-From-Not-Being-Something" in 481, 482, 498, 517, 521
layout and sources of "Substantial Phenomena and Isolate Phenomena" in 696, 729, 757
layout and sources of "The Introductory Presentation of Causes and Effects" in 532, 549, 556, 562, 566, 568, 585, 589, 593, 600
line citations for Tibetan text of 222
masculine pronouns in translation of xx
obeisance in 173-177
on consequences 56
portion of translated in this text xxi
reason for title xiii
sections of xiv-xvii
self-exemplification as the basis for "Substantial Phenomena and Isolate Phenomena" in 695
"Signs and Reasonings" in 35
"Substantial Phenomena and Isolate Phenomena" as a summary chapter in 695, 770
three subsections of each chapter in 171-173
type-generality 630
    compared to collection-generality 680
    defined 630
    regarding the definition of 684

U

ultimate awareness 286, 314
ultimate truth 278
    and conventional truths 284-317, 849-850
    compared to impermanent phenomenon according to Dak-tsang's interpretation 312
    criteria for according to Bel-den-chö-jay 313
    defined 273
    defined according to Dak-tsang's interpretation 308
    identified in relation to an ultimate awareness 315
    phenomena mutually inclusive with 272-279
uncommon empowering condition 218
    and consciousnesses 360, 361
uncomposed
    defined 323
    phenomena mutually inclusive with 325
uncomposed phenomenon
    defined 282
    phenomena mutually inclusive with 279-284
uncomposed space 83
    as an example of a permanent phenomenon 279
unwanted consequence 107

V

Vaibhāṣhika (see Great Exposition School)

Vajrapāṇi 27
valid cognizer/valid cognition 82
   and the translation of *tshad ma*
   as "prime cognizer" 72n.3, 676-
   677
   as establishing phenomena 270,
   407-409
   as the verifier of reasoning xv
   defined 676
   divided into three 19, 178
   divided into two 19
   enumerated definitely as two
   295-297
   unique quality of 19
Vasubandhu xviii
   cited 187
   dates of xviii
vehicles, three 365-367
   reason for name 365
very hidden phenomenon 179, 182
virtue 24
visible form 192-200

W

Wangyal, Geshe 121n.1
water
   defined 211
   manifest as cohesiveness 212
what is to be proven 34
what something is and what
something is not 481, 498-525, 529
   alternative translations of 499
white religious conch 57, 78, 79,
106
   as an element, not a color 253-
   256
   as one of the eight good luck
   symbols 105n.1
Wilson, Joe, Jr. 175n.1

wind 79
   as an element, not arisen from
   the elements 256-258
   as the mount of consciousness
   213
   defined 211
   manifest as motility 213
wisdom 3
   and Mañjushrī 174
   as a true path 5
   as dependent on virtue 24
   as symbolized in the monk's
   clothing 26
   identified 5
   observing selflessness 16
   represented by the left hand 29
Wittgenstein, Ludwig
   on color 62n.1
wrong consciousness
   defined 289
   divided into two 14
wrong view 14
Wylie, Turrell ix

Y

yogic direct perceiver
   as ascertaining the uncommon
   characteristics of impermanent
   phenomena 298
   as realizing selflessness etc. 294,
   358
   development of as purpose for
   reasoning 302

Z

Zahler, Leah 371n.1

Tibetan Text of
"The Introductory Path of Reasoning"
in Pur-bu-jok Jam-ba-gya-tso's
The Presentation of Collected Topics
Revealing the Meaning of the Texts on Valid Cognition,
the Magical Key to the Path of Reasoning

༄། །ཚད་མའི་གཞུང་དོན་འབྱེད་པའི་བསྡུས་གྲྭའི་རྣམ་བཞག་རིགས་ལམ་འཕྲུལ་གྱི་ལྡེ་མིག་ཅེས་བྱ་བ་ལས་རིགས་ལམ་ཆུང་ངུའི་རྣམ་པར་བཤད་པ་བཞུགས་སོ། ། 1

༄། །བླ་མ་དང་མགོན་པོ་འཇམ་པའི་དབྱངས་ལ་ཕྱག་འཚལ་ལོ། །ཡང་དག་དོན་ཀུན་གཟིགས་པའི་སྤྱན་མཆོག་དམ་དེས། །ལེགས་པར་གསུངས་པའི་རིགས་པའི་ལམ་མཚོན་དམ་པར་ཀུན་ལ་མཛད་པ་ཡི། །བདག་ཉིད་ཆེན་པོ་ཕྱོགས་གླང་ཆོས་ 2
གྲགས་སོགས་ལ། [illegible] །འདིར་རིགས་པའི་རིགས་ལམ་གྱི་སྒོ་འབྱེད་བསྡུས་གྲྭའི་རྣམ་བཞག་བཤད་པ་ལ། རིགས་ལམ་ཆུང་ངུའི་རྣམ་བཞག་བཤད་པ། རིགས་ལམ་འབྲིང་གི་རྣམ་
བཞག་བཤད་པ། རིགས་ལམ་ཆེན་པོའི་རྣམ་བཞག་བཤད་པ་དང་གསུམ། དང་པོ་རིགས་ལམ་ཆུང་ངུའི་ནང་ཚན་ཁ་དོག་དཀར་དམར་སོགས་ཀྱི་རྣམ་བཞག་བཤད་པ་ལ། དགག་བཞག་སྤོང་གསུམ་ལས། དང་པོ་ནི། ཁ་
ཅིག་ན་རེ། །ཁ་དོག་ཡིན་ན་དམར་པོ་ཡིན་པས་ཁྱབ་ཟེར་ན། ཆོས་ཅན་དུ་དཀར་པོའི་ཁ་དོག་ཆོས་ཅན། དམར་པོ་ཡིན་པར་ཐལ། །ཁ་དོག་ཡིན་པའི་ཕྱིར། ཁྱབ་པ་ཁས། མ་གྲུབ་ན། ཆོས་ཅན་དུ་དཀར་པོའི་ཁ་དོག་ཆོས་ཅན།
།ཁ་དོག་ཡིན་པར་ཐལ། དཀར་པོ་ཡིན་པའི་ཕྱིར། མ་ཁྱབ་ན། ཆོས་ཅན་དུ་དཀར་པོའི་ཁ་དོག་ཆོས་ཅན། དཀར་པོ་ཡིན་པར་ཐལ། ཆོས་ཅན་དུ་དཀར་པོའི་ཁ་དོག་ཅིག་ཡིན་པའི་ཕྱིར། རྩ་བར་འདོད་ན། ཆོས་ཅན་དུ་དཀར་

༄། །པོའི་ཁ་དོག་ཆོས་ཅན། དམར་པོ་མ་ཡིན་པར་ཐལ། དཀར་པོ་ཡིན་པའི་ཕྱིར། མ་གྲུབ་ན། གྲུབ་པ་ཡོད་པར་ཐལ། དཀར་པོ་དང་དམར་པོ་གཉིས་ཀྱི་གཞི་མཐུན་མེད་པ་ཡིན་པའི་ཕྱིར་ཏེ། དེ་གཉིས་འགལ་བ་ཡིན་པའི་ 3
ཕྱིར། །ཁ་ཅིག་ན་རེ། །ཁ་དོག་ཡིན་ན་དཀར་པོ་ཡིན་པས་ཁྱབ་ཟེར་ན། སངས་རྒྱས་ཚེ་དཔག་མེད་ཀྱི་ཁ་དོག་ཆོས་ཅན། དཀར་པོ་ཡིན་པར་ཐལ། །ཁ་དོག་ཡིན་པའི་ཕྱིར། ཁྱབ་པ་ཁས། མ་གྲུབ་ན། སངས་རྒྱས་ཚེ་
དཔག་མེད་ཀྱི་ཁ་དོག་ཆོས་ཅན། །ཁ་དོག་ཡིན་པར་ཐལ། མདོག་དམར་སྐྱ་ཡིན་པའི་ཕྱིར། མ་གྲུབ་ན། དེ་ལ་གྲུབ་པ་ཡོད་པར་ཐལ། མདོག་དམར་སྐྱ་བ་ཁ་དོག་གི་མཚན་ཉིད་ཡིན་པའི་ཕྱིར། རྩ་བར་འདོད་ན། སངས་
རྒྱས་ཚེ་དཔག་མེད་ཀྱི་ཁ་དོག་ཆོས་ཅན། དཀར་པོ་མ་ཡིན་པར་ཐལ། དམར་པོ་ཡིན་པའི་ཕྱིར། མ་གྲུབ་ན། སངས་རྒྱས་ཚེ་དཔག་མེད་ཀྱི་ཁ་དོག་ཆོས་ཅན། དམར་པོ་ཡིན་པར་ཐལ། སངས་རྒྱས་ཚེ་དཔག་མེད་ཀྱི་
།ཁ་དོག་གི་ལྡོག་པ་ཡིན་པའི་ཕྱིར། མ་གྲུབ་ན། སངས་རྒྱས་ཚེ་དཔག་མེད་ཀྱི་ཁ་དོག་ཆོས་ཅན། ཁྱོད་ཁྱོད་ཀྱི་ལྡོག་པ་ཡིན་པར་ཐལ། ཁྱོད་གཞི་གྲུབ་པའི་ཕྱིར། །ཁ་ཅིག་ན་རེ། །ཁ་དོག་ཡིན་ན། སེར་པོ་ཡིན་པས་ཁྱབ་

བསྡུས་གྲྭ

༄༅། །དཀར་ནག་གཉིས་ཀ་ཆོས་ཅན། བདག་གཉིས་གཅིག་ཡིན་པར་ཐལ། རིགས་གཅིག་ཡིན་པའི་ཕྱིར། ཁྱབ་པ་ཁས། མ་གྲུབ་ན། དེ་ཆོས་ཅན། དེར་ཐལ། ལྡོག་པ་རིགས་པ་གཅིག་ཡིན་པའི་ཕྱིར། མ་གྲུབ་ན། དེ་ཆོས་ཅན། དེར་ཐལ། གང་ཟག་གང་ཞིག···
ཡིན་ན་གང་དང་བར་མ་ཐོང་ཙམ་ཉིད་ནས་དེ་དང་དེའོ་ཞེས་སྣང་བའི་བློ་ངང་གིས་སྐྱེ་རུང་བའི་ཆོས་ཡིན་པའི་ཕྱིར། ཁྱབ་སྟེ། ལྡོག་པ་རིགས་པ་གཅིག་གི་དོན་ཡོད་པའི་ཕྱིར། རྩ་བར་འདོད་ན། དེ་ཆོས་ཅན། བདག་གཉིས་གཅིག་མ་ཡིན་པར་ཐལ། དོན་ཐ་དད་ཡིན་པའི་ཕྱིར་ཏེ། བཤད་རྒྱུན
འབྲེལ་མེད་དོན་ཐ་དད་ཡིན་པའི་ཕྱིར། །ཁ་ཅིག་ན་རེ། དངོས་པོའི་ཉེར་ལེན་གྱི་འབྲས་བུ་ཡིན་ན། དངོས་པོའི་ཉེར་འབྲས་ཡིན་པས་ཁྱབ་ཟེར་ན། དངོས་པོ་ཆོས་ཅན། དངོས་པོའི་ཉེར་འབྲས་ཡིན་པར་ཐལ། དངོས་པོའི་ཉེར་ལེན་གྱི་འབྲས་བུ་ཡིན་པའི་ཕྱིར། ཁྱབ་པ་ཁས། མ་···
གྲུབ་ན། དེ་ཆོས་ཅན། རང་གི་ཉེར་ལེན་གྱི་འབྲས་བུ་ཡིན་པར་ཐལ། ཁྱོད་ཀྱི་ཉེར་ལེན་ཡོད། ཁྱོད་ཀྱི་རྒྱུ་ཡིན་པའི་ཕྱིར། རྩ་བར་འདོད་ན། དེ་ཆོས་ཅན། དངོས་པོའི་ཉེར་འབྲས་མ་ཡིན་པར་ཐལ། དངོས་པོའི་འབྲས་བུ་མ་ཡིན་པའི་ཕྱིར། མ་གྲུབ་ན། དེ་ཆོས་ཅན། ཁྱོད་ཁྱོད་
ཀྱི་འབྲས་བུ་མ་ཡིན་པར་ཐལ། བདག་མེད་ཡིན་པའི་ཕྱིར། གཉིས་པ་རང་གི་ལུགས་ལ། རྒྱུའི་མཚན་ཉིད་ཡོད་དེ། སྐྱེད་བྱེད་དེ་དེ་ཡིན་པའི་ཕྱིར། རྒྱུ་འབྲས་བུ་དངོས་པོ་གསུམ་དོན་གཅིག དངོས་པོའི་རྒྱུའི་མཚན་ཉིད་ཡོད་དེ། དངོས་པོའི་སྐྱེད་བྱེད་དེ་དེ་ཡིན་པའི་ཕྱིར་ཏེ།
དངོས་པོ་ཡིན་ན། ཁྱོད་ཀྱི་སྐྱེད་བྱེད་ཁྱོད་ཀྱི་རྒྱུའི་མཚན་ཉིད་ཡིན་པས་ཁྱབ་པའི་ཕྱིར། དངོས་པོའི་རྒྱུ་ལ་དབྱེ་ན་གཉིས་ཡོད་དེ། དངོས་པོའི་དངོས་རྒྱུ་དང་། དངོས་པོའི་བརྒྱུད་རྒྱུ་གཉིས་ཡོད་པའི་ཕྱིར། དངོས་པོའི་དངོས་རྒྱུའི་མཚན་ཉིད་ཡོད་དེ། དངོས་པོའི་དངོས་སུ་སྐྱེད་བྱེད་དེ། 31

རིགས་ལམ་པ་མཆོག་ཏུ་དགའ་བ

དེ་ཡིན་པའི་ཕྱིར། མཚན་གཞི་ཡོད་དེ། དངོས་པོའི་སྔ་ལོགས་སུ་བྱུང་བ་དེ་དེ་ཡིན་པའི་ཕྱིར། དངོས་པོའི་བརྒྱུད་རྒྱུའི་མཚན་ཉིད་ཡོད་དེ། དངོས་པོའི་བརྒྱུད་ནས་སྐྱེད་བྱེད་དེ་དེ་ཡིན་པའི་ཕྱིར། མཚན་གཞི་ཡོད་དེ། དངོས་པོའི་སྔ་ལོགས་སུ་བྱུང་བའི་སྔ་ལོགས་སུ་བྱུང་བ་དེ
དེ་ཡིན་པའི་ཕྱིར། དེས་ན་དངོས་པོ་ཐམས་ཅད་ཀྱི་དངོས་རྒྱུ་དང་བརྒྱུད་རྒྱུ་ལ་རིགས་འགྲེ། ཡང་དངོས་པོའི་རྒྱུ་ལ་དབྱེ་ན་གཉིས་ཡོད་དེ། དངོས་པོའི་ཉེར་ལེན་དང་དངོས་པོའི་ལྷན་ཅིག་བྱེད་རྐྱེན་གཉིས་ཡོད་པའི་ཕྱིར། དངོས་པོའི་ཉེར་ལེན་གྱི་མཚན་ཉིད་ཡོད་དེ། དངོས་པོ་རང་
གི་རྫས་རྒྱུན་དུ་གཙོ་བོར་སྐྱེད་བྱེད་དེ་དེ་ཡིན་པའི་ཕྱིར། མཚན་གཞི་ཡོད་དེ། དངོས་པོའི་རྒྱུར་གྱུར་པའི་བུམ་པ་དེ་དེ་ཡིན་པའི་ཕྱིར། དངོས་པོའི་ལྷན་ཅིག་བྱེད་རྐྱེན་གྱི་མཚན་ཉིད་ཡོད་དེ། དངོས་པོ་རང་གི་རྫས་རྒྱུན་མ་ཡིན་པར་རྫས་སུ་གཙོ་བོར་སྐྱེད་བྱེད་དེ་དེ་ཡིན་པའི་ཕྱིར། 32
མཚན་གཞི་ཡོད་དེ། དངོས་པོའི་རྒྱུར་གྱུར་པའི་གང་ཟག་དེ་དེ་ཡིན་པའི་ཕྱིར། འབྲས་བུའི་མཚན་ཉིད་ཡོད་དེ། བསྐྱེད་བྱ་དེ་དེ་ཡིན་པའི་ཕྱིར། དངོས་པོའི་འབྲས་བུའི་མཚན་ཉིད་ཡོད་དེ། དངོས་པོའི་བསྐྱེད་བྱ་དེ་དེ་ཡིན་པའི་ཕྱིར། མཚན་གཞི་ཡོད་དེ། དངོས་པོའི་
ཕྱི་ལོགས་སུ་བྱུང་བ་དེ་དེ་ཡིན་པའི་ཕྱིར། དངོས་པོའི་འབྲས་བུ་ལ་དབྱེ་ན་གཉིས་ཡོད་དེ། དངོས་པོའི་དངོས་འབྲས་དང་དངོས་པོའི་བརྒྱུད་འབྲས་གཉིས་ཡོད་པའི་ཕྱིར། དངོས་པོའི་དངོས་འབྲས་ཀྱི་མཚན་ཉིད་ཡོད་དེ། དངོས་པོའི་དངོས་སུ་བསྐྱེད་བྱ་དེ་དེ་ཡིན་པའི་ཕྱིར།
མཚན་གཞི་ཡོད་དེ། དངོས་པོའི་ཕྱི་ལོགས་སུ་བྱུང་བ་དེ་དེ་ཡིན་པའི་ཕྱིར། དངོས་པོའི་བརྒྱུད་འབྲས་ཀྱི་མཚན་ཉིད་ཡོད་དེ། དངོས་པོའི་བརྒྱུད་ནས་བསྐྱེད་བྱ་དེ་དེ་ཡིན་པའི་ཕྱིར། མཚན་གཞི་ཡོད་དེ། དངོས་པོའི་ཕྱི་ལོགས་སུ་བྱུང་བའི་ཕྱི་ལོགས་སུ་བྱུང་བ་དེ་དེ་ཡིན་པའི་ཕྱིར།

བརྩོན་འགྲུས

༄༅། །དེས་ན་དངོས་པོ་གཞན་གྱི་དངོས་འབྲས་དང་བརྒྱུད་འབྲས་ལ་རིགས་འགྲེ། གསུམ་པ་རྩོད་སྤོང་ལ། ཁ་ཅིག་ན་རེ། དངོས་པོའི་ཉེར་ལེན་མེད་པར་ཐལ། དངོས་པོའི་སྔ་ལོགས་སུ་བྱུང་བ་དེ་དེ་མ་ཡིན་པའི་ཕྱིར། མ་གྲུབ་ན། དངོས་པོའི་སྔ་ལོགས་སུ་
བྱུང་བ་ཆོས་ཅན། དངོས་པོའི་ཉེར་ལེན་མ་ཡིན་པར་ཐལ། ཁྱོད་དངོས་པོ་རང་འགྱུར་བ་དེར་མ་ཡིན་པའི་ཕྱིར། མ་གྲུབ་ན། དངོས་པོའི་སྔ་ལོགས་སུ་བྱུང་བ་ཆོས་ཅན། དངོས་པོ་རང་འགྱུར་བ་དེར་མ་ཡིན་པར་ཐལ། དངོས་པོ་རང་འགྱུར་བ་ཞིག་ཡིན་པའི་ཕྱིར་ཟེར་ན་མ་ཁྱབ། མ་···
གྲུབ་ན། དངོས་པོའི་སྔ་ལོགས་སུ་བྱུང་བ་ཆོས་ཅན། དངོས་པོ་རང་འགྱུར་བ་ཞིག་ཡིན་པར་ཐལ། དངོས་པོ་ཡིན་པའི་ཕྱིར། །ཁ་ཅིག་ན་རེ། ཀ་བུམ་གཉིས་ཆོས་ཅན། ཁྱོད་ཀྱི་ཉེར་ལེན་ཡོད་པར་ཐལ། ཁྱོད་དངོས་པོ་ཡིན་པའི་ཕྱིར། ཁྱབ་པ་ཁས། འདོད་ན། ཀ་བུམ་གཉིས··· 33
ཆོས་ཅན། ཁྱོད་དུ་འགྱུར་བ་དེར་ཡོད་པར་ཐལ། ཁྱོད་ཀྱི་ཉེར་ལེན་ཡོད་པའི་ཕྱིར། རྟགས་ཁས། འདོད་ན། ཀ་བུམ་གཉིས་ཆོས་ཅན། ཁྱོད་ཀྱི་ཡིན་པ་ཡོད་པར་ཐལ། ཁྱོད་དུ་འགྱུར་བ་དེར་ཡོད་པའི་ཕྱིར་ཟེར་ན་འདོད་དུ་མ་ཁྱབ། དངོས་པོ་ཡིན་ན། རང་གི་རྒྱུའི་འབྲས་བུ···
ཡིན་པས་ཁྱབ། ཁྱབ་པ་ལ་གནོད་ན་རེ། རང་གི་རྒྱུ་ཆོས་ཅན། དེར་ཐལ། དེའི་ཕྱིར་ཟེར་ན། རྟགས་མ་གྲུབ་སྟེ། རང་གི་རྒྱུ་མེད་པའི་ཕྱིར་ཏེ། རང་རྟག་པ་ཡིན་པའི་ཕྱིར། ཁོ་ན་རེ། བུམ་པ་ཆོས་ཅན། རྒྱུ་འབྲས་ཡིན་པར་ཐལ། རྒྱུ་འབྲས་གཉིས་ཀ་ཡིན་པའི་ཕྱིར།
ཟེར་ན་མ་ཁྱབ་སྟེ། བུམ་པ་ཆོས་ཅན། རྒྱུ་འབྲས་མ་ཡིན་པར་ཐལ། ཐ་དད་མ་ཡིན་པའི་ཕྱིར་ཏེ། གཅིག་ཡིན་པའི་ཕྱིར། ཁ་ཅིག རྟག་པ་ཡིན་ན་རྒྱུ་མ་ཡིན་པས་ཁྱབ་པར་ཐལ། རྒྱུ་ཡིན་ན་རྟག་པ་མ་ཡིན་པས་ཁྱབ་པའི་ཕྱིར་ཟེར་ན། མི་འཐད་དེ། རྒྱུ་ཡིན་ན